Antoinette Schapper
A Grammar of Bunaq

Mouton Grammar Library

Edited by
Georg Bossong
Bernard Comrie
Patience L. Epps
Irina Nikolaeva

Volume 86

Antoinette Schapper

A Grammar of Bunaq

ISBN 978-3-11-163168-4
e-ISBN (PDF) 978-3-11-076114-6
e-ISBN (EPUB) 978-3-11-076137-5
ISSN 0933-7636

Library of Congress Control Number: 2022931834

Bibliographic information published by the Deutsche Nationalbibliothek
The Deutsche Nationalbibliothek lists this publication in the Deutsche Nationalbibliografie;
detailed bibliographic data are available on the internet at http://dnb.dnb.de.

© 2024 Walter de Gruyter GmbH, Berlin/Boston
This volume is text- and page-identical with the hardback published in 2022.
Typesetting: Integra Software Services Pvt. Ltd

www.degruyter.com

Acknowledgements

My initial research for this grammar was made possible by an Australian Postgraduate Award and an Australian National University Supplementary Scholarship, held from 2006 to 2009. That work resulted in a PhD thesis (Schapper 2010b). Subsequent field research on Bunaq was conducted under the auspices of a small grant from the Endangered Languages Documentation Programme. Complete revision of Schapper (2010b) for publication was made possible by the Netherlands Organisation for Scientific Research VENI project "The evolution of the lexicon: Explorations in lexical stability, semantic shift and borrowing in a Papuan language family" and by the OUTOFPAPUA project funded by the European Research Council (grant agreement no. 848532).

My greatest thanks go to the Bunaq people for sharing their language and culture with me. On my first field trip, Jose Louis Barreto, the *loro* Aiasa, and his wife Isabella, kindly introduced me to Ignatius Kali, the *loro* Lamaknen. Ama Nasu and his wife Eme Rosa, along with his daughters, Yati, Yuli, Isi and Dorce as well as *nana* Laura, provided me with every kind of support that I could have ever hoped for. Ama Nasu introduced me to Eme Eta, a retired school teacher in Gewal. She housed me, fed me, and stubbornly spoke only Bunaq to me. Thanks to all the kids of Gewal for all the great times we had, especially Aris, Novi, Ela, Laura, Markus, Diana and Yati. Hironimus Mau worked closely with me for several months in 2007 as did Wili Loe in 2009. Their patient explanations and fine judgements added many details to this work. Agustinus Saik has been a great help to me with his work transcribing and translating Bunaq texts.

I am indebted to John Bowden who first took me on as a PhD student in 2006. Later Wayan Arka became my supervisor and he, together with Nick Evans, patiently read and commented on draft chapters until submission of my thesis at the end of 2009. More recently, I have benefited from the editorial guidance of Bernard Comrie. His comments on my submitted manuscript were insightful and immensely helpful in improving aspects of my argumentation. Many thanks to Allison Adelman for copy-editing the manuscript.

I dedicate this book to the memory of Ludwig. The writing of it took me far from Ludwig, and I never returned. For that, I am immensely sorry.

Contents

Acknowledgements —— V

Abbreviations and glossing conventions —— XXI

Chapter 1
The Bunaq language and its speakers —— 1
1.1 Introduction: locating the Bunaq —— 1
1.2 Language names —— 3
1.3 Historical setting: Extent and dispersal of the Bunaq —— 4
1.3.1 Bunaq in West Timor —— 5
1.3.1.1 Bunaq in northern Belu —— 6
1.3.1.2 Bunaq in southern Belu —— 8
1.3.2 Bunaq in East Timor —— 8
1.3.2.1 Bunaq in Bobonaro and Zumalai —— 8
1.3.2.2 Bunaq in western Covalima —— 9
1.3.2.3 Bunaq in Ainaro and Manufahi —— 10
1.3.3 The Bunaq homeland —— 12
1.4 Sociolinguistic setting: numbers, vitality, and bilingualism —— 13
1.5 Bunaq dialects —— 14
1.6 Genealogical affiliations —— 17
1.6.1 Low-level affiliations —— 17
1.6.2 High-level affiliations —— 19
1.7 Borrowing and influence —— 21
1.7.1 Borrowings from Central Timor —— 22
1.7.2 Tetun borrowings and calques —— 24
1.7.3 Borrowings from unknown Austronesian sources —— 29
1.8 Ritual language: parallelism —— 30
1.9 Linguistic type —— 31
1.9.1 Typological overview —— 31
1.9.2 Bunaq as a Papuan language —— 32
1.10 Previous work —— 36
1.11 This work: Fieldwork and data —— 37
1.11.1 Fieldwork —— 37
1.11.2 Kinds of data —— 38

Chapter 2
Phonology and morphophonology —— 40
2.1 Introduction —— 40
2.2 Phoneme inventory —— 40
2.2.1 Vowel phonemes —— 40

2.2.2	Diphthong phonemes — 41
2.2.3	Consonant phonemes — 43
2.2.3.1	Voiceless stops — 45
2.2.3.2	Voiced stops — 46
2.2.3.2.1	/b/ — 46
2.2.3.2.2	/d/ — 46
2.2.3.2.3	/g/ — 47
2.2.3.3	Fricatives — 48
2.2.3.4	Voiceless palato-alveolar affricate — 49
2.2.3.5	Liquids — 51
2.2.3.6	Nasals — 51
2.2.3.7	Approximant — 52
2.2.3.8	Glottal stop — 53
2.2.4	Phoneme adaptation in loans — 54
2.3	Phonotactics — 57
2.3.1	Syllable structure — 57
2.3.2	Word templates — 58
2.3.3	Phoneme distribution — 60
2.3.4	Cluster constraint violations — 61
2.3.4.1	Consonant clusters in loans — 61
2.3.4.2	Consonant clusters in native words — 62
2.3.5	Vowel sequences — 63
2.3.6	Phonetic glide insertion between VV sequences — 64
2.3.7	Glottal stop as boundary marker — 65
2.4	Stress — 66
2.5	Morphophonology — 69
2.5.1	Prefixation — 69
2.5.1.1	Vowel harmony — 69
2.5.1.2	Vowel deletion — 70
2.5.1.3	Metathesis — 70
2.5.1.4	Loss of initial /h/ — 73
2.5.2	Suffixation with *-wen* — 73
2.5.3	Reduplication — 74
2.5.3.1	Full reduplication and repetition — 74
2.5.3.2	Partial reduplication — 75
2.5.3.3	Reduplication with vowel changes — 76
2.6	Irregularities in prefixation — 77
2.6.1	Irregular prefixes — 77
2.6.2	Irregular roots — 78
2.6.2.1	Root reduction — 78
2.6.2.2	Root mutation — 79

2.6.2.3	Initial consonant alternations —— 80	
2.7	Orthography —— 81	

Chapter 3
Word classes —— 83

3.1	Introduction —— 83	
3.2	Nouns —— 83	
3.2.1	Nominal compounds —— 85	
3.2.1.1	Left-headed compounds —— 85	
3.2.1.2	Right-headed compounds —— 86	
3.2.1.3	Nominal coordinative compounds —— 88	
3.3	Verbs —— 90	
3.3.1	Lack of an adjective class —— 91	
3.3.2	Verbal coordinative compounds —— 94	
3.4	Noun-verb conversion —— 96	
3.5	Minor word classes —— 97	
3.5.1	Pronouns —— 97	
3.5.2	Interrogatives —— 99	
3.5.3	Locationals —— 101	
3.5.4	Determiners —— 104	
3.5.5	Numerals —— 105	
3.5.5.1	Excursus on the numeral *uen* 'one' —— 109	
3.5.6	Postpositions —— 110	
3.5.7	Interjections —— 111	
3.6	Problems in the classification of the lexicon —— 113	
3.6.1	Verbal postpositions —— 113	
3.6.2	Quantificational items in the NP —— 116	
3.6.3	Adverbs —— 117	
3.6.4	Clause conjunctions —— 118	

Chapter 4
The clause —— 121

4.1	Introduction —— 121	
4.2	Verbal clauses —— 121	
4.2.1	Monovalent clauses —— 122	
4.2.2	Bivalent clauses —— 124	
4.2.3	Trivalent clauses —— 126	
4.2.4	Verbal clauses with unmarked obliques —— 128	
4.2.5	Summary —— 130	
4.3	Non-verbal clauses —— 131	
4.3.1	Nominal clauses —— 131	

4.3.2	Postpositional clauses —— 132	
4.3.3	Possessive clauses —— 133	
4.3.4	Clauses with complex predicates of physical, emotional, and character traits —— 134	
4.4	Peripheral constituents in the clause —— 137	
4.5	Negative clauses —— 139	
4.5.1	Clausal negation with *niq* 'NEG' —— 139	
4.5.2	Other negators —— 141	
4.6	Non-declarative clauses —— 142	
4.6.1	Imperatives —— 142	
4.6.1.1	Imperatives and hortatives with *naq* 'PRIOR' —— 143	
4.6.1.2	Invitations/permissions with *mal* 'go' —— 144	
4.6.1.3	Responses to imperatives —— 145	
4.6.2	Questions —— 146	
4.6.2.1	Information questions —— 146	
4.6.2.2	Polar questions —— 148	
4.6.2.2.1	Unmarked polar questions —— 148	
4.6.2.2.2	Questions soliciting agreement with =*e* 'AGREE' —— 149	
4.6.2.2.3	Alternative questions with =*ka* 'OR' —— 149	
4.6.2.2.4	Monitoring the addressee questions with =*to* 'CONF' —— 150	
4.6.2.2.5	Answers to polar questions —— 151	
4.6.3	Exclamatives —— 152	
4.7	Pragmatic variation in the clause —— 154	
4.7.1	Variation in argument realisation —— 154	
4.7.1.1	Anaphoric elision —— 154	
4.7.1.2	Zero pro of generic/non-referential As: a functional passive? —— 157	
4.7.2	Variation in word order —— 160	
4.7.2.1	Dislocation —— 160	
4.7.2.1.1	Left-dislocation —— 162	
4.7.2.1.2	Right-dislocation —— 163	
4.7.2.2	Fronting and other clause-internal word order variation —— 165	
4.7.2.3	Animacy effects on word order —— 168	
4.7.3	Variation in bivalent verb agreement —— 171	
4.7.4	Discourse markers —— 174	
4.7.4.1	Relator enclitics —— 175	
4.7.4.1.1	=*bu* 'GIVEN' —— 175	
4.7.4.1.2	=*be* 'CONTEXP' —— 177	
4.7.4.2	Focus enclitics —— 179	
4.7.4.2.1	=*o* 'AND' —— 180	
4.7.4.2.2	=*sa* 'EVEN' —— 181	
4.7.4.2.3	=*na* 'FOC' —— 182	

Chapter 5
Noun phrases —— 184

5.1	Noun phrase structure —— 184	
5.2	Nominal classification —— 185	
5.2.1	Overview of noun class agreement targets —— 186	
5.2.2	Nouns referring to animates —— 186	
5.2.3	Nouns referring to inanimates —— 188	
5.2.3.1	Nouns referring to entities with animate-like properties —— 189	
5.2.3.2	Nouns referring to edible plant cultivars —— 190	
5.2.3.3	Nouns referring to items of human production —— 192	
5.2.3.4	Nouns referring to oral and written forms of literature —— 193	
5.2.3.5	Nouns referring to items of clothing and jewellery —— 193	
5.2.3.6	Nouns referring to money and currency —— 194	
5.2.3.7	Nouns referring to rocks and hard items —— 195	
5.2.4	Noun class reassignment —— 195	
5.2.4.1	Reassignment in reference to groups of animates —— 195	
5.2.4.2	Reassignment in reference to controlled natural elements —— 196	
5.2.4.3	Reassignment in reference to plants —— 197	
5.3	N_{MOD} modifiers of N_{HEAD}s —— 199	
5.3.1	Inalienably possessed nouns as N_{MOD}s —— 200	
5.3.2	An agreeing N_{MOD} —— 202	
5.4	Attributive verbs and relative clauses —— 203	
5.4.1	Attributive verbs and non-restrictive relative clauses —— 203	
5.4.2	Restrictive relative clauses —— 205	
5.4.3	NP accessibility to relativisation —— 206	
5.4.3.1	Unmarked obliques as RC heads —— 206	
5.4.3.2	NP complements of verbal postpositions as RC heads —— 207	
5.4.3.2	NP complements of postpositions as RC heads —— 207	
5.4.3.4	Possessors as RC heads —— 208	
5.5	Indefiniteness marking —— 208	
5.5.1	*uen* 'one' —— 209	
5.5.2	*bun* 'INDEF' —— 210	
5.6	Nominal quantification —— 212	
5.6.1	Numerals and numeral classifiers —— 212	
5.6.1.1	Numeral classifier construction —— 212	
5.6.1.2	QUANT + *uen* 'one' construction —— 213	
5.6.2	Human plurality: *halaqi* '3PL' —— 214	
5.6.3	Quantificational *mil* 'inside' —— 216	
5.6.3.1	Human collective —— 216	
5.6.3.2	Temporal duration —— 217	
5.6.4	Animate group plural: *g-inil* '3AN-name' —— 218	

5.6.5	Animal group plural: *g-omoq* '3AN-udder' —— 219
5.6.6	Partitive plural: *waqen* 'PART.PL' —— 220
5.6.7	Universal quantification: *hotu~hotu* 'all' —— 221
5.6.8	Quantification of 'kinds' —— 222
5.6.9	Distributive plurality by reduplication —— 224
5.7	Nominal conjunction and disjunction —— 225
5.7.1	Zero conjunction —— 225
5.7.2	Conjunction with =*o* 'AND' —— 226
5.7.3	Conjunction with *halali* '3DU' —— 227
5.7.4	Conjunction with *ai* 'ONLY' —— 228
5.7.5	Disjunction with =*ka* 'OR' —— 228

Chapter 6
Pronouns and person reference —— 230

6.1	Introduction —— 230
6.2	Pronominal person reference —— 230
6.2.1	Pronouns and person prefixes —— 231
6.2.2	Pronoun and determiner combinations —— 234
6.2.3	Dual versus plural number in pronouns —— 235
6.2.4	Additional referential uses of pronouns —— 236
6.2.4.1	Generic reference —— 236
6.2.4.1.1	Generic *i* '1PL.INCL' —— 236
6.2.4.1.2	Generic *eto* '2SG' —— 238
6.2.4.2	Polite reference —— 239
6.2.4.2.1	Superior *nei* '1PL.EXCL' —— 239
6.2.4.2.2	Honorific *i* '1PL.INCL' —— 241
6.2.4.2.3	Respectful *ei* '2PL' —— 243
6.2.4.2.4	Polite *halaqi* '3PL' and *halali* '3DU' —— 243
6.2.4.2.5	Hierarchy of polite pronoun uses —— 244
6.3	Non-pronominal person reference —— 245
6.3.1	Kin terms —— 246
6.3.1.1	With kin —— 247
6.3.1.2	With non-kin —— 249
6.3.2	Personal names —— 251
6.4	Summary —— 253

Chapter 7
Determiners —— 255

7.1	Introduction —— 255
7.2	Overview of determiner functions —— 256
7.3	Proximal demonstrative —— 258
7.3.1	In the nominal domain —— 258

7.3.1.1	Spatial use —— 258	
7.3.1.2	Temporal use —— 259	
7.3.1.3	Anaphoric use —— 259	
7.3.1.4	"Closeness" of relation use —— 261	
7.3.1.5	Non-anaphoric uses —— 263	
7.3.2	In the clausal domain —— 264	
7.3.2.1	Non-embedded use —— 264	
7.3.2.2	Thematic use —— 265	
7.3.2.3	Sentence connective use —— 265	
7.4	Non-proximal demonstrative —— 267	
7.4.1	In the nominal domain —— 267	
7.4.1.1	Spatial use —— 267	
7.4.1.2	Temporal use —— 268	
7.4.1.3	Anaphoric use —— 269	
7.4.1.4	Use in referring to a new discourse participant —— 271	
7.4.1.5	Use in person deixis —— 272	
7.4.2	In the clausal domain —— 275	
7.4.2.1	Non-embedded use —— 275	
7.4.2.2	Thematic use —— 276	
7.4.2.3	Sentence connective use —— 277	
7.5	Specifier demonstrative —— 277	
7.5.1	In the nominal domain —— 278	
7.5.1.1	Spatial use —— 278	
7.5.1.2	Discourse use —— 280	
7.5.2	In the clausal domain —— 281	
7.5.2.1	Non-embedded nominalisation use —— 281	
7.5.2.2	Thematic use —— 283	
7.5.2.3	Sentence connective use —— 283	
7.6	Contrastive demonstrative —— 285	
7.6.1	In the nominal domain —— 285	
7.6.1.1	Contrastive use —— 285	
7.6.1.2	Topic shift use —— 287	
7.6.1.3	Sequential use —— 288	
7.6.2	In the clausal domain —— 290	
7.6.2.1	Thematic use —— 291	
7.6.2.2	Sentence connective use —— 292	
7.7	Counter-expectational demonstrative —— 294	
7.7.1	In the nominal domain —— 294	
7.7.2	In the clausal domain —— 296	
7.8	Article —— 297	
7.8.1	In the nominal domain —— 297	
7.8.2	In the clausal domain —— 300	

Chapter 8
Locationals —— 302

8.1	Introduction —— 302	
8.2	Syntax of locational and N_{HEAD} —— 303	
8.2.1	Pre-N_{HEAD} use —— 303	
8.2.2	Post-N_{HEAD} use —— 305	
8.2.3	No N_{HEAD} use —— 306	
8.2.4	Frequency of locational uses —— 307	
8.3	Semantics of locationals —— 308	
8.3.1	Elevational locationals —— 308	
8.3.1.1	Elevation in real-world place- and path-finding in Lamaknen —— 310	
8.3.2	Place locationals —— 314	
8.3.3	Temporal/discourse locational —— 317	
8.3.4	Addressee locational —— 321	
8.4	Combining locationals —— 323	
8.4.1	Place locationals: here + there —— 323	
8.4.2	Elevational and place locationals —— 324	
8.4.3	Elevational locationals + addressee locational —— 325	
8.4.4	Temporal/discourse locational + addressee locational —— 327	
8.5	Summary —— 328	

Chapter 9
Adnominal possession and related constructions —— 329

9.1	Introduction —— 329	
9.2	Indirect possession —— 330	
9.2.1	Preposed possessors —— 331	
9.2.1.1	Associativity: Indirect possessor constructions without a possessum —— 332	
9.2.2	Postposed possessors —— 334	
9.2.2.1	Possessor as destination —— 335	
9.2.2.2	Possessor as origin —— 336	
9.3	Direct possession —— 338	
9.3.1	Class I —— 339	
9.3.2	Class II —— 341	
9.3.3	Class III —— 344	
9.3.4	Class IV —— 346	
9.3.5	Class V —— 347	
9.4	From possessive phrases to possessive compounds —— 350	
9.5	Double possessor marking —— 352	
9.6	Summary —— 354	

Chapter 10
Verbs —— 356
10.1　　　　　Introduction —— 356
10.2　　　　　Bivalent verbs —— 357
10.2.1　　　　Class I bivalent verbs —— 357
10.2.2　　　　Class II bivalent verbs —— 358
10.2.3　　　　Class III bivalent verbs —— 359
10.2.4　　　　Class IV bivalent verbs —— 361
10.2.4.1　　　h-conjugation verbs —— 362
10.2.4.1.1　　Note on /h/-initial items borrowed from Tetun —— 364
10.2.4.2　　　s-conjugation verbs —— 365
10.2.4.3　　　t-conjugation verbs —— 366
10.2.4.4　　　d-conjugation verb —— 367
10.2.4.5　　　l-conjugation verbs —— 367
10.2.5　　　　Bivalent verb classes with distinct agreement patterns —— 368
10.2.5.1　　　Two transport verbs: *tula* 'move' and *penen* 'shift' —— 369
10.2.5.2　　　Two keeping verbs: *lumaq* 'take care of' and *bilan* 'keep' —— 370
10.3　　　　　Monovalent verbs —— 371
10.3.1　　　　Monovalent verbs without prefixes —— 372
10.3.2　　　　Monovalent verbs with prefixes —— 372
10.4　　　　　Trivalent verbs —— 374
10.4.1　　　　*h-ege* '3INAN-give' —— 374
10.4.2　　　　*h-ini* '3INAN-call' —— 375
10.5　　　　　Labile verbs —— 378
10.5.1　　　　Verbs of setting —— 379
10.5.2　　　　Verb of learning/teaching —— 380
10.5.3　　　　Verbs of mixing —— 381
10.5.4　　　　Causative labile verbs —— 381
10.6　　　　　Verb classes with unmarked obliques —— 383
10.6.1　　　　Saturation verbs —— 383
10.6.2　　　　Existential verbs —— 384
10.6.3　　　　Motion verbs —— 386
10.6.4　　　　Verb of teaching —— 387

Chapter 11
Valency-reducing morphology and deponency —— 388
11.1　　　　　Introduction —— 388
11.2　　　　　Prefixal deponency —— 388
11.3　　　　　Reflexive *dV-* —— 390
11.3.1　　　　Reflexive situations —— 390
11.3.1.1　　　On verbs and verbal postpositions —— 390
11.3.1.2　　　On nouns —— 391

11.3.1.3	Reflexive binding with complement clauses and serial verbs —— 393	
11.3.2	Middle situations —— 395	
11.3.2.1	Spontaneous events —— 395	
11.3.2.2	Self-benefactive events —— 397	
11.3.2.3	Cognitive events —— 399	
11.3.2.4	Body action events —— 400	
11.3.2.5	Impersonal middles —— 402	
11.4	Reciprocal *tV-* —— 403	
11.4.1	Reciprocal situations —— 403	
11.4.1.1	On verbs —— 403	
11.4.1.2	On nouns —— 404	
11.4.2	Symmetrical states —— 405	
11.4.3	Iterative events —— 405	
11.4.4	Situations with plurality of participants —— 406	
11.4.4.1	Fighting events —— 407	
11.4.4.2	Physical contact events —— 407	
11.4.4.3	Gathering events —— 409	
11.4.4.4	Verbs of (un)joining —— 410	
11.4.5	Uses of *tV-* 'RECP' on verbal postpositions —— 410	
11.4.5.1	Joint action *t-erel* 'RECP-INS' —— 411	
11.4.5.2	Uniting of participants: *ti-ta* 'RECP-GL' —— 412	
11.4.5.3	Symmetrical participation: *t-o* 'RECP-SRC' —— 413	
11.5	Anticausative *-wen* —— 415	
11.5.1	Anticausative use —— 415	
11.5.2	Moderative use —— 419	
11.5.3	Similative use —— 420	

Chapter 12
Expressing peripheral NPs —— 422

12.1	Introduction —— 422	
12.2	Postpositions —— 422	
12.2.1	*no* 'OBL' —— 422	
12.2.1.1	Locative function —— 422	
12.2.1.2	Temporal function —— 424	
12.2.2	*gene* 'LOC' —— 425	
12.2.3	*goet* 'LIKE' —— 426	
12.2.3.1	Similative function —— 426	
12.2.3.2	Demonstrative manner function —— 427	
12.2.3.3	Introducing direct speech and thought —— 428	
12.3	Reason *gie* 'BECAUSE' —— 430	
12.4	Verbal postpositions —— 431	
12.4.1	*g-utu* '3-COM' —— 432	

12.4.2	*dele* 'INS' —— 434	
12.4.2.1	Instrument —— 434	
12.4.2.2	Cause —— 435	
12.4.2.3	Manner —— 436	
12.4.2.4	Non-controlling comitants —— 436	
12.4.3	*a-ta* '3INAN-GL' —— 437	
12.4.3.1	Goal —— 438	
12.4.3.2	Interest —— 439	
12.4.3.3	Motive —— 440	
12.4.4	*g-o* '3-SRC' —— 441	
12.4.4.1	Human source —— 441	
12.4.4.2	Point of relation/comparison —— 442	
12.4.4.3	Maleficiary —— 444	
12.4.4.4	Addressee —— 445	
12.4.5	*h-otol* '3INAN-WITHOUT' —— 445	
12.4.6	*h-ege* '3INAN-BEN' —— 447	
12.4.6.1	Beneficiary —— 447	
12.4.6.2	Addressee —— 448	
12.4.6.3	Theme of a cognitive event —— 449	
12.4.7	*h-os* '3INAN-WAIT' —— 450	
12.4.8	*h-onogo* '3INAN-SEPARATE' —— 451	

Chapter 13
Serial verb constructions —— 452

13.1	Introduction —— 452	
13.2	Properties of Bunaq SVCs —— 452	
13.3	Syntactic types of SVCs in Bunaq —— 455	
13.4	Causative serialisation —— 456	
13.5	Resultative serialisation —— 458	
13.6	Manner serialisation —— 459	
13.6.1	Participant-oriented manner serialisation —— 460	
13.6.2	Event-oriented manner serialisation —— 461	
13.7	Intensifying serialisation —— 462	
13.8	Aspectual serialisation —— 464	
13.8.1	Serialisation with *haqal* 'finished' —— 464	
13.8.1.1	Completed action —— 465	
13.8.1.2	Complete state —— 466	
13.8.1.3	"Complete" quantification —— 467	
13.8.2	Serialisation with *liol* 'continue' —— 468	
13.8.2.1	Continuous action —— 469	
13.8.2.2	Immediate action —— 470	
13.8.3	Frequent action with *des* 'still' —— 470	

13.8.4	Persistent action with *ciluq* 'rest' —— 472	
13.9	Motion serialisation —— 472	
13.9.1	Origin-Motion-Goal SVCs —— 473	
13.9.2	Reversive motion SVCs —— 477	
13.9.3	Directional SVCs —— 478	

Chapter 14
Verbal and clausal modifiers —— 481

14.1	Introduction —— 481	
14.2	Preverbal modification —— 481	
14.2.1	Modal adverbs —— 482	
14.2.1.1	*misti* 'must' —— 482	
14.2.1.2	*sala* 'should' —— 483	
14.2.1.3	*asal* 'necessarily' —— 484	
14.2.1.4	*hilaq* 'surprisingly' —— 485	
14.2.1.5	*hele* 'perhaps' —— 486	
14.2.1.6	*kalaq* 'maybe' —— 487	
14.2.1.7	*hani* 'PROH' —— 488	
14.2.2	Manner adverbs —— 489	
14.2.2.1	*nor* 'aimlessly' —— 489	
14.2.2.2	*naqi* 'simply' —— 489	
14.2.3	Temporal adverbs —— 490	
14.2.4	Negative reinforcers —— 491	
14.3	Postverbal modification —— 492	
14.3.1	Postverbal adverbials —— 493	
14.3.1.1	Postverbal nominals —— 493	
14.3.1.1.1	Duration/distance measure nominals —— 493	
14.3.1.2	Temporal/aspectual adverbs —— 495	
14.3.1.3	Adverbs of addition and comparison —— 496	
14.3.1.4	Intensifiers —— 497	
14.3.2	Performative *on* 'DO' —— 498	
14.3.2.1	Emphasis —— 498	
14.3.2.2	Durative/progressive events —— 499	
14.3.2.3	Causation —— 501	
14.3.3	Prospective *gie* 'PROSP' —— 502	
14.3.3.1	*gie oa* 'be about to' —— 504	
14.3.3.2	*gie taq* 'just going to' —— 505	
14.3.4	Restrictive *ai* 'ONLY' —— 505	
14.3.5	Phasal polarity markers —— 507	
14.3.5.1	Continuative *taq* 'still' —— 508	
14.3.5.1.1	*niq taq* 'not yet' —— 509	
14.3.5.2	Iamitive *oa* 'already' —— 509	

14.3.5.2.1	*niq oa* 'no more' —— 511	
14.3.6	Information markers —— 512	
14.3.6.1	Reportative *gin* 'REPORT' —— 512	
14.3.6.2	Informative *nai* 'INFORM' —— 514	
14.3.7	Priorative *naq* 'PRIOR' —— 516	

Chapter 15
Multiclausal constructions —— 518

15.1	Introduction —— 518
15.2	Clause complementation —— 518
15.2.1	NP-replacing complements —— 519
15.2.1.1	Complements as P —— 519
15.2.1.2	Complements as S —— 521
15.2.2	Non-NP replacing complements —— 523
15.3	Clause conjoining —— 526
15.3.1	Clause conjoining by juxtaposition —— 526
15.3.2	Clause conjoining with overt markers —— 528
15.3.2.1	Clause-final conjunctions —— 529
15.3.2.1.1	Reason conjunction: *=si* —— 530
15.3.2.1.2	Sequence conjunction: *soq* and *soq oa* —— 531
15.3.2.1.3	Relator enclitics: *=bu*, *mesaq=bu*, and *=be* —— 533
15.3.2.1.4	Focus enclitics: *=o*, *=sa*, *=na*, and *naq=na* —— 535
15.3.2.2	Borrowed clause-initial conjunctions —— 537
15.3.2.3	Clauses bracketed by multiple initial and final conjunctions —— 538
15.3.2.4	Adverbial clause conjoiners —— 539
15.3.2.5	(Verbal) postpositions used in clause conjoining —— 540
15.3.2.6	Verbs used in clause conjoining —— 541
15.4	Sentence connecting —— 542
15.4.1	Tail-head linkage —— 542
15.4.2	Demonstratives in sentence connecting —— 545
15.4.2.1	Anaphoric demonstratives —— 545
15.4.2.2	Cataphoric demonstratives —— 547
15.4.3	*Tebe* 'return' in sentence connecting —— 548
15.4.4	Sentence connectives —— 549

Text Appendix —— 551

References —— 573

Index —— 583

Abbreviations and glossing conventions

Glosses

1	1st person
2	2nd person
3	3rd person
ADDR	addressee locational
AGREE	agreement question tag/exclamative marker
AN	ANIMATE noun class
AND	additive focus enclitic
ANTIC	anti-causative
ART	article
BEN	benefactive
CAUS	causative
CLF	classifier
COLL	collective plural
COM	comitative
CONF	confirmation question tag
CONT	continuative
CONTR	contrastive demonstrative
CONTEXP	counter-expectational demonstrative/relator enclitic
DO	performative auxiliary
DU	dual
DUR	temporal duration marker
EXCL	exclusive
EXCLAM	exclamative
EVEN	scalar additive focus enclitic
FOC	restrictive focus enclitic
GIVEN	given relator enclitic
GL	goal
GRP	group plural
HERE	proximal place locational
HIGH	elevation higher than DC (deictic centre)
HUM	human
IAM	iamitive
INAN	INANIMATE noun class
INCL	inclusive
INDEF	indefinite
INFORM	information marker
INS	instrumental
INTERJ	interjection
LEVEL	elevation level with DC
LIKE	'like' postposition
LOC	locative postposition
LOW	elevation lower than DC
MODER	moderative
NEG	negative

NOW	temporal/discourse locational
NPRX	non-proximal demonstrative
OBL	oblique postposition
ONLY	restrictive particle
OR	disjunctor/alternative question tag
PART	partitive noun
PL	plural
POSS	possessive (alienable)
PRIOR	priorative
PROH	prohibitive
PROSP	prospective aspect
PROX	proximal demonstrative
REAS	reason
RECP	reciprocal
REDUP	reduplicant
REFL	reflexive
REPORT	reportative marker
SEQ	sequential marker
SIM	similative
SG	singular
SPCPLC	specific place locational
SPEC	specifier demonstrative
SRC	source encoding verbal postposition
THERE	distal place locational

Category labels

A	most agent-like argument of a bi-/trivalent clause
Adv	adverbial
Agr	agreement
Arg	argument
Asp	aspectual particle
Comp	complement
Dem	demonstrative
Det	determiner
Lct	locational
N	noun
N_{HEAD}	semantic head of noun phrase
N_{MOD}	nominal modifier of head of noun phrase
NP	noun phrase
Obl	oblique argument
P	most patient-like argument of a bivalent clause
Peri	peripheral NP constituent
PP	postpositional phrase
Psm	possessum
Pred	predicate
Psr	possessor

QUANT	quantificational item in the NP
R	most recipient-like argument of a trivalent clause
RC	relative clause
S	single argument of a monovalent clause
SA	single agentive argument of a monovalent clause
SP	single patientive argument of a monovalent clause
"subject"	cover term for the single argument of a non-verbal predicate
SVC	serial verb construction
T	most theme-like argument of a trivalent clause
V	verb
VpP	verbal postpositional phrase

Other abbreviations used in the text

AN	Austronesian language(s)
AP	Alor-Pantar languages
DC	deictic centre
fig.	figurative
GWB	Greater West Bomberai languages
k.o.	kind of
lit.	literally
p.o.	part of
PGWB	Proto-Greater West Bomberai
PMP	Proto-Malayo-Polynesian (daughter of Proto-Austronesian)
PTAP	Proto-Timor-Alor-Pantar
s.o.	someone
sp.	species
s.th.	something
TAP	Timor-Alor-Pantar languages

Conventions

SMALLCAPS are used to denote items with grammatical rather than lexical meaning, and reflect that these morphemes are Bunaq-specific. They serve to differentiate the Bunaq from its translation equivalent. Thus, "ANIMACY" denotes the grammatical property of being either of AN(IMATE) or INAN(IMATE) noun class, while "animacy" refers to the semantic property of a referent being either animate or inanimate.

Morphological glossing:
- hyphen "-" separates distinct morphemes within a single morphophonological word
- equals "=" represents the boundary between a clitic and its host

- tilde "~" connects reduplicated elements
- forward slash "/" separates morphemes with two meanings

Intonation unit glossing:
- comma "," non-final rise in pitch, and before right dislocated elements
- full stop "." sentence-final drop in pitch
- exclamation mark "!" sentence-final rise in pitch
- question mark "?" question intonation
- quotation marks "" direct speech/thought

Where a single Bunaq morpheme requires glossing with more than one English word, these are separated by a full stop.

In glosses, noun class may be included after a noun where relevant to the point under discussion, thus: e.g., *zap* 'dog.AN' for an ANIMATE noun and *deu* 'house.INAN' for an INANIMATE noun.

In translations:
- parentheses "()" are used to denote elided material that is not actually present in the text
- curly brackets "{}" denote an approximation of modal or evidential meaning encoded by a Bunaq morpheme in the English translation.

Marking of grammaticality at the beginning of an example:
- asterisk "*" marks utterances which have been judged by speakers to be ungrammatical
- question mark "?" marks utterances that have been judged as only border-line grammatical or for which the grammaticality is questionable for some speakers
- hash "#" marks utterances that have been judged semantically bizarre by speakers

Chapter 1
The Bunaq language and its speakers

1.1 Introduction: locating the Bunaq

This book is a grammar of the Bunaq language as spoken in Lamaknen, West Timor, Indonesia. In this chapter, I introduce the reader to the Bunaq language and its speakers. Following a general orientation (§1.1), I discuss the names by which the Bunaq people and their language are known (§1.2), their dispersal and its historical causes (§1.3), the sociolinguistic setting of the language (§1.4), and dialectal variation (§1.5). I treat issues of genealogical affiliation (§1.6), borrowing and influence (§1.7), ritual language (§1.8) and linguistic type (§1.9). Finally, I discuss previous work on Bunaq (§1.10) and the background to the current work (§1.11).

Bunaq is a Papuan (non-Austronesian) language spoken in the central mountainous region of the island of Timor. Timor is located at the eastern extreme of the Minor Sundic Island chain in the Indian Ocean (Map 1.1). The western half of Timor was formerly a Dutch colony and now is part of Indonesia; the eastern half belonged to Portugal until 1975 and was the province Timor Timur of Indonesia until gaining independence in 2002 as Timor-Leste (henceforth East Timor). Bunaq is spoken on both sides of the modern border.

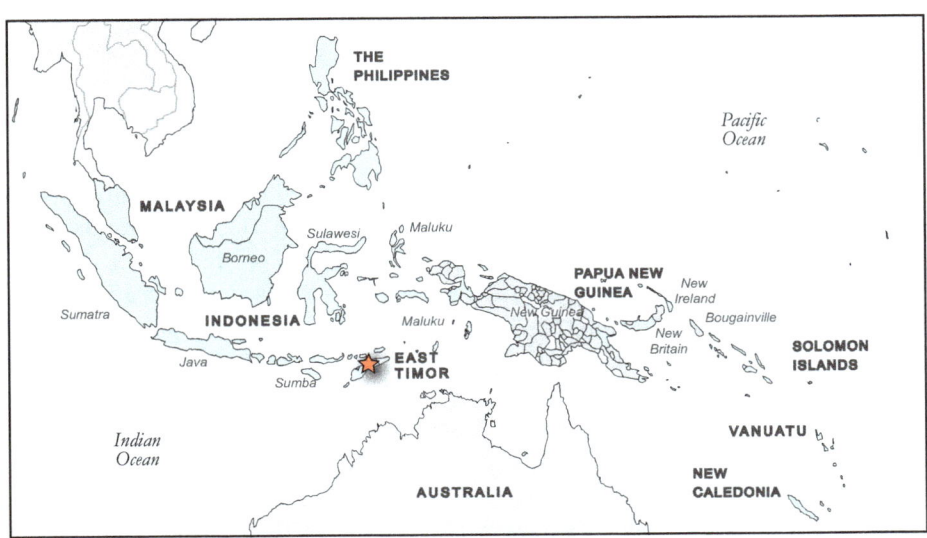

Map 1.1: Bunaq in its wider geographical context.

The Bunaq people are isolated in central Timor by two factors: their language and their social structure. Firstly, they are surrounded on all sides by Austronesian languages: Kemak to the north, Mambae to the east, and Tetun to the south and west (Map 1.2). The other Papuan languages of Timor, Fataluku, Makasae, and Makalero, are located in a contiguous coastal area on the island's eastern tip. The Bunaq language is widely recognised by the Bunaq and their Austronesian neighbours as "different", and, whilst Bunaq is rarely learnt by non-Bunaq, almost all Bunaq are fluent in at least one Austronesian language. See §1.9.2 on Bunaq's place in the Papuan-Austronesian dichotomy.

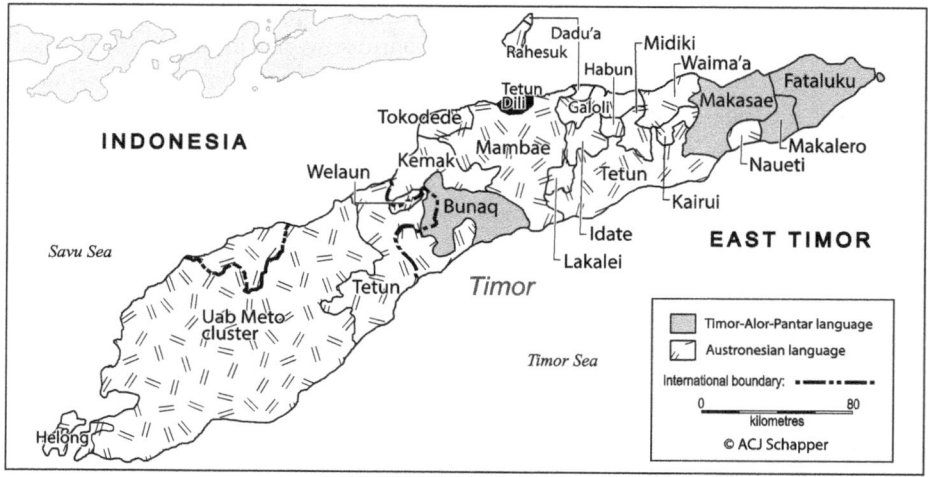

Map 1.2: The languages of Timor.

Secondly, the sense of Bunaq's otherness has been fostered by their socially distinct character. For example, in contrast to the other groups in Timor which are either matrilineal (Wehali Tetun: Therik 2004), or more commonly patrilineal (e.g., Kemak: Renard-Clamagirand 1982), the Bunaq allow both forms of descent and marriage (i.e., cognation, Hicks 1983). Amongst the Bunaq, the woman typically remains in the *deu* 'house' (> lineage group) of her birth; her husband joins her to live in the house of her parents and their children become members of the mother's *deu* (i.e., a matrilineal pattern). However, there is a rarer form of marriage where the woman is "purchased" by the husband's family in a process (distinct from the normal payment of the bride price) known in Bunaq as *paen*, and she along with her children then belong to her husband's *deu* (i.e., a patrilineal situation). See Berthe (1961) for a detailed discussion of Bunaq marriage patterns.

A reputation for pugnacity has also ensured that the Bunaq have remained somewhat apart from their neighbours. The Bunaq are traditionally considered to be an aggressive and argumentative people by the neighbouring Austronesian speaking groups. This belief is reflected in the Bunaq's own traditions, such as the conclusion of the folk story of two brothers Asa Paran and Mau Paran given in (1):

(1) En   Emaq   g-epal   legul. En   Bunaq   g-epal   gol.
    people Kemak   3AN-ear long   people Bunaq   3AN-ear small
    'The Kemak people have long ears. The Bunaq people have small ears.' [Bk-4.098]

The metaphor in (1) reflects the Bunaq's characterisation of the Kemak as quiet and patient (*gepal legul* 'long-eared'), in contrast with themselves who are impatient and short-tempered (*gepal gol* 'small-eared'). This conception of the Bunaq also finds historical support: place-names, oral histories, and the current Bunaq dispersal in central Timor indicate that the Bunaq, driven by a string of conflicts, have progressively expanded eastwards, westwards, and southwards into Tetun and Mambae lands and into uninhabited lands on the southern plain of central Timor (§1.3).

These factors of linguistic non-conformity and social isolation have set the Bunaq apart to some degree. At the same time, they have also led to a very inclusive cultural attitude on the part of the Bunaq, expressed through widespread borrowing and adaptation from Austronesian language and society (§1.7). Of course, such twin efforts to assert their identity and to adapt to the surrounding social milieux may also be seen as a normal outcome of significant and prolonged contact between neighbouring cultural groups.

1.2 Language names

The name of the Bunaq people and their language name has been written variously as *Bunak*, *Buna*, *Bunaq*, *Bunac*, *Bunä*, and *Buna'*. Phonetically the name is [bunaʔ], the final glottal stop being differently (un)transcribed in the orthographies of different authors. The spelling *Bunak* appears to have originated in Portuguese usage where the grapheme <c> is reserved for /k/ and <k> for /ʔ/; the use of the umlaut " ̈" appears to be of Dutch origin and is reflected in some West Timorese texts such as the Bunaq Bible (*Libur por toma tip gie* 1988). *Buna* is found in a number of Indonesian texts, (e.g., Sawardo et al. 1996). In the practical orthography used here, the language and the people are *Bunaq*, following the orthographic conventions established by Berthe (1972) (§2.7).

The name "Bunaq" is recognised and accepted as a term of self-reference for the Bunaq people and their language across the whole of the Bunaq-speaking region. Its origins are unknown, though it has been suggested to be derived from Old Malay *budak* 'slave' (Hull 2004). There is, however, little to support this claim and speakers naturally reject this explanation. There are two additional names used in self-reference by Bunaq people in restricted areas.

In the northeast of the Bunaq-speaking area, Bunaq people refer to themselves and their language is *Gaiq* or *Gaeq*. This term is not used elsewhere and is almost entirely unknown outside the northeast. Bunaq people identifying themselves as *Gaiq* suggested to me that the term goes back to an early Bunaq lineage group name. Another possible etymology for the term is *Mgai*, the Kemak name for the Bunaq. Though the origin of the name is uncertain, a relation between *Mgai* and *Gaiq* seems plausible given that the northeast is an area of intense contact with Kemak people (§1.7.1).

Among the groups of Bunaq speakers in southern Belu of West Timor, the Tetun language name for the Bunaq, *Marae*, has been adopted as a term of self-reference. The origin of *Marae* in Tetun itself is not known, though its formal similarity to Tetun *malae* 'stranger, outsider' suggests a connection between the two, particularly in light of the Bunaq's "other" status in the region. Bunaq speakers from other regions tend to reject the term *Marae*, seeing it as a pejorative outsiders' name. Some Bunaq speakers, however, view the use of the term *Marae* as not so much pejorative as ignorant, arising out of a lack of awareness of the "proper" name for the Bunaq people and their language. Bunaq people in southern Belu seem to be desensitised to any negative connotations in the name *Marae*. The adoption of an exogenous name in self-reference by a group in close contact with speakers of the name's source language is a dynamic which plays itself out frequently in Timor.

1.3 Historical setting: Extent and dispersal of the Bunaq

The Bunaq-speaking area straddles the border between independent East Timor and Indonesian West Timor (Map 1.3). It extends in the north from Maliana in East Timor down to portions of the southern coast; it stretches west from the eastern edges of the southern Belu regency in West Timor to the western edge of Manufahi sub-district in East Timor.[1]

The modern dispersal of Bunaq speakers reflects a long history of migration and expansion into new territory. By their own accounts traditionally a mountain people, the Bunaq have been gradually moving into areas at lower elevations. Excessive pressure on land caused by growing populations and the depletion of soil due to the nature of shifting agriculture have forced the Bunaq to look for new farming land over a period of centuries.

Political factors and governmental ventures have also affected modern Bunaq settlement patterns. Ongoing political turmoil and upheaval from before the Portuguese era and continuing today has caused significant population displacements. The position of the Bunaq on the frontier between separate colonies and later nation states, has exacerbated population movements, with successive waves of Bunaq people crossing the border between East and West Timor in search of asylum from conflict (Schapper

---

[1] Land in Indonesia is officially divided into five levels of administration: province (*provinsi*), regency (*kabupaten*), sub-district (*kecamatan*), village grouping (*desa*), and village (*kampung*). Land in East Timor is officially divided into four levels of administration: district (*distrito*), sub-district (*subdistrito*), village grouping (*suco*), and village (*aldeia*).

1.3 Historical setting: Extent and dispersal of the Bunaq

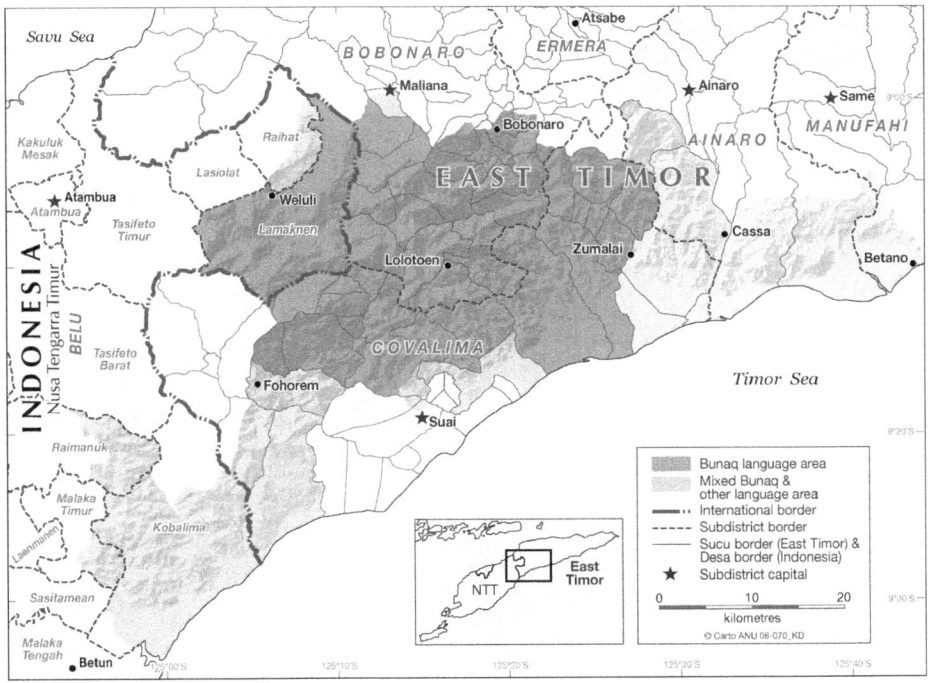

Map 1.3: The geographical extent of the Bunaq-speaking people.

2011a: 30–36). Isolated communities have also been drawn down from the mountains into the region of newly constructed roads, variously, by convenience and by the compulsion of administrators seeking greater access to the populace. Other villages have been relocated to entirely new areas as part of government agricultural development projects.

The extent and dispersal of Bunaq-speaking villages in central Timor are outlined in the following sections. The information presented in this section stems largely from my own survey work on the Bunaq area (see §1.11 on this).

1.3.1 Bunaq in West Timor

In West Timor the Bunaq are located in the Belu regency of Nusa Tenggara Timur province in Indonesia.[2] In the north of Belu, the Bunaq occupy the whole of the Lamaknen sub-district and a small neighbouring area of the Raihat sub-district (Map 1.4). In the

---

[2] In 2012, the southern part of Belu was carved off and made into its own *kabupaten* 'regency'. At the same time, Lamaknen was divided into Lamaknen and Lamaknen Selatan. Here I maintain the traditional names for consistency with the maps, which were drawn in 2009.

Map 1.4: Bunaq villages in Lamaknen and Raihat.

south of Belu the Bunaq occupy a number of settlements of the Kobalima, Malaka Timur, and Raimanuk sub-districts (Map 1.5). Both the Bunaq populations in West Timor have their origins in East Timor.

1.3.1.1 Bunaq in northern Belu

According to their own oral histories, the Bunaq in Lamaknen and Raihat came to the area from somewhere around Bobonaro in the remote past. When they arrived, they found a pre-existing Austronesian people, either Tetun or an Uab Meto group depending on the particular account; they mixed freely with them, gradually absorbing them over time. This view of the past is supported by the many village names in Lamaknen and Raihat which have at least partial Austronesian etymologies: e.g., Duarato > Malay *dua dato* 'two kings', Weluli > Tetun *we luli* 'sacred water'.

Map 1.5: Bunaq villages in southern Belu (West Timor) and southwestern Cobalima (East Timor).

Recent conflict has brought several additional waves of Bunaq from East Timor to Lamaknen and Raihat (Schapper 2011a: 34–36). At the end of World War II, Bunaq people fearing reprisals due to their support for the Japanese arrived in Lamaknen from Lebos and established the village of Lakus which still today maintains distinct elements of a northeast dialect. More refugees arrived in 1975 when the Indonesian army moved into East Timor. Fighting destroyed whole villages in Lamaknen: Claudine Friedberg (pers. comm.) reports that her field site, the village of Abis, had ceased to exist when she returned to Lamaknen after 1975. In 1999, following the vote for independence in East Timor, many more refugees arrived in Lamaknen and Raihat and set up rambling bush huts along the roadsides, many of which remain to this day.

1.3.1.2 Bunaq in southern Belu

In southern Belu, individual Bunaq villages are scattered amongst a majority Tetun population (Map 1.5). At the western extreme of the Bunaq area are Haroe and Welaus (noted by Woertelboer 1955: 172), while to the north are the very isolated villages of Rainawe and Raqakfao. Moving east, Bunaq villages are strung out along the road right up to the *desa* of Alas and Alas Selatan on the border with East Timor.

With one exception, the Bunaq villages in southern Belu have their origins in the Bunaq region of Maukatar north of Suai in East Timor. This area, known as the Maukatar enclave, was subject to ongoing border disputes between the Portuguese and Dutch colonial administrations. In 1860, the enclave was recognised as part of the Dutch territory in Timor.[3] However, in 1904, it was agreed in principle that the enclave would be ceded to Portugal in exchange for other lands (Sowash 1948). Following the 1904 agreement, disputes continued over the demarcation of borders, and in 1911 when Portuguese troops moved into Maukatar, they were met by Dutch forces. Clashes continued throughout 1911, before the Dutch agreed to withdraw as per the agreement of 1904. During the fighting of 1911 and following the ceding of the enclave to Portugal, some 5,000 of the population of Maukatar, mostly Bunaq, decamped to Dutch Timor, in what is now southern Belu (Schapper 2011a: 32–34).

The Bunaq in southern Belu proudly declare themselves the first refugees from East Timor to West Timor and trace themselves back to particular villages in Maukatar. For instance, the Bunaq in Raqakfao trace their origins to Fatuloro in Maukatar and those in Sukabesikun to Belekasak in Maukatar. As in Lamaknen, each of these Bunaq settlements has seen new additions from East Timor during the upheavals of 1975 and 1999.

The village of Namfalus is exceptional in that the Bunaq people here originate from the area of Bobonaro, from where they fled fighting during the Japanese occupation in World War II (discussed in §1.3.2.2). The Bunaq dialect spoken in Namfalus has characteristics which are consistent with Bobonaro Bunaq, but has also been significantly affected by the Maukatar variety of Bunaq that is spoken by the majority.

1.3.2 Bunaq in East Timor

1.3.2.1 Bunaq in Bobonaro and Zumalai

The Bunaq-speaking area in the highlands of the Bobonaro subdistrict and Zumalai, the eastern part of the Cobalima subdistrict, is the probable Bunaq homeland. It is here that we find place names with Bunaq etymologies, e.g., Odelgomo < *odel*

---

[3] The borders of the Maukatar enclave were defined with reference to local, and in particular Bunaq, states. The Dutch claimed Maukatar was theirs on the grounds that it was a part of the Dutch state Lakmaras, in modern day Lamaknen, and was joined by that state to other Dutch territories. The Portuguese, however, claimed that Lakmaras had been taken over since 1859 by the Portuguese state of Lamakhitu, from modern day Bobonaro.

'monkey', *gomo* 'owner'; Mapelai < *mape* 'eagle', *lai* 'set'; and Zoilpoq < *zoil* 'k.o. tree, *Alstonia scholaris*', *poq* 'holy'.

The highlands of Bobonaro and Zumalai are a region of dense settlement and significant land pressure. They have been the source of much of the Bunaq expansion into lower areas which were traditionally uninhabited, with most lowland villages tracing themselves back to a particular upland village. For example, the upland village of Tapo is the origin of the lowland village Tapomemo, situated on the alluvial plains south and east of Maliana.

Similarly, Bunaq villages in the lowland areas of the Zumalai district were all founded as offshoots from upland villages. As in the northwest corner, upland placenames reoccur in lowland areas: for example, Zulotas (lit., 'civet village') has given rise to a twin just north of Zumalai town called Zulokota (lit., 'civet city'). The villages along the south coast east of Zumalai town were established during the Indonesian period with whole villages brought south to the road on the promise of modern housing.

Connections between old and new villages often run deep. For instance, inhabitants of Beco, a village situated on the coastal plain east of Suai, identify themselves as coming from Teda, an upland village not far from Lolotoen. Yet, they had never been to Teda themselves and both they themselves and their parents were born in Beco.[4]

1.3.2.2 Bunaq in western Covalima

In the western part of the Covalima sub-district, the Bunaq people meet the Tetun Fehan or 'lowland Tetun'. Bunaq people dominate the region of the old Maukatar enclave located north of Fohorem (Map 1.5), while to the west and south of the enclave the Tetun are in the majority. Within the former Maukatar enclave, however, placenames indicate a Tetun past for many modern-day Bunaq villages, such as the *sucos* Fatululik < Tetun *fatu* 'stone' *lulik* 'holy', and Datotolu < Tetun *dato* 'nobleman' *tolu* 'three'.

South of Fohorem, Bunaq villages are interwoven with Tetun villages. This Bunaq corridor stretches southwest to the border and coastal area. The Bunaq villages in the lower lands nearer to the border and the coast were resettled by the Indonesian administration from northern Cobalima *sucos* such as Fatululik and Taroman. As part of a program to develop rice agriculture in Timor, the villagers were moved down to the flatter land, provided with houses, and taught wet rice cultivation.

The villages immediately south of Fohorem, such as Wetearba and Salele, are populated by Bunaq people speaking a dialect consistent with that of the Bobonaro region. These villages were established following a massive collective flight from

---

4 Note that <c> in East Timorese place names reflects Portuguese orthography for [k]. Thus, we find the subdistrict <Covalima> in the south eastern corner of East Timor and the adjacent *kecamatan* <Kobalima> on the Indonesian side of the border. The name means 'five lime pouches' in Tetun.

the Japanese army and comprise the most significant displacement of Bunaq dating from World War II. The Japanese had invaded Timor on 20 February 1942 and within days had overwhelmed the small force of Australian and Dutch troops. Some of these managed to evade capture and withdrew into the mountains, from where they waged a guerrilla campaign against the Japanese. The guerrillas spent much of their time in the Bobonaro area and were at different times based in Bobonaro town and Lolotoen. In August 1942, the Japanese carried out a series of reprisals against the population of East Timor who had assisted the guerrillas, with tens of thousands believed to have been killed and many others displaced as in the case of these Bunaq who settled south of Fohorem.

1.3.2.3 Bunaq in Ainaro and Manufahi

To the east of Zumalai, a corridor of Bunaq villages stretches across the southern areas of the subdistrict of Ainaro to Manufahi (Map 1.6). In this area, the Bunaq have intermingled significantly with the Mambae, the Austronesian group native to the area. The Bunaq here are typically bilingual in Mambae and their varieties of Bunaq show the impact of mixing with Mambae. They have also shifted to an entirely patrilineal form of descent, like that of the Mambae.

In Ainaro, the Bunaq occupy the whole of the *suco* of Maununo. Originally Maununo contained three discrete villages, Aileu, Mamalau, and Mausuka. However, during the Indonesian era the villages were brought together to occupy the single location they do today. To the south of Maununo, Bunaq speakers are spread throughout the *suco* of Cassa. There are no apparent differences in the Bunaq spoken in Maununo and Cassa. There are conflicting accounts of the origins of the Bunaq of Maununo and the Cassa group, with some traditions claiming the Bunaq to be the original inhabitants and others that they arrived later. Place names strongly suggest that the Bunaq here moved into an area with a pre-existing Austronesian population. In the Bobonaro region, the Bunaq know Cassa as 'Cassa-Aiasa', reflecting what they see as the origin of the Cassa Bunaq group, i.e., Aiasa, a Bunaq village just west of Bobonaro town.

There is another Bunaq group in Cassa located in two villages, Sivil and Lailima, which are strung along the road south of Ainaro town amongst Mambae settlements. The people of Sivil and Lailima were moved down from the Zumalai area during the Indonesian period. The Bunaq dialect spoken in Sivil and Lailima is still strongly northeast in flavour, consistent with a recent move from Zumalai.

East of Cassa, there are two villages of Bunaq speakers amongst the sea of Mambae villages in the *suco* Leolima, Hutseo and its offspring of the Indonesian period, Hutseo Dua 'Hutseo II'. Further east again, the entire *suco* of Fohoailiku in the southeast of Ainaro is Bunaq. The Hutseo and the Fohoailiku Bunaq claim to have fled from the western part of Ainaro due to a dispute between Bunaq groups there sometime in the Portuguese era. These claims are consistent with the dialectal evidence which shows a set of features in common with Maununo and Cassa Bunaq.

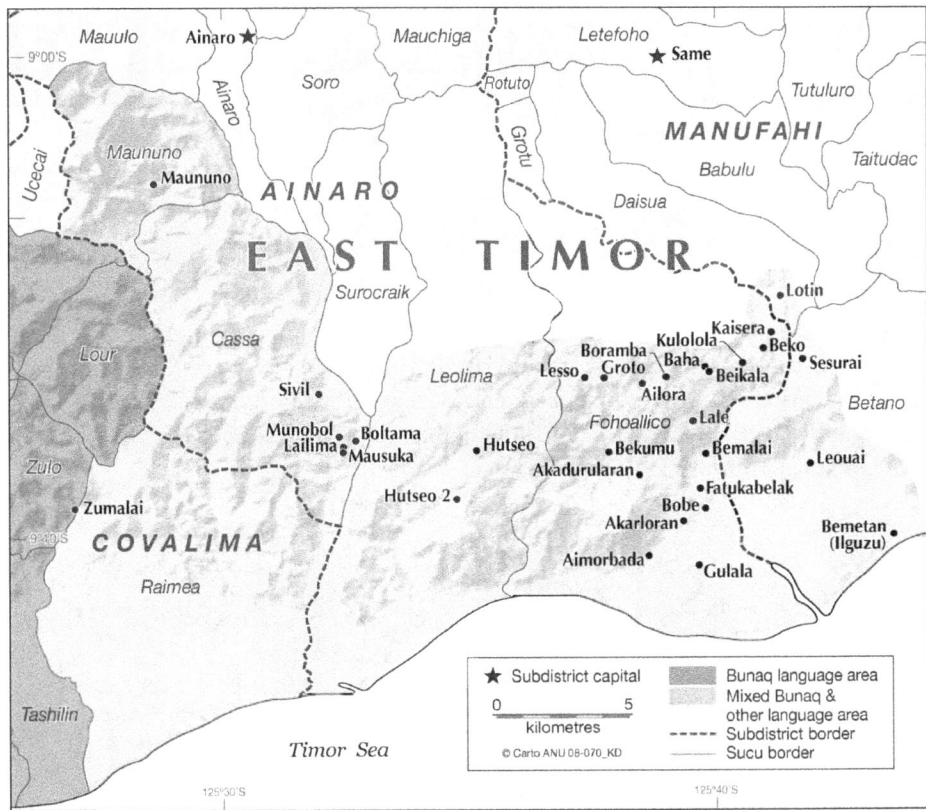

Map 1.6: Bunaq villages in Ainaro and Manufahi.

In Manufahi there are four Bunaq villages scattered along the road south of the main town, Same. The oldest Bunaq village in this area is Lotin. The Bunaq are thought to have moved into the Lotin area sometime in the 1800s from the Bobonaro region following a dispute over the purchase of a bride (Pyone Thu pers. comm.). Following the Boaventura rebellion[5] the Portuguese resettled some of the Lotin Bunaq in lower lands. The modern village of Lotin is some kilometres south of the original village and two further villages, Il Guzu (lit. 'black water' in Bunaq, also calqued in Mambae as Bemetan 'black water') and Leoai, were established for the Lotin Bunaq close to the coast. The three villages share a dialect distinct from all other Bunaq dialects (§1.5).

---

5 Late in 1911, a Manufahi king known as Boaventura had united many of the kingdoms in central and western East Timor in revolt against what was seen as an oppressive and exploitative colonial power. The rebellion came to an end in August 1912. Surrounded and besieged on a mountain top, Boaventura led an unsuccessful breakout following which most of his estimated three thousand supporters were rounded up and slaughtered.

The fourth Bunaq settlement is Sesurai, located on the road between Lotin and Leoai. According to tradition, the Sesurai Bunaq fled from the Zumalai area to Manufahi during the upheavals of the Boaventura revolution. The dialect of Bunaq spoken in Sesurai has characteristics consistent with the Zumalai dialect, but has taken on some traits of Lotin Bunaq.

1.3.3 The Bunaq homeland

Based on the placename distributions, I infer that the Bunaq homeland was likely located in the area of today's central-eastern Bobonaro and northeastern Covalima subdistricts. In this area, placenames have exclusively Bunaq etymologies (see §1.3.2.1). The core Bunaq area that is defined by these placenames is indicated with hatching on Map 1.7.

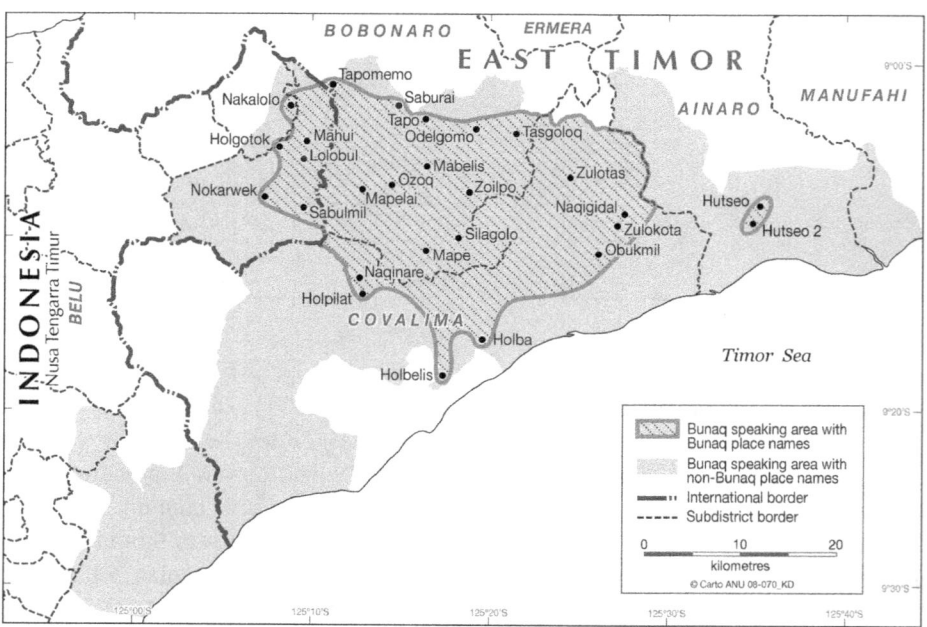

Map 1.7: The dispersal of village names with transparent Bunaq versus Austronesian etymologies.

Outside the core area, we find Bunaq villages with Bunaq placenames alongside Bunaq villages with Austronesian placenames (area defined by grey line on Map 1.7). Bunaq placenames increasingly give way to non-Bunaq ones until all Bunaq villages have non-Bunaq names (grey shaded area). This dispersal of placenames strongly points to the "homeland" of the Bunaq as being in central-eastern Bobonaro and northeastern

Covalima – the geographical centre of the modern Bunaq-speaking area. If the Bunaq were immigrants to the core area, we would expect to find traces of the previous populations left behind in placenames, as we do outside the core.

See Schapper (2011b) for further argumentation about the homeland of Bunaq speakers.

1.4 Sociolinguistic setting: numbers, vitality, and bilingualism

There are roughly 85,000 native speakers of the Bunaq language. Of these, approximately 20,000 are located in Belu province of West Timor. Here, the greatest concentration of speakers, around 16,000 people, is in Lamaknen and the neighbouring Bunaq-speaking villages of southern Raihat (Badan Pusat Statistik Kabupaten Belu 2019). The remaining 4,000 are found in scattered villages in southern Belu (Badan Pusat Statistik Kabupaten Malaka 2019).[6] In the Belunese capital, Atambua, there is also a sizeable Bunaq population based in the southeastern suburb of Fatobenao, but their number is not known. In East Timor, there are approximately 65,000 speakers of Bunaq. Dili also boasts a sizeable community of some 3,000 Bunaq speakers. Table 1.1 presents the number of Bunaq speakers per district taken from the 2020 census figures.

Table 1.1: Bunaq speakers in East Timor (General Directorate of Statistics 2020).

Ainaro	4,703
Bobonaro	24,427
Covalima	31,296
Manufahi	795
Dili	3,136
Other districts	304
Total	64,661

In West Timor, the Bunaq language is vulnerable; significant shift is apparent in the current parent and child generation. Whilst still learnt by many children in the villages in Lamaknen and Raihat, Bunaq is rapidly losing ground to Indonesian, the national language, and to local varieties of Malay. Fifteen years ago, when I started my fieldwork on Bunaq, children were raised bilingual in Bunaq and Malay, switching freely between the two in social interaction with one another. Today, those children

---

6 Note that these figures are population statistics for traditionally Bunaq-speaking villages. In the past, it was reasonable to assume that population size in these places would largely correspond to speaker population size. However, as language shift progresses, the correspondence between the two figures will decline.

are having children of their own, many of whom have only passive competence in Bunaq. In Raihat, Bunaq speakers are also competent in the variety of Tetun Terik spoken in the neighbouring villages, while in Lamaknen most older people have some competence in Tetun. In southern Belu, the shift from Bunaq is more advanced than in Lamaknen. In the eastern villages, such as Haroe and Welaus, many children still acquire the Bunaq language, but in the remaining villages to the east, Bunaq is weak, having lost significant ground to Tetun Terik, the majority language in the region, and Indonesian, the national language. Similarly, in Atambua, the children of Bunaq speakers are rarely full speakers of Bunaq; they are typically most comfortable with Indonesian/Malay and use that language amongst themselves, although they may speak to or be spoken to by their parents in Bunaq.

In East Timor, Bunaq remains vital in the villages of Bobonaro and the Covalima districts. Bilingualism with Tetun Dili, the lingua franca of East Timor, has increased since its pronouncement as an official language along with Portuguese in 2002. But whilst great emphasis is placed upon the acquisition of Tetun Dili as the language of advantage and employment, the vitality of Bunaq does not appear to have been greatly affected. In Ainaro and Manufahi, Bunaq people speak Mambae in addition to Tetun Dili, and their variety of Bunaq shows signs of being significantly influenced by Mambae. Bunaq is strong in Ainaro where there are sizeable groups of Bunaq people, but in Manufahi the switch to Mambae appears to be almost complete with no children below the age of 15 speaking the language in my observation.

1.5 Bunaq dialects

There are a great many features of phonology and lexicon which are not spread uniformly across the Bunaq-speaking area. Among the many criss-crossing isoglosses, five main dialect areas can be distinguished. Their extent is illustrated in Map 1.8.

The dialect areas are:
i. Southwest – a phonologically conservative dialect region extending from Maukatar, just north of Fohorem in East Timor to southern Belu;
ii. Lamaknen – a dialect phonologically and lexically intermediate between the South and the Northeast, sharing features in common with each, but also showing patterns distinct from both;
iii. Northeast – largest dialect, spreading from Maliana east to Bobonaro and down to Zumalai, phonologically most radical;
iv. Ainaro – a dialect characterised by significant Mambae influence, phonologically similar to, but not as advanced in the application of the key sound changes characterising the Northeast dialect;
v. Manufahi – smallest dialect, characterised by radically different lexicon and relatively conservative phonology, features in common with Ainaro due to shared Mambae influence.

1.5 Bunaq dialects

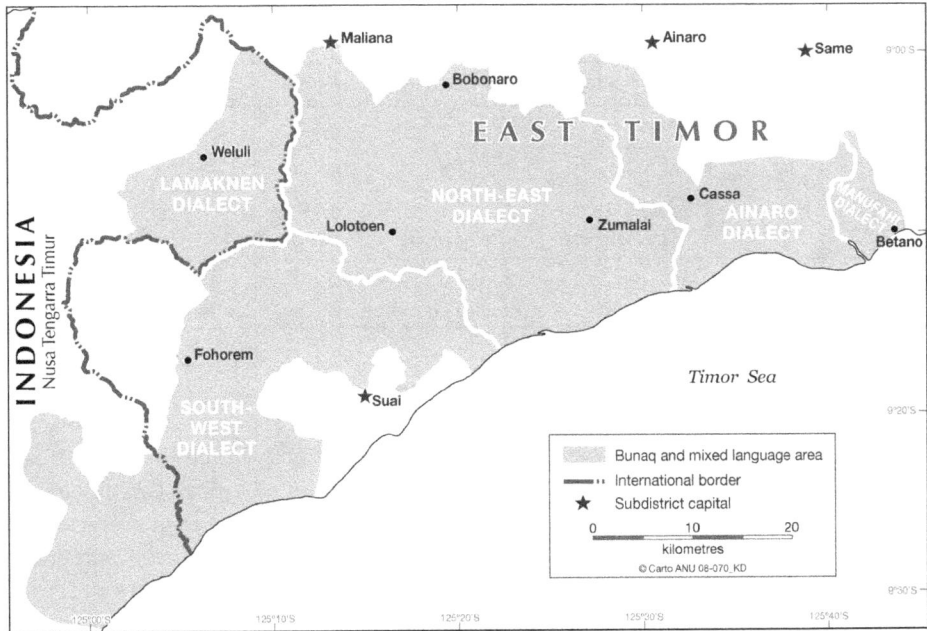

Map 1.8: The major Bunaq dialect areas.

A few examples illustrating the dialect divisions on phonological grounds are provided in Table 1.2. We see that the Southwest and Manufahi dialects preserve *d and *t with that value in all environments. Lamaknen has *d changing to *r* initially and medially, whereas in the Northeast *r* is only an allophone of *d* medially. The Northeast affricates *t before all high vowels both initially and medially. Lamaknen and Ainaro show some limited affrication of initial *t before *i*, with Lamaknen further showing an incipient merger of *tʃ* with *s*. Loss of *w and glottalization of final *r together characterise the three eastern dialects, with subsequent loss of the glottal phoneme in Ainaro and Manufahi. Sporadic loss of initial *h is found in the Northeast and Ainaro dialects. The loss of *ʔ and *w in Ainaro and Manufahi is probably due to the influence of Southern Mambae, which lacks both phonemes.

Table 1.2: Phonological characteristics of Bunaq dialects.

proto-Bunaq	Southwest	Lamaknen	Northeast	Ainaro	Manufahi
*d	d	d ~ r / #_ r / elsewhere	d / #_ r / elsewhere	d / #_ d ~ r / elsewhere	d
*r (final only)	r	d ~ r / #_ r ~ l / elsewhere	ʔ / _# l / elsewhere	ʔ / _# l / elsewhere	ʔ / _# l / elsewhere

Table 1.2 (continued)

proto-Bunaq	Southwest	Lamaknen	Northeast	Ainaro	Manufahi
*ʔ	ʔ	ʔ	ʔ	Ø	Ø
*h	h	h	h ~ Ø / #_	h ~ Ø / #_	h
*t	t	tʃ ~ s / #_i t / elsewhere	tʃ / _ i, u t / elsewhere	tʃ ~ t / #_i t / elsewhere	t
*w	w	w	Ø ~ u / #_ Ø ~ b / elsewhere	Ø ~ u / #_ Ø ~ b / elsewhere	Ø ~ u / #_ Ø ~ b / elsewhere

A prominent difference in phonology between western and eastern dialects of Bunaq is the phonemic contrast between aspirated and unaspirated voiceless stops, /p, pʰ, t, tʰ, k, kʰ/. Across the eastern dialect regions, Bunaq speech is characterised by significant bursts of breath with the release of aspirated stops. This is often a noticeable feature of the speech of Bunaq people from this dialect region even when speaking Tetun Dili. Whilst completely absent in Lamaknen, the phonemic aspiration contrast gradually declines in the Southwest Bunaq region as one moves west into Indonesian West Timor. In Table 1.3 I present some minimal pairs of aspirated and unaspirated voiceless plosives on the basis of Bunaq Bobonaro.

Table 1.3: (Near-)minimal pairs for aspirated versus unaspirated voiceless stop phonemes in Bunaq Bobonaro.

Aspirated		Unaspirated	
pʰi	'trap'	pi	'riverstone, pebble'
pʰit	'throat'	pit	'roll (sth.) over'
pʰol	'stack up, send'	pol	'hand of bananas'
tʰaʔ	'axe'	taʔ	'still, yet'
etʰen	'right-hand'	eten	'want'
otʰa	'stab you'	ota	'over there'
kʰali	'testicle'	kali	'scatter, spread'
kʰoiʔ	'little bit'	koi	'guava'

A phonemic aspiration contrast is not found in any of Bunaq's neighbours or relatives. The contrast in the eastern Bunaq dialects is thus unusual. It remains for future research to determine its origins.

A sample of the many lexical features illustrating the dialect divisions is provided in Table 1.4. The maximal differentiation pattern is illustrated by 'big' with each of the dialect areas having a distinct lexeme. The Southwest is distinct from all other dialects in having two inalienably possessed nouns -*ip* 'wife' and -*enen* 'husband'; the remaining areas simply use 'woman' and 'man' for these concepts. For 'sleep' the Northeast and Ainaro dialects have innovative *malat*, while the Southwest, Lamaknen and Manufahi dialects have *tier* or *tfier*. By contrast, for 'stand', the Southwest and Lamaknen have innovative *duʔat* < *du-huʔat* 'REFL-erect', while Northeast *net*ʰ 'stand' in the other dialects has widespread cognates in related languages. Ainaro and Manufahi share the borrowing *boi* 'not want' from Mambae, while only the Ainaro dialect has borrowed *au* 'I' from Mambae. Both the Ainaro and Manufahi dialects have innovated lexemes for 'not exist', the former from *haziʔ* 'disappear', the latter from *muel* 'be thin'. Finally, Manufahi is distinct from all other dialects in its lexeme for 'exist'.

Table 1.4: Some lexical characteristics of Bunaq dialects.

	Southwest	Lamaknen	Northeast	Ainaro	Manufahi
'big'	*boʔal*	*masak*	*tʰia, masaʔ*	*gemel*	*kaman*
'wife'	*-ip*	*pana*	*pʰana*	*pʰana*	*pʰana*
'husband'	*-enen*	*mone*	*mone*	*mone*	*mone*
'sleep'	*tier*	*tfier*	*malatʰ*	*malatʰ*	*tier*
'stand'	*duʔat*	*duʔat*	*netʰ*	*netʰ*	*netʰ*
'play'	*bukuʔ*	*bukuʔ*	*kʰisaʔ, bukʰuʔ*	*bukʰu*	*neun*
'not want'	*tiaʔ*	*tfiaʔ*	*piaʔ*	*boi*	*boi*
'I'	*neto*	*neto*	*neto*	*au*	*neto*
'not exist'	*hobel*	*hobel*	*hobel*	*hazi*	*muel*
'exist'	*hati*	*hati*	*atfi*	*hati*	*hono*

1.6 Genealogical affiliations

Bunaq is a member of the Timor-Alor-Pantar (TAP) language family. This family is, in turn, a subgroup of the Greater West Bomberai (GWB) family. These languages have no proven genealogical relations to other Papuan languages, though several hypotheses exist in the literature. Bunaq's place in the TAP family is treated in §1.6.1. The wider affiliations of the TAP family are reviewed in §1.6.2.

1.6.1 Low-level affiliations

The Timor-Alor-Pantar family comprises around 25 languages spoken by an estimated 300,000 people in southeastern Indonesia and East Timor (Map 1.9). Members of the family dominate on the islands of Alor, Pantar, and the straits in between. Other members are found interspersed among Austronesian languages on the islands of Timor and Kisar. On Timor, there are four TAP languages: Bunaq straddling the border between West and East Timor, and Makasae, Makalero, and Fataluku occupying a contiguous region at the eastern tip of the island. Close by to the north, again in Indonesia, Oirata is a TAP language spoken on Kisar, an island dominated by the Austronesian language Meher. For a long time, many scholars assumed from the geographical proximity of the TAP languages that they must be related (e.g., Greenberg 1971, Stokhof 1975: 22–24). However, it was only recently, with the publication of Schapper, Huber, and van Engelenhoven (2014), that the relatedness of the TAP languages was demonstrated using the comparative method.

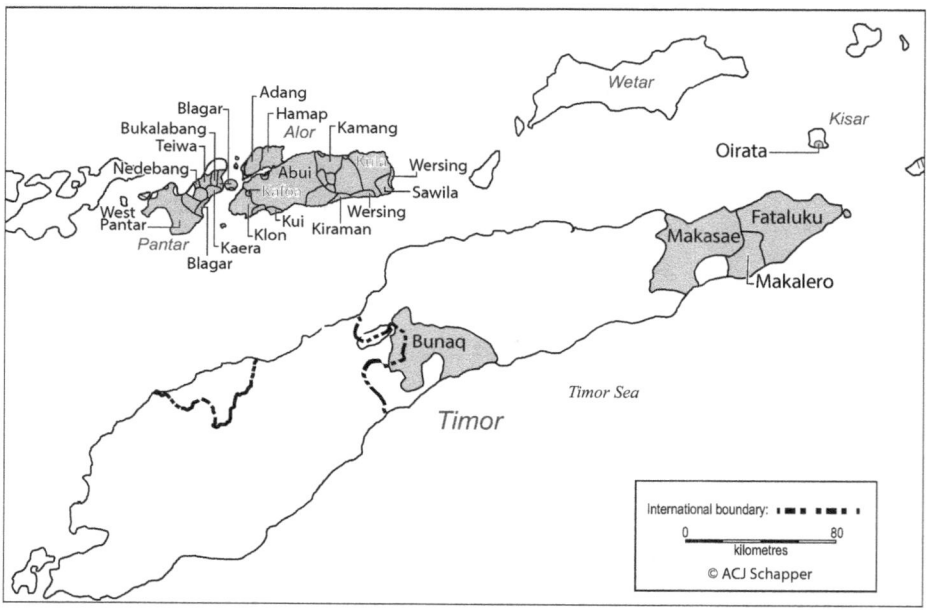

Map 1.9: The languages of the Timor-Alor-Pantar family.

The precise place of Bunaq in the TAP family remains unclear. The two contiguous groups of TAP languages form two clearly defined subgroups, the Alor-Pantar subgroup and the Eastern Timor subgroup. Based on current knowledge of the family, there are two places that Bunaq could fit in the family tree, as set out in Figure 1.1.

The first possibility sees Bunaq subgrouping together with the East Timor languages. Schapper, Huber, and van Engelenhoven (2014) posited this subgrouping, partly because they were comparing the results of separate reconstructive work on the Timor languages (Schapper, Huber, and van Engelenhoven 2012), and on the AP languages (Holton et al. 2012). They identified just one sound change which could be

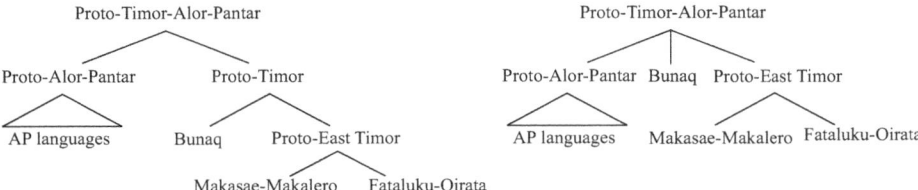

Figure 1.1: Tree diagrams of the possible relationship of the Timor-Alor-Pantar languages.

taken to characterise a Timor subgroup: medial *k > ʔ shared by Bunaq and Proto-East Timor, but not Proto-Alor-Pantar (e.g., PTAP *kaku 'younger sibling' > Bunaq kauʔ 'younger sibling', Proto-East Timor *kaʔu > Makalero kaʔu 'younger, junior relative', Proto-Alor-Pantar *kaku > Blagar kaku 'sibling of same gender, friend', Reta kaku 'friend', Kamang -kak 'younger relative of the same generation', Wersing kaku, Sawila ka:ku 'younger sibling'). If one does not attribute subgrouping value to comparisons of this kind and to this sound change (and it is not exceptionless), then Bunaq must be regarded as constituting its own primary subgroup within the TAP family. This is the view put forward recently by Schapper (2020a) and Usher and Schapper (forthcoming).

1.6.2 High-level affiliations

The Timor-Alor-Pantar languages have a chequered history of classification. Being spoken several hundred kilometres from New Guinea, where most other Papuan languages are found, meant that there were no obvious candidates for historical comparison.

Cowan (1957/58) posited a large 'West Papuan' family taking in most languages of the Bird's Head of New Guinea. In Cowan (1963, 1965) he added Bunaq, Oirata, and Makasae, observing that their closest relatives seemed to be the South Bird's Head languages. Capell (1975: 677–681) maintained Cowan's West Papuan family, but Capell's article is appended with a hasty note from the editor, Stephen Wurm, pointing the reader to the reclassification of TAP languages as part of the newly posited 'Trans-New Guinea' family made in Voorhoeve's (1975) article of the same volume. To date, neither link to the essentially putative West Papuan or Trans-New Guinea families has been demonstrated.

Since 1975, multiple authors have compared lower-level groups in New Guinea to the TAP languages. On the basis of lexicon, Stokhof (1975) suggested a relationship between Alor-Pantar languages and languages of the South Bird's Head of New Guinea. Hull (2004) looked for a TAP relationship to other Papuan languages using the available wordlists for the languages of West Bomberai, South Bird's Head, Mor, and Tanahmerah. Although unsystematic in his comparison and with no attempt to establish sound correspondences, Hull observed particular lexical similarities between TAP and the West Bomberai languages, concluding: 'All that can be said with any certainty is that the matches [to Timor Papuan languages] are much more common with the Onin-Bomberai zone [i.e., West Bomberai languages] than with the South Bird's Head' (Hull 2004: 52). Recently, Holton and Robinson (2014) and Cottet (2015) have echoed Hull's observations, but without the addition of data.

Today the TAP languages are considered to be related to the three West Bomberai languages, Iha, Mbaham, and Kalamang (Map 1.10). Usher and Schapper (forthcoming) demonstrate the link and name the group the Greater West Bomberai family. Building on earlier work reconstructing relevant subgroups (Usher and Schapper 2018; Schapper, Huber, and van Engelenhoven 2012, 2014), they present a reconstruction of around 50 Proto-Greater West Bomberai (PGWB) lexemes and pronominal paradigms, based on a set of largely regular sound correspondences built up subgroup by

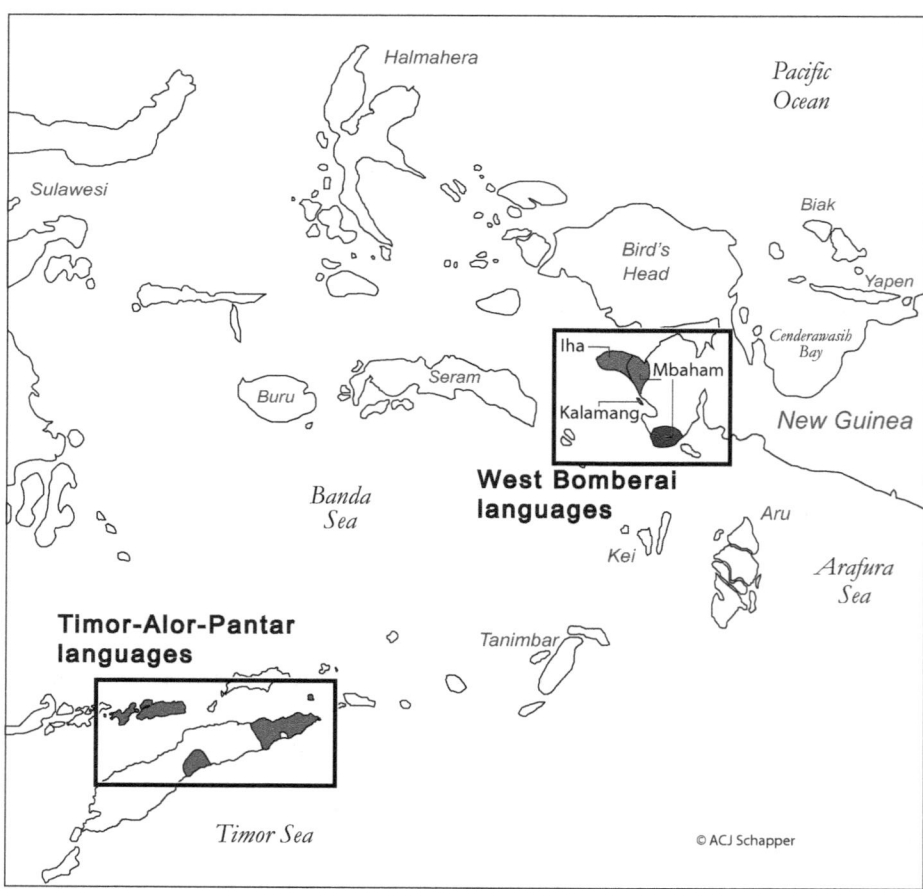

Map 1.10: The Greater West Bomberai languages.

subgroup. Schapper (2020a: 15–16) adds a verbal plural number suffix and a pronominal dual suffix to the PGWB reconstructions, while Schapper (forthcoming) posits a few more lexical reconstructions to PGWB.

Following Usher and Schapper (forthcoming), the Greater West Bomberai family divides into three primary subgroups, as presented in Figure 1.2, of which Timor-Alor-Pantar languages form one.

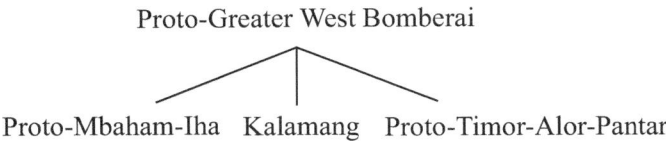

Figure 1.2: Tree diagram of the Greater West Bomberai languages.

This classification implies that PGWB was originally spoken in the vicinity of the Bomberai Peninsula and that the TAP languages were the result of a migration out of, rather than into, New Guinea. The idea of a period of Papuan expansion is at odds with traditional models of population history in New Guinea and, potentially, has radical repercussions for our view of the prehistory of the region. It remains for future research to determine whether the Greater West Bomberai languages are part of the large, but still basically conjectural Trans-New Guinea macro-family.

1.7 Borrowing and influence

Capell (1975) notes that Austronesian loanwords are very common in Papuan languages across eastern Indonesia. The long history of proximity and engagement between speakers of Papuan and Austronesian languages, as well as the centuries of inter-island trade networks and interaction with traders from the Moluccas, Sulawesi, and Java, often using Malay as a lingua franca, have contributed to extensive cross-fertilization of language forms (Bellwood 1998; McWilliam 2007).

In Bunaq, borrowing and adaptation from Austronesian language and society pervades every aspect of the language. It is so extensive that it led Berthe (1959, 1963) to describe Bunaq as being of "mixed" Papuan-Austronesian origin. The sheer number of foreign words and constructions in Bunaq points not merely to millennia of Austronesian contact and multilingualism on the part of the Bunaq, but also to their readiness to borrow linguistic forms from other languages (Schapper 2011a: 36–47).

In Bunaq, lexical items borrowed from Austronesian account for over 30% of the modern lexicon. This includes many supposedly borrowing-resistant items of so-called "core vocabulary"; on a basic 200-item Swadesh wordlist, 40 items are Austronesian in origin.

There are at least two layers of borrowing from Austronesian languages that can be distinguished in Bunaq: (i) borrowings from surrounding Austronesian languages of the Central Timor subgroup (§1.7.1) and (ii) borrowings from Tetun (§1.7.2). It is not always possible to determine which layer a borrowing comes from when it is found in both sets of languages and displays no telling sound changes (e.g., Bunaq *ama* 'father' could be borrowed from any of its neighbours, cf. Kemak, Mambae, Tetun *ama* 'father' < PMP *ama 'father'). In §1.7.3, I discuss a third layer of Austronesian borrowings from unknown sources.

1.7.1 Borrowings from Central Timor

Bunaq has a small but noticeable layer of borrowings from its Austronesian neighbours of the Central Timor subgroup, Kemak, Mambae, Tokodede, and Welaun, or their forerunners. Table 1.5 lists a number of these items. See Berthe (1963) for more. Most of the borrowings that I have identified are from Kemak and to a lesser extent Mambae. This is not a surprising finding given that the expansive northern border of the Bunaq-speaking area runs the length of the Kemak-speaking area.

Table 1.5: Borrowings from Central Timor languages.

Bunaq		Central Timor	
baba	'maternal uncle'	Kemak *baba*, Welaun *baba*	'maternal uncle'
betu	'kick'	Kemak *betu*	'kick'
botus	'meet'	Kemak *botus*	'meet'
bubun	'moist, damp'	Kemak *bubu*	'damp, partly dry'
doʔ	'cut off'	Kemak *doo*, Mambae *do*	'cut, hack, slice'
haru	'shirt, clothes'	Kemak, Mambae *haru*	'clothes'
hasa	'clean, clear out'	Kemak *hasa*	'wash'
huan	'heart'	Kemak *huan*	'heart'
hui	'wild'	Kemak *huii*, Mambae *hui*	'wild'
keleʔ	'frog'	Kemak *kere*	'frog'
le	'light'	Mambae *le ~ lel*	'sun'
ligi	'sleepless'	Kemak *bligi*	'sleepy'
lihur	'thousand'	Kemak *rihur*	'thousand'
lose	'grind'	Kemak *rose*	'rub'

Table 1.5 (continued)

Bunaq		Central Timor	
loi	'good'	Kemak *mloi* Tokodede *bloi*	'good'
lokon	'lake, pond'	Kemak *lokon*	'lake, pool, puddle'
lolo	'mountain'	Kemak *lolo*	'hilly'
lore	'fly, run very fast'	Kemak *lore*	'fly'
lulai	'move'	Mambae *lolai*	'walk'
matas	'old, elder'	Welaun *matas*	'old, adult'
meʔu	'kiss'	Tokodede *meku*	'kiss'
nagi	'swim'	Kemak *nagi*	'swim'
nenuʔ	'greater morinda'	Kemak *nenuʔ*	'greater morinda'
selu	'weave'	Kemak *seru*	'weave'
si	'meat'	Kemak *sii*, Mambae *si ~ sis*	'meat'
tahoʔ	'low cloud'	Kemak *tahoʔ*	'cloud, mist'
teʔa	'pray'	Kemak *teʔa*	'curse'
tiluʔ	'stay, rest'	Kemak *tiluʔ*	'play, rest'
to	'year'	Kemak *to*, Mambae *to ~ ton*	'year'
toek	'talk, tell'	Kemak *toek*	'speak, say'

The lexemes in Table 1.5 are found across all Bunaq dialects. This points to their being present in the proto-language – in other words, present in the Bunaq language before dialect differentiation took place. As such, proto-Bunaq would have had to have been spoken in an area that had intense contact with speakers of Kemak and Mambae, or at least where people were speaking the forerunners of these modern languages. The central-eastern area of Bobonaro and northeastern Covalima subdistricts fit precisely this profile, with Kemak and Mambae both close by, to the north and to the east, respectively. This accords with the placename evidence discussed in §1.3.3.

The borrowing between Papuan languages and Central Timor languages does not appear to have been uni-directional. Central Timor has several lexemes which appear to have been borrowed from Bunaq, a predecessor of Bunaq or a now extinct relative of Bunaq. Most notable are several kin terms that have PTAP and in some cases PGWB etymologies. These are set out in (2).

(2) a. Kemak *nana-* 'older sister' < Bunaq *nana* 'older sister' < PTAP *nana 'older sibling' (Makalero *nana*, Sawila *naːna* Wersing *-naŋ* 'older sibling', Abui *naːna*, Nedebang *-naŋ* 'older sibling') < PGWB *nana 'older sibling'.

b. Kemak *topor-* 'sister, female cousin (male speaking)', Mambae *topo* 'younger sister' < PTAP *tubur 'woman, sister' (Makasae *tufu* 'man's older sister, man's mother's sister's daughter, man's father's brother's daughter, man's father's sister's daughter', Makalero *tufur* 'sister, (female) cousin', Fataluku *tupur(u)* 'woman', Oirata *tuhur(u)* 'woman') < PGWB *tumbur 'female, woman'
c. Kemak *kaʔu* 'young (of a baby)', Mambae *kau* 'younger sibling' < PTAP *kaku 'younger sibling' (Bunaq *kauʔ* 'younger sibling', Makalero *kaʔu* 'younger, junior relative', Blagar *kaku* 'sibling of same gender, friend', Reta *kaku* 'friend', Wersing *kaku*, Sawila *kaːku* 'younger sibling')

Borrowings such as these suggest a complex early history of interaction between speakers of Papuan and Austronesian speakers in central Timor that remains to be to be unravelled.

1.7.2 Tetun borrowings and calques

For several centuries the Bunaq were under the ritual rulership of the Wehali kingdom, a Tetun-speaking group located on the south coast of modern-day West Timor. Prior to the establishment of the European colonies on Timor, the Tetun-speaking Wehali kingdom had risen to significance and its people dispersed northwards into the mountainous interior and along the south coast from their traditional base on the south-central coast (Fox 2003: 20–21; Francillon 1967; Therik 2004). Concomitant with the authority of this Tetun state was their ability to assert influence on other groups. The consequences of this are seen linguistically in the huge quantity of Tetun vocabulary present in the Bunaq lexicon.

Tetun words in Bunaq span all semantic domains of the lexicon. They include a large number of verbs and nouns. Examples of a few of the many Bunaq verbs with Tetun origins are given in Table 1.6. Amongst the examples given, verbs include reference to states, domestic and agricultural practices, and cognitive events.

Table 1.6: Sample of verbs borrowed from Tetun.

Bunaq		Tetun	
bali	'protect'	bali	'treat, heal'
baruʔ	'bored'	baruk	'anger, bored'
belo	'lap up, lick'	belo	'lick'
besik	'exact, precise'	besik	'be close'
bokul	'fat, healthy'	bokur	'fat'
hananu	'sing'	hananu	'sing'

Table 1.6 (continued)

Bunaq		Tetun	
dale	'speak, talk'	dale	'speak, talk'
daʔet	'cross over (river, road)'	daʔet	'pass from one side to another'
dari	'occur, happen'	dadi	'happen, succeed'
kabala	'wear around waist'	kabala	'wear around waist'
kaku	'move back and forth'	kaku	'shake'
koʔus	'cradle (of a child)'	koʔus	'be pregnant'
leʔu	'roll up'	leʔu	'roll'
lete	'step on top of'	lete	'to place oneself upon'
lolar	'prune, trim'	lolar	'prune'
lolok	'follow one after another'	lolok	'follow, pursue'
luku	'wash hair'	luku	'wash hair'
lumaʔ	'raise, look after (animal)'	lumak	'raise, look after (animal)'
mail	'bendy, malleable'	mail	'sag'
mamal	'soft'	mamar	'soft'
meak	'be reddish-brown'	meak	'rust'
meʔi	'dream'	mehi	'dream'
mout	'sink, submerge'	mout	'sink'
piar	'believe'	fiar	'believe'
punu	'war, fight'	funu	'war, fight'
saki	'slice open'	saki	'incise'
sasa	'separate, split up'	sasa	'separate'
seʔo	'sell'	seʔo	'sell'
soro	'mix'	soro	'mix'
sukit	'extract, remove'	sukit	'extract'
taka	'cover'	taka	'cover'
tane	'hold hands out'	tane	'beg, supplicate'
tara	'know'	tada	'know'
tekeʔ	'look at, examine'	ha-teke	'see'
toman	'accustomed, spoilt'	toman	'accustomed'
tun	'fall down, collapse'	tun	'descend, collapse'
tutan	'join, connect'	tutan	'increase, augment'
tutul	'carry on head'	tutur	'carry on head'

In Table 1.7 I list a small number of the very many Bunaq nouns with a Tetun source. These include items of modern material culture, insects and reptiles, plants, and body parts.

Table 1.7: Sample of nouns borrowed from Tetun.

Bunaq		Tetun	
barut	'candlenut, lamp from candlenut'	badut	'candlenut'
bakat	'rhizophore (plant)'	bakat	'rhizophore (plant)'
bebak	'crown of palm'	bebak	'crown of palm'
bereliku?	'bird sp.'	bereliku	'bird sp.'
bi?an	'plate'	bikan	'plate'
boek	'shrimp, prawn (in river)'	boek	'shrimp, prawn'
dama	'bow'	rama	'bow'
dero?	'lime'	delok	'lime'
heran	'pandanus'	hedan	'pandanus'
keboko?	'caterpillar'	kebeko	'caterpillar'
kakibat	'banyan tree'	kakibat	'banyan tree'
labarain	'spider'	labadain	'spider'
lalenok	'mirror'	lalenok	'mirror'
lafae?	'crocodile'	lafaek	'crocodile'
lenuk	'turtle'	lenuk	'turtle'
loron	'road'	luron	'road'
ne?ek	'black ant sp.'	nehek	'ant'
sabi	'key'	sabi	'key'
sakan	'upper leg'	sakan	'thigh'
sela	'saddle'	sela	'saddle'
susu?	'mosquito'	susuk	'mosquito'
suta	'cotton thread'	suta	'thread, silk line'
tais	'cloth'	tais	'cloth'
teki	'skink'	teki	'skink'
tuku	'clock, time'	tuku	'clock, time'
turi?	'knife'	tudik	'knife'
uat	'vein'	uat	'vein'
uran	'rainwater caught in tub'	udan	'rain'

Beyond lexicon, Bunaq has incorporated numerous Tetun grammatical morphemes and constructions by reanalysing them to fit existing Bunaq structures. For example, Bunaq has adapted Tetun verbal agreement prefixes. In Tetun, a verbal prefix co-indexes the S/A argument (van Klinken 1999: 172, illustrated in 3), while in Bunaq, a verbal prefix co-indexes the P argument (4). Bunaq also has different prefixes depending on the animacy of the object: animate 3rd person objects are marked with *gV-* (4a), while inanimate 3rd person objects are marked with *hV-* (4b). This pattern is not present in Tetun.

Tetun
(3) a. *HaʔU k-aree Yati.*
      1SG   1SG-see Yati
      'I see Yati.'
  b. *HaʔU k-aree uma.*
      1SG   1SG-see house
      'I see a house.'

Bunaq
(4) a. *Neto Yati g-azal.*
      1SG   Yati 3AN-see
      'I see Yati.'
  b. *Neto deu h-azal.*
      1SG   House 3INAN-see
      'I see a house.'

Tetun verbs with initial /h/ lose their first consonant where subject prefixes mark the verb. 1st and 2nd person plural subjects are not marked by an agreement prefix and the *h*-initial root is used in these contexts. Bunaq copies this pattern on borrowed *h*-initial Tetun verbs, but replaces the Tetun subject prefixes with its own object prefixes and reanalyses the initial /h/ of the Tetun root as a 3rd person inanimate prefix like that in (4b). Bunaq similarly reanalyses the Tetun causative prefix *ha-* as part of this inflectional paradigm. Table 1.8 illustrates the Tetun prefixation pattern and the reanalysed Bunaq pattern on the Tetun verb *hisik* 'sprinkle'.

Table 1.8: Tetun and Bunaq prefixation of *h*-initial verbs.

Tetun			Bunaq		
1SG	k-isik	'I sprinkle'	1EXCL	n-isik	'sprinkle me/us'
2SG	m-isik	'you sprinkle'	1INCL/2	Ø-isik	'sprinkle us/you'
3SG	n-isik	's/he sprinkles'	3AN	g-isik	'sprinkle him/her'
1PL/2PL	hisik	'we/you sprinkle'	3INAN	h-isik	'sprinkle it'
3PL	r-isik	'they sprinkle'	REFL	d-isik	'sprinkle oneself'

In the domain of quantification, Bunaq both directly borrows quantifiers and calques quantifiers from Tetun. For example, the Tetun quantifier *oiʔ~oik ~ oik~oik*, formed by means of reduplication of *oik* 'face' (5), is borrowed into Bunaq with its quantificational meaning (6a), but is also calqued with a reduplication of Bunaq *gewen* 'face' (6b).

Tetun
(5) *tais   oiʔ~oik*
    cloth   REDUP~face
    'all kinds of cloth'

Bunaq
(6) a. *tais   oik~oik*
       cloth   various.kinds
       'all kinds of cloth'
    b. *tais   gewen~gewen*
       cloth   REDUP~face
       'all kinds of cloth'

Alongside native Bunaq clause conjunctions occurring at the end of the clause, Bunaq has borrowed Tetun clause conjunctions that occur clause-initially. Both clause-final and clause-initial conjunctions can be used independently, as with Bunaq *be* 'but' (7a) and borrowed *mais* 'but' (originally < Portuguese *mas* 'but') (7b). In addition, the borrowed initial clause conjunctions can be combined with Bunaq final ones of similar meaning. This has the effect of bracketing both ends of the dependent clause in a conjoined pair (7c).

(7) a. *Halaʔi   soʔat,   bokul=**be**.*
       3PL   poor   fat=CONTEXP
       'They are poor but well fed.'
    b. *Halaʔi   soʔat,   **mais**   bokul.*
       3PL   poor   but   fat
       'They are poor but well fed.'
    c. *Halaʔi   soʔat,   **mais**   bokul=**be**.*
       3PL   poor   but   fat=CONTEXP
       'They are poor but fat.'

Such bracketing constructions illustrate a propensity found widely in the Bunaq language: rather than give up native structures in favour of foreign ones, Bunaq speakers accommodate them alongside one another.

1.7.3 Borrowings from unknown Austronesian sources

These two layers do not account for all Austronesian borrowings in Bunaq and it seems likely that Bunaq was in contact with at least one other Austronesian language, but possibly more.

There are numerous items in Bunaq that look to have Austronesian etymologies, but that have no likely sources in the surrounding Austronesian languages. For example, Bunaq *buleʔen* 'gold' is almost certainly a borrowing of a reflex of PMP *bulaw-an 'gold', but no Austronesian languages in Timor have a reflex of this item. Similarly, Bunaq *tinik* 'cook in water or juice, boil' presents a good formal and semantic match to PMP *tanek 'cook by boiling'. In this case, not only are there no known reflexes of this item in Timor, but there are none attested anywhere in the whole eastern Indonesian region. Bunaq *piral* 'rice grain' also seems likely to be a borrowing of PMP *pajay 'rice plant', but the nearby languages either do not have reflexes of this item (e.g., Kemak *etu* ~ *eʧu* 'rice plant, food', *mreas* 'unhusked rice'), or show sound changes that exclude them as possible sources (e.g., PMP *p > h or Ø: Tetun *hare* 'rice plant, unhusked rice grain', Kusa-Manea Meto *ane* 'rice plant').

For several Bunaq lexemes with Austronesian etymologies, good formal and semantic matches seem to be present with Proto-Rote-Meto, the common ancestor of most of the Austronesian languages in western Timor and on Rote Island, just off the western tip of Timor. For example, Bunaq *mami* 'tasty' is certainly a borrowing of a reflex of PMP *ma-həmis 'sweet'. While a reflex of this PMP item is not known in any Central Timor language or in Tetun, close matches are found in the Austronesian languages of Rote Island, including Termanu *mami*, Dengka *mamis*, Oenale *mamis* < Proto-Rote-Meto *mamis 'sweet' (Edwards 2021: 244). Another case of this kind is Bunaq *bin* 'seed for planting', which is a clear borrowing of a reflex of PMP *binəhiq 'rice seed, rice set aside for the next planting'. Reflexes of the PMP lexeme are found in Central Timor languages (Kemak *hini*, Mambae *hiin*, Tokodede *wini*) as well as Tetun (*fini*) and Meto (*fini*), but because of the sound changes they display (e.g., *b > f > h), none are plausible sources for the Bunaq form. Many of the languages of Rote, however, retain *b as *b* (e.g., Termanu *bini*, Bokai *bini* < Proto-Rote-Meto *bini 'seed for replanting'; Edwards 2021: 100). This could be taken to suggest that Bunaq was in contact with an early daughter of Proto-Rote-Meto that was lost when speakers of Meto expanded across western Timor (see Schapper and Wellfelt 2018: 99–100 for further discussion of this).

Contact with early speakers of a Rote-Meto language may be argued to be unsupported by the above cases because there are no distinctive sound changes displayed by the Bunaq and the Rote-Meto languages that link the lexemes clearly together to the exclusion of other languages. That is, it is only the geographical proximity of the languages plus the absence of sound changes in the relevant forms that suggest a link. Yet, for other forms, we do find positive evidence supporting the idea of contact between speakers of Bunaq and a Rote-Meto language. Consider Bunaq *mone* 'man, male, husband', a borrowing of a reflex of PMP *ma-Ruqanay 'male'. This PMP lexeme is reflected in Central Timor languages like Kemak and Mambae, and Tetun as *mane* 'man, male', with regular PMP *a > *a*. Whilst *a > o is an expected sound change in native Bunaq vocabulary, it is not found in Bunaq borrowings from Central Timor and Tetun (cf. Tables 1.6 and 1.7). An etymological doublet of *mone and *mane 'man, male' is, however, reconstructed by Edwards (2021: 245, 257) to Proto-Rote-Meto.

Finally, I have identified several shared items between Bunaq and Meto varieties that might suggest that they were both in contact with a third language. For example, Bunaq *habu~habu* 'cloud, fog' is strikingly similar to *habu* 'cloud, fog' in the easternmost Meto variety, Kusa-Manea. The relative proximity of Bunaq and Kusa-Manea Meto and the absence of similar forms in other nearby languages suggests that this shared form (likely ultimately < PMP *kabut 'fog, haze, mist; indistinct, blurry') is a borrowing from another Austronesian language that is no longer extant. See also Edwards' (2021: 67–69) proposal that some of the distinct lexicon of Meto varieties can be accounted for as borrowings from Central Timor languages.

1.8 Ritual language: parallelism

Parallelism is a poetic device that is used in ritual languages in much of eastern Indonesia (Fox 1988). Parallelism is also the basis for the Bunaq ritual language and occupies a position of considerable cultural importance. Parallelism involves the repetition of near identical half-lines. The language is highly formulaic and differs significantly from everyday speech, having a highly divergent vocabulary and a very flexible approach to syntax. It is spoken by specially trained *makoqan* [makoʔan] 'poet, historian', a term borrowed from Tetun, who perform at special events, such as deaths and rituals. The art is in significant decline, with *makoqan* nowadays being typically quite elderly and few and far between. Nevertheless, there is widespread recognition of half-lines: when given a common half-line, most speakers can complete the line, giving its formulaic pair.

The ritual language will not be discussed in this book, but the short stretch of text in (8) is provided to give the reader an impression of the language. The example is an excerpt from a longer performance of a *bei gua* 'ancestor journey' by the *makoqan* of Weluli and records the Bunaq ancestors' building of boats (8a), their journey across the sea (8b–c), their arrival in Timor (8d–f), and their dispersal (8g). A hyphen is used to connect the two half-lines of a parallelism. The translation is very free.

(8) a. biruk   tomak   haqal   -   ro   tetuk   haqal
    boat   whole   finished   vessel complete finished
    'the boats were complete'
  b. irak   ro   saqe   -   irak   biruk saqe
    separate vessel ascend   separate boat   ascend
    'separately they boarded the boats'

c. *meti iti   man - mo raqet   man*
   sea opposite come   sea lined.up come
   'they came one after the other'
d. *pan betak Timor - muk betak Timor*
   sky other Timor   land other Timor
   'to another land, Timor'
e. *hati a-ta   sai - hati a-ta   taru*
   exist 3INAN-GL exit   exist 3INAN-GL appear
   'when they arrived'
f. *hono d-itimik   - hono d-atun*
   there REFL-descend   there REFL-bring.down
   'they disembarked'
g. *waqen   hot taru   - waqen   hot topa*
   PART.PL sun appear   PART.PL sun drop
   'some went east, some went west'   [Bere-07.01]

We see in (8) that parallel constructions are formed by varying one word or, occasionally, two words across half-lines, while keeping the frame in which the words occur constant. Typically, varying words used in adjoined half-lines are (near-)synonyms. They follow a number of patterns. The main pattern in this text is: one synonym from Tetun, one synonym from Bunaq: e.g., Tetun *tomak* 'whole' but Bunaq *tetuk* 'complete, circular' (8a); Tetun *meti* 'sea' but Bunaq *mo* 'sea' (8c). In other cases, dialect synonyms (e.g., *net ~ duʔat* 'stand') or allophones (e.g., [d ~ r]) are used to vary half-lines. Varying words may also be opposites that complement or elaborate on one another, as in: *pan* 'sky' and *muk* 'earth' (8d); *hot taru* 'east' and *hot topa* 'west' (8g).

The interested reader can examine whole texts of ritual speech in the *Bei Gua* published in Berthe (1972).

1.9 Linguistic type

1.9.1 Typological overview

Bunaq is a head-marking language with a basic APV/SV word order and postpositions. The word order shows a significant amount of pragmatic variation, and is also sensitive to factors such as person and animacy in non-agentive clauses. Whilst Bunaq is an APV/SV language, it is not strictly verb-final. Many elements follow the verb, such as the theme argument of a trivalent verb and the clausal negator.

The Bunaq vowel phoneme inventory consists of the five cardinal vowels and three phonemic diphthongs, while the number of consonant phonemes differs between dialects. For instance, the inventory of Bunaq Lamaknen is /p, b, t, d, k, g, ʔ, s, z, h, tʃ, l, r, m, n, w/, while the inventory of Bunaq Bobonaro adds an aspirated stop series /p^h, t^h, kʰ/ to this, but lacks /r, w/. The preferred syllable shape is CV. Consonant clusters are largely prohibited and codas are highly restricted. Stress is not phonemic. Morphophonological processes include metathesis and irregular root mutations.

The language is largely isolating, with the only morphology being a single set of person prefixes, occurring on both verbs and nouns. On verbs, they mark P and less often S; there is no verbal affixation of A. P arguments are differentially marked according to the grammatical noun class ANIMACY of the P argument. On nouns, person prefixes mark possessors.

The NP is predominantly head-initial. Noun heads are followed by modifier (relative clause, num, noun, det), but preceded by locationals and possessors. Noun class is a covert property of nouns reflected in determiner and prefixal agreement on the verb. The two noun classes are ANIMATE and INANIMATE. Free pronouns are marked for person, number (singular, dual, plural), and clusivity, but are unmarked for grammatical role.

Bunaq has an elaborate set of deictic elements, including six determiners and eight locationals. Determiners and locationals are used extensively and in complex ways to locate, identify, and track referents in space, time, and discourse, as well as to mark an array of pragmatic meanings.

Bunaq distinguishes lexical classes of alienably and inalienably possessed nouns. The possessor of an inalienably possessed noun is marked directly on the possessed noun with person prefixes. The possessor of an alienably possessed noun is marked indirectly by a free possessive classifier with a person prefix indexing the possessor.

Bunaq makes extensive use of verb serialisation to express, for instance, manner, cause, and aspect. A set of inflecting, verbal postpositions is used to add a range of peripheral NPs to clauses. Complex events are expressed by conjoined clauses, either juxtaposed or linked by a conjunction. Indigenous conjunctions are clause-final, while borrowed ones are clause-initial; they often combine together to 'bracket' a dependent clause. Tail-head linkage is common.

1.9.2 Bunaq as a Papuan language

The term "Papuan" is a negative category: a language is said to be "Papuan" if it is spoken in the area near New Guinea, and belongs neither to the Austronesian nor Australian language family. "Papuan" thus brings languages of over 60 families under a single label (see Foley 1986: 231–245). The alternative label, "non-Austronesian", is similarly vague and presents other difficulties in so far as Austronesian languages are in geographic contact with several language families, such as Austro-Asiatic languages in mainland South-east Asia, which cannot accurately be identified with the label "Papuan".

While there is no agreement about the existence of a single, unified Papuan linguistic type, a number of features have been proposed as 'typical' of Papuan languages. Foley (1998, 2000), Reesink (2002), Ross (2017), and Schapper (2015a, 2020b) discuss a range of grammatical properties that are found across many, but by no means all, languages of New Guinea. These features are identified as contrasting with the standard typological profile presented by languages of the Austronesian family, although some features are not unique to the Papuan languages of New Guinea.

Given Bunaq's location in the midst of Austronesian languages, its isolation from other Papuan languages, a comparison between standard Austronesian and Papuan features offers a benchmark by which to gauge the character of the language. I will assess the status of Bunaq by comparing its features against the Austronesian and Papuan typological "benchmarks" set out in Foley (1998). Underlining is used to highlight similarities between features in Bunaq and the Austronesian and Papuan types.

Table 1.9 outlines eight defining characteristics of the phonologies broadly "typical" of Austronesian and Papuan languages. Of these, Bunaq has a typologically unexceptional system of five pure vowels. As for feature 2, the Bunaq places of articulation may be taken as typical of either Papuan or Austronesian languages. Bunaq's voicing contrast in the obstruents is more typical of Austronesian than Papuan, while the fricatives of Bunaq are not typical for either Austronesian or Papuan languages. The contrast between two liquids is a feature of Austronesian languages, as is the simple segmental syllable structure, non-phonemic stress, and the lack of tone. Of the assessable phonological features, Bunaq thus scores four clear points for Austronesian and none for Papuan; the remaining features are either typical of both or neither.

Table 1.9: Papuan-Austronesian phonology compared.

	Feature	Austronesian	Papuan	Bunaq
1	Vowels	5 vowels	5 vowels + schwa; front rounding	5 vowels (+ 3 diphthongs)
2	Places	P – T – K (~C)	P – T – (C/s) – K	P – T – (C) – K
3	Manner	P≠B; B = MB	no pattern	P≠B
4	Fricatives	f v – s – ɣ	fricatives = stops p/ɸ/β ; t/r/l; k/g/ɣ few fricatives; often just s	s z – h
5	Liquids	r ≠ l	r = l	r ≠ l
6	Syllables	(C)V	C(C) V C	(C)V
7	Stress	penultimate stress	phonemic stress	penultimate stress
8	Tone	typically no tone	tone present	no tone

Table 1.10 presents eight morphological characteristics of Austronesian and Papuan languages. Morphologically Bunaq is isolating and thus closer to Austronesian than Papuan. Bunaq inflection is not fusional with other grammatical categories, but simply marks person. Consistent with the Papuan type, Bunaq makes extensive use

of serial verbs, but has no applicative or other derivational morphology. In contrast to both Papuan and Austronesian types Bunaq nouns have gender, though this is not marked on them morphologically. There is no morphological case in Bunaq. Bunaq verbal agreement follows neither the Austronesian nor the Papuan pattern. Bunaq TAM marking is by serial verbs or postverbal free morphemes, similar to the Papuan type. Bunaq roots show some categorial indeterminacy in the manner of the Austronesian type. Overall, Bunaq scores four with Austronesian and two with Papuan. However, given that Bunaq has only one productive morphological paradigm, the assignment of figures for morphology will be generous in any direction.

Table 1.10: Papuan-Austronesian morphology compared.

	Feature	Austronesian	Papuan	Bunaq
1	type	close to isolating	agglutinative	isolating
2	inflection	little	strong often fused with TAM	little, person inflection only
3	derivation	applicative suffixes causative prefixes	SVCs suffixal derivational morphology	SVCs no derivational morphology
4	nominal categories	no number or gender	usually no number or gender	gender
5	case	no case	suffixal/enclictic case	no case
6	verbal agreement	S=V=O	O=V=S, V=O=S, V=S=O	O=V, (S=V)
7	TAM	s=TAM=V	V-TAM, SVCs	V TAM, SVCs
8	categoriality	categorial indeterminacy	strict root categories	some categorial indeterminacy

Table 1.11 summarises six contrasting syntactic features of Austronesian and Papuan languages. The syntactic profile of Bunaq is right-headed at the phrasal and clausal level, with SOV word order and two postpositions. Consistent with a right-headed profile, articles as well as demonstratives follow the noun. However, Bunaq is not universally right-headed with relative clauses and numerals following the noun, a feature which is consistent with both the Papuan and Austronesian types. Bunaq has no system of switch-reference. It does have clause-final conjunctions, thus conforming to the overall right-headed profile of the language and differing from that of the Austronesian languages. In terms of syntax, Bunaq scores three for Papuan and none for Austronesian.

Table 1.11: Papuan-Austronesian syntax compared.

	Feature	Austronesian	Papuan	Bunaq
1	phrase	left-headed	right-headed	right-headed
2	clause	SVO	SOV (also OSV)	SOV, (OSV)
3	adposition	PREP N	N POST	N POST
4	article	ART N	no ART	N ART
5	modifiers	N ADJ, N RC	N ADJ, (ADJ N)	N RC, N NUM
6	sentence	CONJ Clause	SS, S-SWITCH	no SS, Clause CONJ

Table 1.12 summarises the features across the three domains. It would appear that, on the basis of Foley's (1998) features, Bunaq belongs convincingly to neither the broad Austronesian nor the so-called Papuan linguistic type, but at the same time has typological characteristics consistent with both. Taken to refer to stable entities, the labels "Papuan", "Austronesian", and "non-Austronesian" would seem thus to be of limited usefulness in describing the typological profile of Bunaq.

Table 1.12: Summary of Bunaq comparative features.

	Feature	Austronesian	Papuan	Neither
1	Phonology	4	0	4
2	Morphology	4	2	2
3	Syntax	0	3	3
	Total (of 22)	8	5	9

However, if we discard the facile view that there is a consistent Papuan linguistic type that extends over the whole area in which Papuan languages are found, then we can examine other possible relations. Recent work has shown that eastern Indonesia broadly, and the Timor region specifically, are areas in which linguistic features have diffused and Sprachbund effects are present. In particular, the Austronesian and Papuan languages have been shown to share characteristics distinct from those of other Austronesian and Papuan languages in different areas (Schapper 2015a), such as:

(i)   stative-active alignment (Donohue 2004; Klamer 2008)
(ii) neuter gender (Schapper 2010a)
(iii) N PSR and PSR N order with semantic differences between orders in the Timor area (Schapper 2009, 2020c)
(iv) metathesis in the Timor-Babar area (Schapper 2015a; Edwards 2020)
(v)   verb serialisations (van Staden and Reesink 2008; Unterladstetter 2020)
(vi) parallelism (Fox 1988; Klamer 2002)

As a language which shares these and other features with both types of language in the area, it is more profitable to view Bunaq as neither an aberrant Austronesian nor non-conformist Papuan, but as displaying a particular "insular eastern Indonesian" linguistic type which cross-cuts the distinction between Papuan and Austronesian.

1.10 Previous work

The earliest documentation of the Bunaq language that I have identified is a Holle word list of "Marae", described as the language spoken in Maukatar, Lamaknen, and Lamakhitu, that was published in Stokhof (1983). The earliest work on Bunaq by a foreign linguist was conducted by Arthur Capell. He worked with Bunaq speakers in a refugee camp outside Dili during World War II. The results of his work in Timor were published in a trilogy of articles in *Oceania* (Capell 1943a, 1943b, 1944). Some additional Bunaq data is presented in Capell (1972, 1975). His fieldnotes are available in Capell and Newton (1999) in the PARADISEC archive.

Bunaq matrilineality attracted the French anthropologist Louis Berthe to Lamaknen in West Timor during the 1950s, with subsequent fieldtrips in the 1960s. He published two articles on the Bunaq language: Berthe (1959) looks at language and metaphor in traditional Bunaq sayings, while Berthe (1963) describes some features of Bunaq inflectional morphology. Berthe's collection of ritual texts describing the origin and lineal transmission of privileges and titles amongst the Bunaq, submitted as a doctoral dissertation at the University of the Sorbonne in 1961, was posthumously published by Claudine Friedberg as Berthe (1972). Friedberg further edited and published a collection of Bunaq folktales collected and translated by Berthe which appeared as Friedberg (1978a). Her preface to this work includes remarks on the Bunaq language including a segmental phonology and notes on a range of word classes. During his fieldwork, Berthe took photographs, made audio recordings and silent moving picture recordings of Bunaq people and culture, and assembled a material culture collection of items used by the Bunaq. Many of these collections are still in existence today and can variously be found in the archives of the Musée du quai Branly – Jacques Chirac, Musée de l'Homme, and Collège de France. After Berthe's death in 1968, Claudine Friedberg deposited the original reel-to-reel tape recordings with the Collège de France, but many were lost. A small number, containing mostly traditional music, survived and have been digitalized by the Centre de Recherche en Ethnomusicologie sound archive (Berthe 2020).

Claudine Friedberg herself conducted extensive fieldwork among the Bunaq people of Lamaknen and published significantly. Her mammoth five-volume doctoral thesis (Friedberg 1982) remains the definitive work on Bunaq society and culture. Volume 3 of the thesis dealt with traditional Bunaq plant classification and was published as Friedberg (1990). Her numerous other publications on aspects of Bunaq ethnobotany include Friedberg (1970, 1971a, 1971b, 1972, 1973b, 1978b, 1979, 1986, 1991).

Her contributions on Bunaq culture and society include Friedberg (1973a, 1978c, 1980, 1989, 1999, 2014).

There are also numerous manuscripts in Bunaq and Indonesian written in the 1970s by A. A. Bere Tallo, the first governor of Belu (where Bunaq is spoken) and the previous *loro* ('king') of the Bunaq area of Lamaknen. The only one of these manuscripts to which I was able to obtain access was Bere Tallo (1978), a collection of 21 *zapal* 'folktales'. With the permission of Dr. Anton Bele, a PDF of the manuscript is archived with the Endangered Languages Archive (ELAR) as part of a wider collection documenting the *zapal* oral literature form (Schapper 2019). This collection also includes 61 *zapal* transcribed by Louis Berthe, for which the reel-to-reel recordings have been largely lost. These are archived with the permission of Claudine Friedberg. On the basis of the collection in the ELAR, two volumes of *zapal* were produced for use in schools in Lamaknen (Schapper 2015b, 2016).

Other works on Bunaq include Sawardo et al. (1996), a short grammatical sketch published under the auspices of Indonesia's national language centre. The sketch was produced by means of a questionnaire answered with the help of Bunaq speakers in Atambua. Finally, a small dictionary of the Lamaknen dialect with Indonesian translations is Bele (2009).

1.11 This work: Fieldwork and data

This work is a completely revised and substantially updated version of my PhD thesis (Schapper 2010b). Where there are differences between that work and this one, the reader should take the information presented here as authoritative.

1.11.1 Fieldwork

This work deals primarily with the Bunaq language as it is spoken in the Lamaknen region of West Timor. The majority of the fieldwork was conducted in the village of Gewal (see Map 1.4). I was resident in this village for two months from September to the end of October 2006, then five months from March to July 2007, and a final one month in May 2009. In addition to this I spent two months surveying the Bunaq-speaking area in East Timor, one month in October 2007 and one month in April 2009. Subsequent to the completion of Schapper (2010b), I returned to Belu and continued further work on Bunaq in 2011, 2012, and 2015 for short fieldtrips of a few weeks.

During my stays in Gewal, I lived with an unmarried retired teacher, Marieta Soi, and her five foster children, Ela, Laura, Novi, Diana and Yuni. The latter two were away during the week attending high school in Weluli. I spoke almost no Indonesian/Malay when I first arrived in the village, and concentrated on learning Bunaq for my first two-month stay in 2006. This was greatly facilitated by living with a group of children who were always keen to answer my questions and tell me what something was called, whilst Eme ('mother') Eta (Marieta Soi) was forever quick to correct my mistakes.

Once I was sufficiently competent in Bunaq, I began recording conversations and texts from different individuals in Gewal and the surrounding villages in Lamaknen. I was at pains to stress to the Bunaq people that I was interested in "everyday Bunaq" and not the ritual language, discussed briefly in §1.8, which had been the concern of Berthe. Towards the end of my second fieldtrip, I began work doing elicitation and getting grammaticality judgements on sentences I constructed on the basis of observations and analyses of textual data. This work was done chiefly with Hironimus Mau of Dirun village who was resident in Gewal at the time, Wili Loe, a retired teacher whom I would visit at his home in Nualain village, and Florentina Bau, also a retired teacher who lived in Gewal. In Atambua, I was also able to consult the extensive knowledge of the *loro Lamaknen* 'king of Lamaknen', Ignatius Kali, and his wife Eme Rosa. In the course of my fieldwork, I consulted with many other speakers.

1.11.2 Kinds of data

The data I have used in developing the analysis of the Bunaq language presented here were collected in a variety of ways over several years. The language examples presented are annotated to indicate their origin. Data type records are shown in square brackets '[ ]' following the free translation. This work makes use of five different kinds of data:

I. **Recorded data:** this refers to data recorded in audio or audiovisual form by myself in Lamaknen between 2006 and 2013. The 90 texts that I collected between 2006 and 2009 and that were used in Schapper (2010b) are designated by 'Bk' (for 'Bunak'), then the text number and finally the line number of the text referred as it appears in Toolbox. For example, '[Bk-28.105]' refers to line 105 of Bunaq text number 28 in the corpus. Details of these texts and their speakers can be found at DOI: 10.5281/zenodo.5535640.

Additional recordings of 43 *zapal* (see §1.10 on this genre of oral literature) were made between 2009 and 2013. These additional texts are referred to by a shortened version of their title plus the line number in Toolbox (e.g., [PipUsik-43] refers to the 43rd line of the *zapal* text *Pip o Usik* 'Goat and Crocodile'. These texts are available online at the ELAR (Schapper 2019).

Texts of Bunaq varieties of East Timor that were recorded during survey work in 2007 are not included in the corpus; texts which I recorded in ritual parallel speech, such as the sample given in (8), are also not included in the corpus used for this work.

II. **Written data:** this refers to texts that I had access to in written forms. Data of this kind come from several sources. In Schapper (2010b), I made extensive use of the texts collected in Lamaknen by Louis Berthe that were published in Friedberg

(1978a). I thoroughly checked these texts with speakers on my first fieldtrip and entered them into Toolbox. They are cited throughout this work as 'LB', followed by the text number (1–10) and the Toolbox line it occurs in, e.g., [LB-06.123]. Subsequent to Schapper (2010b), I gained access to more *zapal* texts transcribed by Louis Berthe and by A. A. Bere Tallo (detailed in §1.10) and made use of them in the present work. These additional texts are also referred to by a shortened version of their title plus the line number in Toolbox. These texts are available online at the ELAR (Schapper 2019).

In addition, I was given two religious texts written by native speakers of Lamaknen Bunaq which I have also made some use of. All examples used have been rechecked with speakers. This first consists of portions of the New Testament of the Bible, published in 1988 by the Pusat Pastoral Keuskupan Atambua (Diocese of Atambua Pastoral Care Centre), printed under the title *Libur por toma tip gie*, literally, 'holy book's new message' (1988). This text where referred to is designated as 'Bib' followed by the page number, e.g., [Bib-64]. The second religious text is a Bunaq prayer book entitled *Tea Buna* printed in 1961. This text where referred to is designated as 'Pray' followed by the page number, e.g., [Pray-4].

III. **Overheard speech:** I kept a pocket notebook on me at all times in which I wrote down speech I happened to overhear or which was said to me in the course of everyday routine. Examples of this kind are designated in language examples with 'OS', and then by the fieldwork trip during which it was heard (06, 07, or 09) and finally the notebook number. Thus '[OS-06.01]' refers to a piece of overheard speech from my first pocket notebook of my fieldwork in 2006.

IV. **Elicited data:** elicited data are data which were produced in elicitation contexts (e.g., can you say X? how do say X?) and/or where speakers spontaneously gave grammaticality judgements or corrected errors in my speech. Language examples of this kind are designated as 'Not', and then by the fieldwork trip during which they were recorded (06, 07, or 09) and finally the notebook number. Thus '[Not-07.03]' refers to a piece of elicited data from my third pocket notebook of my fieldwork in 2007. Formal elicitation was always based upon hypotheses formed through looking at texts.

V. **Facebook group data:** in 2013 I started a public Facebook group, *Proyek Kamus Bahasa Bunaq* [Bunaq language Dictionary Project], in order to gather data for a community dictionary. As of March 2022, the group had 2,100 members, most of whom are native Bunaq speakers. In revising Schapper (2010b) for this publication, I made extensive use of the intuitions of members of the Facebook group to check grammatical distinctions and lexical meanings. Language data from this source are designated as 'FB', followed by the date of the original query posted to Facebook (with the format DDMMYY). Thus, '[FB-220321]' refers to a query put on Facebook on the 22nd of March 2021.

Chapter 2
Phonology and morphophonology

2.1 Introduction

This chapter gives an account of the phonology of Bunaq Lamaknen. The chapter begins with a description of the Bunaq Lamaknen segmental phonology in §2.2. Bunaq phonotactics are dealt with in §2.3 and stress in §2.4. Morphophonology is dealt with in §2.5, while irregularities in morphophonological behaviour are discussed in §2.6. The orthographic conventions according to which the segments will be represented throughout the remainder of this description are given in §2.7.

2.2 Phoneme inventory

There are a total of 24 segmental phonemes in the native phoneme inventory of Bunaq Lamaknen: 5 vowels (§2.2.1), 3 diphthongs (§2.2.2), and 16 consonants (§2.2.3). Non-native phonemes and their adaptation in Bunaq phonology are treated in §2.2.4.

2.2.1 Vowel phonemes

Bunaq has a simple five-vowel system, consisting of two front, two back, and a single low central vowel (Table 2.1).

Table 2.1: Bunaq vowel inventory.

	Front		Back
High	i		u
Mid	e		o
Low		a	

The contrasts between the Bunaq vowel phonemes are demonstrated with the minimal pairs in Table 2.2.

The vowel phoneme /u/ shows minimal allophonic variation. In open syllables /i/ is realised as [i], but in closed syllables /i/ can have a mid-centralised realisation [ɪ], e.g., /pi/ [pi] 'set a trap' versus /pit/ [pɪt] 'throat'. The vowel /a/ is typically realised as [a], except immediately following a stressed syllable where it is typically centralised to [ɐ], e.g., /basu/ ['basu] 'pass over' versus /busa/ ['busɐ] 'cat'.

The mid vowels /e/ and /o/ are usually realised as [ɛ] and [ɔ] respectively, but tend to be realised as slightly higher [e] and [o] in open syllables or when followed

Table 2.2: Vowel minimal pairs.

Item	Gloss
/a/	'eat'
/e/	'salt'
/i/	'1PL.INCL'
/o/	'prawn'
/u/	'grass'

in the next syllable by a high vowel /i/. In stressed syllables of disyllabic words, the mid vowel phonemes /e/ and /o/ may be raised to [i] and [u]. This raising can also be found in graphemic variation between <e> ~ <i> and <o> ~ <u> in native speaker orthographic choices. Items in which such raising is common are given in (1) for /e/ and in (2) for /o/. The variation is a stable feature of female speech and does not appear to represent an ongoing neutralisation of vowel phoneme distinctions.

(1) /sesal/ ['sesal ~ 'sisal] 'bone'
    /sekal/ ['sekal ~ 'sikal] 'potato'
    /heser/ ['heser ~ 'hiser] 'dead'
    /menal/ ['menal ~ 'minal] 'go down'

(2) /hotus/ ['hotus ~ 'hutus] 'woven pattern'
    /moal/ ['moal ~ 'mual] 'lower ground'
    /topi/ ['topi ~ 'tupi] 'owl'
    /loron/ ['loron ~ 'luron] 'road'

The high vowel phonemes /i/ and /u/ are not observed to vary in this way.

2.2.2 Diphthong phonemes

In addition to the five cardinal vowel phonemes, Bunaq has three phonemic diphthongs /a͡i, e͡i, o͡i/. The diphthongs are treated here as two pure vowels in a single-syllable nucleus. The second vowel in the syllable nucleus is /i/ and is realised as a high off-glide, yielding the surface forms [aj, ej, oj] respectively.

The diphthongs contrast with sequences of the same vowels in which each vowel belongs to a separate syllable. (Near) minimal pairs illustrating the contrasts between diphthongs and VV sequences are presented below. The symbol '.' marks a syllable boundary.

(3) /ai͡/   /a.i/
    /sai͡/   ['saj]   'exit'   /sa.i/   ['saʲi]   'be amused'
    /hai͡/   ['haj]   'hey'   /ha.i/   ['haʲi]   'gape'
    /bai͡/   ['baj]   'thing'   /pa.i/   ['paʲi]   'surprise'

(4) /ei͡/   /e.i/
    /tei͡/   ['tej]   'dance type'   /e.i/   ['teʲi]   'stare at'
    /sei͡/   ['sej]   'slide over'   /e.i/   ['seʲi]   'collect (of water)'
    /lei͡/   ['lej]   'eagle sp.'   /e.i/   ['leʲi]   'call out'

(5) /oi͡/   /o.i/
    /poi͡/   ['poj]   'choose'   /lo.i/   ['loʷi]   'good'
    /soi͡/   ['soj]   'rich'   /do.i/   ['doʷi]   'SPEC.AN'
    /koi͡l/ ['kojl] 'whittle'   /ko.in/ ['koʷin] 'burn (of garden)'

The spectrograms below illustrate the difference between diphthongs and VV sequences. Figures 2.1 and 2.2 represent /sai͡/ 'exit' realised with the diphthong [saj], and /sa.i/ 'be amused' realised with the vowel sequence as [saʲi]. In Figure 2.1 we see a smoothly changing spectrum with no steady state developing following the high off-glide. In Figure 2.2 the spectrogram shows two steady states for the two separate

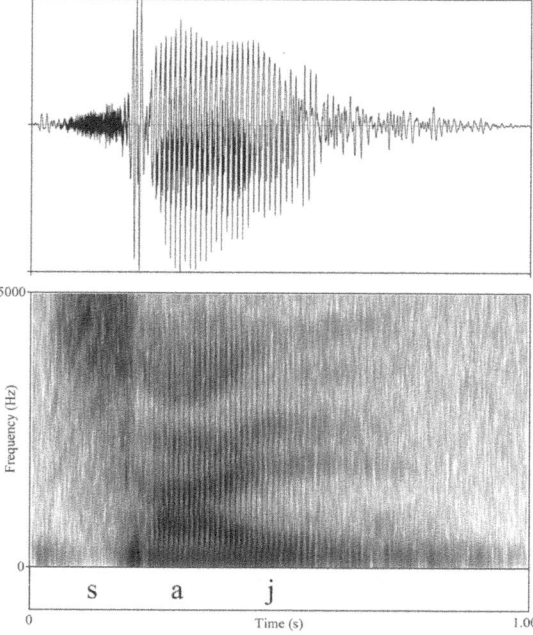

Figure 2.1: Spectrogram of /sai͡/ ['saj] 'exit'.

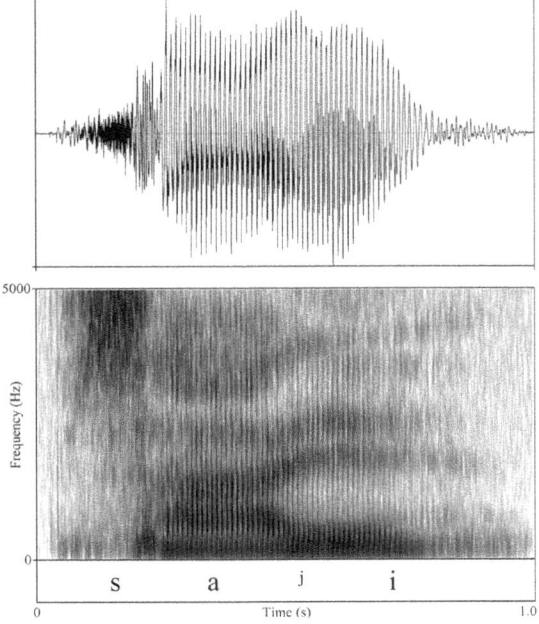

Figure 2.2: Spectrogram of /sa.i/ ['saʲi] 'be amused'.

vowels /a/ and /i/ interrupted by an epenthetic palatal glide [j] (see §2.3.6). It can also be seen that the VV sequence has a longer duration overall than the diphthong.

The contrast between diphthongs and vowel sequences has a low functional load in terms of the whole lexicon: there are 25 tokens of /a͡i/, 7 of /e͡i/, and 12 of /o͡i/, and only 5 of /a.i/, 6 of /e.i/, and 3 of /o.i/. All other vowel sequences are realised as two distinct vowels (§2.3.5).

In an alternative analysis, it may be possible to see the final element in the diphthongs as an underlying /j/ instead of as an allophonic variant of the high vowel /i/. This analysis is not adopted here for the following reasons. For one, the palatal glide is not otherwise evidenced in Bunaq as an independent phoneme, so that an underlying /j/ would mean positing an extra phoneme with a very limited and restricted occurrence. Secondly, whilst the glide analysis would be permissible for open syllables such as /ko͡i/ ['koj] 'bed, cot', in closed syllables such as /ko͡il/ ['kojl] 'whittle, scratch with a knife' it would violate Bunaq phonotactic rules which prohibit two consonants in a coda (§2.3.1).

2.2.3 Consonant phonemes

Table 2.3 presents the sixteen phonemes of the Bunaq consonant inventory.

Table 2.3: Consonant inventory of Bunaq Lamaknen.

	(Bi)labial		Alveolar		Palatal	Velar		Glottal
Plosive	p	b	t	d		k	g	ʔ
Fricative			s	z				h
Affricate					tʃ			
Nasal		m		n				
Trill				r				
Lateral				l				
Approximant		w						

Minimal pairs illustrating the contrasts of consonant phonemes are given in Table 2.4. For minimal pairs with /tʃ/, see §2.2.3.4. The allophones of consonant phonemes are described in the following sections.

Table 2.4: Consonant minimal pairs.

Contrast	Item	Gloss
/p/ ≠ /b/ ≠ /m/ ≠ /w/	/pel/	'rotten'
	/bel/	'wind'
	/mel/	'wake'
	/wel/	'burnt'
/t/ ≠ /d/ ≠ /n/	/ten/	'ready'
	/den/	'dry in sun'
	/nen/	'NEG'
/k/ ≠ /g/	/kal/	'finger'
	/gal/	'rib'
/m/ ≠ /n/	/mo/	'sea'
	/no/	'in'
/l/ ≠ /r/	/mal/	'go'
	/mar/	'farm'
/s/ ≠ /z/	/=si/	'because'
	/zi/	'snake'
/s/ ≠ /h/	/se/	'clear'
	/he/	'run'
/ʔ/ ≠ /k/ ≠ Ø	/seleʔ/	'sand'
	/selek/	'fountain'
	/sele/	'urinate'

2.2.3.1 Voiceless stops

There is no significant allophony for voiceless stops in Bunaq Lamaknen. The phoneme /k/ can be realised either as [k] or as [x]. Typically, [x] is heard intervocalically.

Aspiration of voiceless stops is not phonemic in Bunaq Lamaknen, being erratic and heard only weakly and intermittently. This contrasts with varieties of Bunaq spoken in East Timor where aspiration is phonemic and significant aspiration bursts are audible (see §1.5 on Bunaq dialects).

Word-final voiceless stops are often unreleased or significantly delayed in their release, particularly when they occur at the end of an intonation unit with a falling contour. These allophones are transcribed as [p̚] [t̚] [k̚]. The waveform in Figure 2.3 is illustrative, showing a 31.6 ms delay in the release of the final voiceless alveolar stop /t/ in /mit/ [mɪt̚] 'sit'.

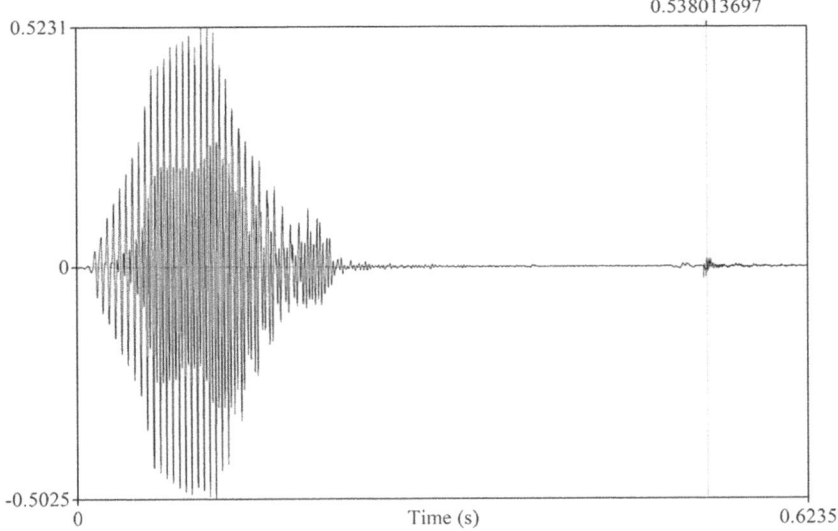

Figure 2.3: Delayed release of final /t/ in /mit/ [mɪt̚] 'sit'.

Voiceless stops appear in syllable onsets, both word-initially and -medially, as well as in codas (Table 2.5).

Table 2.5: Distribution of voiceless stops.

	Initial	Medial	Final
/p/	/pe/ 'be swollen'	/apa/ 'cow'	/op/ 'highland'
/t/	/ten/ 'be ready'	/neto/ '1SG'	/pit/ 'throat'
/k/	/koen/ 'nice'	/naka/ 'mud'	/pak/ 'chop'

Within Lamaknen, there is some variation between villages as to whether a small set of lexemes are realised with a final /k/ or final /ʔ/. In villages in the west of Lamaknen, /ʔ/ can be found finally with the lexemes in (6), while /k/ is used finally elsewhere.

	West	Elsewhere	
(6)	/masaʔ/	/masak/	'large, big'
	/zobeʔ/	/zobek/	'squishy, squashed'
	/damaʔ niʔ/	/damak niʔ/	'not right, not proper'
	/miliʔ/	/milik/	'afraid'

2.2.3.2 Voiced stops

Voiced stops appear in word-medial and word-initial syllable onsets but are excluded from codas. Table 2.6 illustrates the distribution of these consonants.

Table 2.6: Distribution of voiced stops.

	Initial	Medial	Final
/b/	/bin/ 'seed'	/laba/ 'slice'	–
/d/	/de/ 'be right'	/tada/ 'know'	–
/g/	/guzel/ 'charcoal'	/sagal/ 'seek'	–

Each of the voiced stops evidences some allophony, discussed in §2.2.3.2.1 to §2.2.3.2.3.

2.2.3.2.1 /b/

The phoneme /b/ can be realised either as [b] or as [β]. The allophones are in free variation, though [b] is more common than [β], particularly initially. Impressionistically, [β] is most common medially between like vowels.

2.2.3.2.2 /d/

Intervocalically /d/ is realised as either a trill [r] or a flap [ɾ]. Word-initially, the trill and stop realisations are in free variation. Speakers seem largely unaware of the stop ~ rhotic alternation, varying their realisations of the phoneme for one and the same lexical item even within a single utterance. The distribution of the allophones of /d/ is recapitulated in Table 2.7.

The initial stop allophone is undergoing attrition. It is now mainly found in the speech of conservative, older males. The change of $d > r$ has, however, been held back by a strong dispreference for the repetition of a rhotic. Sequences of two rhotics are avoided by speakers such that a small subset of words shows only stop realisa-

Table 2.7: Allophony of /d/.

	Allophone	Environment
/d/	[d] ~ [r]	/ #_
	[r] ~ [r]	/ V_V

tions initially. No rhotic realisations are recorded and in elicitiation speakers either doubted or outright rejected the rhotic realisation. The relevant items in the corpus are listed in (7). Such dissimilation of liquids is a cross-linguistically widely attested process (Alderete and Frisch 2006).

(7) /dar/ [dar, *rar] 'lay out for sale'
    /dada/ [dara, ?rara] 'erect, prepare'
    /dade/ [dare, ?rare] 'all sorts'
    /dadi/ [dari, *rari] 'happen, succeed'
    /dado/ [daro, *raro] 'until'
    /dida/ [dira, *rira] 'fuse a knife blade to its handle'
    /didaʔ/ [diraʔ, *riraʔ] 'dew'

The dispreference for sequences of the rhotic trill is not present where another consonant intervenes. For the examples in (8), we see that speakers judged realisations with either initial [d] or [r] to be well formed.

(8) /digir/ [digir ~ rigir] 'lay out for sale'
    /doter/ [doter ~ roter] 'storm off'

2.2.3.2.3 /g/

Some speakers affricate the voiced velar stop /g/ to [ʤ] word-initially before a high front vowel, /i/, when this vowel is immediately followed by a stressed vowel (see §2.4 on this stress pattern). This is most common amongst younger speakers and it has not been observed at all in older male speakers. The items in (9) illustrate the allophony.

(9) /gia/ [giˈa ~ ʤiˈa] 'eat it/him/her'
    /gie/ [giˈe ~ ʤiˈe] 'his/hers/its'
    /gial/ [giˈal ~ ʤiˈal] 'carry it/him/her'
    /gio/ [giˈo ~ ʤiˈo] 'his/her/its faeces'

The clause-final prospective aspect marker *gie* 'PROSP' (§14.3.3) may be reduced to [ʤe] such that there is an incipient phonemic split between the voiced velar stop and its affricate allophone. The resulting minimal pair is given in (10).

(10) /gie/ [giˈe ~ ʤiˈe ~ ˈʤe] 'PROSP'
 /ge/ [ge] 'tree sp., *Inocarpus fagifer*'

Elsewhere /g/ can be realised as [g] or less commonly as [ɣ]. The allophony of /g/ is summarised in Table 2.8.

Table 2.8: Allophony of /g/.

	Allophone	Environment
/g/	[g] ~ [ʤ]	/ # _iˈV
	[g] ~ [ɣ]	/ elsewhere

2.2.3.3 Fricatives

No special allophony has been noted for the phonemes /s/ and /h/, though [s] is also an allophone of /tʃ/ (§2.2.3.4).

The voiced alveolar fricative /z/ has three allophones: a plain voiced alveolar allophone [z], a voiced alveolo-palatal sibilant affricate allophone [ʥ] and a voiced palato-alveolar affricate allophone [ʤ]. The allophones are in free variation, though some tendencies towards certain realisations in particular environments are observed. The phoneme /z/ tends to be realised as [z] in monosyllabic words of the shape CV and as [ʤ] or [ʥ] before a high front vowel in words of greater size than CV.

The distribution of the fricatives is illustrated in Table 2.9. Whilst /s/ is unrestricted, /z/ and /h/ appear exclusively in onsets. The appearance of /h/ in word-medial codas is very limited with only a handful of instances, most of which can be identified as Tetun borrowings. Final /h/ is only attested in interjections – see §3.5.7.

Table 2.9: Distribution of fricatives.

	Initial	Medial	Final
/s/	/sil/ 'sweat'	/hasaʔ/ 'count'	/hos/ 'bird'
/z/	/zap/ 'dog'	/ozo/ 'shit'	–
/h/	/hien/ 'louse'	/lahan/ 'sty'	(interjections)

Within Lamaknen, there is some variation between villages as to whether a small set of lexemes are realised with an initial /s/ or initial /z/. In villages in the northeast of Lamaknen, /s/ is found with the lexemes in (11), while /z/ is used elsewhere.

	Northeast	Elsewhere	
(11)	/seroʔ/	/zeroʔ/	'spoon out, scoop out'
	/sapal/	/zapal/	'folktale, fable'
	/soroʔ/	/zoroʔ/	'river bank'
	/sa͡ui/	/za͡ui/	'swishing sound'

2.2.3.4 Voiceless palato-alveolar affricate

The voiceless palato-alveolar affricate /tʃ/ is a minor phoneme found word-initially preceding a high front vowel /i/ in a total of 15 lexical items (out of a corpus of 2000+ lexical items), given in (12). Paralleling the allophones of /z/, the affricate phoneme has three allophones in free variation with one another: a voiceless fricative allophone [s], a voiceless alveolo-palatal sibilant affricate allophone [tɕ], and a voiced palato-alveolar affricate allophone [tʃ]. Most speakers show considerable variation, with affricate and fricative realisations co-occuring within a single utterance. For the higher frequency lexical items with /tʃ/, such as /tʃio/ 'who', /tʃie/, and /tʃier/, affricate realisations are rarely heard, with [sio], [sie], and [sier] being the overwhelmingly dominant realisations for each. This points to /tʃ/ being in the course of merging with /s/ in Bunaq Lamaknen.

(12) /tʃia/   [tʃiˈa ~ tɕiˈa ~ siˈa]   'burn'
     /tʃiak/   [tʃiˈak ~ tɕiˈak ~ siˈak]   'extinct'
     /tʃiaʔ/   [tʃiˈaʔ ~ tɕiˈaʔ ~ siˈaʔ]   'not want'
     /tʃie/   [tʃiˈe ~ tɕiˈe ~ siˈe]   'chicken'
     /tʃiel/   [tʃiˈel ~ tɕiˈel ~ siˈel]   'bright'
     /tʃier/   [tʃiˈer ~ tɕiˈer ~ siˈer]   'sleep'
     /tʃiet/   [tʃiˈet ~ tɕiˈet ~ siˈet]   'rip open'
     /tʃila/   [ˈtʃila ~ ˈtɕila ~ ˈsila]   'stomp and shout'
     /tʃileʔ/ [ˈtʃileʔ ~ ˈtɕileʔ ~ ˈsileʔ]   'pour'
     /tʃilon/ [ˈtʃilon ~ ˈtɕilon ~ ˈsilon]   'canine tooth'
     /tʃiluʔ/ [ˈtʃiluʔ ~ ˈtɕiluʔ ~ ˈsiluʔ]   'rest, play'
     /tʃinoʔ/ [ˈtʃinoʔ ~ ˈtɕinoʔ ~ ˈsinoʔ]   'hot'
     /tʃio/   [tʃiˈo ~ tɕiˈo ~ siˈo]   'who'
     /tʃiro/   [ˈtʃiro ~ ˈtɕiro ~ ˈsiro]   'which'
     /tʃiˈwal/ [ˈtʃiwal ~ ˈtɕiwal ~ ˈsiwal]   'flee'

The highly restricted distribution of the phoneme is the result of /tʃ/ once having been a conditioned allophone of /t/. In Bunaq Lamaknen /tʃ/ has gained phonemic status due to an allophonic rule in which /t/ is realised as [tʃ] before /i/ having only been differentially applied to the lexicon. Initially before /i/, /t/ has been retained as [t] in monosyllabic words and where identified as the reciprocal prefix tV- 'RECP'. It was in particular the conservative behaviour of the reciprocal morpheme in relation to affrication that gave rise to three minimal pairs in which /tʃ/ contrasts with /t/. They are given in (13).

(13) /tʃ/
/tʃio/ 'who'
/tʃie/ 'chicken'
/tʃia/ 'burn'

/t/
/tio/ 'each other's faeces'
/tie/ 'each other's'
/tia/ 'eat each other'

In an alternative analysis, the affricate could still be regarded as an allophone of /t/ with the distribution presented in Table 2.10.

Table 2.10: Allophony of /t/.

	Allophone	Environment
/t/	[tʃ] ~ [s]	/ #__i except
	[t]	/#__i(C)#
		/ tV- = 'RECP'
		elsewhere

However, /t/ has also remained [t] in some items which have the appropriate conditioning environment. Examples are provided in (14). As such, the occurrence of the affricate is not entirely predictable and it is thus best viewed as an independent phoneme.

(14) /tili/   [tili, *tʃili]   'bell'
/tilik/ [tilik, *tʃilik] 'bird sp.'
/tigi/   [tigi, *tʃigi]   'drip'
/timi/   [timi, *tʃimi]   'deshelled'

Medial affrication of /t/ is also a feature of the phonology of some children, but it has only been observed in a small number of lexemes. The most common instances are:

(15) /neto/ [neto ~ netʃo] '1SG'
/eto/   [eto ~ etʃo]   '2SG'
/hati/ [hati ~ hatʃi]   'exist'

It is not clear whether affrication in these items is an age-stable variable of Bunaq child phonology or part of a change in progress. The lack of a single consistent conditioning environment is notable. Though not found initially before the mid back vowel /o/, affrication is observed medially before /o/ as well as /i/. If child affrication were related to affrication of /t/ before /i/, then we would expect a simple rule extension whereby the change /t/ > [tʃ] / _i were applied to medial environments in addition to initial ones.

2.2.3.5 Liquids

Bunaq has two liquid phonemes: a rhotic trill /r/ and a lateral approximant /l/.

The lateral phoneme has a voiceless fricative allophone [ɬ] which occurs word-finally in free variation with [l]. The fricative allophone is most common following the high front vowel /i/ and least common following the mid front vowel /e/ and the low central vowel /a/. The distribution of the allophones of /l/ is summarised in Table 2.11.

Table 2.11: Allophony of /l/.

	Allophone	Environment
/l/	[l] ~ [ɬ]	/ _#
	[l]	/ elsewhere

The distribution of the liquid phonemes /r/ and /l/ is illustrated in Table 2.12. The lateral /l/ is unrestricted. The distribution of /r/ is more complicated. Only a handful of /r/-initial words are evidenced in Bunaq Lamaknen and they are for the most part identified as borrowings (see §2.2.4); all other instances of /r/ are final, with medial occurrences of [r] being treated as allophones of /d/.

Table 2.12: Distribution of liquids.

	Initial	Medial	Final
/r/	(/redi/ 'net')	–	/por/ 'holy'
/l/	/lai̯/ 'lay'	/tolo/ 'put in'	/pol/ 'send'

If it were not for the small number of /r/-initial words, it would be best to analyse /d/ and /r/ as constituting a single phoneme /d/ in Bunaq Lamaknen, as they would then have non-overlapping distributions. This analysis is not preferred here as it would mean that the otherwise robust rule that voiced (oral) consonants do not appear in codas is violated (see §2.3.3 on phoneme distributions).

2.2.3.6 Nasals

Bunaq has two nasal phonemes, the bilabial nasal /m/ and the alveolar nasal /n/. No special allophony has been noted for the nasal phonemes /m/ and /n/; both conform closely to the IPA norms for their symbols, showing little, if any, perceptual variation.

Table 2.13 illustrates the distribution of the Bunaq nasals. We see that /n/ is unrestricted, while /m/ cannot appear in codas.

Table 2.13: Distribution of nasals.

	Initial	Medial	Final
/m/	/mo/ 'sea'	/mami/ 'tasty'	–
/n/	/nor/ 'randomly'	/ene/ 'night'	/bon/ 'box bean'

Final /n/ can be dropped in words of more than two syllables, as seen in (16).

(16) /hiloʔon/ [hiloʔon ~ hiloʔo] 'two'
 /goniʔon/ [goniʔon ~ goniʔo] 'three'
 /saruʔan/ [saruʔan ~ saruʔa] 'complain'

Nasal consonants cause some sporadic nasalisation of adjacent vowels. In an onset, a nasal consonant onset can cause nasalisation of the following vowel. In a coda, a nasal can cause nasalisation of the preceding vowel.

2.2.3.7 Approximant

The phoneme /w/ is an approximant and is distinct from the vowel /u/. The vowel phoneme /u/ can carry stress and occurs in syllable nuclei, whereas the phonetically similar consonant phoneme /w/ can occur inter-vocalically and does not form the nucleus of a syllable. Minimal pairs illustrating the contrast are given in (17). Note that initial /u/ before another vowel is consistently unstressed.

```
      /w/                           /u/
(17)  /wal/   ['wal]  'be full'     /ual/   [uˈʷal]  'bend'
      /wer/   ['wer]  'wash'        /uer/   [uˈʷer]  'pot'
      /wi/    ['wi]   'suckle'      /ui/    [uˈʷi]   'spirit'
      /wil/   ['wil]  'dig'         /uil/   [uˈʷil]  'mushroom'
```

The approximant cannot occur in codas. It has the additional restriction that it does not occur adjacent to the back vowel /u/ either in the preceding or same syllable. Co-occurrence of /w/ and /o/ is limited to a handful of items. This distribution is illustrated in Table 2.14.

Table 2.14: Distribution of approximant.

	Initial	Medial
w + a	/wa/ 'discard'	/nawa/ 'head basket'
w + e	/wek/ 'hug'	/zewen/ 'roll out'
w + i	/wit/ 'take'	/diwi/ 'a lot'
w + o	/wo/ 'bulb, corm'	/gowo/ 'womb'

2.2.3.8 Glottal stop

The glottal stop phoneme /ʔ/ contrasts with other phonemes and with zero. I present minimal pairs in which the glottal stop phoneme contrasts with zero in (18) and with other consonants in (19).

(18)
/ʔ/		∅	
/baʔi/	'PROX.INAN'	/ba͡i/	'thing'
/haʔal/	'be finished'	/hal/	'dandruff'
/okoʔ/	'hole'	/oko/	'valley'
/niʔ/	'NEG'	/ni/	'OBL'

(19)
/ʔ/		/C/	
/toʔi/	'hollow out'	/toli/	'be together, be complete'
/leʔa/	'roll up'	/leba/	'carrying pole'
/sieʔ/	'tear'	/sien/	'plait'
/goeʔ/	'be ancient'	/goet/	'be like'

Phonetically, the glottal stop phoneme can also be realised as creak. With a final glottal stop, the creak is realised on the preceding vowel, while, with a medial glottal stop, the creak is realised on the following vowel. There appears to be variation in the realisation of the creak: the creak may affect the entire vowel or just the edge at which the glottal stop occurs, or may be realised as a transition between vowels in medial occurrences. More work is required to establish the full continuum of phonation types with which the glottal stop can be realised.

The glottal stop has a different distribution from that of other stops. While other consonants occur either in onsets or in codas and onsets without any differentiation of word-medial and word-initial positions (see §2.3.3), the glottal stop phoneme only occurs word-finally in codas and word-medially in onsets. In word-initial onsets, it does occur, but then only non-phonemically as a default onset on vowel-initial words. The default glottal stop onset, however, is not used with clitics, which are not independent words. Compare /o/ [ˈʔo] 'prawn' and /=o/ [o] 'also, too' in Bunaq, where the former is a lexical word with a glottal stop onset and the latter a phrasal enclitic without an onset. The non-phonemic appearance of a glottal stop in onsets and the contrastive appearance of a glottal stop between vowels are discussed in §2.3.1 and §2.3.7 respectively.

2.2.4 Phoneme adaptation in loans

In this section I address the way in which phonemes and allophones with distributions not present in Bunaq are adapted when they are borrowed into the language. Table 2.15 presents an overview of the main patterns observed in adapted loans from Tetun Terik and Indonesian/Malay.

Table 2.15: Loan phoneme adaptation.

Source phoneme		Bunaq phoneme
/f/	>	/p/
/d/ & medial /r/	>	/d/ [d~r]
inital /r/	>	/d/ [d~r] or /l/
final /r/	>	/l/ or /r/
medial /h/	>	/h/ or /ʔ/
final /k/	>	/k/ or /ʔ/
final /V/	>	/V/ or /Vʔ/
/VV/	>	/VV/ or /VʔV/
/dʒ/	>	/z/

The phoneme /f/ is most frequent in East Timorese varieties where bilingualism with Tetun is the norm. Older loanwords from Tetun with /f/ have been adapted with the voiceless bilabial stop /p/ (20).

```
       Tetun                              Bunaq
(20)  /faen/   'transfer of female'  >  /paen/
      /foun/   'new'                 >  /poun/
      /funu/   'fight'               >  /punu/
```

The voiceless affricate /tʃ/ in Indonesian/Malay items shows no adaptation and is consistently maintained as such in loanwords.

Tetun loans with a voiced alveolar stop /d/ have been fully adapted to Bunaq native phonology. In accordance with Bunaq allophonic rules, /d/ is realised as [d~r] initially (21) and as [r] medially (22). Borrowings with medial /r/ are kept as [r], presumably representing underlying /d/.

2.2 Phoneme inventory

	Tetun			Bunaq	
(21)	/dale/	'party'	>	/dale/	[dale ~ rale]
	/deal/	'commoner'	>	/deal/	[deal ~ real]
	/daun/	'needle'	>	/daun/	[daun ~ raun]

	Tetun			Bunaq	
(22)	/badak/	'short'	>	/badak/	[barak]
	/tada/	'know'	>	/tada/	[tara]
	/kuda/	'horse'	>	/kuda/	[kura] (or < Malay *kuda*)

Even in borrowings which otherwise show no loan adaptation, there is a tendency for a medial voiced alveolar stop /d/ to be realised as [r] in the casual speech of older Bunaq speakers. Four instances from the corpus are given in (23). Initially, no alternation between [d] and [r] is observed in Indonesian/Malay loans.

	Indonesian			Bunaq
(23)	/adat/	'custom'	>	[adat ~ arat]
	/jadi/	'so'	>	[dʒadi ~ dʒari]
	/adel/	'Adel'	>	[adel ~ arel]

Some Tetun loanwords with initial /r/ are incorporated into the Bunaq lexicon with /d/ (24), others with /l/ (25), and still others, although rare, with /r/ (26). Where /d/ is used for loan adaptation of initial Tetun /r/, there has been a back application of the allophonic rule for /d/, whereby speakers recognise that initial [r] is always an allophone of /d/ and therefore shows [d~r] alternation initially.

	Tetun			Bunaq	
(24)	/renu/	'commoner'	>	/denu/	[denu ~ renu]
	/ro/	'boat'	>	/do/	[do ~ ro]
	/roos/	'brush, wipe'	>	/dos/	[dos ~ ros]
(25)	/rade/	'duck'	>	/lade/	[lare]
	/rai/	'lay down'	>	/l͡ai/	
	/resin/	'more'	>	/lesin/	
(26)	/redi/	'fishing net type'	>	/redi/	[reri] (*dedi)

Tetun loanwords with a final rhotic /r/ are typically adapted into Bunaq Lamaknen with the liquid phoneme /l/ (27), but some retain /r/ (28).

	Tetun			Bunaq
(27)	/bokur/	'fat'	>	/bokul/
	/kahur/	'mix'	>	/kahul/
	/mamar/	'soft'	>	/mamal/
	/hanaur/	'burn'	>	/hanaul/
(28)	/fiar/	'believe'	>	/piar/
	/fetor/	'chief'	>	/petor/

Tetun loans with medial /h/ are either retained as /h/ (29) or adapted with /ʔ/ (30) in Bunaq.

	Tetun			Bunaq
(29)	/dahur/	'celebration'		/dahul/
	/hahu/	'begin'	>	/hahu/
	/luhan/	'stable'	>	/luhan/
(30)	/mehi/	'dream'	>	/meʔi/
	/nehek/	'black ant'	>	/neʔek/
	/tatehan/	'reflect'	>	/tateʔan/

Tetun final /k/ is in some items adapted with /ʔ/ (31). Vowel-final words borrowed from Tetun are often adapted with a final /ʔ/ in Bunaq (32). Vowel sequences in borrowed Tetun words are also frequently interrupted by /ʔ/ in their Bunaq adaptations (33).

(31)	/lumak/	'tame'	>	/lumaʔ/
	/susuk/	'mosquito'	>	/susuʔ/
	/tudik/	'knife'	>	/tudiʔ/ [turiʔ]
(32)	/hateke/	'see'	>	/tekeʔ/
	/keboko/	'grub'	>	/kebokoʔ/
	/kanko/	'water spinach'	>	/kankoʔ/
(33)	/buar/	'summon'	>	/buʔar/
	/dean/	'scold'	>	/deʔan/
	/doit/	'money'	>	/doʔit/

Indonesian/Malay items with /dʒ/ tend to retain their native phonology when used in Bunaq. In a few items, Indonesian/Malay /dʒ/ in initial position has been adapted into the Bunaq lexicon with /z/; these items show the corresponding allophony of this phoneme, as in (34).

	Indonesian/Malay		Bunaq	
(34)	/dʒaga/	'guard' >	/zaga/	[zaga ~ dʑaga ~ dʒaga]
	/dʒawa/	'Java' >	/zawa/	[zawa ~ dʑawa ~ dʒawa]
	/dʒepit/	'clip' >	/zepit/	[zepit ~ dʑepit ~ dʒepit]

Bunaq also adapts nasals in some borrowings, but generalisations are not possible due to the small number of items involved. For example, Bunaq does not allow /m/ in codas (§2.3.3). Accordingly, Malay *lem* 'glue' (< Dutch *lijm*) is adapted in Bunaq as /len/ 'glue'. The same adaptation of /m/ as /n/ in a coda, however, does not occur in Bunaq /kampo/ 'village' via Tetun and/or Malay, perhaps on account of the following bilabial stop. In the case of Bunaq /sondaru/ 'soldier' (< Tetun *soldadu* < Portuguese *soldado*), /l/ is adapted as /n/ in a coda, thereby limiting consonant clusters in the language to nasal+obstruent. See §2.3.4 for further discussion and illustration of violations of the Bunaq cluster constraint.

2.3 Phonotactics

This section describes the constraints on the permissible combinations of phonemes in Bunaq, including possible syllable structures, consonant clusters, and vowel sequences.

2.3.1 Syllable structure

As is evident from the vowel minimal pairs presented at the beginning of this chapter in Table 2.2, there is no minimal word constraint in Bunaq. Thus, the minimal syllable and word consists of a single vowel, represented as V, or diphthong, V + [i]; the maximal syllable is CVC.

Consonant clusters are prohibited both within a single syllable and across syllables. Accordingly, codas are strictly word final. The respective structures of non-final and final syllables are illustrated in Figures 2.4 and 2.5.

(C1)   V (i)   **Figure 2.4:** Non-final syllable structure.

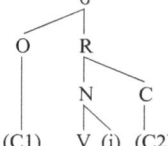

Figure 2.5: Final syllable structure.

Vowel-initial words have a glottal stop onset. This is a default onset and the glottal stop in this position is entirely predictable and, thus, non-contrastive. This suggests that the structure of the initial syllable in Bunaq should be differentiated from that of the medial and final syllable: initial syllables require an onset, whereas medial and final ones do not. See §2.3.7 for discussion of the glottal stop as a boundary marker in Bunaq.

2.3.2 Word templates

The arrangement of C and V illustrated in mono-morphemic words of different syllables is exemplified in this section. The marginal diphthong phonemes will not be dealt with here; their distribution is discussed in §2.3.3. The arrangements of C and V possible for monosyllabic words are given in (35).

(35) V   : /u/   'live'
      CV   : /to/   'year'
      VC   : /il/   'water'
      CVC   : /man/ 'come'

Disyllabic words show the arrangements of C and V presented in (36).

(36) V.V   : /u.i/   'spirit'
      V.CV   : /i.pi/   'rice (plant)'
      V.VC   : /u.er/   'pot'
      V.CVC   : /o.del/ 'monkey'
      CV.V   : /te.o/   'where'
      CV.CV   : /lo.lo/ 'mountain'
      CV.VC   : /ko.en/ 'nice'
      CV.CVC : /ho.tel/ 'tree'

The vast majority of Bunaq words are either monosyllabic or disyllabic. There are no words of 5 syllables in the (2000+ item) corpus and only twelve words of 4 syllables, while a total of 65 items in the corpus are trisyllabic.

The majority of trisyllabic words can be identified as borrowings, derived words (either historically compounded or affixed forms), or onomatopoeias. Of the trisyllabic words which cannot be identified as belonging to any one of these categories, there are not enough examples to generalise on each potential combination of syllables, though the preference for CV is obvious. Some representative examples are given in (37).

(37) V.V.CVC   : /o.a.lak/   'wretch'
     CV.CV.V   : /ni.su.i/   'sniff'
     CV.CV.CV   : /ge.le.ni/   'howl'
     CV.CV.CV   : /ka.ko.lo/   'drift'
     CV.CV.CVC   : /me.lo.koʔ/ 'wander'

One noticeable pattern in trisyllabic items is that the glottal stop appears as the onset to the last syllable very frequently. Examples are given in (38).

(38) CV.V.ʔV   : /bu.a.ʔi/   'yarn'
     CV.CV.ʔV   : /ba.li.ʔa/   'plant sp., *Momordica charantia*'
     CV.CV.ʔV   : /ba.ni.ʔa/   'guest'
     CV.CV.ʔV(C) : /sa.du.ʔan/ 'complain'
     CV.CV.ʔVC   : /bu.le.ʔen/ 'red'

Trisyllablic onomatopoeic words are composed according to a general template $[C_1V_1.C_2V_2.C_2V_2ʔ]$ in which the second syllable is reduplicated in the third syllable with the addition of a glottal stop in coda position (39).

(39) CV.CV.CVʔ   : /ka.ka.kaʔ/ 'cackle'
     CV.CV.CVʔ   : /ke.ke.keʔ/ 'giggle'
     CV.CV.CVʔ   : /ka.da.daʔ/ 'crackle, pop'
     CV.CV.CVʔ   : /ko.do.doʔ/ 'hoorah, cheer'
     CV.CV.CVʔ   : /tu.lu.luʔ/ 'squelch'
     CV.CV.CVʔ   : /si.gu.guʔ/ 'sizzle, whizz'

In all but one item the vowel is identical throughout, yielding a template of this kind: $[C_1V_1.C_2V_1.C_2V_1ʔ]$. In two items, it is not only the vowel which is identical across all three syllables but also the consonant, yielding the template $[C_1V_1.C_1V_1.C_2V_1ʔ]$.

Of the dozen 4-syllable words in the corpus, only five cannot be identified as Tetun borrowings. They are given in (40). Of these, two look to be derived: *kudukudu* seems likely to be a reduplicated form, while *gomolale* appears to be derived from *molal* 'domesticated'. The remaining three are likely historical compounds.

(40) V.CV.CV.C   : /a.ma.de.ʔu/   'plant sp., *Solanum verbascifolium*'
    V.CV.CV.VC   : /a.ti.to.uʔ/   'bird sp.'
    CV.CV.CV.CV   : /go.mo.la.le/ 'persuade'
    CV.CV.CV.CV   : /ku.du.ku.du/ 'game type'
    CV.CV.CV.CVC : /hi.le.de.noʔ/ 'two days prior'

2.3.3 Phoneme distribution

All vowel phonemes may appear as a syllable nucleus and are attested word-initially, -medially, and -finally. An illustration is given in Table 2.16.

Table 2.16: Distribution of vowel phonemes.

	Initial	Medial	Final
/a/	/an/ 'grass'	/matas/ 'old'	/apa/ 'cow'
/e/	/el/ 'crawl'	/selek/ 'spring'	/ene/ 'night'
/i/	/in/ 'onion'	/sipik/ 'sharpen'	/ipi/ 'rice plant'
/o/	/op/ 'highlands'	/lotoʔ/ 'noisy'	/oko/ 'hole'
/u/	/ul/ 'pull out'	/puluk/ 'spit'	/uku/ 'tip out'

The diphthong phonemes (D) appear as a syllable nucleus of both open and closed syllables. They appear in the syllable nuclei of both stressed and unstressed syllables. An illustration is given in Table 2.17.

Table 2.17: Distribution of diphthong phonemes.

	/ai/	/ei/	/oi/
/D/	/ai/ 'only'	/ei/ '2PL'	/oi/ 'INTERJ'
/CD/	/bai/ 'thing'	/dei/ 'further'	/poi/ 'choose'
/CDC/	/dain/ 'bind'	/beik/ 'dumb'	/toiʔ/ 'flat'
/(C)DCV(C)/	/aibaʔ/ 'eD'	--	/goiga/ 'guava'
/CVCD/	/lulai/ 'move'	/kawei/ 'sit cross-legged'	/moroi/ 'sleepy'

The distribution of the individual consonant phonemes was discussed in §2.3.3. An overview of the distribution is provided in Table 2.18. The restricted nature of the coda position relative to onset positions is conspicuous: the only consonants able to appear in codas are voiceless obstruents, /n/, the two liquids, and the glottal stop phoneme. Other obvious asymmetries in the distribution of consonant phonemes include that of the voiceless affricate in relation to the other obstruents and the liquids in relation to one another.

Table 2.18: Distribution of consonant phonemes.

	p	b	t	d	k	g	n	m	s	z	h	tʃ	r	l	w	ʔ
word-initial (onset)	+	+	+	+	+	+	+	+	+	+	+	+	+	+	+	−
word-medial (onset)	+	+	+	+	+	+	+	+	+	+	+	+	−	−	+	+	+
word-final (coda)	+	−	+	−	+	−	+	−	+	−	−	−	+	+	−	+

2.3.4 Cluster constraint violations

There are a handful of items in the Bunaq lexicon which violate the constraint set out in §2.3.1 that prohibits consonant clusters. These are, for the most part, loanwords.

2.3.4.1 Consonant clusters in loans

The constraint on medial codas is violated in a few loans which have medial nasal codas. These are mostly from Portuguese, typically via Tetun or Malay, as set out in (41).

(41) /ban.de.ra/ < Tetun *bandera* < Portuguese *bandeira* 'flag'
 /kam.po/ < Tetun *kampo* < Malay *kampuŋ* 'village'
 /kan.koʔ/ < Tetun *kanko* < Malay *kaŋkuŋ* 'water spinach'
 /kan.se.da/ < Portuguese *canseda* 'weariness, salary'
 /kin.tal/ < Malay *kintal* < Portuguese *quintal* 'yard'
 /kon.ta/ < Tetun *konta* < Portuguese *contar* 'tell, recount'
 /lan.ta.ro/ < Malay *lamtara* ~ *lamtoro* 'plant sp., *Leucaena leucocephala*'

With Bunaq /son.da.ru/ < Tetun *soldadu* < Portuguese *soldado* 'solider', a medial coda in /l/ is adapted in Bunaq as /n/, thereby keeping to the nasal+obstruent pattern that is permitted for the above loans.

In my data, there are three loans with a s+t cluster in Bunaq. These are set out in (42).

(42) /kas.ti.gu/ < Tetun *kastigu* < Portuguese *castigo* 'punishment, curse'
 /misti/ < Tetun *misti* < Malay *mesti* 'must, have to'
 /pes.ta/ < Malay *pesta* < Portuguese *festa* 'celebration, party'

Finally, Bunaq has three items with medial clusters in which /k/ or /ʔ/ occurs in the medial coda (43). It seems likely that these represent loans of Tetun verbs marked with the causative prefix *hak-* (a reflex of PMP *paka-) (cf. §2.2.4 where it is shown that Tetun /k/ can be adapted in Bunaq as /k/ or /ʔ/). However, this hypothesis is problematic in that I have not been able to identify Tetun sources for these items.

(43) /hak.bi.lan/   'deceive, cheat'
      /hak.bok/   'bother'
      /haʔ.men/   'glorify, worship'

2.3.4.2 Consonant clusters in native words

Consonant clusters in native Bunaq words are, in accordance with the rules set out in the previous sections, near non-existent, apparently limited to historical compounds.

A notable group is formed by the items ending in /-ter/ given in (44). The semantic commonalities plus the irregular pattern of final stress on these items suggests that they originate in compounds headed by a now no-longer-extant item *ter. See §2.4 on stress in Bunaq.

(44) /hulakter/   [ˌhu.lak.ˈter]   'step across, step over'
      /palakter/   [ˌpa.lak.ˈter]   'kick'
      /sosalter/   [ˌso.sal.ˈter]   'jerk (of legs), kick uncontrollably'
      /ulter/   [ul.ˈter]   '(spread one's legs to) expose one's genitals'

A further two items, given in (45), optionally delete their stressed /e/. This reduction results in a cluster of /d/ and /n/ across syllables and a shift in stress to the new penultimate syllable. These items are certainly historical compounds. For example, /hiledenoʔ/ is transparently a compound of /hilede/ [hiˈlere] 'day after tomorrow' plus /noʔ/ 'ago', as in /to uen noʔ/ 'one year ago'.

(45) /edenoʔ/   [eˈrenoʔ ~ ˈernoʔ]   'day before, yesterday'
      /hiledenoʔ/   [ˌhileˈrenoʔ ~ hiˈlernoʔ]   'two days prior'

Finally, there are two native Bunaq words with a medial nasal coda. The first item is /metensi/ 'just now' realised as [metensi ~ metenti]. The second item /gontʃiet/ 'five' is typically realised as [ˌgon.tʃi.ˈet] with a consonant cluster across the syllable boundary. For some speakers it may also be realised as [ˌgo.ni.ˈtʃet] 'five', while for still others it can be further realised as [ˌgo.in.ˈtʃet]. The cluster of /n/ and /tʃ/ appears to be the result of a compound in which the first component historically may reflect *g-on* '3AN-hand', a formative also reflected in the numerals /goniʔon/ 'three' and /goniʔil/ 'four'.

2.3.5 Vowel sequences

All vowels occur in VV sequences. Vowels in VV sequences belong to separate syllables. All sequences are attested except for homorganic sequences of vowels. Table 2.19 presents the 20 possible VV sequences and the number of times a particular VV sequence is attested in a lexicon of approximately 2000 words with an example of each.

Table 2.19: Bunaq vowel sequences.

	/a/	/e/	/i/	/o/	/u/
/a/	–	a.e (7) /aen/ 'shy'	a.i (5) /sai/ 'be amused'	a.o (2) /tao/ 'pound'	a.u (6) /laun/ 'fast'
/e/	e.a (2) /mea?/ 'virgin'	–	e.i (5) /mei/ 'bleat'	e.o (7) /teo/ 'where'	e.u (5) /deu/ 'house'
/i/	i.a (6) /sia/ 'burn'	i.e (19) /hien/ 'louse'	–	i.o (7) /niol/ 'sound'	i.u (3) /iu/ 'maggot'
/o/	o.a (5) /moal/ 'earth'	o.e (12) /goet/ 'be like'	o.i (2) /loi/ 'good'	–	o.u (12) /kou/ 'slip'
/u/	u.a (12) /dua/ 'indeed'	u.e (19) /kuel/ 'worm'	u.i (11) /hui/ 'wild'	u.o (2) /uor/ 'vegetable'	–

From the overview offered by Table 2.19, it is obvious that some sequences occur much more frequently than others. I find that:
(i) though /ie/ and /ue/ are the most common vowel sequences, high frequency is not necessarily related to the high vowels, with the sequence /oe/ also having a high number of tokens;
(ii) vowels in sequence need not be maximally different and there seems to be no preference for maximal contrasts in height and frontness, and;
(iii) there is no strong restriction in direction (e.g., high before non-high), cf. /ia/ occurs 6 times and /ai/ 5 times, though it must be noted that /uV/ and /Ve/ are altogether more frequent than /Vu/ and /eV/ respectively.

Vowel sequences may be stressed on the first vowel or the second vowel in the sequence. All cases of stress of the second vowel are where the first is a high vowel. However, not all high vowels that are first in a sequence are unstressed. See §2.4 on the details of stress in Bunaq.

In addition to sequences of two simple vowels, a diphthong may occur following a simple vowel, but then not in the same syllable. The sequence VD (where D stands for diphthong) is only a marginal pattern, occurring in a total of 5 items, presented in (46).

(C)VD
(46) /u.a͡i/   [uʷaj]   'moo'
      /ke.a͡i/   [keʲaj]   'wail'
      /te.a͡i/   [teʲaj]   'stare at'
      /ko.e͡i/   [koʷej]   'squeal'
      /te.o͡i/   [teʲoj]   'thwack'

2.3.6 Phonetic glide insertion between VV sequences

Non-phonemic glides are regularly inserted between sequences of vowels. Glide epenthesis is most frequent and most distinct where the height and backness values of the vowels in sequence differ most. Following front vowels, modifications are in the direction of the palatal glide, and following back vowels in the direction of the bilabial glide. Epenthesis of each of these is illustrated in (47) and (48) respectively. Note that glide epenthesis is observed with both finally and penultimately stressed roots.

       [ʲ] insertion
(47) /tʃia/   [tʃiʲa ~ siʲa]   'burn'
      /deu/   [ˈdeʲu]   'house'
      /tʃio/   [tʃiʲo ~ siʲo]   'who'
      /lokomea?/   [lokoˈmeʲa?]   'eagle sp.'

       [ʷ] insertion
(48) /uor/   [uˈʷor]   'vegetable'
      /guel/ [guˈʷel]   'light'
      /loi/   [ˈloʷi]   'good'
      /kou/   [ˈkoʷu]   'slip'

Glide insertion may be seen as a low-level phonetic process or a rule creating well-formed CV syllables. That is, epenthetic glides may be taken as the default onsets of medial syllables with an underlying shape V(C). If this view is taken, then an epenthetic glide parallels the glottal stop, which performs the same function word-initially (cf. §2.3.7).

2.3.7 Glottal stop as boundary marker

In §2.2.1 we saw that the glottal stop appears non-phonemically as a default onset for vowel-initial words in Bunaq. That is, the glottal stop functions as a kind of 'boundary marker' delimiting one word from another.[1] There is evidence to suggest that, although synchronically phonemic, the medial glottal stop may historically have also been a non-contrastive boundary marker.

Table 2.20 presents the attested vowel sequences with an intervening glottal stop, the number of attestations of each and an example. Forms exhibiting a medial glottal stop may be compared with the corresponding sequences of vowels without a glottal stop presented in Table 2.19. Most obvious in comparing the two tables is that, while the glottal stop regularly appears between sequences of identical vowels, these same homorganic vowel clusters are absent without the glottal stop. That is, the glottal stop can be interpreted as being an epenthetic consonant medially; it may have been inserted to distinguish the boundaries of syllables with identical vowels in adjacent positions, i.e., where the first syllable has the shape (C)V and the second V(C).

Additional phenomena pointing to the glottal stop being a boundary phenomenon come from historically suffixed forms. For instance, consider the pronouns /halaʔi/ '3PL' and /halali/ '3DU', which are historically composed of a root *hala suffixed with *-i 'PL' and *-li 'DU', and the demonstratives /baʔi/ 'NPRX.AN' and /baʔa/ 'NPRX.INAN', which are historically built by adding *-i and *-a to the PTAP demonstrative *ba (Schapper 2007). The glottal stop in these items appears at the morpheme boundary between vowel-final roots and vowel-initial affixes seemingly to prevent a sequence of vowels. The glottal stop was similarly seen in loans, such as the examples in (33) of §2.2.4, to appear breaking up vowel sequences where the source had no glottal stop.

Table 2.20: Vowel sequences interrupted by a glottal stop.

	/a/	/e/	/i/	/o/	/u/
/a/	aʔa (8) /taʔa/ 'close'	aʔe (8) /aʔen/ 'wear'	aʔi (6) /baʔis/ 'much'	aʔo (2) /paʔol/ 'maize'	aʔu (8) /naʔut/ 'wear'
/e/	eʔa (4) /teʔa/ 'pray'	eʔe (8) /beʔen/ 'ripe'	eʔi (2) /deʔin/ 'near by'	eʔo (3) /weʔon/ 'shack'	eʔu (2) /heʔu/ 'whistle'

---

[1] Trubetzkoy (1936) posited the notion of *Grenzsignale* 'boundary signals' that serve delimitative functions in a language and occur at the boundaries of units of meaning, such as morphemes, in relation to the appearance of the glottal stop in German.

Table 2.20 (continued)

	/a/	/e/	/i/	/o/	/u/
/i/	iʔa (4) /iʔal/ 'advance'	iʔe (0) –	iʔi (7) /siʔil/ 'insert'	iʔo (1) /goniʔon/ 'three'	iʔu (3) /piʔu/ 'ever'
/o/	oʔa (9) /boʔal/ 'great'	oʔe (4) /goʔet/ 'other'	oʔi (3) /hoʔi/ 'peanut'	oʔo (6) /noʔok/ 'enough'	oʔu (2) /toʔuk/ 'question'
/u/	uʔa (4) /tuʔal/ 'swap'	uʔe (3) /huʔe/ 'here'	uʔi (0) –	uʔo (0) –	uʔu (5) /puʔup/ 'peak'

In sum, whilst the glottal stop in Bunaq is both non-contrastive initially and contrastive non-initially, there is evidence to suggest that in the past it may also have had non-contrastive functions word-medially.

2.4 Stress

In the vast majority of Bunaq words, stress falls on the penultimate syllable of the phonological word, as in the following disyllabic (49) and trisyllabic words (50).

(49) /tekeʔ/ [ˈte.keʔ] 'look at'
    /pana/ [ˈpa.na] 'woman'
    /bini/ [ˈbi.ni] 'steal'
    /loi/ [ˈlo.ʷi] 'good'

(50) /buleʔen/ [bu.ˈle.ʔen] 'gold, red'
    /honogo/ [ho.ˈno.go] 'be separate'
    /nisui/ [ni.ˈsu.i] 'sniffle'
    /zebelak/ [ze.ˈbe.lak] 'beam'

In words of four syllables, primary stress also falls on the penultimate syllable. Additionally, there is secondary stress that falls on the initial syllable (51). Syllables with secondary stress are perceptually louder than unstressed syllables. However, I have not been able to establish the exact phonetic correlates of secondary stress and how they differ from those of primary stress, due to the very small number of items with four syllables.

(51) /sidubisu/ [ˌsi.ru.ˈbi.su] 'work'
/bedeliku?/ [ˌbe.re.ˈli.ku?] 'bird sp.'
/hiledeno?/ [ˌhi.le.ˈre.no?] 'two days prior'
/gomolale/ [ˌgo.mo.ˈla.le] 'persuade'

Final stress is a minor pattern found in two sets of items. The first set, listed in (52), are trisyllables which were historically compounds (as treated in §2.3.4.2). These have secondary stress on their initial syllable.

(52) /goni?on/ [ˌgo.ni.ˈ?on] 'three'
/goni?il/ [ˌgo.ni.ˈ?il] 'four'
/gontʃiet/ [ˌgon.tʃi.ˈet] 'five'
/hulakter/ [ˌhu.lak.ˈter] 'step across, step over'
/palakter/ [ˌpa.lak.ˈter] 'kick'
/sosalter/ [ˌso.sal.ˈter] 'jerk (of legs), kick uncontrollably'

The second, larger set with final stress contains items with a vowel sequence where the first vowel is a high vowel and the second a non-high vowel. Examples of items of this type are set out in (53).

(53) /gia/ [giˈʲa] 'eat it/him/her'
/gie/ [giˈʲe] 'his/hers/its'
/gial/ [giˈʲal] 'carry it/him/her'
/giel/ [giˈʲel] 'its nest'
/giep/ [giˈʲep] 'chop it/him/her'
/gio/ [giˈʲo] 'his/her/its faeces'
/giol/ [giˈʲol] 'his/her/its voice'
/gua/ [guˈʷa] 'his/her footsteps'
/gue/ [guˈʷe] 'hit him/her'
/guel/ [guˈʷel] 'light'
/guen/ [guˈʷen] 'grow back, regenerate'
/guol/ [guˈʷol] 'back of the knee'
/iel/ [iˈʲel] 'multiply, populate'
/kuek/ [kuˈʷek] 'dead'
/kuel/ [kuˈʷel] 'worm'
/luel/ [luˈʷel] 'skin, peel'
/muel/ [muˈʷel] 'thin, skinny'
/niat/ [niˈʲat] 'beginning'
/tʃia/ [tʃiˈʲa] 'burn'
/tʃiak/ [tʃiˈʲak] 'extinct'
/tʃia?/ [tʃiˈʲa?] 'not want'
/tʃie/ [tʃiˈʲe] 'chicken'

/tʃiel/	[tʃiˡiel]	'bright'
/tʃier/	[tʃiˡier]	'sleep'
/tʃiet/	[tʃiˡiet]	'rip open'
/tʃio/	[tʃiˡio]	'who'
/tuek/	[tuˡʷek]	'heavy'
/tuen/	[tuˡʷen]	'when'
/uor/	[uˡʷor]	'vegetable'

As mentioned in §2.3.5, not all vowel sequences of this kind have final stress. The result is that stress in items with VV sequences with an initial high vowel must be considered contrastive. To date, I have, however, only identified a single stress-based minimal pair: /d-uˈa/ [duˡʷa ~ dʷa] REFL-footstep 'one's own footstep' versus /ˈdua/ [ˈdu.ʷa] 'truly, indeed'. Thus, the functional load carried by stress in this context is low.

Bunaq stress is sensitive to prefixation (§2.5.1) in certain environments, but never to suffixation (§2.5.2). Prefixation does not affect stress placement on vowel-initial monosyllabic roots or on disyllabic roots. The items in (54) illustrate prefixation of vowel-initial monosyllabic roots (of which there only a small number) and in (55) of disyllabic roots with the 3ʳᵈ person ANIMATE prefix *gV-* '3AN-'.

		Bare root				Prefixed root	
(54)	/al/	[ˈal]	'stand up'	>	/gV-al/	[ˈgal]
	/il/	[ˈil]	'water'	>	/gV-il/	[ˈgil]
	/ul/	[ˈul]	'extract'	>	/gV-ul/	[ˈgul]
(55)	/iwal/	[ˈiwal]	'pick'	>	/gV-iwal/	[ˈgiwal]
	/ube/	[ˈube]	'block'	>	/gV-ube/	[ˈgube]
	/tekeʔ/	[ˈtekeʔ]	'look'	>	/gV-tekeʔ/	[geˈtekeʔ]
	/mobel/	[ˈmobel]	'like'	>	/gV-mobel/	[goˈmobel]

But where a monosyllabic root with the shape CV(C) is prefixed, the vowel of the prefix bears the stress, as can be seen with the examples in (56). This pattern means that the preference for penultimate stress is preserved.

		Bare root				Prefixed root	
(56)	/po/	[ˈpo]	'foam'	>	/gV-po/	[ˈgopo]
	/tin/	[ˈtin]	'price'	>	/gV-tin/	[ˈgitin]
	/wa/	[ˈwa]	'discard'	>	/gV-wa/	[ˈgawa]
	/ziʔ/	[ˈziʔ]	'write'	>	/gV-ziʔ/	[ˈgiziʔ]

2.5 Morphophonology

As a language with relatively isolating word structure, Bunaq morphophonology is quite simple. This section deals with the morphophonology of prefixation (§2.5.1), suffixation (§2.5.2) and reduplication (§2.5.3).

2.5.1 Prefixation

The majority of morphophonological processes in Bunaq centre around the paradigm of prefixes, given in Table 2.21. These prefixes mark person (but not number – see §6.2.1 on use of pronouns to specify number), as well as reflexivity and reciprocity. No more than one prefix can occur on any root. Prefixes appear on nouns indexing possessors and on verbs, typically, indexing P arguments.

Table 2.21: Person prefixes.

1EXCL	nV-
1INCL/2	V-
3AN	gV-
REFL	dV-
RECP	tV-

The person prefixes are analysed as having an unspecified vowel segment, represented by V. An alternative analysis would see the prefixes as consisting simply of consonantal roots and the vowel as epenthetic, occurring to break up disallowed consonant clusters. This latter analysis is not favoured here for the reason that there is no consonant associated with the 2nd and 1st person inclusive inflection, so the single vowel characterising inflections in these persons cannot be explained away as simply epenthetic.

The productive synchronic processes associated with person prefixes in Bunaq are vowel harmony (§2.5.1.1), vowel deletion (§2.5.1.2), consonant-vowel metathesis (§2.5.1.3), and the optional loss of initial /h/ under prefixation (§2.5.1.4). Prefixation is also subject to a wide range of irregularities on certain roots. This is discussed separately in §2.6.

2.5.1.1 Vowel harmony

On prefixation to consonant initial roots, the vowel of the prefix takes its specifications for height and backness from that of the initial vowel of the root. Prefixal vowel harmony is illustrated in (57) with the noun /bol/ 'value' and in (58) with the class II bivalent verb (§10.2.2) /wit/ 'fetch'.

(57) /nV-/ + /bol/ 'value'   > ['nobol]   '1EXCL-value'
    /V-/   ['obol]   '1INCL/2-value'
    /gV-/   ['gobol]   '3AN-value'
    /dV-/   ['dobol]   'REFL-value'
    /tV-/   ['tobol]   'RECP-value'

(58) /nV-/ + /wit/ 'fetch'   > ['niwit]   '1EXCL-fetch'
    /V-/   ['iwit]   '1INCL/2-fetch'
    /gV-/   ['giwit]   '3AN-fetch'
    /dV-/   ['diwit]   'REFL-fetch'
    /tV-/   ['tiwit]   'RECP-fetch'

Note that there are a handful of cases where the prefixal vowel is not harmonised with that of the root. These are regarded as older prefixal vowels that have been irregularly retained from before vowel harmony was at work in the language. They are described in §2.6.1.

2.5.1.2 Vowel deletion

Where the root is vowel-initial, the prefixal vowel is deleted. The prefix *V-* '1INCL/2' is realised as zero and is thus indistinguishable from the unprefixed, vowel-initial roots. This is illustrated in (59) with the noun *il* 'water' and in (60) with the verb *obon* 'hang'.

(59) /nV-/ + /il/ 'water'   > ['nil]   '1EXCL-water'
    /V-/   ['il]   '1INCL/2-water'
    /gV-/   ['gil]   '3AN-water'
    /dV-/   ['dil]   'REFL-water'
    /tV-/   ['til]   'RECP-water'

(60) /nV-/ + /obon/ 'hang up' > ['nobon]   '1EXCL-hang'
    /V-/   ['obon]   '1INCL/2-hang'
    /gV-/   ['gobon]   '3AN-hang'
    /dV-/   ['dobon]   'REFL-hang'
    /tV-/   ['tobon]   'RECP-hang'

2.5.1.3 Metathesis

Synchronic metathesis of segments in a root in particular morphophonological and syntactic contexts is a characteristic shared by many languages of the Timor region (Schapper 2015a). Morphophonologically conditioned metathesis is found in Bunaq on prefixation of roots with two distinct shapes in Bunaq.

2.5 Morphophonology

The first root shape with which metathesis occurs is $CV_1'V_2C$, where V_1 is high (/i/ or /u/) and unstressed, while V_2 is non-high and stressed. Metathesis involves V_1 swapping places with the initial consonant when a prefix is added; stress remains on the second syllable, i.e., $CV[+HIGH]_1'V_2[-HIGH]C > -V[+HIGH]_1'CV_2[-HIGH]C$. Examples of this metathesis are presented with the noun /luel/ 'peel' in (61) and with the verb /sieʔ/ 'rip' in (62). Note that the unprefixed, unmetathesised forms of these items are used where the former has an INANIMATE possessor (§9.3.5) and the latter an INANIMATE P (§10.2.2).

(61) /nV-/ + /luel/ [lu'el] 'peel' > [nu'lel] '1EXCL-peel'
     /V-/   [u'lel] '1INCL/2-peel'
     /gV-/   [gu'lel] '3AN-peel'
     /dV-/   [du'lel] 'REFL-peel'
     /tV-/   [tu'lel] 'RECP-peel'

(62) /nV-/ + /sieʔ/ [si'eʔ] 'rip' > [ni'seʔ] '1EXCL-rip'
     /V-/   [i'seʔ] '1INCL/2-rip'
     /gV-/   [gi'seʔ] '3AN-rip'
     /dV-/   [di'seʔ] 'REFL-rip'
     /tV-/   [ti'seʔ] 'RECP-rip'

The number of items with the appropriate phonological shape for this pattern of metathesis to occur is small. In the corpus there are a total of eight items (Table 2.22). Some roots of the appropriate shape for metathesis do not take prefixes and therefore do not show metathesis, e.g., /muel/ [mu'el] 'thin' does not take prefixes.

Table 2.22: $CV_1'V_2C$ roots with metathesis.

Unprefixed form	3rd ANIMATE prefixed form	Gloss
luel	g-ulel	'skin, peel'
mien	g-imen	'immediately, customarily'
niat	g-inat	'first (one)'
nuas	g-unas	'stink'
nuke	g-unek	'smelly'
sieʔ	g-iseʔ	'rip'
tuek	g-utek	'heavy'
ziek	g-izek	'fry'

Since it is the most morphologically unmarked form of the verb, I regard the $CV_1'V_2C$ form of metathesising items as basic. However, it might be possible to argue that the form $V_1'CV_2C$ is basic and that $CV_1'V_2C$ is the metathesised form. This analysis might be tenable if metathesis to the form $CV_1'V_2C$ could be perceptually motivated, for instance, if the first consonant were a better signaller of the word edge (e.g., a stop) than the V_1, (disregarding the presence of a phonetic glottal stop on vowel-initial words). The test of this hypothesis is whether there are words with a surface shape V_1CV_2C where the first consonant is not a good signaller of the word edge in comparison to those in words with metathesis. There are only three roots of the appropriate V_1CV_2C shape in Bunaq, but they all have penultimate stress and therefore cannot be equated with the metathesising roots. Accordingly, there is little to support a hypothesis which sees the form $V_1C'V_2C$ of metathesising words as basic.

The second pattern of metathesis in Bunaq involves roots of the shape CV_1CV_1, where both vowels have the same quality and stress falls regularly on the penultimate syllable. On prefixation, the vowels and consonants of both syllables metathesise, while stress stays on the penultimate syllable, i.e., $'CV_1CV_1 > -'V_1C\ V_1C$. The pattern is illustrated in (63) and (64).

(63) /nV-/ + /dele/ ['dele] 'INS' > ['nerel] '1EXCL-with'
 /V-/ ['erel] '1INCL/2-with'
 /gV-/ ['gerel] '3AN-with'
 /dV-/ ['derel] 'REFL-with'
 /tV-/ ['terel] 'RECP-with'

(64) /nV/ + /tuʔu/ ['tuʔu] 'strike' > ['nutuʔ] '1EXCL-strike'
 /V-/ ['utuʔ] '1INCL/2-strike'
 /gV-/ ['gutuʔ] '3AN-strike'
 /dV-/ ['dutuʔ] 'REFL-strike'
 /tV-/ ['tutuʔ] 'RECP-strike'

The four items in the corpus that display this pattern of metathesis are presented in Table 2.23.

Table 2.23: $'CV_1CV_1$ roots with metathesis.

Unprefixed form	3rd ANIMATE prefixed form	Gloss
tuʔu	g-utuʔ	'beat'
buʔu	g-ubuʔ	'bite'
mene	g-emen	'empty into'
dele	g-erel	'INS'

Not all items with the appropriate root shape display this pattern of metathesis under prefixation. Many roots that do not participate in metathesis can be identified as loans. This indicates that the pattern of metathesis is not a productive one in Bunaq today. But it seems likely to have applied more widely in the past. Bunaq has many obligatorily possessed roots with the shape -'VCVC (see §9.3.1 on these nouns) that appear to be the result of metathesis of original CVCV roots.

2.5.1.4 Loss of initial /h/

Verbal roots with initial /h/ may have this segment optionally deleted on prefixation. This is an occasional feature of rapid speech and not a hard and fast morphophonological rule in the language; in careful speech initial /h/ is always retained. The example in (65) illustrates the optional deletion of the initial /h/ with the verb *hukat* 'lift'.

(65) /nV/   + /hukat/ ['hukat] 'lift' >   [nuˈhukat ~ ˈnukat]   '1EXCL-lift'
      /V-/   [uˈhukat ~ ˈukat]   '1INCL/2-lift'
      /gV-/   [guˈhukat ~ ˈgukat]   '3AN-lift'
      /dV-/   [duˈhukat ~ ˈdukat]   'REFL-lift'
      /tV-/   [tuˈhukat ~ ˈtukat]   'RECP-lift'

Optional /h/ deletion and associated syllable reduction in such examples as (65) is distinct from that found with verbs of the h-conjugation (see §2.6.2.3).

2.5.2 Suffixation with *-wen*

Bunaq has only one productive suffix /-wen/. This is chiefly used as an anticausative marker on agentive bivalent verbs (see §11.5 for a full description of its functions). The suffix has two allomorphs, [-wen] occurring on verbal roots in all environments and [-ʔen] occurring on verbal roots ending in a back vowel. In (66) the allomorphy rule for /-wen/ is presented along with examples.

(66) /-wen/ >   [-wen ~ -ʔen] / V[+back]#_   e.g., /lelu-wen/ [lelu-wen ~ lelu-ʔen]
                                                                                                                                 'twist-ANTIC'
            [-wen]   / elsewhere   e.g., /dara-wen/ [dara-wen]
                                                                                                                        'erect-ANTIC'

The allomorph [-ʔen] appears to be a further expression of the Bunaq dispreference for /w/ to occur adjacent to back vowels, as described in §2.2.3.7. The appearance of the glottal stop in the allomorph is also a manifestation of the boundary-marking function of [ʔ] in Bunaq, discussed in §2.3.7.

2.5.3 Reduplication

Reduplication refers to the repetition of phonological material within a word for semantic or grammatical purposes. Bunaq makes some use of both full (§2.5.3.1) and partial reduplication (§2.5.3.2). There is a third, extremely marginal pattern of reduplication with vowel changes (§2.5.3.3).

2.5.3.1 Full reduplication and repetition

Bunaq uses full reduplication to express a range of grammatical concepts (summarised in Table 2.24).

Table 2.24: Constructions in which reduplication takes place.

Domain of reduplication	Function of reduplication
– Verbal domain	
stative V	intensity
post-verbal numeral	distributivity
– Nominal domain	
N_{HEAD}	distributivity
modifier of N_{HEAD}	distributivity

In full reduplication, the reduplicant matches the base from which it is copied without phoneme changes or additions. Paralleling partial reduplication, the reduplicant precedes the base. The base attracts primary stress and the reduplicant attracts secondary stress. This pattern of stress is what allows the base to be distinguished from the reduplicant. In (67) some examples of reduplication are presented.

	Root			Reduplicated form	
(67)	/tas/	['tas]	'village'	[ˌtas~'tas]	'village after village'
	/unu/	['unu]	'quiet'	[ˌunu~'unu]	'really quiet'
	/hiloʔon/	[hi'loʔon]	'two'	[hiˌloʔon~hi'loʔon]	'two by two'

Because there is little morphology in Bunaq, it is difficult to distinguish between reduplication and repetition (a problem treated in detail in Gil 2005). Like reduplication, repetition involves the iteration of linguistic material. However, unlike reduplication, repetition may involve between one and three copies; more than three copies are not attested. Repetition is used to encode iteration and durativity, as in the examples in (68) from the corpus.

	Root			Repeated form	
(68)	/liol/	[liˈol]	'continue'	[liˈol liˈol]	'keep going'
	/mele/	[ˈmele]	'walk'	[ˈmele ˈmele ˈmele]	'keep walking on and on'
	/pie/	[piˈe]	'steam'	[piˈe piˈe piˈe]	'keep steaming on and on and on'

The phonological differences between reduplication and repetition in Bunaq remain to be investigated. Impressionistically, there is no prosodic difference between reduplications and repeats. This suggests that what I have called repetition here may in fact be a form of multiple word reduplication, involving two or more copies, such as that described for Thao by Blust (2001).

Against the reduplication analysis is the fact that we find other types of phrasal predicates repeated with iterative meaning. For instance, predicative postpositional phrases (§4.3.2), such as those in (69), occur repeated with the same kinds of iterative meanings as the verbs in (68).

	Phrase		Repeated phrase	
(69)	g-ua gene	'3AN-footprint LOC'	gua gene gua gene	'keep following X'
	'follow X'(lit., 'in X's footprints')			
	baʔa goet	'NPRX.INAN LIKE'	baʔa goet baʔa goet	'like that over and over'
	'(do) like that'			

That these are clearly phrases and not roots suggests that the copying of linguistic material to express iterativity/durativity is discourse-level repetition and not word-forming reduplication.

For the purposes of keeping apart instances of copying only involving one copy and those allowing more than one copy, I will use the following terminology in this work: I reserve the term 'reduplication' (glossed 'REDUP' and with the copied form connected by a tilde '~') for instances of copying where there can be no more than one copy; and I use the term 'repetition' (with each element glossed separately and with no hyphen, etc., connecting copies) for instances of copying denoting iteration/durativity where there can be more than one copy.

2.5.3.2 Partial reduplication

Partial reduplication is a minor pattern found only with onomatopoeias of the shape CV.(C)V.i. In this pattern the final syllable /i/ is not copied, i.e., CV(C)Vi > CV(C)V~CV(C)Vi. Reduplicated forms denote sounds which are iterated. Table 2.25 presents the onomatopoeias known to show this pattern of reduplication.

Table 2.25: Onomatopoeias allowing partial reduplication.

Unreduplicated form	Reduplicated form	Gloss
garui	garu~garui	'sound made when eating something hard or crunchy'
geoi	geo~geoi	'sound of clinking made by ceramics or glass'
geroi	gero~geroi	'sound of something rattling inside something else'
heqoi	heqo~heqoi	'sound of panting, shortness of breath'
mui	mu~mui	'sound of indistinct chatter or a machine in the distance'
naui	nau~naui	'sound of grumbling, discontent'
nisui	nisu~nisui	'sound of sniffing, sniffling, and whimpering'
pakai	paka~pakai	'sound of a horse's hooves'
parai	para~parai	'sound of cracking or crunching as made by someone walking on dry leaves'
pasui	pasu~pasui	'sound of chewing, smacking of mouth'
pokoi	poko~pokoi	'sound of breaking or cracking of something hard like dry wood'
sagui	sagu~sagui	'sound of whispering'
saui	sau~saui	'sound of plastic or similar crinkling; sound of someone/thing moving through grass/bushes'
teoi	teo~teoi	'sound of knocking or banging of wood'
toloi	tolo~toloi	'sound of a crowd of people, bustle, throng'
tikui	tiku~tikui	'sound of splashing as made by an object falling into water or a person swimming'
tupui	tupu~tupui	'heavy thudding sound, sound of a drum, sound of thunder'

2.5.3.3 Reduplication with vowel changes

In the Bunaq corpus, there are three instances of full reduplication with replacement of one vowel between base and reduplicant. Table 2.26 presents these reduplicated words with bolding of the changing vowel. This pattern of reduplication is lexicalised; the bases do not exist independently of the reduplicants, at least not with clearly relatable meanings.

Table 2.26: Reduplication with vowel changes.

Reduplicated form	Gloss
tusan~tusun	'order each other around, push each other around'
wiku~waku	'be a tramp, homeless'
wiru~waru	'be indecisive, unconcentrated, change one's mind or one's work frequently'

2.6 Irregularities in prefixation

Bunaq has a collection of lexical items which show irregularities in their prefixation. There are two main types of irregularity: (i) the form of the prefixal vowel differs from that predicted by the above outlined rules (§2.6.1); and (ii) the root changes form on prefixation (§2.6.2). Their treatment here is justified as they can be seen to exist, on the one hand, as the result of the incomplete application of synchronic morphophonemic processes and, on the other, as remnants of earlier productive morphophonemic and morphological processes.

2.6.1 Irregular prefixes

While the productive shape of person prefixes in Bunaq is (C)V- with harmony and deletion rules applying as already described, there are several roots which do not conform to this pattern of prefixation and for which the prefixal vowel is already specified, either as (C)i- or (C)a-.

Similar to many other Papuan languages, PTAP used "vowel grades" to indicate number in person paradigms: *a for singular and *i for plural (Ross 2005). In Bunaq, this number distinction has been lost in person inflections due to the effects of vowel harmony on unstressed prefixal vowels (cf. §2.5.1.1). However, several items irregularly retain the high vowel *i of the plural person in the person prefixes of a small number of high frequency items, albeit without any number value. Table 2.27 presents the four items that display this pattern: two transitive verbs, a verbal postposition and the indirect possessive classifier. The 3rd person inanimate forms of these items reflect the unprefixed roots.

In a second set of items, an /a/ vowel is used in the prefixes of the two verbs given in Table 2.28. Note that 1st and 2nd person agreement forms are rare as these verbs are used prototypically in reference to domestic animals. In additional to their forms, the agreement patterns and semantics associated with prefixation differ from the norm (§10.2.5).

Table 2.27: Inflected forms with an irregular /i/ prefix.

	'eat'	'carry'	'GOAL'	'POSS'
1EXCL	nia	nial	nita	nie
1INCL/2	ia	ial	ita	ie
3AN	gia	gial	gita	gie
3INAN	a	zal	ata	---

Table 2.28: Inflected forms with an irregular /a/ prefix.

	'care for'	'raise'
1EXCL	nalumaʔ	nabilan
1INCL/2	alumaʔ	abilan
3AN	galumaʔ	gabilan
3INAN	lumaʔ	bilan

The aberrance of the vowel in the prefixes on the items in Table 2.28 appears to be due to the fact that the prefix was originally the Tetun causative prefix *ha-* (cf. van Klinken 1999: 59–66). This is suggested by the fact that both verbs are Tetun borrowings: *lumaʔ* < Tetun *lumak* 'be domestic', and possibly *bilan* < Tetun Belu *bila* 'transact'. See §10.2.4.1.1 on the incorporation of Tetun h-initial words into the Bunaq verb classes.

2.6.2 Irregular roots

There is a group of verbs which on prefixation undergo changes to their roots. Though the changes are not predictable, several different patterns can be discerned, suggesting that they go back to earlier productive morphophonological processes.

2.6.2.1 Root reduction

Disyllabic verb roots of the form $BV_1LV_1(k)$ – where B stands for any (bi)labial consonant, V_1 for any identical vowel and L for the liquid phoneme /l/ – typically delete the medial LV syllable in the manner represented in (70).

      Prefix   Root
(70) (C)V   + $BV_1LV_1(k)$ > $(C)V_1BV_1(k)$

Table 2.29 presents all the roots in the corpus to which this applies. All roots showing the reduction are transitive verbs. There are two roots in the corpus with the appropriate shape which do not show the reduction of the medial liquid-initial syllable. They are: /wilik/ 'fan' but [giwilik] '3AN-fan' not *giwik, and /pelek/ 'plant' but [gepelek] '3AN-plant' not *gepek.

Table 2.29: Roots with medial liquid reduction.

Unprefixed form	3rd ANIMATE prefixed form	Gloss
belek	gebek	'turn'
bilik	gibik	'bind'
bolok	gobok	'cover'
palakter	gapakter	'kick'
pili	gipi	'break'
walak	gawak	'carry'
welek	gewek	'hug'

Note also that in the corpus there is one instance of reduction of this kind, *bini* 'steal', where the consonant of the deleted syllable is /n/ and not /l/: *bini / gibi* 'steal'. There are no other prefixing roots with the appropriate form from which to establish whether there is a similar trend of reduction with /n/ as with /l/.

2.6.2.2 Root mutation

Table 2.30 presents the forms of the small number of transitive verb roots that show a change in form under prefixation. There is no easily generalisable pattern of mutation in these forms, with additional consonants and vowels appearing unpredictably. Suppletion may also play a role in the difference between *uti* 'bite' and *g-i* '3AN-bite'.

Table 2.30: Verbs with root mutation.

Unprefixed form	3rd ANIMATE prefixed form	Gloss
bagal	gagabal	'split'
binun	gibibun	'gather'
buʔu	gububu	'chew meat'
ili	gigili	'wash'
pilaʔ	gipiala	'tell'
uti	gi	'bite'

2.6.2.3 Initial consonant alternations

Bunaq has a small group of transitive verbs (described in §10.2.4) whose initial consonant alternates with person prefixes of other persons when prefixed. Items showing initial consonant alternation are divided into conjugation classes according to the particular initial consonant they have. Table 2.31 presents the five different conjugations with an example of each. We see that with a 3rd person ANIMATE agreement controller, typically P, the initial consonant of the 3rd person INANIMATE agreement form is replaced by the 3rd person ANIMATE prefix.

Table 2.31: Bunaq initial consonant alternation conjugations.

Conjugation class	Example		
	3rd INANIMATE	3rd ANIMATE	Gloss
h-class	hazal	gazal	'see'
s-class	sagal	gagal	'seek'
t-class	tinik	ginik	'cook'
d-class	doenik	goenik	'forget'
l-class	lual	gual	'bend'

The initial consonant alternation observed with these verbs is not a regular morphophonological process in the language. Each of the classes has only a small number of non-predictable members relative to the whole lexicon; the vast majority of items with the consonants at issue do not show any alternation of their initial consonant under prefixation. Examples of these are presented in Table 2.32.

Table 2.32: Examples of items with initial consonants identical to conjugation-marking consonants.

Initial consonant	Example		
	3rd INANIMATE	3rd ANIMATE	Gloss
/h/-initial	hukat	guhukat	'lift'
/s/-initial	sarat	gasarat	'drag'
/t/-initial	tiba	gitiba	'order'
/d/-initial	daʔu	garaʔu	'rip'
/l/-initial	lete	gelete	'step on'

Throughout this grammar, on verbs such as those in Table 2.31 I segment the initial consonants that are replaced by another person prefix as 3rd person INANIMATE prefixes. Thus, the inflections of an s-class verb like *sagal* 'seek' and a t-class verb like *tinik* 'cook' will respectively be glossed and segmented as follows: *n-agal* '1EXCL-seek',

Ø-*agal* '1INCL/2-seek', *g-agal* '3AN-seek' and *s-agal* '3INAN-seek'; *n-inik* '1EXCL-cook', Ø-*inik* '1INCL/2-cook', *g-inik* '3AN-cook' and *t-inik* '3INAN-cook'. The fact that I segment these initial consonants as if they were inflectional prefixes should not be taken to mean that they are actually segmentable in this way historically. The comparative data make clear that the initial consonants on these items are, for at least the /s/, /t/, and /l/ classes, part of the historical verb roots (see §10.2.4 for more in-depth discussion of each of these classes). Nonetheless, I elect here to segment them from the root on verbs where they are replaced by prefixes because the replacement of the initial consonants on verb roots is not a synchronically productive process in Bunaq. The ahistorical segmentation, therefore, serves to differentiate the roots with the "replacive" inflectional pattern from those without it.

A small number of nouns also show replacement of their initial consonants on prefixation with a person prefix indicating a possessor. Two nouns with initial /t/ have that consonant replaced on prefixation: see §9.3.4 for discussion and illustration. A second, slightly larger class of nouns have initial /h/ that is replaced under prefixation. These are discussed in §9.3.2.

2.7 Orthography

The orthographic conventions used throughout this work for Bunaq consonant phonemes are given in (71).

(71) Phonemic: p b t d   k g ʔ h s z tʃ   l r m n w
      Orthographic: p b t d~r k g q h s z c~s   l r m n w

Where an allophone of a phoneme is itself also an independent phoneme, the orthographic form used is that of the surface realisation and not that of the underlying form. For example, /tʃio/ may be realised as [tʃio] or [sio]. When the speaker produces the former, the orthography is <cio>, and when the latter, <sio>. This convention is in accordance with native speaker preferences. It is also practical given that the ongoing mergers of /d/ into /r/ and /tʃ/ into /s/ mean that speakers are not typically able to identify surface realisations with underlying forms if the latter are represented in the orthography. For example, speakers struggle to recognise <tada> as a Bunaq orthographic representation of /tada/ because it always surfaces as [tara], hence <tara> is used.

The orthographic conventions used throughout this work for Bunaq vowel and diphthong phonemes are given in (72).

(72) Phonemic: a e i o u a͡i e͡i o͡i
      Orthographic: a e i o u ai ei oi

The vowel sequences /a.i/, /e.i/, and /o.i/ and the contrasting diphthongs /a͡i/, /e͡i/, and /o͡i/ are written simply as <ai>, <ei>, and <oi> in accordance with speaker preferences. All other vowel sequences do not have diphthongs from which they must be distinguished and are written without any special marking, e.g., /pa.u/ 'k.o. bean' is written simply as <pau>.

Spelling conventions for phonemes which are absent in Bunaq, but which are found in unadapted loanwords from Indonesian/Malay and Tetun, are given in (73). Words with these phonemes are invariably identified as non-Bunaq items by Bunaq speakers and their use is taken here to represent code-switching and not borrowing.

(73) Phonemic: f d͡ʒ ŋ j
     Orthographic: f j ng y

Note that the [d͡ʒ] allophone of /z/ in Bunaq is only represented as <z> in the orthography used here. This is done in order to distinguish it from non-adapted Indonesian/Malay words with a palato-alveolar affricate, represented as <j>, which is distinct in that it lacks the allophony of Bunaq /z/ (§2.2.3.3).

Chapter 3
Word classes

3.1 Introduction

This chapter offers an overview of the word classes in Bunaq on the basis of their morphosyntactic distribution. Many of the word classes described here are discussed in greater detail in subsequent chapters. See individual sections for referral onwards to these later discussions.

Bunaq has two major word classes, nouns (§3.2) and verbs (§3.3). These have for the most part open membership, but each includes some small closed subclasses. There is also a sizeable group of roots that may appear without derivation as either nouns or verbs (§3.4).

The remaining word classes are minor and, for the most part, closed classes (§3.5). These classes show less internal division and have much smaller membership than the major classes. The members of minor classes also often lack isolatable meaning, having only a general, abstract grammatical function in specific constructions.

In addition to these well-defined classes, there are many items in Bunaq which cannot be easily categorised. §3.6 discusses issues complicating the categorisation of items into individual classes in the lexicon and relates them to processes of grammaticalisation and borrowing.

3.2 Nouns

The class of nouns in Bunaq is defined by the ability of its members to occur in the following syntactic constructions. The heads of NPs are nouns. NP heads (N_{HEAD}) may be modified by an attributive noun (N_{MOD}: §5.3), relative clause (RC: §5.4), and/or lexical item indicating quantity (QUANT: §3.6.2 and §5.6). Example (1) illustrates the use of a noun as the head of an NP with two nominal attributes, a restrictive RC and a quantifier.

	N_{HEAD}	N_{MOD}	N_{MOD}	RC	QUANT
(1)	**en**	**pana**	**gol=na**	**koen**	**ginil**
	person	female	small=FOC	pretty	GRP

'group of girls who are pretty'

Nouns can also be possessed (PSR = possessor: §9) and modified by a locational (LCT: §3.5.3 and §8), both occurring prior to the head of the NP (2).

	LCT	PSR		N~HEAD~
(2)	*ola*	*Markus*	*gie*	***zo***
	LOW	Markus	3.POSS	mango

'Markus' mangoes down there'

A noun can occur as an argument of a predicate and a complement of a postposition. In (3) the noun *hol* 'stone' is the S argument of a monovalent verb, while in (4) the nouns *bel* 'wind' and *mok* 'banana' are, respectively, the A and P arguments of a bivalent verb. In (5) the noun *deu* 'house' is the complement of the locative postposition *gene* 'LOC'.

(3) **Hol** *topol*.
    stone fall
    'The stone fell.'

(4) **Bel mok** *pili*.
    wind banana bend
    'The wind bent the banana tree.'

(5) *Eme* **deu** *gene*.
    mother house LOC
    'Mother is at home.'

Nouns are specified for ANIMATE or INANIMATE noun class (see §5.2 for a summary of assignment rules). Noun class specification manifests itself in grammatical agreement on determiners (6–7) and verbal prefixes (8–9).

(6) **en** *pana gol koen ginil* **bi**
    person.AN female child pretty GRP ART.AN
    'the group of pretty girls'

(7) **zo**=*na neto a* **ba**
    mango.INAN=FOC 1SG eat ART.INAN
    'the mangoes which I ate'

(8) *Yati* **en** **ge**-*sen*.
    Yati person.AN 3AN-point.to
    'Yati pointed to the person.'

(9) *Yanti* **zo** *sen*.
    Yati mango.INAN point.to
    'Yati pointed to the mango.'

Nouns can occur in possessive constructions. In (10) there are nouns denoting both the possessor and the possessed item.

(10) **en**   gie   **zap**
     person 3.POSS dog
     'a person's dog'

Bunaq has a closed subset of inalienably possessed nouns marked with a prefix denoting a possessor. Subsets of prefixed nouns are distinguished according to the array of prefixes which the individual nouns take and are discussed in §9.3. See also the discussions of pronouns (§3.5.1) and interrogatives (§3.5.2), both classes with similar distributions to nouns.

3.2.1 Nominal compounds

The Bunaq nominal lexicon contains a large number of nominal compounds. A compound is a lexeme composed of two roots. The individual roots in a compound cannot be separated from one another by other lexemes and cannot be independently inflected or marked in any way without a change in meaning. Nominal compounds are of three types: left-headed compounds (§3.2.1.1), right-headed compounds (§3.2.1.2), and coordinative compounds (§3.2.1.3).

3.2.1.1 Left-headed compounds

Left-headed compounds are nominal compounds which consist of either noun+verb (NV) or noun+noun (NN). The left-hand noun is the head of the compound. It is this noun which carries the compound accent (realised by higher pitch and intensity) and which determines the noun class of the compound. The INANIMATE noun *deu* 'house' and the ANIMATE noun *sekal* 'potato' head the NN (a) and NV (b) compounds in (11) and (12), respectively. The respective heads give their noun class to each of the compounds as a whole, making those in (11) INANIMATE and those in (12) ANIMATE.

(11) a. N   N
         deu   *hoto*
         house.INAN   fire.INAN
         'traditional thatched house'
         N   V
     b. *deu*   *memel*
         house.INAN   sick
         'hospital'

(12) a.   N   N
       sekal   *mun*
       potato.AN rope.INAN
       'sweet potato'

       N   V
   b. *sekal*   *a*
      potato.AN eat
      'kind of edible potato'

Instances of left-headed nominal compounds composed of NN differ from instances of N_{HEAD} modified by an N_{MOD}. Whereas in a left-headed NN compound it is not possible to have multiple modifying Ns, two N_{MOD}s coordinated by =*o* 'AND' can modify a single N_{HEAD}. See §5.3 for exemplification of Bunaq N_{MOD}.

3.2.1.2 Right-headed compounds

Right-headed nominal, or "possessive" compounds are NN compounds in which the right-hand noun is the head. Unlike left-headed compounds, which are frequently not semantically decomposable, right-headed compounds are lexically productive, compositional, and semantically transparent. Right-headed compounds are used in the expression of part–whole relations where the left-hand N denotes the whole (N_{WHOLE}) to which the head is part. Whole–part modification only occurs where both N_{HEAD} and the modifying N have non-specific, inanimate referents, as in (13).

(13) N_{WHOLE} N_{HEAD}
   a. *deu*   *puqup*
      house roof
      'house('s) roof'

    N_{WHOLE} N_{HEAD}
   b. *oto*   *mil*
      car   inside
      'car('s) inside'

    N_{WHOLE} N_{HEAD}
   c. *hotel* *wa*
      tree   top
      'tree top'

    N_{WHOLE} N_{HEAD}
   d. *mar*   *alan*
      garden border
      'garden('s) border'

That the right-hand noun is the head is indicated by the fact that it takes the compound accent and gives its noun class to the compound as a whole (see §5.3 for further illustration and discussion). In (14) and (15) we see that the article agrees in noun class with the right-hand noun. In (14a) where the head noun is INANIMATE *puqup* 'roof' the article takes the form *ba* 'ART.INAN', while in (14b) where the head noun is ANIMATE *liqas* 'carving', the article takes the form *bi* 'ART.AN'. In (15) we see that the INANIMATE head noun *mil* 'inside' controls agreement on the article, even where the modifying noun changes from INANIMATE *oto* 'car' in (15a) to ANIMATE *sabul* 'orange' in (15b).

(14) a. INAN INAN
    deu   *puqup*   *ba*   /   *bi
    house   roof   ART.INAN   ART.AN
    'the house('s) roof'

   b. INAN AN
    deu   *liqas*   *bi*   /   *ba
    house   drawing   ART.AN   ART.INAN
    'the house('s) carvings'

(15) a. *oto*   *mil*   *ba*   /   *bi
    car   inside   ART.INAN   ART.AN
    'car('s) inside'

   b. *sabul*   *mil*   *ba*   /   *bi
    orange   inside   ART.INAN   ART.AN
    'orange('s) inside'

That these constructions are compounds is furthermore suggested by the fact that no more than one N can modify a single N$_{HEAD}$ in a right-headed compound. In (16), the coordination of multiple N$_{WHOLE}$s with =*o* 'AND' results in ungrammaticality. Coordinated possessors can only be expressed through the inclusion of the indirect possessive classifier, *gie* '3AN.POSS' (§9.2).

(16) a. **deu=o*   *gereja*   *puqup*
    house=AND   church   roof
    'house's and church's roof'

   b. **oto=o*   *reu*   *mil*
    car=AND   house   inside
    'car's and house's inside'

   c. **hotel=o*   *lolo*   *wa*
    tree=AND   mountain   top
    'tree and mountain top'

      d. *mar=o   zol   alan
          garden AND river border
          'garden's and river's border'

Secondly, the left-hand N denoting the whole must be a simple N and cannot be expanded to a full NP in which it is modified and/or determined independent of the N_{HEAD}. Thus, (17a) is ungrammatical. In order for (17a) to be grammatical, the possessor of the N_{HEAD} must be just a simple N, *deu* 'house'. If the possessor is expanded to include a determiner, then the indirect possessive classifier must occur between the possessor and *puqup* 'roof', as in (17b).

(17) a. *deu   koen   baqa   puqup
         house nice   NPRX.INAN roof
         'the pretty house roof'
      b. *deu*   *koen* *baqa*   *gie*   *puqup*
         house   nice   NPRX.INAN 3.POSS roof
         'the pretty house's roof'

See §9.4 for further discussion of possession, including part–whole and spatial relations of the type discussed here, as expressed by compounding in Bunaq.

3.2.1.3 Nominal coordinative compounds

Bunaq also has NN compounds in which the relation between members is like one of coordination (known also as "dvandva" compounds: Matthews 2005: 77, or "co-compounds": Wälchli 2005). Coordinative compounds most commonly involve referents occurring in natural pairs, and can semantically be equated to general cover terms in other languages: *eme ama* 'mother father' > 'parents' (18a); *kauq kaqa* 'younger sibling older sibling' > 'siblings' (19a); and *g-on g-iri* '3AN-arm 3AN-leg' > 'limbs' (20a). The order of nouns is fixed and switching results in ungrammaticality as seen in the (b) examples below. Where both nouns are inalienably possessed, as is the case of (20), they must be inflected for the same person; compare the grammaticality of (20a) and (20d) with that of (20c).

(18) a. *eme*   *ama*
         mother father
         'parents'
      b. **ama* *eme*
         father mother

(19) a. *kauq*   *kaqa*
         yS   eS
         'siblings'

    b. *kaqa   kauq
         yS   eS

(20) a. g-on   g-iri
         3AN-arm   3AN-leg
         'his limbs'
     b. *g-iri   g-on
         3AN-leg   3AN-arm
     c. *g-on   n-iri
         3AN-arm   1EXCL-leg
     d. n-on   n-iri
         1EXCL-arm   1EXCL-leg
         'my limbs'

The analysis of these items as compounds is supported by the fact that the elements of the pairs occur within a single intonation contour; no pause may intervene between the two Ns. Additionally, no element may intervene between Ns, and they cannot be independently modified or determined without a change in meaning. For instance, where the nouns *eme* 'mother' and *ama* 'father' are overtly coordinated with =*o* 'AND' (§5.7.2), each noun has a referent distinct from the other, 'mother' and 'father', and not a shared one 'parents' (21a). Accordingly, each of the nouns in the coordinated pair may be a full NP and independently modified, determined, and possessed (21b).

(21) a. eme=o   ama
         mother=AND   father
         'mother and father'
     b. nie   eme   memel bari=o   gie   ama   bokul
         1EXCL.POSS   mother   sick   PROX.AN=AND   3.POSS   father fat
         baqi
         NPRX.AN
         'my sick mother here and his healthy father there'

As mentioned above, coordinative compounds most often form a general cover term for a unitary category for referents in natural pairs (e.g., *pana mone* 'all the people, everyone' < *pana* 'woman', *mone* 'man'). In other cases, two nouns coordinatively compounded create a term denoting plurality of kinds. This typically involves compounding a noun with a generic denotation together with a noun with a specific denotation, such as in *ho tir* 'all kinds of legume' < *ho* 'legume (generic), *tir* 'legume sp., *Cajanus cajan*' and *bora pil* 'all kinds of mats' < *bora* 'mat made of pandanus', *pil* 'mat (generic)'. Where there is no generic term, as is the case for many trees, two nouns with specific reference can be compounded together, as in *pur kabokeq* 'all kinds of fig tree' < *pur* 'fig sp., *Ficus benjamina*', *kabokeq* 'fig sp., *Ficus septica*'.

In all of the instances given thus far, coordinative compounds have denoted a plurality of referents. There is, however, one coordinative compound in my Bunaq data that does not have such plural reference, but rather denotes a generic category: *meaq gol* is the only way to express 'child (non-kin), young person'. The compound is composed of the noun *meaq* 'nubile girl' plus the inalienably possessed noun *g-ol* '3AN-child (kin)'. The prefix on this second noun is invariable in the compound. This high frequency noun can be used in both singular (e.g., *meaq gol uen* 'one/a child') and plural reference (e.g., *meaq gol tomol* 'six children').

3.3 Verbs

Syntactically, verbs are those items that typically function as the predicate head in the clause. Each verb has lexically specified valency and licences a specific number of arguments. In (22) *tuek* 'heavy' acts as predicate and licences a single S argument. In (23) *tekeq* 'watch, look at' is the sole predicate of the clause and licences two arguments, an A and a P, in the clause.

(22) Zo **tuek**.
 mango heavy
 'The mango (is) heavy.'

(23) *Meaq gol baqi zo* **tekeq**.
 child NPRX.AN mango watch
 'The child looks at (the) mango.'

Morphologically, verbs may take a prefix which is coreferent with an argument in the clause. In (24a), the verb *tuek* 'heavy' takes a 1st person prefix coreferent with the S argument. In (25a) the verb *tekeq* 'watch' takes a 3rd person ANIMATE prefix coreferent with the P argument of the clause. Verbs allow the elision of their arguments (24b and 25b) under conditions described in §4.7.1.1, as well as fronting of non-S/A arguments in the case of polyvalent verbs (25), the pragmatics of which are discussed in §4.7.2.2.

(24) a. *Neto* **n-utek**.
 1SG 1EXCL-heavy
 'I (am) heavy.'
 b. *N-utek*.
 1EXCL-heavy
 '(I am) heavy.'

(25) a. *Neto meaq gol **ge-tekeq**.*
       1SG child   3AN-watch
       'I watched the child.'
   b. *Ge-tekeq.*
       3AN-watch
       '(I) watched (the child).'
   c. *Meaq gol   neto **ge-tekeq**.*
       child 1SG   3AN-watch
       'The child, I watched her.'

Verbs are divided into classes on the basis of two criteria: (i) valency, i.e., whether the verb takes one, two, three or a variable number of arguments with a secondary division as to the kind of argument (core versus oblique), and (ii) inflectional prefixes, i.e., what prefixes does the verb take. These two criteria typically intersect to robustly define individual classes of verbs. A detailed treatment of Bunaq verb classes is found in Chapter 10.

3.3.1 Lack of an adjective class

There is no distinct adjective class in Bunaq. The items encoding Dixon's (1982) "adjectival notions" – value, age, colour, dimension, speed, physical property, and human propensity – are monovalent stative verbs in Bunaq. The reasons for not seeing these items as constituting a separate word class are outlined below.

In Bunaq all verbs can occur attributively. That is, regardless of whether a verb is stative or active, monovalent or bivalent, it can occur modifying the head of an NP. In (26) we see that the head of the NP, *en* 'person', is modified without constructional difference by a monovalent stative non-agentive verb (26a), a monovalent dynamic non-agentive verb (26b), a monovalent agentive verb (26c), a bivalent verb in the A role (26d), and a bivalent verb in the P role with agreement on the verb (26e).

(26) a. *en   matas   bi*
        person old   ART.AN
        'the old person'
   b. *en   topol   bi*
        person fall   ART.AN
        'the fallen person'
   c. *en   sok   bi*
        person swear   ART.AN
        'the swearing person'
   d. *en   bai   seqo   bi*
        person thing   sell   ART.AN
        'the selling person'

e. *en ge-seqo bi*
   person 3AN-sell ART.AN
   'the sold person', i.e., 'the person (who was) sold' [Not.06-01]

In Bunaq, there is no difference in the adverbials that can apply to a class of adjectives rather than verbs, as is found in many languages with an adjective–verb distinction, e.g., English 'very'. In Bunaq all verbs can occur with intensifiers, such as *los* 'very', irrespective of whether they are used attributively (27) or predicatively (28). The translations given in (27) and (28) do not pretend to be idiomatic English, but seek to preserve something of the flavour of the Bunaq original in which *los* 'very' indicates merely that the action or situation denoted by the verb was carried out or experienced with intensity. Whether the intensity indicated by *los* 'very' refers to severity, quantity, frequency, etc. is disambiguated by context. More natural English translations, e.g., 'a lot', 'a long way', 'greatly', etc., would force a particular reading of the nature of the intensity which is not present in the Bunaq.

(27) a. *en matas los bi*
     person old very ART.AN
     'the very old person'
   b. *en topol los bi*
     person fall very ART.AN
     'the very fallen person', i.e., 'the person (who) fell badly'
   c. *en sok los bi*
     person swear very ART.AN
     'the very swearing person', i.e., 'the person (who) swears a lot'
   d. *en bai seqo los bi*
     person thing sell very ART.AN
     'the very selling person', i.e., 'the person (who) sells a lot'
   e. *en ge-seqo los bi*
     person 3AN-sell very ART.AN
     'the very sold person', i.e., 'the person (who gets) sold a lot' [Not.06-01]

(28) a. *En baqi matas los.*
     person NPRX.AN old very
     'That person (was) very old.'
   b. *En baqi topol los.*
     person NPRX.AN fall very
     'That person fell badly.'
   c. *En baqi sok los.*
     person NPRX.AN swear very
     'That person swore a lot.'

d. *En   baqi   bai   seqo   los.*
   person NPRX.AN   thing   sell   very
   'That person sold a lot.'

e. *En   baqi   ge-seqo   los.*
   person NPRX.AN   3AN-sell   very
   'That person (was) sold a lot.' [Not.06-01]

Textual examples of the use of *los* 'very' with stative and active verbal predicates are given in (29) and (30), respectively.

(29) *En   bari   neto=na   g-osok   los.*
      person PROX.AN   1SG=FOC   3AN-receive very
      'I really took in a lot of these people.' (lit., 'These people, I received a lot.')
      [Bk-2.024]

(30) *Sore   baqa   koen   raza   los.*
      machete   NPRX.AN   nice   different   very
      'That machete is especially beautiful.' (lit., 'That machete was really differently nice.') [Bk-24.039]

Similarly, the marker of a comparative is not limited to occurring with stative and active predicates, such as might be expected were there a class of adjectives separate from verbs. We see that the comparative adverb *lesin* 'more' occurs with both active verbs, such as *a* 'eat' (31) and *mele* 'walk' (32), as well as 'adjectival notions', such as *baqis* 'much' (33) and *koen* 'nice' (34). See §14.3.1.3 for more on comparatives in Bunaq.

(31) *Le ai~le ai,   nei   paqol=na   gi-a   lesin.*
      everyday   1PL.EXCL   maize=FOC   3AN-eat   more
      'Day in day out, it is maize that we eat more (than anything else).' [Bk-24.033]

(32) *En   gereja   gie   ukon   dele=na   mele   lesin.*
      person   church   3.POSS   govern   INS=FOC   walk   more
      'People follow the teachings of the church more.' [Bk-62.030]

(33) *Halali   gie   u   bilik   baqis   lesin.*
      3DU   3.POSS   herbaceous.plant   bound   much   more
      'Those two's bound grass was much more.' [Bk-12.013]

(34) *Huqe   gene   koen   lesin.*
      HERE   LOC   nice   more
      'Here is nicer.' [Bk-30.092]

Verbs encoding 'adjectival notions' differ from other kinds of verbs in the way that they combine with aspect markers. However, this different behaviour arises not from any word class distinction, but simply because of semantic and pragmatic restrictions on combinatorics. For instance, consider how the prospective aspect marker *gie* 'PROSP' (§14.3.3) combines with the different verbs in (35). In (35a) *gie* 'PROSP' combines with the agentive monovalent verb *mal* 'go' to denote the intentionality and volitionality of the S to carry out the event. In (35b) the marker is also acceptable with the prototypically non-agentive dynamic verb, *topol* 'fall', to suggest that the falling is about to happen. However, (35c), combining *gie* 'PROSP' with the stative monovalent verb, *moroi* 'sleepy', is judged to be semantically bizarre. This is because the use of *gie* 'PROSP' cannot be used by itself for prospective entry into a state, but rather needs to combine with verbs denoting relatively punctual events.

(35) a. *Yati mal gie.*
    Yati go PROSP
    'Yati is about to go.'
  b. *Yati topol gie.*
    Yati fall PROSP
    'Yati is about to fall down.'
  c. #*Yati moroi gie.*
    Yati sleepy PROSP
    ?'Yati is about to be(come) sleepy.' [Not.06-01]

Finally, there are no morphological grounds for distinguishing verbs from adjectives. For the most part, monovalent verbs, regardless of whether they refer to an "adjectival notion" or a dynamic event, take no prefixal marking of their participant. Of the very small number of monovalent verbs which do take prefixes, all have a non-agentive S, and only some of these are covered under the rubric "adjectival notion", such as 'stinky' and 'heavy', but not 'lost, disappeared' (see §10.3.2).

In sum, none of the morphological or syntactic tests which we have applied shows any difference amongst verbs which are sufficient to confirm the existence of an adjective word class separate from that of verbs.

3.3.2 Verbal coordinative compounds

Compounding of verbs is not a feature made much use of in Bunaq. However, there are some verbal coordinative compounds in which near-synonymic verbs are compounded together to denote an intensified state or situation.

As with the nominal coordinative compounds discussed already in §3.2.1.3, the pairing of items in verbal coordinative compounds is lexically fixed, as is the order of items in the compounds. The verbs of a coordinative compound occur within a single intonation contour; no pause may intervene between the two Vs compounded together. They also cannot be independently modified or determined and the component verbs cannot be coordinated with =*o* 'AND' without a change in meaning. For example, the coordinative compound *cia lili* is composed of the intransitive verbs, *cia* 'burn' and *lili* 'be aflame, blaze' and denotes 'burn brightly, intensely' (36a). Flipping the order of items results in speakers rejecting the utterance (36b). It is possible to have =*o* 'AND' intervene between the two verbs, but the meaning changes; the coordinated verbs do not denote an intense burning as in the coordinative compound, but separately describe characteristics of the fire (36c).

(36) a. *Hoto cia lili.*
    fire burn aflame
    'The fire burns brightly.'
  b. **Hoto lili cia.*
    fire aflame burn
    'The fire burns brightly.'
  c. *Hoto cia=o lili.*
    fire burn=AND aflame
    'The fire burns and is flaming.' [FB-131220]

Most verbal coordinative compounds in my Bunaq data have one member, typically the second member, that does not occur independently outside of the compound. In these cases, speakers typically say that the non-independent member "means the same thing" as the other item in the compound. Examples are given in (37). A question mark "?" indicates that the item does not occur outside the compound.

(37) *pe sululuq* 'very swollen' < *pe* 'swollen', *sululuq* ?
  uku dukut 'very curly (of hair)' < *uku* ?, *dukut* 'curly'
  laga baka 'very stupid' < *laga* 'stupid', *baka* ?
  buta kusuq 'very blind, completely blind' < *buta* 'blind', *kusuq* ?
  masak kati 'very large' < *masak* 'large', *kati* ?
  mal dotok 'very bitter' < *mal* 'bitter', *dotok* ?

Because one of their members has no meaning independent of the compound, it is not possible with these compounds to have =*o* 'AND' intervene between the two verbs in normal speech. In some cases, however, the elements of these compounds can appear split over parallel half lines of ritual speech. See §1.8 on the use of synonyms in the parallelism of Bunaq ritual speech.

3.4 Noun-verb conversion

Noun-verb conversion refers to roots that can appear in the syntactic frame of a noun or that of a verb without any morphological change where noun and verb have related senses. The number of roots which are ambiguous in this way in Bunaq is relatively small in comparison to the whole lexicon.

Bunaq noun-verb roots of this kind refer to inanimates. They are divisible into two main categories:
(i) verbs denoting an event/state and a noun denoting the associated instrument, result, or patient of that event
(ii) verbs denoting an event/state and a noun denoting that same event/state

Examples are given in (38).

	Root	Noun	Verb
(38)	*inel*	'rain'	'rain, be raining'
	ilok	'flood'	'flood, be flooding'
	teqa	'prayer'	'pray, be praying'
	lili	'flame'	'be aflame, blaze'
	luma	'competition'	'compete'
	luni	'pillow'	'put head down to rest'
	ari	'grinding stone'	'grind on a stone'
	sil	'sweat'	'sweat, be sweaty'
	memel	'sickness'	'be sick'
	potok	'blister'	'be blistered'
	luqes	'wound'	'be wounded'
	bouq	'swelling'	'be swollen, swell up'
	tues	'fine'	'be fined'
	huruk	'cold'	'be cold'
	cinoq	'heat, fever'	'be hot, feverish'

The question raised here is: what is the status of these roots? Should they be interpreted as pre-categorial, being neither noun nor verb? Alternatively, should one be derived from the other, and if so, is noun or verb basic? Or do we simply have two distinct lexical entries, one as noun one as verb, of a homophonous form? This is a question that has challenged many researchers of languages showing such patterns (see Vonen 2001 for an overview of the debate in Polynesian languages). It is beyond the scope of this grammar to deal with these questions in depth. As a matter of descriptive convenience, I will label items, such as *memel* 'sick/ness' and others in (39), "noun" when they appear in a nominal frame, i.e., as an NP head (39a), and "verb" when they appear in a verbal frame, i.e., as a predicate (39b).

(39) a. *Nie* **memel** *bare* *loi*.
      1EXCL.POSS sick/ness PROX.INAN good
      'This sickness is better.' [Bk-40.017]

   b. *Neto* **memel**.
      1SG sick/ness
      'I'm sick.' [Bk-40.001]

3.5 Minor word classes

3.5.1 Pronouns

Pronouns distinguish singular, dual, and plural numbers and have three persons, including an inclusive–exclusive distinction in both non-singular numbers. The complete set of free pronouns is presented in Table 3.1. Note that there is no 3rd singular personal pronoun; demonstratives are used in this role (see §7.4.1.5).

Table 3.1: Pronouns.

	SG	DU	PL
1EXCL	neto	neli	nei
1INCL		ili	i
2	eto	eli	ei
3	--	halali	halaqa

Like nouns, pronouns function as the head of NPs and fill argument slots in the clause. Also, in the manner of nouns, they can be modified by relative clauses (40), determiners (41), and locationals (42).

(40) [**Halaqi**=na *meten* *no* *en* *g-ebeqen*=o *bai* *bi*]
     3PL=FOC past OBL person 3AN-kill=AND thing ART.AN
     en *g-utu* *sesuq*.
     person 3-COM argue
     'They who in the past were killing people and so on were arguing with people.' [Bk-66.045]

(41) [**Halali** *baqi*] *t-erel* *mele*.
     3DU NPRX.AN RECP-INS walk
     'The two of them went off together.' [Bk-38.009]

(42) Gie   pie   [ola **nei**]   n-o   pir   doe.
     3.POSS steam LOW   1PL.EXCL   1EXCL-SRC reach SPEC.INAN
     'The smell (lit., its steam) reached us down there just now.'   [Bk-69.021]

Pronouns differ from nouns, however, in that they cannot be modified by a preceding possessor. In (43a), we see that nouns are used to denote both the possessor and the possessed item in an indirect possessor construction (§9.2). Yet, whilst it is possible for a pronoun to encode a possessor (43b), it is not possible for it to encode the possessum (43c). This restriction holds even when *halaqi* '3PL' occurs modifying the head noun in (43d) (see §5.6.2).

(43) a. **en**   gie   zap
        person   3.POSS   dog
        'a person's dog'
     b. **halaqi**   gie   zap
        3PL   3.POSS   dog
        'their dog'
     c. *en   gie   **halaqi**
        person   3.POSS   3PL
     d. *en   gie   mila   **halaqi**
        person   3.POSS   slave   3PL   [Not.07-01]

The restriction on possessors modifying a pronoun may be taken to indicate that pronouns occupy a syntactic position other than N_{HEAD}. For instance, pronouns could be seen as occupying the possessor position (§5.1) followed by null N_{HEAD}. In an alternative analysis, the restriction could be seen as pragmatically motivated: if a possessor is viewed as functioning to identify the referent of N_{HEAD} by locating it relative to a possessor,[1] then pronouns do not require marking with a possessor since the use of a pronoun implies that the referent is identifiable within the speech context (cf. Ewing 2005: 126–127). This analysis would mean that pronouns are a closed class within the larger class of nouns. See Chapter 6 for discussion of the use of pronouns in Bunaq.

---

1 Possessors and related categories are often regarded as "pragmatic anchors" (Fraurud 1990; Hawkins 1981; Koptjevskaja-Tamm 2001) or "reference-points" (Langacker 1993).

3.5.2 Interrogatives

Interrogatives are lexical items that occur in questions indicating what part of the proposition the asker wishes to know about (Sadock and Zwicky 1985: 185). Table 3.2 gives the basic Bunaq interrogative words.

Table 3.2: Basic interrogatives.

cio	'who?'
ciro	'which (person)?'
nego	'what?'
tero	'which (thing)?'
teo	'where?'
tuen	'when?'

All basic Bunaq interrogative words are nominal and can occur in an NP either as N_{HEAD} or modifying an N_{HEAD} (i.e., as an N_{MOD}: §5.3). This is illustrated in (44) with the interrogative *tuen* 'when?'. In (44a) *tuen* 'when' stands alone as the complement of the oblique postposition *no* 'OBL', while in (44b) *tuen* 'when' modifies the N_{HEAD} *hul* 'moon, month' for the NP that forms the complement of *no* 'OBL'.

(44) a. *Eto* **tuen** *no man?*
    2SG when OBL come
    'When are you coming?'
  b. *Eto* **hul** *tuen no man?*
    2SG month when OBL come
    'What month are you coming?' [Not.07-02]

In questions, an interrogative cannot be modified by a relative clause or a determiner. This restriction is pragmatic: in questions interrogatives refer to entities with unidentified referents, whereas referents encoded with determiners are by their very marking signalled as identifiable and definite. Thus, in questions an interrogative marked with a determiner is uninterpretable in Bunaq. Compare the grammaticality of the examples in (45).

(45) a. *Nego loi niq?*
    what good NEG
    'What is not good?'
  b. *#Nego ba loi niq?*
    what ART.INAN good NEG
    'The what is not good?' [Not.07-02]

That the restriction is not syntactic is evident from the fact that all basic interrogatives can also be used in "wh"-embedded interrogative clauses and, in this function, they are modified by a restrictive relative clause and, optionally, by a determiner, as in (46–47).

(46) [**Nego**=na i   Gewal gene t-erel   h-oqon
     what=FOC 1PL.INCL Gewal LOC RECP-INS 3INAN-do
     ba]   hani   r-oenik.
     ART.INAN PROH   3INAN-forget
     'Don't forget that which we did together in Gewal.' [Bk-14.010]

(47) [**Sio**=na dato gol] gie   si   det   ga-lai.
     who=FOC noble small 3.POSS meat alone 3AN-set
     'Whoever is a lower-ranked noble also gets their meat set aside.' [Bk-70.190]

Schachter (1985: 34) observes that "[t]he set of interrogative pro-forms typically cuts across other part-of-speech classes". This is true of Bunaq interrogatives as they occur in interrogative phrases. The interrogative phrases used in Bunaq Lamaknen are given in Table 3.3.

Table 3.3: Non-basic interrogatives.

tuen~tuen	REDUP~when	'how much/many (time/quantity)?'
tuen goet on	when LIKE DO	'how?', 'in what manner?'
teo goet on	where LIKE DO	'how?', 'in what manner?'
nego on	what DO	'why?', 'for what reason?'

Unlike the basic interrogatives, *tuen~tuen* only occurs adnominally, either with common nouns questioning quantity (48a) or with temporal nouns questioning duration (48b) (see §14.3.1.1 on the postverbal position of temporal duration nominals). The equivalents without a head noun are ungrammatical (48c–d).

(48) a. Eto [zo   **tuen~tuen**] a?
        2SG   mango   how.much   eat
        'How many mangoes did you eat?'
     b. Eto mit [hul   **tuen~tuen**]?
        2SG sit month how.much
        'How many months did you stay?'
     c. *Eto **tuen~tuen** a?
         2SG how.much   eat
        'How many did you eat?'

d. *Eto mit **tuen~tuen**?
   2SG sit how.much
   'How long did you stay?' [Not.07-01]

Interrogative phrases questioning reason and manner can occur either as predicates or as clausal adverbs in clause-initial or clause-final position. These three positions are illustrated with the interrogative phrase *tuen goet on* in the examples in (49).

(49) a. En   Makasai **tuen goet on**?
       person Makasae when LIKE DO
       'What are the Makasae people like?' [Bk-61.071]
   b. **Tuen goet on** suku bari   hati?
      when   LIKE DO   clan PROX.AN exist
      'How did these clans come to exist?' [Bk-70.024]
   c. A bokal   h-oqon   **tuen goet on**?
      porridge 3INAN-make   when   LIKE DO
      'How (do you) make porridge?' [Bk-44.015]

Finally, two interrogatives can occur with non-interrogative indefinite meaning.[2] The interrogative *nego* 'what?' is used non-interrogatively to mean 'whatever (thing/s)'. The interrogative *tuen* 'when?' occurs in two phrases where it has non-interrogative indefinite meaning. *Tuen~tuen uen* 'REDUP~when one' is a mid-scalar quantifier meaning 'several' and has the same distribution as its interrogative source expression, *tuen~tuen* 'how much/many?, how long (time)?'. *Tuen noq* 'when ago' is used as a temporal adverb referring to an indefinite past time.

3.5.3 Locationals

Locationals occur in the NP denoting a location which acts as the ground for the referent of the NP head as figure. There are four distinct sets of locationals in Bunaq (Table 3.4), specifying elevation, place, addressee location, and temporal/discourse location.

---

[2] Discussing Australian languages, Mushin (1995) calls items which are polysemous, being both interrogatives and indefinites, "epistemes".

Table 3.4: Locationals.

Elevational Locationals	ola	'LOW'
	ota	'LEVEL'
	esen	'HIGH'
Place Locationals	huqe	'HERE'
	haqe	'THERE'
	hoqe	'SPCPLC'
Temporal/Discourse Locational	mete	'NOW'
Addressee Locational	o	'ADDR'

Locationals occupy a distinct syntactic position in the NP preceding the N_{HEAD} and its possessor (50a); a position following the possessor results in ungrammaticality (50b and 50c).

(50) a. ola   Yati   gie   reu
       LOW   Yati   3.POSS house
       'Yati's house down there'
    b. *Yati   ola   gie   reu
        Yati LOW   3.POSS house
    c. *Yati   gie   ola   reu
        Yati 3.POSS LOW house   [Not.07-01]

That locationals are distinct from possessors is seen in their ability to co-occur with a pronoun. Whilst pronouns cannot be possessed (§3.5.1), they can have their location specified by a locational. We see in (51) that the elevational locational *ola* 'LOW' modifies *nei* '1PL.EXCL', while in (52) the discourse locational *mete* 'NOW' modifies *halaqi* '3PL'.

(51) Gie   pie   [**ola** nei]   n-o   pir   doe.
     3.POSS steam   LOW   1PL.EXCL 1EXCL-SRC reach SPEC.INAN
     'Its smell (lit., its steam) reached us down there just now.'   [Bk-69.021]

(52) [**Mete** halaqi guni   gene   roi]=na   ate   gene...
      NOW   3PL   outside   LOC   SPEC.AN=FOC   far   LOC
      'Now those (people) who were on the outside are far away...'   [Bk-15.013]

Locationals are part of the NP; this is manifest in several features of their behaviour. First, prosodically, a locational occurs in a single intonational unit with the NP; there can be no pause or break in intonation between the locational and the NP. Second, a locational can follow the N_{HEAD} whose location it refers to; in this position it occurs to the left of the determiner, i.e., within the NP (see §8.2.2 for illustration). Third, it is unacceptable to have a locational simply appear in a clause without it being associated with an NP slot. For instance, (53) is unacceptable as *ola* 'LOW' is not associated with an NP position: the verb *mele* 'walk' takes a single S, encoded in this case by the pronominally used determiner *baqi*, and the locational occurs to the right of the NP periphery marked by the determiner, thus necessarily outside the NP.

(53) **Baqi   ola   mele.*
     NPRX.AN   LOW   walk
     'S/he walks down there.'   [Not-06-03]

Locationals can be used independently to denote locations, but they still must be associated with an NP slot in the clause. That is, they can be used on their own without an N$_{HEAD}$ to indicate a vague location, as in (54a). Used in this way, the locational can only be modified by a determiner (54b). Unlike an N$_{HEAD}$, the locational cannot be modified by a (restrictive/non-restrictive) relative clause (54c) or a possessor (54d), though there is no apparent pragmatic motivation for the restriction.

(54) a. *ola*
        LOW
        '(location) down (there)'
     b. *ola   baqa*
        LOW   NPRX.INAN
        'that (location) down (there)'
     c. **ola(=na)   ate*
        LOW=FOC   far
        'far (location) down (there)'
     d. **nie   ola*
        1EXCL.POSS   LOW
        'my (location) down (there)'

The addressee locational is distinct from the other locationals in that it is syntactically dependent and requires other elements to be expressed in the NP along with it, while the other Bunaq locationals do not, and are able to stand alone in the NP. See Chapter 8 for a full discussion of Bunaq locationals.

3.5.4 Determiners

The set of determiners in Bunaq encompasses the demonstratives and the anaphoric article (Table 3.5).[3] Like locationals discussed in the previous section, determiners are used for locating and identifying entities. However, whereas locationals refer to the location of an entity, determiners refer to an entity by locating it in space, time, or the discourse.

Table 3.5: Bunaq Lamaknen determiners.

		ANIMATE	INANIMATE
DEMONSTRATIVES			
PROXIMAL	'PROX'	*bari*	*bare*
NON-PROXIMAL	'NPRX'	*baqi*	*baqa*
SPECIFIER	'SPEC'	*doi*	*doe*
CONTRASTIVE	'CONTR'	*himo*	*homo*
COUNTER-EXPECTATIONAL	'CONTEXP'	*beri*	*bere*
ARTICLE	'ART'	*bi*	*ba*

Syntactically, determiners appear at the right periphery of the NP. All elements of the NP must occur to the left of the determiner, as in (55a). We see in (55b) that where *mamal* 'soft' occurs to the right of the determiner *baqa* 'NPRX.INAN', it is not part of the NP, but can only be interpreted as the predicate of a clause. Only one determiner is permitted in the NP (55c) and no NP is syntactically required to be marked by a determiner (55d).

(55) a. *zo   mamal baqa*
       mango soft   NPRX.INAN
       'that soft mango'
    b. *zo   baqa   mamal*
       mango NPRX.INAN   soft
       'that mango is soft', not good for *'that soft mango'
    c. **zo   mamal baqa   ba*
       mango soft   NPRX.INAN   ART.INAN

---

[3] In using the label "determiner" here, I do not posit the existence of a "determiner phrase" as in the "DP hypothesis" of Abney (1987). There are many unresolved issues concerning the idea that determiners are heads of DPs with NPs as their complements (outlined in Matthews 2007: 11–26 & 61–78), particularly in languages such as Bunaq that do not syntactically *require* a determiner.

d. *zo   mamal*
   mango   soft
   '(a/the) mango'

As mentioned above, determiners are of two syntactic types: (i) demonstratives, which can occur syntactically independently of a noun, where the referent can be understood from the context or identified from the preceding discourse (56), and (ii) the article, which is syntactically dependent and cannot occur as the only element in the NP (57).

(56) a. *zo   baqa*
        mango   NPRX.INAN
        'that mango'
     b. *baqa*
        NPRX.INAN
        'that (mango)'

(57) a. *zo   ba*
        mango   ART.INAN
        'the mango'
     b. **ba*
        ART.INAN

Morphologically, determiners are characterised by being marked for noun class. Each determiner has an ANIMATE and an INANIMATE form and agrees in noun class with the head of the NP, as in (58).

(58) a. *zo   bare   / *bari*
        mango.INAN   PROX.INAN   PROX.AN
        'this mango'
     b. *en   bari   / *bare*
        person.AN   PROX.AN   PROX.INAN
        'this person'

Determiners may also be used to determine clauses. This use along with a detailed description of the individual functions of Bunaq determiners is found in Chapter 7.

3.5.5 Numerals

Bunaq numerals constitute their own word class with distributional properties distinct from other classes. The basic members of the set of numerals are listed in Table 3.6.

Numerals 7 through 9 as well as terms for 100, 1,000, and 10,000 are borrowed from neighbouring Austronesian languages.

Table 3.6: Numerals.

1	*uen*	one
2	*hiloqo(n)*	two
3	*goniqo(n)*	three
4	*goniqil*	four
5	*gonciet*	five
6	*tomol*	six
7	*hitu*	seven
8	*walu*	eight
9	*siwe*	nine
10	*sogo*	tens
11-19	*sogo gal +*	teens
20+	*sogo +*	tens of
100+	*atus +*	hundreds of
1,000+	*lihur +*	thousands of
10,000+	*beqin +*	tens of thousands of

Bunaq numerals are verb-like in that they may be used both predicatively (59a) and attributively (59b). Yet, they differ from verbs in that they may be reduplicated with a meaning different from that of reduplication in other word classes (§2.5.3). Numerals appear following a predicate in reduplicated form to denote distributivity (59c), a common cross-linguistic pattern (Gil 2008). Also, unlike verbs, numerals may be zero-coordinated to denote approximate quantity, in both their predicative (59d) and attributive use (59e).

(59) a. Predicative numeral
    *Pana   bi   **hiloqon**.*
    female ART.AN two
    'The women are two.', i.e. 'There are two women.'
  b. Attributive numeral
    *pana   **hiloqon** bi*
    female two   ART.AN
    'the two women'

c. Reduplicated numeral
   *Pana   bi   man   **hiloqon~hiloqon**.*
   female ART.AN   come   REDUP~two
   'The women came two by two.'
d. Zero-coordinated predicative numeral
   *Pana   bi   **hiloqon   goniqon**.*
   female ART.AN   two   three
   'The women were two (or) three.', i.e., 'There were two (or) three women.'
e. Zero-coordinated attributive numeral
   *pana   **hiloqon   goniqon**   bi*
   female two   three   ART.AN
   'the two (or) three women'

With the exception of *uen* 'one', which has some unique referential and morphosyntactic properties among numerals (§3.5.5.1), no difference in behaviour (and thus word class membership) has been found between higher and lower numerals.

Finally, only numerals can fill slots in the formula for a complex numeral. The formula for the formation of complex numerals is given in (60). The term 'DIGIT' is used to refer to numerals from 1–9. Examples are given below.

	10,000s	1,000s	100s	10s	plus	1–9
(60)	(*beqin* DIGIT)	(*lihur* DIGIT)	(*atus* DIGIT)	(*sogo* DIGIT)	(*gal*)	DIGIT

Sogo 'ten' is the base of all numerals between eleven and ninety-nine. Numerals from 11 to 19 are formed with *sogo* 'ten' + *gal* + a DIGIT (61).[4] The items *sogo* 'ten' and *gal* typically collapse and are realised as a single phonological word, *sogal* 'teens', in normal rapid speech, but may be kept separate in careful speech.

(61) a. *sogo*
        10
        'ten'
     b. *sogo   gal   uen*   [ˈsogo ˈgal uˈen ~ soˈgal uˈen]
        10   plus   1
        'eleven'
     c. *sogo   gal   hiloqon*   [ˈsogo ˈgal hiˈloʔon ~ soˈgal hiˈloʔon]
        10   plus   2
        'twelve'

---

4 In East Timorese dialects, *resi(n)* 'more', a borrowing from Tetun, is used in the place of *gal*. Bunaq Lamaknen also borrows this but as *lesin* 'more'. However, it does not use *lesin* in numeral constructions, but rather limits it to comparatives – see §14.3.1.3 on the coding of comparative constructions.

d. *sogo gal   goniqon* ['sogo 'gal goni'ʔon ~ so'gal goni'ʔon]
   10   plus 3
   'thirteen'
e. *sogo gal   goniqil* ['sogo 'gal goni'ʔil ~ so'gal goni'ʔil]
   10   plus 4
   'fourteen'

Numerals of twenty and above are formed with *sogo* plus a numeral with *gal* introducing a DIGIT (62). Sequences of [go], as in *sogo goniqon* '30', are optionally reduced in rapid speech. The final vowel of *sogo* is dropped and the velar consonant devoiced resulting in *sok goniqon* '30', *sok goniqil* '40', *sok gonciet* '50'.

(62) a. *sogo hiloqon*
        10   2
        'twenty'
     b. *sogo hiloqon gal   uen*
        10   2   plus 1
        'twenty-one'
     c. *sogo hiloqon gal   hiloqon*
        10   2   plus 2
        'twenty-two'

Atus 'hundred', *lihur* 'thousand', and *beqin* 'ten thousand' are the bases for units of numerals for hundreds, thousands, and tens of thousands, respectively. These bases are always accompanied by a DIGIT: e.g., *atus uen* 'one hundred' not **atus* '100'. Their use is illustrated in (63). Note also that when a numeral involves a base plus a simple unit of ten, *sogo* 'ten' must be accompanied by *uen* 'one', thus *sogo* '10', but *atus uen sogo uen* '110' and not **atus uen sogo*.

(63) a. *atus   goniqon   sogo hiloqon   gal tomol*
        100   3   10   2   +   6
        '326'
     b. *lihur   uen   atus   siwe   sok goniqil   gal gonciet*
        1000   1   100   9   10   4   +   5
        '1945'
     c. *beqin   tomol lihur   hitu   sogo uen*
        10000   6   1000   7   10   1
        '67010'

Some older speakers insist that, when counting from 1 to 9 following a unit of a hundred, *kereq* 'single' must introduce a unit of 1 to 9, as in (64). Above 10, *kereq* 'single' is not used (65). The star '*' in these examples is for older speakers; younger speakers, particularly those more influenced by Indonesian/Malay, produce the starred phrases below.

(64) a. *atus uen kereq uen* / *atus uen uen
    100 1   single 1   100 1   1
    '101'

   b. *atus uen kereq hiloqon* / *atus uen hiloqon
    100 1   single 2   100 1   2
    '102'

(65) a. *atus uen sogo uen* / **atus uen kereq sogo uen*
    100 1   10   1   100 1   single 10 1
    '110'

   b. *atus uen sogal uen* / **atus uen kereq sogal uen*
    100 1   teens 1   100 1   single teens 1
    '111'

3.5.5.1 Excursus on the numeral *uen* 'one'

The numeral *uen* 'one' is not simply used to denote that an entity has a quantity of precisely one. It also has particular referential properties and syntactic combinational properties that set it apart from the other numerals.

Firstly, *uen* 'one' can co-occur with other quantificational items in the NP, often with non-singular reference. Following other numerals and quantification verbs in the NP, *uen* 'one' denotes that the plurality of participants referred to form a single unit together. In (66) and (67), *uen* 'one' occurs after the numeral *hiloqon* 'two' and quantificational verb *deal* 'be many', respectively.

(66) [*En   pana   **hiloqon uen**]   higal.*
     person female   two   one   laugh
     'Two girls were laughing together as one.'   [Bk-4.054]

(67) [*Mau Paran en   **real   uen**] gi-ta   sai.*
     Mau Paran person   many   one   3AN-GL   exit
     'Mau Paran came upon a large (group of) people.'   [Bk-4.014]

Secondly, when reduplicated, *uen* 'one' does not have the meaning 'one by one' as would be predicted from the meaning of other reduplicated numerals. Rather, it means 'same, identical'. Reduplicated *uen* 'one' not only appears following a main verb (68), but also may itself be an independent predicate (69).

(68) En   gol   baqi   memel   **uen~uen**   teni.
     person small NPRX.AN   sick   REDUP~one   again
     'The child was sick just the same again.'   [Bk-39.047]

(69) Tubi raka=na   baqa.   Tubi s-alak   baqa
     k.o.cake=FOC   NPRX.INAN   cake 3INAN-roast   NPRX.INAN
     uen~uen.
     REDUP~one
     'That was raka cakes. Roasted cakes are the same (as raka cakes).'   [Bk-76.036-37]

Finally, as in many languages, *uen* 'one' is used in NPs to express indefiniteness. This function is discussed and illustrated in §5.5.1.

3.5.6 Postpositions

The class of postpositions in Bunaq has three members, the oblique (locational and temporal) postposition *no* 'OBL' (and its dialectal variant *ni* 'OBL'), the locational postposition *gene* 'LOC', and the similative postposition *goet* 'LIKE'.

Postpositions occur as the heads of postpositional phrases. The complement of a PP is an NP. A postposition can head a predicate (70) or introduce an NP with a peripheral thematic role into the clause (71).

(70) Neto reu   gene.
     1SG   house LOC
     'I (am) at home.'   [Not-07.03]

(71) Neto reu   gene mit.
     1SG   house LOC   sit
     'I sit at home.'   [Not-07.03]

Unlike verbs (§3.3) and verbal postpositions (§3.6.1), postpositions do not take prefixes and require an overt *in situ* NP complement. We see in (72) that the postposition *goet* 'LIKE' has the same form, regardless of whether its NP complement is 1st person (72a) or 3rd person (72b).

(72) a. Baqi   neto   goet.
        NPRX.AN 1SG   LIKE
        'S/he is like me.'
     b. Baqi   gie   ama   goet.
        NPRX.AN 3.POSS father LIKE
        'S/he is like his/her father.'   [Not-07.03]

Example (73b) is ungrammatical because the postposition's complement, *tas* 'village' from (73a), is missing.

(73) a. *Neto   tas   gene.*
       1SG   village LOC
       'I (am) in the village.'
   b. **Neto   Ø   gene.*
       1SG   LOC
       'I (am) in (the village).'   [Not-07.03]

When the complement of a locative postposition, whether *no* 'OBL' or *gene* 'LOC', is relativised, the postposition is deleted from the relative clause (see §5.4.3.3). Example (74) shows *reu* 'house' as the head of a relative clause based on (71). We see that, with the extraction of *reu* 'house' as head to the front of the relative clause, the postposition, *gene* 'LOC' marking the locative role of *reu* 'house' is obligatorily deleted in the RC.

(74) *Baqi*   [*reu*_{HEAD}=*na*   [*neto*   Ø   *mit*]_{RC}]_{NP}   *h-azal.*
     NPRX.AN house=FOC   1SG   sit   3INAN-see
     'She saw the house that I was sitting (in).'   [Not-07.03]

See §4.4 for an overview of the position of postpositional phrases in the clause and §12.2 for a full discussion of the semantics of postpositions.

3.5.7 Interjections

Interjections are small, independent words expressing an emotion or reaction on the part of the speaker. They are a class of words which constitute utterances by themselves; they do not enter into phrases or constructions with words belonging to other word classes or with other interjections. Morphologically, interjections are invariable, that is, they never take inflectional prefixes or valency-reducing affixes.

Interjections are typically words of one or two syllables. Phonologically, interjections differ from other word classes in Bunaq in that many have a final /h/, a phoneme normally only found initially in native Bunaq words (cf. §2.2.3.3). They are characterised by a sharply rising pattern of intonation, indicated here by an exclamation mark, such as in examples (75) to (77).

(75) **Eqi!**   *Nie*   *deu*   *buleqen*   *haqal*   *oa!*
     INTERJ 1EXCL.POSS house gold   finished IAM
     'Wow! My house is all of gold.'   [BeiUer.046]

(76) **A!**   Ei   hani   naq!
      INTERJ 2PL   PROH   PRIOR
      'Oh! Don't!'   [ApaGiriKereq.049]

(77) **Wah!** Neto mit   sal   oa.
      INTERJ   1SG   sit   wrong IAM
      'Oh no! I have been sitting the wrong way.'   [BeiZap.043-44]

Table 3.7 presents a selection of interjections from the Bunaq corpus with a characterisation of their approximate meaning. The interjections listed are what are known as 'primary' interjections in the typological literature (see, e.g., Ameka 1992). That is, they are only used as interjections and have no known lexical meaning beyond their interjective one. Despite this, the class seems not to have been static or closed. For example, *hainaq* 'wait!' likely originated in a verb plus the priorative marker *naq* (see §14.3.7), but because *hai* is not found as an independent verb today, it is considered a primary interjection here. *Adeh* 'ow, oh no!' is a borrowing of the Malay interjection *aduh* of similar meaning.

I have observed few secondary interjections (i.e., items co-opted as interjections from other parts of speech) in Bunaq. The only clear example in the corpus to date is the noun *eme* 'mother', which may be used as an interjection meaning something like English 'oh dear!'.

Table 3.7: Selection of interjections.

abeh	interjection expressing alarm, concern, or regret
adeh	interjection expressing a feeling of pain or regret arising from an error or accident
ae	interjection expressing the need for caution or attention in the presence of a danger or hazard
ah ~ a	interjection expressing annoyance or disappointment
aiga	interjection expressing physical pain
arin	interjection expressing doubt or scepticism
eh	interjection used to indicate a negative reaction to what was previously said or suggested
eqi	interjection expressing surprise or amazement
hai	interjection to attract the attention of someone
hainaq	interjection asking someone to wait or stop what they are doing
ho	interjection expressing acknowledgement of and compliance with an order, often begrudgingly
o	interjection expressing acknowledgment or understanding of a statement
wah	interjection expressing surprise or shock
wei	interjection expressing disbelief or astonishment
wou	interjection expressing disagreement or difference of opinion

3.6 Problems in the classification of the lexicon

In every language there are problems in the absolute interpretation of the place of individual items in the lexicon. Processes of language change lead to some members of the lexicon moving between word classes, or showing some properties consistent with one word class and others with another. Borrowing of lexical items from other languages may also contribute to categorial confusion, particularly where the loanwords are transferred with the source language's syntactic features, which differ from that of the target language. This section briefly addresses the problem of the representation in the lexicon of items with ambiguous categorial status. Four cases in point from Bunaq are briefly summarised below: §3.6.1 looks at verbal postpositions, §3.6.2 at items with a quantificational function in the NP, §3.6.3 at items with an adverbial function, and §3.6.4 at clause conjoiners.

3.6.1 Verbal postpositions

"Verbal postpositions"[5] is the label used here to describe a set of lexical items that display characteristics consistent in different ways with two other word classes, verbs (§3.3) and postpositions (§3.5.6).[6] Table 3.8 presents an overview of the morphosyntactic properties of postpositions and verbal postpositions from least verbal to most verbal for comparison.

Bunaq verbal postpositions appear to have their origins in serial verbs which functioned to introduce NPs with peripheral thematic roles into the clause.[7] We see from Table 3.8 that whilst some of the items used as verbal postpositions are still very much verbal, others are not. Verbal postpositions have morphosyntactic properties consistent with verbs (§3.3), such as inflecting for person, e.g., (78a) versus (78b), and allowing the elision or fronting of their NP complement (78c).

---

[5] The term "verbal postposition" is adapted here from "verbal preposition" in the Austronesian literature, especially Durie (1988). The switch from "pre-" to "post-" reflects Bunaq's head-final syntactic typology in contrast to the typical head-initial one of Austronesian. Other labels for these items include "prepositional verbs" and "verboids".

[6] See Enfield (2006) for a discussion of a similar classificatory problem.

[7] The diachronic emergence of adpositions from serial verbs is a well-described grammaticalisation path, e.g., Lichtenberk (1991) and Pawley (1973). Inflecting adpositions have also been known to arise through the fusion of pronouns and adpositions, e.g., in Irish and Hungarian. The possibility of a similar process having occurred in Bunaq cannot be entirely excluded. However, there does appear to be good internal evidence, as well as comparative etymologies, to support the view that verbal postpositions developed from verbs. These are discussed in the individual sections on the verbal postpositions in §12.4.

Table 3.8: Verbal and non-verbal properties of postpositions and verbal postpositions.

				Elision/ fronting of NP COMP?	Person inflection?	ANIMATE / INANIMATE inflection?	Independent predicate?	Sharing A/S?
Postpositions		no / ni	'OBL'	X	X	X	✓	--
		gene	'LOC'	X	X	X	✓	--
		goet	'LIKE'	X	X	X	✓	--
Verbal postpositions	Least verb-like	g-utu	'3-COM'	✓	✓	X	X	X
		dele	'INS'	✓	✓	✓	X	✓
		a-ta	'3INAN-GL'	✓	✓	✓	(✓)†	X ‡
		g-o	'3-SRC'	✓	✓	X	(✓)†	X ‡
		h-otol	'3INAN-WITHOUT'	✓	✓	✓	(✓)†	✓
		h-ege	'3INAN-BEN'	✓	✓	✓	✓	✓
		h-os	'3INAN-WAIT'	✓	✓	✓	✓	✓
	Most verb-like	h-onogo	'3INAN-SEPARATE'	✓	✓	✓	✓	✓

† Independent use of the verb attested synchronically, but appears unrelated to postpositional use.
‡ Reciprocal-marked form only (see §11.4.5).

(78) a. *Baqi* **ni-ta** *man.*
    NPRX.AN 1EXCL-GL come
    'S/he came to me.'
  b. *Baqi* **i-ta** *man.*
    NPRX.AN 1INCL/2-GL come
    'S/he came to you.'
  c. **Baqi** *neto* **gi-ta** *man.*
    NPRX.AN 1SG 3AN-GL come
    'I came to *her*.'

However, verbal postpositions often lack the crucial verbal property of being able to appear finally as the independent main predicate of a clause. And where they can act as a main predicate in the clause, there may be little or no connection between their meaning as a main final verb and that as a medial verbal postposition. Compare the meanings of *ni-ta* as a goal-encoding verbal postposition in (79a) and *ni-ta* as a final, independent verb meaning 'shoot' in (79b).

(79) a. *Baqi* **ni-ta** *man.*
    NPRX.AN 1EXCL-GL come
    'S/he came to me.'
  b. *Baqi* **ni-ta**.
    NPRX.AN 1INCL/2-shoot
    'S/he shot me.'

Some verbal postpositions lack distinct 3rd person ANIMATE/INANIMATE inflections. For example, *g-utu* is an invariable 3rd person inflection used with both animate (80a) and inanimate (80b) NP complements. Additionally, we see that some verbal postpositions may lack the A/S sharing properties of verbs in core serialisation (§13.3), with some also sharing P. This is also illustrated with the examples in (80), where *g-utu* shares the S with *man* 'come' in (80a), but does not share the A with *kahul* 'mix' in (80b).

ANIMATE / S SHARING
(80) a. *Neto* **baqi** *g-utu* *man.*
    1SG NPRX.AN 3-COM come
    'I came with her/him.'
INANIMATE / P SHARING
  b. *Neto* *tun* **mok** *baqa* *g-utu* *kahul.*
    1SG flour banana NPRX.INAN 3-COM mix
    'I mix banana with that flour.'

The exact mix of verbal characteristics varies from item to item, such that what we see is an apparent process of grammaticalisation from full lexical verb into postposition involving the step-by-step attrition of verbal features. However, the inability of verbal postpositions to occur as a predicate head also makes them unlike postpositions, since postpositions can do so (§3.5.6). Verbal postpositions thus only functionally resemble Bunaq postpositions in so far as they add peripheral NPs to a clause. Bunaq's verbal postpositions do not appear to be on a grammaticalisation cline between verb and postposition, but rather look as if they are forming into a word class distinct from that of the existing postpositional class in Bunaq.

See §12.4 for a description of the functions of the individual verbal postpositions and other items functioning to introduce peripheral NPs.

3.6.2 Quantificational items in the NP

A quantifier is a lexeme that expresses the number or amount of an NP's referent. Gil (2001) observes that "[t]here is probably no language within which there is a formal category consisting exactly of all quantifiers but no other expressions." In Bunaq also, there is not a coherent set of morphosyntactic properties that can be identified as defining a class of quantifiers. In fact, the items performing quantificational functions in the NP are a "mixed bag", showing significant diversity in their distributional properties. Table 3.9 presents an overview of the morphosyntactic properties of quantificational items in the NP. We see that each of the items differs as to which other items it can occur with in the NP and where it occurs relative to them.

In the right-most column of Table 3.9, we see that the majority of the NP quantifiers can be traced back to members of another word class. Their morphosyntactic heterogeneity is the result of multiple construction-specific grammaticalisations from a diverse range of word classes (as per Croft 2005).[8] This miscellany has been added to by a range of borrowings from Tetun, which have retained aspects of their original syntax. For instance, *naran* in Tetun occurs before the noun and this syntax has been kept in Bunaq although it contrasts with all the other quantificational items which follow. These two points, constructional grammaticalisation and borrowing, mean that the distributional properties and combinatorics of items are on a construction-by-construction basis, with few generalisations to be made across all items. See §5.6 for a description of the different items used as non-numeral quantifiers in Bunaq.

---

[8] For obvious reasons of space, it is not possible here to describe each individual grammaticalisation path from lexeme to NP quantifier.

Table 3.9: Distributional properties of quantificational items in the NP.

	Pre-N_HEAD or Post-N_HEAD?	Without N_HEAD?	With other modifiers?	With other QUANT?	Position in NP?	Source?
halaqi 'PL'	post	✓	RC, Det	numeral	post-num, pre-RC	< pronoun halaqi '3PL'
mil 'COLL'	post	X	X	uen 'one' / ginil 'GRP'	--	< noun mil 'inside'
ginil 'GRP'	post	X	RC, Det	only mil 'COLL'	post-RC	< inalienably possessed noun g-inil '3AN-name' calqued from Tetun
gomoq 'GRP. ANIMAL'	post	X	RC, Det	X	post-RC	< inalienably possessed noun g-omoq '3AN-udder'
waqen 'PART.PL'	post	✓	RC, Det	X	pre-RC	< Tetun wa?in 'many'
hotu~hotu 'all'	post	X	X	X	--	< Tetun hotu 'all'
naran 'every, various'	pre	X	RC, Det	X	--	< Tetun naran 'name, any'
gewen~gewen 'all sorts'	post	✓	RC, Det	X	pre-RC	< inalienably possessed noun g-ewen '3AN-face' calqued from Tetun
oik~oik 'all sorts'	post	✓	RC, Det	X	pre-RC	< Tetun oi?~oik 'REDUP~face'

3.6.3 Adverbs

In the absence of an adjective class, adverbs are defined here as modifiers of constituents in the clause other than nouns. Cross-linguistically, defining a class of adverbs morphosyntactically is often extremely problematic (Schachter and Shopen 2007: 20). It is also not easy typologically to identify a semantic prototype for adverbs (Ramat and Ricca 1994).

In Bunaq, the designation of a single adverbial class is similarly problematic. Items serving to modify non-nominal constituents in the clause are a massively heterogeneous bunch. Only a few negative morphosyntactic attributes can be used to narrow down the field: adverbs cannot head predicates, have no valency (unless one considers the clause their argument, cf. the "ambient" serialisation discussed in §13.3), and cannot be modified.

Furthermore, the group of Bunaq adverbs isolated by this definition still encompasses significant variance in distributional properties. In particular, adverbs in Bunaq vary as to whether they occur preceding or following the predicate. Yet, even within the pre-predicate group and post-predicate group, there are noteworthy syntactic differences: in the preverbal group, for instance, a modal adverb, such as *misti* 'must', can occur without a predicate where the event denoted by the predicate can be contextually retrieved, whilst a participant-oriented adverb, such as *nor* 'randomly', cannot have its predicate omitted.

As suggested by the labels "modal" and "participant-oriented" used in the previous paragraph, some broad semantic subsets can be discerned amongst adverbs in the pre-predicate and post-predicate groups. Within these semantic subsets, there are also typically syntactic differences between members. For instance, whilst some modal adverbs can precede an A/S argument, others cannot.

In sum, there is little to unite "adverbs" into a single group in Bunaq. What is more, there are often few characteristics which are shared in common between smaller semantic subsets of adverbial items. See Chapter 14 on clausal modification for further discussion and illustration of the various kinds of "adverbs" in Bunaq.

3.6.4 Clause conjunctions

Bunaq does not have a united class of clause conjunctions. Rather, there are at least three classes of dedicated conjunctions displaying different distributional properties. They are: (i) postverbal conjunctions that have no functions outside of clause conjoining, (ii) clause-initial conjunctions that are mostly borrowed, and (iii) adverbial clause conjunctions that also have adpositional functions. Even within these three groupings there is little internal consistency. See §15.3.2 for detailed discussion of the clause conjunctions used in Bunaq.

Bunaq has only two dedicated postverbal clause conjunctions: *=si* 'REAS' and *soq* 'SEQ'. While *=si* 'REAS' is enclitic to the last element of a clause in the same way as the Bunaq enclitic discourse markers (§4.7.4), *soq* 'SEQ' occurs in a position preceding the iamitive phasal polarity marker *oa* 'IAM'. Compare the position of *oa* 'IAM' and the different postverbal clause conjoiners in (81) and (82).

(81) *Neto   dokter   g-ege   seq   mina,   n-osil*
     1SG   doctor   3AN-BEN   call   come.LOW   1EXCL-breath
     hobel   gie   goet   o=si.
     not.exist   PROSP   LIKE   IAM=REAS
     'I called for the doctor to come, because it was as if I couldn't breathe.'

[Bk-40.008]

(82) G-awa gini hul goniqon, g-ubeqen g-inil,
 3AN-feed moon four 3AN-squeeze 3AN-try
 lenuk bokul porsa **soq oa.**
 turtle fat very SEQ IAM
 '(We will) feed it for fourth months, (and then we will) try and pinch it, as soon as the turtle is very fat.' [OrelHalaliLenuk.038]

The conjunctions =si 'REAS' and soq 'SEQ' are discussed further in §15.3.2.1.1 and §15.3.2.1.2, respectively.

Clause-initial clause conjunctions are frequently used in Bunaq and are all identifiable as borrowings. An example with *mais* 'but' (< Portuguese via Tetun) is given in (83). Clause-initial conjoiners always occur at the left edge of the clause.

(83) ..., apa kereq bari neto gi-tin selu heta,
 cow single PROX.AN 1SG 3AN-price replace able
 mais neto perlu si g-ume gie.
 but 1SG need meat 3AN-kill PROSP
 '..., I afford this cow, but I do need to kill it for meat.' [OrelBusaKawak-61]

See §15.3.2.2 for more information and illustration of clause-initial conjoiners.

Finally, Bunaq has two adverbial clause conjoiners, *helo* 'since' and *daurau* 'until', used to locate an event by referring to a period of time or to another event. Adverbial clause conjoiners differ from the other clause conjoiners in that they can take a clause, an NP, or a PP as their complement. For example, *helo* 'since' is shown with a clausal complement in (84), an NP complement in (85), and a PP complement in (86). The ability to introduce an NP makes adverbial clauses conjoiners superficially similar to postpositions. But unlike postpositions, adverbial clauses conjoiners cannot act as an independent clausal predicate (cf. §3.5.6 on the distributional properties of postpositions).

(84) [N-iri tol] **helo**, neto mele lomar niq.
 1EXCL-leg broken since 1SG walk straight NEG
 'Since I broke my leg, I don't walk right.' [OS-07.03]

(85) [Hari Senin] **helo**, gie ama g-aziq.
 Tuesday since 3.POSS father 3AN-not.seen
 'Since Tuesday, his father has not been seen.' [OS-07.01]

(86) Baqi [Maret no] **helo** Timor gene.
 NPRX.AN March OBL since Timor LOC
 'She's been in Timor since March.' [OS-07.02]

While *helo* 'since' occurs following the clause or phrase it introduces, *daurau* 'until' (or its variants, *darau* and *daro*) appears preceding the elements it introduces. This is illustrated with a clausal complement in (87), an NP complement in (88), and a PP complement in (89).

(87) Muk   bula,   **darau**   [matas   mil   nie   ama   halaqi   g-ege
     land pasture until   old   COLL   1EXCL.POSS   father   3PL   3AN-give
     solat   h-one], ...
     strong   3INAN-hold
     'The land was pasture, until the elders gave it to my father and his associates to garden, ...'   [Bk-29.072]

(88) Jadi   nei   h-one   h-oqon   **daro**   [bare].
     so   1PL.EXCL   3INAN-hold   3INAN-make   until   PROX.INAN
     'So we kept on doing this until this (time).'   [Bk-8.034]

(89) Baqi   saqe   **daurau**   [pan   gene].
     NPRX.AN   ascend   until   sky   LOC
     'He went up until the sky.'   [FB-140821]

The clause-conjoining functions of *helo* 'since' and *daurau* 'until' are illustrated further in §15.3.2.4.

Chapter 4
The clause

4.1 Introduction

This chapter is concerned with the structure of the clause in Bunaq. Following an overview of clause structure in §4.1, I look at the different kinds of clauses in Bunaq: verbal clauses are considered in §4.2, and non-verbal clauses in §4.3. Peripheral constituents in the clause are treated in §4.4, and the construction of negative clauses in §4.5. Non-declarative clauses are dealt with in §4.6, while pragmatic variation in the clause is treated in §4.7.

A basic independent clause consists of a predicate (PRED) and its arguments (ARG). Arguments are realised by morphosyntactically unmarked NPs subcategorised for by the predicate. Depending on the predicate type, a predicate can have between one and three arguments. Predicates with one or two arguments have their arguments preceding the predicate, while predicates with a third argument have it following the predicate.

NPs in postpositional (§12.2) and verbal postpositional (§12.4) phrases are peripheral constituents (PERI) (or "external" NPs in the terms of Andrews 2007: 152); that is, they are not subcategorised for by the predicate. Peripheral constituents can occur, according to their function, in any position before, after, or between the predicate and its arguments. Finally, the clausal negator (NEG) follows the predicate and any postverbal arguments or adjuncts.

Figure 4.1 gives an overview of the clause structure as just outlined. Optional elements are given in brackets. The slash "/" introducing the right-most peripheral constituent reflects the fact that there are no predicates in Bunaq, which allow both a postverbal third argument and a postverbal peripheral NP. The ordering of elements in the clause formula can be manipulated for pragmatic effect, while obligatory arguments can also be elided where they are contextually understood (§4.7.1).

(PERI) ARG$_1$ (PERI) ARG$_2$ (PERI) PRED ARG$_3$ (/PERI) (NEG)

Figure 4.1: Bunaq clause formula.

Throughout this chapter, the above clause formula will be discussed and elaborated.

4.2 Verbal clauses

The most frequent clause type is one with a verb as predicate. Subtypes of verbal predicate are distinguished by the number of arguments of the verb (1 to 3). The arguments

of the Bunaq verbal clause will be discussed in terms of the following semantic–syntactic roles (after Comrie 1978, and Dryer 1986):
S: single argument of a monovalent clause
A: most agent-like argument of a bi-/trivalent clause
P: most patient-like argument of a bivalent clause
R: most recipient-like argument of a trivalent clause
T: most theme-like argument of a trivalent clause

In the subsequent sections, we will further define each of the above argument types in the verbal clause as they behave in regards to the following:
(i) unmarked word order;
(ii) agreement on the verb;
(iii) restriction of the floating quantifier *gaqal* 'all.AN' (§13.8.1.3);
(iv) syntactic pivot of the causative predicate *h-ini* '3INAN-CAUS' (§10.4);
(v) binding of the reflexive *dV-* 'REFL' (§11.3.1).

On the basis of the behaviour of Bunaq arguments in the above constructions, I will propose the existence of an additional category of argument, the unmarked oblique (OBL). This argument type has properties distinct from P and occurs with a limited, non-predictable set of verbs. In the following sections we will also see that the various morphosyntactic properties of S align it variably with both A and P, and that T has syntactically more in common with the OBL argument than with P or R.

Monovalent verbs are discussed in §4.2.1, bivalent verbs in §4.2.2, trivalent verbs in §4.2.3, and verbs with an unmarked oblique in §4.2.4. Finally, §4.2.5 summarises the results.

4.2.1 Monovalent clauses

The single argument of a monovalent verbal clause is S and precedes the verb. Monovalent verbs typically do not take an agreement prefix and their single argument is realised exclusively by independent constituents (1).

(1) a.   S   V
     Neto memel.
     1SG   sick
     'I'm sick.'
     S   V
  b. *Manek zemal.*
     Manek go.LOW
     'Manek went down.'

There is a small group of seven verbs whose single S argument is indexed on the verb by a person prefix, as in (2). Relevant to these verbs is the contrast between S_A, referring to an agentive argument of a monovalent verb, and S_P, the non-agentive argument of a monovalent verb. Monovalent verbs with prefixation only take S_P and not S_A arguments. See §10.3.2 on these verbs.

(2)   S   S-V
    a. *Neto n-utek.*
        1SG   1EXCL-heavy
        'I (am) heavy.'
        S   S-V
    b. *Manek g-utek.*
        Manek   3AN-heavy
        'Manek (is) heavy.

The plural ANIMATE S of a monovalent verb binds the floating universal quantifier *gaqal* 'all.AN'. This is the case with monovalent verbs that occur both with and without an agreement prefix for S, as in (3a) and (4a). The examples in (3b) and (4b) show that a singular S is unacceptable with *gaqal* 'all.AN'.[1]

(3)   a. *Nei   memel gaqal.*
          1PL.EXCL sick   all.AN
          'We all are sick.'
   b. **Neto memel gaqal.*
          1SG   sick   all.AN
          'I all am sick.'

(4)   a. *Nei   n-unas   gaqal.*
          1PL.EXCL 1EXCL-stink all.AN
          'We all stink.'
   b. **Neto n-unas   gaqal.*
          1SG   1EXCL-stink all.AN
          'I all stink.'

The underlying S becomes the matrix P of the causative predicate *h-ini* '3INAN-CAUS' for all monovalent verbs, regardless of whether or not they are prefixed (5).

---

[1] Note that one informant suggested that (3b) and (4b) were acceptable in Bunaq, where the singular S is interpreted as referring to 'I (with others we) all'. Such a use of *gaqal* 'all.AN' with a grammatically singular S pronoun was not accepted by any other speakers in elicitation and does not occur in any texts in the corpus.

(5) *Markus nei n-ini memel.*
  Markus 1PL.EXCL 1EXCL-CAUS sick
  'Markus made us sick.'

An S can be the antecedent of the reflexive prefix *dV-* 'REFL'. Example (6) is thus grammatical: the peripheral NP introduced by the instrumental verbal postposition *dele* 'INS' (§12.4.2) is marked reflexive and has the S as its antecedent.

   S INS V
(6) *Neto d-erel mele.*
   1SG REFL-INS walk
   'I went walking with myself.'

4.2.2 Bivalent clauses

The two arguments of a bivalent verb are A and P. The basic pragmatically unmarked constituent order of the bivalent clause is A-P-V (7a), though the P can be fronted to a position before A (7b).

    A P V
(7) a. *Neto zo zal.*
    1SG mango carry
    'I carried the mango.'
    P A V
  b. *Zo neto zal.*
    mango 1SG carry
    'The mango I carried.'

On bivalent verbs, prefixes agree with P; there are no bivalent verbs for which prefixes agree with A. While 1st and 2nd person Ps are consistently realised with *nV-* '1EXCL' and *V-* '1INCL/2' respectively, 3rd person Ps are differentially marked: 3rd person ANIMATE Ps are indexed on the verb with *gV-* '3AN' (8a), while 3rd person INANIMATE Ps receive no verbal indexing (8b).[2] Fronting of P does not affect agreement (8c–8d).

---

[2] This is the majority pattern. See §10.2 for further details on the prefixal patterns of indexing 3rd person P arguments on the verb.

INANIMATE P, no verbal prefixing
(8) a. *Markus zo poi.*
Markus mango choose
'Markus chose a mango.'
ANIMATE P, verbal prefixing with *gV-*
b. *Markus zap go-poi.*
Markus dog 3AN-choose
'Markus chose a dog.'
Fronted INANIMATE P, no verbal prefixing
c. *Zo Markus poi.*
mango Markus choose
'A mango Markus chose.'
Fronted ANIMATE P, verbal prefixing with *gV-*
d. *Zap Markus go-poi.*
dog Markus 3AN-choose
'A dog Markus chose.'

An ANIMATE P argument binds the floating quantifier (9a), even when the P is fronted (9b). The A cannot bind the floating quantifier.[3]

(9) a. *Nei zap go-poi gaqal.*
1PL.EXCL dog 3AN-choose all.AN
'We choose all the dogs.' not 'We all choose the dogs.'
b. *Zap nei go-poi gaqal.*
dog 1PL.EXCL 3AN-choose all.AN
'All the dogs we choose.' not 'The dogs we all choose.'

Only the underlying A of the bivalent verb can be the matrix P of the causative predicate *h-ini* '3INAN-CAUS' (10a) and never the underlying P (10b).

(10) a. *Markus nei n-ini zap go-poi.*
Markus 1PL.EXCL 1EXCL-CAUS dog 3AN-choose
'Markus made us choose the dogs.'
b. **Markus zap g-ini nei go-poi.*
Markus dog 3AN-CAUS 1PL.EXCL 3AN-choose
'Markus made the dogs be chosen by us.'

---

[3] The NP-internal quantifier, *hotu~hotu* 'all', would be used in this context to universally quantify A – see §5.6.7.

In a bivalent verbal clause, the reflexive is bound by A and not P. In (11) we see that the possessor of the peripheral NP introduced by the instrumental verbal postposition *dele* 'INS' (§12.4.2) is encoded with the reflexive *dV-* 'REFL'. The antecedent for this reflexive possessor prefix can only be the referent of A, i.e., Markus, and not that of P, i.e., Ela.

(11)
    A   P   INS   P-V
    Markus Ela d-on dele go-hoqat.
    Markus Ela REFL-hand INS 3AN-strike
    'Markus struck Ela with his own hand.'
    *'Markus struck Ela with her own hand.'

4.2.3 Trivalent clauses

This section deals with the sole Bunaq trivalent verb: *h-ege* '3INAN-give'. While *h-ini* '3INAN-call/cause' takes three arguments and behaves in many respects much the same as *h-ege* '3INAN-give', it is not considered to be a true trivalent verb as its third argument is itself an argument-taking predicate. See §10.4 on the differences between the two Bunaq trivalent verbs. In this section, I focus on *h-ege* '3INAN-give'.

The three arguments of the trivalent verb are A, R, and T. The basic constituent order of the trivalent clause is A-R-V-T (12a). T can also appear in a diverse range of preverbal positions (12b & 12c) or can be fronted (12d). Neither A nor R can appear in a post-verbal position within the clause.

(12)
       A   R   R-V   T
a. *Eta nei n-ege paqol.*
    Eta 1PL.EXCL 1EXCL-give maize
    'Eta gave us maize.'
       A   R   T   R-V
b. *Eta nei paqol n-ege.*
    Eta 1PL.EXCL maize 1EXCL-give
    'Eta gave us maize.'
       A   T   R   R-V
c. *Eta paqol nei n-ege.*
    Eta maize 1PL.EXCL 1EXCL-give
    'Eta gave us maize.'
       T   A   R   R-V
d. *Paqol Eta nei n-ege.*
    maize Eta 1PL.EXCL 1EXCL-give
    'Eta gave us maize.'

R can also be fronted to a position before A (12e). If R is fronted, T occurs post-verbally, presumably to avoid pragmatic overload. Thus, (12f) and (12g) are not accepted.

	R	A	R-V	T
e.	*Nei*	*Eta*	*n-ege*	*paqol.*
	1PL.EXCL	Eta	1EXCL-give	maize
	'We were given maize by Eta.'			
	R	A	T	R-V
f.	**Nei*	*Eta*	*paqol*	*n-ege.*
	1PL.EXCL	Eta	maize	1EXCL-give
	R	T	A	R-V
g.	**Nei*	*paqol*	*Eta*	*n-ege.*
	1PL.EXCL	maize	Eta	1EXCL-give

Of the trivalent verb's three arguments, only R is indexed on the verb. As with the P of a bivalent verb, 1st and 2nd person Rs are realised with *nV-* '1EXCL' and *V-* '1INCL/2' respectively, while 3rd person Rs are differentially marked: an ANIMATE 3rd person R is prefixed with *g-* '3AN' (13a), while an INANIMATE 3rd person R is signalled by *h-* '3INAN' (13b), the marker of the h-conjugation (mentioned already in §2.6.2.3 and described in further detail in §10.2.4.1).

		A	R	R-V	T
(13)	a.	*Nei*	*Markus*	*g-ege*	*tumel.*
		1PL.EXCL	Markus	3AN-give	money
		'We gave Markus money.'			
		A	R	R-V	T
	b.	*Nei*	*gereja*	*h-ege*	*tumel.*
		1PL.EXCL	church	3INAN-give	money
		'We gave the church money.'			

An ANIMATE R argument binds the floating quantifier (14). Neither A nor T can bind the floating quantifier.

	A	R	R-V	T	QUANT
(14)	*Halaqi*	*nei*	*n-ege*	*zap*	*gaqal.*
	3PL	1PL.EXCL	1EXCL-give	dog	all.AN
	'They gave all of us dog(s).' Not good for: *'All of them gave us the dogs.', *'They gave us all of the dogs.'				

Only the underlying A of a trivalent verb can be the matrix P of the causative verb *h-ini* '3INAN-CAUS' (15a) and never the underlying R (15b), or the underlying T (15c).

(15) a. *Markus   nei   n-ini   ei   Ø-ege   zap.*
       Markus   1PL.EXCL   1EXCL-CAUS   2PL   1INCL/2-give dog
       'Markus made us give the dogs to you.'
    b. **Markus   ei   Ø-ini   nei   Ø-ege   zap.*
       Markus   2PL   1INCL/2-CAUS   1PL.EXCL   1INCL/2-give dog
       'Markus made you be given the dogs by us.'
    c. **Markus   zap   g-ini   nei   ei   Ø-ege.*
       Markus   dog   3AN-CAUS   1PL.EXCL   2PL   1INCL/2-give
       'Markus made the dogs be given to you by us.'

With a trivalent verb, the reflexive is bound only by the A. Consider the clause in (16) where the possessor of the T is encoded with the reflexive on the indirect possessive classifier, *die* 'REFL.POSS'. The antecedent for this reflexive-marked possessive can only be the referent of A, Markus, and not that of R, Ela.

(16) *Markus   Ela   g-ege   die   zap.*
     Markus   Ela   3AN-give   REFL.POSS   dog
     'Markus gave Ela his dog.' Not good for: *'Markus gave Ela her dog.'

4.2.4 Verbal clauses with unmarked obliques

The term "unmarked oblique" (OBL)[4] is used here to refer to an NP that is not a P, but that occurs in the clause headed by a limited set of verbs without any overt marking, such as a postposition. Table 4.1 provides an overview of the small range of verb types that have unmarked obliques. Unmarked obliques are arguments, that is, they are subcategorised for by the verb and part of the lexical information entered for the verb. The reason for seeing unmarked obliques as subcategorised for by the verb is: whilst unmarked obliques are part of the predictable semantics of the verb they occur with (e.g., that a motion has a goal), the ability of a verb to take an unmarked oblique is not predictable merely from the semantics of a verb (e.g., not all motion verbs take an unmarked goal oblique). What is more, while some verbs taking unmarked obliques always have the unmarked oblique present, others only take an unmarked oblique in one of their subcategorisation frames with a difference in verb meaning between the frame with the oblique and that without.

---

4 Note that the category label 'OBL' refers to a non-core argument, and contrasts with the gloss 'OBL', the postposition *no/ni*, which introduces NPs with locative and temporal roles (§12.2.1).

Table 4.1: Verbs taking unmarked obliques.

VERB SEMANTICS	ROLE OF OBL	EXAMPLE (OBL = bold)
Saturation verbs	location of saturation	ho **n-on** pegar blood 1EXCL-hand bloodied 'Blood is covering my hand.'
Existential verbs	possessed item	nei **il** hobel 1PL.EXCL water not.exist 'We have no water.'
Motion verbs	goal of motion	baqi **tas** mal NPRX.AN village go 'S/he goes to the village.'
Verbs of teaching/learning	taught thing	baqi **inggris** hanorin NPRX.AN English teach/learn 'S/he learns English.'

Unmarked obliques occur with monovalent verbs in the immediately preverbal position (17a). They can be fronted, occurring before the S in the manner of a P (17b). However, we also see in the examples in (17) that, unlike an ANIMATE P but like a T, an ANIMATE OBL is not indexed on the verb.

(17)   S   OBL   V
    a. Neto kura saqe.
        1SG   horse ascend
        'I ascended the horse.'
        OBL   S   V
    b. Kura neto saqe.
        horse 1SG   ascend
        'The horse I ascended.'

An unmarked oblique is distinguishable from a P in that the floating quantifier cannot quantify the OBL as it would a P. Rather *gaqal* 'all.AN' refers to an ANIMATE S (18a), even when the OBL is fronted (18b), again similar to T.

(18)   S   OBL   V   QUANT
    a. Nei   kura   saqe   gaqal.
        1PL.EXCL house ascend all.AN
        'We all ascended the horse(s).', *'We ascended all the horses.'
        OBL   S   V   QUANT
    b. Kura   nei   saqe   gaqal.
        1PL.EXCL horse ascend all.AN
        'The horse(s) we all ascended.', *'All the horses we ascended.'

As with monovalent verbs, only the S of a verb with an unmarked oblique can be the P of the causative predicate *h-ini* '3INAN-CAUS' (19a) and not the OBL (19b).

(19) a. *Markus   nei   n-ini   kura   saqe.*
       Markus   1PL.EXCL   1EXCL-CAUS horse   ascend
       'Markus made us ascend the horse.'
    b. **Markus kura   g-ini   nei   saqe.*
       Markus   horse 3AN-CAUS   1PL.EXCL   ascend
       'Markus made the horse be ascended by us.'

Also like the S of a monovalent verb, the only S of a verb with an unmarked oblique can be the antecedent for the reflexive prefix *dV-* 'REFL'. In (20) the NP complement of the instrumental verbal postposition *dele* 'INS' has a possessor marked with the reflexive. This can only have the S as its antecedent and not the unmarked oblique.

(20) *Neto kura   d-iri   dele saqe.*
     1SG   horse REFL-leg   INS   ascend
     'I mounted the horse using my legs' (lit., 'I ascended the horse with my own legs.', *'I ascended the horse with its legs.')

See §10.6 for further description of the individual properties of subclasses of verbs with unmarked obliques.

4.2.5 Summary

Table 4.2 summarises the properties of the arguments for each type of verbal predicate that have been seen in the preceding sections.

Table 4.2: Overview of properties of Bunaq arguments.

	PRE–V	INITIAL	AGR	QUANT FLOAT	CAUS PRED	REFL
A	+	+	−	−	+	+
S	+	+	− / (+)	+	+	+
P	+	−	+	+	−	−
R	+	−	+	+	−	−
T	−	−	−	−	−	−
OBL	+	−	−	−	−	−

The arguments A and S pattern together in that they appear as the first in a pragmatically neutral ordered clause, while P, R, and OBL all come later. T is set apart from all other argument types in that it alone occurs post-verbally.

In terms of verbal agreement, P and R pattern together in taking verbal agreement prefixes. S patterns mainly like A, T, and OBL in lacking agreement on the verb; however, a subset of Ss are like P in taking agreement (§10.3.2).

S, P, and R pattern together in terms of restricting reference of the floating quantifier in contrast to A, T, and OBL which do not. Finally, causative serialisation and reflexive binding target the highest argument in a clause, picking out A or S.

In sum, there is some evidence for a "subject" grouping of A and S in Bunaq, but it is weakened by the fact that S also shares properties in common with P and R. The "object" grouping of P and R (so-called "secundative" alignment: Dryer 1986) is robust. The T is defined by the absence of any of the properties displayed by any other of the arguments, and may be better characterised as an OBL, a category with which it shares more properties in common.

On account of the fuzziness in the behaviour of S, throughout this grammar I will avoid the labels "subject" and "object" in reference to the arguments of verbal clauses. Instead, I will continue to refer to semantic–syntactic roles: S, A, P, etc.

4.3 Non-verbal clauses

There are four types of clauses with non-verbal predicates in Bunaq: clauses with nominal predicates (§4.3.1), clauses with predicates headed by postpositions (§4.3.2), clauses with predicates headed by the indirect possessive classifier (§4.3.3), and clauses with complex "character" predications (§4.3.4).

Each of these predicate types takes a single non-predicative NP. This NP will for descriptive convenience be called "subject". It evidences the same control behaviour as that shared in common by A or S. That is, it controls the reflexive and occurrs as the P of the causative verb in causative constructions.

4.3.1 Nominal clauses

Two NPs, of which the second is the predicate, can be juxtaposed to express a relationship of identity between two entities. In Bunaq there is no copula intervening between the two NPs.

Two kinds of identity relationship are expressed by nominal clauses (Dryer 2007: 233–236): clauses of equation, where the first NP has one and the same referent as that of the second, predicative NP (21), and clauses of "proper inclusion" (also known as "ascriptive" clauses), where the first NP has a referent that is among the class of entities specified by the second NP (22).

(21) *Timor   bare   nie   muk.*
     Timor   PROX.INAN   1EXCL.POSS   land
     'Timor here is my (home)land'. [OS-07.01]

(22) *En   bari   en   Islam.*
     person   PROX.AN   person   Islam
     'This person is a Muslim person.' [Bk-37.051]

The two different kinds of nominal clause differ as to their reversibility. Reversal of the ordering of equative NPs is permissible: because the NPs of (21) are entirely coreferential, their reversal in (23) is grammatical. This is not the case for clauses of proper inclusion where reversal results in bizarre semantics and questionable grammaticality: in the reversal of (22) given in (24) there is a disparity of referentiality between the NPs, with the class-identifying NP preceding the specific and referential NP.

(23) *Nie   muk   Timor   bare.*
     1EXCL.POSS   land   Timor   PROX.INAN
     'My (home)land is Timor here.' [Not-07.01]

(24) #/?*En   Islam   en   bari.*
     person   Islam   person   PROX.AN
     'A Muslim person is this person.' [Not-07.01]

There is a subtype of equational clause used in presentational contexts. In this, the predicative NP is fronted to a position before the other NP. The fronted NP is marked with the restrictive focus marker =*na* 'FOC' (§4.7.4.2.3), while the following NP is encoded by a demonstrative, as in (25) and (26)

(25) *En   rato=o   renu   gie   raza=na   baqa.*
     person   noble=AND   commoner   3.POSS   difference=FOC   NPRX.INAN
     'The differences between nobles and commoners are those.' [Bk-18.050]

(26) *Nie   rale=na   bare   ai.*
     1EXCL.POSS   talk=FOC   PROX.INAN   ONLY
     'My speech is this only.' [Bk-7.026]

4.3.2 Postpositional clauses

Postpositional clauses are clauses in which the predicate is headed by one of the three Bunaq postpositions: *no* 'OBL', *gene* 'LOC', and *goet* 'LIKE' (see §3.5.6 on the morphosyntactic properties defining postpositions). Postpositional predicates headed by *no* 'OBL' and *gene* 'LOC' specify the location of an NP, while those headed by *goet* 'LIKE' express the entity to which an NP is similar. The NP expressing the entity that is located/likened precedes the predicative postpositional phrase, consisting of an NP plus the postposition governing it, as in the examples in (27) to (29).

(27) *Il   kokoq   no   niq.*
     water   bucket   OBL   NEG
     'Water is not in the bucket.', i.e., 'There is no water in the bucket.'   [Bk-6.026]

(28) *Neto   reu   memel   gene.*
     1SG   house   sick   LOC
     'I (was) in hospital.'   [Bk-2.018]

(29) *Baqi   gie   ama   goet.*
     NPRX.AN   3.POSS   father   LIKE
     'He is like his father.'   [OS-07.03]

See §4.4 for an overview of the placement of postpositional phrases when encoding peripheral constituents, and §12.2 for more on the semantics of the postpositions.

4.3.3 Possessive clauses

Possessive clauses are those in which the predicate is headed by an inflection of the indirect possessive classifier (see §9.2), plus any cross-referencing NP. The predicate expresses the possessor, while the NP preceding it expresses the possessed item, as in (30) and (31).

(30) *Atis=o   liqul   ba   halaqi   gie.*
     loom.bar=AND   weaving.sword   ART.INAN   3PL   3.POSS
     'The loom bar and weaving swords are theirs.'   [LB-1.058]

(31) a. *Homo   nei   gunung   nie.*
        CONTR.INAN   1PL.EXCL   mountain   1EXCL.POSS
        'That (type of cake) is ours, us mountain people's.'   [Bk-76.039]
     b. *Tubi   s-alak   roe   en   ewi   gie.*
        cake   3INAN-roast   SPEC.INAN   person   stranger   3.POSS
        'Those roasted cakes belong to the foreigners.'   [Bk-76.040]

Possessive clauses are also used to encode location of origin. In this function, *gie* '3.POSS' heads the predicate and takes an NP denoting a location as its complement;

the preceding NP denotes the entity whose origin location is being referred to. Examples of possessive clauses denoting an origin location are given in (32–33).

(32) *Neto Gewal gie.*
    1SG Gewal 3.POSS
    'I am from Gewal.' [Bk-68.010]

(33) *Halaqi Timor-Leste gie.*
    3PL East Timor 3.POSS
    'They are from East Timor.' [Bk-11.013]

Possessive predicates with the indirect possessive classifier *-e* '-POSS' are derived from an adnominal possessive strategy discussed in chapter 9.

4.3.4 Clauses with complex predicates of physical, emotional, and character traits

Physical, emotional, and character traits are typically expressed in Bunaq by means of complex predicates composed of either noun+noun or noun+monovalent verb. For brevity, I will refer to these as "complex character predicates". Table 4.3 presents a selection of some of the more lexicalised complex character predicates in the Bunaq corpus. Many complex predications have little or no flexibility in the lexical identity of their components and their denotational basis is often semantically opaque.

Table 4.3: A selection of lexicalised complex character predicates.

INALIENABLY POSSESSED NOUN + NOUN		
g-ewen buk	3AN-face flower	'be dizzy'
gu-bul bel	3AN-head brain/marrow	'be smart'
g-agar zo	3AN-mouth mango	'be sweet-toothed'
gu-bul hol	3AN-head stone	'be stubborn'
ALIENABLY POSSESSED NOUN + VERB		
tueq lilak	alcohol crazy	'drunk, drunken'
pit saq	throat dry	'thirsty'
INALIENABLY POSSESSED NOUN + VERB		
g-al baruq	3AN-rib bored	'be lazy'
g-al koleq	3AN-rib tired	'be tired, worn out'
g-epal koke	3AN-ear deaf	'be deaf'
g-ewen tomak	3AN-face complete	'be unknown'
g-ewen danu	3AN-face layered	'be insane'

Table 4.3 (continued)

g-iral bulu	3AN-eye blind	'be blind'
g-imil loi	3AN-inside good	'be happy'
g-on laun / rono	3AN-hand fast / slow	'be good / bad workers'
g-otok saqe	3AN-liver ascend	'get angry'
g-otok wel	3AN-liver burnt	'be angry'

At the same time, there are also some compositional, semantically transparent complex character predicates in Bunaq. Such complex character predicates are productive formations that allow varying of the verb (e.g., *aruq dukut* hair curly 'be curly-haired', *aruq legul* hair long 'be long-haired') or noun (e.g., *sakan memel* thigh sick 'be hurt [with respect to one's] thigh', *but hinal* knee sick 'be hurt [with respect to one's] knee').

Clauses with complex character predicates consist of the predicate plus the subject NP denoting the referent who displays the characteristic. The constituents of a complex predicate cannot be prosodically separated from one another. Syntactically, there can also be no separation of the constituents. The initial noun in a complex character predicate is always a simple N (34a). It cannot be independently modified or determined in any way (34b). It also cannot be fronted to a position before the NP encoding the subject of the predication (34c), nor can any item, such as an adverb, intervene between the constituents of the complex predicate (34d).

(34) a. *Neto* [*tueq lilak*]_{PRED}.
    1SG   alcohol crazy
    'I'm drunk.' (lit., 'I'm alcohol-crazy')
  b. **Neto tueq bare lilak.*
    1SG   alcohol PROX.INAN crazy
    'I'm crazy (with) this alcohol.'
  c. **Tueq neto lilak.*
    alcohol 1SG crazy
    '(For) alcohol I'm crazy.'
  d. **Neto tueq nor lilak.*
    1SG   alcohol without.reason crazy
    'I craze alcohol without reason.'

Where the first noun in a complex character predicate is inalienably possessed, the prefix on the noun agrees in person with the subject (35a). The reflexive prefix cannot be used on an inalienably possessed noun in a complex predication (35b). This would be possible were *-otok* 'liver' a P or an unmarked oblique argument, rather than part of the predicate. See §11.3.1 on reflexive binding.

(35) a. *Neto   n-otok   saqe.*
       1SG   1EXCL-liver   ascend
       'I'm angry' (lit., 'I'm raised as to my liver.')
    b. **Neto   d-otok   saqe.*
       1SG   REFL-liver   ascend
       I'm raised as to my own liver.'

Where a complex predicate contains a monovalent verb that takes a prefix (applicable in the case of *nuas* 'stink' and *nuek* 'smell'; see §10.3.2), agreement is with the subject of the clause (36a) and not with the noun of the predication (36b).

(36) a. *Neto   ikan   n-unas.*
       1SG   fish   1EXCL-smell
       'I smell fishy (i.e., like fish).'
    b. **Neto   ikan   g-unas.*
       1SG   fish   3AN-smell

It is also possible to relativise on the subject of a complex character predicate, as in (37). If *en* 'person' were a possessor NP dependent on *g-iwiq* '3AN-skin' rather than the subject of the RC, relativisation, as in (37), would not be possible (see §5.4.3).

(37) [*En*_{HEAD} [*g-iwiq   belis*]_{RC}]_{NP} *Timor   mil   tama.*
     person   3AN-skin white   Timor   inside enter
     'The people who were white-skinned entered Timor.'   [Bk-29.002]

Where the initial noun of a complex predicate is not inalienably possessed, the use of a complex predication to express a characteristic is frequent, but only optional. Compare the clauses in (38). In (38a) we have a clause with a complex predication involving the noun *aruq* 'hair' and with a subject expressed by the pronoun *neto*. By contrast in (38b), *aruq* 'hair' is the head of the NP expressing the S of the simple monovalent verb *legul* in predicate function; a 1st person exclusive inflection of the indirect possessive classifier encodes the person whose hair is at issue.

(38) a. [*Neto*]_{NP} [*aruq   legul*]_{PRED}.
       1SG   hair   long
       'I have long hair.' (lit., 'I am long-haired')
    b. [*Nie   aruq*]_{NP} [*legul*]_{PRED}.
       1EXCL.POSS   hair   long
       'My hair is long.'

While semantically similar in content, the two clauses in (38) differ pragmatically in that the complex predicate in (38a) denotes a situation or state that characterises a human referent, while the clause in (38b) is a verbal predication describing a property of the hair. This difference means that constructions with complex predicates with alienably possessed nouns seem to be preferred in certain situations over the equivalent verbal clauses and are even subject to some lexicalisation. For example, I have consistently heard the complex character predicate in (39a) used by the Bunaq to express 'thirsty'. It is possible to construct a verbal clause such as that in (39b), where *pit* 'throat' is not part of the predicate, but rather an S argument. However, on questioning, speakers said that whereas the clause in (39a) denoted that the speaker was thirsty, (39b) did not necessarily describe thirst, because a dry throat could be caused not only by thirst, but also by sickness. That is, (39b) does not denote a specific situation experienced by the speaker in the same way as the predicate in (39a), which has lexicalised to mean 'thirsty'.

(39) a. [*Neto*]$_{NP}$ [*pit*   *saq*]$_{PRED}$.
          1SG   throat dry
          'I'm thirsty.' (lit., 'I am dry-throated.')
      b. [*Nie*   *pit*]$_{NP}$ [*saq*]$_{PRED}$.
          1EXCL.POSS throat   dry
          'I have a dry throat.'

4.4 Peripheral constituents in the clause

As mentioned in §4.1, there are no predicates that absolutely require an NP expressed in a postpositional phrase (PP) or verbal postpositional phrase (VERBAL PP). I have labelled NPs encoded in such phrases as "peripheral constituents" (PERI).[5] A peripheral constituent can be expressed in any clause where it is semantically compatible with the event denoted by the clause. In this section, I give a brief overview of the basic positions of peripheral constituents with different roles.

Table 4.4 summarises the position of peripheral constituents relative to the predicate and its arguments. No post-verbal peripheral co-occurs with a post-verbal T argument of a trivalent clause (ARG$_3$). The lists for peripherals given in the table are complete, except for the position between ARG$_1$ and ARG$_2$, which presents only a sample of the most common items appearing in this position.

---

[5] Note that there are cases in which, although the verbal postpositional phrase is not obligatorily required by the verb, the verb seems to control the semantic role of the NP in the verbal postpositional phrase, making it difficult to decide between an oblique and adjunct status for the verbal postpositional phrase. This problem is known in many languages (see discussions in, e.g., Gawron 1986; Jackendoff 1990; Wechsler 1995). See §12.4 for a description of the semantics of individual Bunaq verbal postpositions and their combinatorics with verbs.

Table 4.4: Positions of peripheral constituents in the clause.

Peri	Arg₁	Peri	Arg₂	Peri	Pred	Peri/Arg₃
Locative PP (setting)		Locative PP (motion origin)		Locative PP (goal Arg₂)		Locative PP (motion goal)
		Comitative Verbal PP		Similative PP		Similative PP
		Origin Verbal PP		Comitative Verbal PP		
		Benefactive Verbal PP		Goal Verbal PP		
		Instrument Verbal PP				
		...				

As can be seen from Table 4.4, locative PPs (§12.2.1–§12.2.2) have the greatest flexibility in their placement, with different positions having different functions. Preceding Arg₁, a locative PP encodes a setting, information about the time/location of the event denoted by the clause, as in (40) with *no* 'OBL' (§12.2.1; see also fn. 4 in §4.2.4 on this gloss). A locative PP following Arg₁ and preceding Arg₂ encodes the origin location of a motion (41). A locative PP following the Arg₂ (P of a bivalent verbal clause) encodes the goal location for the referent of P in non-motion events (42). Finally, a locative PP following the predicate encodes the goal location of a motion (43).

(40) **Baqa** **no,** neto holon.
    NPRX.INAN OBL 1SG cry
    'At that (point) I cried.'

(41) Neto **mar** **no** zo zal reu mal.
    1SG garden OBL mango carry house go
    'I carried the mango home from the garden.'

(42) Neto il **botil** **no** t-olo.
    1SG water bottle OBL 3INAN-put.in
    'I put the water in the bottle.'

(43) Neto zemal **tas** **no.**
    1SG go.LOW village OBL
    'I go down to the village.'

The placement of a similative PP (§12.2.3) before or after a predicate makes no difference to the meaning of a clause. With verbs of speaking, a similative PP cataphorically refers to a complement clause encoding what is spoken, and typically occurs before the predicate (44), but can also follow it (45). In bivalent verbs where a P is expressed, the similative PP follows the predicate.

(44) Pana   gol   hitu   baqi   t-ege   roe   goet   sasi.
     female small   seven NPRX.INAN RECP-BEN   SPEC.INAN   LIKE   say
     'Those seven girls spoke like this to each other.'   [Bk-6.028]

(45) En   pana   hiloqon sasi roe   goet.
     person female   two   say   SPEC.INAN   LIKE
     'The two females spoke like this.'   [Bk-4.054]

An NP introduced by the comitative verbal postposition *g-utu* '3-COM' (§12.4.1) directly follows the NP to whose referent it is concomitant. Other peripherals do not intervene, as in (46) where the instrumental NP marked by the verbal postposition *dele* 'INS' (§12.4.2) follows the comitative.

(46) Asa Paran **Mau Paran** **g-utu** zap   g-erel   mele.
     Asa Paran Mau Paran   3-COM   dog   3AN-INS   walk
     'Asa Paran with Mau Paran went walking taking dogs.'   [BK-4.065]

See Chapter 12 for a description of the range of functions of postpositions and verbal postpositions.

4.5 Negative clauses

4.5.1 Clausal negation with *niq* 'NEG'

Clauses are negated by means of the clausal negator *niq* 'NEG' placed following the predicate. *Niq* 'NEG' is used to negate a clause irrespective of the type of predicate, as illustrated in the examples in (47) to (50).

VERBAL CLAUSE
(47) G-ot=sa   wel   niq.
     3AN-fur=EVEN   burnt   NEG
     'Not even his fur was burnt.'   [Bk-50.020]

NOMINAL CLAUSE
(48) Nei   milisi   niq.
     1PL.EXCL militia NEG
     'We are not militia.'   [Bk-61.044]

POSTPOSITIONAL CLAUSE
(49) Neto ota   gene niq.
     1SG   LEVEL LOC   NEG
     'I was not over there.'   [Bk-29.068]

POSSESSIVE CLAUSE
(50) Hot esen bi   nie   niq.
     sun HIGH ART.AN 1EXCL.POSS   NEG
     'The (person belonging to) the sun is not mine.'   [LB-10.017]

Whilst it always follows the main verb, *niq* 'NEG' very readily occurs to both the right and the left of other postverbal elements and may even intervene between the elements of an ambient serial verb construction (§13.3). Different postverbal positions of *niq* 'NEG' correspond to differences in scope and meaning. For instance, compare the relative ordering *niq* 'NEG' and the verb *liol* 'continue' in examples (51) and (52). In (51) *liol* 'continue' is V$_2$ in a serial verb construction providing aspectual specification (§13.8.2) for the V$_1$, *h-oqon* '3INAN-do'. *Niq* 'NEG' follows the VV sequence and has scope over both verbs; it denotes the *non-continuance of doing* (an event). Again in (52) *liol* 'continue' is V$_2$ in a serial verb construction with the V$_1$, *h-oqon* '3INAN-do', but this time we see that *niq* 'NEG' intervenes between the verbs. Here *niq* 'NEG' only has scope over the verb to its left, *h-oqon* '3INAN-do', while the verb to its right, *liol* 'continue', has scope over the whole clause. By contrast, this ordering denotes the *continuance of not doing* (an event).

(51) Gie   ama   heser o=si,   baqa   h-oqon   liol
     3.POSS father dead   IAM=REAS NPRX.INAN 3INAN-do   continue
     niq.
     NEG
     'Because her father had already died, (she) didn't continue to do that.'
                                                                            [Bk-70.128]

(52) Sirubisu baqa   neto h-oqon   **niq** liol   toqo
     work   NPRX.INAN 1SG   3INAN-do NEG   continue until
     mete bare.
     NOW   PROX.INAN
     'That work I continued to not do until this very day.'
     (i.e., 'I have never done such work again.')   [Bk-12.023]

A further example of the flexible positioning of *niq* 'NEG', this time relative to the postverbal floating quantifier *gaqal* 'all.AN' (§13.8.1.3), is given in (53) and (54). In (53) *niq* 'NEG' follows the verb *kou* 'slip' and *gaqal* 'all.AN' and has scope over both to denote 'some toppled over, some didn't'. By contrast, in (54) *niq* 'NEG' follows and has scope over the verb *re* 'strike' and is followed by *gaqal* 'all.AN' referring to the P, *sogo baqi* 'those ten'. The quantifier has scope over *niq* 'NEG' and denotes that 'all (of the ten) were not struck', i.e., 'none'. See §14.3 on the ordering of postverbal elements.

(53) Sogo   baqi   kou   gaqal   niq.
     ten   NPRX.AN slip all.AN   NEG
     'Those ten didn't all topple over.'   [Bk-10.012]

(54) Halaqi sogo baqi   re   niq   gaqal.
     3PL   ten   NPRX.AN strike NEG   all.AN
     'They didn't strike any of those ten.'   [Bk-10.020]

4.5.2 Other negators

In addition to the clausal negator, *niq* 'NEG', there are four items in Bunaq used in the expression of negative polarity. These will be mentioned here briefly before the reader is referred on to other sections for more information.

Firstly, *hani* 'PROH' is used to express prohibition. That is, it indicates that the action denoted by the main verb is not permitted (55) and is used to form negative imperatives (56). See §4.6.1 and §14.2.1.7 for further illustration of *hani* 'PROH'.

(55) Ini   mesaq=bu, hoto hani   rene.
     set.alight GIVEN   fire   PROH spread
     'When burning (the fields), the fire is not permitted to spread.'   [Bk-3.023]

(56) Hani   nei   n-oenik!
     PROH 1PL.EXCL 1EXCL-forget
     'Don't forget us!'   [Bk-14.003]

Secondly, the negative existential verb, *hobel* 'not exist', is the negative polarity verb matching the existential verb *hati* 'exist' (§10.6.2). For instance, in (57) we see that *hobel* 'not exist' is used in a negative response to a question with *hati* 'exist'; the formulation *hati niq 'exist NEG' is not acceptable in Bunaq Lamaknen.

(57) A. Hele   hosu   hati?
        perhaps other exist
        'Perhaps there is something else?'   [Bk-44.014]

B. *Hobel   oa.*
   not.exist IAM
   'No, that's it.'   [Bk-44.015]

Finally, Bunaq has two negative reinforcers, *ozol* 'NEG' and *nen* 'NEG'. They occur pre-verbally in a clause marked with the standard negator *niq* 'NEG'. The adverbs function to reinforce the negation in relation to the particular constituent in the clause which they directly precede. In (58) and (59) *ozol* 'NEG' and *nen* 'NEG' emphasise the negation of the following NPs headed by *nego* 'what'. See §14.2.4 for further illustration of the negative reinforcers.

(58) *Nei   homo   **ozol** nego uen=o   bai   **niq**.*
     1PL.EXCL   CONTR.INAN   NEG   what one=AND   thing NEG
     'We didn't do anything at all.' (lit., 'We didn't do not a thing.')   [Bk-1.046]

(59) *G-ege   **nen** nego uen=sa   dari   **niq** ai.*
     3AN-BEN   NEG   what one=EVEN   succeed NEG   ONLY
     'Nothing at all turned out right for him.' (lit., 'For him not even a thing was successful.')   [LB-2.010]

4.6 Non-declarative clauses

4.6.1 Imperatives

Imperatives are clauses that function to issue commands, directives, and requests. Positive imperatives in Bunaq do not have to have any overt syntactic marker of the fact that they are imperative. They may be marked simply by a rising intonation clause-finally. An NP/pronoun encoding the addressee may or may not be included in an imperative. (60) gives an example of an imperative without explicit encoding of the addressee and (61) with the 2nd person pronoun encoding the addressee.

(60) *N-ege   sasi!*
     1EXCL-BEN say
     'Tell me!'   [OS-07.04]

(61) *Eto   tebe   on   oa!*
     2SG   return DO   IAM
     'You go back now!'   [Bk-63.008]

As mentioned in §4.5.2, negative imperatives are encoded with the prohibitive modality adverb, *hani* 'PROH', as in (62). See §14.2.1.7 for further illustration of this form.

(62) Hani   wa!
     PROH   discard
     'Don't throw (it) out!'   [OS-07.03]

There are two items used to mark different types of commands: *naq* 'PRIOR' for imperatives and hortations (§4.6.1.1) and the verb *mal* 'go' for giving permission and offering invitations (§4.6.1.2).

4.6.1.1 Imperatives and hortatives with *naq* 'PRIOR'

The priorative marker *naq* 'PRIOR' is used as a postverbal imperative-hortative marker. It is used to denote imperatives, that is, in an appeal to the addressee(s) to make the state of affairs true, as in the examples in (63) to (65).

(63) Nu-bul   kumu   **naq**!
     1EXCL-head   massage   PRIOR
     'Massage my head!'   [Bk-43.074]

(64) N-ege   ga-saqe   **naq**!
     1EXCL-BEN   3AN-ascend PRIOR
     'Bring him up for me!'   [Bk-69.051]

(65) Eto   hali   **naq**!
     2SG   go.ahead   PRIOR
     'You go first!'   [Bk-50.021]

Naq 'PRIOR' is also used in the expression of hortations, that is, appeals to make a state of affairs true that are directed at individuals who are not only the addressee (van der Auwera, Dobrushina, and Goussev 2013). Hortations may include the addressee(s), as in (66), or exclude the addressee, as in (67). There are no examples of hortations with 3rd persons (i.e., 'let him', etc.) in the corpus.

(66) I   rasal   **naq**!
     1PL.EXCL   stop   PRIOR
     'Let's stop!'   [Bk-37.097]

(67) Nei   mal   **naq**!
     1PL.EXCL   go   PRIOR
     'Let's go!'   [OS-07.02]

Naq 'PRIOR' also appears with *hani* 'PROH', the negative imperative marker (§4.5.2). This is illustrated in (68).

(68) A!   Ei   **hani**   **naq**!
      INTERJ   2PL   PROH   PRIOR
      'Oh! Don't!'   [ApaGiriKereq-49]

The functions of the priorative marker are discussed further in §14.3.7.

4.6.1.2 Invitations/permissions with *mal* 'go'

The verb *mal* 'go' is an imperative marker used to issue invitations and to grant permission to proceed with an action. In this function, *mal* 'go' follows the main verb of the clause and is only used with 2nd person S/As.

Examples (69) and (70) illustrate the use of *mal* 'go' to extend invitations to the addressee. In (69) *mal* 'go' marks *man* 'come' to express an invitation for the addressee to join the speaker in West Timor. In (70), the invitation of speaker A to ride their horses is rejected by speaker B for themselves, but speaker A is invited to get the accompanier of speaker B to get on the horse; this invitation is signalled by *mal* 'go'.

(69) a. *Ei*   *man*   ***mal!***
         2PL   come   go
         'Go ahead and come!'   [Bk-66.062]
     b. *Nei*   *ei*   *Ø-osok.*
         1PL.EXCL   2PL   1INCL/2-receive
         'We will receive you.'   [Bk-66.063]

(70) A. *Mama*   *hiloqon,*   *ota*   *kura*   *bari=na*   *saqe*   *oa.*
         mother   two   LEVEL   horse   PROX.INAN=FOC   ascend   IAM
         '(You) two ladies, mount these horses over here.'   [Bk-37.083]
     B. *Hani,*   *neli*   *roe=bu*   *mele=o*   *han.*
         PROH   1DU.EXCL   SPEC.INAN=GIVEN   walk=AND   no.problem
         'Don't, for us walking is not a problem!'   [Bk-37.084]
     B. *En*   *gol*   *bari=na*   *g-ini*   *kura*   *saqe*   ***mal!***
         person   small   PROX.AN=FOC   3AN-CAUS   horse   ascend   go
         'Get this person to ride the horse!'   [Bk-37.085]

Examples (71) and (72) illustrate the use of *mal* 'go' to indicate to the addressee that they have permission to proceed. In (71) speaker B uses *mal* 'go' with *sasi* 'speak' to grant permission for speaker A to say something following her request to do so. In (72), following an assertion by speaker A that there is a person wanting to walk with speaker B, speaker B responds favourably using *mal* 'go' with *mina* 'come.HIGH' to signal that she is permitted to come up and join them.

(71) A. *Naqi,   neto   toek   bare,   i   Ø-ege*
       royal   1SG   talk   PROX.INAN   1PL.INCL   1INCL/2-BEN
       sasi=bu   loi=ka   niq?
       speak=GIVEN   good=OR   NEG
       'Sire, I am talking, (am I) permitted to speak to you or not?'   [LB-8.025]
    B. *Eme   sasi   **mal**!*
       mother   speak   go
       'Go ahead and speak, mother!'   [LB-8.026]

(72) A. *Baqi=o   mele   gie   heten.*
       NPRX.AN=AND   walk   PROSP   want
       'She also wants to walk.'   [Bk-37.023]
    B. *O=baqi   mele   heta=bu,   mina   **mal**!*
       ADDR=NPRX.AN   walk   can=GIVEN   come.HIGH   go
       'If she near you is able to walk, (she should) go ahead and come up!'
       [Bk-37.024]

4.6.1.3 Responses to imperatives

The addressee(s) of an imperative typically responds with the interjection *ho* 'ok', when expressing compliance with it, as in (73) and (74). *Ho* 'ok' is also used by an addressee to acknowledge a call to them. *Ho* 'ok' is not normally used in positive responses to questions.

(73) A. *Ibu,   eto   bai   a   naq!*
       mother   2SG   thing   eat   PRIOR
       'Mrs, you eat something!'   [Bk-37.056]
    B. ***Ho**!   Loi,   ibu.*
       INTERJ   good   mother
       'Ok! (That's) fine, Mrs.'   [Bk-37.058]

(74) A. *Eli   mal   sai   kolun   ba   leqat   naq.*
       2DU   go   go.to.garden   fallow.garden   ART.INAN   inspect   PRIOR
       'You to go to the garden (and) check out the fallow!'   [LB-2.014]
    B. ***Ho**!*
       INTERJ
       'Ok!'   [LB-2.015]

Orders with which the addressee is not compliant may go unanswered or will use *hani* 'PROH', as in the response of speaker B in (70).

4.6.2 Questions

4.6.2.1 Information questions

Information (or constituent, "wh"-) questions make use of the class of interrogatives which are discussed in §3.5.2. Basic interrogatives typically occur *in situ*, i.e., filling the syntactic position in the question as the answer would in the statement corresponding to the question. In (75) *nego* 'what?' questions the T of the trivalent verb *h-ini* '3INAN-call' and accordingly occurs following the verb (§4.2.3). In (76) *cio* 'who?' questions the possessor of the house and accordingly occurs in the position of a possessor NP introduced by *gie* '3.POSS' (§9.2).

(75) Toren wa h-ini **nego**?
 ceiling top 3INAN-call what
 'What's the ceiling top called?' [Bk-47.123]

(76) Eto **cio** gie reu gene?
 2SG who 3.POSS house LOC
 'You are in whose house?' [Bk-43.071]

In the examples in (77), *teo* 'where?' occurs as the complement of the postposition *no* 'OBL'. We see that the PP occurs in different positions in the clause depending on the type of location questioned, as described for declarative clauses in §4.4. In (77a) the preverbal position of the PP questions the origin location of the motion. In (77b) the position of the PP between P and V questions the goal of the P in the action (77b). Finally, in (77c) the postverbal position of the PP questions the goal location of the motion.

(77) a. Eto **teo** no man?
 2SG where OBL come
 'Where did you come from?' [Bk-61.029]
 b. Eto il **teo** no t-olo?
 2SG water where OBL 3INAN-put.in
 'Into where did your pour the water?' [OS-07.01]
 c. Eto zemal **teo** no?
 2SG go.LOW where OBL
 'Where did you go down to?' [OS-07.02]

Interrogatives or the phrases in which they occur can be optionally focused with the restrictive focus particle *=na* 'FOC' (§4.7.4.2.3). Focused interrogatives must occur in a non-final position. This is illustrated with a focused interrogative questioning the T of a trivalent verb in (78), and with a focused interrogative questioning manner

(79). In (78c) and (78c), respectively, we see that these interrogatives can occur finally when not focused.

(78) a. **Nego=na** Ø-ege?
    what FOC 1INCL/2-give
    'What did (they) give to you?' [Bk-4.036]
  b. *Ø-ege **nego=na**?
    1INCL/2-give what=FOC [Not-09.01]
  c. Ø-ege **nego**?
    1INCL/2-give what
    '(They) gave you what?' [Not-09.01]

(79) a. **Teo** goet on=na pelek?
    where LIKE DO=FOC plant
    'How is it that (you) plant (them)?' [Bk-65.080]
  b. *Pelek **teo** goet on=na?
    plant where LIKE DO=FOC [Not-09.01]
  c. Pelek **teo** goet on?
    plant where LIKE DO
    'How (do you) plant (them)?' [Not-09.01]

Examples (78) and (79) represent the most frequent natural language pattern: when a focused interrogative is present in a clause, no other clausal constituent apart from the verb is typically expressed. When other elements are expressed, in particular the S/A of the clause, the focused interrogative still typically occurs *in situ*, like the locative PP in (80a: 8 similar tokens in the corpus). It is infrequent but possible for such a locative PP to occur before the clausal S/A (80b: 1 similar token in the corpus).

(80) a. Eto **teo gene=na** mit gie?
    2SG where LOC=FOC sit PROSP
    'You are going to live where?'
  b. **Teo gene=na** eto mit gie?
    where LOC=FOC 2SG sit PROSP
    'Where are you going to live?' [Not-09.01]

There are no natural language examples of questions containing more than one interrogative word. In elicitation, speakers approved of examples such as (81) with two interrogatives.

(81) Sio nego h-oqon?
    who what 3INAN-do
    'Who did what?' [Not-07.02]

4.6.2.2 Polar questions

Polar questions are ones to which the expected answer is the equivalent of 'yes' or 'no' (sometimes called yes-no questions). Polar questions in Bunaq can be syntactically unmarked (§4.6.2.2.1), or marked by means of one of three question tags, =e 'AGREE' (§4.6.2.2.2), =ka 'OR' (§4.6.2.2.3), or =to 'CONF' (§4.6.2.2.4). The latter two Bunaq question tags are borrowed from Tetun and/or Malay. Question tags always appear as the last element in a clause. The question tags are accompanied by rising intonation. They sometimes also appear in non-interrogative clauses, where they retain their rising intonation pattern. Answers to polar questions are discussed in §4.6.2.2.5.

4.6.2.2.1 Unmarked polar questions

Polar questions may be denoted by rising intonation clause-finally and no change of word order. Unmarked polar questions of this kind have neutral polarity, that is, there is no expectation on the part of the speaker that the answer will be either positive or negative. Examples (82) and (83) illustrate Bunaq unmarked polar questions.

(82) *Niat ni ei teras h-oqon ba, teras koen=na*
first OBL 2PL terrace 3INAN-make ART.INAN terrace nice=FOC
h-oqon gimen?
3INAN-make immediately
'In the beginning when you made terraces, were they good terraces straightaway?' [Bk-65.066]

(83) *Taq Topol ola zol mil gene?*
Taq Topol LOW river inside LOC
'Is Taq Topol down there in the river?' [Bk-29.055]

It is unusual for an unmarked polar question to include the standard negator *niq* 'NEG'. In the corpus, there are only three unmarked polar questions in the negative. All three instances come from a single speaker in a single text. The questions appear to have weak negative polarity, and all three are answered in the negative. One of the three is presented in (84).

(84) A. *Ei Ø-azal soq, baqi ei i-ta man niq?*
2PL 1INCL/2-see SEQ NPRX.AN 2PL 1INCL/2-GL come NEG
'Having seen you, she didn't come towards you?' [Bk-47.026]
B. *Man niq.*
come NEG
'(She) didn't come.' [Bk-47.027]

4.6.2.2.2 Questions soliciting agreement with =e 'AGREE'

The enclitic =e 'AGREE' is used in polar interrogatives in situations where the speaker expects the proposition denoted by the clause to be true and invites the agreement of the addressee. Examples of questions tagged with =e are given in (85) and (86). Questions tagged with =e 'AGREE' such as these may or may not elicit a response from the addressee, being used by the speaker to ensure the compliance of the addressee. The tag, which attaches to the final element in a clause, is accompanied by a sharply rising intonation.

(85) Ei   milisi=**e**?
     2PL   militia=AGREE
     'You're militia, right?'   [Bk-47.027]

(86) D-ol   o=bi   g-ege   sasi=**e**?
     REFL-child   ADDR=ART.AN   3AN-BEN   say=AGREE
     '(You're) going to say (something) to your kid, right?'   [Bk-22.006]

Polar questions soliciting active confirmation from the addressee are marked by =e 'AGREE' followed by niq 'NEG', as in (87) and (88).

(87) Ei   matas mil   heten=**e**   **niq**?
     2PL   old   COLL   want=AGREE   NEG
     'You parents want to, don't you?'   [Bk-38.077]

(88) Eto   n-igo   bare   h-azal   milik=**e**   **niq**?
     2SG   1EXCL-beak   PROX.INAN   3INAN-see   afraid=AGREE   NEG
     'You are afraid of this beak of mine, aren't you?'   [Bk-49.020]

The agreement tag is also used in a range of non-interrogative functions: marking certain kinds of exclamative clauses (see §4.6.3) and, although rare, nominal disjunction (see §5.7.5).

4.6.2.2.3 Alternative questions with =ka 'OR'

Bunaq uses =ka 'OR' to mark alternative questions. This item is borrowed from Malay, possibly via Tetun, where it has similar functions marking alternative questions. An alternative question "presents two or more possible answers and presupposes that only one is true" (Quirk et al. 1985: 823). The two alternatives may be specified, in which case they are conjoined by =ka 'OR', as in (89) to (91), or may be left unspecified, in which case =ka 'OR' appears finally (92).

(89) *Biqan esen ba h-apal sal on=**ka** de on?*
     plate HIGH ART.INAN 3INAN-open wrong DO=OR right DO
     '(Did you) open up the plates up there wrong or right?' [LB-2.147]

(90) *Eto na-tara=**ka** na-tara niq?*
     2SG 1EXCL-know=OR 1EXCL-know NEG
     'Do you know me or not?' [Bk-43.065]

(91) *Domba hati=**ka** niq?*
     sheep exist=OR NEG
     'Are there sheep or not?' [OS-07.03]

(92) *Ei ie mar gene rik=o balo hati=**ka**?*
     2PL 1INCL/2.POSS garden LOC cassava=AND taro exist=OR
     'Is there cassava and taro in your garden or not?' [Bk-6.042]

See §5.7.5 on the use of *=ka* to mark disjunction in the nominal domain.

4.6.2.2.4 Monitoring the addressee questions with *=to* 'CONF'

The question tag *=to* 'CONF' functions in Bunaq to monitor the attention and understanding of the addressee by soliciting a confirming answer (typically in the form of a gesture) from the speaker.[6] In accordance with this "understanding monitoring" function, the majority of examples of *=to* 'CONF' in the corpus mark a clause in which the speaker repeats information that they have already given in a prior clause, as in (93) and (94).

(93) a. *Baqi boqal oa.*
         NPRX.AN grown.up IAM
         'She was grown up now.' [Bk-69.062]
     b. *Baqi boqal oa=**to**?*
         NPRX.AN grown.up IAM=CONF
         'She was grown up now, you know?' [Bk-69.064]

(94) a. *G-ebu memel.*
         3AN-bottom sick
         'Her bottom was sore.' [Bk-37.129]
     b. *G-ebu memel=**to**?*
         3AN-bottom sick=CONF
         'Her bottom was sore, you know?' [Bk-37.130]

---

6 In my experience, *=to* is also used in local Malay varieties spoken in Timor and elsewhere in eastern Indonesia with similar functions to what I describe here. It is originally from Dutch *toch*.

There is one clear use of the question tag =*to* 'CONF' to ask a question in my corpus. Given in (95), here =*to* functions to confirm a piece of information with the addressee about the whereabouts of a sought item.

(95) *O=yang   wa   los   baqa=to?*
    ADDR=that.which top   very   NPRX.INAN=CONF
    'You mean that thing at the very top, yeah?'   [Bk-47.126]

4.6.2.2.5 Answers to polar questions

Positive answers to positive polar questions typically echo the predicate, as in (96); there is no word for 'yes' as such. Negative answers to positive polar questions either echo the verb of the question with *niq* 'NEG' following (97) or have just the negative particle (98).

(96) A. *G-azal?*
       3AN-see
       '(Did you) see (her)?'   [Bk-47.014]
    B. *G-azal.*
       3AN-see
       '(We) saw (her).'   [Bk-47.015]

(97) A. *Asrama   gene   loi?*
       boarding.school   LOC   good
       '(Is it) good in the boarding school?'   [Bk-30.071]
    B. *Loi   niq.*
       good   NEG
       '(It's) not good.'   [Bk-30.072]

(98) A. *Aruq   g-ewen   taqa?*
       hair   3AN-face   close
       'Was hair covering her face?'   [Bk-47.076]
    B. *Niq.*
       NEG
       'No.'   [Bk-47.077]

Negative answers to negative polar questions also echo the verb and *niq* 'NEG', as in (99), or just *niq* 'NEG' (100).

(99) A. *Ei   Ø-azal   soq,   baqi   ei   i-ta   man   niq?*
       2PL   1INCL/2-see   SEQ   NPRX.INAN   2PL   1INCL/2-GL   come   NEG
       'After (she) saw you, she didn't come towards you?'   [Bk-47.026]

B. *Man niq.*
   come NEG
   '(She) did not come (towards us).' [Bk-47.027]

(100) A. *Eto heten niq?*
   2SG want NEG
   'Do you want to?'
   B. *Niq.*
   NEG
   'No (I don't want to).' [OS-09.01]

See example (57) in §4.5.2 on negative responses to questions with *hati* 'exist'.

4.6.3 Exclamatives

Exclamatives are clauses expressing strong assertion or emotion on the part of the speaker. In Bunaq, exclamative clauses have a sharply rising pattern of intonation (indicated here by an exclamation mark); they can be marked with either the clause-final exclamative enclitic =*o* 'EXCLAM' or the agreement enclitic =*e* 'AGREE'.

The enclitic =*o* 'EXCLAM' is not very common in my corpus, with only a handful of examples. Two of them are provided in (101) and (102). In (101), =*o* marks an exclamation in which the speaker expresses their great surprise at how little the addressee knows about anything. In (102), =*o* marks an exclamative clause expressing the speaker's excitement at the prospect of soon eating meat.

(101) *Eto bai tara niq masak=***o***!*
   2SG thing know NEG big=EXCLAM
   'You really don't know anything!' [OS-07.04]

(102) *Goniqon, i si bari gi-a gie=***o***!*
   three 1PL.INCL meat PROX.AN 3AN-eat PROSP=EXCLAM
   'Another three days and we will be eating this meat!' [OrelHalaliLenuk.41]

While exclamative-marking =*o* is identical in form to the Bunaq additive focus enclitic =*o* 'AND' (§4.7.4.2.1), I do not view them as different functions of the same item. Exclamative =*o* is widely found in local Malay varieties spoken in Timor and appears to have been adopted from there, in the same way as =*to* 'CONF' (discussed in §4.6.2.2.4). Additive focus =*o* 'AND' is not known in local Malay and, therefore, is kept distinct in the analysis here.

The agreement enclitic =e 'AGREE' is more common marking exclamative clauses than =o 'EXCLAM', and is used in a wider range of exclamative contexts. Like =o, =e marks clauses as having the force of an exclamatory statement, typically with an emotive overlay. In (103), =e marks an exclamative clause in which the speaker expresses how cold she is feeling as she is being swallowed by a python. In (104), =e marks an exclamative clause describing the dramatic end of the anthropomorphised Wax, who was burnt to a crisp after falling into a fire.

(103) *Ai,   bai   uen roi   huruk=e!*
      INTERJ thing one SPEC.AN   cold=AGREE
      'Wow, whatever this thing is, it's cold!'   [Bk-71.025]

(104) *Hoto sinoq gie,   wel   o=e!*
      fire hot   BECAUSE   burn   IAM=AGREE
      'From the heat of the fire, (he) was all burnt up!'   [LuaWezun2.057]

Additionally, =e marks emphatic affirmative answers to questions of both positive (105) and negative (106) polarity.

(105) A. *Baqa   beqo?*
         NPRX.INAN pulped
         'That was pulped?', i.e. 'That (head) was squashed to pulp?'   [Bk-52.035]
      B. *Beqo=e!*
         pulped=AGREE
         '(It was) so pulped!'   [Bk-52.036]

(106) A. *Hele   muk   g-omo   niq?*
         perhaps   earth 3AN-owner   NEG
         'Perhaps it wasn't a spirit (lit., an earth owner)?'   [Bk-47.072]
      B. *Muk   g-omo   on=e!*
         earth 3AN-owner   DO=AGREE
         '(It was) so a spirit (lit., an earth owner)!'   [Bk-47.073]

It can also be used to mark imperative clauses encouraging compliance from the addressee and in statements reminding the addressee of a point which is obvious, as in (107) and (108).

(107) *Dia Laho, ni-ta   tuk   teni   naq=e!*
      Dia Laho   1EXCL-GL   pile.up   again   PRIOR=AGREE
      'Dia Laho, pile (it) up onto me again, won't you?'   [Bk-50.023]

(108) *Bapaq,   eto   tumel   roe   r-oenik   o=e!*
      Mr   2SG   money   SPEC.INAN   3INAN-forget   IAM=AGREE
      'Mr, you have forgotten this money, haven't you?'   [Bk-50.023]

4.7 Pragmatic variation in the clause

In this section I give a brief overview of some patterns of pragmatic variation in the clause. §4.7.1 looks at variation in the realisation of arguments, peripheral constituents, and predicates. §4.7.2 examines patterns of word order variation in which the arguments and peripherals are ordered differently from the typical order shown in Figure 4.1. §4.7.3 looks at variation in bivalent verb agreement. Finally, §4.7.4 treats Bunaq discourse marking enclitics, the relators (§4.7.4.1), and focus markers (§4.7.4.2).

Subtopics relevant to pragmatic marking in the clause that are not discussed here are: the use of determiners (§7.2) and the temporal/discourse locational (§8.3.3), which has reference-tracking functions.

4.7.1 Variation in argument realisation

4.7.1.1 Anaphoric elision

Neither arguments nor the complements of verbal postpositions are overtly realised by NPs in every clause. That is, they may be covertly referenced through zero anaphora. A lack of any overt reference signals that the hearer should identify the elided argument as a participant that has already been referred to in the preceding discourse. For example, in (109), after his initial mention, *Ama Mau Kasu* (bolded) is not overtly expressed again. A second participant is understood from the preceding events in the narrative and is not realised by NPs, but is signalled by the obligatory agreement prefixes on the verbal postpositions, *dele* 'INS' (§12.4.2) in (109a) and *g-ege* '3AN-BEN' (§12.4.6) in (109b–d). NPs are used to signal the goal of the motion, i.e., *hober* 'cave' in (109a–b), and new participants, i.e., the stolen items in (109c–d).

(109) a. **Ama   Mau Kasu**=na   *g-erel*   *hober*   *tubuk*   *mal.*
         father Mau.Kasu=FOC   3AN-INS   cave   burrow   go
         'It was father Mau Kasu who took (her) to a cave.'   [Bk-68.013]
      b. *Hober   tubuk   tama,   homo=na,   g-ege...*
         cave   burrow   enter   CONTR.INAN=FOC   3AN-BEN
         '(He) entered the cave, then, for (her)...'   [Bk-68.014]
      c. *G-ege   su   il   bini.*
         3AN-BEN   breast   water   steal
         '(He) stole milk for (her).'   [Bk-68.015]

d. *G-ege si g-ibi.*
   3AN-BEN meat 3AN-steal
   '(He) stole meat for (her).' [Bk-68.016]

When a participant maintains the same role, it is not typically overtly mentioned after the initial reference. However, participants are often overtly referenced at points of change, i.e., where there is discontinuity of both identity and/or argument type. That is, where a clause intervenes in which a different participant is in that grammatical function, an established participant may receive an overt mention in order to clarify that the relevant relation has switched back to them. For instance, in (110a), the A argument, *polisi* 'police', is overtly realised but then zero-mentioned in the following clause where it has the same relation. In the first clause of (110b), however, there is a different A, such that in the second clause, where *polisi* 'police' is again the A, it receives another overt mention. Now established again as A, *polisi* 'police' is elided in (110c), but is overtly mentioned in the second clause of (110d), due to the first clause having a different S, *nei* '1PL.EXCL'.

(110) a. *Kalo **polisi** nei n-one, nei n-ini*
       if police 1PL.EXCL 1EXCL-grab 1PL.EXCL 1EXCL-CAUS
       bui tama.
       prison enter
       'If the police catch us, (they) put us in jail.' [Bk-11.012]
   b. *Kalo halaqi Timor-Leste gie=na man, **polisi** halaqi*
      if 3PL East Timor 3.POSS=FOC come police 3PL
      g-one.
      3AN-grab
      'If they come from East Timor, the police catch them.' [Bk-11.013]
   c. *Homo soq, halaqi g-ini bui tama.*
      CONTR.INAN SEQ 3PL 3AN-CAUS prison enter
      'Then, (the police) put them in jail.' [Bk-11.014]
   d. *Nei Timor-Leste gene, halaqi gie **polisi** nei*
      1PL.EXCL East Timor LOC 3PL 3.POSS police 1PL.EXCL
      n-one.
      1EXCL-grab
      '(If) we are in East Timor, their police catch us.' [Bk-11.015]

A switching of function does not necessarily entail an overt mention of a participant with an NP, so long as there is no possibility of ambiguity in the reference. In (111a) *Palatina Soi* is established as the topical S with a non-proximal demonstrative, *baqi* 'NPRX.AN' (§7.4.1.5). Following this, the referent is elided throughout the remaining string, despite the fact that the referent shifts to a peripheral role as the complement of *g-ege* '3AN-BEN' with the introduction of a new S participant in (111c; bolded).

Identification of the elided argument is supported here by the fact that there are no other participants mentioned in the text such that the earlier S is the only possible referent for the prefix on *g-ege* '3AN-BEN'. When *Palatina Soi* becomes S again in (111e) it is also without overt mention, since the reference is clear from the fact that she is the underlying S of *man* 'come' in the causative construction in (111d).

(111) a. **Palantina Soi, baqi** Malaysia gene.
Palantina Soi NPRX.AN Malaysia LOC
'Palantina Soi, she was in Malaysia.' [Bk-43.002]
b. *Malaysia mal.*
Malaysia go
'(She) went to Malaysia.' [Bk-43.003]
c. *Homo=na,* **gie en** huqe gene g-ege hape honal.
CONTR.INAN=FOC 3.POSS person HERE LOC 3AN-BEN mobile.phone go.LEVEL
'Then, her people here called (her) by mobile.' [Bk-43.004]
d. *SMS honal, g-ini man gie.*
SMS go.LEVEL 3AN-CAUS come PROSP
'(They) texted across, to get (her) to come.' [Bk-43.005]
e. *Homo=na, man Kupang pir.*
CONTR.INAN=FOC come Kupang reach
'Then, (she) came to Kupang.' [Bk-43.006]

Highly animate subjects with "topical continuity" (Givón 1983) in Bunaq tend not to be continuously elided, but are typically realised by a succession of free pronouns. The repetition of the pronoun typically occurs at points of change and narrative advancement and is most obvious with first-person narrators. In (112) the first-person narrator is established with the pronoun *neto* '1SG' at the beginning of the narrative (112a) and then reoccurs throughout the story when something new happens in the narrative, as bolded in (112c), (112d), and (112e).

(112) a. **Neto** memel.
1SG sick
'I was sick.' [Bk-40.001]
b. *Meten no loi~loi.*
before OBL REDUP~good
'Before (that I was) fine.' [Bk-40.002]
c. **Neto** cier honal loi~loi.
1SG sleep go.LEVEL REDUP~good
'I went to sleep fine.' [Bk-40.003]

d. *Ene   no   tekil~tekil,* **neto** *meqi,   en=na   sarat*
   night OBL   suddenly   1SG   dream   person=FOC limp
   honal   sarat man.
   go.LEVEL   limp   come
   'In the night, all of a sudden I dreamt there was a person was limping to and fro.' [Bk-40.004]
e. *Baqa   haqal,   le gie   mel,*   **neto** *mel, . . .*
   NPRX.INAN finish   next.day wake   1SG   wake
   'Then, the next morning, I got up, . . .' [Bk-40.005]

4.7.1.2 Zero pro of generic/non-referential As: a functional passive?

In descriptions of procedures, the speaker may make no reference to a human actor in the A role, without ever establishing a referent for it. This is permitted as the actions described are event-oriented and generic, being done in the same way independent of the identity of the actor. I will call this "zero pro" of A.

Example (113) comes from the beginning of a text describing the manner in which *tubi lemet* 'lemet cakes' are made. As in this excerpt, at no point in the text is an A mentioned. The bivalent verbs *parut* 'peel', *kumu* 'squeeze', and *ha-sai* '3INAN-take out' occur only with Ps.

(113) a. *Pertama, rikotel   parut.*
         first   cassava grate
         'First, (one) grates the cassava.' [Bk-82.001]
     b. *Rikotel   parut, g-ini   baqis   haqal,   homo*
         cassava grate   3AN-CAUS   much   finished CONTR.INAN
         haqal   soq, g-il   kumu.
         finished   SEQ 3AN-water   squeeze
         '(One) grates the cassava, after (one) has made a lot, after that, (one) squeezes its water out.' [Bk-82.002]
     c. *G-il   homo   ha-sai   haqal,   homo*
         3AN-water   CONTR.INAN   3INAN-exit   finished   CONTR.INAN
     d. *naq=na,   mok   nor   wa   no.*
         PRIOR=FOC   banana   leaf   top   OBL
         'After (one) has taken the water out, once that is done, (put it) on top of banana leaves.' [Bk-82.003]

In some procedural texts, a generic A is encoded in one of the opening clauses either with the generic noun *en* 'person' (114) or the generic pronoun *i* '1PL.INCL' (§6.2.4.1.1) (115), but then it is elided throughout the remaining text.

(114) a. **En**   tani   sirubisu, mar=na   h-oqon.
       person farmer   work   garden=FOC   3INAN-make
       '(When) farmers work, it is gardens (that they) make.'   [Bk-3.002]

   b. Mar   h-oqon   roe   goet   on.
      garden   3INAN-make   SPEC.INAN   LIKE   DO
      '(One) makes a garden like this.'   [Bk-3.002]

   c. Mar   h-iqil   to   goniqon   goniqil   oa,
      garden   3INAN-leave   year   three   four   IAM
      mar   baqa   hatak.
      garden   NPRX.INAN   ripe
      '(After one has) left the garden for four (or) five years, that garden is ready.'
      [Bk-3.003]

   d. Mar   hatak   oa=si,   mar   baqa   se   oa.
      garden   ripe   IAM=REAS   garden   NPRX.INAN   cut   IAM
      'Because the garden is already ready, (one) now cuts the garden.'
      [Bk-3.004]

(115) a. Paqol   g-ureq   gie   mal,   tebe   i   g-ohiq
       maize   3AN-pick   PROSP   go   return   1PL.INCL   3AN-strip
       g-erel   man.
       3AN-INS   come
       'Going to pick maize, we come back with (it) to strip (it).'   [Bk-44.001]

   b. G-ohiq   haqal,   g-apiq,   g-ini   pisi~pisi.
      3AN-strip   finished   3AN-sort   3AN-CAUS   REDUP~clean
      'After (one) strips (it), (one) sorts (it), (one) makes (it) very clean.'
      [Bk-44.002]

   c. G-otol   il   dara.
      3AN-WITHOUT   water   prepare
      '(One) leaves (the maize) to the side to prepare the water.'   [Bk-44.003]

An A may be realised as "zero pro" in contexts where the focus of the discourse is on the referent of P and attention to the A is downgraded. Whilst this is functionally like a passive, syntactically it is not; the valency of the verb does not change and the P remains P with the associated syntactic properties, as outlined in §4.2.2. Consider the examples in (116a–b) with the bivalent verb *ha-susar* '3INAN-afflict'.[7] Example (116a) has overtly expressed A and P arguments, whilst (116b) has only a P expressed, with

---

[7] The verb is a borrowing of the monovalent Tetun verb *susar* 'be in difficulties' plus the Tetun causative prefix *ha-* 'CAUS'. This prefix appears in Bunaq on borrowed Tetun verbs as a transitiviser, cf. §10.2.4.1.1.

no retrievable referent for A. In (116a) the clause denotes an agentive event in which the A, *eme* 'mother', wilfully imposes suffering upon the P. By contrast, in (116b), the non-referential A is realised as "zero pro". The pragmatic force of (116b) is on the effect on the P, with the connotation that their predicament is being actively imposed upon the P by an external force.

(116) a. *Ei   ie   eme   na-susar.*
         2PL   1INCL/2.POSS   mother   1EXCL-afflict
         'Your mother gives me a hard time.'   [Bk-30.053]
    b.   *I   bare   a-susar   masak.*
         1PL.INCL   PROX.INAN   1INCL/2-afflict   big
         'We here are greatly afflicted.'   [Bk-19.037]

The construction in (116b) in turn differs from (116c–d) with the related stative monovalent verb *susar* 'afflicted'. Examples (116c–d) depict a stative monovalent verbal predicate (§4.2.1) and a locative postpositional predicate (§4.3.2), respectively, in which a condition simply holds without any implication of an effector.

    c.   *Mama   susar.*
         mum   afflicted
         'Mum is afflicted.'   [Bk-22.004]
    d.   *Neto   susar   ni.*
         1SG   afflicted   OBL
         'I am in affliction.'   [Bk-61.021]

A further example of a "zero pro" realisation of an A is given in (117), the continuation of the answer to the question given in (97). We see that in the reply to the question, the speaker tells of the regular beatings that are endured by the inmates of the boarding school. However, at no point in the discourse is the referent of A, who conducted the beatings, identified. The verb *g-ue* '3AN-hit' only occurs with an overt encoding of P. English non-referential 'they' is used in the translation to represent this.

(117) a. *I   Ø-ue   ruquk.*
         1PL.INCL   1INCL/2-hit   always
         '(They) are always hitting us.'   [Bk-30.073]
    b.   *I   pukul   terus*
         1PL.INCL   hit   continue
         '(They) hit us continually.'   [Bk-30.074]
    c.   *I   Ø-ue.*
         1PL.INCL   1INCL/2-hit
         '(They) hit us.'   [Bk-30.075]

d. I   aturan   ikut   niq=bu,   i   Ø-ue.
    1PL.INCL   rules   follow NEG=GIVEN   1PL.INCL   1INCL/2-hit
    'When we don't follow the rules, (they) hit us.'   [Bk-30.076]

"Zero pro" of an A in generic and non-referential contexts is pervasive in Bunaq discourse; there are no apparent restrictions on A elision given the appropriate discourse situation.

4.7.2 Variation in word order

We have seen throughout this chapter that the pragmatically neutral word order in Bunaq is: ARG₁ ARG₂ PRED ARG₃. In addition to this unmarked order, there are a number of pragmatically marked word order constructions, in which a phrase that is pragmatically prominent appears in another position in the clause, typically, at the front or back of the clause.

In the following sections, I present an overview of the main patterns of word order variation observed in Bunaq. In §4.7.2.1, I look at dislocation, while in §4.7.2.2 fronting and other types of clause-internal word order variation are discussed. In §4.7.2.3, I deal with animacy effects on word order in non-agentive clauses.

See Chapter 14 on variation in the placement of preverbal adverbs relative to arguments, and postverbal elements relative to one another, and the differences in scope entailed by different orderings.

4.7.2.1 Dislocation

Dislocation refers to the distinct prosodic treatment of a phrase (so-called "comma intonation", Payne 1997: 274–275) at the left or right periphery of a clause. In the case of left-dislocation, the dislocated phrase typically involves a slightly rising terminal pitch (i.e., a rise on the last syllable of the phrase) and is followed by a pause, before the speaker continues (Figure 4.2). In the case of right-dislocation, the dislocated phrase follows a falling terminal pitch and is itself characterised by such a falling contour (Figure 4.3).

Dislocation may also involve copying. Copying refers to the coreference of a left- or right-dislocated constituent with a pronominal or demonstrative element within the clause.

Left-dislocation (§4.7.2.1.1) is associated with the pragmatic property of "topic", i.e. what the proposition expressed by a clause is "about" (Lambrecht 1994: 118). Right-dislocation (§4.7.2.1.2) is associated with an element expressing "afterthought topicalisation" (Payne 1997: 275), i.e., clarification of reference in a clause that the speaker sees as unclear.

4.7 Pragmatic variation in the clause — 161

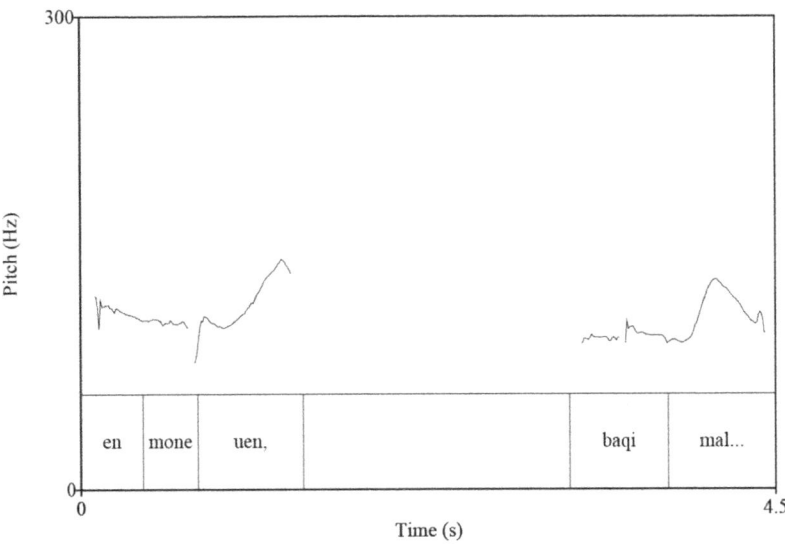

Figure 4.2: Pitch traces of left-dislocation in example (119).

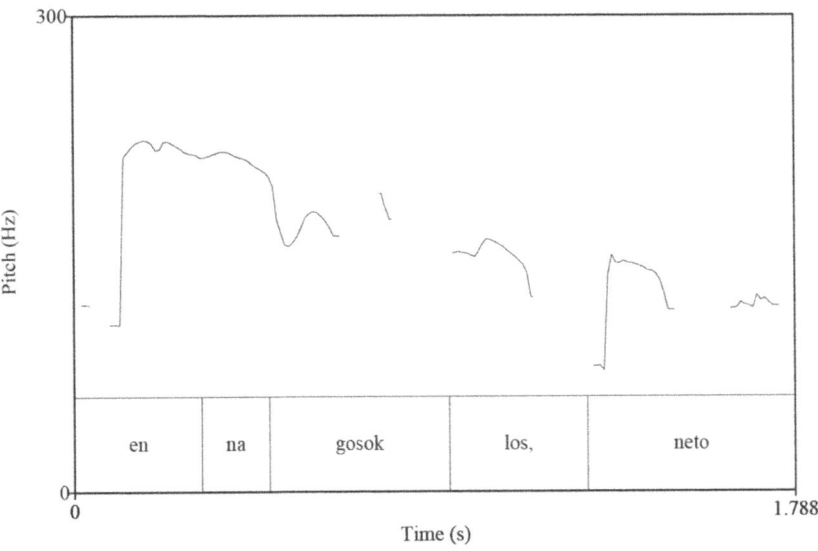

Figure 4.3: Pitch traces of right-dislocation in example (127).

4.7.2.1.1 Left-dislocation

Topical elements of the clause frequently appear in the left-dislocated position. The constituents most commonly encountered in the left topicalised position are NPs. A left-dislocated phrase can occur with or without resumption of the topicalised phrase in the clause, though bound agreement markers on the verb cannot be omitted under any circumstances.

Left-dislocated topics typically make use of the non-proximal demonstrative (§7.4.1), either marking the topic itself, as with the left-dislocated P in (118), or representing the topic in the clause as resumptive, as with the left-dislocated S in (119).

(118)   ***Nie***   *u*   *baqa,*   *halaqi=na*   *d-ege*   *seqo*   *ai.*
       1EXCL.POSS   grass   NPRX.INAN   3PL=FOC   REFL-BEN   sell   ONLY
       'As for my grass, they sold (it) for themselves.'   [Bk-12.021]

(119)   ***En***   *mone*   *uen,*   *baqi*   *mal...*
       person   man   one   NPRX.AN   go
       '(There was) a guy, he went...'   [Bk-21.003]

Left-dislocated topics are not only marked by the non-proximal demonstrative, but may be marked with any of the determiners depending on the type of topic (see Chapter 7 for a description of the individual determiners and their functions). In (120), we see a contrastive demonstrative marking the left-dislocated topic encoding the T, and in (121) a definite article marking an A. Finally, in (122) we see that there is no determiner marking the left-dislocated topic. This example is unusual for the fact that the dislocated element encodes a peripheral role, the NP complement of the instrumental verbal postposition *dele* 'INS', which is left behind in the clause.

(120)   ***Misa masak homo,***   *en*   *linkungan*   *g-ege.*
       mass   big   CONTR.INAN   person   connection   3AN-give
       'The big mass (by contrast), it's given to people with obligations.'
                                                                       [Bk-38.038]

(121)   ***Mone*** *mete*   *g-inat*   *bi,*   *baqi=na*   *h-oqon*   *bare.*
       male   now   3AN-earliest   ART.AN   NPRX.AN=FOC   3INAN-do   PROX.INAN
       'The boy mentioned just now, the oldest, it is him who's building (this).'
                                                                       [Bk-46.067]

(122)   ***Turiq soq,***   *nei*   *n-ini*   *rele*   *mona*   *baqa*
       machete.type   1PL.EXCL   1EXCL-CAUS   INS   forest   NPRX.INAN
       h-ose   *gie.*
       3INAN-clear   PROSP
       'Heavy machetes, we were made to clear the forest with (them).'   [Bk-65.055]

In the preceding examples, the left-dislocated topics were either argument NPs or peripheral NPs in the clause. However, a left-dislocated topic does not necessarily have to have even a peripheral role in the clause, but can have a general "scene-setting" function, referring to "a spatial, temporal or individual framework within which the main predication holds" (Chafe 1976: 50). In (123) the predicative numeral can only take a single argument *leteq* 'step'; *reu* 'house' is a left-dislocated topic which functions to orient the hearer as to where the seven steps presented in the clause are. In (124) *hol okoq* 'stone hole' is a left-dislocated topic, referring to the game which the speaker then begins to describe in the following bivalent verbal clause.

(123) **Reu baqa,** leteq hitu.
house NPRX.INAN step seven
'The house, (its) steps are seven.' [Bk-6.032]

(124) **Hol okoq baqa,** i okoq=na wil tut.
stone hole NPRX.INAN 1PL.INCL hole=FOC dig first
'(As for the game) stone-hole, we dig a hole first.' [Bk-9.001]

In addition to NPs with no clear grammatical role in the clause, left-dislocated topics can be whole clauses. A clausal topic denotes an event which sets the scene for the following clause. Topicalised clauses are nominalised with a determiner; as with NP topics, the choice of which determiner is dependent on the type of setting the topical clause is providing. In (125) the topical clause is nominalised with the definite article, while in (126) the specific demonstrative is used. The use of determiners to nominalise clauses and create "domains" (Reesink 1994) is discussed further in Chapter 7.

(125) **En hiloqo heser ba,** neto rai~rai niq.
person two dead ART.INAN 1SG be.anything NEG
'Two people died, (but) I was not affected at all.' [Bk-61.003]

(126) **I reu a-ta mal roe,** bai a mami.
1PL.INCL house 3INAN-GL go SPEC.INAN thing eat tasty
'When we came home just now, we ate tasty food.' [Bk-30.092]

4.7.2.1.2 Right-dislocation

A right-dislocated element is added to a clause in order to disambiguate the referent of a particular role from a range of possible referents in the discourse (Foley 2007: 446). Right-dislocation is not used to establish new topics in the discourse. A right-dislocated element is never contrastive, but it is somewhat emphatic, in so far as it functions to highlight either the identity of a referent or something about the nature of the referent. The use of right-dislocation is not limited to clarifying the identity or nature of a referent in the discourse; it may also be used to clarify a temporal setting of an event or something about the event itself as described in the clause.

In the examples in (127) and (128), the referent of the right-dislocated element is not overtly mentioned with an NP in the clause, and the right-dislocated element functions to clarify who is meant in the role. In (127) the A is the right-dislocated element, in (128) the P.

(127) *En=na*   *g-osok*   *los,*   **neto**.
       person=FOC   3AN-receive   very   1SG
       'Taking people in a lot, I (was).'   [Bk-2.019]

(128) *Neli*   *g-otol,*   **baqi**.
       1DU.EXCL   3AN-take.care.of   NPRX.AN
       'We two were looking after (her), her (it was).'   [Bk-43.073]

Phrases encoding peripheral roles are also frequently found to be right-dislocated. In (129) a verbal postposition encoding an addressee with *g-o* '3-SRC' (§12.4.4) is right-dislocated, while in (130), a verbal postposition encoding a beneficiary with *g-ege* '3AN-BEN' (§12.4.6) is right-dislocated.

(129) *En*   *Gewal*   *no*   *bari*   *nona*   *gu-sura*   *ruquk,*   **eme**
       person   Gewal   OBL   PROX.AN   girl   3AN-ask   always   mother
       Eta   **g-o**.
       Eta   3-SRC   [Bk-14.011]
       'These people in Gewal ask after you constantly, mother Eta (they ask).'

(130) *Wendi*   *bari*   *g-iri*   *kumu,*   **g-ege**.
       Wendi   PROX.AN   3AN-leg   massage   3AN-BEN
       'Wendy here was massaging his leg, for him (she did it).'   [Bk-43.052]

A right-dislocated NP is occasionally coreferent with an NP in the clause. In (131), *zo* 'mango' appears in the clause both encoding the P as well as right-dislocated where the description of the mango as ripe is added. In (132), the right-dislocated NP clarifies the identity of *halaqi* '3PL'.

(131) *Nei*   **zo**   *zal,*   **zo**   **za**.
       1PL.EXCL   mango   carry   mango   ripe
       'We carried a mango, a ripe mango.'   [Bk-37.072]

(132) **Halaqi** mos t-o   koko baqa   goet, **makoqan~makoqan**
       3PL   also RECP-SRC test NPRX.INAN LIKE, REDUP~poet
       bi.
       ART.AN
       'They also tested each other like that, the different poets (did).' [Bk-70.037]

Temporal settings (§4.4) occasionally appear right-dislocated, where the speaker seeks to clarify the time-reference of the clause, as in (133). Finally, predicates also occasionally appear right-dislocated, where the speaker seeks to clarify the nature of the verb. In (134), *pesiar* 'stroll' appears with *t-erel* 'RECP-INS' (§11.4.5.1) in a right-dislocated position where it elaborates on the nature of the joint motion denoted by *t-erel* 'RECP-INS' in the clause.

(133) Uen tekeq,   **nei**   **n-on**   **no.**
       one look.at 1PL.EXCL 1EXCL-hand OBL
       'One would watch (it), in our time (lit., in our hand).' [Bk-38.072]

(134) Halaqi=na t-erel,   **t-erel**   **pesiar**.
       3PL=FOC   RECP-INS   RECP-INS   stroll
       'It is they who (go) together, (that is) stroll together.' [Bk-38.020]

4.7.2.2 Fronting and other clause-internal word order variation

Non-dislocation, or clause-internal word order variation, is defined by the absence of "comma intonation" and copying. In this section, I will discuss fronting of elements to a position before the S/A and movement of elements to a preverbal position. These positions are associated with the pragmatic property of focus, which functions to present "new" information. A focused position may provide new information and fill a perceived gap in the hearer's knowledge (Dik 1989: 392), or pick out prominent new information, which is often in contrast to some other piece of information (Choi 1996).

Throughout §4.2, it was seen that NPs encoding the arguments of a verbal predicate could be reordered such that a non-S/A argument could appear before the S/A. This was called "fronting" and is only relevant to non-S/A arguments, since S/A typically precede other arguments in an unmarked clause order. The examples in (135) and (136) present instances of P-fronting. In (135b) the P (bolded) is fronted, as it constitutes new information which completes the hearer's understanding of the conditions under which a young couple could go walking together as described in (135a). The clause in (135c) then further explains the new information given in (135b).

(135) a. *T-erel*   mele   mos.
           RECP-INS walk also
           '(We) would walk together as well.' [Bk-38.037]

b. **Meaq gol uen** nei gi-al.
   child one 1PL.EXCL 3AN-take
   'A child we would take along.' [Bk-38.038]
c. Ret mele niq, tut.
   alone walk NEG past
   '(We) didn't walk (together) alone back then.' [Bk-38.039]

In (136c) we see P-fronting used to pick out a prominent piece of new information (bolded). In the preceding discourse, illustrated in (136a–b), the speaker relates the quickness to anger he observed in the Makasae and Fataluku, in response to a question about what those peoples were like. In (136c), he changes tack in his description, offering a new characterisation of the people and their language.

(136) a. Bai gol uen, t-oqon, t-ota baqa goet los.
   thing small one RECP-do RECP-stab NPRX.INAN LIKE very
   'A little thing, (and they) fight (and) stab each other like that.' [Bk-61.074]
b. En Makasai en Fataluku, baqi=na
   person Makasae person Fataluku NPRX.INAN=FOC
   baqa goet.
   NPRX.INAN LIKE
   'Makasae people (and) Fataluku people, they are like that.' [Bk-61.075]
c. **En halaqi g-iol** i tara soqat.
   person 3PL 3AN-voice 1PL.INCL know hard
   'Their language we can only learn with difficulty.' [Bk-61.085]

The example in (137) illustrates a very unusual instance involving fronting of a peripheral. In (137a) the peripheral NP introduced by the comitative *g-utu* '3-COM' (§12.4.1) is fronted, as a phrase asserting prominent new information on the basis of which the predication is to be understood. The proposition denoted by (137a) in turn contrasts with that denoted by (137b), since the young midwife is not so used to walking in sandals on muddy ground. This is the only example of its kind in the corpus.

(137) a. Homo, **sendel g-utu** nei roe toman
   CONTR.INAN sandal 3-COM 1PL.EXCL SPEC.INAN accustomed
   oa, mele.
   IAM walk
   'Yet, with sandals we here were already accustomed, (to) walk (that is).'
   [Bk-37.033]

b. *Mete   en   gol   bidan   Jawa   gie   roi*
   NOW   person small midwife Jawa   3.POSS   SPEC.INAN
   woa   mele   kou.
   woa   walk   slip
   'Now this young midwife from Java was -woooh- walking (and) slipping.'
   [Bk-37.035]

In addition to fronting, Bunaq uses the immediately preverbal position to express focus. As in many verb-final languages, the preverbal position is associated with unmarked focus (Kim 1988). Unlike fronting which focuses a P or much less frequently a peripheral element in a clause where the only other element expressed is an A or an S, respectively, preverbal focus affects the ordering of P/R, T, and peripheral NPs relative to one another and requires that more than one of these occur in the clause. Some examples are discussed below.

In §4.2.3, we saw that the T of a trivalent verb could, in addition to its unmarked postverbal position, occur in a position before the verb. Example (138) illustrates this. In (138a) both the P (him) and the T (water) of *g-ege* '3AN-give' are elided under anaphora from the preceding discourse. In (138b), we see that the T occurs in the preverbal focus position: the water in the bucket that was given is in contrastive focus with the water which was not given in the previous clause.

(138) a. *Waqen   g-ege   heten   niq.*
         PART.PL   3AN-give   want   NEG
         'Some didn't want to give (him any water).'   [Bk-6.025]
      b. *Pana   gol   uen=na   rie   il   kokoq   no*
         female small   one=FOC   REFL.POSS   water   bucket   OBL
         ba   *g-ege.*
         ART.INAN   3AN-give
         'It was one girl who gave (him) the water in her bucket.' [Bk-6.026]

In §4.4, we saw that the unmarked position of most peripheral constituents is following the ARG₁ (S/A of a verbal clause) and preceding the ARG₂ (P or OBL of a verbal clause) where one is expressed. The unmarked word order is illustrated in (139) with benefactive *g-ege* '3AN-BEN' (§12.4.6) preceding the P. By contrast, (140) shows a marked word order, with *g-ege* '3AN-BEN' following the P. This preverbal position functions to place focus on the beneficiary, emphasising that the oranges were picked just for him. Note that the 3rd person ANIMATE agreement on the predicate *iwal* 'pick' is with the P headed by the ANIMATE noun *sabul* 'orange'.

(139) **G-ege**   *tuat   bolu   uen   h-oqon.*
      3AN-BEN   cake   ball   one   3INAN-make
      '(She) made a cake for him.'   [LB-8.127]

(140) *Sabul   bolu   hiloqon   bi   **g-ege**   g-iwal.*
      orange ball   two   ART.AN   3AN-BEN   3AN-pick
      '(They) picked the two oranges for him.'   [Bk-4.042]

Finally, in (141) and (142) we see that *no* 'OBL' introduces an NP referring to the goal location of a P as part of the act of setting and dividing, respectively. Example (141) represents the unmarked word ordering, with P preceding the locative PP. In (142) the ordering is marked, with the locative PP preceding the P; the P is focused, highlighting the pragmatically unusual point that the participants are eating uncooked rice grains, as opposed to cooked rice.

(141) *Baqa   **hoto**   wa   no   lai.*
      NPRX.INAN   fire   top   OBL   set
      '(You) set that on top of the fire.'   [Bk-76.069]

(142) *Halaqi   **bogeq~bogeq**   no   piral   t-ege   ge-neq.*
      3PL   REDUP~plate   OBL   grain   RECP-BEN   3AN-divide
      'They divide up the grain onto plates for each other.'   [Bk-6.036]

4.7.2.3 Animacy effects on word order

The A of a bivalent verb always comes as the first NP expressed in the clause in a pragmatically neutral ordering, regardless of the animacy of the participants. So, for instance, (143) is a pragmatically unmarked clause in which an inanimate A occurs before an animate P. Were the P, *en* 'person', to precede the A, i.e., be fronted, then the referent of P would be pragmatically focused in the clause.

```
        A         P       PERI            P-V
(143)  Tues   ba     en      hik    a-ta       g-ebek      niq.
       fine   ART.INAN person path   3INAN-GL   3AN-turn    NEG
```
'The fines don't put people on the right path (lit., turn people to the path).'
[Bk-53.102]

However, in the absence of an agentive predicate, the pragmatically unmarked linear ordering of NPs in a clause is determined by person and animacy, as per the hierarchy in Figure 4.4 (after the first animacy hierarchy proposed by Silverstein 1976). The hierarchy says that local (i.e., 1st and 2nd) persons are more eligible for clause-initial position than non-local (3ʳᵈ) persons, and that semantically animate 3ʳᵈ persons are more eligible for clause-initial position than semantically inanimate 3ʳᵈ persons.[8]

1ˢᵗ & 2ⁿᵈ persons > animate 3ʳᵈ persons > inanimate 3ʳᵈ persons

Figure 4.4: Hierarchy for ordering of non-agentive clauses.

Cross-linguistically, the role that animacy plays in determining the ordering of arguments in (di)transitive sentences is well known, with the principle that an animate entity should occur at the beginning of a sentence being referred to as the "Animate First principle" (e.g., Bock and Warren 1985; Tomlin 1986; van Nice and Dietrich 2003). The Bunaq reflex of this principle is interesting, because it does not apply to bivalent (or transitive) clauses as in many languages, but only to clauses in which the predicate does not involve an agentive argument, e.g., in experiencer constructions (cf. similar examples in Foley 1986: 121–127, 190–194; Pawley 2000). In this section, I will briefly illustrate the ways in which the hierarchy affects the ordering of non-agentive clauses in Bunaq.

Consider the ordering of NPs in (144) and (145). Both examples have non-agentive monovalent verbal predicates with the S *memel* 'sickness'; the NPs encoded by a verbal postposition, *ni-ta* '1EXCL-GL' and *g-o* '3-SRC', respectively, denote the experiencer of the sickness. The verbal postpositions occur between the S and the predicate as would be expected from the description in §4.4. However, the independent nominal constituents encoding the nominal complement of the verbal postpositions, i.e., *neto* '1SG' and *baqi* 'NPRX.AN', precede the S. This is because the 1ˢᵗ person and 3ʳᵈ person ANIMATE referents respectively are higher on the above hierarchy than the S. Where the complement of the verbal postposition is expressed by independent nominal constituents, this ordering is the pragmatic neutral ordering; placing the S clause-initially is pragmatically marked.

(144)   PERI   S   PERI-VERBPP   V
        Neto   memel   **ni-ta**   topol.
        1SG   sickness 1EXCL-GL   fall
        'Sickness fell to me.', i.e., 'I fell sick.'   [Bk-46.057]

(145)   PERI   S   PERI-VERBPP   V
        Baqi   memel   **g-o**   re.
        NPRX.AN   sickness 3-SRC   right
        'Sickness righted against her', i.e. 'She was struck down sick.'   [Bk-70.084]

---

[8] The local versus non-local person distinction plays a role in other parts of Bunaq grammar, namely, the obligatoriness of pronouns co-indexing prefixes (§6.2.1) and the availability of determiners with pronouns (§6.2.2).

A similar ordering phenomenon can be observed in (146) and (147). Both examples have the non-agentive verbal predicate *kaeq* 'filled', which subcategorises for an S and an OBL (§10.6.1). Both S and OBL have inanimate referents and are ordered neutrally with respect to one another, that is, with the S preceding the OBL. However, in each case, the OBL is a "bound" or inalienably possessed noun (§9.3) whose possessor is animate. These animate possessors are expressed by NPs that occur in clause-initial position, preceding the S. Again, this clause-initial position of the animate possessor is unmarked in these clauses, since the other participants are neither animate nor agentive.

(146)   PSR   S   PSR-OBL   V
       Ola himo   keke   **g**-on   kaeq.
       LOW CONTR.INAN   bracelet   3AN-hand   filled
       'That one down there's hands were filled with bracelets.'   [Bk-68.066]

(147)   PSR   S   PSR-OBL   V
       Bui Guloq   sele   **g**-iwiq   kaeq   oa.
       Bui Guloq   sand   3AN-body   filled   IAM
       'Bui Guloq's body was filled with sand.'   [LB-5.123]

In the previous examples, we have seen a 1st person outranking a 3rd person INANIMATE and a 3rd person animate outranking a 3rd person inanimate. Example (148) illustrates a 1st person outranking a 3rd person animate: the initial NP, *neto* '1SG', refers to the possessor of a "bound" inalienably possessed noun that is the NP complement of the predicative postposition, *no* 'OBL'. Example (149) illustrates a 2nd person outranking a 3rd person animate: the initial pronoun, *eto* '2SG', refers to the possessor of the "bound" inalienably possessed noun, the predicate of the equative clause.

(148)   PSR   SUBJECT   [PSR-NP   POSTPOSITION]_{PRED}
       Neto   Yati   bari   **n**-oq   no   taq.
       1SG   Yati   PROX.AN   1EXCL-womb   OBL   CONT
       'This Yati was still in my womb.', i.e., 'I was still pregnant with Yati.'
                                                                                                                                                [Bk-2.002]

(149)   PSR   SUBJECT   [PSR-NP]_{PRED}
       Eto   eme   Ø-owo.
       2SG   mother   1INCL/2-womb
       '(Your) mother was your womb.' (i.e., 'your mother bore you')   [OS-07.03]

There are no examples in which a 1st person and a 2nd person co-occur in a non-agentive clause. It remains to be seen how they are ordered relative to one another.

4.7.3 Variation in bivalent verb agreement

Under normal circumstances, only 3rd person P arguments belonging to the ANIMATE noun class are indexed on bivalent verbs with the agreement prefix *gV-* '3AN' (see §10.2 on the different inflectional classes of bivalent verbs). For example, the prefix agrees with the ANIMATE noun class noun *eme* 'mother' with an animate referent in (150a), and with the ANIMATE noun class noun *paqol* 'maize' with an inanimate referent in (150b).

(150) a. *Neto   eme   gi-wit.*
          1SG   mother.AN   3AN-fetch
          'I fetched mother.'
      b. *Manek   paqol   gi-a.*
          Manek   maize.AN   3AN-eat
          'Manek ate maize.'

However, prefixal agreement on bivalent verbs can also be manipulated in some limited ways on pragmatic grounds in Bunaq. Specifically, there is a minor pattern of variation whereby Ps with inanimate referents of INANIMATE noun class (see §5.2 on noun class assignment) can occasionally be indexed with a 3rd person ANIMATE prefix *gV-* '3AN'. The variation in agreement patterns for INANIMATE Ps appears to correlate with differing degrees of semantic transitivity in a clause (cf. Hopper and Thompson 1980): the presence of a '3AN' prefix with an INANIMATE class noun signals that the clause is high in transitivity. That is, in the absence of a P with an animate referent, the '3AN' prefix may be taken to not so much encode any particular property of the P argument, but rather the overall transitivity of the clause. Table 4.5 summarises the observed variations in the environments in which '3AN' prefixation occurs with an INANIMATE noun. "High" semantic transitivity is associated with increased agentivity on the part of the A and/or increased affectedness on the part of the P, as well as the realisation of the event denoted by the clause.

Table 4.5: Transitivity-based alternations in P agreement.

	Animate referent	ANIMATE noun with inanimate referent	INANIMATE noun with inanimate referent
3rd person ANIMATE prefix	obligatory	default	high transitivity
3rd person INANIMATE prefix/no prefix	ungrammatical	default	default

Transitivity-based variation in semantically inanimate 3rd person P agreement appears to be very rare in Bunaq. In the vast majority of speech that I analysed, the default pattern of agreement according to the grammatical ANIMACY of P is followed. Only a few examples where it was not were identified in the corpus. More frequently, I noticed these unexpected agreement patterns in overheard speech. It remains to be seen to what extent these variations might be the result of online production errors. At the same time, speakers gave consistent judgements of the differences between the variable prefixal agreement forms in elicitation, suggesting that the phenomenon is indeed real. In what follows I set out the variations I am aware of and their apparent, albeit tentative, explanations.

Increased agentivity can be used to explain the differences between the clauses in (151) with the INANIMATE noun *musik* 'music' as P. In (151a) where no prefix for P is used, the music is heard in passing from a distance. But in (151b) where the 3rd ANIMATE prefix is used, the music has the speaker's positive and undivided attention according to the intuitions of the speakers I worked with.

(151) a. *Neto   musik   **mak**.*
         1SG   music.INAN   hear
         'I hear music.'
      b. *Neto   musik   **ga-mak**.*
         1SG   music.INAN   3AN-hear
         'I listen to music.'   [OS-06.01]

More frequently, it appears to be the affectedness of the inanimate referent of P that seems to impact whether the 3rd ANIMATE prefix is used. For example, in (152a) the P is the INANIMATE noun *kursi* 'chair' and the verb follows the default "zero" agreement pattern for such Ps. However, in (152b), where the animate agreement prefix is used, it implies that the chair is struck repeatedly, i.e., it is more affected.

(152) a. *Yati   kursi   **dere**.*
         Yati   chair.INAN   knock
         'Yati struck the chair.'
      b. *Yati   kursi   **ge-rere***
         Yati   chair.INAN   3AN-knock
         'Yati struck the chair repeatedly.'   [Not-06.02]

The iterative reading of (152b) appears to fall out from the punctual *Aktionsart* of the clausal verb, *dere* 'knock'. In other examples of ANIMATE agreement for inanimate Ps, the high affectedness of P is reflected in the extended duration that an event has. This is, for example, seen in (153) where ANIMATE agreement is used on the verb *h-one* '3INAN-hold' with the INANIMATE P *do* 'boat'.

(153) **Do**   ba   **g-one**   goniqo mil   oa=sa,   do
      boat.INAN ART.INAN   3AN-hold   three   DUR   IAM=EVEN   boat
      mele   loi   niq.
      walk   good   NEG
      'Even after holding on and on to the boat for three days, the boat couldn't sail.'
      [OrelBusaKawak-082]

The above example also illustrates an important point about variable prefixal agreement with INANIMATE Ps. We see in (152a) that the determiner marking *do* 'boat' takes the INANIMATE agreement form. This means that we cannot view the change in agreement as variable assignment of the noun to the ANIMATE or INANIMATE class (although this is found with some nouns, but then with different semantics and also impacting determiner agreement: see §5.2.4).

The specificity of the P also appears to be a dimension of high clausal transitivity. This is illustrated by the variable verbal agreement in (154) with the INANIMATE noun *uor* 'vegetable'. In (154a) reference is to the vegetables is general and indefinite, and the clause shows the default agreement with no prefix. By contrast, in (154b) the speaker is referring to specific vegetables that were at the time being held by the addressee, and there is co-indexing with the 3rd person ANIMATE prefix.

(154) a. *Gereja*   *g-ewen*   *no*   *eto*   *uor*   **wit**   *loi.*
          church   3AN-face   OBL   2SG   vegetables   fetch   good
          'In front of the church, you can buy vegetables.'   [OS-06.02]
      b. *Neto*   *uor*   **gi-al**   *gie.*
          1SG   vegetables   3AN-carry   PROSP
          'I'll carry (these here) vegetables.'   [OS-06.01]

Finally, complement clauses filling the position of a P argument, while normally taking INANIMATE agreement, can also occur with an ANIMATE prefix of the verb in contexts of high semantic transitivity. Two such examples are given in (155) and (156). The ANIMATE agreement on *h-azal* '3INAN-see' in (155) appears to have to do with the realis status of the event; it is an affirmation that the speaker has himself seen the lights. Similarly, in (156) the speaker informs the addressee that the owl hooting is what he hears and this is accompanied by ANIMATE agreement on *mak* 'hear'.

(155) *Ene*   *no*   *lolo*   *wa*   *gene*   *eto*   [*listrik*   *sia*]$_{COMP}$ **g-azal**.
      night OBL   mountain   top   LOC   2SG   electricity   burn   3AN-see
      'At night on top of the mountain you see the lights.'   [OS-06.01]

(156) Neto [topi bi   doqon]ᴄᴏᴍᴘ ga-mak, ...
      1SG owl ART.AN hoot   3AN-hear
      'I hear the hooting of the owl, ...'   [EnLoiEnPuanMoen-020]

See §15.2.1 on complement clauses taking NP argument positions.

4.7.4 Discourse markers

The Bunaq discourse markers are a class of high frequency enclitics signalling that one part of the discourse is dependent on another. The discourse markers are presented in Table 4.6. I divide them into two functional types: relator enclitics (§4.7.4.1) and focus enclitics (§4.7.4.2).

Table 4.6: Discourse markers.

Given relator	=bu	'GIVEN'
Counter expectational relator	=be	'CONTEXP'
Restrictive focus	=na	'FOC'
Additive focus	=o	'AND'
Scalar additive focus	=sa	'EVEN'

Discourse markers are in a paradigmatic relationship with one another and do not co-occur marking one and the same constituent. They can mark an NP, a PP, or a clause. They attach to the right edge of one of these units, as illustrated with =na 'FOC' in the examples in (157). They cannot attach to an embedded phrase; for instance, a discourse marker cannot mark an NP which is the complement of a postposition, but must mark the PP as whole.

(157) a. Marking NP
         Suta   baqa=**na**   rele tebe   a-ta   suta   hosu ruil.
         thread NPRX.INAN=FOC   INS return 3INAN-GL thread other spin
         'It is that thread with which (you) in turn spin it together with another thread.'   [Bk-35.021]
      b. Marking PP
         Neto Hulul gene=**na** zol.
         1SG Hulul LOC=FOC   originate
         'It is Hulul where I come from.'   [Bk-1.002]

c. Marking clause
*Malaysia gene man=**na**, tebe lilak teni.*
Malaysia LOC come=FOC return crazy again
'It was (when) she came back from Malaysia, (that) she went back to being crazy.' [Bk-43.037]

In what follows, I describe the functions of the discourse markers marking phrases within the clause, i.e., NPs and PPs. The reader is referred to Chapter 15 for illustration and explanation of their functions in clause combining.

4.7.4.1 Relator enclitics
Relator enclitics are pragmatic markers indicating a relation between the phrase which they mark and the larger linguistic unit in which they are embedded (Trask 1993: 84). Encliticising to an NP or PP, a relator denotes the manner of relation between the referent and the situation or event denoted by the clause in which it is found. They can also be used to conjoin clauses. For discussion and illustration of the further functions conjoining clauses, see §15.3.2.1.3.

4.7.4.1.1 =*bu* 'GIVEN'
The relator =*bu* 'GIVEN' marks "given" relations, i.e., "given X then Y holds". With an NP or PP, =*bu* marks an "as for" topic, that is, it establishes the background against which the information in the clause holds (cf. Haiman 1978). For example, =*bu* 'GIVEN' marks a topical NP in (158) and a topic PP headed by *no* 'OBL' in (159).

(158) *Nona=**bu** nei n-ege loi los*
 girl=GIVEN 1PL.EXCL 1EXCL-BEN good very
 '**As for the girl**, she was always very good to us.' [Bk-14.002]

(159) *Ni-mil no=**bu**, ei Ø-ini nie muk gie.*
 1EXCL-inside OBL=GIVEN 2PL 1INCL/2-CAUS 1EXCL.POSS land 3.POSS
 r-ige.
 REFL-teach
 '**It is my intention** (lit., in my mind) to teach you about my land.' [Bk-24.041]

While a =*bu*-marked constituent can itself be left-dislocated as in (159), it may also appear within the clause and even co-occur with a left-dislocated "scene-setting" topic marked with a determiner (discussed in §4.7.2.1.1). For example, in (160) we see that the left-dislocated topic establishes that there were four people and the use of =*bu* in the clause singles out two of them as good workers.

(160) *Nei   goniqil   ba   na-lak   no,   en*
      1PL.EXCL   four   ART.INAN 1EXCL-between   OBL   person
      *hiloqon=**bu** g-on   laun   porsa.*
      two=GIVEN   3AN-hand quick   very
      'Between the four of us, **two people** were very quick workers (lit., 'had quick hands).'   [Bk-12.011]

Whilst no contrastive meaning is entailed by the use of =*bu*, it is a frequent implicature of the relator's function to mark the participant in respect to whom the information in the clause holds. For example, we see in (161) that =*bu* marks successive topics in the discourse for whom different situations apply: the first in (161a) is a goat, who would not be able to escape hunting dogs, and the second in (161d) is a monkey, who would not be troubled by their arrival.

(161) a. *Neto=**bu**   en   g-azal   milik.*
         1SG=GIVEN   people   3AN-see   scared
         '**As for me**, (I am) scared of humans.'   [OrelNisPipLoko-06]
      b. *Baqi   man=bu,   die   zap   gi-al.*
         NPRX.AN   come=GIVEN REFL.POSS   dog   3AN-carry
         'If they were to come, they would bring their dogs.'
                                                           [OrelNisPipLoko-07]
      c. *Zap   ili   Ø-i   heser   oa.*
         dog   1DU.INCL   1INCL/2-bite   dead   IAM
         'The dogs would bite us to death immediately.'   [OrelNisPipLoko-08]
      d. *Eto=**bu**   loi-wen,   laun~laun   hotel   saqe   loi=si.*
         2SG=GIVEN   good-MODER   REDUP~quick   tree   ascend   good=REAS
         '**As for you**, (you) would be just fine, because you can quickly climb a tree.'
                                                           [OrelNisPipLoko-09]

The relator =*bu* is often found marking an NP in a negated clause adjacent to a positive polarity clause with an NP marked by the restrictive focus marker =*na* (§4.7.4.2.3). In these situations, =*bu* could be regarded as having a contrastive meaning, but this is again an implicature arising out of the juxtaposition of the positive and negative clauses. For instance, in (162a) =*bu* marks the P of the negated verb *seq* 'call', signalling that the calling did *not* happen with respect to the referent of P. In (162b) the person who was called is marked as a focused participant with =*na* 'FOC'.

(162) a. *Neto   eto=**bu**   Ø-ege   seq   niq.*
         1SG   2SG=GIVEN   2/1INCL-BEN   call   NEG
         'I wasn't calling **you**.'   [OrelPipMokBini-036]

b. *Neto   rie   moen   pip=**na**   g-ege   seq!*
   1SG   REFL.POSS   friend   goat=FOC   3AN-BEN   call
   'It was my friend Goat that I was calling.'   [OrelPipMokBini-037]

The relator =*bu* not only occurs with NPs and PPs, but can also mark a clause so long as there is a following clausal marker in relation to which the =*bu*-marked clause is understood. In the corpus, there are two attested clausal markers that follow a =*bu*-marked clause. The first is the verb *loi* which signals possibility when used with clausal complements (see §15.2.1.2 on this kind of S-complementation) and is exemplified with a =*bu*-marked clause in (163). The second is the clausal negator *niq* which signals that the proposition denoted by the =*bu*-marked clause does not hold, as in (164).

(163) *Nei=o   neq=**bu**   loi,...*
      1PL.EXCL=AND   divide=GIVEN   good
      'As for us dividing (the food), (that is) possible, ...'   [HulTopol-070]

(164) *Roti=na   a   los=**bu**   niq.*
      bread=FOC   eat   very=GIVEN   NEG
      'As for eating bread a lot, (they) don't.'   [Bk-70.169]

Finally, related to its temporal meaning when coordinating clauses, =*bu* can occur on a temporal noun or adverb, as in (165) and (166).

(165) *Mon=**bu**   tebe   zal   pir.*
      afternoon=GIVEN   return   carry   come.from.garden
      'When it's afternoon, return bringing them up from the garden.'
      [Bk-4.011]

(166) *Lain=**bu**   meren   s-ileqen.*
      past.times=GIVEN   gun   3INAN-let.down
      'In the past, (they) fired guns.'   [Bk-18.034]

4.7.4.1.2 =*be* 'CONTEXP'

The relator =*be* 'CONTEXP' primarily marks that a counter-expectational or unexpected relation holds between the marked constituent and the proposition denoted by the clause. Because of its semantics of unexpectedness, =*be* frequently conveys surprise on the part of the speaker and is typically accompanied by rising intonation.

The most common constituent marked by =*be* is an NP, where it functions similar to the counter-expectational demonstrative (§7.6).⁹ On an NP, =*be* marks a referent whose relation to the proposition denoted by the clause is contrary to expectation or unexpected. That is, it is not the =*be*-marked NP which is specifically unexpected in the speech context, but rather its relation to the event denoted by the clause. For example, in (167) =*be* 'CONTEXP' marks the NP *sele* 'sand', signalling that it was unexpected to have found Bui Guloq's body full of sand such a short time after her drowning in the water. The equative clause in (168) has the NP *cier goloq* 'bed' marked with =*be*, expressing that the bed's being made of precious metal was unexpected given that its owner is a slave.

(167) Bui Guloq sele=**be**   g-iwiq   kaeq~kaeq   oa.
       Bui Guloq sand=CONTEXP 3AN-body REDUP~fill IAM
       'Bui Guloq's body was already completely full of sand!'   [LB5.123]

(168) Gie   cier   g-oloq=**be**   tumel, ...
       3.POSS sleep 3-place=CONTEXP metal
       'Her bed was (made of) precious metal!'   [LB5.077]

Clauses with an NP marked with =*be* frequently have negative polarity. In such cases, =*be* signals that the referent of the marked NP was expected to have a positive polarity relation to the proposition. For instance, the example in (169) comes from a text in which the speaker describes her difficulties in giving birth to her first child. The marking of *n-ol* 'my child' with =*be* expresses the unexpectedness of the child having still not been delivered after a long time in labour. Similarly, the use of =*be* in (170) to mark the NP headed by *en* 'person' signals that the speaker did not expect that no one would come to help her when she fell and broke her arm.

(169) N-ol=**be**   hobel.
       1EXCL-child=CONTEXP not.exist
       'My child had not come!'   [Bk-58.010]

(170) En   bolu   uen=**be**   n-ege   taru   niq.
       person CLF one=CONTEXP 1EXCL-BEN appear NEG
       'Not a person came to my aid.'   [Bk-46.056]

---

9 =*be* 'CONTEXP' is the historical base of the counter-expectational demonstrative (Schapper 2007). Synchronically, they are still very close in meaning and do not co-occur although they appear in different syntactic positions. That their non-co-occurrence is not a syntactic constraint is seen in that the counter-expectational relator can mark NPs determined by other demonstratives and that the counter-expectational demonstrative can occur with the relator =*bu* 'GIVEN'.

Unlike =*bu* 'GIVEN', the counter-expectational relator can also occur in a clause-final position without a following clause or clausal marker. Examples are presented in (171) and (172). In these cases, =*be* marks the clause as exclamatory and expresses that the event or situation denoted by the clause is contrary to the speaker's expectations.

(171) *Kebokoq   uen   roi   koen=**be**!*
      caterpillar one   SPEC.AN   beautiful=CONTEXP
      'This one grub is beautiful!'   [Bk-30.037]

(172) *Nei   n-ini   d-ege   bai   a   inil   o=**be**!*
      1PL.EXCL   1EXCL-CAUS   REFL-give   thing   eat   try   IAM=CONTEXP
      'If only we were told to share food among ourselves too!' [BaiANeq-021]

Finally, there is a minor, secondary use of =*be* where it functions to contrast participants with differing points of view in the discourse. This use is recognisable in that it involves =*be* marking multiple NPs with referents in similar roles over successive clauses. For instance, in (173) there are two participants, the monkey and the mouse, who need to decide who, as part of a bravery competition, will be the first to have the garden cuttings piled on top of them (173a), and while the monkey (= Dia Karawa) is willing (173b), the mouse (= Dia Laho) is not (173c). The use of =*be* on *Dia Karawa* in (173b) and *Dia Laho* in (173c) functions to contrast the positions taken by the two animals.

(173) a. *Ti-ta   zipil   kama,   halali   ti-mil   sura.*
         RECP-GL   garden.cuttings   pile.up   3DU   RECP-mind   ask
         'When it was time to pile up the garden cuttings on one another, the two of
         them asked one another what they wanted to do.'   [Bk-50.010]
      b. *Dia Karawa=**be**,   himo   gi-ta=na   kama   tutu   gie.*
         Dia Karawa=CONTEXP   CONTR.AN   3AN-GL=FOC   pile.up   first   PROSP
         'Dia Karawa, for his part, wanted to have piling up done to him first.'
                                                                       [Bk-50.011]
      c. *Dia Laho=**be**   niq.*
         Dia Laho=CONTEXP   NEG
         'Dia Laho, by contrast, did not (want to be first).'   [Bk-50.012]

4.7.4.2 Focus enclitics

Focus enclitics serve to evaluate the meaning of a proposition relative to a set of alternatives (König 1991: 58). There are three focus enclitics in Bunaq: the additive focus enclitic =*o* 'AND' (§4.7.4.2.1), the scalar additive focus enclitic =*sa* 'EVEN' (§4.7.4.2.2), and the restrictive focus enclitic =*na* 'FOC' (§4.7.4.2.3). Like the relator enclitics dealt with in the previous sections, focus enclitics can attach to an NP or to a PP. These uses are dealt with in the following sections. They can also be used to conjoin clauses (see §15.3.2.1.4 on that use). Individual enclitics may have additional functions; these are mentioned in the specific sections.

4.7.4.2.1 =o 'AND'

The additive focus enclitic =o 'AND' expresses *additivity*, evoking alternatives for which the proposition denoted by the clause holds. In (174) =o marks *tumel* 'money' as being additional to the *ipi* 'rice' named in the preceding clause. In (175) =o marks the complex NP headed by *en* 'person', but the set to which these wild people in the forest are additional is contextually assumed; it is understood that there were also people living normal settled lives. The clause in (176) comes after a description of how to make *tubi raka* 'raka cakes' with banana; the use of =o on the phrase headed by the verbal postposition *dele* 'INS' expresses the alternative of making the cakes with cassava.

(174) Ipi   hober kaeq, tumel=**o**   kaeq   los   oa.
       rice   cave   full   money=AND   full   very   IAM
       'The cave was full of rice, it was also very full of money.'   [Bk-68.021]

(175) En   hui   hotel   mil   gene=**o**   baqis   taq.
       person wild   tree   inside   LOC=AND   many   CONT
       'There were also still many people (living) wild in the forest.'   [Bk-61.019]

(176) Dikotel   dele=**o**   tubi raka   baqa   h-oqon   loi.
       cassava   INS=AND   cake.type   NPRX.INAN   3INAN-make   good
       'It's also possible to make these *raka* cakes with cassava.'   [Bk-76.049]

When marking an NP, the enclitic =o often combines with the free form *mos* 'also' (a borrowing of Tetun *moos* 'also'). The stacked combination has the effect of slightly intensifying the additive meaning. The enclitic =o always attaches to *mos* as illustrated in (177) and (178).

(177) En   Bunaq   **mos=o**   da-tara.
       person   Bunaq   also=AND   REFL-know
       'The Bunaq also know themselves.'   [Bk-15.012]

(178) Neli   **mos=o**   rebel.
       1DU.EXCL   also=AND   descend
       'We also went down.'   [Bk-1.023]

In negative polarity contexts the additive particle can yield a scalar reading whereby the associate of the focus particle constitutes the expected or high scalar alternative which is unusually or very much *not* the case. In (179) the use of =*o* on the noun *hik* 'path' emphasises the speaker's surprise at having to walk to their destination, when no car came to pick them up.

(179) *Hik=o   tara   niq.*
      path=AND know   NEG
      '(I) didn't even know the way.'   [Bk-61.014]

The use of =*o* 'AND' as a medial connective in NP coordination is discussed in §5.7.2.

4.7.4.2.2 =*sa* 'EVEN'

The scalar additive enclitic =*sa* is the least frequent of the Bunaq focus particles. In my analysis, the use of =*sa* presupposes the existence of a scale of likely alternatives and locates the constituent it marks at the extreme bottom of this scale. For example, in (180), two children describe how their aunts beat them (180a); =*sa* on -*iwiq* 'skin' expresses that the result was so extreme that their whole bodies[10] were bruised and swollen (180b).

(180) a. *Nei   nie   eme   tomol uen neli   n-ue.*
         1PL.EXCL   1EXCL.POSS   mother six   one 1DU.EXCL   1EXCL-hit
         'Our six aunts beat the two of us.'   [LB1.054]
      b. *Neli   n-iwiq=sa   pe.*
         1DU.EXCL   1EXCL-skin=EVEN   swell
         'Even our bodies were swollen.'   [LB1.055]

Similarly, in (181) =*sa* marks the PP headed by the locative postposition *gene* and expresses that, in addition to the usual locations, animals are *even* kept in gardens. Normally, animals would assiduously be kept away from gardens for fear that they would destroy food crops.

(181) *Apa=o   pip,   kura   bi   ga-bilan   soq,   en   gie*
      cow=AND goat,   horse   ART.AN   3AN-keep   SEQ   person   3.POSS
      mar   h-iqil,   mil   gene=sa   kaleq   go-lola   gaqal.
      garden   3INAN-leave   inside LOC=EVEN   tree.sp. 3AN-strip all.AN
      '(People) keep cows, goats, and horses, then leave (the animals) in people's gardens, (and) even there (in the gardens) they strip all *kaleq* trees bare.'
                                                                   [Bk-19.001]

---

10 Note that in Bunaq -*iwiq* 'skin' is also used to refer to the body in its entirety.

The scalar additive marker occurs more frequently within the scope of the negator *niq* than =*o* 'AND', but there is little difference in the translation meaning between the two in these contexts. Examples (182) and (183) illustrate the use =*sa* in a negative clause.

(182) Neto   bare   en   uen=**sa**   n-utu   bukuq niq.
      1SG   PROX.INAN   person   one=EVEN   1EXCL-COM   play   NEG
      'Not even one person will play with me.'   [LB5.017]

(183) Gereja=**sa**   dara   niq   taq.
      church=EVEN   build   NEG   CONT
      'Not even the church was built yet.'   [Bk-23.028]

In the corpus, there are a few occurrences of =*sa* in clause-final position. For example, in (184) =*sa* denotes that in addition to the normal traffic of relatives visiting the house as discussed in the preceding text, the Australian ambassador came to the house and that the event was unusual. Example (185) comes from a text describing the unhappiness experienced by the speaker at a particular time; =*sa* is used to emphasise that this unhappiness was unusual, given that he had a job and money at the time.

(184) Deu   bare   duta   Australia   man   mos=o
      house   PROX.INAN   ambassador   Australia   come   also=AND
      g-osok=**sa**.
      3an-receive=EVEN
      'This house even welcomed the ambassador of Australia when he too came.'
                                                                              [Bk-2.032]

(185) Baqa   no   ba,   neto   susar   ni=**sa**.
      NPRX.INAN   OBL   ART.INAN   1SG   be.in.difficulties OBL=EVEN
      'Even at that (time) I was suffering.'   [Bk-61.021]

4.7.4.2.3 =*na* 'FOC'

The restrictive focus enclitic =*na* 'FOC' is the most frequent of the Bunaq focus markers. While the additive and scalar focus markers include some alternative(s) as possible value(s) for the variable of their scope, =*na* implies that none of the alternatives satisfies the proposition, such that the referent of the focus-marked constituent cannot be substituted for by any other variable. The use of =*na* to mark an NP is illustrated in (186); it is used to mark a postpositional phrase in (187), and to mark a verbal postpositional phrase in (188).

(186) Nei   Bunaq=**na**   sasi.
      1PL.EXCL Bunaq=FOC   speak
      'It is Bunaq that we speak.'   [Bk-7.011]

(187) Nei   Halewen   gene=**na** a-ta   sai.
      1PL.EXCL Halewen   LOC=FOC   3INAN-GL   find
      'It was in Halewen that we found it [i.e., work]).'   [Bk-12.003]

(188) Eli il   cinoq   pie~pie   rele=**na** gi-ta   uku.
      2DU water hot   REDUP~steam   INS=FOC   3AN-GL   pour
      'It is boiling hot water which you two (must) pour onto him.' [Bk-4.083]

The restrictive focus enclitic frequently appears in contrastive contexts. In these, the constituent marked with =na expresses the particular referent at issue as opposed to some stated alternative which is explicitly excluded in a preceding clause with negative polarity. This kind of contrast with =na is illustrated in (189).

(189) a. Halaqi baqa   gene misa niq oa.
         3PL   NPRX.INAN   LOC   mass NEG IAM
         'They don't (hold) mass in that place (i.e., the old church).' [Bk-34.058]
      b. Reu   por   baru gene=**na** misa h-oqon   oa.
         house holy   new   LOC=FOC   mass 3INAN-make   IAM
         'It is the new church in which they do the mass now.' [Bk-34.059]

Other functions of =na 'FOC' already discussed in this chapter are its use in presentational clauses (§4.3.1) and marking fronted phrases with interrogative words (§4.6.2.1). The restrictive focus marker is also used to mark restrictive relative clauses – see §5.4.2.

Chapter 5
Noun phrases

5.1 Noun phrase structure

This chapter describes the noun phrase (NP) in Bunaq. The NP is prototypically a referring expression, that is, it is used to refer to entities in a possible world. As mentioned in §3.2, NPs chiefly serve as the arguments of predicates.

The template for the Bunaq NP is given in Figure 5.1. The figure represents a maximally "extended" NP that includes locationals (LCT) at the left periphery of the NP, followed by a possessor (PSR), and a determiner (DET) occurring at the right periphery of the NP. At the "core" of the Bunaq NP is the head noun (N_{HEAD}), followed by a range of optional modifiers elaborated on in Figure 5.2. The N_{HEAD} of an NP can be a noun (§3.2), a pronoun (§3.5.1), or an interrogative (§3.5.2). Determiners agree with N_{HEAD}. Nouns in Bunaq belong to either the INANIMATE or ANIMATE noun class; the N_{HEAD} gives its noun class to the whole of the NP.

LCT PSR [N_{HEAD} ...]CORE DET

Figure 5.1: Template of the extended NP.

The NP core consists of an N_{HEAD} and its modifiers. Figure 5.2 presents an overview of the elaborated template of the NP core that has been described here. Different aspects of this template will be discussed and exemplified throughout this chapter.

QUANT N_{HEAD} N_{MOD} N_{MOD} V_{ATTR} RC/QUANT

Figure 5.2: Elaborated template of the NP core.

An N_{MOD} may directly follow the N_{HEAD}. An N_{MOD} is a noun describing a property of the referent of an N_{HEAD}, such as its shape, sex, or size. Up to two N_{MOD}s can modify a single N_{HEAD}, though the second N_{MOD} is lexically restricted to *gol* 'small' < '3AN-child'.

Following an N_{MOD}, a simple, single-word, verb can occur attributively (V_{ATTR}). A verbal attribute is posited as a separate slot here because it is possible to have a simple attribute in V_{ATTR} followed by another verbal modifier in the RC slot. An RC may be non-restrictive (head unmarked) or restrictive (head marked with =*na* 'FOC').

Relative clauses do not normally co-occur with a quantifier (QUANT) in my data and so they are regarded here as sharing a postnominal slot. By quantifier, I mean non-numeral quantifier; numerals are regarded as verbs and are analysed as occurring in either the V_{ATTR} or the RC slot of the template. One quantifier, *naran* 'every sort', occurs before the N_{HEAD}. More than one quantifier may occur in an NP. The indefinite marker *bun* also occurs in the QUANT slot, but does not permit co-occurrence with quantifiers.

No item in the NP is obligatory, and the N$_{HEAD}$ is readily elided where its referent is contextually or anaphorically retrievable. However, in some cases, the presence of one item syntactically requires the presence of another constituent in the NP. The following syntactic constraints are observed:

(i) if an N$_{MOD}$ is expressed, then an N$_{HEAD}$ must be overtly expressed (see §5.3);
(ii) if an RC is restrictive, the N$_{HEAD}$ must be overtly expressed (see §5.4.2);
(iii) if the indefinite marker *bun* occurs in the quantifier slot, the N$_{HEAD}$ must be overtly expressed (see §5.5.2);
(iv) if the article occurs as a determiner, then another NP constituent must be expressed (see §7.8);
(v) if an addressee-centred locational occurs, then another NP constituent must be expressed (see §8.3.4).

In §5.2 I discuss noun class as a property of N$_{HEAD}$s and look at the division of nominals into the ANIMATE and INANIMATE noun classes. In §5.3 I deal with N$_{MOD}$. §5.4 looks at the expression of verbal attributes and relative clauses, while §5.5 looks at indefiniteness marking. §5.6 is concerned with non-verbal quantificational strategies in the NP. Finally, §5.7 looks at different functional strategies for the conjunction and disjunction of nominals. Several topics relevant to the NP are discussed in subsequent chapters: Chapter 6 discusses pronouns and other forms of person reference; Chapter 7 describes the functions and meanings of determiners; Chapter 8 treats the class of locationals; and Chapter 9 describes the different types of adnominal possessive constructions.

5.2 Nominal classification

Bunaq has a category "noun class" (also known as "gender"). That is, nouns are lexically specified for the noun class they are assigned to, with distinct agreement patterns associated with each noun class.

The Bunaq nominal classification system involves a two-way class distinction of ANIMATE versus INANIMATE noun class, similar to that found in other languages in the region (Schapper 2010a). The system has a strong semantic basis, that is, in most cases it is sufficient to know the meaning of a noun in order to determine its noun class. However, the basic pattern is complicated by the inclusion of entities that lack discernible semantic animacy in the ANIMATE noun class on the basis of their association with real-world animates. That is, whilst all nouns denoting animates are of ANIMATE noun class, a small set of nouns denoting inanimates are also of ANIMATE noun class; the remaining (majority of) inanimates belong to the INANIMATE noun class (Table 5.1).

Table 5.1: Bunaq noun class assignment.

		Semantic animacy	
		animate	inanimate
NOUN CLASS	ANIMATE	✓✓✓	✓
	INANIMATE	--	✓✓

In this description, small caps "ANIMATE" and "INANIMATE" are used in reference to the grammatical classification of nouns in Bunaq, while lower case "animate" and "inanimate" are used in reference to the real-world, semantic animacy of referents. Throughout §5.2, agreement targets and their controllers are bolded. Following a brief overview of noun class agreement in §5.2.1, I discuss the classification of animates in §5.2.2 and inanimates in §5.2.3. Finally, I look at cases of noun class reassignment in §5.2.4.

5.2.1 Overview of noun class agreement targets

Noun class is a covert property of Bunaq nouns. It is reflected on two agreement targets, prefixes on verbs (§10.1) and determiners (§7.1).[1]

In (1a), the INANIMATE noun *zo* 'mango' is modified by the INANIMATE form of the article and does not trigger agreement on the verb (see §4.2.2 on differential P agreement). In (1b), the ANIMATE noun *zap* 'dog' is modified by the ANIMATE form of the article and triggers the agreement prefix *gV-* '3AN-' on the verb.

(1) a. Neto **zo** **ba** tekeq.
  1SG mango.INAN ART.INAN watch
  'I'm watching the mangoes.'
 b. Neto **zap** **bi** **ge**-tekeq.
  1SG dog.AN ART.AN 3AN-watch
  'I'm watching the dog.' [Not-06.01]

5.2.2 Nouns referring to animates

Classification of nouns with animate referents is relatively uncomplicated: all nouns with sentient, animate referents, both higher (humans, mammals, etc.) and lower

---

[1] There are two further individual items that agree with controllers on the basis of noun class: the noun *niat* 'earliest' (§5.3.2) and the floating quantifier *gaqal* 'all.AN' (§13.8.1.3).

animates (reptiles, insects, etc.), belong to the ANIMATE noun class. There are no biologically sentient entities that are classified as INANIMATE.

Example (2) illustrates ANIMATE agreement with a noun with a human referent on the determiner *baqi* 'NPRX.AN' (as opposed to *baqa* 'NPRX.INAN'; §7.4). In (3) and (4) we see verbal ANIMATE agreement with nouns denoting higher animates (e.g., mammals) and lower animates (e.g., amphibians, reptiles), respectively.

(2) **En**   **baqi**   Bunaq.
    person   NPRX.AN   Bunaq
    'That person is Bunaq.'   [Bk-15.006]

(3) *Asa Paran   Mau Paran   g-utu   **zap**   **g**-erel   mele,   **zon**=o*
    Asa Paran   Mau Paran   3-COM   dog   3AN-INS   walk   wild=AND
    zulo   ***g***-agal.
    civet   3AN-seek
    'Asa Paran with Mau Paran went walking, taking along dogs, looking for wild (pigs) and civets.'   [Bk-4.065]

(4) *G-otol   **keleq**   **ga**-lalin,   **tokoq**   **gi**-wit.*
    3AN-WITHOUT   frog   3AN-bring   gecko   3AN-fetch
    '(The children) without (their parents knowing) brought frogs (and) fetched geckos.'   [LB-4.201]

Whilst a noun belonging to the ANIMATE noun class is strongly tied to having an animate referent, ANIMATE agreement is not dependent on the sentience of the referent, but rather is a lexical property of the noun. Nouns referring to animates take ANIMATE agreement regardless of whether the referent is living or dead. Thus, in (5–6), although their referents are dead, as seen by the context, the ANIMATE nouns *en* 'person' and *zon* 'wild (pig)' take the ANIMATE determiner forms *bi* 'ART.AN' and *himo* 'CONTR.AN' (as opposed to *ba* 'ART.INAN' and *himo* 'CONTR.INAN'), respectively.

(5) **En**   **heser bi**   bei   g-utu   ti-ta   bolu   niq.
    person   dead   ART.AN   ancestor   3-COM   RECP-GL   united   NEG
    'The dead person is not together with his ancestors.'   [Bk-18.019]

(6) **Zon**   **himo**   heser   oa.
    wild   CONTR.AN   dead   IAM
    'The pig was already dead.'   [LB-4.134]

Finally, noun class is a category relevant to 3rd persons only; local (1st and 2nd) persons are not specified for noun class. As such, although the referents of 1st and 2nd

person pronouns are almost always animate and prototypically human, NPs headed by a 1st and 2nd person pronoun take INANIMATE determiner forms, as in (7) and (8).²

(7) **Neto roe** gi-ta zaga.
    1SG SPEC.INAN 3AN-GL watch.over
    'I watched over him.' [Bk-1.026]

(8) **Ei bare** teo gene man?
    2PL PROX.INAN where LOC come
    'Where have you here come from?' [LB-3.020]

By contrast, ANIMATE determiners are used with noun phrases headed by a 3rd person pronoun, as in (9).

(9) **Halaqi hitu bi** d-opil no d-oter gie.
    3PL seven ART.AN REFL-power LOC REFL-snatch PROSP
    'They tried with all their might to tear themselves away.' [Bk-6.051]

See §6.2.2 for more on pronoun–determiner combinations.

5.2.3 Nouns referring to inanimates

Nouns with inanimate referents are split between the INANIMATE and ANIMATE noun classes. That is, whilst all INANIMATE nouns have inanimate referents, some nouns with inanimate referents belong to the ANIMATE noun class. Although items of this kind do not form a very significant proportion of the class of nouns in Bunaq, included amongst them are many high-frequency nouns, such that their departure from the obvious semantic animacy principle underlying noun class assignment is very salient.

The assignment of nouns referring to inanimates to the ANIMATE noun class is not random. ANIMATE nouns with inanimate referents are not typically semantically isolated instances of the ANIMATE noun class, but rather cluster into sets with semantically similar members. And there is evidence to suggest that the assignment of inanimates to the ANIMATE noun class has a semantic basis. For one, children acquiring the language do not appear to have to learn the noun class of items individually.³ Additionally,

---

2 An alternative approach would be to say that 1st and 2nd person pronouns are specified as INANIMATE. This is not favoured here as it would mean positing a very limited and unprincipled exception to the otherwise exceptionless rule that animate referents belong to the ANIMATE noun class.
3 This is based on my own observations of noun class assignments amongst children. I lived in a household with five children between the ages of 6 and 16, and helped at the local pre-school that

loanwords are directly assigned to the same noun class independently by different speakers, both within and across dialects. For instance, the nouns *buku* 'book' (< Indonesian *buku* 'book' < Dutch *boek* 'book') in West Timorese Bunaq dialects and *libru* ~ *libur* 'book' (< Tetun *libru* 'book' < Portuguese *livro* 'book') in East Timorese Bunaq dialects are both assigned to the ANIMATE noun class (§5.2.3.4).

In the most general terms, assignment of inanimates to the ANIMATE class is based on "association": nouns whose inanimate referents are associated with the animate world may be assigned to the ANIMATE noun class. There are diverse ways in which an inanimate entity can be associated with animates and become part of the ANIMATE class. In Bunaq, the following associations have been observed:

(i) physical or behavioural resemblance to animates;
(ii) belonging to or consisting of animates;
(iii) being modified, controlled, or fixed in place by animates;
(iv) occupying an important role in the livelihood of animates;
(v) mythological connection to animates.

Any individual one or combination of these five different association types can be seen to play into the assignment of an inanimate to the ANIMATE noun class. However, noun class assignment by association is a guiding principle only, not an absolute; it does not explain all instances of ANIMATE noun class assignment for inanimate referents, nor why some inanimate referents are not assigned ANIMATE. What is more, an association which allows a noun to be assigned ANIMATE may be indirect: a semantic pattern in the assignment of ANIMATE to inanimate referents often appears to be the result of clustering around an initial member/set of members which has a direct association with animates (a phenomenon described, e.g., in Lakoff 1987).

In §5.2.3.1–§5.2.3.7, I look at the main semantic categories of ANIMATE nouns with inanimate referents and consider the basis of their association with animates. Since culture-specific abstractions must be seen as at least partly responsible for the classifications, it is best to think of the following discussion as an attempt to distill various aspects of the way in which the Bunaq taxonomise their environment.

5.2.3.1 Nouns referring to entities with animate-like properties

Nouns referring to entities displaying human-like or animal-like properties in either their form or manner of conduct belong to the ANIMATE noun class.

Association of this kind includes nouns referring to members of the spirit world such as: *melo* 'soul', *mugen* 'ghost', *ui* 'spirit', *muk gomo* 'earth spirit' (literally, 'earth owner'). Bunaq animist belief centres on the idea that spirits of the dead, both human and animal, occupy portions of their environment. The ANIMATE classification of

---

met once a week for children between the ages of 3 and 6. So I had ample opportunity to observe children's speech.

nouns denoting these referents is thus a reflection of their status as animate in the mortal world.

ANIMATE classification is also given to any item made in the image of an animate entity, such as *aitos* 'wooden/stone figure', *liqas* 'carving of human on house', and *hutus* 'weaving motif'. The ANIMATE classification of *hutus* 'weaving motif' is based on the fact that traditional weaving motifs depicted only animal figures, most typically lizards and geckos (cf. *hutus tokoq* 'gecko motif'). Modern floral themes in weaving motifs (e.g., *hutus paen*) are of recent European origin (Yeager and Jacobson 2002: 85). Although they lack the direct association with animates that is characteristic of the original weaving motifs, because they belong to the class of *hutus*, these motifs are still assigned to the ANIMATE class.

A final, high frequency, member of this semantic group is the ANIMATE noun *si* 'meat'. Meat is naturally associated with the animal it comes from and its ANIMATE classification reflects this association. In Bunaq we can talk of eating the meat of an animal, as in (10a) where the P is *si* 'meat' N$_{HEAD}$ with *sael* 'pig' as its N$_{MOD}$, or we can eat the animal, as in (10b) where the P is headed by *sael* 'pig'.

(10) a. En   g-utu   si   sael=na   gi-a.
        person 3-COM   meat.AN   pig.AN=FOC   3AN-eat
        '(He) would eat pig meat with people.'   [Bk-70.171]
    b. Sael   gi-wit,   en   g-utu   sael   baqi   gi-a.
        pig   3AN-buy   person   3-COM   pig.AN   NPRX.AN   3AN-eat
        '(He) would buy (the pig), (and) eat that pig with people.'   [Bk-70.172]

5.2.3.2 Nouns referring to edible plant cultivars

Whilst members of the plant kingdom are typically classified as INANIMATE in Bunaq, a small number of nouns referring to the edible products of cultivars belong to the ANIMATE noun class. Example (11) illustrates the different agreement patterns of ANIMATE *paqol* 'maize' and INANIMATE *ipi* 'rice'.

(11) Baqi   paqol   g-ota=ka,   ipi   h-ota=ka, ...
     NPRX.AN   maize.AN   3AN-plant=OR   rice.INAN 3INAN-plant=OR
     'They plant maize or (they) plant rice, ...'   [Bk-3.034]

Table 5.2 presents the most frequently occurring nouns for edible plant cultivars and how they divide between the ANIMATE and INANIMATE noun classes. A variety of factors appear to be behind the differential classification of edible cultivars. Immediately apparent is that cultivars of the ANIMATE noun class on the whole tend to be more recent introductions into Timor (cf. Fox 1991; Oliveira 2008). However, more broadly, the most significant appears to be the extent of a plant's domestication, the intensity of its agriculture, and its general importance as a crop. In the ANIMATE class are nouns referring to maize, potato, and pumpkin, foods which are at the centre of the diets of the Bunaq people and are the focus of agricultural production. By contrast, the crops of INANIMATE noun class items, such as taro and rice, are on the whole much less significant in the livelihoods of the Bunaq.

Other ANIMATE nouns, such as onions and papayas, are not such important food sources but are plants which do not grow wild in Timor, and whose presence must have resulted from human introduction and deliberate cultivation. By contrast, INANIMATE nouns, such as the tubers *me* and *telo*, are not typically cultivated but are found wild, while other INANIMATE nouns grow in a semiwild state and do not require replanting from year to year, such as bananas and mangoes, and, in the case of coconut and betel, readily self-multiply.

Table 5.2: ANIMATE – INANIMATE split in edible plant cultivars.

ANIMATE		INANIMATE	
paqol	'maize'	*balo*	'taro'
dila	'papaya'	*uor*	'leafy green, vegetable'
ope	'pumpkin, cucumber'	*mok*	'banana'
kulo	'jackfruit'	*hoza*	'coconut'
keliq	'soybean'	*ipi*	'rice (plant)'
goiga	'k.o. guava'	*zo*	'mango'
sekal	'potato'	*pao*	'legume spp.'
in	'onion'	*me*	'tuber sp., *Amorphophallus paeoniifolius*'
dikotel	'cassava'	*telo*	'tuber sp., *Tacca leontopetaloides*'
hoqi	'peanut'	*dik*	'tuber spp., *Dioscorea* spp.'
sabul	'orange'	*ho*	'legume, bean'
mura	'pomelo'	*molen*	'sago'
deloq	'lemon'	*ma*	'bamboo'
masin	'lime'	*molo*	'betel vine'

Citrus fruits all have ANIMATE classification in Bunaq, potentially arising out of a mythological association. In Bunaq folktales, *sabul* 'orange' represents women. In my corpus alone there are three separate stories in which oranges transform into women. This association appears to underlie the assignment of *sabul* 'orange' to the ANIMATE noun class, with the classification extended to other nouns referring to citrus on account of their similarity to oranges, although they do not themselves have a direct association with an animate. There are no INANIMATE nouns that refer to citrus fruits.

Bunaq systematically allows the reassignment of INANIMATE nouns referring to plants to the ANIMATE class where the reference is to a plant as a living organism. This is discussed in §5.2.4.3.

5.2.3.3 Nouns referring to items of human production

Items produced by humans are split between the ANIMATE and INANIMATE noun classes. Although there are many exceptions, the broad pattern of assignment appears to be that natural items, such as earth and wood, that are modified and/or controlled by humans tend to be classified as ANIMATE, while less human influenced things are generally INANIMATE. For instance, INANIMATE *hut* 'thatch' refers to a dried palm leaf still in its natural state before it is tied to a roof, while ANIMATE *esaq* 'palm leaf rib' denotes a palm leaf that has been stripped of its leaves. The latter ANIMATE noun is changed in form directly at the hands of a human, while the former INANIMATE noun retains its natural shape and is changed in form by the sun.

Table 5.3 presents some of the most common nouns illustrating the opposition in the classifications of items of human production. Included in the ANIMATE class are nouns referring to elements such as earth, wood, and plant matter, parts of the natural non-human world, which have been processed by humans into forms for their own use. By contrast, INANIMATE class nouns refer to cultural items which are inherently associated with the human world, including semantic fields such as food preparation, shelter, clothing, and metal tools.

Table 5.3: ANIMATE – INANIMATE split in goods of human production.

ANIMATE		INANIMATE	
hasan	'water drain, gutter'	*uer*	'pot (earthen/metal)'
kanu	'rice-paddy bank'	*bogeq*	'wooden bowl'
solo	'drain, gutter'	*suluq*	'spoon (wood/metal)'
keu	'stake, wedge'	*deu*	'house'
teuq	'ground stake'	*tazuq*	'door'
hequ	'whistle'	*tais*	'cloth'
kurus	'cross, crucifix'	*mun*	'rope'
kuteq	'spinning top'	*turiq*	'machete'
satan	'crossbeam'	*nut*	'k.o. metal hoe'
sabi	'key'	*taka*	'woven basket'
oe	'rattan'	*hoto*	'fire'
magap	'bamboo fire torch'	*wilik*	'fan'
wetin	'firesticks, torch'	*le*	'daylight'
barut	'candlenut (lamp)'	*guel*	'morning light'

One further group of nouns assigned to the ANIMATE class refers to small portable, modern appliances, such as *tifi* 'TV', *radio* 'radio', *kaset* 'cassette', and *kabel* 'electrical cable'. By contrast, large modern items are INANIMATE, e.g., *satelit* 'satellite dish', *genset* 'generator', *pesawat* 'aeroplane', etc. These words are all borrowed from Indonesian.

5.2.3.4 Nouns referring to oral and written forms of literature

Nouns referring to forms of oral literature and writing, including any implement involved in the activity of writing, are classified as ANIMATE, such as: *zapal* 'folktale', *libur por* 'bible' (literally, 'holy book'), *sejara* 'history', *carita* 'story', *surat* 'letter', *buku* 'book', *pena* 'pen'. We can see that many nouns of this class are borrowings from Indonesian. ANIMATE agreement for items of this set is illustrated in (12).

(12) Hot   baq   no   **zapal**   **ga**-sasi   niq.
      sun   noon   OBL   folktale.AN   3AN-say   NEG
      'During the day (we) don't tell folktales.'   [Bk-70.102]

The connection between the diverse elements of this class appears to stem from the fact that traditional forms of storytelling are closely associated with the animate entities that are characters in them. *Zapal* 'folktales' are associated with one or more animate referents and are typically named after them: for instance, *Zapal Suri Guloq* 'Story (of) Suri the Youngest', or *Zapal Bui o Mau* 'Story (of) Bui and Mau'. I suggest that due to the close association between folktales and their animate subjects, the noun *zapal* is classified as ANIMATE.

Similarly, the notion of history for the Bunaq people is centred around the identification of ancestors and description of their journeys (cf. Berthe 1972). This association between ancestors and the telling of history appears to underlie the ANIMATE class assignment of borrowed words in this semantic field – for instance, with Indonesian *sejara* 'history', illustrated in (13).

(13) Neto   **sejara**   tut   gie   **g**-apal   tanan   loi   niq.
      1SG   history.AN   past   3.POSS 3AN-open   too   good   NEG
      'I can't reveal too much of the history of the past.'   [Bk-67.021]

5.2.3.5 Nouns referring to items of clothing and jewellery

The total number of ANIMATE items in the domain of clothing and jewellery is small. Table 5.4 presents a complete list of ANIMATE items in the corpus identified for this domain with some representative examples from the INANIMATE class to illustrate the oppositions involved.

The split between ANIMATE and INANIMATE in the domain of clothing and jewellery is based upon boundness to the body. Items which are closely fitted to or around the body are classified as ANIMATE, whereas items which are open in form and which do not themselves grasp the body firmly are INANIMATE. In particular, items which are fixed around the waist are always ANIMATE. Thus, trousers and cloths that are fastened around the waist either with a belt or by means of being sewn closed or having their own fastening are ANIMATE. By contrast, clothing which remains unfastened at the waist such as shirts and open cloths that are folded and tucked in around the waist are INANIMATE.

The basis of the association between tightly fitting or fixed items and animates seems to be that they are physically fastened or bound tightly to an animate and are thus in a sense also animate. By indirect association, items which are used in fastening clothing and jewellery, such as buttons, zips, and belts, are also classified as ANIMATE.

Table 5.4: ANIMATE – INANIMATE split in clothing/jewellery.

ANIMATE nouns		INANIMATE nouns	
dikit	'ring'	kaebauk	'k.o. metal headdress'
kabata	'earring for men'	lesu	'k.o. metal headdress'
karubu	'earring for women'	peq	'necklace'
keke	'tight bracelet'	kabitun	'forearm clasp'
kacamata	'glasses'	luketon	'upper arm clasp'
boru / celana	'trousers'	lipa	'k.o. white ikat'
doq tiq	'cloth sewn in a tube'	kaluk	'pocket, bag'
bolas	'wide male belt'	jaket	'jacket'
butan	'button'	tais	'cloth'
tarik	'zip'	haru	'shirt, clothes'

5.2.3.6 Nouns referring to money and currency

Nouns denoting types of money and currency are classified as ANIMATE, such as: *hatak* 'gold coin', *dolar* 'dollar', *rupia* 'rupiah', *nota* 'bill', *doqit* 'cash', and *uang* 'money'. These nouns all appear to be borrowed either from Indonesian/Malay or Tetun. The noun *sasikun* 'hairpin' is assigned to the ANIMATE class, because hairpins are made from a *hatak* 'gold coin'. The ANIMATE classification of currency nouns is illustrated in (14), with *dolar* taking an ANIMATE determiner, and with *uang* taking ANIMATE agreement on *h-osok* '3INAN-receive'.

(14) **Dolar himo** tebe tuqal, neto **uang**
dollar.AN CONTR.AN return exchange 1SG money.AN
Indonesia gie **g**-osok.
Indonesia 3.POSS 3AN-receive
'Once those dollars are changed, I get Indonesian money.' [Bk-11.006]

The ANIMATE classification of currency nouns probably resulted from a general association between the cash economy and developed human culture. This is suggested by the fact that, while ANIMATE class items refer to introduced currencies, traditional forms of payment in Bunaq culture that pre-date the modern cash economy are classified as INANIMATE, such as: *tumel* 'metal' (but now also used to mean 'money'), *belak* 'silver chest plate', *tain* 'silver plate', *buleqen* 'gold, red', and *belis* 'silver, white'.

5.2.3.7 Nouns referring to rocks and hard items

Nouns referring to different types of rocks are classified as ANIMATE in Bunaq, for instance: *hol* 'stone, rock', *bosok* 'large rounded stone pile representing an ancestor', *mot* 'stone ritual area containing a *bosok*', *ari* 'grinding stone', and *bon* 'gaming stone made from a box bean'. This assignment is illustrated in (15).

(15) **Bon**   *baqi*   heser **gaqal**.
 box.bean.AN NPRX.AN dead all.AN
 'The gaming stones are all knocked over (lit., dead).'   [Bk-10.017]

In Bunaq mythology, the apical ancestors are believed to have turned into stone upon death, and rock features in the landscape are often identified as ancestral personages. *Mot* are stone ceremonial areas where rituals worshipping ancestors are carried out; they are not only icons for the lineage groups, the ancestors, and their descendants, but also typically contain several *bosok*, stones believed to represent various ancestors.[4] The mythological association between ancestral identities and stones appears to have meant that nouns referring to those stones are classified as ANIMATE, and so by extension are other nouns referring to stones.

5.2.4 Noun class reassignment

INANIMATE class nouns from a small number of semantic fields can occasionally be reassigned to the ANIMATE noun class in order to highlight a particular association between the referent and animacy.

5.2.4.1 Reassignment in reference to groups of animates

Nouns referring to lineage groups are typically INANIMATE, but can be construed as ANIMATE where emphasis is placed on the fact that the lineage group is composed of humans. Nouns showing this variation include *deu* 'house', *suku* 'lineage group',

---

[4] This is a feature of traditional religion across Timor, and multiple anthropological studies have recognised the importance of 'rock' in the ancestral religion of Timor (e.g., Fox 1989; Fox 2006; McWilliam 2006).

and *turunan* 'descent'. The examples in (16) illustrate the variation with *suku* 'lineage group'. In (16a), *suku* refers to the names of the lineage groups that the referent of *baqi* 'NPRX.AN' sought; the lack of ANIMATE agreement on *s-agal* '3INAN-seek' shows the INANIMATE classification of *suku*. In (16b), *suku* refers to the members of the lineage groups that had come to sit together; the form of the determiner *baqi* 'NPRX.AN' shows the ANIMATE classification.

(16) a. **En   gie   suku~suku,   baqi   s-agal.**
       person 3.POSS REDUP~lineage.group NPRX.AN 3INAN-seek
       'Those people's lineage groups, he sought.'   [Bk-70.023]
   b. **Suku   baqi   mit   soq   oa.**
       lineage.group NPRX.AN sit   SEQ   IAM
       'Those lineage group (members) now sat.'   [Bk-23.018]

Agreement variation of this kind is also observed in reference to vehicles that can carry a group of people, such as *bis* 'bus', *oto* 'car', and *kreta* 'train'. These nouns are typically INANIMATE, as in (17a), but are very occasionally reassigned ANIMATE, as in (17b), when there is emphasis on the vehicle containing a collection of human individuals.

(17) a. **Bis   ba   mele   oa.**
       bus   ART.INAN walk   IAM
       'The bus is gone.'
   b. **Bis   bi   mele   oa.**
       bus   ART.AN   walk   IAM
       'The bus (carrying people) is gone.'   [Not.07-03]

5.2.4.2 Reassignment in reference to controlled natural elements
In §5.2.3.3 we saw that nouns referring to items made of natural elements had a tendency to belong to the INANIMATE noun class, whereas things made of naturally occurring products that are subject to greater manipulation by humans were classified as ANIMATE. There are also instances where an INANIMATE noun is reassigned to the ANIMATE noun class when humans have modified the referent or brought it under their control in some way.

The two pairs of sentences in (18) and (19) illustrate the contrasting classifications possible for the nouns *g-iri* '3AN-leg' and *il* 'water'. In (18a) *g-iri* '3AN-leg' refers to the leg of a human individual and is classified as INANIMATE, while in (18b) it refers to the supporting posts of a house and is ANIMATE.[5]

---

[5] Note that Bunaq does not systematically use body-part nouns in reference to parts of inanimate things. *G-iri* '3-leg' is one of the few nouns used with both animate (human or animal) possessors and inanimate possessors (tables, houses, traps, etc.).

(18) a. **G-iri baqa** tugal.
     3-leg NPRX.INAN break
     'That leg of his was broken.' [Bk-1.024]
   b. **G-iri** hiloqon **himo** **g**-al.
     3-leg two CONTR.AN 3AN-erect
     '(We) erect the two legs (of the trap).' [Bk-32.008]

Similarly, in (19a) *il* 'water' refers to water in a bucket drawn from a river and is INANIMATE. However, where directed through irrigation channels, *il* 'water' is treated as ANIMATE. For example, in (19b) we see ANIMATE agreement on the verb with *il* 'water', because here it is being used to irrigate a rice paddy.

(19) a. Pana gol uen=na rie **il** kokoq no
     female small one=FOC REFL.POSS water bucket OBL
     ba **g**-ege.
     ART.INAN 3AN-give
     '(There was) one girl who gave him the water in her bucket.' [Bk-6.026]
   b. Ipi pelek haqal soq=bu, i **il**
     rice plant finished SEQ=GIVEN 1PL.INCL water
     ga-tama oa.
     3AN-bring.in IAM
     'Once the rice is all planted, then we bring in the water.' [Bk-51.018]

A significant factor contributing to the reassignment to the ANIMATE noun class appears to be not simply human control, but the fixing in place of an item. That is, items which are fixed in place by humans and are immovable are typically treated as ANIMATE, while comparable or component items made from the same materials that can move freely are INANIMATE. For example, *tazuq* 'door, doorway' is an INANIMATE noun in Bunaq, but when we look at its component parts, we see an ANIMACY split: *tazuq nor* (lit., door leaf) referring to the opening and closing part of a door is INANIMATE, while *tazuq gamal* (lit., male door) referring to the doorframe is ANIMATE. A similar divide in ANIMACY between clothing items that were loose fitting (INANIMATE) and clothing and other worn items that were fastened (ANIMATE) was seen in §5.2.3.5.

5.2.4.3 Reassignment in reference to plants

In §5.2.3.2 we saw that Bunaq nouns referring to plants are split between those assigned to the INANIMATE class and those assigned to the ANIMATE class. In fact, nouns referring to plants that are normally INANIMATE can be treated as grammatically ANIMATE when the speaker wants to particularly emphasise the semantic animacy of the referent, that is, that the referent plant is a living, growing organism. The reassignment of INANIMATE nouns referring to plants is often manipulated to create various subtle discourse effects.

Consider the agreement forms found with the Bunaq noun *mok* 'banana' in examples (20) and (21). In its default assignment, *mok* is INANIMATE, as can be observed in the inflection on the goal-marking verbal postposition in (20). This contrasts with the default ANIMATE assignment shown by *dikotel* 'cassava' later in the same utterance.

(20) En   gie   **mok**=sa   **a-ta**   g-in   gie,   en
     person 3.POSS   banana=EVEN   3INAN-GL   3AN-tie   PROSP   person
     gie   **dikotel** **gi-ta**   apa   g-in   gie,   kura   g-in   gie.
     3.POSS   cassava   3AN-GL   cow   3AN-tie   PROSP   horse   3AN-tie   PROSP
     '(They) will just tie it up to someone else's banana (tree), (or) tie up their cow or horse to someone's cassava (tree).' [Bk-19.023]

The examples in (21), by contrast, show *mok* 'banana' used throughout with ANIMATE agreement. In doing so, the speaker emphasises that the banana tree in question is alive. This is important for the story's plot, as Frog goes on to plant the tree and get fruit from it, much to the chagrin of Monkey.

(21) a. *Bukuq~bukuq   homo   ni,   nare-wen,   ilok*
        REDUP~play   CONTR.INAN   OBL   long.time-MODER   flood
        mete   zol   no   sai   ba,   mok   bul   uen
        NOW   river   OBL   exit   ART.INAN   banana   base   one
        ***gu-surut**,   **g-erel**   wil   halali   go-totok   no.*
        3AN-sweep.along   3AN-INS   come.LOW   3DU   3AN-row   OBL
        'After (Monkey and Frog) had been playing for a while, a flood rose in the river and swept down a banana tree, bringing it down to a position alongside the two of them.'   [OrelKeleqMoenHoqon-031]
     b. *Homo=na,   Bei   Keleq   sikit   honal*
        CONTR.INAN=FOC   grandfather   frog   leap   go.LEVEL
        *ba,   **mok**   bi   **ga-sarat**,   **g-erel***
        ART.INAN   banana   ART.AN   3AN-pull   3AN-INS
        teten   a-ta   saqe.
        dry.land   3INAN-GL   ascend
        'Then, when the Frog leaped across, he pulled the banana tree over and brought it up onto dry land.'   [OrelKeleqMoenHoqon-034]

The Bunaq noun *hotel*, meaning variously 'tree' or 'wood', displays particularly variable ANIMACY assignment, but it follows the broad pattern described already for *mok* 'banana'. When the referent is growing, *hotel* is assigned to the ANIMATE noun class, as in (22). When the referent is dead or is a part separated from the living tree, *hotel* is assigned to the INANIMATE noun class. We see this, for instance, in (23) where *hotel* refers to old, fallen wood and in (24) where *hotel* refers to green, freshly chopped wood.

(22) **Hotel himo** g-iep.
    tree CONTR.AN 3AN-chop
    '(They) chop those trees down.' [Bk-3.010]

(23) Halaqi goniqon die **hotel ba** dele tebe.
    3PL three REFL.POSS wood ART.INAN INS return
    'The three of them return with their own wood.' [LB5.013]

(24) **Hotel**=na wit=o, **h**-ini ugar minak.
    wood=FOC fetch=AND 3INAN-call green complete
    '(She) fetched wood and (her mother) said it was all green.' [Bk-6.004]

The assignment of noun class to *hotel* is also used to create effects more subtle than those captured in English by the independent lexemes 'tree' and 'wood'. In (25) a child in despair addresses the trees surrounding him as he searches for the parts of his mother's loom: in (25a) *hotel* is treated as INANIMATE, but then in (25b) it is treated as ANIMATE. According to native speaker introspections about this variation, the initial INANIMATE classification implies that the child addresses the trees but does not believe that they can hear him, while the later ANIMATE assignment suggests that they are sentient and that the child expects a response to his imploration.

(25) a. **Hotel ba** g-o die eme gie
       tree ART.INAN 3-SRC REFL.POSS mother 3.POSS
       atis=o nolu sura.
       loom.bar=AND weaving.sword ask
       '(The child) asked the trees about his mother's loom bar and weaving swords.' [Bk-49.010]
    b. Atis=o nola sura, **hotel bi**
       loom.bar=AND weaving.sword ask tree ART.AN
       g-ege baqa goet on, ...
       3AN-BEN NPRX.INAN LIKE DO
       'In asking about the loom bar and weaving swords, (he) spoke like this to the trees, ...' [Bk-49.011]

5.3 N$_{MOD}$ modifiers of N$_{HEAD}$s

An N$_{MOD}$ is a noun which modifies an N$_{HEAD}$, describing a property of it, such as shape, sex, or size. An N$_{MOD}$ occurs directly following the N$_{HEAD}$. An N$_{MOD}$ cannot occur without an explicit N$_{HEAD}$. Examples of an N$_{MOD}$ modifying an N$_{HEAD}$ are:

(26) a. *en   pana*
       person   female
       'female person'
    b. *sael   zon*
       pig   wild.animal
       'wild pig'

Unlike NN compounds (§3.2.1), multiple N$_{MOD}$s conjoined by =*o* 'AND' can modify a single N$_{HEAD}$. Examples of multiple N$_{MOD}$s are provided in (27).

(27) a. *en   [pana=o   mone]*$_{MOD}$
       person female=AND   male
       'females and males'
    b. *sael   [zon=o   hina]*$_{MOD}$
       pig   wild.animal=AND   domestic.animal
       'wild and domestic pigs'

That N$_{MOD}$s can be conjoined with =*o* 'AND' shows that N$_{MOD}$s are not simply a modifying N in an NN compound. Instead it indicates that N$_{MOD}$s occur on the same syntactic level as verbal modifiers, since they can also be conjoined in this manner (§5.7.2).

5.3.1 Inalienably possessed nouns as N$_{MOD}$s

A few bound nouns (§9.3) are used in their 3rd person form as an N$_{MOD}$. For instance, *g-ol* '3AN-child' in (28a) and *g-amal* '3AN-male animal' in (29a) must be in the 3rd person form inflection; the other person inflections in (28b) and (29b) are ungrammatical.

(28) a. *mone   g-ol*
       male   3AN-child
       'boy' or 'small man'
    b. **mone   n-ol*
       male   1EXCL-child

(29) a. *sie   g-amal*
       chicken   3AN-male.animal
       'rooster' (lit., 'male chicken')
    b. **sie   Ø-amal*
       chicken   1INCL/2-male.animal

The use of inalienably possessed nouns as an N_MOD is distinguishable in a number of ways from possessive constructions in which the inalienably possessed noun is the N_HEAD and the preceding noun a possessor. Firstly, constructions in which an inalienably possessed noun is an N_MOD and those in which it is an N_HEAD have different semantics. Compare the examples in (30) below representing identical sequences of the words *ama* and *g-ol*. The N_HEAD N_MOD sequence in (30a) literally means 'small father' and is a kin term denoting 'father's younger brother', while the PSR N_HEAD in (30b) denotes the possessive relationship 'father's child'.

(30)   N_HEAD   N_MOD
    a.   *ama*   *g-ol*
       father   3AN-child
       'father's younger brother'
       PSR   N_HEAD
    b.   *ama*   *g-ol*
       father   3AN-child
       'father's child'

Secondly, prosodically an N_HEAD is more prominent than an N_MOD or a possessor. In (31a) the first element *ama* 'father' is the N_HEAD and is realised with a higher pitch and greater intensity, while the second element *g-ol* '3AN-child' is an N_MOD characterised by lower pitch and intensity. In (31b) the second element *g-ol* '3AN-child' is the N_HEAD realised with a higher pitch and greater intensity, while the first element *ama* 'father' is a possessor cross-referenced by the 3rd person animate prefix on the N_HEAD and is lower in pitch and intensity.

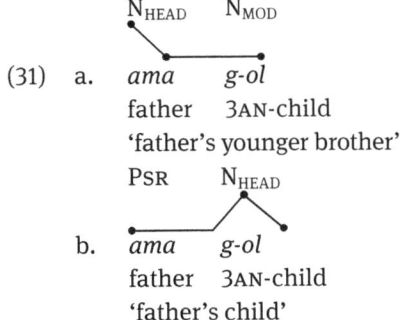

(31)   a.   *ama*   *g-ol*
       father   3AN-child
       'father's younger brother'

    b.   *ama*   *g-ol*
       father   3AN-child
       'father's child'

Thirdly, an N_HEAD controls agreement, which neither an N_MOD nor a PSR does. Compare the agreement patterns shown by the NPs containing *g-ol* '3AN-child' in (32). In (32a) the N_HEAD is the INANIMATE noun *turiq* 'knife', showing INANIMATE agreement on the determiner *homo* 'CONTR.INAN', while in (32b) the ANIMATE N_HEAD, *en* 'person', triggers ANIMATE agreement on the determiner *roi* 'SPEC.AN'. By contrast, in (32c) we have a possessive construction in which INANIMATE *iskola* 'school' is a possessor cross-referenced by the prefix on *g-ol* '3AN-child', the N_{HEAD}. In accordance with its N_{HEAD} status, *g-ol* '3AN-child' controls agreement, as shown by the ANIMATE agreement on the verb, *sura* 'ask'.

(32) a. [Gie   turiq_{HEAD}   g-ol_{MOD}   homo]_{NP}   ret golaq   topol.
      3.POSS   machete.INAN   3AN-child   CONTR.INAN   all.alone   fall
      'His knife fell all on its own.'   [Bk-1.043]
   b. Nego   on=na   [en_{HEAD}   g-ol_{MOD}   roi]_{NP}   topol?
      what   DO=FOC   person.AN   3AN-child   SPEC.AN   fall
      'Why did this child fall?'   [Bk-1.034]
   c. Baqi   [iskola_{PSR}   g-ol_{HEAD}]_{NP}   gu-sura.
      NPRX.AN   school.INAN   3AN-child   3AN-ask
      'He asked for a school's child.' i.e., 'He propositioned a school child.'
                                                                              [Bk-21.003]

Elsewhere in this work, where an inalienably possessed noun is used as an N_{MOD} the possessor prefix is not segmented. So, for instance, the N_{MOD} *gol* is glossed 'small', while the homophonous N_{HEAD} is glossed *g-ol* '3AN-child'. As an N_{HEAD}, *g-ol* '3AN-child' can occur in any of its person inflections and does not have the meaning 'small'. Note also that *gol* is also the only N_{MOD} which is attested as being able to follow another N_{MOD}, as in (33).

(33) Baqi   [en_{HEAD}   pana_{MOD}   gol_{MOD}   bi]_{NP}   g-utu   cier   gie.
     NPRX.AN   person   female   small   ART.AN   3-COM   sleep   PROSP
     'He wanted to sleep with the girl (lit., small female person).'   [Bk-21.004]

5.3.2 An agreeing N_{MOD}

Niat is a temporal noun denoting 'earliest time, beginning', as in (34) where it appears in a PP headed by *no* 'OBL':

(34) Niat   no   halali   ta-tara   oa.
     earliest   OBL   3DU   RECP-know   IAM
     'In the beginning the two of them would get to know one another.' [Bk-38.001]

Niat can also appear as an N_{MOD} where it agrees in ANIMACY with the N_{HEAD}; it is the only N_{MOD} that shows agreement in this way. Compare the agreement patterns shown by the NPs containing *niat* 'earliest' in (35). In (35a) the N_{HEAD} is the INANIMATE noun *misa* 'mass' and is modified by the N_{MOD} *niat* 'earliest' which does not show any agreement with the N_{HEAD}. In (35b) where the N_{HEAD} is the ANIMATE noun *kaqa* 'older brother', *niat* 'earliest' takes the ANIMATE prefix *gV-* '3AN-' (see §2.5.1.3 on the metathesis shown by this noun).

(35) a. Misa   niat   iskola   g-ol   g-ege.
        mass   earliest   school   3AN-child   3AN-give
        'The earliest mass is given to the school children.'   [Bk-34.077]
    b. Nie   kaqa   g-inat   nie   eme
       1EXCL.POSS   older.brother   3AN-earliest   1EXCL.POSS   mother
       g-olep   no.
       3AN-abdomen   OBL
       'My oldest brother was in my mother's tummy.'   [Bk-29.067]

5.4 Attributive verbs and relative clauses

Attributive verbs and relative clauses (RCs) are modifiers of the N$_{HEAD}$ within the NP. While attributive verbs are individual lexemes, RCs are clauses which modify the N$_{HEAD}$. There are two types of RC in Bunaq: non-restrictive RCs (§5.4.1), and restrictive RCs (§5.4.2). NPs of almost any role can be relativised on; §5.4.3 discusses the few restrictions on the 'accessibility' of participants of different roles to the head position within an RC and the distribution of the different RC types across them.

5.4.1 Attributive verbs and non-restrictive relative clauses

Attributive verbs and non-restrictive RCs do not aid in the identification of the referent of the head, but only provide information about it, fulfilling the function of adjectives in other languages (cf. §3.3.1 on the absence of an adjectival class in Bunaq). In some respects, there is little to distinguish an attributive verb from a non-restrictive RC in Bunaq. An attributive verb could in fact be seen as a non-restrictive RC, albeit a simple one, consisting of a single word. I posit two different modifying slots to accommodate the fact that if an N$_{HEAD}$ is modified by a simple verb and a clause then the simple verb must come first. Compare the grammaticality of the NPs in (36).

(36) a. zap   [guzu]$_{VATTR}$ [mar   gene]$_{RC}$ baqi
        dog   black   garden   LOC   NPRX.AN
        'those black dogs in the garden'
    b. *zap   [mar   gene]$_{RC}$ [guzu]$_{VATTR}$ baqi
        dog   garden   LOC   black   NPRX.AN

Where two simple verbs appear modifying a single N$_{HEAD}$, I regard the first as the attributive verb and the second as an RC. This analysis finds support in that, as with a simple verbal attribute plus a non-restrictive RC, the second verb has scope over the N_{HEAD} and the V_{ATTR} (36c) in the same way as the RC does in (36a).

    c.   zap   [guzu]$_{VATTR}$ [hiloqon]$_{RC}$ baqi
        dog   black   two   NPRX.AN
        'those two black dogs'

Where a modifier consists of more than one word, I regard it as a non-restrictive relative clause. Examples are given in (37) and (38). In (37) the RC is a possessive predicate (§4.3.3), while in (38) it is a locative postpositional predicate (§4.3.2).

(37)   [Mak-leqat$_{HEAD}$ [soron   goniqil   gie]$_{RC}$]$_{NP}$ go-poi   gie.
      overseer   land.division four   3.POSS   3AN-choose PROSP
      '(You) are going to elect the overseers from the four areas.'   [Bk-19.026]

(38)   Eli   [zipil$_{HEAD}$ [mar   g-ebu   no]$_{RC}$]$_{NP}$ ini   naq!
      2DU   garden.cuttings garden 3AN-bottom OBL   burn   PRIOR
      'You two go burn the leaves which are at the bottom of the garden!'   [LB2.019]

With both a verbal attribute and a non-restrictive RC, the N_{HEAD} may be elided. We see this with a verbal attribute in (39) and (40), and with a non-restrictive relative clause in (41) and (42).

(39)   Hele   [Ø$_{HEAD}$ [hosu]$_{VATTR}$]$_{NP}$ hati?
      perhaps   other   exist
      'Perhaps there is another (thing)?'   [Bk-44.014]

(40)   Adat   gie,   [Ø$_{HEAD}$ [hiloqon]$_{VATTR}$]$_{NP}$ mit, . . .
      tradition BECAUSE   two   sit
      'Because of tradition, two (people) would sit, . . .'   [Bk-38.070]

(41)   [Mete   Ø$_{HEAD}$ [rie   rale]$_{RC}$ bi]$_{NP}$ ola   gene
      NOW   REFL.POSS speak   ART.AN   LOW   LOC
      r-obon   heser   haqal.
      REFL-hang   dead   finished
      'The (one mentioned just) now talking of himself hanged himself dead down
      there.'   [Bk-23.045]

(42)   [Ø$_{HEAD}$ [Ate   gene]$_{RC}$ roi]$_{NP}$=na   toek   ta-tara   niq   taq, . . .
            far   LOC   SPEC.AN=FOC talk   RECP-know   NEG   CONT
      'Those (people) at a distance don't know each other's language yet, . . .'
                                                                                              [Bk-15.013]

5.4.2 Restrictive relative clauses

A restrictive RC functions to identify the referent in question, restricting the noun's scope of reference to a single entity or set of entities.

The head of a restrictive RC occurs at the front of the RC marked with the restrictive focus enclitic =*na* 'FOC' (§4.7.4.2.3). As with non-restrictive RCs, the head is gapped, that is, is missing from inside the RC itself. Unlike non-restrictive RCs, restrictive RCs cannot be headless. The structure of the restrictive RC is presented in (43).

(43) Restrictive RC structure
 N_{HEAD}=*na* [...]_{RC} (DET)

Some examples of restrictive RCs are given below. In (44) and (45) the head of the RC has the S and the P role in the RC, respectively. In (46) the RC has a postpositional predicate.

(44) [*En*_{HEAD}=*na*   [*talu*   *kororoq*]_{RC}]_{NP}   *tara*   *niq*.
 person=FOC   gamble   cheer   know   NEG
 'People who gamble merrily don't know'   [Bk-23.037]

(45) [*U*_{HEAD}=*na*   [*nei*   *h-ozep*]_{RC}   *baqa*]_{NP}   *hot*   *mil*
 herbaceous.plant=FOC   1PL.EXCL   3INAN-cut   NPRX.INAN   sun   DUR
 sabtu   *no=na*   *oto*   *rele*   *tula*.
 Saturday   OBL=FOC   car   INS   transport
 'The grass which we cut (we) transported on Saturday with the car.'   [Bk-12.015]

(46) [*Keke*_{HEAD}=*na*   [*en*   *heser*   *g-on*   *no*]_{RC}   *bi*]_{NP}   *kasu*   *oa*.
 bracelet=FOC   person   dead   3AN-hand   OBL   ART.AN   remove   IAM
 'The bracelet which was on the hand of the dead person is now removed.'
 [Bk-18.009]

The head of a restrictive RC may be an interrogative (§3.5.2); RCs headed by an interrogative are never non-restrictive. In (47) *nego* 'what' is the RC head and has the P role in the RC. In (48) *cio* (~*sio*) 'who' is the head of the RC and has the A role in the RC.

(47) [*Nego*_{HEAD}=*na*   [*i*   *Gewal*   *gene*   *t-erel*   *h-oqon*]_{RC}
 what=FOC   1PL.INCL   Gewal   LOC   RECP-INS   3INAN-do
 ba]_{NP}   *hani*   *r-oenik*.
 ART.INAN   PROH   3INAN-forget
 'Don't forget what we did in Gewal.'   [Bk-14.06]

(48) Tiap malam [sio_HEAD=na [teqa ikut niq]_RC]_NP g-ue.
every evening who=FOC pray follow NEG 3AN-hit
'Every evening, whoever doesn't go to prayers is hit.' [Bk-30.076]

5.4.3 NP accessibility to relativisation

Figure 5.3 represents the noun phrase Accessibility Hierarchy (AH), an implicational scale that "expresses the relative accessibility to relativisation of NP positions in a simplex main clause" (Keenan and Comrie 1977: 66). The AH predicts that if an NP of a particular role is accessible to relativisation, then NPs higher on the hierarchy (i.e., to the left) are also accessible to relativisation.

SUBJECT > OBJECT > INDIRECT OBJECT > OBLIQUE > GENITIVE

Figure 5.3: The Noun Phrase Accessibility Hierarchy.

In Bunaq, there are no restrictions on the relativisation of arguments (S/A, P/R, or T of verbal clauses) corresponding to 'subject', 'object', and 'indirect object' in Keenan and Comrie's (1977) terms. In the following sections, I look at restrictions on the relativisation of the Bunaq equivalents of Keenan and Comrie's "oblique" and "genitive". Bunaq has several categories of NP equivalent to "oblique": unmarked oblique NPs (§5.4.3.1), NP complements of verbal postpositions (§5.4.3.2), and NP complements of postpositions (§5.4.3.3). "Genitive" corresponds to Bunaq NPs encoding possessors (§5.4.3.4). We will see that the line for NP accessibility to relativisation in Bunaq falls to the right of NP complements of verbal postpositions and to the left of possessor NPs, with the NP complements of different postpositions behaving differently, as represented in Figure 5.4.

CORE ARG > OBLIQUE ARG > COMP OF VPP > ‖COMP OF PP‖> PSR

Figure 5.4: The Bunaq NP Accessibility Hierarchy.

5.4.3.1 Unmarked obliques as RC heads

A participant with an unmarked oblique argument function (defined in §4.2.4) in an RC may be the head of an RC, either restrictive or non-restrictive. In (49) the unmarked goal oblique *kura* 'horse' of the RC predicate *saqe* 'ascend' is the head of the restrictive RC. In (50) the unmarked locative oblique *nawa* 'head basket' of the RC predicate *kaqe* 'fill' is the head of a non-restrictive RC.

(49) [Kura_HEAD=na [neto saqe]_RC bi]_NP he laun los.
horse=FOC 1SG ascend ART.AN run fast very
'The horse that I mounted runs really fast.' [Not-01.07]

(50) [Nawa_{HEAD}   [paqol   kaqe]_{RC}   homo]_{NP}   h-aziq.
    head.basket   maize   fill   CONTR.INAN   3INAN-disappear
    'The head baskets filled with maize have disappeared.'   [Not-01.07]

5.4.3.2 NP complements of verbal postpositions as RC heads

The complements of verbal postpositions (§3.6.1) can also occur as the heads of non-restrictive (51) and restrictive (52) RCs. In both examples, the RC head is the gapped NP complement of the goal-marking verbal postposition *a-ta* '3INAN-GL'.

(51) [Hik_{HEAD}   [i   a-ta   mit]_{RC}   bare]_{NP}   h-azal   oa.
    path   1PL.INCL   3INAN-GL   sit   PROX.INAN   3INAN-see   IAM
    '(We) now see this path we are sitting at.'   [Bk-23.064]

(52) [Sirubisu_{HEAD}=na   [nei   a-ta   sai]_{RC}   baqa]_{NP}
    work=FOC   1PL.EXCL   3INAN-GL   go.out   NPRX.INAN
    h-ini   apa   g-ege   u   h-ozep.
    3INAN-call   cow   3AN-BEN   herbaceous.plant   3INAN-cut
    'The work that we found involved (lit., was called) cutting grass for cows.'
    [Bk-12.004]

5.4.3.2 NP complements of postpositions as RC heads

Where the complement of a locative postposition, either *gene* 'LOC' or *no* 'OBL' (§3.5.6), is the head of an RC, the postposition is deleted in the RC. Example (53a) represents a clause with a locative postpositional predicate with an NP complement, while (53b) presents a clause in which the locative NP of (53a) is the head of an RC. It can be seen that on relativisation the locative NP is extracted out of the RC to a position at its front, while the postposition is deleted. Context serves to disambiguate the role of the locative encoding NP in the RC. RCs of this kind can also be non-restrictive, as in (53c).

(53) a.   *Paqol   meja   no   lai.*
        maize   table   OBL   lie
        'The maize was lying on the table.'
    b.   *Yati   [meja_{HEAD}=na   [paqol   lai]_{RC}   ba]_{NP}   h-ini   late.*
        Yati   table=FOC   maize   lie   ART.INAN   3INAN-CAUS   bad
        'Yati broke the table (on) which the maize was lying.'
    c.   *Yati   [meja_{HEAD}   [paqol   lai]_{RC}   ba]_{NP}   h-ini   late.*
        Yati   table   maize   lie   ART.INAN   3INAN-CAUS   bad
        'Yati broke the table the maize was lying (on).'   [Not-07.01]

The similative postposition, *goet* 'LIKE', does not allow the relativisation of its complement at all. In (54a) the similative postposition heads the predicate. In (54b) we see that it is not possible to relativise on *domba* 'sheep', the NP complement of *goet* 'LIKE' in (54a); rather, *domba* 'sheep' must be the 'subject' of the non-verbal RC in order for (54b) to be grammatical.

(54) a. *Markus domba goet.*
    Markus sheep LIKE
    'Markus is like a sheep.'
  b. [*Domba*_{HEAD}(=*na*)] [*Markus goet*]_{RC}]_{NP} *heser.*
    sheep(=FOC)   Markus   LIKE   dead
    'The sheep which is like Markus is dead.', not *'The sheep which Markus is like is dead.' [Not-09.01]

5.4.3.4 Possessors as RC heads

Functionally equivalent to 'GENITIVE' in Keenan and Comrie's AH hierarchy are Bunaq NP encoding possessors. Possessors are of two types in Bunaq: indirect (§9.2) and direct (§9.3). There are no instances in the corpus of the possessor of an indirectly possessed noun or a directly possessed noun being the head of an RC. In elicitation also, speakers invariably rejected attempts to relativise possessors for both restrictive and non-restrictive RCs, as illustrated in (55).

(55) a. *[*Mone*_{HEAD}(=*na*)] [*gie reu koen*]_{RC} *bi*]_{NP} *Atambua mal.*
    man=FOC   3.POSS house nice   ART.AN   Atambua go
    'The man whose house is nice went to Atambua.'
  b. *[*Mone*_{HEAD}(=*na*)] [*neto gu-bul pak*]_{RC} *bi*]_{NP} *heser oa.*
    man=FOC   1SG 3AN-head chop   ART.AN   dead   IAM
    'The man whose head I struck is dead.' [Not-09.01]

5.5 Indefiniteness marking

Indefiniteness marking is not obligatory in the Bunaq NP, but indefiniteness can be signalled with: (i) the numeral *uen* 'one' (§5.5.1), and (ii) the non-specific indefinite marker *bun* 'INDEF' (§5.5.2). Both are used adnominally, but *uen* 'one' can also be used pronominally. More common as indefinite pronouns are the interrogatives *nego* 'what' and *tuen~tuen* 'how much' (§3.5.2), and the noun *en* 'person' (discussed in §5.5.1 also).

5.5.1 *uen* 'one'

The Bunaq numeral *uen* 'one' is used in the expression of specific indefiniteness in the context of a new participant being introduced into the narrative. *Uen* marks an N$_{HEAD}$ referring to the new participant on its first mention in a text when it persists in the subsequent discourse. Thus, in (56) the N$_{HEAD}$ *en* 'person' referring to the participant at the centre of the sun and the wind's competition is initially introduced with *uen* 'one' (56a), but in its subsequent mention in (56b) the referent of *en* 'person' is tracked with a demonstrative. A noun referring to a non-topical entity, such as *tais* 'cloth' in (56), will not be introduced with *uen* 'one'.

(56) a. **En uen** man   tais   rele ru-hukut.
       person one   come cloth INS   REFL-wrap
       'A person came along wrapped up in a blanket.'   [Bk-16.002]
   b. Bel   halali hot   t-ege   sasi,   sio=na   **en**
      wind   3DU   sun   RECP-BEN say   who=FOC   person
      bari   g-ini   tais   h-apal,   baqi=na   solat   lesin.
      PROX.AN   3AN-CAUS cloth 3AN-open   NPRX.AN=FOC strong   more
      'The sun and the wind said to each other, whoever makes this person take off his blanket, he is the stronger.'   [Bk-16.003]

Another example of the new participant-introducing function of *uen* is given in (57), which presents the first three utterances of a narrative. In (57a), the speaker introduces the subject matter 'a problem' using *uen* to mark the N$_{HEAD}$ *masala* 'problem'. In its subsequent mention in (57b) *masala* is then marked with a demonstrative. When the topic changes to a new participant in (57c), *uen* is used for the first mention of the referent, but then again, the demonstrative is used in its subsequent mention.

(57) a. Erenoq   **masala uen** hati.
       yesterday problem one   exist
       'Yesterday there was a problem.'   [Bk-21.001]
   b. **Masala baqa**   huqe   tas   mil   Gewal   gene.
      problem NPRX.INAN   HERE   village inside Gewal   LOC
      'The problem was here within the village of Gewal.'   [Bk-21.002]
   c. **En   mone   uen**, **baqi**   mal   en   iskola   g-ol
      person male   one   NPRX.AN   go   person school   3AN-child
      gu-sura.
      3AN-ask
      'There was a man, he went and propositioned a school girl.'   [Bk-21.003]

Uen can also be used pronominally in indefinite contexts where a human referent is uniquely identified. For example, in (58) and (59) *uen* 'one' occurs without an N$_{\text{HEAD}}$ to denote a specific but unidentified human referent, in the manner of the English pronoun 'someone', who is mentioned only once in the discourse.

(58) **Uen**   gie   tazuq   gene   tama.
      one   3.POSS   door   LOC   enter
      '(She) went into someone's house.'   [Bk-43.030]

(59) **Uen**   g-ini   mal   matas   mil   gi-wit.
      one   3AN-CAUS   go   old   COLL   3AN-fetch
      'Someone was made to go fetch the parents.'   [Bk-1.026]

In its pronominal use, *uen* is similar, but not identical, in meaning to the indefinite pronominal use of the noun *en* 'person'. Compare the two utterances in (60). With *uen* 'one', reference is to just a single person and implies that the speaker has some knowledge of the referent, while the use of *en* 'person' is vaguer as to the identity of the referent.

(60) a. *Pana*   baqi   **uen**   gie   mone   g-utu   cier.
         woman   NPRX.AN   one   3.POSS   man   3-COM   sleep
         'The woman slept with someone's (one person's) husband.'
      b. *Pana*   baqi   **en**   gie   mone   g-utu   cier.
         woman   NPRX.AN   person   3.POSS   man   3-COM   sleep
         'The woman slept with someone's (some person's) husband.'   [FB-090121]

5.5.2 *bun* 'INDEF'

Bun 'INDEF' is a dedicated marker of non-specific indefiniteness in the NP. Syntactically, *bun* differs from *uen* in that while *uen* can appear independently without any other NP element, *bun* never does. Semantically, its use implies that either the speaker or the hearer lacks knowledge as to the precise identity of the referent. The difference between the two indefiniteness markers in Bunaq can be illustrated with the contrastive utterances in (61). Whereas the use of *uen* 'one' with *hot mil* 'day' in (61a) implies that the speaker has a particular day in mind, *bun* 'INDEF' in (61b) signals that the speaker does not know precisely what day it was that the people departed.

(61) a. **Hot**   **mil**   **uen**,   halaqi   mal   mele   liol   liol.
         sun   DUR   one   3PL   go   walk   continue   continue
         'One (particular) day, they left and kept walking.'

b. **Hot mil bun,** halaqi mal mele liol liol.
   sun DUR INDEF 3PL go walk continue continue
   'One day (precise day not known), they left and kept walking.' [FB-090121]

Marking with *bun* is by no means always associated with the identity of the referent being unknown to the speaker. Thus, in (62) *bun* is used with *pengalaman* 'experience', even though it is clear that the speaker has knowledge of the event he is about to recount. Instead, here it is the hearer who is considered not to have the knowledge. A further example of *bun* used in the context of a lack of hearer knowledge is provided in (63). Here the speaker is recounting the story of the founding of Lakus village to me. Whilst the speaker knew the identity of the mountain after which Lakus was named, I did not, and so *bun* was used. Similarly, in (64), the speaker knows their identity of his friend, but I do not, hence the use of *bun*.

(62) Neto nei nie pengalaman **bun** rale gie.
     1SG 1PL.EXCL 1EXCL.POSS experience INDEF speak PROSP
     'I'm going to recount an experience of ours' [Bk-1.007]

(63) Lakus bare tan lolo masak **bun** esen gene
     Lakus PROX.INAN because mountain big INDEF HIGH LOC
     h-ini Lakus.
     3INAN-call Lakus
     '(This village was given the name) Lakus because there's a big mountain up there called Lakus.' [Bk-29.022]

(64) Sampai ene nie moen **bun** nei t-erel
     until night 1EXCL.POSS friend INDEF 1PL.EXCL RECP-INS
     bis mil gene.
     bus inside LOC
     'I was in the bus together with a friend of mine until night.' [Bk-61.084]

The most frequent use of *bun* in my data is in content questions, where it marks the interrogative word. For example, *bun* marks *nego* 'what' in (65), *sio* 'who' in (66), and *teo* 'where' in (67). By using *bun* in these questions, the speaker makes it clear to the hearer that they have no idea as to the identity of the questioned referent or location.

(65) **Nego bun**=na nuas late porsa ba?
     what INDEF=FOC smell bad very ART.INAN
     'Whatever is it that smells so bad?' [OrelZulo-021]

(66) **Sio bun**=o   rale   higal   bi?
     who INDEF=AND speak   laugh   ART.AN
     'Whoever is it that is giggling?' [Bk-4.053]

(67) A   Berek=o   Mauk,   eli   zipil   **teo**   **bun**
     INTERJ Berek=AND   Mauk   2SG   garden.cuttings   where   INDEF
     ni=na   ini?
     OBL=FOC set.alight
     'O Berek and Mau, wherever are the garden cuttings you will burn?' [LB-3.008]

5.6 Nominal quantification

Nouns are unmarked for number in Bunaq. Number may be optionally expressed through the use of items with quantificational meaning, specifying the amount of the referent. Typically, only a single, if any, quantifier is used in an NP. There are, however, some highly restricted combinations of quantifiers which are discussed in the individual sections below. Issues concerning the use of numeral quantifiers are discussed in §5.6.1. Bunaq does not have a morphosyntactically coherent class of non-numeral quantifiers (discussed in §3.6.2), but a diverse array of items that perform a quantificational function in the NP. In §5.6.2 to §5.6.9, I illustrate the functions and behaviour of the most frequent (non-verbal, non-numeral) quantificational items.

5.6.1 Numerals and numeral classifiers

The properties of numerals, including their attributive function, have been discussed in §3.5.5. Here I only deal with a small number of outstanding descriptive matters.

5.6.1.1 Numeral classifier construction
Sortal numeral classifiers are a very marginal phenomenon in Bunaq; most numerals used in NPs appear without any classificatory element. Where a classifier is used, it appears between the N$_{HEAD}$ and the numeral. In my data, there are two sortal numeral classifiers, *bolu* and *bul*, and they are used chiefly with respect to trees and their fruits. Because lexemes such as *zo* 'mango' and *sabul* 'orange' can refer to both the tree and its fruit, a classifier serves to disambiguate between the two related referents in enumeration.

Bolu is used together with numerals quantifying nouns chiefly referring to small round items, as in (68) and (69). *Bolu* is only found in NPs with a numeral; it is not used as an independent noun in my data, but it does appear as a verb meaning 'be in a group, be united'.

(68) **Sabul** **bolu** **hiloqon** bi g-ege g-iwal.
orange CLF two ART.AN 3AN-BEN 3AN-pick
'(They) picked the two oranges for him.' [Bk-4.042]

(69) G-ege **tuat** **bolu** uen h-oqon.
3AN-BEN cake CLF one 3INAN-make
'(She) made a cake for him.' [LB-8.127]

Occasionally, *bolu* is used with a numeral in an NP referring to a person. In the small number of examples of this kind in the corpus, *bolu* seems to emphasise the referent not as a human person, but rather as an enumerated "unit". Examples are given in (70) and (71).

(70) ..., **en** **bolu** **uen** g-ia gaqal o=si.
person CLF one 3AN-eat all.AN IAM=REAS
'..., because (he) had completely eaten a whole person.' [BaloBi-056]

(71) **En** **bolu** **uen**=be n-ege taru niq.
person CLF one=CONTEXP 1EXCL-BEN appear NEG
'Not even a single person came for me.' [Bk-46.056]

The second classifier is *bul*. It is used in NPs together with numerals quantifying nouns referring to trees, as in (72) and (73). *Bul* is also a noun meaning 'base' and, unlike *bolu*, need not co-occur with a numeral in the NP.

(72) G-olo soq, **dilu** **bul** **goniqon** g-olo.
3AN-bury SEQ lontar CLF three 3AN-bury
'Once he was buried, (he) planted three lontar trees.' [BeiLera-08]

(73) Hol Taqol baqa no nei nie zo **masak**
Hol Taqol NPRX.INAN OBL 1PL.EXCL 1EXCL.POSS mango big
bul **hiloqo**.
CLF two
'At Hol Taqol, we had two big mango trees.' [Bk-1.015]

5.6.1.2 QUANT + *uen* 'one' construction

The numeral *uen* 'one' can co-occur with other quantificational items in the NP, often with non-singular reference. Following other numerals and verbs with quantificational meaning in the NP, *uen* 'one' denotes that the plurality of participants referred to form a single unit together. In (74) and (75), *uen* 'one' occurs after the numeral *hiloqon* 'two' and quantificational verb *deal* 'be many', respectively. Both of these quantificational items make clear that the referent of the NP is plural.

(74) [En   pana   **hiloqon**   **uen**]   higal.
     person   female   two   one   laugh
     'Two girls were laughing together as one.'   [Bk-4.054]

(75) [Mau   Paran   en   **real**   **uen**]   gi-ta   sai.
     Mau   Paran   person   many   one   3AN-GL   exit
     'Mau Paran came upon a large (group of) people.'   [Bk-4.014]

5.6.2 Human plurality: *halaqi* '3PL'

The pronoun *halaqi* '3PL' (§6.1) can be used to mark plurality chiefly with human referents. In (76) *halaqi* '3PL' marks an N_{HEAD} with a plural human referent. In (77) there is no N_{HEAD}, the pronoun follows an attributive verb *saqe* 'ascend' and is itself followed by an anaphoric demonstrative as determiner.

(76) [Tani   **halaqi**]   mar=na   h-oqon.
     farmer   3PL   garden=FOC   3INAN-do
     'The farmers make gardens.'   [Bk-7.013]

(77) [Saqe   **halaqi**   himo]   tebe   g-ete, ...
     ascend   3PL   CONTR.AN   return   3AN-throw
     'Those ascending (people) go back to throwing, ...'   [Bk-6.016]

In addition to human referents, *halaqi* is often used to mark plurality in NPs with anthropomorphised animals. This, for instance, is common in *zapal*, a genre of fable-like oral literature which often has animals as the principal participants. Examples (78) and (79) are taken from two different *zapal*.

(78) Orel   **halaqi**   il   a.
     monkey   3PL   water   eat
     'The monkeys drank the water.'   [OreloZul-066]

(79) Baqa   goet=na,   zulo   **halaqi**   boto   gaqal   oa,
     NPRX.INAN   LIKE=FOC   civet   3PL   disperse   all.AN   IAM
     g-i   g-oli.
     3AN-bite   3AN-chase
     'As a result, all the civets dispersed, being snapped at and chased away.'
                                                                   [BaiANeq-052]

Halaqi '3PL' can also be used to form associative plurals with human or anthropomorphic animal reference. That is, *halaqi* may follow a nominal which has unique reference, usually a person's name or a kin term, to denote 'X and other people associated with X'. Examples (80) and (81) illustrate this associative use.

(80) [*Eme   Eta   **halaqi***]   *gereja   mal,   teqa   gie.*
     mother Eta   3PL   church   go   pray   PROSP
     'Mrs Eta and her associates (in the prayer group) went to the church to pray.'
     [OS-09.01]

(81) ..., *gie   ama   roi   mar   mal,   [gie   eme   **halaqi**]*
          3.POSS   father   SPEC.AN   garden   go   3.POSS   mother   3PL
     ret.
     alone
     '... when their father went to the garden, they and their mother were alone.'
     [KakaqHitu-016]

Halaqi '3PL' in the examples seen thus far is not strictly a quantifier in the NP, but constitutes an appositional N$_{HEAD}$. There may be a pause before *halaqi*, as is often possible between different elements in appositions. What is more, *halaqi* can take its own modifier, which suggests that it is the N$_{HEAD}$ of a separate phrase within the extended NP. In (82) *en* 'person' is modified by the verb *saqe* 'ascend', while *halaqi* '3PL' is modified by *gonciet* 'five'. These two phrases are then determined by a single demonstrative. In (83), *pana* 'female' is modified by the N$_{MOD}$ *gol* 'small', while *halaqi* '3PL' is modified by *hitu* 'seven'.

(82) [*En*$_{HEAD}$ *saqe*]   [*halaqi*$_{HEAD}$ *gonciet*] *himo*]$_{NP}$ *tebe*   *g-ete.*
     person   ascend   3PL   five   CONTR.AN   return   3AN-throw
     'Those five ascending (people) go back to throwing.'
     [Bk-6.015]

(83) [*Pana*$_{HEAD}$ *gol*]   [*halaqi*$_{HEAD}$ *hitu*]]$_{NP}$ *kauq-nana, ...*
     female   small   3PL   seven   younger.sibling-older.sister
     'Those seven girls were siblings, ...'
     [KeleqMainu-03]

In casual speech, plural-marking *halaqi* '3PL' is sometimes reduced, encliticising to the preceding NP as unstressed *=i*, glossed here as 'HUM.PL'. Example (84) illustrates *=i* marking a human referent as plural, while (85) shows it with an NP with a unique human referent to mark associative plurality.

(84) [*Pana   koen*]$_{NP}$*=i*   *n-azal   oa.*
     woman   pretty=HUM.PL   1EXCL-see   IAM
     'The pretty girls have seen me already.'
     [Not-09.01]

(85) [Paq Desa]~NP=i~   g-o   gene=na   ciluq   gin.
     Mr   village=HUM.PL 3-SRC   LOC=FOC   stay   REPORT
     'Apparently (she) hangs out at the house of the village head and his family.'
     [Bk-63.032]

While the range of plural-marking meanings of the enclitic appears to be the same as that of the full pronominal form, the enclitic form =i 'HUM.PL' cannot take its own numeral modifier, as seen with *halaqi* in (82) and (83).

5.6.3 Quantificational *mil* 'inside'

The topological noun *mil* 'inside' is used in the NP with two different quantificational functions: human collective marker (§5.6.3.1) and temporal duration marker (§5.6.3.2).

5.6.3.1 Human collective

Mil can be used as an N_{MOD} to express that a set of human referents is referred to collectively as a single unit without enumeration of individuals that make up the collective. In this function, *mil* is glossed as 'COLL'.

In (86), marking with *mil* indicates that there is a collective tendency for *pana* 'women' to swear in contrast with the collective avoidance of swearing by *mone* 'men'. Similarly, in (87) the use of *mil* denotes that the referents of the N_{HEAD}, *moen* 'friend', pray as a collective.

(86) a. [Pana   **mil**]~NP~ sok   ebel.
        woman COLL   swear   strongly
        'Women swear greatly.'   [Bk-30.037]
     b. [Mone   **mil**]~NP~ g-otok   saqe=bu,   nor   sok   niq.
        man   COLL   3AN-liver ascend=GIVEN   without.reason   swear   NEG
        'When men get angry, (they) don't normally swear.'   [Bk-30.038]

(87) Akirnya, [nie   moen   **mil**]~NP~ nei   t-erel   teqa   on.
     finally   1EXCL.POSS   friend   COLL   1PL.EXCL   RECP-INS   pray   DO
     'In the end, my friends and I, we prayed together.'   [Bk-40.011]

Mil 'COLL' can co-occur with other quantificational items in the NP as well as with determiners. In (88) *mil* occurs together with the group marker *ginil* 'GRP' (§5.6.4), while example (89) shows *mil* together with the proximal demonstrative determiner modifying the inalienably possessed noun *n-ol* '1EXCL-child'.

(88) *Mone* **mil** **ginil** *haru r-on legul=na t-olo.*
man COLL GRP shirt REFL-arm long=FOC 3INAN-put.on
'All the men put on shirts with long sleeves.' [Bk-24.027]

(89) *Nei n-ol* **mil** **bari** *g-utu ciluq heten niq.*
1PL.EXCL 1EXCL-child COLL PROX.AN 3-COM relax want NEG
'(He) didn't want to hang out with our kids' [Bk-22.06]

In (90a) the numeral *uen* 'one' combines with *mil* to give the partitive meaning 'one of a collective'. However, it is ungrammatical for any higher numerals to occur with *mil* (90b).

(90) a. *Naqi* **mil** *uen heser.*
royal COLL one dead
'One of the royals died.' [Bk-68.011]
b. **Naqi* **mil** *hiloqon / goniqon heser.*
royal COLL two three dead
'Two/three of the royals died.' [Not-09.01]

5.6.3.2 Temporal duration

There are two schemas in which *mil* 'inside' is used with temporal nouns to express temporal duration. This use of *mil* 'inside' is glossed as 'DUR'.

The first schema expresses 'for the duration of X' and involves a temporal noun followed by *mil* and then a quantificational verb or numeral. In (91) and (92), the absence of *mil* between the temporal noun and the numeral would mean that the NPs headed by the temporal nouns would be interpreted not duratively, but punctually as 'in the fourth year, in year four' and 'at one o'clock', respectively.

(91) *Halaqi* [*to* **mil** *goniqon*]~NP~ *Lebos bare gene.*
3PL year DUR three Lebos PROX.INAN LOC
'They were here in Lebos for three years.' [Bk-29.005]

(92) *Mele* [*tuku* **mil** *uen*]~NP~ *lesin ai.*
walk hour DUR one more ONLY
'(We) only walked for a little more than an hour.' [Bk-34.042]

Bunaq has no single dedicated lexical item referring to the temporal concept of 'day'. Whilst East Timorese dialects have typically borrowed the Tetun *loro* 'sun, day', Bunaq Lamaknen has a collocation of *hot* 'sun' followed by *mil* to express 'the duration of a sun', i.e., 'day'. *Hot mil* is used in (93) to refer to the expanse of a single day in particular, while in (94) it refers to a series of days.

(93) [**Hot mil** minggu]ₙₚ no, misa hiloqon.
sun DUR Sunday OBL mass two
'On Sunday, there are two masses.' [Bk-34.076]

(94) Baqi Gewal ni [**hot mil** tuen~tuen uen]ₙₚ.
NPRX.AN Gewal OBL sun DUR how.much one
'He was in Gewal for several days.' [Bk-70.006]

The second temporal schema with *mil* 'DUR' expresses 'during the period X'. In this schema, a temporal noun is followed by a modifier defining the temporal period referred to, then *mil* and the oblique postposition. This is illustrated in (95) to (97).

(95) [[*Hot mil* tomol **mil**] **no**] nei n-ege rale.
sun DUR six DUR OBL 1PL.EXCL 1EXCL-BEN say
'Over six days, (they) talked to us.' [Bk-65.073]

(96) Hot mil uen no [[to 1987 **mil**] **no**], neto nie
sun COLL one OBL year 1987 DUR OBL 1SG 1EXCL.POSS
moen goniqon g-utu, nei sirubisu s-agal.
friend three 3-COM 1PL.EXCL work 3INAN-seek
'One day during 1987, my friends and I, we were looking for work.' [Bk-12.001]

(97) Halaqi ti-ta bei g-ua tuir bare,
3PL RECP-GL ancestor 3AN-footprint follow PROX.INAN
[[minggu uen **mil**] **no**].
week one DUR OBL
'They followed the path of the ancestors over a week.' [Bk-70.035]

5.6.4 Animate group plural: *g-inil* '3AN-name'

The 3ʳᵈ person inflection of the inalienably possessed noun *g-inil* '3AN-name' is used quantificationally in the NP to denote that the referent forms a group in which there is internal diversity between members. Glossed here as 'GRP', *ginil* is most often used in reference to humans (98), but can also be used in reference to animals (99).

(98) Nei nu-bul n-ege tugas bendahara kansera
1PL.EXCL 1EXCL-head 1EXCL-give task boss salary
h-one, [guru **ginil**]ₙₚ gie kansera h-one.
3INAN-hold teacher GRP 3.POSS salary 3INAN-hold
'My boss gave me the task of being in charge of the salary, (so I) got the pay of the group of the teachers.' [Bk-52.08]

(99) Lele   [ie   apa **ginil**]ₙₚ baqis   o=si   muzuk
      nowadays   1INCL/2.POSS cow GRP   much   IAM=REAS   earth
      h-arat   gie.
      3INAN-destroy   PROSP
      'These days because you have a lot of herds of cows, the land is being destroyed.'   [Bk-19.022]

Ginil 'GRP' occurs within the NP. This can be seen in (100), where *ginil* occurs to the left of the determiner *baqi* that marks the right edge of the NP.

(100) ..., [Bei   Busa gie   g-ol   g-atal   **ginil**
             grandfather   cat   3.POSS 3AN-child 3AN-grandchild   GRP
       baqi] rawaq,   r-io   bere   harus a-ta
       NPRX.AN   defecate REFL-faeces CNTEXP.INAN   must   3INAN-GL
       muk   tuk, ...
       earth   pile.on
       '..., when the diverse descendants of the ancestral cat defecate, they must cover their faeces with earth, ...'   [BeiZapBeiBusa-32]

Ginil very frequently occurs in reduplicated form, as in (101). This is part of a wider pattern where reduplication is used to denote quantification of kinds (see §5.6.8).

(101) Uer gol   ba   dara   piqu kereq,   [bai   a
       pot small ART.INAN prepare   all.together   thing   eat
       ginil~ginil]   hati   mohu.
       REDUP~GRP   exist   complete
       'It was prepared all together in the small pot, and there were all sorts of food.'   [EnBaruq-63]

The group plural can occasionally be used together with another non-numeral quantifier in the NP, as seen already with *mil* 'COLL' in (86) in §5.6.3.1. *Ginil* 'GRP' can also co-occur with *naran* 'every sort, all sorts', which is also based on a lexeme 'name', albeit borrowed from Tetun (see §5.6.8).

5.6.5 Animal group plural: *g-omoq* '3AN-udder'

The inalienably possessed noun *g-omoq* '3AN-udder' is infrequently used in the NP as an animal group marker denoting a number of animals of one kind, feeding or travelling in company, glossed here as 'GRP.ANIMAL'. Although chiefly applied to domestic animals kept together under the charge of one or more persons, such as cows, goats, or horses (102), it can also be used for an assemblage of monkeys (103).

(102) [Apa **gomoq** bi] g-aziq.
 COW GRP.ANIMAL ART.AN 3AN-disappear
 'The herd of cows have disappeared.' [LB9.044]

(103) ..., homo=be, [orel **gomoq** masak]
 CONTR.INAN=CONTEXP monkey GRP.ANIMAL big
 ma mil gene, guzup nap no.
 bamboo inside LOC settlement beside OBL
 '..., but there was a big group of monkeys living in the bamboo by the settlement' [OrelMaMil-03]

5.6.6 Partitive plural: *waqen* 'PART.PL'

Waqen 'PART.PL' expresses partitive plurality in Bunaq. That is, it is used to modify a noun where the referent represents a part of some total number or whole amount. The use of *waqen* with a count noun as N_{HEAD} is illustrated in (104), and its use with a mass referent but not overtly expressed as an N_{HEAD} is illustrated in (105).

(104) Tapi [tas **waqen**] gene baqa goet dari niq
 but village PART.PL LOC NPRX.INAN LIKE happen NEG
 'But in some villages, it doesn't happen like that.' [Bk-62.006]

(105) Il kokoq no baqa a, [**waqen**] leleq rebel.
 water bucket OBL NPRX.INAN eat PART.PL flow descend
 '(He) drank the water in the bucket (and) some (water) dribbled down.' [Bk-6.027]

The above instances of *waqen* have inanimate referents; the partitive also occurs with human referents, both with an N_{HEAD} (106) and without (107).

(106) [En **waqen**] mar hobel.
 person PART.PL garden not.exist
 'Some people don't have gardens.' [Bk-24.007]

(107) [**Waqen**] g-one oa.
 PART.PL 3AN-hold IAM
 'Some had already been caught.' [Bk-29.030]

Waqen...waqen 'PART.PL...PART.PL' is often used in the contrasting of two partitive sets of a single group of entities with the meaning 'some...others'. This is illustrated in (108).

(108) **Waqen** a, **waqen** dele tuat h-oqon.
 PART.PL eat PART.PL INS rice.cake 3INAN-make
 '(They) eat some (of the rice), and with some they make rice cakes.' [LB7.013]

5.6.7 Universal quantification: *hotu~hotu* 'all'

Hotu~hotu 'all' is used in reference to any count noun. Unlike the floating universal quantifier *gaqal* 'all.AN' (§13.8.1.3), *hotu~hotu* 'all' can be used with animate, as in (109) and (110), and inanimate referents (111).

(109) [En **hotu~hotu**] haqe gene=na il ho.
 person all THERE LOC=FOC water draw
 'The people all fetch water there.' [Bk-7.022]

(110) [En **hotu~hotu**] gie mar hati.
 person all 3.POSS garden exist
 'All the people have a garden.' [Bk-24.006]

(111) Nie muk bare [muk **hotu~hotu**] g-o lesin
 1EXCL.POSS land PROX.INAN land all 3-SRC more
 liol.
 continue
 'My land here is better than all other lands.' [Bk-24.042]

Hotu~hotu 'all' is not restricted to marking NPs of certain roles or ANIMACY in the way that *gaqal* 'all.AN' is (§13.8.1). In (109) *hotu~hotu* 'all' modifies an A, in (110) a possessor NP, and in (111) a peripheral NP, all types of NPs that *gaqal* 'all.AN' cannot quantify. However, *hotu~hotu* 'all' and *gaqal* 'all.AN' are not in complementary distribution; they can occur in overlapping domains. In (112a) we see that *hotu~hotu* 'all' modifies the S of a monovalent clause, and that in (112b) *gaqal* 'all.AN' modifies the same argument. In (112c) we see that the two universal quantifiers do not occur together marking the same argument.

(112) a. [Halaqi hotu~hotu] teai.
 3PL all amazed
 'They all were amazed.'
 b. [Halaqi] teai gaqal.
 3PL amazed all.AN
 'They were all amazed.'

c. *Halaqi   hotu~hotu   teai   gaqal.
   3PL   all   amazed   all.AN   [Not-07.03]

Hotu~hotu also cannot be used in combination with any determiners. This restriction is seen here to be semantic and pragmatic, not syntactic, as hotu~hotu 'all' lacks the syntactic properties of determiners (§3.5.4). Determiners are used in order to identify the referent. Universal quantification means that *all* members of the referent set are identified, such that a determiner identifying a particular referent would be not merely redundant, but also in conflict with the universal quantifier (cf. Gil 2001: 1278). *Hotu~hotu* 'all' also cannot occur without an overt N$_{HEAD}$.

5.6.8 Quantification of 'kinds'

Bunaq has several quantificational items associated with reference to 'all kinds'. I give each of them distinct glosses here in order to separate them from one another, e.g., 'all sorts' and 'every sort', but they are very close in meaning.

The most common quantifier in this group is *gewen* 'all sorts', originating in the lexeme *g-ewen* '3AN-face'. This quantifier is commonly used in reduplicated form, as in (113). But *gewen* occurs in unreduplicated form in a fixed combination with *nego* 'what' (114).

(113) Suri Guloq   dik,   balo,   sekal,   [**gewen~gewen**   baqa]
       Suri Guloq   yam   taro   potato   REDUP~all.sorts   NPRX.INAN
       s-alak.
       3INAN-roast
       'Suri Guloq roasted the yams, taros, potatoes, all those sorts of things.'
       [Bk-6.050]

(114) Neto   n-opol-wen   haqal,   [**gewen**   nego]   hobel   oa.
       1SG   1EXCL-scoop.up-ANTIC   COMPL   all.sorts   what   not.exist   IAM
       'Once I awoke suddenly, everything was gone.'

Two other quantifiers of kinds always come in reduplicated form: *oik~oik* 'all sorts' (115) and *dai~dai* 'all kinds'[6] (116). *Oik~oik* is borrowed from Tetun where it is a reduplication of the noun *oik* 'face', paralleling Bunaq *gewen* 'face'.

---

6 *Dai-dai* 'all kinds' is realised variously as [ˈdai~dai, ˈdai~rai, ˈdare, ˈrare].

(115) [Tumel **oik~oik**] neto h-osok loi.
money all.sorts 1SG 3INAN-receive good
'I can accept all sorts of money.' [OS.07-03]

(116) [Bai **dai~dai**] deu mil no baqis.
thing all.kinds house inside OBL many
'There were many things of all kinds in the house.' [LB1.079]

Also in this class is *naran* 'every (sort), all different sorts'. *Naran* differs from other quantificational modifiers in the NP in that it is never reduplicated and it occurs before the N$_{HEAD}$. This order is taken over from Tetun where *naran*, a lexeme meaning 'name', appears in a prenominal position in its quantificational use (cf. Bunaq *g-inil* '3AN-name', discussed in §5.6.4, which is postnominal when used quantificationally). *Naran* cannot occur by itself in the NP but must always be followed by either an N$_{HEAD}$ or a determiner. In the Bunaq example in (117) we see that *naran* modifies the N$_{HEAD}$, *nego* 'what'. In (118) we see that *naran* is distinct from a locational in that it appears following a possessor and not prior to it (see §8.1 on the syntax of locationals).

(117) [**Naran** nego=na Suri Guloq h-oqon ba], gie
every.sort what=FOC Suri Guloq 3INAN-do ART.INAN 3.POSS
eme h-ini sal minak.
mother 3INAN-call wrong complete
'Everything (lit., every what) that Suri Guloq did, his mother said was completely wrong.' [Bk-6.005]

(118) [Gie **naran** ipi] reu kaeq.
3.POSS every.sort rice house filled
'He had rice of every sort filling the house.' [Bk-68.083]

Naran can also co-occur in an NP with the quantifiers *gewen* 'every sort' (119) and *ginil* 'GRP' (120). This has the effect of bracketing the N$_{HEAD}$, with *naran* preceding it and the native Bunaq quantifier following. Similar bracketing constructions are observed with clauses where native clause-final and borrowed clause-initial conjunctions are combined (see §15.3.2.3).

(119) ..., i en bare [**naran** bai **gewen**]
1PL.INCL person PROX.INAN every.sort thing all.sorts
muk wa no bare g-utu t-iol tara taq.
earth top LOC PROX.INAN 3-COM RECP-voice know CONT
'We humans could still talk to all different kinds of creatures on the earth.'
[HulTopol-01]

(120) H-azal,   [naran   hina   ginil~ginil]   lotoq   dele   d-on
      3INAN-see   every.sort animal   REDUP~GRP   noise   INS   REFL-arm
      pas   higal.
      clap   laugh
      'When they saw it, all the different animals laughed and clapped noisily.'

[BaiANeq-39]

In fact, quantifiers of kinds are often stacked together where they serve to reinforce one another, as in (121).

(121) [Naran   dai~dai   gewen~gewen]   hobel   taq.
      every.sort   all.kinds   REDUP~all.sorts   not.exist   CONT
      'Absolutely everything was gone.'   [LuaWezun3-10]

5.6.9 Distributive plurality by reduplication

Nominal reduplication is used in contexts of distributive plurality, where individual members of a set of like referents are to be regarded or treated separately. Distributive reduplication is not grammatically required in any context; the choice to reduplicate is made according to whether the collection of plural objects is to be regarded as constituting a more or less uniform mass, in which case there is no reduplication, or made up of a number of discrete objects, in which case reduplication may take place. Examples of nominal reduplication from the corpus include:

(122) Suri Guloq   hoto   witin   baqa   [reu~reu]   a-ta   neq.
      Suri Guloq   fire   stick   NPRX.INAN   REDUP~house   3INAN-GL   divide
      'Suri Guloq distributed the fire torches to the different houses.'   [Bk-6.064]

(123) Halaqi [mete   kelompok~kelompok   baqi]   ta-tara   niq   taq.
      3PL   NOW   REDUP~group   NPRX.AN   RECP-know   NEG   CONT
      'They, those different groups, don't know each other yet.'   [Bk-15.004]

Where a noun with an individuated multitude of referents is modified, the modifier may be reduplicated in place of the head noun (124), but this is not obligatory (125).

(124) [En   matas~matas]   g-ubak.
      person   REDUP~old   3AN-collect
      'The different elders gathered.'   [Bk-21.012]

(125) [**Tas~tas** hosu] gene halaqi h-oqon niq oa.
REDUP~village other LOC 3PL 3INAN-do NEG IAM
'In the other villages they don't do it anymore.' [Bk-8.036]

Interrogatives may also be reduplicated where the identities of multiple individuals in a single role are being questioned. For instance:

(126) Jenis kain baqa [**nego~nego**]?
kind cloth NPRX.INAN REDUP~what
'What are the different kinds of weavings?' [Bk-8.036]

(127) [En **sio~sio**] g-azal?
person REDUP~who 3AN-see
'Who were the different people (you) saw?' [OS-07.01]

5.7 Nominal conjunction and disjunction

There is no single dedicated nominal conjunction in Bunaq. There are four strategies for conjunction of nominals: zero conjunction (§5.7.1); conjunction with the additive focus enclitic =o 'AND' (§5.7.2); conjunction with halali '3DU' (§5.7.3); and conjunction with ai 'ONLY' (§5.7.4). Disjunction with =ka 'OR' is discussed in §5.7.5. Patterns of agreement resolution with conjoined nominals of different noun classes will be discussed where relevant in the following sections.

5.7.1 Zero conjunction

Zero conjunction or the juxtaposition of NPs is used in reference to sets of two or more referents which the speaker regards as grouping together in a particular context. A pause separates zero-conjoined elements. Zero conjunction occurs only on the level of the NP; constituents within the NP cannot be zero conjoined, e.g., two zero-conjoined N_{HEAD}s cannot be determined by a single determiner.

In (128) we have three zero-conjoined nominals, each independently marked with a possessor. In (129), three bare nouns with a P role are zero conjoined.

(128) Baqi gie kaqa, gie kauq, g-intili mil
NPRX.AN 3.POSS older.brother 3.POSS younger.sibling 3AN-cousin COLL
g-azal milik.
3AN-see scared
'He was scared of his siblings and cousins.' [Bk-21.03]

(129) Rik   balo   sekal   gi-wil   / *wil.
      yam   taro   potato   3AN-dig   dig
      '(They) dug up cassava, taro, potato.'   [Bk-6.048]

Bunaq noun class resolution rules follow a principle of closest conjunct agreement. In a string of zero-conjoined nouns of differing noun classes, agreement is calculated on the value of the final nominal. Notice in (129) the ANIMATE agreement on the verb, *wil* 'dig'. This is because the final noun, *sekal* 'potato', is ANIMATE, while the other nouns further to the left, *dik* 'yam' and *balo* 'taro', are INANIMATE.

5.7.2 Conjunction with =o 'AND'

The additive focus enclitic =*o* 'AND' (§4.7.4.2.1) can function as a medial connective in the construction 'X AND Y'. The enclitic typically conjoins on the level of the NP, as in (130) to (132).

(130) [Pana   bi]=**o**   [mone   bi]   tueq   lilak.
      female   ART.AN=AND   male   ART.AN   alcohol   crazy
      'The woman and the man were drunk.'   [Bk-43.060]

(131) [Nie   eme]=**o**   [nie   ama]   ton.
      1EXCL.POSS   mother=AND   1EXCL.POSS   mother   marry
      'My mother and my father married.'   [Bk-29.066]

(132) *Halali*   *g-ini*   [*Manek Tuas*]=**o**   [*Bere Soro*].
      3DU   3AN-call   Manek Tuas=AND   Bere Soro
      'Those two were called Manek Tuas and Bere Soro.'   [Bk-12.012]

The additive =*o* 'AND' can also conjoin constituents within the NP. It can conjoin two N$_{MOD}$s that have a single N$_{HEAD}$, as in (133) and (134).

(133) [*En*$_{HEAD}$ *rato*$_{MOD}$=**o**   *renu*$_{MOD}$]   *gie*   *raza*=*na*   *baqa*.
      person   noble=AND   commoner   3.POSS   difference=FOC   NPRX.INAN
      'The nobles and the commoners have these differences.'   [Bk-18.050]

(134) [*Bai*$_{HEAD}$ *buleqen*$_{MOD}$=**o**   *belis*$_{MOD}$ *ba*]   *tumel*   *minak*.
      thing   gold=AND   silver   ART.INAN   metal   complete
      'The gold and silver things were all precious metal.'   [Bk-24.035]

It is also possible for two N$_{HEAD}$s to share a single modifier and/or determiner and to be conjoined with =*o* 'AND', as in (135) and (136). Notice also in (136) the agreement resolution of the determiner: the article that determines the two N_{HEAD}s of the NP agrees not with the first noun, ANIMATE *paqol* 'maize', but with the second noun, INANIMATE *ipi* 'rice'.

(135) *Halaqi [dik$_{HEAD}$=o balo$_{HEAD}$ s-alak$_{RC}$ baqa]*
      3PL   yam=AND   taro   3INAN-roast   NPRX.INAN
      t-erel   a.
      RECP-INS eat
      'They ate the roasted yam and taro together.' [Bk-6.057]

(136) *Halali   haqe   gene   [paqol$_{HEAD}$=o   ipi$_{HEAD}$ topol$_{RC}$ ba]*
      3DU   THERE LOC   maize=AND   rice   fall   ART.INAN
      h-ek.
      3INAN-pick.up
      'The two there picked up the maize and the rice that had fallen.' [LB7.011]

The additive particle is not normally used to conjoin more than two elements. Where more than two elements are conjoined, *=o* 'AND' typically conjoins only the first and second, while the third noun is juxtaposed; there is not usually a pause between second and third conjuncts. Examples from the corpus are given in (137) and (138).

(137) *[Apa=o   pip   kura   bi]   ga-bilan.*
      COW=AND goat horse ART.AN   3AN-keep
      '(People) keep cows, goats, and horses.' [Bk-19.001]

(138) *Neli   [Bora=o   Tahon   Builalu]   mal   gie.*
      1DU.EXCL   Bora=AND   Tahon   Builalu   go   PROSP
      'We two are going to Bora, Tahon, and Builalu.' [OS.09-01]

5.7.3 Conjunction with *halali* '3DU'

Where reference is to exactly two entities, the pronoun *halali* '3DU' may conjoin two NPs to stipulate that those two entities are being referred to exclusively. Whilst the pronoun can typically only refer to humans (§6.1), when conjoining NPs it can conjoin nouns that have human (139) or non-human referents (140). Unlike *=o* 'AND', *halali* '3DU' cannot conjoin constituents within the NP.

(139) Dato Gol halaqi   [Louis Berthe]$_{NP}$ **halali** [g-otil]$_{NP}$ g-ege
       Dato Gol 3PL   Louis Berthe   3DU   3AN-spouse   3AN-BEN
       tumel   ha-tama.
       money   3INAN-bring.in
       'The people of *Dato Gol* got Louis Berthe together with his wife to contribute money.' [Bk-70.121]

(140) Tapi   i   adat   h-ua   gene   on,
       but   1PL.INCL tradition 3INAN-footprint LOC   DO
       [hutus morok]$_{NP}$ **halali** [lak gol   roe]$_{NP}$.
       cloth.type   3DU   cloth.type SPEC.INAN
       'But according to tradition, the (traditional kinds of Bunaq weaving) are the *hutus morok* cloth together with the *lak gol* cloth.' [Bk-35.98]

5.7.4 Conjunction with *ai* 'ONLY'

In the nominal domain, the restrictive particle *ai* 'ONLY' is used to conjoin NPs; it does not conjoin constituents within the NP. *Ai* 'ONLY' appears in two constructions conjoining NPs in which it is iterated: (i) X *ai* Y *ai*, meaning 'both X and Y' (141); and (ii) X *ai* X *ai*, meaning 'every X', where X is a temporal noun (142). Each *ai* 'ONLY' in these constructions prosodically brackets with the preceding NP. An NP marked by *ai* 'ONLY' does not stand alone, but is always followed by another marked by *ai* 'ONLY'.

(141) [Mok   **ai**] [mete=o   tun   **ai**] kahul.
       banana   ONLY   NOW=ADDR   flour ONLY   mix
       '(You) mix both the banana and the flour (mentioned just) now together.' [Bk-76.016]

(142) [To   **ai**] [to   **ai**] baqa   goet   h-oqon   des.
       year   ONLY   year   ONLY   NPRX.INAN   LIKE   3INAN-do   constantly
       'Year after year (we) do like that constantly.' [Bk-8.048]

See §14.3.4 on the use of *ai* in the verbal domain.

5.7.5 Disjunction with =*ka* 'OR'

In §4.6.2.2.3, we saw that =*ka* 'OR' could be used as an alternative question tag, and it was also mentioned that =*ka* 'OR' can be used to mark disjunction in declarative clauses. As in its interrogative function, =*ka* 'OR' brackets prosodically with the preceding constituent and is accompanied by a rising pitch. Examples are given in (143) and (144).

(143) *Tasu late=**ka** hol beseq hoto wa baqa no lai.*
wok bad=OR stone flat fire top NPRX.INAN OBL set
'Set an old wok or a flat stone on top of the fire.' [Bk-76.028]

(144) *Biasa en sogo=**ka** sogo lesin t-ege g-asaq.*
usually person ten=OR ten more RECP-BEN 3AN-count
'Usually, 10 or more than 10 people count out (the stones) for each other.'
[Bk-8.012]

Whilst =*ka* 'OR' is by far the most common marker of disjunction in Bunaq, =*e* is also occasionally used for this purpose.

Chapter 6
Pronouns and person reference

6.1 Introduction

This chapter discusses the patterns of person reference and address in Bunaq. There are multiple pronominal and non-pronominal options for referring to persons. This chapter will consider how factors such as politeness and familiarity influence the manner of person reference in Bunaq. Pronominal options for person reference, including the syntax of pronouns, will be addressed in §6.2. Non-pronominal strategies of person reference, using kin terms and names, are treated in §6.3.

6.2 Pronominal person reference

The Bunaq pronouns are given in Table 6.1. Pronouns distinguish three numbers: singular, plural, and dual. First person dual and plural pronouns show a distinction between inclusive (i.e., including the addressee) and exclusive (i.e., excluding the addressee). Third person pronouns only refer to humans (though see §5.6.2). There are no singular 3rd person pronouns; demonstratives are used for this purpose (§7.4.1.5).

Table 6.1: Bunaq pronouns.

	SG	DU	PL
1EXCL	neto	neli	nei
1INCL	--	ili	i
2	eto	eli	ei
3	--	halali	halaqi

Each person in the pronominal paradigm is associated with a different initial formative: 1st person exclusive is characterised by [ne]; 1st person inclusive by [i]; 2nd person by [e]; and 3rd person by [hala]. Similarly, each number has its own final formative with which it is associated in the pronominal paradigm: singular number is characterised by [to]; dual number by [li]; and plural by [i]. Before the restrictive focus marker =na 'FOC', the final [to] of the 1st and 2nd person singular pronouns is optionally deleted, as illustrated in (1).

(1) *Baqa*   *goet*   *dele,* **ne=na**   *seq.*
    NPRX.INAN   LIKE   INS   1SG=FOC   call
    'In that manner I did call.' [Bk-22.017]

The pronouns presented in Table 6.1 are not marked for any case or pragmatic function, and so can appear in any syntactic or pragmatic role called for. This can be seen in the following examples, which show the same pronoun, *nei* '1PL.EXCL', appearing as S (2a), A (2b), P (2c), and 'subject' of a nominal clause (2d).

(2) a. ***Nei**=na*   *honal.*
       1PL.EXCL=FOC go.LEVEL
       'We go across.'   [Bk-11.015]
    b. ***Nei***   *t-ege*   *bai*   *g-olo.*
       1PL.EXCL RECP-BEN thing 3-bury
       'We bury things for each other.'   [Bk-11.010]
    c. *Polisi*   ***nei***   *n-one.*
       police   1PL.EXCL 1EXCL-arrest
       'The police arrest us.'   [Bk-11.012]
    d. ***Nei***   *Indonesia.*
       1PL.EXCL Indonesia
       'We are Indonesia.', i.e., 'We are people of Indonesia.'   [Bk-11.022]

In the following sections, I will discuss various aspects of the syntax and reference of the Bunaq pronouns: §6.2.1 looks at pronoun and person prefix agreement; §6.2.2 looks at agreement restrictions between pronouns and determiners; §6.2.3 looks at the obligatoriness of using dual versus plural pronouns in reference to two referents; and §6.2.4 deals with referential extensions of individual pronouns in Bunaq.

6.2.1 Pronouns and person prefixes

As discussed in §2.5.1, prefixes are bound person markers. Table 6.2 presents the three person prefixes (valency reducing prefixes excluded; see §11.1). Unlike pronouns, person prefixes are unmarked for number and do not distinguish between 1st person inclusive and 2nd person. Person prefixes can occur agreeing with the argument on a verb (§4.2), on the complement of a verbal postposition (§3.6.1), and on the possessor of an inalienably possessed noun (§9.3). They are obligatory in the presence of the appropriate agreement trigger and cannot be omitted under any circumstances.

Table 6.2: Person prefixes.

1EXCL	nV-
1INCL/2	V-
3AN	gV-

Person prefixes regularly co-index pronouns. In 1ˢᵗ and 2ⁿᵈ person singular reference, a person prefix is used without a co-indexing pronoun. The examples in (3) can only be interpreted as having singular reference.

(3) a. *Baqi* **na**-*tara*.
    NPRX.AN 1EXCL-know
    'S/he knows me.', *'S/he knows us (excl.).'
   b. *Baqi* **a**-*tara*.
    NPRX.AN 1INCL/2-know
    'S/he knows you (SG).', *'S/he knows us (INCL)', *'S/he knows you (DU/PL).'

For 1ˢᵗ and 2ⁿᵈ person non-singular reference, the prefix must be co-indexed by the appropriate non-singular pronoun, as in (4).

(4) a. *Baqi* nei **na**-*tara*.
    NPRX.AN 1PL.EXCL 1EXCL-know
    'S/he knows us (EXCL).'
   b. *Baqi* eli **a**-*tara*.
    NPRX.AN 2DU 1INCL/2-know
    'S/he knows you (DU).'

With a 3ʳᵈ person prefix, non-singular readings are available without a pronoun. That is, it is not obligatory for a non-singular 3ʳᵈ person pronoun to occur with the prefix in non-singular reference. Once the non-singular referent is clearly established, the use of a 3ʳᵈ person pronoun is optional. Consider the pronoun use in (5). After the establishment of the two girls as topic in (5a), the referents are tracked with the 3ʳᵈ person dual pronoun *halali* co-indexed by the prefix on *zal* 'carry' in the first clause of (5b). However, in the second clause of (5b), there is no *halali* and the girls are only referenced by the prefix on the instrumental *dele* 'INS' (§12.4.2).

(5) a. **Pana gol koen** *hiloqon*=*na* *homo* *no*.
    female small beautiful two=FOC CONTR.INAN OBL
    'There were just two beautiful girls there.' [Bk-4.057]
   b. *Mau Paran* **halali gi**-*al*, **g**-*erel* *reu* *mal*.
    Mau Paran 3DU 3AN-carry 3AN-INS house go
    'Mau Paran took them, (and) went home with (them).' [Bk-4.058]

Although rare, it is possible to explicitly co-index a 1ˢᵗ or 2ⁿᵈ person prefix with a singular pronoun. This has the pragmatic effect of placing contrastive focus on, or emphatically asserting the identity of, the referent. In (6a) and (6b) the pronouns *neto* '1SG' and *eto* '2SG' are respectively co-indexed by the appropriate inflections of the indirect possessive classifier (§9.2). The inclusion of the pronouns serves to emphatically contrast the speaker's and the addressee's claims of possession over the disputed child and the conditions under which the dispute will be settled.

(6) a. *Hul   gu-tul   g-awas   no   hati,   **neto   nie**.*
         moon   3AN-part   3AN-forehead   OBL   exist   1SG   1EXCL.POSS
         '(If) there's a crescent moon on his forehead, (he's) *mine*.'   [LB-10.022]
    b.   *Hul   gu-tul   hobel,   **eto   ie**.*
         moon   3AN-part   not.exist   2SG   1INCL/2.POSS
         '(If) there's no crescent moon, (he's) *yours*.'   [LB-10.023]

In (7a) *neto* '1SG' is co-indexed by the agreement prefix on the goal-marking verbal postposition *a-ta* '3INAN-GL' (§12.4.3). The pronoun emphasises the fact that the spirit did not go towards the speaker, but rather ran away (7b).

(7) a. *G-ini   ciaq   **neto   ni**-ta   man.*
         3AN-CAUS   not.want   1SG   1EXCL-GL   come
         '(The prayer) made (the spirit) not want to come to *me*.'   [Bk-47.135]
    b.   *Baqi   g-ini   he.*
         NPRX.AN   3AN-CAUS   run
         '(Rather it) made (him) run away.'   [Bk-47.136]

We see in (8) that the additional singular pronoun co-indexing an agreement prefix on a verb is often fronted, as is common for focused participants (§4.7.2.2). Fronting is not obligatory and the pronoun can occur directly beside the inflected verb, as in (9). The pronouns head their own NPs and can be marked by enclitics, as for example in (10).

(8) ***Neto***   *eto   **n**-inil, . . .*
     1SG   2SG   1EXCL-look.at
     'Look at *me*, . . .'   [OrelLenuk-071]

(9) *Homo=si,   nie   bai   a   **eto   i**-a*
     CONTR.INAN=REAS   1EXCL.POSS   thing   eat   2SG   1INCL/2-eat
     bare.
     PROX.INAN
     'Because of this, my food is to eat *you*.'   [LareKeleq-06]

(10) *A,   eto   bare,   **eto**=bu   Ø-ege   seq   niq!*
     INTERJ   2SG   PROX.INAN   2SG=GIVEN   1INCL/2-BEN   call   NEG
     'Ah you, I wasn't calling you.'   [OrelPip-036]

6.2.2 Pronoun and determiner combinations

NPs headed by pronouns can occur with a determiner. Determiners agree with personal pronominal heads in terms of ANIMACY and distance specification. 1st (inclusive and exclusive) and 2nd person pronouns can be determined by proximal demonstrative determiners, but not non-proximal demonstrative determiners; the agreement form with these persons of the proximal determiner must be INANIMATE. By contrast, 3rd person pronouns can be determined by non-proximal determiners, but not proximal determiners; they must also take ANIMATE agreement forms of the determiner. Table 6.3 summarises these patterns.

Table 6.3: Pronoun and determiner combinations.

	Distance specification of DET	Noun class specification of DET
1st persons	Proximal	INANIMATE
2nd persons	Proximal	INANIMATE
3rd persons	Non-proximal	ANIMATE

The patterns displayed in the table are exemplified in (11).

(11) 1ST PERSON
    a. ***Nei bare*** *moroi porsa.*
       1PL.EXCL PROX.INAN sleepy really
       'We here are really sleepy.' [Bk-4.017]

  2ND PERSON
    b. ***Ei bare*** *teo gene man?*
       2PL PROX.INAN where LOC come
       'You there, where have you come from?' [LB-2.212]

  3RD PERSON
    c. ***Halaqi baqi*** *g-ege tumel gol uen.*
       3PL NPRX.AN 3AN-give money small one
       'Those people give (them) a little money.' [Bk-18.011]

As discussed in §5.2.2, the INANIMATE agreement of 1st and 2nd persons arises out of the fact that noun class is only assigned to 3rd persons in Bunaq. Thus, despite prototypically having animate referents, 1st and 2nd persons take INANIMATE agreement as the least marked, default agreement pattern.

The difference between the way in which pronouns combine with distance-marked demonstratives can be explained by the (non-)participation of their referents in the speech situation. 1st and 2nd persons are local persons, that is, they are participants present in the speech situation and are therefore construed as proximal. By contrast,

6.2.3 Dual versus plural number in pronouns

Dual pronouns are pervasive in everyday Bunaq speech. However, marking for dual number is not obligatory in the pronominal system. Instead of dual pronouns, plural pronouns may be used in reference to only two participants, and this is often seen once dual reference has already been established in the discourse. For instance, in (12a) the 3rd person dual pronoun is used initially, but the pair are subsequently referred to with 3rd person plural (12b).

(12) a. ***Halali*** mal liol.
   3DU   go   continue
   'They both went on...'   [LB-3.175]
   b. *Jadi baqa* ni ***halaqi*** loi gene mit oa.
   so   NPRX.INAN   OBL   3PL   good   LOC   sit   IAM
   'So, in that place, they lived in comfort.'   [LB-3.180]

In (13) we see the same pattern of the initial use of a dual pronoun, in this case *ili* '1DU.INCL', to establish dual reference, followed by the plural *i* '1PL.INCL' in reference to the same participants. Similarly, in (14) the A is expressed by *neli* '1DU.EXCL', yet the same referent is encoded with *nei* '1PL.INCL' when referring to the possessor introduced by *nie* '1EXCL.POSS'.

(13) ***Ili***   t-erel,   en   ***i***   a-tara   oa.
   1DU.INCL   RECP-INS   person   1PL.INCL   1INCL/2-know   IAM
   '(If) we two (go) together, people will recognise us.'   [LB-8.215]

(14) ***Neli***   *nei*   *nie*   *eme=o*   ***nei***
   1DU.EXCL   1PL.EXCL   1EXCL.POSS   mother=AND   1PL.EXCL
   nie   *ama*   *g-agal?*
   1EXCL.POSS   father   3AN-search
   'We two are searching for our mother and our father.'   [LB-2.045]

Whilst dual number may not be an obligatory part of the Bunaq number system, dual pronouns are nevertheless very common in Bunaq speech. In fact, it is rare for two entities to be referred to with a plural pronoun. The variations observed here appear to be governed by stylistic considerations, namely, that the repetition of a pronoun should be avoided.

That dual and plural pronouns occur without feature clashes in these examples indicates that the plural pronouns could be analysed to be not marked as plural, i.e., referring to 3 or more, as would be expected in a pronominal system with dual (Corbett 2000: 20), but rather as non-singular, i.e., referring to 2 or more.

6.2.4 Additional referential uses of pronouns

The previous sections have discussed uses of pronouns that are in accordance with their "normal" meaning based on the sum of their feature specifications for person and number, e.g., a 3rd person plural pronoun refers to a plural entity that is not a speech participant. However, in Bunaq, as in many languages, some pronouns do not have the same referential properties in every context in which they are used. In this section, I examine the use of Bunaq pronouns in generic reference (§6.2.4.1) and in polite reference (§6.2.4.2).

6.2.4.1 Generic reference
Generic reference is reference to a whole class, rather than to individual and specified members of it. Bunaq uses the pronouns *i* '1PL.INCL' (§6.2.4.1.1) and *eto* '2SG' (§6.2.4.1.2) in generic reference.

6.2.4.1.1 Generic *i* '1PL.INCL'
The pronoun *i* '1PL.INCL' may be used with generic reference in the description of general and hypothetical situations, typical practices, and cultural norms. The generic *i* '1PL.INCL' may be used even where neither the speaker nor the hearer is intended in the class of people under discussion.

Example (15) comes from a procedural text. We see here the generic use of *i* '1PL.INCL' to detail the steps which 'one' would go through in making maize porridge, without suggesting that either speaker or hearer would be doing so.

(15) a. *I   paqol   g-ao.*
        1PL.INCL maize   3AN-pound
        'We pound the maize.'   [Bk-45.006]
    b. *Paqol   g-ao,   i   g-apiq   taq.*
        maize   3AN-pound 1PL.INCL 3AN-sift CONT
        '(After) pounding the maize, we keep sifting it.'   [Bk-45.007]

See also §4.7.1.2 on the elision of NP elements referring to A/S participants in "generic" situations.

Bunaq uses *i* '1PL.INCL' also to express generalisations holding over of a group of people (such as social standards or cultural norms). In (16) *i* '1PL.INCL' is used to indicate that this is how all siblings ought to behave to one another, regardless of who they are. In (17), a male speaker uses *i* '1PL.INCL' in telling a woman that it is not acceptable for a person to marry the child of their own maternal uncle. As both speaker and hearer are already married, there is no question of the situation applying to either of them.

(16) *I* *kauq-kaqa* *g-ege* *loi.*
1PL.INCL younger.sibling-older.sibling 3AN-give good
'We (should) be good to our brothers and sisters.' [Bk-4.096]

(17) *I* *rie* *baba* *g-ol* *g-utu=na* *ton,*
1PL.INCL REFL.POSS maternal.uncle 3AN-child 3-COM=FOC marry
ton *baqa* *koen* *niq.*
marry NPRX.INAN nice NEG
'(If) it is our mother's brother's child that we marry, it's [Bk-62.011]
not a good marriage.'

Generic *i* '1PL.INCL' can also be used in situations where reference is in fact exclusive, typically to a 1st person singular. By employing the 1st person inclusive, a speaker signals their inclusion of the hearer in the discourse. In (18) the speaker begins with *nei* '1PL.EXCL' (18a) before switching in the second clause (18b) to the pronoun *i* '1PL.INCL' in recognition of the hearer's shared status as Catholic, even though she did not actually take part in the prayer on this occasion.

(18) a. *Akirnya,* *nie* *moen* *mil* *nei* *t-erel* *teqa* *on.*
finally 1EXCL.POSS friend COLL 1PL.EXCL RECP-INS pray DO
'In the end, I prayed together with friends.' [Bk-40.011]
b. *Teqa,* *i* *rie* *piar* *h-alolo.*
pray 1PL.INCL REFL.POSS believe 3INAN-follow
'We prayed (and thereby) followed our own beliefs.' [Bk-40.012]

In (19) the speaker gives voice to his feelings of isolation living in the east of Timor; he switches from talking about himself in the 1st person exclusive in (19a) to using the generic *i* '1PL.INCL' in (19c) to arouse sympathy in his hearer regarding his lonely predicament, and to generalise his experience beyond himself.

(19) a. *Hot* *saqe* *a-ta* *mal* *ba=na,* **ni**-*mil*
sun ascend 3INAN-GL go ART.INAN=FOC 1EXCL-inside
susar.
afflicted
'When I went east, I felt sad (lit., my insides were afflicted).' [Bk-61.007]

b. *En   keluarga   hobel.*
   person   family   not.exist
   'There was no family.'   [Bk-61.008]

c. *I   en   ga-tara=o   hobel.*
   1PL.INCL   person   3AN-know=AND   not.exist
   'There was no one we knew.'   [Bk-61.009]

In utterances with two participant roles involving non-specific referents, generic *i* '1PL.INCL' is used for one role and the noun *en* 'person' is used for the other, as in (20) and (21).

(20) *I   en   g-ege   late   h-oqon=bu,   i=o*
     1PL.INCL   person   3AN-BEN   bad   3INAN-do=GIVEN   1PL.INCL=AND
     late   a-ta   sai.
     bad   3INAN-GL   exit
     'If we do harm to someone, we too will meet with harm.'   [Bk-4.097]

(21) *Kalo i   en   g-ini   puan,   en   i*
     if   1PL.INCL   person   3AN-call   cannibal   person   1PL.INCL
     Ø-o   hosok   niq.
     1INCL/2-SRC   reply   NEG
     'If we call someone a cannibal, they won't talk to us.'   [Bk-39.015]

6.2.4.1.2 Generic *eto* '2SG'

The pronoun *eto* '2SG' is also used with generic reference in Bunaq. It is used in familiar, informal contexts by a speaker to enliven the discourse by making the addressee a participant, although the pronoun does not refer to the actual addressee in the speech act. Generic uses of *eto* '2SG' are less frequent in the corpus than generic *i* '1PL.INCL'.

Example (22) comes from a text describing the traditional prohibition against unmarried men and women spending time together. The speaker describes what used to happen to a man who violated the prohibition, putting the hearer in the role of the offender by using *eto* '2SG'. The past time setting and that the fact that the hearer is female show that the pronoun here is not being used with strict 2nd person reference.

(22) a. *Kalo tut   baqa   goet,   eto   mone   Ø-ini   tues.*
        if   past   NPRX.INAN   LIKE   2SG   man   1INCL/2-CAUS   fine
        'In the past it was like that, you as a man were fined.'   [Bk-38.022]

    b. *Nor   en   gol   pana   g-utu   mele   niq.*
       without.reason   person   small   female   3-COM   walk   NEG
       '(You) didn't just walk around with a girl.'   [Bk-38.023]

c. *En   gol   pana   g-on   h-one   niq.*
   person small female 3AN-hand   3INAN-hold   NEG
   '(You didn't just) take a girl by the hand.'   [Bk-38.024]
d. *G-on   hone, **eto** g-ubeqen   bare   goet, en*
   3AN-hand   hold   2SG   3AN-squeeze   PROX.INAN   LIKE   person
   Ø-erel   huk.
   1INCL/2-INS   shout
   'If (you) take her by the hand (and) you squeeze like this, people would shout at you.'   [Bk-38.025]
e. ***Eto** tues   masak.*
   2SG   be.fined   big
   'You would be fined a lot.'   [Bk-38.026]

Similarly, in (23) the generic *eto* '2SG' is used to bring the hearer into the discourse. Whilst demonstrating the spinning of cotton, the speaker describes what she is doing. Although the addressee is not himself (going to be) spinning, generic *eto* '2SG' is used to cast the hearer as a participant in the process.

(23) a. *H-ini   nigi gie,   pese.*
        3INAN-CAUS   fine PROSP   press
        'To make (the thread) fine, squeeze (it).'   [Bk-64.012]
     b. *Pese,   **eto**.*
        press   2SG
        'Squeeze, you (do).'   [Bk-64.013]

6.2.4.2 Polite reference

The most common non-prototypical uses of pronouns involve the expression of a social relation between the speaker and the addressee or the people the speaker refers to, such as respect or superiority. Particularly important for politeness is the avoidance of directness of reference, which can be considered confronting and rude depending on the discourse context. As is typologically common (cf. Cysouw 2003; Head 1978), Bunaq uses pronominal features such as (in)clusivity, non-singular number, and the 3rd person to circumvent direct person reference.

6.2.4.2.1 Superior *nei* '1PL.EXCL'

The pronoun *neto* '1SG' is often substituted with *nei* '1PL.EXCL' in order to avoid repeated direct reference to one's self as "I". The *nei* '1PL.EXCL' pronoun is felt to bring more dignity and authority to a speaker and to be characteristic of *g-iol nigi* '3AN-voice fine' or 'refined language'. This use of *nei* '1PL.EXCL' is most common in the speech of formally educated Bunaq speakers and may be a result of the influence of Indonesian and varieties of Malay, which also use the 1st person plural exclusive in polite self-reference (e.g., Donohue and Smith 1998).

The interaction between direct self-reference with *neto* '1SG' and indirect self-reference with *nei* '1PL.EXCL' is often complex. Example (24) comes from a text in which the speaker frequently switches between referring to herself with *neto* '1SG' and *nei* '1PL.EXCL'. The use of *neto* '1SG' (24b) and the absence of a plural pronoun cross-referencing the person-marking on *mil* 'inside' (24a) reflect the intimacy and personal importance of the events to the speaker. The switch to *nei* '1PL.EXCL' in (24c) in introducing a portion of direct speech indicates the social distance between the speaker and *Pator Rot* 'Father Rot' and the formal setting of their meeting. That is, just as the speaker and *Pator Rot* would have addressed one another indirectly in their conversation, so the speaker recreates the distance between them by referring to herself indirectly with *nei* '1PL.EXCL' in reporting those events.

(24) a. **Ni**-*mil=bu*   res   niq   los.
     1EXCL-inside=GIVEN still NEG   very
     'I felt so very unsettled.'   [Bk-85.102]

   b. **Neto** misti suster tama.
      1SG   must   nun   enter
      'I had to enter the convent.'   [Bk-85.103]

   c. Baqi,   pastor   Rot   bi,   en   Jerman   gie
      NPRX.AN priest   Rot   ART.AN person   Germany   3.POSS
      bi,   baqi   **nei**   n-ege   Hailulik
      ART.AN   NPRX.AN 1PL.EXCL   1EXCL-BEN   Hailulik
      gene sasi...
      LOC   speak
      'He, Father Rot, the person from Germany, he said to me in Hailulik...'
                                                    [Bk-85.104]

The use of *nei* '1PL.EXCL' with singular reference frequently signals the speaker's sense of social superiority over the addressee. Example (25) is an excerpt from a public speech made by a *dato* 'noble' to villagers; the speaker uses *nei* '1PL.EXCL' to assert himself and silence the chattering populace, which he addresses directly with *ei* '2PL'. In (26), the use of *nei* '1PL.EXCL' contrasts with the two earlier instances of the possessive where it is absent. The appearance of *nei* '1PL.EXCL' at the end indicates the forceful insistence of the speaker that the meat belongs to him, distinct from the earlier uses of *nie* '1EXCL.POSS', which are neutral statements of 1st person possession.

(25) **Nei**   toek, ei=o   rale=bu,   man.
     1PL.EXCL   talk   2PL=AND speak=GIVEN   come
     'I'm talking, if you also want to speak, then come (here).'   [Bk-19.025]

(26) *Kakaq=na*   **nie**   *haru*   *zal*   *ba=na,*   *si*
    cockatoo=FOC   1EXCL.POSS   shirt   bear   ART.INAN=FOC   meat
    bari   **nei**   **nie**.
    PROX.AN   1PL.EXCL   1EXCL.POSS
    'Cockatoo was wearing my clothes, (so) this meat must be *mine*.'   [Bk-78.086]

6.2.4.2.2 Honorific *i* '1PL.INCL'

First person plural inclusive pronouns are cross-linguistically frequent in 2nd person honorific address (Cysouw 2005). This pattern is attested in both the Austronesian (e.g., Tetun: van Klinken 1999: 111) and non-Austronesian languages of eastern Timor (Makasae: Correia 2011: 10). Bunaq also uses *i* '1PL.INCL' for honorific address of high-ranked individuals. In (27) and (28) the speaker respectfully addresses members of the royal class with *i* '1PL.INCL'.

(27) *Naqi,*   *o=sael*   *masak*   *zigi*   *no*   *bi*   *i*
    royal   ADDR=pig   large   beneath   OBL   ART.AN   1PL.INCL
    g-ini   *bin*   *lai*   *oa.*
    3AN-CAUS   seed   set   IAM
    'Lord, your pig down there, please make him go for the seeds.'   [LB4.016]

(28) *Neto*   *toek*   *bare,*   *i*   *Ø-ege*   *sasi=bu,*
    1SG   talk   PROX.INAN   1PL.INCL   1INCL/2-BEN   speak=GIVEN
    loi=ka   *niq?*
    good=OR   NEG
    'Is it permitted for me to talk to you like this?'   [LB8.025]

God and other biblical figures are addressed in prayers and the Bunaq Bible (*Libur por toma tip gie* 1988) with *i* '1PL.INCL'. Example (29) is taken from the Bunaq 'Our Father' or *Nei nie Ama* '1PL.EXCL 1EXCL.POSS father' and shows the use of *i* '1PL.INCL' in the address of 'God'. Example (30) comes from the Bunaq 'Hail Mary' or *Tabe Maria* 'greet Maria' and similarly exhibits the use of honorific *i* '1PL.INCL' in the address of Mary.

(29) *Nei*   *nie*   *Ama*   *pan*   *esen*   *gene,*   *i*
    1PL.EXCL   1EXCL.POSS   father   sky   HIGH   LOC   1PL.INCL
    Ø-inil   *h-atetu*   *gie.*
    1INCL/2-name   3INAN-worship   PROSP
    'Our father who are art in heaven, hallowed be thy name.'   [Bk-Pray.2]

(30) Tabe   Maria, huruk bulas kaeq, Hot   Esen   i   Ø-utu
      greet   Maria   bless   full   sun   HIGH   1PL.INCL   1INCL/2-COM
      ti-ta.
      RECP-GL
      'Hail Mary, full of grace, the Lord is with you.'   [Bk-Pray.3]

I masaq '1PL.INCL big' is used for honorific second person address in Bunaq. The construction is found in many Timorese languages and is probably calqued from the Tetun honorific 2nd person address form *ita boot* '1PL.INCL big' (Williams-van Klinken and Hajek 2006: 11–12). The *zapal* texts collected by Louis Berthe evidence occasional use of the construction in the address of royalty, as in (31). The Bunaq prayer book uses *i masaq* in reference to God; this is seen, for example, in the first line of the Bunaq version of the Apostles' Creed given in (32).

(31) Naqi,   perdua, i   **masaq** nei   nie   deu
      royal   pardon   1PL.INCL big   1PL.EXCL   1EXCL.POSS   house
      ola   sael   g-iel   goet   bere   tama   gie=ka?
      LOW   pig   3AN-nest   LIKE   CONTEXP.INAN   enter   PROSP=OR
      'Lord, excuse me, does your greatness really wish to enter our house which is like a pig's sty down there?'   [LB-6.029]

(32) Neto   piar,   i   **masaq** naqi   pan=o   muk   g-omo.
      1SG   believe   1PL.INCL big   royal   sky=AND   earth   3AN-owner
      'I believe in God, the Father Almighty, Creator of Heaven and earth.' (lit., I believe your greatness is the lord of the heavens and earth.')   [Bk-Pray.10]

Today, *i masaq* seems to be an old-fashioned form of reference. In the course of my fieldwork, I never heard *i masaq* used by Bunaq speakers. It only occurs in one text in my corpus, a *zapal* told by a nun from Gewal village. She uses the form *i masak*, illustrated in (33). The difference between *masak* and *masaq* is dialectal: the form with the velar stop [k] is used in Gewal and other villages of eastern Lamaknen, while the form with the final glottal stop is used in Dirun, where Louis Berthe did much of his fieldwork.

(33) Hai!   Neto   i   **masak** bare   e-tekeq=bu   bai
      INTERJ   1SG   1PL.INCL big   PROX.INAN   1INCL/2-watch=GIVEN   thing
      susar   *des.*
      suffer   constantly
      'I saw that your highness was sad.'   [KeleqMainu-06]

6.2.4.2.3 Respectful *ei* '2PL'

In addressing a 2ⁿᵈ person singular referent, a Bunaq speaker may use *ei* '2PL' in order to express respect and deference to the addressee's experience or knowledge over the speaker's own. In (34), *ei* '2PL' is used respectfully by children in the address of an elderly snake in an attempt to coax information from him on the whereabouts of their mother and father.

(34) a. Zi   uen   g-utu   botus, g-o   sura:
        snake one   3-COM   meet   3-SRC ask
        '(They) met with a snake, (and) asked him:'   [LB-1.022]
    b. "Bei   zi,   bei   zi,   ei   hele
        grandparent snake grandparent snake 2PL perhaps
        nei   nie   eme   nei   nie   ama
        1PL.EXCL 1EXCL.POSS mother 1PL.EXCL 1EXCL.POSS father
        g-azal?"
        3AN-see
        '"Mr Snake, Mr Snake have you perhaps seen our mother and our father?"'
                                                                    [LB-1.023]

In (35) *ei* '2PL' is used in recognition of the singular addressee's knowledge of events questioned. The addressee is shown deference in this way because it was his forefathers who did the work and, although the addressee was not yet born and so not part of the group of individuals who farmed the land in the beginning, he is seen to have greater knowledge of events.

(35) Muk   bare   ei   h-oqon   koen?
     earth PROX.INAN 2PL   3INAN-do   nice
     'Could you work the land here well?'   [Bk-29.070]

6.2.4.2.4 Polite *halaqi* '3PL' and *halali* '3DU'

The 3ʳᵈ person non-singular pronouns, *halaqi* '3PL' and *halali* '3DU', may also be used in polite 2ⁿᵈ person address. The plural pronoun can be used in singular or plural 2ⁿᵈ person address, while the dual pronoun is restricted to the address of exactly two individuals. Not attested in texts but frequent in everyday speech, this form of address is reserved for calling out from a distance and is common in this context even amongst children. It is considered coarse to call out to someone using either a 2ⁿᵈ person pronoun or their name. Thus, indirect address with *halaqi* '3PL' and *halali* '3DU' are neither honorific nor respectful *per se*, but they are polite in so far as they function to mitigate the rudeness associated with the act of calling out to someone.

In (36) the eldest child of a family calls for her two younger siblings to come and eat using *halali* '3DU', while in (37), using *halaqi* '3PL', a woman calls from her house to a single person passing by on the road, enquiring as to his destination. In (38), *halaqi* '3PL' is used to call out to a group of people.

(36) Hei, **halali**, man naq! Bai a gie oa.
INTERJ 3DU come PRIOR thing eat PROSP IAM
'Hey you two, come on! We're about to eat.' [OS-07.01]

(37) Teo mal, **halaqi**?
where go 3PL
'Where are you off too?' [OS-07.03]

(38) **Halaqi** mar mal=ka?
3PL garden go=OR
'Going to the garden, are you?' [OS-07.02]

In (39) we see the use of a 3rd person pronoun in speaker A calling out to speaker B. When speaker B (me) approaches to talk, speaker A switches to a different form of address, the kin term *aibaq* 'eldest daughter' (see §6.3.1). The use of *halaqi* '3PL' in address once the addressee has approached would be semantically bizarre.

(39) A. **Teo** mal gie, **halaqi**?
where go PROSP 3PL
'Where to, you lot?'
B. Lakus mal gie.
Lakus go PROSP
'(I'm) going to Lakus.'
A. Baqa=bu, n-ege hoqi gi-al,
NPRX.INAN=GIVEN 1EXCL-BEN peanut 3AN-carry
aibaq?
eldest.daughter
'If that's (the case), will you take some peanuts for me, daughter?'
[OS-07.01]

6.2.4.2.5 Hierarchy of polite pronoun uses

Table 6.4 presents polite uses of pronouns in a ranking from least respectful and most informal to most respectful and most formal terms. The ranking is approximate in that not all pronominal forms may be available in a given speech act, e.g., the polite 2nd person address use of 3rd person pronouns is restricted to contexts of calling out to the addressee.

Table 6.4: Politeness ranking of pronouns.

ADDRESSEE	less polite				more polite
1st person singular	*neto* '1SG'				*nei* '1PL.EXCL'
2nd person singular	*eto* '2SG'	*ei* '2PL'	*halaqi* '3PL'	*i* '1PL.INCL'	*i masaq* '1PL.INCL'
2nd person dual	*eli* '2DU'	–	*halali* '3DU'	"	"
2nd person plural	*ei* '2PL'	–	*halaqi* '3PL'	"	"

We see that indirect forms of reference are preferred over direct reference. Most polite are 1st person plural forms of address and self-reference, while least polite are forms in which the referent is directly identified by the pronoun. In between these poles, plurality in 2nd person singular address and 3rd person in 2nd person address are used to create moderately polite forms.

Outside this hierarchy are, of course, forms of non-pronominal address, which can also be used to avoid direct address. These forms of address are discussed in §6.3.

6.3 Non-pronominal person reference

In Bunaq the major options for non-pronominal person reference and address are kin terms (§6.3.1) and/or personal names (§6.3.2). Similar systems of personal reference and address exist in Indonesian and varieties of Malay (cf. Sneddon 1996: 160–163), and in Tetun Dili (cf. Williams-van Klinken and Hajek 2006), languages which have in the past exerted, and continue to exert, significant influence on the different dialects of Bunaq.

Table 6.5 presents an overview of the relative politeness of non-pronominal address forms. As with pronominal address, we see that indirect forms of address and reference are preferred over direct forms. Address by name is equivalent to direct address with a 2nd person pronoun. Address with a kin term, with or without a name, is familiar but polite, while address with titles, equivalent to English 'Mr' and 'Mrs', etc., is formal and polite.

Table 6.5: Politeness ranking of non-pronominal address forms.

less polite		more polite
name / (*eto* '2SG')	kin term / kin term + name	borrowed generic titles
		bapaq/ibu/nona etc. 'Mr/Mrs/Miss' (WT)
		señór/señora/senhorita 'sir/madam/miss' (ET)

In the following sections, I will exemplify and elaborate on forms of non-pronominal person reference in Bunaq. Because of the great variety of non-pronominal terms of person reference available, this section is limited to describing the general pattern of non-pronominal address and cites only the most common terms.

6.3.1 Kin terms

Table 6.6 presents the basic terms of Bunaq kinship; it does not include extensions and multi-word terms. Basic Bunaq kin terms are grammatically of two types: those nouns that are inalienably possessed nouns and therefore directly possessed, cited here with the possessor prefix *g-* '3AN-' (§9.3); and nouns that are alienably possessed and do not directly host possessor prefixes (§9.2). Many of the directly possessed items in Table 6.6 denote body parts in the first instance, and on the basis of a body part metaphor have extended to denote kin relations. For instance, *g-otil* denotes both the body part 'cheek' and the kin relation 'spouse'.

Table 6.6: Basic Bunaq kinship terms.

Kin term		Address?
tataq	'great grandparent'	
bei	'grandparent'	✓
eme	'mother', 'parent's sister'	✓
ama	'father', 'father's brother'	✓
g-otil	'spouse' (lit., 'cheek')	
g-ip	'wife' (southwest dialect)	
g-enen	'husband' (southwest dialect)	
baba	'mother's brother'	
naqi	'mother's older brother' (honorific of *baba*)	✓
kela	'brother-in-law'	
ai	'sister-in-law'	
kaqa	'older brother'	✓
nana	'older sister'	✓
kauq	'younger sibling'	✓
g-ol	'child'	✓
g-intili	'cross-cousin, member of same generation but opposite sex'	
apaq	'eldest child (male)'	✓
aibaq	'eldest child (female)'	✓

Table 6.6 (continued)

Kin term		Address?
pou	'second child'	✓
uzu	'third child'	✓
uka	'fourth child'	✓
g-uloq	'fifth child' (lit., 'tail')	✓
buaq	'child(ren) following the g-uloq esp. for a male child'	✓
g-atal	'grandchild'	
gu-buk	'great grandchild' (lit., 'flower')	
g-alel	'great great grandchild'	

Kin terms are the most widely used non-pronominal terms of address in Bunaq. Kin terms can be employed both within the family to denote respect and deference, and outside of it to lessen distance and formality, as well as emphasise solidarity between interlocutors. Only a few of the kin terms in Table 6.6 have been observed in address and these are marked as such. The kin terms used most frequently in address are those for people in the parent, grandparent, and child/sibling generations. I will focus on the use of these in the following sections.

In §6.3.1.1, I look at some patterns in the use of kin terms with kin, and in §6.3.1.2, with non-family. We will see that kin terms can be used in a range of contexts where they do not refer to relationships of actual biological kinship. These uses of kin terms often have the purpose of lowering or raising the status of the referent, and of expressing supplication or sarcasm.

6.3.1.1 With kin

Within the family, kin terms are more common in the address of family members than pronouns or names. This pattern is, however, asymmetrical across generations. Children and younger family members typically address their elders with the appropriate kin term. Older family members address younger ones either by the kin term referring to their birth-rank in the case of parents, or by name, or by the familiar pronoun *eto* '2SG'.

Whilst kin terms referring to birth-rank strictly encode a relation between parent and child, these terms may also be used between siblings in contexts in which use of a name or pronoun is dispreferred, such as calling out to someone (see §6.2.4.2.4). For instance, this occurs in (40) where the *pou* 'second child' calls out to her younger sister, the third of five children.

(40) **Uzu,** nei mal oa.
third.child 1PL.EXCL go IAM
'Third one, we are going now!' [OS-07.02]

By using a kin term different from that appropriate to the kin relationship between speaker and addressee, a speaker can express supplication to or sarcasm towards a person of lower status. For example, a kin term above the kin status of the addressee may be used. In (41) a parent sarcastically addresses their children as *eme* 'mother' after the children disobeyed the order from the mother not to cook the cassava; this form of address is sarcastic, signalling that the children are wilful and demanding beyond their status. Similarly, in (42) the bossy *uzu* 'third child' is addressed with the higher kin term *aibaq* 'eldest female child', highlighting the irony of a younger sibling running the evening meal preparation.

(41) **Eme,** eli=bu belan=o balun=na mal oa!
mother 2DU=GIVEN one.half=AND other.half=FOC go IAM
'Mother, you can get lost (lit., you two go to the one half or the other).'
[Bk-69.022]

(42) **Aibaq** t-inik gie loi.
eldest.daughter 3INAN-cook PROSP good
'Oldest sister can go ahead and cook.' [OS-07.02]

Kin terms are also frequent in self-reference, with the kin term chosen according to the relationship between speaker and addressee. Self-reference with a kin term is familiar but polite, as it avoids direct reference. For instance, in (43) a parent addresses her child by name, but refers to herself as *eme* 'mother', sweetly attempting to cajole the child into eating more. By contrast, kin terms are omitted in favour of more direct person reference strategies when a speaker is angry or annoyed. For instance, in (44) a mother expresses anger at – what she sees as – her parasitic children, addressing them directly with *ei* '2PL' and referring to herself directly with *neto* '1SG'.

(43) Uzu bai a baqis, **eme** mobel.
third.child thing eat much mother like
'(When) you (third child) eats a lot, mother likes (it).' [OS-07.03]

(44) **Ei** bai a los. **Neto** n-ini koleq.
2PL thing eat very 1SG 1EXCL-CAUS tired
'You lot eat so much. It wears me out.' [OS-07.03]

6.3.1.2 With non-kin

Bunaq kin terms are regularly extended to non-family members. Incorporation of outsiders into the kin system by means of address with kin terms indicates familiarity and solidarity between interlocutors.

Young people may use the Bunaq kin terms *eme* 'mother' or *ama* 'father' in the address of non-kin adults with whom they have a respectful relationship. The term *bei* 'grandparent, ancestor' is also common as a term of respectful address to the elderly. Example (45) was overheard on a bus: as an elderly man was getting off the bus, a teenage girl gently reminded him about a sack he had left behind, addressing him courteously with *bei*. In (46) we see *bei* used in respectful third person reference to a car owner.

(45) **Bei**,   hani   karon   uen   roe   r-oenik.
     grandparent PROH   sack   one   SPEC.INAN 3INAN-forget
     'Elder, don't forget this one sack.'   [OS-07.02]

(46) Oto   saqe,   oto **Bei**   Mikael   ota=o   Fulur no...
     car   ascend   car grandparent   Mikael   LEVEL=ADDR   Fulur OBL
     '(I) got into a car, (the) car (of) Elder Mikael over there in Fulur...'
                                                                 [Bk-58.13]

In East Timor, Bunaq speakers often use *abo* 'ancestor' (< Tetun Dili *avo* 'grandparent' < Portuguese *avô/avó* 'grandfather/grandmother') in much the same manner as *bei* in West Timor.

Sibling kin terms *kauq* 'younger sibling', *kaqa* 'older brother', and *nana* 'older sister' are often used to indicate solidarity between non-kin referents. In (47) the children in Gewal village familiarly refer to themselves as my little brothers and sisters. In (48) compound sibling kin terms (see §3.2.1.3) are used to encourage split communities to come together again despite disputes.

(47) Nei   ie   **kauq**   mil   Ø-ege   tabe
     1PL.EXCL   1INCL/2.POSS   younger.sibling   COLL   1INCL/2-BEN   greet
     baqis~baqis.
     REDUP~much
     'We your little brothers and sisters greet you heartily.'   [Bk-14.007]

(48) Ei   **kauq-kaqa**,   ei   **kauq-nana**.
     2PL   younger.sibling-elder.brother   2PL   younger.sibling-elder.sister
     'You are brothers, you are sisters.'   [Bk-66.050]

In place of Bunaq sibling kin terms, Tetun Dili *maun* 'older brother' and *mana* 'older sister' and Indonesian/Malay *kakak* 'older sibling' are often used in non-kin peer reference in East Timor and West Timor, respectively.

In non-kin reference, many kin terms can be used with broader reference, including a wider range of ages than would normally be acceptable within the family. Native and borrowed kin terms of higher and lower status can alternate in elaborate ways to create particular pragmatic effects. The text in (49) illustrates both these patterns. In the excerpt, I am being addressed by an old woman who describes to me the difficulties of her life since she broke her wrist, and asks for help. Consider the variety of kin terms used in address:

(49) a. *Kou   haqal,   neto   huqe   a-ta   wil*
        slip finished 1SG   HERE   3INAN-GL   come.LOW
        ba,   ie   bapaq roi   ie
        ART.INAN 1INCL/2.POSS father SPEC.AN 1INCL/2.POSS
        kauq   n-os,   roe   no.
        younger.sibling 1EXCL-wait SPEC.INAN   OBL
        'After I slipped, I came down here and your father and younger siblings were waiting in this place.'   [Bk-46.056]

   b. *N-on   han   leqak-wen   roe   goet on,*
        1EXCL-hand no.matter bend-ANTIC SPEC.INAN LIKE DO
        aibaq.
        eldest.daughter
        'My hand was just all twisted up like this, oldest daughter.'   [Bk-46.057]

   c. *Neto bai   h-oqon   loi   niq, ri-ta   paksa,*
        1SG thing 3INAN-do good NEG   REFL-GL   force
        r-on   suel   rele,   nie   eme.
        REFL-hand left-hand INS   1EXCL.POSS   mother
        'I couldn't do a thing, I forced myself to use my left hand, my mother.'   [Bk-46.058]

Throughout this text, the speaker addresses me using a range of kin terms. The variety of kin terms used here creates multiple perspectives on my position, on the one hand, placing me in reference to other people present and, on the other hand, indicating that I am someone for whom the speaker has respect. In (49a) the kin terms, *bapaq* 'father' (< Malay *bapak*) and *kauq* 'younger sibling', are directed to me as addressee with the appending of the 2nd person form of the possessor *ie* '1INCL/2.POSS'. At the same time the use of *kauq* 'younger sibling' rather than *kaqa* 'older brother' or *nana* 'older sister' indicates respect as they place me as addressee above the referents of *kauq* 'younger sibling', some of whom were substantially older than me. The familiarity of this address is a function of the personal nature of the story and the pleading tone with which it was told. It is also striking as it was the first time that I had met the speaker. In (49b) the speaker addresses me as *aibaq* 'eldest daughter', a term which again suggests a degree of acquaintance between speaker and hearer, but also respect. Finally, in (49c) the speaker becomes entirely deferential, addressing me, her much younger hearer, as 'my mother'.

6.3.2 Personal names

Bunaq people have multiple given names. Bunaq personal names are of three types: Christian names, ancestral (and clan) names, and nicknames.

Christian names (referred to as *g-inil serani* '3AN-name Christian' or *g-inil agama* '3AN-name religion' in Bunaq Lamaknen) are of either Dutch or Portuguese origin. In Bunaq as in Malay/Indonesian, Christian names are typically shortened: e.g., *Hironimus* > *Hiro*; *Ignatius* > *Nasu*; *Johanis* > *Anis*; *Florentina* > *Tina*; and *Marieta* > *Eta*. The use of a Christian name in address indicates familiarity between interlocutors, and is most common amongst children and close adult friends, or by older people to younger people. Amongst adults, a first name may be coupled with a kin term or title in more polite, respectful address, e.g., *Ama Nasu* 'father Nasu', though zero address may be favoured over this.

Christian names are followed by an ancestral name. Table 6.7 lists some of the male and female ancestral names amongst the Bunaq of Lamaknen. An ancestral name is composed of any two of these names. The first element appears as in the table, while the second, if vowel-final, takes a final glottal stop. Thus, we find the male names *Bau Maliq* and *Mali Bauq*, but not any of the following: **Maliq Bau*, **Bauq Mali*, **Bau Mali*. In everyday speech, only the first element of the two elements in a name is typically ever used. It is often coupled with a kin term, e.g., *Loe Uzu* 'Loe the third child'.

Table 6.7: Sample of Bunaq names in Lamaknen.

MALE		FEMALE	
Ati	Loe	Balok	Lawa
Atok	Luan	Belak	Lese
Bau	Mali	Biaq	Lika
Bauk	Mau	Boeq	Lilo
Bere	Mauk	Bui	Mako
Hale	Nak	Ili	Mare
Hasuk	Nali	Irik	Motu
Koli	Seran	Koeq	Soi

As it was explained to me, the process of giving an ancestral name traditionally involved saying an ancestor's name to a new-born child and then offering the mother's breast to it. If the child took the breast, then the ancestor's name also became the child's name. If not, a new name must be selected and the process is repeated until the child takes the mother's breast. Today this system of name-giving has largely broken down and ancestral names are passed down as surnames from father to child.[1]

As mentioned above, Bunaq speakers do not normally use each other's names in address. A variety of address strategies involving constructed names exist for the avoidance of simple given names. One strategy I observed was that some traditional names had a conventionalised substitute name used when calling out to someone. Table 6.8 presents the traditional names (left) and their replacements (right). These replacement names only substitute for the first of an individual's two Bunaq names. The use of the substitute name when calling out to someone is considered polite, but is also a signal of familiarity between caller and callee. The replacement names vary to some extent from village to village. For example, my language consultant, Hironimus Mau, could only name one replacement pair for female names (*Bui* → *Lotu*) that was used in Dirun village, but speakers from elsewhere could adduce other examples in use in other villages. In the case of the male names *Bere* and *Tai*, different substitute names are used in different villages.

Table 6.8: Bunaq name replacements.

MALE		FEMALE	
Asa →	Keri	Bia →	Koles
Bau →	Lole	Boe →	Bokes
Bere →	Manus ~ Leki	Bui →	Lotu
Hale →	Boles	Motu →	Kuru
Koi →	Kalis	Soi →	Suk
Mali →	Taus		
Mau →	Sinas		
Mela →	Koles		
Tai →	Lolis ~ Mau		
Talo →	Leos		

---

1 In addition to given names, individuals may be also identified by the name of their Bunaq *deu* 'house'. House names themselves often invoke the name of the apical ancestor, for instance, *Tes g-atal* 'Tes 3AN-grandchildren' 'Descendants of Tes' or *Loe g-atal* 'Loe 3AN-grandchildren' 'Descendants of Loe'. Other house names seem to refer to a founding group, such as *Mone Sogo* 'Ten Men', and *Bein Goniqil* 'Four Chiefs', or to a founding event, such as *Tama Op* 'Enter Highlands', a Bunaq Bobonaro house name. Within each *deu* 'house', there are multiple named lineage groups, called *gamal* (lit., 'male'). Whilst house and lineage group names are important for locating an individual within the complex networks of kinship relations, they are not used in address.

Another Bunaq speaker, Anselmus Tallo, described a pattern of name avoidance formerly present in the village of Loonuna, whereby a woman could be politely addressed with a special construction that involved an amalgamation of her first given name and her eldest child's first given name. In this, the child's name is suffixed with *-na* (a morpheme not known outside of this construction) and then followed by the mother's name. For example, where a mother is called *Ili* and her eldest child *Luruk*, the mother may be referred to as *Lurukna Ili*. If the child's name ends in a vowel, this is deleted on suffixation with *-na*; thus, where a mother is called *Lawa* and her eldest child *Talo*, she may be referred to as *Talna Lawa*. This deletion rule does not apply in the case of final diphthongs; thus, where a mother is called *Olo* and her eldest child *Soi*, she may be referred to as *Soina Olo*. This construction is not available for naming fathers. Anselmus Tallo observes that this teknonym-like naming practice was common in Loonuna in the past, but that it is not used anymore.

Across Lamaknen, many individuals are known widely only by a nickname, and can only be identified by their proper names with difficulty. For instance, a young boy in Gewal village was known to everyone as *Bibel* 'morning star, Venus' and not his Christian name *Markus*. Nicknames often draw on some physical property of the individual. Nicknames I encountered for older males used *bei* 'ancestor' followed by a modifier, such as *Bei Rukut* 'elder curly', referring to the referent's very curly hair, and *Bei Giral* 'elder 3AN-eye' in homage to the referent's intelligence. These names were not normally used in address.

Nicknames of noble-ranked individuals are prefixed by *bete* for females and *manek* for males. Both terms are of Tetun origin: Tetun *bete* 'dear one' and *manek* probably from Tetun *mane* 'man'. Nicknames with these elements, particularly for women, draw on a physical characteristic of the referent, such as in *Bete Koen* 'dear beautiful' and *Bete Lalenok* 'dear mirror', both used in reference to girls who were considered pretty. In some cases, individuals are referred to simply with *bete* and *manek* without an additional epithet or in combination with the individual's Christian name. For instance, one of my informants had the Christian name *Vinsensius*, but was always referred to simply as *Manek*, while another was known as *Manek Rofinus*, using his Christian name also.

6.4 Summary

A wide range of person reference and address strategies, both pronominal and non-pronominal in nature, are available to Bunaq speakers. The Bunaq system of person reference has been significantly complicated and enriched by other languages, most recently Indonesian/Malay in the west and Tetun Dili in the east. This has resulted in a very pliable system of person reference, in which, in any given situation, there is more than one way to address or refer to an individual. The choice of forms of person reference is governed by factors such as the relative status of interlocutors, their familiarity, and the formality of the setting. Address forms inappropriate according to these considerations may also be chosen in order to express different effects, such as sarcasm, censure, or esteem.

Chapter 7
Determiners

7.1 Introduction

Determiners are pervasive in Bunaq speech. Although they are not obligatory in any context, almost every utterance contains at least one determiner. Determiners function to locate entities and events in space, time, and discourse (cf. Anderson and Keenan 1985; Levinson 2003), or to encode pragmatic and knowledge-related meanings including specificity, contrast, and counter-expectation (cf. Himmelmann 1996, 1997; Levinson 2004).

Bunaq dialects vary considerably in their determiner inventories and the categories these encode. This chapter deals only with the determiners of the Bunaq Lamaknen dialect (Table 7.1). The set of determiners includes five demonstratives and one article. While the article is used to determine an overtly expressed NP/clause, only demonstratives can substitute for an NP/clause. Each determiner has two forms, an ANIMATE and an INANIMATE form. ANIMATE forms of determiners are characterised by the presence of a high front vowel /i/, which in all but one case occurs finally; INANIMATE forms of determiners are characterised by the absence of the high front vowel. Determiners are in a paradigmatic relationship with one another; they never co-occur to mark one and the same constituent.

Table 7.1: Bunaq Lamaknen determiners.

		ANIMATE	INANIMATE
DEMONSTRATIVES			
PROXIMAL	'PROX'	*bari*	*bare*
NON-PROXIMAL	'NPRX'	*baqi*	*baqa*
SPECIFIER	'SPEC'	*doi*	*doe*
CONTRASTIVE	'CONTR'	*himo*	*homo*
COUNTER-EXPECTATIONAL	'CONTEXP'	*beri*	*bere*
ARTICLE	'ART'	*bi*	*ba*

In this chapter, I describe each determiner's spatial, temporal, discourse, pragmatic, and knowledge-related functions in detail. In §7.2, I provide an overview of the different morphosyntactic contexts and the associated functions of determiners. The uses of the different determiners are then described in detail: the proximal demonstrative (§7.3), the non-proximal demonstrative (§7.4), the specifier demonstrative (§7.5), the contrastive demonstrative (§7.6), the counter-expectational demonstrative (§7.7), and the article (§7.8).

https://doi.org/10.1515/9783110761146-007

Sub-topics relevant to determiners discussed elsewhere are: §3.5.4, treating the properties that define determiners as a word class; and §6.2.2, dealing with how determiners combine with pronouns of different persons. Cross-references to other sections of the grammar that touch on demonstratives can be found in the relevant sections of this chapter.

7.2 Overview of determiner functions

Determiners occur at the right periphery of the NP or, less commonly, of the clause. Determiners have different functions and agreement behaviour in these two situations. When determining an NP, determiners agree in ANIMACY with the N_{HEAD}; while determining a clause, only the INANIMATE form of the determiner is used. Only demonstratives can occur pronominally and proclausally.

The syntactic functions of determiners (DET) and the sub-set of demonstratives (DEM) are summarised schematically in Table 7.2. Not all determiners can appear in all functions listed in the table. Each of these functions is briefly overviewed in the remainder of this section.

Table 7.2: Overview of syntactic functions of demonstratives.

DOMAIN		SYNTACTIC SCHEMA	
Nominal	Adnominal	[. . . DET]$_{NP}$	referring expression
	Pronominal	[DEM]$_{NP}$	referring expression
Clausal	Adclausal	[$_{CLAUSE}$ . . . DET]	non-embedded nominalised clause
	Adclausal	[$_{CLAUSE}$ . . . DET], [$_{CLAUSE}$ . . .]	nominalised thematic clause
	Proclausal	[$_{CLAUSE}$ . . .]. DEM, [$_{CLAUSE}$ . . .]	anaphoric sentence connective
	Proclausal	[$_{CLAUSE}$ . . . DEM *goet*]. [$_{CLAUSE}$ . . .]	cataphoric sentence connective

The most common use of Bunaq determiners is to determine NPs, that is, as part of a referring expression in the clause. In this context, the determiner directs the hearer's attention to the NP referent within a domain, often relative to a deictic centre. The domains in respect to which Bunaq determiners serve to locate an NP referent are spatial, temporal, pragmatic, or discourse information, as well as expectation. All determiners are used in NPs.

When determining a clause, determiners do not refer to a participant in the clause, but have scope over the clause as a whole. There are two kinds of uses for adclausal determiners. First, an adclausal determiner marking a free-standing clause forms a non-embedded nominalisation (Schapper and San Roque 2011). Non-embedded nominalisations are exclamatory clauses in which the speaker asserts a stance concerning the state of affairs denoted by the clause. The demonstratives used in non-embedded nominalisations carry different temporal and knowledge-related (e.g., visibility, certainty, expectation) meanings related to their uses in the nominal domain. The proximal, non-proximal, specifier, and counter-expectational demonstratives are attested in Bunaq non-embedded nominalisations.

Second, an adclausal determiner can mark a clause that is conjoined to another, following clause. These are thematic clauses (de Vries 2006; Haiman 1978) that function as "domain-creators" (Reesink 1994) – that is, they denote an event frame in terms of which the event in the conjoined clause is to be understood (see §15.3.1 on this and other types of clause conjoining by juxtaposition). Thematic clauses are often, but not necessarily, used as part of tail-head linkage structures (§15.4.1). The demonstratives marking thematic clauses carry temporal and pragmatic meanings related to their uses in the nominal domain. The proximal, non-proximal, specifier, and contrastive demonstratives, as well as the article, are used to create thematic clauses.

Proclausal uses of demonstratives are text cohesion devices that connect the event or situation in one sentence with those in another sentence. Proclausal demonstratives may be anaphoric (referring back) or cataphoric (referring forward). The constructions and typical demonstratives for these two directions of reference are not identical. A proclausal demonstrative used anaphorically occurs in a sentence-initial position, often in combination with a (verbal) postposition (such as those discussed in §15.3.2.5) and/or a post-verbal conjunction (§15.3.2.1) separated by a small break in intonation from the rest of the sentence. The contrastive demonstrative is the unmarked choice of demonstrative in this function, but the proximal and non-proximal demonstratives can also be used.

A proclausal demonstrative used cataphorically is always the complement of the postposition *goet* 'LIKE' (see §12.2.3 on the broader functions of this postposition). In cataphoric use, a demonstrative points forward to either a following sentence or, more broadly, to the following discourse as a whole. The most frequent use of cataphoric demonstratives with *goet*, however, is to introduce direct speech and thought (§12.2.3.3). While the non-proximal, proximal, and contrastive demonstratives all may be used for proclausal cataphora, the specifier demonstrative is by far the most common demonstrative used with this function.

In the remainder of this chapter, each of Bunaq's determiners is discussed with relation to the functions described here. While I present a detailed classification of determiner use, it should be borne in mind by the reader that not all uses are well understood; many factors, including attention, prior knowledge and belief, and the ongoing interaction itself, as well as the physical arrangement of participants, are all features of context that simultaneously influence the choice of a determiner.

7.3 Proximal demonstrative

In the nominal domain, the proximal demonstrative is used to refer to items which are spatially, temporally, or metaphorically close to the speaker, as well as anaphorically and non-anaphorically in discourse deixis (§7.3.1). In the clausal domain, it is used in non-embedded nominalisations, in thematic constructions, and as a sentence connective (§7.3.2).

7.3.1 In the nominal domain

7.3.1.1 Spatial use

The proximal demonstrative picks out a referent close to the speaker in space. The position of the addressee is immaterial to the use of the proximal. In (1), *bare* 'PROX.INAN' marks an entity held by the speaker, and which is thus proximal to the speaker but not the addressee. In (2) the speaker and addressee are both in, and thus equally proximal to, the village referred to with *bare* 'PROX.INAN'. The example in (3) comes from a letter and here it is only the speaker who is proximal to the *en* 'people' marked by *bari* 'PROX.AN'.

(1)   Eli   hiloq   **bare**   zal.
       2DU   oil   PROX.INAN   carry
       'You two, take this oil.'   [Bk-4.071]

(2)   Halaqi   mina,   tas   **bare**   a-ta.
       3PL   come.HIGH   village   PROX.INAN   3INAN-GL
       'They came up to this here village.'   [Bk-29.020]

(3)   En   Gewal   no   **bari**   nona   gu-sura   ruquk.
       person   Gewal   OBL   PROX.AN   girl   3AN-ask   always
       'These people here in Gewal always ask after Nona.'   [Bk-14.011]

Example (4) shows the use of the proximal in contrast to that of the non-proximal demonstrative. Speaker A queries the name of the item spatially removed from him using *baqa* 'NPRX.INAN'. Speaker B responds by taking hold of the thread and confirming it as the thread in question using a demonstrative description with the proximal *bare* 'PROX.INAN'.

(4)   A.   Suta   **baqa**   h-ini   nanun?
              thread   NPRX.INAN   3INAN-call   heddles
              'Those threads are called the heddles?'   [Bk-35.091]

B. *Suta   gol   **bare**   h-ini   nanun.*
   thread   small   PROX.INAN   3INAN-call   heddles
   'These threads are called the heddles.'   [Bk-35.092]

See §7.5.1.1 on the use of the proximal with the specifier in contrastive proximal deixis.

A noun marked with the proximal demonstrative cannot refer to a referent that is proximal to the hearer but not the speaker. This is seen in the impossibility of combining the proximal demonstrative with the addressee locational *o* 'ADDR' (§8.3.4), as in (5).

(5) **Nego   o   **bare**?*
    what   ADDR   PROX.INAN
    'What's this you have?'   [Not-07.04]

The INANIMATE form of the proximal demonstrative, *bare* 'PROX.INAN', is frequently used on its own to refer to the speaker's current location. In this function, *bare* 'PROX.INAN' occurs as the complement of a postposition. In (6) the speaker refers to her present location with *bare* 'PROX.INAN' as the complement of *no* 'OBL'.

(6) *Ene   uen   no   neli   **bare**   no.*
    night   one   OBL   1DU.EXCL   PROX.INAN   OBL
    'One night, the two of us were in this (place).'   [Bk-43.050]

7.3.1.2 Temporal use

The INANIMATE proximal, *bare*, appears in contexts of temporal deixis to denote present time. With this meaning, the proximal may appear marking a temporal noun, as in (7), or on its own without any nominal, as in (8).

(7) ***Lele   bare**   i   en   g-ini   puan   gie, ...*
    nowadays   PROX.INAN   1PL.INCL   person   3AN-call   cannibal   PROSP
    'These days now, (if) we want to call a person a cannibal, ...'   [Bk-39.068]

(8) *Jadi   nei   h-one   h-oqon   daro   **bare**.*
    so   1PL.EXCL   3INAN-hold   3INAN-make   until   PROX.INAN
    'Thus, we have held on to (the custom) until this (time).'   [Bk-8.034]

7.3.1.3 Anaphoric use

In narratives, the proximal demonstrative is used to track anaphoric referents which are less expected as topics in the discourse, typically in contexts where there is low referential distance. Topic marking with the proximal is infrequent in comparison to that with the non-proximal demonstrative, which is used to mark referents that are expected and/or continuing topics in the discourse (§7.4.1.3). Unlike the non-proximal demonstrative, the proximal is not used to track different topics in successive clauses, or to track a single topic over multiple clauses.

Topics marked by the proximal demonstrative are digressive; they function to bring the referent temporarily to the foreground of the discourse in contexts where they are not expected to persist in the discourse. In (9a) and (10a) *zo* 'mango' and *Belu* 'Belu (province)' respectively are introduced into the discourse without any demonstrative marking, and in their subsequent mentions (9b) and (10b) these nouns are marked with the proximal demonstrative. Both form asides to the main narrative, in which the speaker digresses to explain a point about the new referents *zo* 'mango' and *Belu* 'Belu (province)' before returning to the central storyline.

(9) a. Nei **zo** za zal.
    1PL.EXCL mango ripe carry
    'We were carrying a ripe mango.' [Bk-37.073]

b. Bai a haqal, g-ini zo **bare**=na
    thing eat finished 3AN-CAUS mango PROX.INAN=FOC
    a ai.
    eat ONLY
    'After eating, (we) made her eat this mango.' [Bk-37.074]

(10) a. Hoqe gene en **Belu**.
    SPCPLC LOC person Belu
    'Here are Belu people.' [Bk-66.100]

b. **Belu bare** h-ini moen.
    Belu PROX.INAN 3INAN-call friend
    'Belu means "friend".' [Bk-66.101]

The second anaphoric function of the proximal demonstrative is in summative contexts, where it marks the topic of the preceding discourse in a speaker's concluding remarks. The antecedents of the proximal in these contexts are less expected in that they are discontinuative, i.e., they do not continue the narrative forward, but break it off by referring back to the beginning of the narrative. For instance, in (11) *teras* 'terrace' is established in (11a). The noun does not occur again until (11d) where it is marked with the proximal as part of the speaker's summing up of his explanation of the need for the terraces.

(11) a. Kalo i **teras** h-oqon niq, muk g-io
    if 1PL.INCL terrace 3INAN-make NEG earth 3AN-faeces
    il zal haqal.
    water carry finished
    'If we didn't make terraces, the nutrients in the earth (lit., the earth's shit) would all be carried away by the water.' [Bk-65.024]

b. *Dele muk toiq gene haqal,   i   ie*
   INS earth flat LOC finished 1PL.INCL 1INCL/2.POSS
   muk roe   muk tewe=si.
   earth SPEC.INAN earth slope=REAS
   '(It would be carried) with (it) and all (end up) on the flat land, because this land of ours is sloping land.' [Bk-65.025]

c. *Homo=bu,   bai   a   loi niq oa.*
   CONTR.INAN=GIVEN   thing eat good NEG IAM
   'If that's so (that the earth is carried down), (we) cannot eat anymore.' [Bk-65.026]

d. *Homo   gie=na,   teras   bare   h-oqon.*
   CONTR.INAN   3.POSS=FOC   terrace PROX.INAN 3INAN-make
   'For this reason, (we) build these terraces.' [Bk-65.027]

Another example of the summative proximal is given in (12). This example occurs at the end of a text describing the cycle of the agricultural year. *Bare* 'PROX.INAN' marks *bai* 'thing', which refers not to a particular referent in the preceding discourse, but rather sums up, referring to all the various stages of the agricultural cycle described in the preceding text.

(12) ***Bai   bare***   *bei   mil   g-on   no h-oqon   mien.*
     thing PROX.INAN   ancestor COLL 3AN-hand OBL 3INAN-do routinely
     'These things were done routinely in the time of the ancestors.' [Bk-8.033]

7.3.1.4 "Closeness" of relation use

A proximal demonstrative may also appear marking a discourse participant on its first mention. In these cases, the proximal demonstrative description is licenced by a non-spatial 'close' association between the speaker and the referent. That is, the proximal can be used to identify that the entity being referred to is figuratively proximal to the speaker, since the 'proximity' to the speaker acts as the anchor by which the referent can be identified.

In (13) and (14), *bari* 'PROX.AN' marks a first mention of a proper name referring to a kin member of the speaker. In (15), *bare* 'PROX.INAN' marks a first mention of the speaker's clan name. In each case the referent of the proximal-marked NP is absent from the speech situation. The presence of the proximal serves to clarify that the referent of the proper name is a relative of the speaker who has the specified name, thereby excluding other persons of that name as possible referents.

(13) *Neto* ***Yati bari***   *n-oq   no   taq.*
     1SG   Yati PROX.AN   1EXCL-waist OBL CONT
     'Yati (my daughter) was in my womb still', i.e., 'I was still pregnant with Yati.' [Bk-2.002]

(14) **Wendy bari**=na gu-bul kumu.
Wendy PROX.AN=FOC 3AN-head massage
'It was this (i.e., my daughter) Wendy who massaged his head.' [Bk-43.052]

(15) Nie reu **Rato Alin bare.**
1EXCL.POSS house Rato Alin PROX.INAN
'My house is this Rato Alin.' [Bk-67.281]

Use of the proximal demonstrative in contexts of figurative closeness does not always introduce a new participant, but may also apply to referents with an antecedent in the discourse. In (16) the proximal is used to denote the already mentioned referent *dik* 'yam', but it does not track the referent. The first use of *bare* 'PROX.INAN' marking *dik* 'yam' in (16a) is licenced by spatial closeness to the speaker: the mother points out the *dik* 'yam' to the children as the one they are not allowed to eat. In the text, the mother then goes to the garden, leaving the yam with the children, which they decide to cook and eat. In this part of the discourse we see that *dik* 'yam' is not (and cannot) be tracked by the proximal, but rather by the contrastive, *homo* 'CONTR.INAN' (§7.6.1.3). When the mother smells the cooking yam and exclaims that the children are cooking her yam, the proximal is again used to mark *dik* 'yam' in (16e) and (16f). However, it is not conditioned by spatial nearness (since the mother is in the garden), but denotes that the *dik* 'yam' are figuratively near the speaker on account of being the mother's property. The proximal marking on *meaq gol* 'child' in (16e) is also licenced by the close association between parent and child.

(16) a. "**Dik buleqen bare** eli hani t-inik.
yam red PROX.INAN 2DU PROH 3INAN-cook
'"This red yam you two don't cook (it).' [Bk-69.009]
b. Eli bai hosu=na t-inik."
2DU thing other=FOC 3INAN-cook
'You two cook something else."' [Bk-69.010]
c. Homo haqal soq, halaqi mar mal.
CONTR.INAN finished SEQ 3PL garden go
'Then, they went to the garden.' [Bk-69.012]
d. Meaq gol hiloqon himo dopol~d-opol
child two CONTR.AN REDUP~REFL-lead
dik buleqen homo=na t-inik.
yam red CONTR.INAN=FOC 3INAN-cook
'Those two children did as they pleased, cooking that red yam.' [Bk-69.013]

e. *Gie pie homo leleq, gie eme gie ama*
   3.POSS steam CONTR.INAN float 3.POSS mother 3.POSS father
   g-o pir.
   3-SRC reach
   'That steam wafted, reaching their mother and their father.' [Bk-69.015]

f. *Homo=na,* **"*Meaq gol hilogon bari*** *ciaq,*
   CONTR.INAN=FOC child two PROX.AN refuse
   g-ini ***dik bare*** *t-inik.*
   3AN-CAUS yam PROX.INAN 3INAN-cook
   'Then (the mother said), "These two children refuse to not cook these yams.' [Bk-69.016]

g. *Halali* ***dik bare*** *t-inik oa."*
   3DU yam PROX.INAN 3INAN-cook IAM
   'They are cooking this yam already."' [Bk-69.017]

7.3.1.5 Non-anaphoric uses

Bunaq also has a minor pattern in which the proximal demonstrative is used on the first mention of a referent. I have identified only a few instances of this in the corpus. The function of the proximal demonstrative is not clear in all of these cases.

In a few examples, the proximal demonstrative is used at the beginning of a narrative and appears to be cataphoric in function. For example, in (17) the marking of *hik* 'path' with *bare* refers forward to the following text in which the speaker describes the route to Nualain village.

(17) *Neto Nualain mal* ***hik~hik bare****=na h-alolo.*
     1SG Nualain go REDUP~path PROX.INAN=FOC 3INAN-follow
     'When I go to Nualain, I take this route (lit., follow these paths).' [Bk-34.001]

But not all non-anaphoric uses of the proximal demonstrative are clearly cataphoric. An example is provided in (18), where it marks *tumel* 'money'. In the preceding utterances, the speaker describes his experiences as a child, when he would take bottles to sell in Weluli. In (18) he explains that he did this because he wanted to make money for his family. We see that *tumel*, in this, its one and only mention in the text, is determined with the proximal demonstrative; the subsequent text, after (18), does not elaborate on the money.

(18) *Neto gol taq no, sirubisu* ***bare*** *h-oqon,*
     1SG small CONT OBL work PROX.INAN 3INAN-make
     nie eme=o ama gi-ta tulun, tan otas
     1EXCL.POSS mother=AND father 3AN-GL help because age

baqa **tumel bare** *susar.*
NPRX.INAN money PROX.INAN difficult
'When I was small, I did this work (to) help my parents, because at that time money was difficult.' [Bk-13.012]

Because the number of examples of this kind is so small, it is not clear at this stage what motivates the use of the proximal demonstrative in non-anaphoric contexts.

7.3.2 In the clausal domain

7.3.2.1 Non-embedded use

Marking a non-embedded nominalisation, *bare* 'PROX.INAN' indicates that the event is in the immediate experience of the speaker. For instance, in (19) the speaker uses *bare* to assert that the process of building the house is ongoing, as it is present and visible at the time of speaking. The example in (20) comes from a text in which the speaker describes a prolonged illness that she experienced. The clause-final *bare* marking the second clause denotes that her good health has continued since she recovered from the illness and is plain to see in the present time. In both cases, the non-embedded nominalisation with *bare* directs attention to the proposition and its current actuality; that is, the fact that the speaker (and, by extension, the addressee) can see its truth in the here and now.

(19) *Mone mete g-inat bi, baqi=na h-oqon* **bare.**
man NOW 3AN-earliest ART.AN NPRX.AN=FOC 3INAN-make PROX.INAN
'My first son, it is him who is building (the house) {as can be seen}.'
[Bk-46.067]

(20) *Homo naq=na, neto mele loi, jadi neto loi*
CONTR.INAN PRIOR=FOC 1SG walk good so 1SG good
bare.
PROX.INAN
'After that, I could walk, and so I am better {as can be seen}.' [Bk-40.014]

Non-embedded nominalisations with *bare* are also used to vivify past time events. Example (21) comes from a text in which children recount to an adult an encounter they had with a *muk gomo* 'earth spirit' the day before. The adult hearer is sceptical about the story and suggests that it was not a *muk gomo* that they saw (Speaker A in 21). One of the children reacts against this suggestion, pointing out that the sighted individual had her face covered in blood (a characteristic implied to be inconsistent with those of a normal person). She uses a *bare*-marked clause to assert that the event is true, by construing it as if it can be seen in the 'here and now' and is therefore evident (Speaker B in 21).

(21) A. *Hele*   *muk*   *g-omo*   *niq?*
         perhaps   earth   3AN-master   NEG
         'Perhaps it was not an earth spirit?'   [Bk-47.072]
     B. *Muk*   *g-omo*   *on=e!*
         earth   3AN-master   DO=AGREE
         'It was an earth spirit!'   [Bk-47.073]
     C. *Baqi*   *hasi*   *g-ewen*   *ho~ho*   *on*   ***bare***.
         NPRX.AN   thus   3AN-face   REDUP~blood   DO   PROX.INAN
         'Her face was all bloodied thus {it's true}.'   [Bk-47.074]

7.3.2.2 Thematic use

Where a clause marked by *bare* 'PROX.INAN' is used thematically as the first in a conjoined pair, it provides a present ongoing frame for the event described in the following clause. In (22) the speaker comments that the child's present riding of the horse is the setting for (and by implication the cause of) the event described in the second clause, namely the child's fatigue. Example (23) is spoken as the speaker demonstrates the playing of the *hol okoq* 'stone hole' game; the initial clause marked with the proximal denotes the playing of the game as the setting during which the gaming pebbles are put into the holes.

(22) *En*   *gol*   *bari*   *kura*   *saqe*   ***bare***,   *setenga*   *mati*.
     person   small   PROX.AN   horse   ascend   PROX.INAN   half   dead
     'In riding a horse, this young person has become completely worn out (lit., half dead).'   [Bk-37.099]

(23) *I*   *bukuq*   ***bare***,   *hol*   *g-oq*   *baqi*
     1PL.INCL   play   PROX.INAN   stone   3AN-seed   NPRX.AN
     g-olo,   *g-olo*,   *g-olo*,   *g-olo*.
     3AN-put.in   3AN-put.in   3AN-put.in   3AN-put.in
     'With us playing (like) this, (we) put the pebbles in (the holes) again and again.'
                                                                            [Bk-9.003]

7.3.2.3 Sentence connective use

The proximal demonstrative *bare* 'PROX.INAN' is able to be used pronominally in connecting sentences both anaphorically and cataphorically, but is not frequent in either function.

An example of the proximal demonstrative used anaphorically to refer back to an event or information in the preceding sentence is given in (24). We see that in (24b) *bare* occurs sentence-initially and refers back to the stubbornness described in (24a). The use of *bare* as the sentence connective here serves to pick out this stubbornness as the immediate cause for the speaker's threat in (24b).

(24) a. *Hilaq=sa   eto   n-ege   u-bul   hol   gie   oa.*
         surprise=EVEN 2SG 1EXCL-BEN 1INCL/2-head stone PROSP IAM
         'It's surprising that you are starting to be so stubborn (lit., are stone-headed) with me.'   [OrelNisPipLoko-56]

   b. ***Bare***   ***gie=na****,   eto   hosok   teni,   eto   bai*
      PROX.INAN   BECAUSE=FOC   2SG   reply   again 2SG   thing
      h-azal   tepel oa,   neto ozol   Ø-utu   bukuq   niq.
      3INAN-see   true   IAM   1SG   NEG   1INCL/2-COM   play   NEG
      'Because of this (i.e., stubbornness), if you talk back again, you will see, I won't play with you at all.'   [OrelNisPipLoko-57]

Like the non-proximal demonstrative, the proximal demonstrative only encodes topical anaphora in connecting sentences and is a marked choice of demonstrative in these contexts. Unlike *homo* 'CONTR.INAN' (§7.6.2.2), *bare* cannot connect strings of sentences together.

The example in (25a) shows *bare* 'PROX.INAN' used cataphorically with the postposition *goet* 'LIKE' to refer forward to a following sentence denoting direct speech and thought (25b).

(25) a. *Halali t-awaq   t-erel   bukuq, Orel   d-opol*
         3DU   RECP-befriend RECP-INS play   monkey REFL-force
         bare   ***goet*** *on.*
         PROX.INAN   LIKE   DO
         'When the two of them had made friends, monkey plucked up the courage to say this:'   [OrelLenuk-03]

   b. *"A,   moen!   Ili   bei   gie   mok   a   gie*
         INTERJ friend 1DU.INCL grandfather 3.POSS banana eat   PROSP
      oa!"
      IAM
      '"Ah friend! Let's go and eat the man's bananas."'   [OrelLenuk-04]

The specifier demonstrative is more typical in such cataphoric contexts – see §7.5.2.3.

7.4 Non-proximal demonstrative

In the nominal domain, the non-proximal demonstrative is used for items which are spatially, temporally, or metaphorically removed from the speaker, as well as being used both anaphorically and non-anaphorically in discourse deixis (§7.4.1). In the clausal domain, it is used in non-embedded nominalisations, in thematic constructions, and as a sentence connective (§7.4.2).

7.4.1 In the nominal domain

7.4.1.1 Spatial use

The non-proximal demonstrative contrasts with the proximal demonstrative; it is not distal, but rather is used to pick out entities which are viewed as not proximal to the speaker. It is an unmarked term in that it can be used to refer to things just about anywhere in space, except where reference is very proximal, e.g., when the speaker is holding the item.

The use of the non-proximal in spatial deixis is illustrated in (26) and (27), which are text excerpts from a videotaped conservation about weaving. Speaker B is sitting on the ground strapped into a back-strap tension loom, while speaker A sits just beside the loom on a chair. In each excerpt, speaker A queries speaker B as to the name of a part of the loom: respectively, *nanun* 'heddles', situated directly in front of the speaker A, and *hasarai* 'embroidery frame', located halfway up the loom.

Example (26) shows the use of the non-proximal in contrast to that of the specifier and proximal demonstrative. Speaker A uses *baqa* 'NPRX.INAN' with a pointing gesture to query the identity of an item, and speaker B responds using the specifier *roe* 'SPEC.INAN' to denote that it is the questioned item in particular that is called *nanun* 'heddle'. Speaker A queries the name of the item using *baqa* 'NPRX.INAN' again, to which speaker B responds by taking hold of the thread and confirming it as the thread in question using a demonstrative description with the proximal *bare* 'PROX.INAN'.

(26) A. ***Baqa***   h-ini   nego?
       NPRX.INAN 3INAN-call what
       'What's that called?'   [Bk-35.089]

    B. *Roe*   h-ini   nanun.
       SPEC.INAN 3INAN-call heddles
       'These are called the heddles.'   [Bk-35.090]

    A. *Suta* ***baqa***   h-ini   nanun?
       thread NPRX.INAN 3INAN-call heddles
       'Those threads are called the heddles?'   [Bk-35.091]

B. *Suta   gol   bare   h-ini   nanun.*
   thread small PROX.INAN 3INAN-call heddles
   'These small threads are called the heddles.'   [Bk-35.092]

Example (27) illustrates how the non-proximal demonstrative can be used to point to any item outside of the very immediate personal space of the speaker. Speaker A uses the non-proximal *baqa* 'NPRX.INAN' to query a part of the loom which he labels *g-on g-iri* '3AN-arm 3AN-leg'. Speaker B again responds using the specifier *roe* 'SPEC.INAN', with speaker A then repeating the item's name in confirmation, again using the non-proximal to refer to it. Speaker B confirms the name and now herself uses the non-proximal *baqi* 'NPRX.AN'; this is accompanied by a pointing gesture to clarify that it is the embroidery loom that she is referring to. Although the loom is closer to speaker B than speaker A, speaker B can refer to it with the non-proximal demonstrative, as does speaker A, because the item is not in her immediate space and even when pointing she is still removed from the item.

(27) A. *Homo   gie   g-on   g-iri   **baqa***
        CONTR.INAN 3.POSS   3AN-hand   3AN-leg   NPRX.INAN
        h-ini   nego,   g-on   g-iri=na   rele   bai
        3INAN-call what   3AN-hand   3AN-leg=FOC   INS   thing
        *selu   gie   **baqa**.*
        weave   PROSP   NPRX.INAN
        'What is that bit called, that bit with which you weave?'   [Bk-35.022]
     B. *G-on   g-iri   hasarai.*
        3AN-hand   3AN-leg   embroidery.frame
        'The bit is the embroidery frame.'   [Bk-35.023]
     B. *Hasarai=na   roe.*
        embroidery.frame=FOC   SPEC.INAN
        'This is the embroidery frame.'   [Bk-35.024]
     A. ***Baqi***   *g-ini   hasarai?*
        NPRX.AN   3AN-call   embroidery.frame
        'That's called *hasarai*?'   [Bk-35.025]
     B. ***Baqi***   *g-ini   hasarai.*
        NPRX.AN   3AN-call   embroidery.frame
        'That's called *hasarai*.'   [Bk-35.026]

7.4.1.2 Temporal use

The non-proximal demonstrative *baqa* 'NPRX.INAN' can mark temporal nouns referring to past events/times, such as *waktu* 'time' in (28) and *otas* 'age' in (29).

(28) Halaqi   he   gaqal,   tan   **waktu**   **baqa**   pas   neto
     3PL   run   all.AN   because   time   NPRX.INAN   exactly   1SG
     halaqi   g-azal,   neto   langsung   ri-mil   h-ukat.
     3PL   3AN-see   1SG   immediate   REFL-inside   3INAN-lift
     'They all ran away, because at that time when I saw them, I immediately sent my thoughts up (i.e., to God).'   [Bk-47.115]

(29) ...,   nie   eme=o   ama   gi-ta   tulun,   tan
             1EXCL.POSS   mother=AND   father   3AN-GL   help   because
     otas   **baqa**   tumel   bare   susar.
     age   NPRX.INAN   money   PROX.INAN   difficult
     '..., (to) help my parents, because at that time money was difficult.'   [Bk-13.012]

7.4.1.3 Anaphoric use

The non-proximal demonstrative is used anaphorically in topic-comment structures to mark the topicality of the referent. This high-frequency pattern is illustrated in (30) and (31). In their first mention, *sore* 'machete' (30a) and *guru* 'teacher' (31a) are not marked by a demonstrative. But in their next occurrence in the following sentence, both occur clause-initially determined by the non-proximal demonstrative (30b & 31b). The determiner marks the referents as topical and the clausal predication acts as a comment on them.

(30) a. *Nie*   *ama*   **sore**   *legul*   *uen*   *r-oq*   *ni*
        1EXCL.POSS   father   machete   long   one   REFL-waist   OBL
        t-olo.
        3INAN-put.in
        'My father puts a long machete in his belt.'   [Bk-24.037]
     b. **Sore**   **baqa**   *koen*   *raza*   *los.*
        machete   NPRX.INAN   beautiful   different   very
        'That machete is so very beautiful.'   [Bk-24.038]

(31) a. *Nei*   *nie*   **guru**   *uen*   *g-ini*   *Donatus Mau.*
        1PL.EXCL   1EXCL.POSS   teacher   one   3AN-call   Donatus Mau
        'One of our teachers was called Donatus Mau.'   [Bk-70.094]
     b. **Guru**   **baqi**   *g-utu*   *t-erel*   *mele.*
        teacher   NPRX.AN   3-COM   RECP-INS   walk
        'That teacher went walking with her.'   [Bk-70.095]

In contrast to the anaphoric use of the proximal demonstrative (§7.3.1.3), the non-proximal marks an anaphoric referent whose topicality is expected in the discourse. "Expected" here means not simply that the topicality of the referent is predictable from the immediately preceding discourse, as that could also hold for topic-comment structures with the proximal. Rather, the topicality of the referent marked by the non-proximal is neither surprising nor emphatic, but part of the predictable course of the advancement of the narrative. In accordance with this, the non-proximal can track a different topic from clause to clause as new thematically prominent referents enter the discourse. In (32), after two non-topical mentions in (32a) and (32b), *mar* 'garden' is then made topic with marking by the non-proximal in (32d). In the comment on topical *mar* 'garden', the place name *Hol Taqol* is mentioned for the first time, becoming the non-proximal marked topic in (32e). In turn, the *zo* 'mango' mentioned in the comment on topical *Hol Taqol* in (32e) (and earlier in the discourse) becomes the topic with non-proximal marking in (32f).

(32) a. *Hot mil uen no, nei nie moen mil*
sun DUR one OBL 1PL.EXCL 1EXCL.POSS friend COLL
*g-utu nei goniqo ola **mar** mal.*
3-COM 1PL.EXCL three LOW garden go
'One day, we – my friends (and I) – we three went down to a garden.'
[Bk-1.011]

b. *Nei **mar** gene zo a gie.*
1PL.EXCL garden LOC mango eat PROSP
'We were going to eat mangoes in the garden.' [Bk-1.012]

c. *Le gie mel, kira-kira tuku hitu, nei*
next.day wake approximately hour seven 1PL.EXCL
kampung gene sai.
village LOC exit
'The next morning, around 7 o'clock, we left the village.' [Bk-1.013]

d. ***Mar baqa**, mar ate h-ini Hol Taqol, ola*
garden NPRX.INAN garden far 3INAN-call Hol Taqol LOW
zol alan gene.
river side LOC
'That garden was a garden far away called Hol Taqol, down by the river.'
[Bk-1.014]

e. ***Hol Taqol baqa** no nei nie zo*
Hol Taqol NPRX.INAN OBL 1PL.EXCL 1EXCL.POSS mango
masak bul hiloqo.
big trunk two
'At that (place) Hol Taqol, we had two big mango trees.' [Bk-1.015]

f. ***Zo baqa** za haqal oa.*
mango NPRX.INAN ripe finished IAM
'Those mangoes were already all ripe.' [Bk-1.016]

The anaphoric use of the non-proximal demonstrative can also track a single, continuing topical referent across clauses. Consider the example in (33). *Mar* 'garden' is introduced into the discourse in (33a) without a determiner. Subsequently, in the thematic clauses in (33b) and (33c), sentence-initial *mar* continues to be undetermined because these clauses provide only background information for the following clauses. In (33b) and (33c), *mar* 'garden' is topical and tracked with the non-proximal demonstrative.

(33) a. ***Mar*** h-oqon roe goet on.
 garden 3INAN-make SPEC.INAN LIKE DO
 'Making a garden is like this.' [Bk-3.002]
 b. ***Mar*** h-iqil to goniqon goniqil oa, ***mar***
 garden 3INAN-leave.behind year three four IAM garden
 baqa hatak oa.
 NPRX.INAN ripe IAM
 '(Once) a garden has been left behind for three (or) four years, that garden is then ready.' [Bk-3.003]
 c. ***Mar*** hatak oa=si, ***mar*** ***baqa*** se oa.
 garden ripe IAM=REAS garden NPRX.INAN cut.back IAM
 'Because a garden is ready, that garden is now cut back.' [Bk-3.004]

7.4.1.4 Use in referring to a new discourse participant

The non-proximal demonstrative is used non-anaphorically to refer to entities that are definite and identifiable to the speaker and hearer. The referent of an NP marked by a non-proximal demonstrative in non-anaphoric use constitutes new information that is thematically prominent in the discourse, in that it is part of the narrative advancement.

In (34) and (35), the non-proximal is used non-anaphorically to mark *mar* 'garden' and *zobuq* 'forest', respectively, on their first mention in the discourse. The referents of *mar* 'garden' and *zobuq* 'forest' are inferentially retrievable: in (34c), the referent of garden is inferred as those gardens owned by *nei* '1PL.EXCL'; and in the response of speaker B in (35), because the hearer knows the location of the water, the referent of 'forest' follows from their knowledge of the surroundings of the water. In both cases, the referent introduced with the non-proximal determiner constitutes new information which advances the narrative: *mar* 'garden' in (34) is the location in which the planned terraces are to be built, as the speaker goes on to describe; *zobuq* 'forest' in (35) refers to the latest location towards which the participant moves in a series of movements which are described in the discourse.

(34) a. *Niat no ti-ta mit=na tut.*
 earliest OBL RECP-GL sit=FOC first
 'In the beginning (we) sit together first.' [Bk-65.005]

b. *Homo=si,   nei   rale.*
   CONTR.INAN=REAS   1PL.EXCL   talk
   '(We do this) so that we (can) talk.'   [Bk-65.006]

c. *Ti-ta   bolu   haqal,   homo   soq,   le gie*
   RECP-GL   united   finished CONTR.INAN   SEQ   next.day
   *mel   nei   mulai   **mar**   **baqa**   h-amos.*
   morning   1PL.EXCL   begin   garden   NPRX.INAN   3INAN-clear
   'After (we've sat) together, then, the next morning we begin to clear those gardens.'   [Bk-65.007]

(35) A. *Il   ni   mal,   hosu   mal? Il   ni   sai?*
        water   OBL   go   other   go   water   OBL   exit
        'From the water, (she) went to another (place)? (She) left the water?'   [Bk-47.038]

     B. *Baqi   **zobuq**   **baqa**   a-ta   mal.*
        NPRX.AN   forest   NPRX.INAN   3INAN-GL   go
        'She went to that forest.'   [Bk-47.039]

Where there are few inferential or contextual clues for identifying the non-anaphoric referent of NPs marked with the non-proximal, a relative clause often provides the information needed to identify the referent ("establishing modifiers" in Himmelman's [1996: 217] terms). In (36) the referent of *kale=o hotel gol* 'small plants and trees' is identifiable via the relative clause locating them in the garden. Similarly, in (37) the *a noq* 'food' referred to is delimited in a relative clause as that of the speaker's liking. As in the previous examples, (34) and (35), the marking with the non-proximal in (36) and (37) indicates that the referents of the relevant NPs constitute thematically prominent new information which will persist in the discourse.

(36) *Uen   [kale=o   hotel   gol   [mar   mil   no]$_{RC}$ **baqi**$_{NP}$*
     one   plant.sp=AND   tree   small   garden   inside   OBL   NPRX.AN
     g-iep.
     3AN-cut
     'One cuts back those plants and small trees inside the garden.'   [Bk-3.006]

(37) *[A   noq=na   [neto   mobel]$_{RC}$ **baqa**]$_{NP}$ g-ini   paqol.*
     eat   seed=FOC   1SG   like   NPRX.INAN   3AN-call   maize
     'That food which I like is called maize.'   [Bk-24.031]

7.4.1.5 Use in person deixis

In §6.2 it was observed that Bunaq has no personal pronouns in the 3rd person singular. The non-proximal demonstrative fills this gap: the ANIMATE form of the non-proximal, *baqi* 'NPRX.AN', is regularly used pronominally to track persisting topics with a singular human referent, as in (38).

(38) a. Tuan   Bert,   Luis   Bert,   **baqi**   man.
        master Berthe Louis   Berthe NPRX.AN   come
        'Mr Berthe, Louis Berthe, he came.'   [Bk-70.001]
    b. Pertama **baqi**   man,   hoqe   muk   Lamaknen   tama.
        first   NPRX.AN   come   SPCPLC land   Lamaknen   enter
        'The first time he came, (he) entered Lamaknen here.'   [Bk-70.002]
    c. Bobonaro   gene=na   man,   **baqi**.
        Bobonaro   LOC=FOC   come   NPRX.AN
        '(He) came from Bobonaro, he (did).'   [Bk-70.003]
    d. Bobonaro   gene   man,   Aiasa   Honaru gene   man.
        Bobonaro   LOC   come   Aiasa   Honaru LOC   come
        '(He) came from Bobonaro, came from Aiasa Honaru.'   [Bk-70.004]
    e. **Baqi**   Gewal   ni.
        NPRX.AN   Gewal   OBL
        'He was in Gewal.'   [Bk-70.005]
    f. Gewal   ni   haqal, **baqi**   Gewal   ni   hot   mil
        Gewal   OBL   finish NPRX.AN   Gewal   OBL   sun   DUR
        tuen-tuen   uen   haqal, **baqi**   langsung   Lakmaras   mal.
        how.many   one   finish NPRX.AN   directly   Lakmaras   go
        'Being finished in Gewal, finished after several days in Gewal, he went directly to Lakmaras.'   [Bk-70.006]

A count in a sample of fifty texts shows that the tendency for pronominal *baqi* 'NPRX.AN' to be used in singular reference is strong. The results are summarised in Table 7.3. We see that, whilst adnominal *baqi* 'NPRX.AN' is relatively frequent in both singular and plural reference, there is a clear skewing to singular reference in pronominal use. In the same fifty-text sample, there was no skewing in the marking of singular versus non-singular referents across adnominal and pronominal uses for the INANIMATE form of the non-proximal, *baqa* 'NPRX.INAN'. What is more, adnominal and pronominal uses of *baqa* 'NPRX.INAN' were equally common.

Table 7.3: Type count of reference of *baqi* 'NPRX.AN' in 50 texts.

Pronominal		Adnominal	
SG ref	PL ref	SG ref	PL ref
123	5	63	33

Of the five pronominal uses of *baqi* 'NPRX.AN' with plural reference, only one, given in (39), has human plural reference. There is, however, some ambiguity in the example: *tani* 'farmer', the apparent antecedent of *baqi* 'NPRX.AN', is unusually distant, occurring some twenty lines earlier with no subsequent mention prior to *baqi* 'NPRX.AN' itself. As such, it is not entirely clear that the speaker had *tani* 'farmer' in mind as the antecedent of the later pronominal *baqi* 'NPRX.AN'.

(39) a. *Nei   tani.*
       1PL.EXCL farmer
       'We are farmers.'   [Bk-3.001]

   b. *En   tani   sirubisu, mar=na   h-oqon.*
       person   farmer   work   garden=FOC   3INAN-make
       '(When) farmers work, it is gardens that they make.'   [Bk-3.002]

   c. *Kalo   koin   haqal   oa,   inel   man   mien,*
       if   burn.garden   finished   IAM   rain   come   usually
       baqi   *h-ota*   *los*   *oa.*
       NPRX.AN   3INAN-plant   very   IAM
       '(When) the garden burning is finished, (when) the rain comes as usual,
       they plant like mad.'   [Bk-3.021]

The remaining examples of pronominal *baqi* 'NPRX.AN' with plural reference have animal, not human referents. The two instances are given in (40) and (41).

(40) a. *Jadi **sael** biasa   paqol   gi-a,   **orel**   biasa   paqol*
       so   pig   usually   maize   3AN-eat   monkey   usually   maize
       gi-a...
       3AN-eat
       'So pigs and monkeys usually eat maize.'   [Bk-8.007]

   b. *Jadi   **baqi**   g-erel   huliliq.*
       so   NPRX.AN   3AN-INS   planting.festival
       'So (we) do the *huliliq* festival (to scare) them.'   [Bk-8.018]

   c. *Homo=na,   **baqi**   hani   paqol   g-arat.*
       CONTR.INAN=FOC NPRX.AN   PROH   maize   3AN-destroy
       'Then they don't destroy the maize.'   [Bk-8.019]

(41) a. *Sael   makao   g-epal   legul   baqa   goet.*
       pig   Macao   3AN-ear   long   NPRX.INAN   LIKE
       'Macao pigs have longs ears like that.'   [Bk-47.101]

b. ***Baqi*** g-epal legul baqa goet.
   NPRX.AN 3AN-ear long NPRX.INAN LIKE
   'They have long ears like that.' [Bk-47.102]

In sum, *baqi* 'NPRX.AN' appears to be in the course of specialising in its pronominal use for 3rd person singular referents, while *baqa* 'NPRX.INAN' is still frequent in pronominal and adnominal reference. The strong tendency of *baqi* 'NPRX.AN' to be used pronominally in singular human reference appears to arise out of pressure to fill the gap in the pronominal paradigm caused by the fact that the 3rd person personal pronouns, *halaqi* '3PL' and *halali* '3DU', only refer to non-singular humans.[1]

7.4.2 In the clausal domain

7.4.2.1 Non-embedded use

The non-proximal demonstrative *baqa* 'NPRX.INAN' is used in non-embedded nominalisations to assertively refer to past events. In (42) the use of the non-embedded nominalisation marked with *baqa* emphasises that the speaker *did* plant beans despite having broken her right hand.

(42) D-on suel bare rele neto ho gapa gol
   REFL-hand left PROX.INAN INS 1SG bean.type small
   uen h-ota ***baqa!***
   one 3INAN-plant PROX.INAN
   'I planted a few beans with this left hand of mine {I did}.' [Bk-46.016]

A non-embedded nominalisation with *baqa* can also be used for clauses denoting events in the present where the information is considered to be obvious, that is, an established fact from the speaker's perspective. For example, the context for (43) is that the speaker is sent by her parents to fetch water, but on the way comes across Big Ears (Bunaq *Gepal Masaq*), who requests that she stop and delouse him. Her exclamatory response using a non-embedded nominalisation marked by *baqa* in (43) suggests impatience, signalling that she is obviously in a hurry and naturally cannot accommodate the request.

(43) Tataq, neto hei bun nai ***baqa***.
   great.grandparent 1SG hurry INDEF INFORM NPRX.INAN
   'Grandfather, I am in a bit of a hurry {I am}.' [GepalMasaq-15]

---

[1] Givón (1984: 353–360) has shown that pronominal demonstratives often develop into 3rd person pronouns. In Bunaq, whilst *baqi* 'NPRX.AN' has become de-stressed and is used to track persisting topics in the manner of a 3rd person pronoun (Diessel 1999: 120), it is still syntactically a determiner.

7.4.2.2 Thematic use

Where a clause marked by *baqa* 'PROX.INAN' is used thematically as the first in a conjoined pair, it provides a topical frame for the event described in the following clause. Most commonly the thematic clause–marking use of *baqa* forms part of tail-head linkage constructions, but it can also include additional topical information. For example, the thematic clause marked with *baqa* in (44b) repeats the final verb *pelek* 'plant' from (44a), but also includes additional information about where the cloth should be placed. *Baqa* marks the clause as the topical frame in terms of which the information in the following clause is to be understood.

(44) a. Tais   tul   wit,   roq   pelek.
cloth piece take cut.off plant
'Get a bit of cloth, cut it off, and plant it.' [Bk-23.062]

b. **Hik** **gene** **pelek** **haqal** **baqa**, i
path LOC plant finished NPRX.INAN 1PL.INCL
Ø-ewen ler oa.
1INCL/2-face bright IAM
'Once the (bit of cloth) is planted in the path, then we can find our way (lit., our faces brighten).' [Bk-23.063]

Occasionally, a thematic clause marked by *baqa* will not repeat final elements of the preceding sentence, but will rely on information from the preceding discourse. For instance, the examples in (45) come from a text in which two children search for food. In this episode of the narrative they travel deep into a forest until they reach a grove of seven trees (45a & 45b). In (45c), the thematic clause marked by *baqa* refers to the journey the two had taken, without using any of the words from the preceding sentences. The thematic clause sets their journey as the topical frame in which their following a dog is to be understood.

(45) a. Halali hotel otan hitu h-o pir.
3DU tree tree.sp seven 3INAN-SRC reach
'The two of them reached seven *otan* trees.' [Bk-69.031]

b. Hotel otan ba hitu.
tree tree.sp ART.INAN seven
'There were seven *otan* trees.' [Bk-69.032]

c. Halali mal **baqa**, zap gol uen g-ua gene mal.
3DU go NPRX.INAN dog small one 3AN-footprint LOC go
'In going (to the grove of seven trees), the two of them had followed a small dog.' [Bk-69.033]

7.4.2.3 Sentence connective use

The non-proximal demonstrative *baqa* 'NPRX.INAN' is regularly used as an anaphoric sentence connective to refer back to an event or information in the preceding sentence, as in (46) and (47).

(46) a. *Il   muk   mil   a-ta   tama   on, hani   leleq.*
       water earth inside 3INAN-GL enter DO   PROH flow
       '(When) the water enters the soil, it should not flow away.'   [Bk-65.109]
   b. ***Baqa***   *gie=na*,   *nei   sekal   g-olo,   dikotel=o*
       NPRX.INAN BECAUSE=FOC 1PL.EXCL potato 3-bury   casava=AND
       g-olo.
       3-bury
       'Because of that, we plant potatoes and cassava too.'   [Bk-65.110]

(47) a. *Heser   oa.*
       dead   IAM
       '(You) are dead.'   [Bk-9.004]
   b. ***Baqa=bu,***   *rasal.*
       NPRX.INAN=GIVEN stop
       'If that's the case, (we) stop (playing).'   [Bk-9.005]

Like the proximal demonstrative, the non-proximal demonstrative is limited to encoding topical anaphora in connecting sentences and is a marked choice of demonstrative. Unlike *homo* 'CONTR.INAN' (§7.6.2.2), *baqa* cannot connect strings of sentences together.

Occasionally, *baqa* is used cataphorically with the postposition *goet* 'LIKE' to refer forward to a following sentence denoting direct speech or thought. An example is given in (48).

(48) a. *En   pana   gie   matas mil   **baqa**   goet.*
       person female 3.POSS old   COLL NPRX.INAN LIKE
       'The woman's parents (say) this:'   [Bk-38.005]
   b. *"Kalo   eto   n-ol   bari   g-akara   tepel, ..."*
       if   2SG   1EXCL-child PROX.AN 3AN-love true
       '"If you really love this child of mine, ..."'   [Bk-38.006]

7.5 Specifier demonstrative

The specifier demonstrative indicates that the referent is exactly the entity or set of entities at issue. In the nominal domain, the specifier demonstrative has spatial and discourse deictic functions (§7.5.1). In the clausal domain, it is used in non-embedded nominalisations, in thematic constructions, and as a cataphoric sentence connective (§7.5.2).

In rapid speech, specifier demonstratives often show phonological reduction when used adnominally. When unstressed their /o/ vowel either reduces to a weak schwa or drops out entirely, thus *doe* and *doi* can be realised as [r(ə)e] and [r(ə)i], respectively.

7.5.1 In the nominal domain

7.5.1.1 Spatial use

The specifier demonstrative is distance-neutral in spatial deixis. However, like distance-marked demonstratives, the specifier demonstrative may be used to focus the hearer's attention on entities in the surrounding situation, with or without an accompanying pointing gesture.

Examples of the situational use of the specifier demonstrative were already given in (26) and (27), where it contrasted with the proximal and non-proximal demonstratives. Example (49) further exemplifies the specifier demonstrative's situational use from the same text as (26) and (27). In this part of the text, the speaker is going through the different names for the parts of the loom as she weaves. We see that each new item that the speaker takes hold of in the process of weaving is marked with the specifier demonstrative, bringing referents into the attentional focus of the hearer and specifying that only that referent is meant in the context.

(49) a. *Homo   haqal   soq, roi   g-ini   rosan.*
        CONTR.INAN   finish   SEQ   SPEC.INAN   3AN-call   loom.part
        'And then, this is called *rosan*.'   [Bk-35.033]

   b. ***Rosan   roe**=na   mete   suta   huqe   gene*
        loom.part   SPEC.INAN=FOC   NOW   thread   HERE   LOC
        homo   h-ake-wen   gie   h-ini.
        CONTR.INAN   3INAN-push-ANTIC   PROSP   3INAN-CAUS
        'It is this *rosan* which is made to be put through in the thread here.'
                                                                                  [Bk-35.034]

   c. *Homo   haqal   soq, roi   g-ini   g-iri   gol.*
        CONTR.INAN   finished   SEQ   SPEC.AN   3AN-call   3AN-leg   small
        'And then, this (the heddle rod) is called "little leg".'   [Bk-35.035]

   d. ***G-iri   gol   roi**=na   i   nanun*
        3AN-leg   small   SPEC.AN=FOC   1PL.INCL   heddles
        ***roe**   no   g-olo.*
        SPEC.INAN   OBL   3AN-put
        'It is this "little leg" that is put into these heddles.'   [Bk-35.036]

e. **Nanun roe** no t-olo.
 heddles SPEC.INAN OBL 3INAN-put
 'It's put into these heddles.' [Bk-35.037]
f. Homo haqal soq, h-iqit.
 CONTR.INAN finished SEQ 3INAN-lift
 'And then, it's lifted.' [Bk-35.038]
g. Homo naq=na, **nolu roe**
 CONTR.INAN PRIOR=FOC weaving.sword SPEC.INAN
 i t-olo.
 1PL.INCL 3INAN-put.in
 'Then, this weaving sword is inserted.' [Bk-35.039]

The specifier demonstrative is also found in contexts of contrastive proximal spatial deixis, as illustrated in (50). The proximal demonstrative is used to introduce the first item, and the specifier demonstrative, the second, contrasting item; both may be accompanied by a pointing gesture.

(50) **Tais bare** tais mone, **tais roe** tais pana.
 cloth PROX.INAN cloth man cloth SPEC.INAN cloth woman
 'This cloth is a man's cloth, this cloth is a woman's cloth.' [OS-06.01]

The use of the specifier demonstrative in contrastive proximal deixis appears to be a relic of the specifier demonstrative's historical derivation from a proximal demonstrative.[2] Synchronically in Bunaq Lamaknen, the specifier demonstrative otherwise retains no distance-bound situational deictic meaning. This is seen in the fact that, in addition to referring to speaker-proximal items, the specifier demonstrative readily combines with elevational locationals (51; see §8.3.1), and the addressee locational (52; see §8.3.4).

(51) Muk **ota roe**, en baqi negara uen oa.
 land LEVEL SPEC.INAN person NPRX.AN country one IAM
 'That land over there, those people are a country now.' [Bk-11.021]

(52) Nego **o=roe**?
 what ADDR=SPEC.INAN
 'What's that you've got?' [OS-06.01]

---

2 This is seen in the fact that in the conservative southwestern Bunaq dialect (§1.5), the specifier demonstrative is used in proximal reference. The proximal demonstratives *bare/bari* in Bunaq Lamaknen do not exist in southern Bunaq.

7.5.1.2 Discourse use

In discourse deictic referent tracking, the specifier demonstrative may be used either anaphorically or non-anaphorically to pick out a referent as the specific one being referred to in the discourse.

In (53) and (54) we observe the use of the specifier demonstrative in non-anaphoric reference. In (53) the speaker is comparing different words for 'eat' in Timorese languages he knows. After comparing the words in Meto and Makasae, he notes that he does not know the word for 'eat' in Kemak, a new referent in the discourse. The headless NP referring to Kemak in (53d) is determined by the specifier demonstrative in order to define the scope of the reference to Kemak specifically (see §9.2.1.1 on possessive constructions with no head).

(53) a. *Dawan=na* mua.
Meto=FOC eat
'The Meto (word for eat is) *mua*.' [Bk-61.095]

b. *Baqa* *uen~uen,* Makasai.
NPRX.INAN same Makasae
'That's the same, (as in) Makasae.' [Bk-61.096]

c. *Kalo* nua, *haqe* *gene* mua.
if eat THERE LOC eat
'Well (it's) *nua* (in Makasae), there (in Meto) it's *mua*.' [Bk-61.097]

d. [Kemak *gie* **roe**] neto tara niq.
Kemak 3.POSS SPEC.INAN 1SG know NEG
'That of Kemak I don't know.' [Bk-61.098]

In (54) there are two NPs marked by the specifier demonstrative. In the first, the specifier demonstrative marks a pronominally headed NP referring to a new discourse referent and denotes that it is specifically the people geographically removed from the Bunaq people that call them by the name Marae. The second NP determined by the specifier demonstrative is appositional to the first and elaborates on the content of the first in order to ensure that the reference is clear.

(54) a. *Marae, en* *Bunaq* *mos=o* *da-tara.*
Marae person Bunaq also=AND REFL-know
'Marae, the Bunaq people also know themselves (as that).' [Bk-15.012]

b. *Halaqi en* *Bunaq, tapi mete* [*halaqi guni* *gene*
3PL person Bunaq but NOW 3PL outside LOC
roi]=*na,* [*ate gene* **roi**]=*na* *toek.*
SPEC.AN=FOC far LOC SPEC.AN=FOC talk
'They are Bunaq people, but now it is those (people) on the outside, those at a distance that talk (like this, calling Bunaq people "Marae").'
[Bk-15.013]

In (55) the specifier demonstrative is used anaphorically, referring to an entity whose identity is clear from the events previously described in the text. On its first mention in (55a), *g-otil* '3AN-spouse' occurs without a determiner, but on its second mention in (55b) it is marked by the specifier demonstrative, emphasising that the wife of the dead man is the precise entity in question.

(55) a. **G-otil**=na man.
 3AN-spouse=FOC come
 'It was his wife who came.' [Bk-70.088]
 b. **G-otil** roi, baqi gie jurisan hosu, botani.
 3AN-spouse SPEC.AN NPRX.AN 3.POSS discipline other botany
 'This wife of his, her discipline was different, (it was) botany.' [Bk-70.089]

Since it is used to pick out an individual referent or particular set of referents, contrastive meaning can be a contextual implicature of the specifier demonstrative's use, but it is by no means entailed by it. For instance, contrastiveness of the specifier demonstrative–marked argument is suggested in (53d) above, where, having just given the lexemes for 'eat' in the Meto and Makasae languages, the speaker proceeds to profess his ignorance of it in Kemak. Another example of the specifier demonstrative's apparent contrastiveness is given in (56). In (56b) the speaker describes how he was left behind to care for his injured friend, while in (56a) his other friend went to fetch the adults. In this example, the contrastiveness arises out of the juxtaposition of different referents within the discourse and does not come from the specifier demonstrative itself, which functions merely to circumscribe the reference to a single entity.

(56) a. Uen g-ini mal matas mil gi-wit.
 one 3AN-CAUS go old COLL 3AN-fetch
 'One was made to go fetch the parents.' [Bk-1.026]
 b. Neto **roe** gi-ta zaga, baqa no.
 1SG SPEC.INAN 3AN-GL watch.over NPRX.INAN OBL
 'I specifically watched over him there.' [Bk-1.027]

The contrastive demonstrative *homo/himo* is the determiner which is argued to have inherently contrastive semantics – see section §7.5.1 for illustration and discussion.

7.5.2 In the clausal domain

7.5.2.1 Non-embedded nominalisation use

Non-embedded nominalisations marked with the INANIMATE form of the specifier demonstrative are most commonly found with past time events which have clear and ongoing implications in the present. In (57) *doe* indicates that the death of Mau Paran had occurred shortly before the time of utterance, while in (58) the snake has just been blinded. The non-embedded nominalisations function to highlight the speakers' exasperation at these recent events.

(57) *Tuen   goet   on   oa,   Mau Paran   heser   haqal   **roe**?*
     how   LIKE   DO   IAM Mau Paran   dead   finish SPEC.INAN
     'What (should we) do now that Mau Paran has died?'   [Bk-4.069]

(58) *N-iral=sa   bulu   on   oa   **roe**!*
     1EXCL-eye=EVEN   blind   DO   IAM SPEC.INAN
     'Now I am blind!'   [BuIkunBeiLoa-82]

Doe is also used to create non-embedded nominalisations with respect to events which are, or ought to be, known to both the speaker(s) and addressee(s). Example (59) is from the text, already sampled earlier, in which two children cook the yams their parents had explicitly told them not to cook. The nominalising demonstrative *doe* indicates that the smell of the cooking yams had recently reached the parents (the speakers in this example), and furthermore that it was obvious that it would, and the children must have known that this would happen. In (60), the speaker exclaims to his friend that they did not bring food with them to the garden. The implication of the non-embedded nominalisation with *doe* is that they could have known they would need food.

(59) *Gie   pie   ola   nei   n-o   pir   **doe**!*
     3.POSS steam   LOW   1PL.EXCL 1EXCL-SRC   reach   SPEC.INAN
     'Its smell (lit., steam) reached us down below {as we all knew it would}.'
                                                             [Bk-69.021]

(60) *A,   moen!   [Ili   mete   buakae   zal   niq   **roe**]!*
     INTERJ friend   1DU.INCL   NOW   provisions   carry   NEG   SPEC.INAN
     'Friend! We didn't bring any provisions {as we should have known to}!'
                                                           [LuaWezun1-22]

Doe can even be used to form non-embedded nominalisations with clauses denoting events that occurred in the distant past so long as they denote situations that still hold and are generally known to be the case in the present. Example (61) describes an event, the discovery of fire, that occurred in the mythical past. Similarly, (62) describes an event of the mythical past in which the crow had to wear black feathers, after the theft of his white feathers by the cockatoo. In both examples, the use of the non-embedded nominalisation with *doe* construes the clause as referring to an event for which the effects are still being felt in the present day and which constitute general knowledge.

(61) *Homo   no=na,*   [*tas   mil   gene   reu   hoto   hati*
    CONTR.INAN   OBL=FOC   village   COLL   LOC   house   fire   exist
    roe].
    SPEC.INAN
    'And so, there were henceforth fires in houses in the villages {as we know to be so today}.' [Bk-6.066]

(62) *Homo   ni=na,*   [*bei   laqo   g-ot   guzu   roe*].
    CONTR.INAN   OBL=FOC   Mr   crow   3AN-body.hair   black   SPEC.INAN
    'Since then, the crow has had black feathers {as we know to be so today}.' [LaqoKakaq-17]

7.5.2.2 Thematic use

Where a clause marked by *doe* 'SPEC.INAN' is used thematically, it provides a recent past frame for the event described in the following clause. In (63), the recent event of returning from boarding school meant that the speaker got to eat good food. In (64) the recent request that the referent come and carry pumpkins went unheard.

(63) [*I   reu   a-ta   mal   roe*],   *bai   a   mami.*
    1PL.INCL   house   3INAN-GL   go   SPEC.INAN   thing   eat   tasty
    'When we came home just now, we ate tasty food.' [Bk-30.092]

(64) [*Ope   gi-al   gie   roe*]=*bu,*   *mak   niq.*
    pumpkin   3AN-carry   PROSP   SPEC.INAN=GIVEN   hear   NEG
    'When there were pumpkins to be carried recently, (he) didn't hear (the call).' [Bk-22.021]

A final, more unusual example of the specifier demonstrative marking a recent past event is given in (65). Here *doe* marks a clause referring to a recent past event which is a fronted complement acting as the P of *dale* 'tell' in the following clause.

(65) [*Ibu   tara   roe*],   *mete   paq   Donatus   bi=na   ibu*
    Mrs   know   SPEC.INAN   NOW   Mr   Donatus   ART.AN=FOC   Mrs
    g-ege   rale.
    3AN-BEN   speak
    'That which Mrs knows (and told) just now, it was this Mr Donatus who told it to Mrs.' [Bk-70.101]

7.5.2.3 Sentence connective use

In the Bunaq corpus that I have assembled, *doe* 'SPEC.INAN' is only used pronominally as a sentence connective with the postposition *goet* 'LIKE'. In these uses, *doe* is cataphoric, referring forward to a following sentence, typically denoting direct speech or thought. This cataphoric use of *doe goet* is illustrated in (66) with a verb, and in (67) without.

(66) a. *Homo   no,   Bei Keleq g-o   sura **doe**   **goet**.*
         CONTR.INAN OBL   Mr   Frog   3AN-SRC   ask   SPEC.INAN   LIKE
         'At that, Frog asked him this:'   [OrelKeleqMoenHoqon-60]
     b. *"Ie   teo   goet   on?   Ie=o   heser=e?"*
         1INCL/2.POSS   where   LIKE   DO   1INCL/2.POSS=AND   dead=AGREE
         '"What is yours doing? Is it also dead?"'   [OrelKeleqMoenHoqon-61]

(67) a. *Orel   mil   **roe**   **goet**   on.*
         monkey   COLL   SPEC.INAN   LIKE   DO
         'The monkeys (thought) this:'   [OrelZul2-44]
     b. *"Tuen   goet   on   oa,   ota   roi?"*
         how   LIKE   DO   IAM   LEVEL   SPEC.AN
         '"What's he doing?"'   [OrelZul2-45]

In other cases, *doe goet* occurs at the beginning of an explanation of a procedure or manner in which something is done or came about. Here, *doe* 'SPEC.INAN' points forward to the whole of the following text and not specifically to the following sentence. For example, (68) and (69) occur as the first utterances in their respective speakers' narratives.

(68) *Aturan   bon   g-ete   gie,   **roe**   **goet**   on.*
     rule   box.bean   3AN-throw   PROSP   SPEC.INAN   LIKE   DO
     'The rules of (the game) *bon gete* are like this.'   [Bk-10.001]

(69) *A,   **roe**   **goet**   on.*
     INTERJ   SPEC.INAN   LIKE   DO
     'Ah, (the founding of Lakus village) occurred like this.'   [Bk-29.001]

Although the non-proximal, proximal, and contrastive demonstratives may all be used cataphorically with *goet*, the specifier demonstrative is notable for being by far the most common demonstrative used in this function. I can find no examples where the specifier demonstrative is unambiguously anaphoric; in all cases, *doe goet* could be taken to refer either forwards or backwards.

7.6 Contrastive demonstrative

The contrastive demonstrative has no spatial deictic meaning and cannot be used situationally. In the nominal domain, it is used extensively in discourse to contrast referents, and to a lesser extent, to mark a topic shift or track referents through a sequence (§7.6.1). In the clausal domain, the contrastive demonstrative is the unmarked choice of demonstrative for thematic constructions, particularly in tail-head linkage structures, and as an anaphoric sentence connective (§7.6.2).

7.6.1 In the nominal domain

7.6.1.1 Contrastive use

The contrastive demonstrative refers to an entity in the discourse and contrasts it, either implicitly or explicitly, with another entity. The entity referred to by the contrastive may be anaphoric or non-anaphoric, illustrated in (70) and (71), respectively. In (70b) the contrastive demonstrative marks *dolar* 'dollar' after it has already been established in the discourse (70a) and sets up a contrast between the dollars and the *uang Indonesia gie* 'money from Indonesia' which the speaker will get in exchange for the dollars.

(70) a. *En   halaqa   n-ege   roqit   **dolar**.*
        person   3PL   1EXCL-give   cash   dollar
        'Those people give me dollars.'   [Bk-11.005]

   b. ***Dolar   himo***   *tebe   tuqal,   neto   uang   Indonesia*
        dollar   CONTR.AN   return   exchange   1SG   money   Indonesia
        gie   g-osok.
        3.POSS   3AN-recieve
        'In turn (I) exchange these dollars, (and) I get Indonesian money.'
                                                                  [Bk-11.006]

In (71c) *homo* 'CONTR.INAN' marks a new discourse referent *WC* 'toilet'. The contrastive demonstrative signals a juxtaposition of the toilet's stinking with the general mess of the boarding house described in the preceding clauses, a sample of which are given in (71a–b). That is, the contrast here does not involve direct opposition between different entities, but rather involves entities being juxtaposed with one another in order to pragmatically highlight one referent over another in the discourse.

(71) a. *Nego   bare   baqis   los.*
        what   PROX.INAN   much   very
        '(In the boarding house, there is) lots of this kind of junk (lit., what).'
                                                                  [Bk-30.101]

b. *Lobot.*
   fine.dirt
   'It's dirty.' [Bk-30.102]
c. *Apa   lagi,   **WC**   **homo**   seleq   nuas.*
   what   again   toilet   CONTR.INAN   urine   stink
   'And also, the toilets stink of urine.' [Bk-30.103]

Anaphoric and non-anaphoric uses of the contrastive demonstrative differ in their frequency, with non-anaphoric uses being only marginal in comparison to the anaphoric uses. Syntactically, there is also a distinction between anaphoric and non-anaphoric uses: whereas an anaphoric contrastive demonstrative can be used either adnominally or pronominally, non-anaphoric instances of the contrastive demonstrative are always adnominal. This is an obvious corollary of the fact that, where the referent is previously unmentioned, it requires explicit identification with a nominal. Example (72a) illustrates the pronominal use of the contrastive demonstrative in anaphoric reference. In (72b) the contrastive demonstrative is used pronominally to refer back to the road heading toward Lakus, which is mentioned in (72a). The contrast denoted by the contrastive demonstrative here is implicit. The presence of the fork in the road means that there must be two choices of road, even though only the branch leading to Lakus is mentioned.

(72) a. *Zemal   hik   sorun   Lakus   a-ta   mal.*
        go.LOW   path   fork   Lakus   3INAN-GL   go
        'Go down to the Lakus fork in the road.' [Bk-34.007]
     b. ***Homo***   *h-alolo.*
        CONTR.INAN   3INAN-follow
        'Follow this one (and not the other fork in the road).' [Bk-34.008]

Whereas in (72) the item that is being contrasted with that marked by the contrastive demonstrative is contextually implicit, there may also be explicit juxtapositioning of two referents that are both marked with the contrastive demonstrative. In (73) the two wronged women are contrasted with one another by being marked adnominally with *himo* 'CONTR.AN' (73b–c).

(73) a. *En   mone   baqi   g-ini   sal   hiloqon.*
        person   male   NPRX.AN   3AN-CAUS   wrong   two
        'That man was said to have done wrong in two ways.' [Bk-21.028]
     b. *Pana   gol   **himo**   tebe   g-ariqa.*
        female   small   CONTR.AN   return   3AN-repair
        '(He must) repair the girl on the one hand.' (i.e., repair the wrong he did the girl). [Bk-21.029]

c. ***Die*** **pana *himo*** tebe g-ewen h-ariqa.
REFL.POSS female CONTR.AN return 3AN-face 3INAN-repair
'(He must) repair the (lost) face of his wife on the other hand.' [Bk-21.031]

Similarly, in (74) *homo* 'CONTR.INAN' is used pronominally with anaphoric reference to the differing sums received for the bottles of contrasting size (74b–c). There are never more than two contrasting entities in such uses of the contrastive demonstrative.

(74) a. Botil uen h-ini nota sogal gonciet.
bottle one 3INAN-CAUS note tens five
'One bottle is (worth) 15 notes.' [Bk-13.011]
b. ***Homo*** botil legul gie.
CONTR.INAN bottle tall 3.POSS
'That's for a big bottle.' [Bk-13.012]
c. Nota sogo, ***homo*** botil barak gie.
note ten CONTR.INAN bottle short 3.POSS
'10 notes, that's for a small bottle.' [Bk-13.013]

7.6.1.2 Topic shift use

The contrastive demonstrative is also used anaphorically to mark a shift in topic to an NP with a less topical referent in the preceding discourse. For instance, in (75) the man is established first as the topical referent and is tracked by the expected non-proximal *baqi* 'NPRX.INAN' in (75a–b), while the girl is a backgrounded participant marked by the article (75b) after her first mention without demonstrative marking in (75a). In (75c) where the focus of the discourse shifts from the man to the girl, the contrastive demonstrative is used to mark the girl as the new topical participant. Note that the INANIMATE contrastive demonstrative, *homo* 'CONTR.INAN', at the beginning of (75c) marks the sequence in which the events took place (§7.6.2.2).

(75) a. En mone uen, baqi mal en iskola gol
person man one NPRX.AN go person school small
gu-sura.
3AN-ask
'(There was) a man, he went and propositioned a school kid.' [Bk-21.003]
b. Baqi en pana gol bi gu-sura g-utu cier
NPRX.AN person female small ART.AN 3AN-ask 3-COM sleep
gie.
PROSP
'He asked the girl to sleep with him.' [Bk-21.004]

c. *Homo=na,* **en** **pana** **himo** *milik,* *die*
   CONTR.INAN=FOC person female CONTR.AN scared REFL.POSS
   tazuq ube, ...
   door close
   'Then, this girl out of fear locked herself in her room, ...' [Bk-21.005]

Similarly, in the extract given in (76) the discourse initially concentrates on the various tasks performed by a range of participants in order to get the injured boy back to the village. In this part of the discourse (76b), the boy is referred to only by agreement on the verbal postposition *gi-ta* '3AN-GL' (cf. §4.7.1.1 on NP elision). When the discourse attention shifts back to the boy himself in (76d), the contrastive demonstrative marks the *en topol* 'fallen person' as a less topical antecedent and functions to reactivate the referent as the topic of the discourse.

(76) a. *Uen g-ini mal matas mil gi-wit.*
       one 3AN-CAUS go old COLL 3AN-fetch
       'One (of us) went to get the parents.' [Bk-1.026]
    b. *Neto roe gi-ta zaga, baqa no.*
       1SG SPEC.INAN 3AN-GL watch.over NPRX.INAN OBL
       'I myself kept an eye on him there.' [Bk-1.027]
    c. *Kira~kira tuku uen, matas mil Gewal gene sai.*
       approximately hour one old COLL Gewal LOC exit
       'About one o'clock, the parents left Gewal.' [Bk-1.028]
    d. **En** **topol** **himo** *g-ukat.*
       person fall CONTR.AN 3AN-lift
       'That one who had fallen was lifted.' [Bk-1.029]

See also §8.3.3 on the use of the temporal/discourse locational *mete* 'NOW' with the contrastive demonstrative in topic shifts.

7.6.1.3 Sequential use

In §7.6.1.1 we saw that the contrastive demonstrative was used to contrast one entity with another or to shift topicality from one entity to another. In this function the contrastive demonstrative was seen to mark only one or two NPs in the discourse. However, there are also examples of the contrastive demonstrative marking multiple NPs over a stretch of discourse. In these contexts, the contrastive demonstrative marks sequentiality of one or more referents, e.g., 'the (next/in turn)'. Two types of multiple NP marking with the contrastive demonstrative can be distinguished.

First, the contrastive demonstrative can mark multiple NPs with different referents, where there is sequentiality in the occurrence of the marked NPs in the discourse. This is illustrated in (77), a partial route description naming the sequence of place encountered when travelling from Gewal to Nualain village. We see that as each new place name enters into the discourse, it is determined by the contrastive demonstrative. The places are not being directly contrasted with one another; rather, the contrastive demonstrative functions to mark the fact that they occur in a sequence where each location is followed by, and takes the place of, another along the route between villages.

(77) a. *Pie Asa Toiq a-ta zemal.*
Pie Asa Toiq 3INAN-GL go.LOW
'Go down towards Pie Asa Toiq.' [Bk-34.016]

b. *Pie Asa Toiq a-ta zemal haqal soq,* **Pie Asa Toiq**
Pie Asa Toiq 3INAN-GL go.LOW finish SEQ Pie Asa Toiq
homo *no zemal.*
CONTR.INAN OBL go.LOW
'Once finished going down to this Pie Asa Toiq, go down from this Pie Asa Toiq.' [Bk-34.017]

c. *Mele mele mele daro esen o=***Duarato** **Pur Bul**
walk walk walk until HIGH ADDR=Duarato Pur Bul
homo *pir.*
CONTR.INAN reach
'Keep walking until (you) reach this Duarato Pur Bul up there.' [Bk-34.018]

d. **Duarato Pur Bul homo** *no menal,*
Duarato Pur Bul CONTR.INAN OBL go.HIGH
Leto Sun a-ta sai.
Leto Sun 3INAN-GL exit
'From this Duarato Pur Bul go up, (and) come out to Leto Sun.' [Bk-34.019]

e. **Leto Sun homo** *no menal teni.*
Leto Sun CONTR.INAN OBL go.HIGH again
'From this Leto Sun go up again.' [Bk-34.020]

Second, there is an infrequent use of the contrastive demonstrative in which it determines multiple NPs that have a single referent, or rather tracks different phases of a single referent over several clauses. This is seen in (78) where *g-oq* '3AN-seed', referring to 'cotton', is the topical discourse entity tracked by *himo* 'CONTR.INAN' across three separate clauses (78c), (78d), and (78f). The contrastive demonstrative indicates that the cotton goes through a sequence of events and is changed in form from stage to stage in the process of being made into thread.

(78) a. *Bei mil g-on homo, suta hobel taq.*
ancestor COLL 3AN-hand CONTR.INAN thread not.exist CONT
'In the time of the ancestors, there was no (store-bought) thread.' [Bk-35.002]

b. *Homo=si,   nei   g-oq   g-erel=na*
   CONTR.INAN=REAS 1PL.EXCL 3AN-seed 3AN-INS=FOC
   h-oqon.
   3INAN-make
   'Because of this, it was with cotton (lit., seed) that we made (thread).'
   [Bk-35.003]

c. ***G-oq   himo***   *nei   mar   gene   kali.*
   3AN-seed   CONTR.AN   1PL.EXCL   garden   LOC   scatter
   'This cotton (seed) we scattered in the garden.'   [Bk-35.004]

d. *Kalo   pan   porat,   nei   **g-oq   himo***
   if   season   dry   1PL.EXCL 3AN-seed   CONTR.AN
   g-iwal.
   3AN-pick
   'When it is dry season, we pick this cotton.'   [Bk-35.005]

e. *G-iwal,   g-erel   man.*
   3AN-pick   3AN-INS   come
   'Having picked (it), (we) take (it) home.'   [Bk-35.006]

f. *Nei   **g-oq   himo***   *g-amos.*
   1PL.INCL 3AN-seed   CONTR.AN 3AN-clean
   'We clean this cotton.'   [Bk-35.007]

The sequence-marking function of the contrastive demonstrative is best not regarded as distinct from its contrastive-marking function. It is, rather, an application of the demonstrative's contrastive semantics to a sequential series of referents. While there is no direct opposition between the roles played by referents, the referents are contrastive in so far as one takes the place of the other. This is also the case with the use of the contrastive demonstrative as the default demonstrative in connecting sentences, as will be discussed in the following section.

7.6.2 In the clausal domain

The INANIMATE form of the contrastive demonstrative, *homo* 'CONTR.INAN', is used extensively in linking sentences denoting sequential events in a narrative. In this function, the contrastive demonstrative is the unmarked demonstrative, and, unlike the sentence-connecting function of the proximal and non-proximal demonstratives, does not denote that the propositions being referred to are in any way topical. This linking use of *homo* is found in thematic constructions and in pronominal sentence connective constructions. The contrastive demonstrative is not known to be used for marking non-embedded nominalisation constructions.

7.6.2.1 Thematic use

In its thematic use, a nominalised clause marked by *homo* 'CONTR.INAN' repeats information from the previous sentence and links it to the following clause either using clause-final conjunctions or, more commonly, using simple juxtaposition of clauses. The clause marked by *homo* is typically an (almost) verbatim repetition of the previous clause, as in (79).

(79) a. *Inanoq   nei   bai   pies   gie   mal.*
       last.night 1PL.EXCL   thing   clean   PROSP   go
       'Last night we went to go wash things.'   [Bk-47.001]
   b. [*Nei   bai   pies   **homo**],   nei   n-erel*
       1PL.EXCL thing clean   CONTR.INAN   1PL.EXCL   1EXCL-INS
       mon.
       afternoon
       '(As) we were washing things, we were overtaken by nightfall.' [Bk-47.002]
   c. [*Nei   n-erel   mon   **homo**],   nei   milik.*
       1PL.EXCL   1EXCL-INS afternoon CONTR.INAN   1PL.EXCL   afraid
       'Having been overtaken by nightfall, we became scared.' [Bk-47.003]

Recapitulative tail-head linkage of this kind is widely used in Bunaq and particularly common in texts with a clear sequence of events, such as narratives and procedurals. Further discussion and illustration of tail-head linkage can be found in §15.4.1.

Sometimes, a thematic clause marked by *homo* 'CONTR.INAN' is not a (near) replica of the final clause of the previous sentence, but can be regarded either as a reformulation of the clause or, more broadly, as drawing on information contained in it. For example, the thematic clause marked by *homo* in (80b) can be understood as a reformulation of the final clause of the sentence in (80a) in the sense that knowing one another's language is part of getting to know one another.

(80) a. *Halaqi mete kelompok~kelompok baqi   ta-tara   niq   taq.*
       3PL   NOW   REDUP~group   NPRX.AN RECP-know   NEG   CONT
       'Now these groups, they don't know (about) each other yet.' [Bk-15.005]
   b. [*Daro   t-iol   tara   **homo**]   naq=na,   en*
       until   RECP-voice   know   CONTR.INAN   PRIOR=FOC   person
       baqi   Bunaq=o   niq.
       NPRX.AN   Bunaq=AND   NEG
       'Once people know each other's languages, then (they recognise that) the person is not even Bunaq.' [Bk-15.006]

In (81) we see a more indirect relationship between the thematic clause and the preceding sentence. In (81a) a monkey wonders to himself how he can cross the river.

The thematic clause marked with *homo* in (81b) sets up the thought processes of the monkey as the context for the arrival of the monkey in the conjoined clause.

(81) a. *"Nego   goet   on?"*
         what   LIKE   DO
         '"How to do it?"'   [OrelKeleqMoenHoqon-11]
     b. [*Ret   rimil~r-imil   **homo**]   no,   nare-wen*
         alone   REDUP~REFL-think   CONTR.INAN   OBL   long.time-MODER
         Bei   Keleq   g-azal.
         Mr   frog   3AN-see
         'While he was thinking, after a while, Frog came along.'
                                                                      [OrelKeleqMoenHoqon-12]

7.6.2.2 Sentence connective use

The contrastive demonstrative is also used with very high frequency as a proclausal sentence connective, linking sequential phases or events in a process or narrative. These sentence-initial appearances of *homo* typically occur in combination with a range of clause-conjoining devices. In (82) we see that *homo* 'CONTR.INAN' is used to refer back to the proposition of the preceding clause and links it with that of the next. *Homo* 'CONTR.INAN' combines with the reason clause conjunction =*si* 'REAS' (82b), the completive verb *haqal* 'finish' (82c), and a combination of *naq* 'PRIOR' and the restrictive focus particle =*na* 'FOC') denoting 'once X, (then Y)' in (82e).

(82) a. *Ho gapa   hati,   soro.*
         bean.type   exist   mix
         '(If) there are beans, mix (them) in.'   [Bk-44.006]
     b. ***Homo**=si,   mami.*
         CONTR.INAN=REAS   tasty
         'That's (so as to make it) tasty.'   [Bk-44.007]
     c. ***Homo**   haqal,   i   g-ini   ten.*
         CONTR.INAN   finish   1PL.INCL   3AN-CAUS   ready
         'After that, we ready (the maize).'   [Bk-44.008]
     d. *G-ini   koen~koen.*
         3AN-CAUS   REDUP~nice
         '(We) make (it) really nice.'   [Bk-44.009]
     e. ***Homo**   naq=na,   i   g-erel   reu   mil*
         CONTR.INAN   PRIOR=FOC   1PL.INCL   3AN-INS   house   inside
         a-ta   tama.
         3INAN-GL   enter
         'Once that's (done) we bring it into the house.'   [Bk-44.010]

Further examples illustrating this sentence-connecting use of *homo* are given in §15.4.2. See also §15.3.2.1 on the different conjoining elements that are regularly used in Bunaq to conjoin clauses.

Occasionally, the contrastive demonstrative is used as a sentence connective without any accompanying conjoining element. On its own, clause-initial *homo* 'CONTR.INAN' links the preceding sentence together with the following sentence in a loose way, with pragmatics supplying the additional inferences about the relation between the propositions in the two sentences, and with a small intonation break following *homo*. In (83) *homo* links the following sentence to the preceding one, with the latter providing a reason for the event referred to in the former.

(83) a. Il   zal   niq,   nei.
        water carry NEG   1PL.EXCL
        'We didn't take water with us, we didn't.'   [Bk-37.068]
    b. **Homo**,   nei   biasa   Lakaqan   bul   gene
        CONTR.INAN 1PL.EXCL usually   Mt.Lakaan base   LOC
        Il Diraq   gene=na   il   a.
        Il Diraq   LOC=FOC   water   eat
        'That (is because) we were used to drinking water from [the spring] Il Diraq at the foot of Mount Lakaqan.'   [Bk-37.069]

It is important to bear in mind that thematic and pronominal uses of *homo* in connecting sentences are not truly distinct. They are part of one and the same sentence-connecting function and are frequently to be found alternating with one another. For example, in (84b) we see a thematic use of *homo* in a tail-head linkage construction, while in (84c) we have a pronominal sentence-connecting use of it.

(84) a. ..., ciwal   sai.
              flee   exit
        '..., (she) ran off (from home).'   [Bk-43.056]
    b. [Ciwal sai   **homo**],   en   huqe   tueq   lilak   g-utu   botus.
        flee   exit CONTR.INAN person HERE   alcohol crazy   3-COM meet
        'Having ran off, (she) met a drunk from here.'   [Bk-43.057]
    c. [**Homo=na**],   halali   t-asal,   "eto   tueq   gie?"
        CONTR.INAN=FOC   3DU   RECP-cross 2SG   alcohol PROSP
        'Then, when they crossed paths, (the drunk asked) "do you want some alcohol?"'   [Bk-43.058]

Occasionally, *homo* is used cataphorically with the postposition *goet* 'LIKE' to refer forward to a following sentence denoting direct speech or thought. An example is given in (85).

(85) a. *Homo=na,   Bei Orel   g-ege   **homo   goet**.*
       CONTR.INAN=FOC Mr monkey   3AN-BEN   CONTR.INAN   LIKE
       'Then, Monkey said this to him:'   [OrelKeleqMoenHoqon-74]
    b. *"Hai   moen, eto   laun   naq!"*
       INTERJ   friend 2SG   quick PRIOR
       '"Hey mate, hurry up!"'   [OrelKeleqMoenHoqon-7]

The specifier demonstrative is much more commonly used in this cataphoric function – see §7.5.2.3.

7.7 Counter-expectational demonstrative

The counter-expectational demonstrative is the least frequent of the Bunaq determiners. It has no spatial, temporal, or discourse deictic meaning. It denotes that the marked element, either an NP (§7.7.1) or a clause (§7.7.2), contradicts the presupposition that is expected to hold in the given speech situation. Where the incompatibility is with respect to the expectations or beliefs of the speaker, the use of a counter-expectational demonstrative often conveys surprise on the part of the speaker. Where the incompatibility is with respect to the expectations or beliefs of the hearer, the counter-expectational demonstrative may be used by the speaker as an emphatic marker to assert the truth of what they are saying, where there is an expectation that the hearer is unlikely to believe them.

The counter-expectational demonstrative shows obvious similarity in form and function to the counter-expectational relator enclitic *=be* 'CONTEXP'. A counter-expectational demonstrative and relator enclitic cannot co-occur marking one and the same NP or clause. This is not a syntactic constraint; *=be* can mark NPs and clauses with other determiners and a counter-expectational demonstrative can co-occur with the given relator *=bu* 'GIVEN'. The constraint is more likely semantic and diachronic; both the counter-expectational demonstrative and relator enclitic contain the earlier demonstrative base *be (Schapper 2007), and although there are some constructional uses that differ between them, both basically denote shades of counter-expectationality. For the uses of *=be* 'CONTEXP', see §4.7.4.1.2 on its NP-marking function and §15.3.2.1.3 on its clause-marking function.

7.7.1 In the nominal domain

Marking an NP, the counter-expectational demonstrative denotes that the referent of the NP has an unexpected referent in relation to the proposition denoted by the clause. In (86), the counter-expectational marking *mila* 'slave' expresses the speaker's surprise at the identity of her accompanier, it being contrary to normal expectation that a master would walk together with their own slave. Similarly, in (87) the counter-expectational is used to express the speaker's surprise and indeed disbelief at the addressee's identifying *gios* as the Bunaq word for 'sinew', equivalent to Indonesian *urat*. As the speaker subsequently explains, her own dialect has *uat*, a Tetun borrowing, for 'sinew'.

(86) *Neto* [*die mila gol* **beri**] *g-utu mele.*
  1SG REFL.POSS slave small CONTEXP.AN 3-COM walk
  'What am I doing walking around with my own slave {I can't believe it}!'
  [LB-6.010]

(87) *Ama=e!* [*G-ios* **bere**] *urat on o=e!*
  father=AGREE 3-sinew CONTEXP.INAN sinew DO IAM=AGREE
  'Sir! *Gios* (Bunaq = sinew) means *urat* (Indonesian = sinew) {I can't believe it}!'
  [FB-210821]

In the corpus, the counter-expectational demonstrative is frequently found determining NPs headed by personal pronouns. In (88) the speaker laments the difficulties of her life. Here, the use of *bere* 'CONTEXP.INAN' marking the 1st person singular pronoun signals that the speaker never expected to experience such things. In (89), when his orders are defied, the speaker tells the addressee that she is stupid before giving her new instructions to follow. The use of *bere* with the 2nd person singular pronoun suggests that the addressee's stupidity is counter to her own belief about herself.

(88) [*Neto* **bere**] *muk wa no susar bare, hoto*
  1SG CONTEXP.INAN earth top OBL afflicted PROX.INAN fire
  naraka mil gene goet on.
  hell inside LOC LIKE DO
  'I am hard up on this earth {I can't believe it's happening to me}, (it's) like being in the fires of hell.' [Bk-46.053]

(89) [*Eto* **bere**] *en beik.*
  2SG CONTEXP.INAN person stupid
  'You are stupid {you just don't know it}.' [BeiUer-16]

In some cases, the counter-expectational demonstrative seems to be used in situations where the speaker wishes something to be true but does not expect it to be. For example, upon getting thirsty, the speaker states in (90) that she and her companions would like to drink some water. *Bere* marks the 1st person plural inclusive pronoun to signal that the speaker does not expect them to be able to have a drink.

(90) A!   [I   **bere**]   il   uen   a=na   loi!
      INTERJ 1PL.INCL   CONTEXP.INAN   water   one   eat=FOC   good
      'Ah! If only we could drink some water!'   [LB-5.005]

7.7.2 In the clausal domain

In the clausal domain, the counter-expectational demonstrative is not attested in the Bunaq corpus with thematic or sentence connective functions. It can, however, be used in non-embedded nominalisations, where it conveys that the event or situation denoted by the clause was contrary to expectation or belief.

For most clause-final uses of a counter-expectational demonstrative, the cognitive locus is either the speaker's expectation or a generalised expectation. The utterance in (91) comes from a story of an accident in which the car carrying the speaker flipped and became jammed between the banks of a river. Clause-final *bere* 'CONTEXP.INAN' signals that this event was generally unexpected and an incredible thing to have happen in a crash. In (92) a man-eating caterpillar pushes for marriage after a girl admits feeling some affection for him. Clause-final *bere* expresses how surprising and unexpected it is for the speaker that she likes him.

(91) Oto   zol   lak   gene   h-abit-wen   on   **bere**,
      car   river between   LOC   3INAN-wedge-ANTIC   DO   CONTEXP.INAN
      zol   lak   gene.
      river between LOC
      'The car just got wedged in the middle of the river {it's unbelievable}, between the river banks!'   [Bk-52.039]

(92) Jadi   mete=bu   harus   ili   ton   on   oa,
      so   NOW=GIVEN   must   1DU.INCL   marriage   DO   IAM
      eto=na   no-mobel   **bere**!
      2SG=FOC   1EXCL-like   CONTEXP.INAN
      'So now we must marry, seeing as you like me! {I can't believe it}'
                                                                   [BaloBiEnGakirik-19]

Clause-final *bere* may also be used with the addressee or hearer's expectations in mind, particularly where the speaker seeks to pre-emptively contradict or dismiss them. For example, the exclamation in (93) was made by the woman I was living with in Gewal to a group of other women in the village. Clause-final *bere* in (93) acts to pre-empt the disbelief of the hearers about the truth of statement (i.e., that a Westerner would be able to speak Bunaq). The example in (94) comes from a story in which the cockatoo borrows the feathers of the crow in order to attend a party. The crow is reluctant to lend out his feathers, but when he voices his concern, the cockatoo puts pressure on him and tells the crow not to be worried because, after all, they are friends. The use of clause-final *bere* in (94) seeks to pre-empt a refusal on the crow's part, suggesting that the crow ought to know that they are friends, but that he seems not to. Crow's hesitation to lend his property is cast here as a violation of the covenant of friendship.

(93) *Baqi*   *Bunaq sasi*   ***bere!***
      NPRX.AN   Bunaq speak   CONTEXP.INAN
      'She speaks Bunaq {can you believe it?}!'   [OS-09.01]

(94) *Hani=e!*   *I*   *moen*   ***bere!***
      PROH=AGREE   1PL.INCL   friend   CONTEXP.INAN
      'Oh, don't! We are friends {don't you know?}!'   [KakaqLaqo-26]

7.8 Article

In Bunaq the article is used primarily as a marker of anaphoricity in reference tracking, but also has some non-anaphoric functions. It can be used with both NPs (§7.8.1) and clauses (§7.8.2). It cannot be used in spatial deixis or accompanied by a pointing gesture. The article is not grammatically obligatory in any context.

The article (*ba/bi*) is similar in form to the non-proximal demonstrative (*baqa/baqi*) and a diachronic relationship seems likely.[3] The article is very close in function to the discourse uses of the non-proximal demonstrative, and speakers typically accept the article in all contexts where the non-proximal is used in discourse. However, the two determiners differ in that, whereas the non-proximal demonstrative marks topical or thematically prominent new information, the article tends to mark less important or backgrounded information.

7.8.1 In the nominal domain

The Bunaq article is used to track referents of NPs that constitute less important, backgrounded information in the discourse context. The article may be used in contexts

---

3 A formal relationship between 'that' and 'the' has been observed in many languages (Schachter and Shopen 2007: 39) and has been claimed to the result of the 'that' demonstrative reducing in unstressed article function: see Greenberg (1978) for the original proposal, and Diessel (1999: 128), and references therein for subsequent descriptions of this pathway. However, Schapper (2007) argues that the synchronic Bunaq article is not a reduction of the synchronic non-proximal demonstrative, but is rather the historical non-proximal demonstrative, while the synchronic non-proximal demonstrative is a reinforced form of the historical non-proximal demonstrative, now article. This process of demonstrative renewal by stacking is also widely observed in the languages of the world, and is also described in Greenberg (1978).

of both anaphoric and non-anaphoric reference. Of these, the anaphoric use is more common.

In its anaphoric use, the article marks an NP whose referent is typically less topical and de-accented in the discourse. This function contrasts with anaphoric uses of the non-proximal demonstrative which has thematically prominent continuing topics as referents. Consider the use of determiners in (95). We see *bai buleqen=o belis* 'gold and silver' occur without a determiner when first introduced into the discourse in (95a). On its second, thematically prominent mention, topical *bai* 'thing' (coreferent with *bai buleqen=o belis* 'gold and silver' in the previous clause) is marked with the non-proximal demonstrative in (95b). On its third mention in (95c), *bai buleqen o belis* 'gold and silver' are simply tracked with the article.

(95) a. *Halaqi=o* [***bai buleqen=o belis***] *t-olo.*
 3PL=AND thing red=AND white 3INAN-put.in
 'They also put on gold and silver things (i.e., jewellery).' [Bk-24.021]
 b. [*Bai* ***baqa***] *ru-bul gie, kalaq gie=o*
 thing NPRX.INAN REFL-head 3.POSS neck 3.POSS=AND
 r-on gie.
 REFL-hand 3.POSS
 'Those things (i.e., those pieces of jewellery) are put on the head, the neck, and the hands.' [Bk-24.022]
 c. ***Bai buleqen=o belis ba*** *tumel minak.*
 thing red=AND white ART.INAN metal complete
 'The gold and silver things are made entirely of precious metal.' [Bk-24.023]

Compare also the use of the non-proximal and contrastive demonstratives and the article in (96) repeated from (75). *En mone* 'man' is the topical participant in the discourse and is tracked with the non-proximal after the first mention. By contrast, *en pana gol* 'girl' constitutes less topical information and is marked with the article in (96b), following her undetermined first mention in (96a). Only when the focus of the discourse switches to her is the article replaced by the contrastive demonstrative in (96c).

(96) a. *En mone uen, baqi mal* ***en*** *iskola* ***gol*** *gu-sura.*
 person man one NPRX.AN go person school small 3AN-ask
 '(There was) a man, he went and propositioned a school kid.' [Bk-21.003]
 b. *Baqi* ***en pana gol bi*** *gu-sura g-utu cier*
 NPRX.AN person female small ART.AN 3AN-ask 3-COM sleep
 gie.
 PROSP
 'He asked the girl to sleep with him.' [Bk-21.004]

c. *Homo=na,* **en pana himo** *milik, die*
   CONTR.INAN=FOC person female CONTR.AN scared REFL.POSS
   tazuq ube, ...
   door close
   'Then, this girl out of fear locked herself in her room, ...' [Bk-21.005]

As well as having a direct antecedent in the discourse, the use of the article may be licenced by a "bridging" antecedent.[4] Consider the use of the article on *mil* 'inside' and *lal* 'problem' in (97) and (98), respectively. In neither case is there a direct antecedent for those nouns. The use of the article is supported by a given referent or event in the preceding text. The referent of *mil* 'inside' in (97b) is identifiable as it is part of the previously introduced *mar* 'garden' in (97a). The arresting of a man in (98a) presupposes that a crime has been committed and that the *lal* 'problem' of that crime in (98b) must be resolved.

(97) a. *Nie matas mil gie mar nolaq.*
       1EXCL.POSS old COLL 3.POSS garden wide
       'My parents' garden is expansive.' [Bk-24.007]
   b. ***Mil ba*** *no halali paqol g-ota.*
       inside ART.INAN OBL 3DU maize 3AN-plant
       'Inside (it) they plant maize.' [Bk-24.008]

(98) a. *Mone baqi g-one haqal, g-erel tas mil gene.*
       man NPRX.AN 3AN-hold finish 3AN-INS village inside LOC
       'After the man was arrested, he was taken to the village.' [Bk-21.011]
   b. *En matas g-ubak, homo=si,* ***lal ba***
       person old 3AN-gather CONTR.INAN=REAS problem ART.AN
       urus.
       manage
       'The elders were gathered together to deal with the crime.' [Bk-21.012]

Non-anaphoric uses of the article are largely limited in Bunaq to immediate situational uses in which the physical situation of the speaker and hearer contributes to the identifiability of the referent of the NP. For instance, in (99) both speech participants are able to identify the referent of *esen* 'HIGH', since within the village – their current location – there is only one elevated area, and it is familiar and immediately visible to all.

---

4 Lyons (1999) used the term "bridging cross-reference" for this manner of article licencing. Hawkins (1978) referred to this use as the "associative anaphoric".

(99) A. *Teo   mal?*
       where go
       'Where (are you) going?'
    B. ***Esen   ba***   *mal.*
       HIGH   ART.INAN   go
       '(I'm) going up the top.'   [OS-07.02]

In non-anaphoric uses where situational information and the article alone may not be sufficient to identify the referent, NP modifiers are frequently used as an anchor by which the scope of possible referents for the NP head is restricted. For instance, in (100) *kura* 'horse' is mentioned for the first time in the text, with the article marking the referent of the noun as unique. A restrictive RC is also appended to *kura* 'horse' in order to assist in the correct identification of the referent. The most frequent anchors to aid identification when using an article in first mentions are possessors and locations, as in (101).

(100) *Neto nie   ama   g-utu   mal gie   mobel, tan*
      1SG   1EXCL.POSS father 3-COM   go   PROSP like   because
      *nei   [kura=na   he   laun   los   **bi**]=na   saqe.*
      1PL.EXCL   horse=FOC   run   fast   very ART.AN=FOC ascend
      'I like to go with my father (to town), because we ride the horse which runs really fast.'   [Bk-24.036]

(101) *[Halaqi gie   il   kokoq   no   **ba**]   Suri Guloq   a*
      3PL   3.POSS   water   bucket   OBL   ART.INAN   Suri Guloq   drink
      gie   sura.
      PROSP ask
      'Suri Guloq asked to drink some of the water of theirs that was in the bucket.'
                                                                        [Bk-6.024]

7.8.2 In the clausal domain

In the clausal domain, the article *ba* 'ART.INAN' can be used in thematic constructions, that is, marking a clause nominalised by *ba* that forms the 'setting' for an event in a following clause. In my Bunaq corpus there are no unambiguous examples of the article being used in non-embedded nominalisation constructions. Because the article cannot stand on its own, it also has no sentence connective functions.

Consider the clauses determined by *ba* 'ART.INAN' in the following examples. In (102), the *ba*-marked setting clause encodes the habitual location and activity of the men, when they engage in the activity, eating *raka* cakes, denoted in the next clause.

In (103), the *ba*-marked clause encodes the context, the death of two people, in which the "alrightness" of the speaker denoted in the next clause is to be understood.

(102) *Mona   gene   zon   g-oli   **ba**,   tubi   raka=na   a.*
       forest   LOC   wild   3AN-hunt   ART.INAN   cake   cake.type=FOC   eat
       '(When) in the bush hunting pigs, it is *raka* cakes that (they) eat.'   [Bk-76.044]

(103) *En   hiloqo   heser   **ba**,   neto   rai~rai   niq.*
       person   two   dead   ART.INAN   1SG   anything   NEG
       '(Although) two people died, I wasn't hurt at all.'   [Bk-61.003]

A clause determined by *ba* 'ART.INAN' may also be a complement of the postposition *no* 'OBL'. The event encoded by the postpositional phrase constitutes the time at which the event in the following clause takes place. The event encoded by the article-marked clause may be anaphorically retrievable from the discourse, as in (104) where the death of Mau Paran has just been described, or be identifiable on the basis of the uniqueness of the time period named, as in (105) where the speaker can only have been ten years old once in his life.

(104) *Mau Paran   heser   **ba**   no,   halali   h-oqon   tuen   goet   on?*
       Mau Paran   dead   ART.INAN   OBL   3DU   3INAN-make   how   LIKE   DO
       'What did those two do at the time of Mau Paran's death?'   [Bk-4.081]

(105) *Nie   to   sogo   taq   **ba**   no,   nie*
       1EXCL.POSS   year   ten   CONT   ART.INAN   OBL   1EXCL.POSS
       nana   hatak   kawen.
       older.sister   ripe   marry
       'When I was still ten years old, my nubile older sister married.'   [Bk-24.037]

See §15.3.2.5 for more discussion and illustration of thematic clauses marked by *no* 'OBL'.

Chapter 8
Locationals

8.1 Introduction

This chapter is concerned with the description of Bunaq locationals. Like determiners, locationals are used in locating and identifying the referent of an NP. However, whereas a determiner refers to an entity by locating it in space, in time, or in the discourse, a locational denotes a location relative to which a referent can be identified in space or in the discourse. That is, a locational is referential to a location which acts as the ground for a figure.

Table 8.1 presents the set of Bunaq locationals. There are four distinct subsets of locationals, each denoting the location of the referent of an NP head according to different parameters: elevation, distance from present location, location in time or discourse, and proximity to addressee.

Table 8.1: Locationals.

ELEVATIONAL LOCATIONALS	*ola*	'LOW'
	ota	'LEVEL'
	esen	'HIGH'
PLACE LOCATIONALS	*huqe*	'HERE'
	haqe	'THERE'
	hoqe	'SPCPLC'
TEMPORAL/DISCOURSE LOCATIONAL	*mete*	'NOW'
ADDRESSEE LOCATIONAL	*o*	'ADDR'

The addressee locational is distinct among locationals in that it is syntactically dependent and requires other elements to be expressed in the NP along with it. The other locationals are able to stand alone in the NP. The addressee locational also differs in that it is monosyllabic, while the other locationals are disyllabic. In these respects, the addressee locational is the locational equivalent of the anaphoric article (§7.4) which differs from the other members of the determiner class in the same ways.

Section §8.2 discusses the different syntactic positions in which locationals occur relative to the N_{HEAD}. §8.3 deals with the semantics of the individual locationals. §8.4 looks at the syntax and semantics of various combinations of locationals. A summary of locationals follows in §8.5. See §3.5.3 for an overview of the morphosyntactic properties that define locationals as a word class.

8.2 Syntax of locational and N$_{HEAD}$

In this section I deal with the syntax of locationals relative to the N$_{HEAD}$ of an NP. Locationals are found in three syntactic contexts with reference to an N$_{HEAD}$: the basic pre-N$_{HEAD}$ position (§8.2.1); a marked post-N$_{HEAD}$ position (§8.2.2); and without an N$_{HEAD}$ (§8.2.3). Finally, in §8.2.4, I look at the frequency of locationals across the different uses.

8.2.1 Pre-N$_{HEAD}$ use

In the NP template in §5.1, we saw that locationals precede the N$_{HEAD}$ whose referent's location they denote. This is the most frequent and unmarked position of locationals. In (1) *esen* 'HIGH' marks the location of the seminary as being higher in elevation than the speaker's current location. In (2) *o* 'ADDR' denotes the location of the book as proximal to the addressee. In (3) *huqe* 'HERE' denotes the location of the village as being that of speaker's current location. In all three examples the locational precedes the N$_{HEAD}$.

(1) Neto [**esen** seminari] gene iskola.
    1SG HIGH seminary LOC school
    'I was at school in the seminary up there.' [Bk-37.014]

(2) [**O** buku baqi] nego?
    ADDR book NPRX.AN what
    'What's that book you've got?' (lit., 'That book at you is what?') [OS-07.03]

(3) Masala baqa [**huqe** tas mil] gene.
    problem NPRX.INAN HERE village inside LOC
    'That problem was within the village here.' [Bk-21.002]

Where a possessor is also included in the NP, the locational occurs to the left of the possessor, as illustrated in (4) and (5). Placing the locational after the possessor is ungrammatical: **Markus gie ola* 'Markus 3.POSS LOW' and **rie ota* 'REFL.POSS LEVEL'.

(4) Neto [**ola** Markus gie mok bul] h-azal.
    1SG LOW Markus 3.POSS banana trunk 3INAN-see
    'I see Markus' banana tree down there.'
    *'I see the banana tree of Markus (who is) down there.' [Not-09.01]

(5) Halaqi [*ota* *rie*] gene mit gaqal oa.
 3PL LEVEL REFL.POSS LOC sit all.AN IAM
 'They are all in their own (homes) over there.'
 *'They are all in (being) over their own (homes).' [Bk-2.025]

Where a possessor co-occurs with a locational in the NP, the locational cannot be interpreted as referring to the location of the possessor, but must refer to that of the referent of the N$_{HEAD}$ of the NP which is possessed. In order to express the location of a possessor with a locational, the possessor must appear as the head of a separate NP removed from the NP encoding the possessum, as in (6) (see §4.7.2.3 on the word order of this clause), or the possessor must be postposed to be the predicate of a relative clause, as in (7) (see §9.2.2 on predicative possessors).

```
       PSR            PSR-NHEAD
(6) [Ola  himo]   keke   [g-on]    kaeq.
    LOW   CONTR.INAN  bracelet 3AN-hand  filled
```
 'That one down there's hands were filled with bracelets.' [Bk-68.066]

```
    NHEAD        PSR
(7) [En   tuan   [ota   Eropa   gie]=na   zal   mina.
    person master LEVEL Europe 3.POSS=FOC carry come.HIGH
```
 'It was the priests from over there in Europe who brought up (the stuff).' [Bk-34.062]

Locationals can substitute for the head of an NP where the referent is anaphorically retrievable. In (8), *ola* 'LOW' in its first use provides the location for *zol* 'river'. In its subsequent appearance, *ola* 'LOW' stands alone with *zol* 'river' elided, since it is understood from the preceding clause. In (9) the contextually understood referent 'street' is not mentioned in the first NP, but is substituted with the locational *ota* 'LEVEL' determined by *ba* 'ART.INAN', literally, 'the one over there'.

(8) Hik iti gene zemal, [*ola* zol masak] a-ta
 path opposite LOC go.LOW LOW river big 3INAN-GL
 sai, [*ola*] a-ta sai.
 exit LOW 3INAN-GL exit
 'From the other side (of the road) go down to the big river down below, until you come to (it) down below.' [Bk-29.057]

(9) [*Ota* ba] h-ini jalan Apodeti.
 LEVEL ART.INAN 3INAN-call street political.party.name
 'The (street) over there is called Apodeti street.' [Bk-2.033]

8.2.2 Post-N$_{HEAD}$ use

A locational may also directly follow the N$_{HEAD}$ whose location it denotes. A post-N$_{HEAD}$ locational is pragmatically marked, focusing on the location of the referent. It aids in the identification of the referent by restricting the referential scope of the preceding N$_{HEAD}$ to the one in the location denoted by the locational. A postposed locational is typically not the last element in the NP, but is usually followed by a determiner and/or an RC.

Example (10) presents a pair of minimally different sentences as to the positioning of the locational *esen* 'HIGH' in the initial setting NP. In (10a), where the locational follows the N$_{HEAD}$, the referent of *lolo* 'mountain' is identified as being specifically the one located on *esen* 'HIGH', as opposed to any other mountain. In (10b), where the locational precedes the N$_{HEAD}$, the location of the referent of *lolo* 'mountain' is referred to as being located on *esen* 'HIGH'. In this position, the locational does not aid in the identification of the referent of the N$_{HEAD}$, but only provides information about its location.

(10) a. [Lolo **esen** ba] no halaqi goniqon
mountain HIGH ART.INAN OBL 3PL three
ru-huqat.
REFL-stand.up
'The three of them stood on the mountain (that is) up there.' [Bk-29.051]
b. [**Esen** lolo ba] no halaqi goniqon
HIGH mountain ART.INAN OBL 3PL three
ru-huqat.
REFL-stand.up
'The three of them stood up there on the mountain.' [Not-07.01]

The distinction between postposed and preposed locationals is thus functionally similar to that between restrictive and non-restrictive relative clauses (§5.4). Postposed locationals, however, show several different syntactic properties setting them apart from restrictive RCs. I will illustrate this using textual examples with the temporal/discourse locational *mete* 'NOW', which occurs very frequently in combination with relative clauses. As mentioned above, where an RC is included in an NP with a postposed locational, the locational precedes the RC as does =*na* 'FOC' in a restrictive RC (11). Unlike a restrictive RC, the N$_{HEAD}$ preceding a postposed locational may be omitted where the referent is retrievable (12). Although infrequent, it is also possible for the restrictive RC marker particle =*na* 'FOC' to co-occur with a postposed locational. In this case, the locational follows =*na* 'FOC' (13).

(11) [En **mete** jaga himo], himo=na ge-sen.
person NOW watch.over CONTR.AN CONTR.AN=FOC 3AN-point.to
'The person who was just now overseeing, it is him (you must) point to.'
[Bk-10.030]

(12) [En   **mete** g-ete   himo]   tebe   karaq.   [**Mete**
       person NOW   3AN-throw   CONTR.AN return   stand.up NOW
       himo]   karaq   tebe   saqe.
       CONTR.AN   stand.up   return   ascend
       'The person who was just now throwing goes back to standing up. (The person) who has just now standing up (the stones) goes back up (to throwing).'
       [Bk-10.014-15]

(13) En   atus~atus,   [en=na   **mete**   g-ini   Melus   bari].
       person   REDUP~hundred   person=FOC   NOW   3AN-call   Melus   PROX.AN
       'There were hundreds and hundreds of the people, these people who were just now named as the Melus.'   [Bk-67.156]

8.2.3 No N_HEAD use

Locationals can also be used without an N_HEAD or a discourse antecedent. In this function, the locational refers to a general location or time. Locationals used in this manner cannot be analysed as an N_HEAD, as they cannot be preceded by a possessor and cannot be modified by an N_MOD (§5.3) or RC (§5.4). See §3.5.3 for illustration of this.

Examples (14) and (15) illustrate the independent use of an elevational locational and a place locational, respectively. In each, contextual and situational information disambiguates the locations referred to by *esen* 'HIGH' and *haqe* 'THERE'.

(14) Kalo   lele   halaqi,   baqa=bu,   h-oqon   kuran~kuran.
       if   nowadays   3PL   NPRX.INAN=GIVEN   3INAN-make   REDUP~less
       Tentu,   nona   [**esen**]   gene   h-azal.
       assuredly   Miss   HIGH   LOC   3INAN-see
       'Nowadays they, as for that (bride price ceremony), do it much less. Certainly, Miss saw it up there [in the mountains where the Bunaq live].'   [Bk-38.028-29]

(15) Milik   baqa   gie=na,   en   baqis   loi   he   [**haqe**]
       scared   NPRX.INAN   BECAUSE=FOC   person   many   good   run   THERE
       a-ta   mal.
       3INAN-GL   go
       'Because of that fear, a great many people ran away to there.'   [Bk-66.013]

The temporal/discourse locational *mete* 'NOW' may also be used independently to refer to a temporal location. This temporal location denoted by *mete* 'NOW' is not necessarily the time of speaking, but may be a narrative-internal "present" time, as in (16).

(16) Uen   man   g-iwal   gie,   g-ereq   niq.   Tebe   rebel.
    one   come 3AN-pick   PROSP 3AN-reach   NEG   return descend
    Daro [**mete**], pana gol   bi   gi-ta sai   niq.
    until NOW   female small ART.AN   3AN-GL exit   NEG
    'Someone came to grab (her), (but he) didn't reach (her). (He) went back down.
    Until now (i.e., this point in the narrative), the girl had not been got to.'
                                                                   [Bk-72.037-39]

Of the locationals, only the addressee locational *o* 'ADDR' is syntactically dependent and cannot occur independently without any other NP constituent; it is the locational equivalent of the article, a determiner which is similarly syntactically dependent (cf. §7.8). In (17a) we see that *o* 'ADDR' occurring by itself is ungrammatical, while in (17b), where the locational occurs with another NP constituent, in this case a determiner, it is grammatical.

(17) a. *o
        ADDR
        '(location/thing) near you'
    b. o   ba
        ADDR   ART.INAN
        'the (location/thing) near you'

8.2.4 Frequency of locational uses

The different sets of locationals occur with different frequencies across the three different positions/functions discussed in the preceding sections. Table 8.2 presents the results of a count of the positions/functions in the corpus for one locational from each of the sets in the corpus.

Table 8.2: Frequency of use of locationals in the corpus.

		Pre-N_{HEAD}	Post-N_{HEAD}	No N_{HEAD}	Total
ota	'LEVEL'	31	6	25	62
haqe	'THERE'	4	5	40	49
mete	'NOW'	98	29	5	132
o	'ADDR'	33	16	--	49

From the table, we see that place locationals, represented in the count by *haqe* 'THERE', are overwhelmingly most frequent in the function without an N_{HEAD}, with both ad-N_{HEAD} uses being roughly equally infrequent (together approximately 20% of occurrences). Elevational locationals, represented in the count by *ota* 'LEVEL', are slightly more frequent in their pre-N_{HEAD} function (50% of occurrences) than in their function without an N_{HEAD} (40% of occurrences), while their post-N_{HEAD} use is relatively infrequent (roughly 10% of occurrences). Both *mete* 'NOW' and *o* 'ADDR' show significant skewing towards the pre-N_{HEAD} uses (roughly 75% and 70% of occurrences, respectively). The majority of the remaining uses of *mete* 'NOW' are post-N_{HEAD}, while *mete* occurs without an N_{HEAD} in just 5% of its uses. In sum, type frequencies across the sets confirm that the basic use of locationals is in the pre-N_{HEAD} adnominal function, with the post-N_{HEAD} adnominal function following as the marked variant position.

The tendency for some locationals to be used more often without an N_{HEAD} is semantically motivated. As we will see in §8.3, elevational and place locationals have clear situational referentiality and can therefore be used in reference to a location in space without ambiguity in most speech situations. By contrast, the temporal/discourse locational typically functions to activate referents in the discourse and thus requires explicit reference to that referent in order for its activation to be successful.

8.3 Semantics of locationals

A locational denotes a physical or temporal location which, when used adnominally, acts as the ground for the referent of the NP. Several locationals also have extensions of their core meaning. In this section, I will look at the semantic ranges of the different sets of locationals, including how they combine with other items in Bunaq used in deixis and encoding location.

8.3.1 Elevational locationals

Elevational locationals denote locations on an elevational plane relative to the deictic centre (DC), typically the speaker. Referents are located on an elevation lower than the deictic centre (*ola* 'LOW': 18), approximately level with the deictic centre (*ota* 'LEVEL': 19), or higher than the deictic centre (*esen* 'HIGH': 20).

(18) Mar   baqa   ate, [*ola* zol   alan] gene.
     garden   NPRX.INAN   far   LOW   river side   LOC
     'The garden is far away, down by the side of the river.'   [Bk-1.014]

(19) Hele   [*ota*   Deloq Toi]   no=na   g-iwil.
     perhaps   LEVEL   Deloq Toi   OBL=FOC   3AN-pick
     'Perhaps (they) picked (the pumpkins) in Deloq Toi.'   [Bk-22.018]

(20) Mele, nei   [**esen** Lakaqan bul]   h-one   on.
     walk 1PL.EXCL HIGH   Lakaqan   base   3INAN-hold   DO
     'Walking along, we kept to the base of Mount Lakaqan up there.'
                                                                        [Bk-37.009]

Bunaq elevational locationals encode global elevation (Burenhult 2008), that is, the use of an elevational locational projects general search domains below, above, or at the same level as the deictic centre. These locationals are not tied to elevation as manifested in features of the geophysical environment, such as *uphill* or *downhill*. This can be seen, for instance, in (21) where *esen* 'HIGH' is used to locate *pan* 'sky' as at a higher global elevation than the speaker.

(21) Neto bi   **esen** pan   gene   ge-tekeq   gie   taq!
     1SG   star HIGH   sky   LOC   3AN-look.at   PROSP   CONT
     'I am going to have a look at the stars up in the sky.'   [FB-160221]

Associated with the general search domains projected by Bunaq elevational locationals is a restriction on the locative postpositions with which they can occur in isolation. That is, an elevational locational that is used as the sole element of an NP to denote a location (i.e., there is no referent, expressed or unexpressed, for N_{HEAD}, see §8.2.3) cannot occur in a postpositional phrase with the specific location postposition *no* 'OBL', but can occur with the general location postposition *gene* 'LOC' (see §12.2.2). Thus, (22a) is ungrammatical or at least semantically bizarre for the speakers I consulted, whereas (22b) is accepted. Only where there is a referent for N_{HEAD} can an elevational locational occur in a postpositional phrase headed by *no* 'OBL', as illustrated in (23) below.

(22) a. */?*ola*   no
         LOW   OBL
         'in (location) down there'
     b. *ola*   *gene*
         LOW   LOC
         'in (location) down there'

This restriction is also found with the place locationals discussed in §8.3.2.

Bunaq elevational locationals are not used in encoding topological relations like 'top' and 'bottom' in reference to items that are roughly person-sized or smaller. For this, the topological nouns *wa* 'top' and *bul* 'base, bottom' (see §9.3.5) are used. These topological nouns can be combined with elevational locationals in reference to larger items, as illustrated in (23). In these examples, the elevational locational signals the location of the referent relative to the DC, while the topological noun denotes the relevant part of the NP referent.

(23) a. ***esen*** *hotel wa no*
      HIGH tree top OBL
      'up in the top of the tree'
   b. ***ola*** *lolo bul no*
      LOW mountain base OBL
      'down at the foot of the mountain' [FB-160221]

Elevational locationals are not distance marked. However, on account of their global locational reference, they are not typically used in relation to items that are very close to a speaker. Considering this, we might think that the elevational locationals would not mark an N_{HEAD} that is determined by the proximal demonstrative (§7.3), but only the non-proximal demonstrative (§7.4) and distance-neutral determiners. In elicitation, the use of the proximal demonstrative in combination with an elevational locational was rejected by some speakers, e.g., **ola bare* 'LOW PROX.INAN'. Yet, there are examples in the corpus in which an elevational locational and a proximal demonstrative do mark one and the same N_{HEAD} with a kind of "mediated" semantic. For instance, in (24) the elevational locational, *ota* 'LEVEL', and a proximal demonstrative, *bari* 'PROX.INAN', modify one and the same noun, *kura* 'horse'. This combination indicates that the horses are distant from both the speaker and the addressee but that they are closer to the speaker than the addressee (and level with the speaker).

(24) *Mama hiloqon,* [*ota kura bari*] *saqe naq!*
    mother two   LEVEL horse PROX.AN ascend PRIOR
    '(You) two ladies, mount these horses over there!' [Bk-37.083]

See §8.4.3 for discussion of elevational locationals in combination with the addressee locational.

8.3.1.1 Elevation in real-world place- and path-finding in Lamaknen

In addition to elevational locationals, Bunaq has a set of elevationally marked motion verbs expressing that a motion occurs on a trajectory at a certain elevation either towards or away from the deictic centre (*go up, come down, go across*, etc.). The full set of elevationally marked items is set out in Table 8.3. Although etymologically unrelated to one another (Schapper 2017: 10), these locationals and motion verbs are organised around the same three-way elevation distinction of LOW, LEVEL, and HIGH. Such a shared elevational "semplate" (Levinson and Burenhult 2009) across verbal and non-verbal items is typical of TAP languages (Schapper 2014).

Reference to elevation by way of the items in Table 8.3 is ubiquitous in place- and path-descriptions among the Bunaq of Lamaknen (see Text 2 'Directions to Nualain' in the Text Appendix). However, it is often subject to "ultimate orientation" effects (Haugen 1957). That is, in the use of elevational locationals and elevational motion verbs, strict measures of elevation are often overridden by contextual factors and conventionalised topographies that exist at different scales of place- and path-finding. There are three main instances of this in my elevational data for Bunaq Lamaknen.

Table 8.3: Elevationally marked items.[1]

	LOCATIONAL	MOTION VERB	
		To DC	From DC
LOW	ola	wil	zemal
LEVEL	ota	(man) †	honal
HIGH	esen	mina	menal

† *Man* 'come' is actually neutral with respect to elevation, but it is included here because it is always paired together with *honal* 'go.LEVEL' in reference to motion back and forth on a level plane.

First, locations significantly beyond Lamaknen, the area where the Bunaq dialect from which these examples are taken is spoken, are treated as LEVEL regardless of their actual elevation. That is, the default elevation of the world significantly outside of the Bunaq-speaking area is LEVEL. Thus, locations at a great distance, such as the Philippines in (25) and Europe in (26), are designated as *ota* 'LEVEL'.

(25) *Baqa   gie   ba,   [ota   Filipina]   gene   Kardinal*
    NPRX.INAN 3.POSS ART.INAN LEVEL   Philippines   LOC   cardinal
    Sin   dokter   bai   go-wol   man,   dokter   perawat   en   sogo
    Sin   doctor   thing   3AN-send   come   doctor   nurse   person   ten
    hiloqon   lesin.
    two   more
    'Because of that, from over there in the Philippines Cardinal Sin sent doctors and so forth here, (it was) more than twenty people, doctors and nurses.'
    [Bk-66.031]

(26) *En   tuan   [ota   Eropa]   gie=na   zal   mina.*
    person   master   LEVEL   Europe   3.POSS=FOC   carry   come.HIGH
    'It was the priests from over there in Europe who brought up (the stuff).'
    [Bk-34.062]

---

1 The non-deictic directional verbs, *debel* 'descend' and *saqe* 'ascend', could also be considered elevationally marked, but because they do not have a LEVEL term they are not included in this table. They are used instead of the deictic motion verbs given in Table 8.3 where vertical displacement is greater than horizontal displacement, e.g., when climbing a tree, getting out of a truck, or even ascending a very steep path.

For reference to areas within Timor that are outside Lamaknen, the default LEVEL elevation is also used. For example, consider the use of *ota* 'LEVEL' in (27). In this text, the speaker describes how the United Nations arranged reconciliation meetings between East Timorese refugees in West Timor and people from the East Timorese villages they fled. Located at the time of speaking in Atambua, a town in West Timor at around 350m above sea level, the speaker uses *ota* 'LEVEL' to locate Aiasa, a village over 850m above sea level. See §8.4.2 on the co-occurrence of the elevational and place locationals.

(27) ..., en [*ota* hoqe Aiasa] gie bi en halaqi
 person LEVEL SPCPLC Aiasa 3.POSS ART.AN person 3PL
 sogo g-inil=na hoqe ziq bare, baqi
 ten 3AN-name=FOC SPCPLC write PROX.INAN NPRX.AN
 g-utu man.
 3AN-COM come
 '..., here are the names of 10 people which have been written down by the people from over there in Aiasa, bring them with you.' [Bk-66.118]

An exception to the default rule treating areas in Timor beyond Lamaknen as LEVEL occurs with respect to Atambua, the main town of Belu situated on the Central Timorese plains in the Tetun-speaking area. The elevational differential between Atambua and Lamaknen is highly salient; travel between Lamaknen and Atambua involves traversing the steep escarpment which rises to the east of Atambua leading up to Lamaknen. Thus, Bunaq speakers from Lamaknen consistently treat Atambua as LOW in relation to Lamaknen, and Lamaknen as HIGH in relation to Atambua, as seen from the use of elevational motion verbs describing motion between villages in Lamaknen and Atambua in (28) and (29).

(28) Neto hoqe gene Gewal gene **zemal** Atambua gene
 1SG SPCPLC LOC Gewal LOC go.LOW Atambua LOC
 bai wit.
 thing fetch
 'I go down from here, from Gewal, and go shopping in Atambua.' [Bk-11.003]

(29) Nie tas, Atambua gene **menal** kilo sogo
 1EXCL.POSS village Atambua LOC go.HIGH kilometre ten
 goniqon.
 three
 'My village, it's about 30km going up from Atambua.' [Bk-7.007]

The second domain in which strict measures of elevation are overridden is on an axis extending eastwards from Weluli across Lamaknen. Speakers from villages roughly located on this imaginary axis to the east of Weluli consistently characterise Weluli as HIGH even when it is at a lower elevation relative to the speaker's location. For instance, the context for the examples in (30) and (31) is that the respective speakers of each text are located in Gewal at above 900m elevation, whereas Weluli is just below 800m above sea level. Yet in both examples, the speakers use *esen* 'HIGH' in locating Weluli.

(30) *Lain   tutu   neli   mama Eta   esen   SMP   Weluli*
     long   past   1DU.EXCL   mother Eta   HIGH   high.school   Weluli
     gene   en   g-ige.
     LOC   person   3AN-teach
     'Long ago Mama Eta and I taught up there in the high school in Weluli.'
     [Bk-37.001]

(31) *Weluli   gene   baruq.   Huqe gene   tifi   nonton.   Esen   gene*
     Weluli   LOC   boring   HERE LOC   TV   watch   HIGH   LOC
     i   tifi   nonton   niq.   Esen   gene   baruq.
     1PLINCL   TV   watch   NEG   HIGH   LOC   boring
     'In Weluli (it's) boring. Here (we) watch TV. Up there you don't get to watch TV. Up there (it's) boring.'
     [Bk-30.096-99]

An explanation of why Weluli is treated as HIGH might be sought in social status. In other words, the motivation for treating Weluli as HIGH could be viewed as arising out of the town's importance as Lamaknen's administrative and commercial centre. However, reference to other important places, such as Atambua, the capital of Belu, are not treated as HIGH. What is more, within Lamaknen, treatment of Weluli as HIGH is itself limited to villages lying roughly on the axis extending eastward from Weluli, including Gewal, Fulur, Lolobul, Leowalu, and Lakus. As one moves away from the east–west axis, reference to Weluli as HIGH decreases and is overridden by strict measures of elevation. For instance, whilst speakers in Duarato categorially treat Weluli as HIGH, in Nualain and Ekin, located further south but still east of Weluli, reference is variable, with both HIGH and LOW being heard. In Dirun, located southwest of Weluli and at a considerably higher elevation, Weluli is categorially treated as LOW. These factors indicate that status cannot adequately explain Weluli's treatment as HIGH. A speaker of Bunaq suggested the following alternative explanation to me. Weluli is located just west of a deep river valley. Anyone coming from villages directly eastwards of Weluli must climb the steep path up from the river to reach the town, whereas from other directions there is no steep hike up from the river valley to be tackled. For at least one Bunaq speaker, this significant climb at the end of the journey was what determined the treatment of Weluli as HIGH for those coming from a due east direction.

Thirdly, within the house, elevational terms are used without elevational meaning in my observations of Bunaq Lamaknen speech. That is, elevation terms are apparently not used according to the terrain beyond the house's walls, but instead are fixed to a conventionalised topography in which the front of the house is HIGH and the back of the house is LOW. Thus, in (32) the speaker calls two children to come to the back part of the house using the LOW-marked verb *wil*. Similarly, when standing in the back of the house, my question as to the whereabouts of Hiro received the response in (33B), locating him in the front of the house, *esen* 'HIGH'.

(32) Halali, **wil** naq!
 3DU come.LOW PRIOR
 'You two, come down (i.e., to the back of the house).' [OS-07.02]

(33) A. Hiro teo gene?
 3DU where LOC
 'Where's Hiro?'
 B. **Esen** gene.
 HIGH LOC
 '(He's) up (i.e., in the front of the house).' [OS-07.02]

This conventionalised topography is also used in locating items within the space of the house. This was seen in a structured elicitation setting where I placed several glasses on a table inside the house and arranged for my consultant Hiro to get one of the children that I lived with to hand him the glass he asked for. The one closest to the front of the house, for example, he referred to as *galas esen gene baqa* glass HIGH LOC NPRX.INAN 'that glass up there', i.e., 'at the front of house'.

8.3.2 Place locationals

Place locationals refer to a general location relative to the distance from the speech participants. Whilst most often used without an N_{HEAD} (§8.2.3), place locationals are also used adnominally, most typically with place names. They are not used adnominally to locate bounded entities, small or large, such as a house or a person. Paralleling the three-way opposition in demonstratives used in spatial deixis (§7.1), place locationals are divided into proximal *huqe* 'HERE', distal *haqe* 'THERE', and specific and distance-neutral *hoqe* 'SPCPLC'. However, unlike demonstratives which are speaker-anchored, the locations referred to by the distance-specified place locationals *huqe* 'HERE' and *haqe* 'THERE' may be anchored not only to the speaker but also to the addressee.

Huqe 'HERE' refers to the current location of the speech participants. In (34), *huqe* 'HERE' indicates the location of the village Gewal to be where both the speaker and addressee are located at the time of speaking. Similarly, in (35) *huqe* 'HERE' refers to the place at which both the speaker and hearer are located.

(34) Aturan r-agar balas baqa [***huqe*** Gewal] gene.
 rules REFL-mouth slap NPRX.INAN HERE Gewal LOC
 'Those are the rules of making amends (lit., slapping one's own mouth) here in Gewal.' [Bk-21.021]

(35) Gie en [***huqe***] gene g-ege hape honal.
 3.POSS people HERE LOC 3AN-BEN mobile.phone go.LEVEL
 'Her people here rang her.' [Bk-43.004]

In the above examples *huqe* 'HERE' denotes the speaker's and hearer's location, and not one or the other. Where only the speaker's location is intended, the proximal demonstrative is used (§7.3.1). Though it does not necessarily exclude the addressee, the proximal demonstrative differs from the proximal locational *huqe* 'HERE' in that its meaning makes no mention of the addressee. Thus, there is no direct semantic conflict between the proximal demonstrative and proximal locational; they simply differ in the scope of what they include in "hereness". That is, while *huqe* 'HERE' refers to a vaguely defined *here* place, the proximal demonstrative refers to a specific *here* space anchored to the speaker.

Consider the use of the proximal demonstrative and the proximal place locational in the examples below. Example (36) comes from a letter written to me from Timor when I was in Australia. *Huqe* 'HERE' is not and cannot be used since I was not present at the location referred to, while the proximal demonstrative can be used in reference to *en* 'person' as the referents are in the same location as the speaker. By contrast, in (37) *huqe* 'HERE' can be used as it refers to a place where both the speaker and the addressee are located, while the proximal demonstrative is also permissible determining the N_{HEAD} *ei* '2PL' as it refers to a speech participant (see §6.2.2). Crucially, however, in this example, *huqe* 'HERE' and the proximal demonstrative do not modify one and the same N_{HEAD}.

(36) [En Gewal no ***bari***] nona gu-sura ruquk, eme Eta
 person Gewal OBL PROX.AN Miss 3AN-ask always mother Eta
 g-o.
 3-SRC
 'These people in Gewal ask after you constantly, (they ask) Eme Eta.'
 [Bk-14.011]

(37) [Ei ***huqe*** gene ***bare***] reu tuen~tuen?
 2PL HERE LOC PROX.INAN house how.many
 'How many houses of you here in this place were there?' [Bk-29.059]

Haqe 'THERE' typically refers to a place removed from the location of the speech participants. The place referred to by *haqe* 'THERE' is identified either through being explicitly mentioned, as in (38) where the place referred to is overtly expressed, *Pie Bulak*, or through being retrievable from the surrounding discourse, as in (39) where *haqe* 'THERE' refers anaphorically to Mrs Yip's place, mentioned in the previous clause.

(38) [Esen **haqe** o Pie Bulak] gene wil Nualain mal.
HIGH THERE ADDR Pie Bulak LOC come.LOW Nualain go
'(I) came down from there at Pie Bulak to Nualain.' [Bk-34.096]

(39) Cinoq dele neto ibu Yip g-o mal, [**haqe**] gene r-ota.
hot INS 1SG Mrs Yip 3-SRC go THERE LOC REFL-stab
'Feverish, I went to Mrs Yip's place and there I got an injection.' [Bk-40.005]

Where there is no antecedent as a referential anchor for its use, *haqe* 'THERE' takes the addressee as its referential anchor. That is, the place referred to by *haqe* 'THERE' is interpreted as being associated with the addressee, such as being their place of residence or origin. In (40) *haqe* 'THERE' is used together with *ota* 'LEVEL' to refer to a distal place for which there is no anaphorically retrievable locational referent. As such, the place referred to must be interpreted as referring to a place associated with the addressee, in this case, Australia, my country of origin (see §8.3.1.1 on the use of *ota* 'LEVEL' as the default location for wider world locational reference). By contrast, in (41) and (42) where there is no association between me as the addressee and the places referred to, only the elevational locational *ota* 'LEVEL' is possible, with speakers consistently rejecting the use of *haqe* 'THERE'.

(40) [Ota **haqe**] gene en roti a los=ka?
LEVEL THERE LOC person bread eat very=OR
'Do people over there eat bread a lot?' [OS-07.01]

(41) En tuan [**ota** Eropa] gie=na zal mina.
person master LEVEL Europe 3.POSS=FOC carry come.HIGH
'It was the priests from over there in Europe who brought up (the stuff).'
[Bk-34.062]

(42) Neto [**huqe**] gene hoto tuka, [**ota**] gene niq.
1SG HERE LOC give.birth LEVEL LOC NEG
'I gave birth here and not over there.' [Bk-29.068]

Hoqe 'SPCPLC' is the place locational equivalent of the specifier demonstrative (§7.5), denoting that the place it refers to is exactly the one at issue. The location denoted by *hoqe* 'SPCPLC' may either include or exclude the speech participants. In

(43) *hoqe* 'SPCPLC' is used twice: in its first use, *hoqe* 'SPCPLC' refers to Aiasa, a place far from the speech participant, as signalled by the elevational locational *ota* 'LEVEL' marking the same N$_{HEAD}$ (see §8.4.2); and in its second use, *hoqe* 'SPCPLC' marks the N$_{HEAD}$ *g-inil* '3AN-name' as being in a place proximal to the speaker, as is clear from the proximal demonstrative determining the N$_{HEAD}$.

(43) ..., en   ota   **hoqe**   Aiasa gie   bi   en   halaqi
         person   LEVEL SPCPLC   Aiasa 3.POSS ART.AN person 3PL
     sogo g-inil=na   **hoqe**   ziq   bare,   baqi   g-utu   man.
     ten 3AN-name=FOC   SPCPLC   write PROX.INAN NPRX.AN 3AN-COM come
     '. . ., here are the names of 10 people which have been written down by the people from over there in Aiasa, bring them with you.' [Bk-66.118]

Note that many speakers do not appear to have a distinction between *hoqe* 'SPCPLC' and *huqe* 'HERE', with the functions of both being subsumed under the form *huqe*. This merger is probably the result of the frequently observed raising of /o/ to [u] (see §2.2.1).

8.3.3 Temporal/discourse locational

In §8.2.3 it was seen that used independently without a referent for N$_{HEAD}$, the locational *mete* 'NOW' refers to the present time. When marking an NP with a referent, *mete* 'NOW' is not strictly temporal in meaning, but serves to locate and activate a referent that is not currently in the focus of the discourse. In other words, *mete* 'NOW' is used to direct the hearer's attention to a referent in the discourse, announcing either the introduction of a new referent or the resumption of reference to an old one.

Mete 'NOW' is used most often to activate a referent already established in the discourse. For instance, in (44a) the *orel* 'monkey' is introduced into the discourse for the first time, indicated by the marking with *uen* 'one' (see §3.5.5.1). The monkey is backgrounded in (44c) as the narrative focuses on the search that the parents conduct for their missing child. In (44d) *mete* 'NOW' is used to reactivate *orel* 'monkey', functioning to connect the referent of the marked *orel* 'monkey' with the *orel* 'monkey' introduced earlier. This redirecting of the hearer's attention to the monkey correlates with the topic shifting to the monkey, as marked by the contrastive demonstrative (§7.6).

(44) a. Homo=na,   **orel**   **uen** man.
         CONTR.INAN=FOC   monkey   one   come
         'Then, a monkey came.'   [Bk-68.006]

b. *Man,   kasu   g-ibi   gi-al.*
   come   remove   3AN-steal   3AN-carry
   '(He) came, removed (and) stole (the child), carrying him off.'
   [Bk-68.007]

c. *Gie   eme   gie   ama   g-agal=o   g-azal   niq.*
   3.POSS   mother   3.POSS   father   3AN-search=AND   3AN-see   NEG
   'His mother (and) his father searched for him and didn't find him.'
   [Bk-68.008]

d. *Hilaq   [**mete**   orel   himo]   g-ini   gie.*
   surprisingly   NOW   monkey   CONTR.AN   3AN-CAUS   3.POSS
   'What a surprise, it was this monkey just now who had made (the child) his.'
   [Bk-68.010]

In (45) and (46) we see similar uses of *mete* 'NOW' to direct the attention of the hearer towards a particular referent already established in the discourse. In (45) there is similarly a correlation between marking with *mete* 'NOW' and a shift in topic. Here the use of *mete* 'NOW' ensures that the referent of *en* 'person' is correctly identified as coreferential with the dead person established earlier in the discourse and not the *en* 'person' of the immediately preceding clause which has generic reference.

(45) a. *Kalaq   **en**   uen   heser,   biasanya   lal   h-oqon.*
        if   person   one   dead   usually   matter   3INAN-do
        'When a person dies, usually the matter is dealt with.'   [Bk-18.018]

   b. *Lal   h-oqon   niq   mesaq=bu,   en   piar,   [**mete**   en*
      matter   3INAN-do   NEG   if=GIVEN   person   believe   NOW   person
      heser   bi]   bei   g-utu   ti-ta   bolu   niq.
      dead   ART.AN   ancestor   3-COM   RECP-GL   united   NEG
      'Should the matter (i.e., a proper burial) not be dealt with, people believe that this person now who died will not be united with the ancestors.'
      [Bk-18.019]

In (46) *mete* 'NOW' marks a right-dislocated NP (§4.7.2.1.2) and functions to clarify the identity of the referents of the pronoun *halali* '3DU' in the preceding clause. The locational functions to direct the hearer to connect the earlier mentioned couple of Louis Berthe and his wife with the referents of this NP.

(46) *Jadi,   waktu   matas   roi   heser,   heser   niq   taq,   **halali***
     so   time   old   SPEC.AN   die   die   NEG   CONT   3DU
     *t-ege   por   h-oqon,   [**mete**   Luis   Bert   halali].*
     RECP-BEN   holy   3INAN-make   NOW   Louis   Berthe   3DU
     'So, at the time this old (man) was dying, before (he was) dead, they two did the exchanging of blessings, (that is,) Louis Berthe and his wife.'   [Bk-70.115]

An NP marked by *mete* 'NOW' need not have a direct antecedent in the discourse, but may be licenced by a "bridging" antecedent. In (47) the referent of the NP with *mete* 'NOW' has not previously been mentioned, but is understood from the preceding discussion of *makoqan* 'poets' to be one of their number. In (47b) *mete* 'NOW' is used to activate a new referent in the discourse.

(47) a. *Halaqi mos t-o koko baqa goet,*
      3PL also RECP-SRC test NPRX.INAN LIKE
      makoqan~makoqan bi.
      REDUP~poet ART.AN
      'They also tested each other like that, the poets (did).' [Bk-70.037]

   b. [**Mete** *Gewal gie bi] pintar liol.*
      NOW Gewal 3.POSS ART.AN clever continue
      'Now the one from Gewal was really clever.' [Bk-70.038]

   c. *Matas baqi Gewal gie uen.*
      old NPRX.AN Gewal 3.POSS one
      'This old (guy) was one of Gewal's (poets).' [Bk-70.039]

An NP marked by *mete* 'NOW' may also introduce an entirely new referent into the discourse where it develops or progresses the narrative. In (48) the NP marked by *mete* 'NOW' has no direct or indirect antecedent in the discourse. In (48c), *mete* 'NOW' serves to shift the hearer's attention to the new referent whose introduction marks a new stage in the discourse, i.e., the progression from spinning to dyeing the yarn. In the translations of *mete* 'NOW' in the following examples, I use English 'now' in an attempt to preserve something of the flavour of the Bunaq original, and as English *now* has a similar discourse function (Aijmer 2002). The translation, however, should not be taken to mean that Bunaq *mete* 'NOW' is adverbial in the same way as English *now*; in the examples *mete* 'NOW' continues to be a constituent of the NP.

(48) a. *Hulun h-ini masak.*
      yarn.ball 3INAN-CAUS big
      'Make the ball of yarn big.' [Bk-64.032]

   b. *Homo soq naq=na, tebe ola ba no*
      CONTR.INAN SEQ PRIOR=FOC return LOW ART.INAN OBL
      putar teni.
      turn again
      'Then once that's done, turn it down there again.' [Bk-64.033]

c. *Lale haqal soq, tebe [**mete** taun hotel nor baqa],*
   spin finish SEQ return NOW indigo tree leaf NPRX.INAN
   baqa no t-olo.
   NPRX.INAN OBL 3INAN-put.in
   'After the spinning, then, now put (the yarn) in those leaves of the indigo tree.' [Bk-64.034]

Finally, example (49) illustrates *mete* 'NOW' being used to direct a hearer's attention both to a new referent and to an old one. In its first use *mete* 'NOW' in (49d) marks an NP with a new referent, whose introduction marks a progression in the described procedure, namely the preparation of *tubi* 'cakes'. The second use of *mete* 'NOW' in (49f) is with an NP whose referent is already established, and signals that the hearer should return their attention to the referent.

(49) a. *Homo haqal soq, mogor nor suel gene*
   CONTR.INAN finished SEQ banana.leaf leaf left-hand LOC
   homo h-ekal.
   CONTR.INAN 3INAN-fold
   'Then after that, fold the banana leaf on the left.' [Bk-76.067]

b. *Heten gene homo h-ekal.*
   right-hand LOC CONTR.INAN 3INAN-fold
   'Fold (it) on the right.' [Bk-76.068]

c. *Homo haqal soq, baqa no lai.*
   CONTR.INAN finished SEQ NPRX.INAN OBL set
   'Then after that, set (the cake) there.' [Bk-76.070]

d. *H-otol, [**mete** hol masak]=ka, atau niq=o,*
   3INAN-WITHOUT NOW stone big=OR or NEG=AND
   ola o tasu, tasu late.
   LOW ADDR wok wok bad
   'Leaving (the cake) to one side, now take a big stone, or (if there) isn't (one), a wok, an old wok.' [Bk-76.071]

e. *Baqa hoto wa no lai.*
   NPRX.INAN fire top OBL set
   'Put it on the fire.' [Bk-76.072]

f. *Tasu=o hol baqa cinoq oa, [**mete** tubi*
   wok=AND stone NPRX.INAN hot IAM NOW cake
   mogor nor no homo] haqe gene lai.
   banana.leaf leaf OBL CONTR.INAN THERE LOC set
   '(When) the wok or stone is hot, now put the cake on there in the banana leaf.' [Bk-76.073]

8.3.4 Addressee locational

The addressee locational *o* 'ADDR' differs not only in syntax from the other sets of locationals, but also semantically in that the deictic meaning of *o* 'ADDR' is functionally linked to the addressee. That is, *o* 'ADDR' makes use of the location of the addressee as a reference point, or deictic anchor, for locating the referent of the NP.

In (50) the speaker uses *o* 'ADDR' to question the identity of an item held by the addressee. In (51) *o* 'ADDR' refers to the location of the referent as close to the addressee, while the determiner *baqi* 'NPRX.AN' points to the referent as being not proximal to the speaker. In (52) *o* 'ADDR' is used by the speaker to point out that the *ope* 'pumpkin' they require is located proximal to the addressee. In (53) the speaker questions the identity of the individual mocking him and uses *o* 'ADDR' to indicate that he knows the addressee is the one who is laughing.

(50) Nego [*o* roe]?
what ADDR SPEC.INAN
'What's that you've got there?' [OS-07.03]

(51) [*O* baqi] mele heta=bu, mina mal.
ADDR NPRX.AN walk can=GIVEN come.HIGH go
'If she near you can walk, then come on up.' [Bk-37.024]

(52) [*O* ope baqi] g-ini man naq!
ADDR pumpkin NPRX.AN 3AN-CAUS come PRIOR
'Pass over that pumpkin near you!' [OS-07.04]

(53) Cio bun [*o* rale higal bi]?
who INDEF ADDR talk laugh ART.AN
'Who are you, laughing one?' [Bk-4.053]

The addressee locational thus allows an additional deictic anchor to be overlaid on top of the speaker-anchored demonstrative system. Due to their feature clash, the addressee-anchored locational *o* 'ADDR' cannot occur with the speaker-anchored proximal demonstrative. The addressee locational, however, freely combines with all other demonstratives, such as the non-proximal as in (51) and (52) above.

The addressee locational has associative extensions whereby it can be used to denote a closeness in association between the addressee and the referent of the NP (see §7.3.1.4 on similar extensions of the proximal demonstrative). Most often an associative *o* 'ADDR' refers to a referent which is the property of the addressee. For example, in (54) the marking of *buku* 'book' with *o* 'ADDR' is licenced by the fact that the referent belonged to the addressee, although it was being held by the speaker at the time of utterance. In (55) the speaker refers to the livestock possessed by the addressee; the possessive relationship between the addressee and the possessum is signalled by *ie* '1INCL/2.POSS'. Although no livestock are present at the time of speaking, *o* 'ADDR' is included in the NP to signal that the referent is located not at the addressee themselves, but on the addressee's property. Making the distinction between straightforward possession by the addressee and the location of the referent relative to the addressee in this way is important in the context of the text, which deals with the problem of people's crops being destroyed as a result of their tethering livestock in their gardens.

(54) [Buku   *o*   bi]   koen.
     book   ADDR   ART.AN   nice
     'This book of yours is nice.'   [OS-07.03]

(55) [*O*   ie   kereq=o   hiloqon]   g-osok   on.
     ADDR   1INCL/2.POSS   single=AND   two   3AN-receive   DO
     'The one or two you have were given (to you).'   [Bk-19.012]

The addressee locational has extensions into further non-spatial domains. *O* 'ADDR' may be used of a referent that is non-visible and removed from the speech situation, but identifiable to one or more speech participants on the basis of their knowledge of the parameters of the speech event. Example (56) is an overheard utterance in which the speaker informs the addressee that a *suster* 'nun' had come by earlier in the day looking for the addressee when she was not at home. The speaker uses *o* 'ADDR' in the NP referring to the nun, with the implication that the identity of the nun is known to the addressee.

(56) [Suster   *o*   bi]   man.
     nun   ADDR   ART.AN   come
     'The nun of yours {who you presumably know} came by.'   [OS-07.03]

The extension of the addressee locational's referential domain is possible because, by construing an unseen entity as being at the addressee's location, the speaker suggests the availability of the identity of the referent to the addressee. The implication of shared knowledge can arise, in turn, because by indicating that the referent is known to the addressee, the speaker establishes a speaker–addressee common ground (cf. Clark, Schreuder, and Buttrick 1983: 257), since it is assumed that if a speaker refers to an entity, then the entity is also known to the speaker.[2] For example,

---

[2] Thus, addressee location plays a crucial role in referent identification. This is consistent with Sacks and Schegloff's (1979) maxim of recipient design, which states that speakers tailor their utterances so that addressees are not required to make reference to information that the speaker knows or assumes they do not have access to.

(57) comes from a text in which *Matas Bere* 'Old Man Bere' comes at night singing threateningly to families locked inside their homes. He is referred to with predicative *o bi* 'ADDR ART.AN' as he is not visible to the speaker and hearer but can be identified by his voice. In (58) *o bi* 'ADDR ART.AN' cannot be taken as coreferential with the referent of *baqi* 'NPRX.AN' in the immediately preceding discourse, but must refer to a referent not present in the surrounding situation, namely, the *kepala desa* 'village head' referred to in an early part of the text as having left the village to collect evidence about the theft. The village head is referred to here with *o bi* 'ADDR ART.AN' by the speaker because he is not personally known to the hearer, but can be identified as the referent due to the contextual knowledge of the situation provided by the speaker in the discourse.

(57) Matas   Bere=na   [*o*   bi]   oa.
     old   Bere=FOC ADDR ART.AN IAM
     'That's old Bere {you hear}.' [Bk-73.041]

(58) Baqi   tenaq piqu   niq.   Baqi   laga.   Nor
     NPRX.AN thief   experience NEG   NPRX.AN dumb   reasonless
     toek   niq.   Homo=na,   [*o*   bi]   urus   taq.
     talk   NEG   CONTR.INAN=FOC ADDR ART.AN manage CONT
     'He had never thieved before. He's dumb. He doesn't talk. So he (i.e., the village head) has still got to decide [what punishment to deal out to the thief].'
     [Bk-55.016]

Further identificational uses of *o* 'ADDR' are discussed in §8.4.3 and §8.4.4.

8.4 Combining locationals

In the NP template in §5.1, only a single locational position was included. But in fact, once more unlike determiners, more than one locational can mark a single NP, though the possible combinations are relatively restricted. This section describes commonly observed combinations of locationals and their functions.

8.4.1 Place locationals: here + there

Locationals of the same set cannot simultaneously mark a single NP due to the resulting semantic clash. The one exception to this is a restricted combination of the distal and proximal place locationals: *haqe huqe* 'THERE HERE' is the only permitted combination of place locationals. Even the reversing of the order to **huqe haqe* 'HERE THERE' is ungrammatical.

In (59) *haqe huqe* 'THERE HERE' occurs as the last element in the NP, denoting that reference is to both parts or parties in a symmetrical relationship. In (60) *haqe huqe* 'THERE HERE' appears adverbially, indicating the multidirectional manner of the dirt dispersal.

(59) [Mar   belan **haqe   huqe**] ni   halali ini   haqal   oa.
     garden half   THERE   HERE   OBL   3DU   light.fire finished IAM
     'On the here and there (i.e., both) halves of the garden, the two of them had already finished lighting fires.' [LB2.030]

(60) Dia Laho   o   gene   t-ipi   ba,   lobot
     Dia Laho nowhere   LOC   RECP-shake   ART.INAN   ash
     titiq   tasal,   **haqe   huqe**   boto.
     disperse.in.air be.opposite   THERE   HERE   disperse
     'When Dia Laho appeared out of nowhere shaking, ash went flying all over the place, being dispersed here and there.' [Bk-50.019]

8.4.2 Elevational and place locationals

An elevational locational and a place locational, either distal or specific, are frequently found marking a single referent within the same NP. The order of the elevational locational and the place locational is free, though it is more usual for the elevational locational to precede the place locational. This pattern is illustrated in (61), while the place locational preceding the elevational locational is illustrated in (62). In these examples, the elevational and place locational are coreferential to a location; they do not modify one another.

(61) Hik   hiloqon   [**ola   hoqe**   Salele]   gene,   Suai   gene.
     path   two   LOW   SPCPLC   Salele   LOC   Suai   LOC
     '(I) was twice down (in) that place Salele, in Suai.' [Bk-66.069]

(62) G-agal,   i   [**haqe   ota**]   gene   UNHCR   g-ege
     3AN-seek 1PL.INCL   THERE   LEVEL   LOC   UNHCR   3AN-BEN
     sasi, ...
     say
     'Searching for (them), we would (be) over there (and) say to the UNHCR, ...' [Bk-66.117]

8.4.3 Elevational locationals + addressee locational

A location may be referred to with an elevational locational followed by an addressee locational in "symbolic" spatial deixis (Fillmore 1971: 63; Levinson 1983: 66). That is, these locationals are used together without a pointing gesture and where the location referred to is not visible. Identification of the location relies on the speech participants' knowledge of the location and the spatial parameters of the speech event for the identification. The combination of elevational locational and addressee locational signals that the speaker knows precisely the location referred to and believes the hearer to know it, too. In the corpus, elevational locationals followed by an addressee locational mark place names, i.e., are used in reference to precise locations.

Example (63) illustrates the symbolic combination of an elevational locational and an addressee locational. Speaker and addressee are located inside a house and there is no gesture accompanying the reference. The reference to Duarato as *esen* 'HIGH' is relative to the location of the speech participants in the village of Lakus, located on the valley floor. The addition of *o* 'ADDR' indicates to the hearer that the speaker is activating knowledge about the communicative situation and the location of Duarato beyond what is immediately visible. For *o* 'ADDR' to be absent from (63), Duarato would have to be immediately visible to the speech participants with the possibility of an accompanying pointing gesture.

(63) Neto [**esen o** Duarato] gene en g-ige.
     1SG HIGH ADDR Duarato LOC person 3AN-teach
     'I teach up in Duarato.' [Bk-61.052]

Example (64) comes from a detailed description of the route between Gewal and Nualain village, in which we see elevational locationals and the addressee locational used together in symbolic deixis. That we are dealing with symbolic deixis in this example is clear from the "deictic projection" (Lyons 1977: 579) on the part of the speaker: the elevational locationals are not relative to the location of the speech participants, but to the point in the route which the speaker has reached in the description. The two locations referred to with locationals in (64) would in non-symbolic, gestural deixis all be referred to with *ota* 'LEVEL', as to the eye they are roughly at the same elevation as Gewal, the location of the speech participants. However, in the description we also find *esen* 'HIGH', for example, in (64b) because the path leading to Duarato descends into a deep saddle on the ridge with a substantial climb ensuing up to the village.

(64) a. *Tebe   Sele Lolo   gene   zemal,   honal   [ota   o*
       return Sele Lolo   LOC   go.LOW go.LEVEL LEVEL ADDR
       Bele Boso Nokar]   gene   tama.
       Bele Boso Nokar   LOC   enter
       'Then going down from Sele Lolo, go across (and) enter Bele Boso Nokar over there.' [Bk-34.006]

   b. *Mele, mele, mele   daro   [esen   o   Duarato Pur Bul*
      walk   walk   walk   until   HIGH   ADDR   Duarato Pur Bul
      homo]   pir.
      CONTR.INAN   reach
      'Walk (and) walk until (you) reach that Duarato Pur Bul up there.' [Bk-34.0017]

The elevational locational *ola* 'LOW' is often found with the addressee locational in contexts where it cannot be interpreted as referring to a location of lower elevation, as it does in (61) above. The combination *ola o* 'LOW ADDR' is often used as an assertive discourse marker, indicating that clear evidence is available for an assertion such that it is generally agreed upon. For instance, in (65) the referent is identified as at a higher elevation location by the question of speaker A. Thus, in the response of speaker B, the *ola* 'LOW' in *ola o* 'LOW ADDR' is clearly not spatial in meaning. Rather *ola o* 'LOW ADDR' as a unit denotes that the identity of the referent as the child of Mr Mateus is evidenced and not open to dispute, or "beneath" dispute as it were.

(65) A. *[En   esen   bi]   sio?*
        person   HIGH   ART.AN   who
        'Who's the person up there?'

   B. *En   esen   baqi   [ola   o   Paq   Mateus   g-ol].*
      person   HIGH   NPRX.AN LOW   ADDR   Mr   Mateus   3AN-child
      'That person up there is {known with certainty to be} the child of Mr Mateus.' [Not-07.04]

The development of *ola o* 'LOW ADDR' to denote the availability of evidence for an assertion is the result of a metaphorical extension of a spatial sense of *ola* 'LOW' in symbolic deictic contexts. The motivating metaphor here appears to be a converse to the well-known metaphor UP is CONTROL, whereby an entity with power is equated with being in a higher elevational position. In Bunaq, the metaphor DOWN is BEING SUBJECT TO CONTROL has allowed *ola* 'LOW', in combination with shared speaker–addressee knowledge implied by *o* 'ADDR', to be interpreted as denoting evidential availability, since that which is accessible to an individual is, in a sense, under their power.[3]

---

[3] Cross-linguistically such metaphors are very common. Lakoff and Johnson (1980) show the precise relations among spatial senses, and describe metaphorical extensions of the spatial senses based on a more detailed investigation of English 'over'.

The interpretation of *ola o* 'LOW ADDR' depends on contextual information as to the nature of the evidence for an assertion: namely, whether it comes from background knowledge or through personal perception or experience. In (66) *ola o* 'LOW ADDR' occurs in an imperative clause, where it acts as a reminder to the hearer of something that it was possible for them to know, i.e., that they should have been able to work out on their own, namely that the mat needs to be spread. Similarly, in (67) *ola o* 'LOW ADDR' denotes an event that the speaker did not witness, but whose truth is not subject to debate, because it is understood from general knowledge that medical treatment is given out in hospitals. In (68) *ola o* 'LOW ADDR' denotes certainty in the availability of evidence for the utterance that is based on the speaker's own witnessing of the event.

(66) **Ola o** pil zewen oa!
LOW ADDR mat spread.out IAM
'{It is clear} the mat is to be spread out now!' [OS-07.03]

(67) Reu memel gene **ola o** perawat g-ege hetel.
house sick LOC LOW ADDR nurse 3AN-give medicine
'In the hospital, nurses {it is clear} gave him medicine.' [Bk-1.049]

(68) Baqi **ola o** zo gene topol.
NPRX.AN LOW ADDR mango LOC fall
'He {definitely} fell from the tree.' [Bk-1.038]

8.4.4 Temporal/discourse locational + addressee locational

The temporal/discourse locational *mete* 'NOW' is frequently followed by the addressee locational *o* 'ADDR'. This combination is pragmatically only very mildly different from that when *mete* 'NOW' independently marks an NP, as described in §8.3.3. *Mete o* 'NOW ADDR' appears in the same contexts in which *mete* 'NOW' is found on its own, namely, activating a new referent (69) or reactivating an old one not currently in the focus of the discourse (70). The addition of *o* 'ADDR' signals hearer orientation on the part of the speaker. That is, its inclusion emphasises that the speaker sees that the referent is located in the hearer's memory and is thus identifiable and retrievable to them. Thus, in (69) and (70) the speaker accentuates with *o* 'ADDR' the fact that the referents of *Makasai* 'Makasae' and *tun* 'flour' which he is activating are known to the hearer.

(69) A. Bai a h-ini nego?
thing eat 3INAN-call what
'What's (the word for) 'eat'?' [Bk-61.089]

B. *Bai   a   h-ini   mace, kalo hoqe   Lospalos*
thing   eat   3INAN-call   eat   if   SPCPLC   Lospalos
*gie.   Kalo   [**mete o**   Makasai] ya   h-ini   nua.*
3.POSS   if   NOW   ADDR   Makasae   yes 3INAN-call eat
'(The word for) eat is *mace*, that's in Lospalos (i.e., in the Fataluku language). As for {you know} Makasae here, (the word for eat) is *nua*.'
[Bk-61.090-91]

(70) a. **Tun**   *homo*   *mok*   *za*   *g-utu*   *kahul.*
flour   CONTR.INAN   banana   ripe   3-COM   mix
'That flour is mixed with ripe banana.' [Bk-76.012]

b. *T-o   pir,   t-o   pir   oa.*
RECP-SRC reach RECP-SRC reach IAM
'Fold them in to one another, fold them in to one another.'   [Bk-76.014]

c. *Mok   ai   [**mete   o**   tun]   ai   kahul   t-o   pir.*
banana   both   NOW   ADDR   flour   both   mix   RECP-SRC   reach
'Both the banana and this here flour get mixed into one another.'
[Bk-76.015]

8.5 Summary

Bunaq locationals are a class of items used to refer to the location of an entity in space, time, and/or discourse. Elevational locationals refer to the location of the referent according to their elevation relative to the deictic centre, with some conventionalised, "ultimately oriented" uses in particular contextual domains. Place locationals refer to a general location relative to the distance from the speech participants. The temporal/discourse locational refers to the present time and functions to activate referents in the discourse. The addressee locational refers to the location of the referent as at the addressee with extensions to denote a referent's association with the addressee and shared knowledge between the speaker and addressee.

In pragmatically neutral position, locationals precede the N$_{HEAD}$ whose location they refer to, but they can follow the N$_{HEAD}$ in restrictive identificational contexts. Locationals can also occur independently without a referent for an N$_{HEAD}$ where they denote a location. Multiple locationals can modify a single NP to locate a referent according to a range of complex criteria. In one case, we saw that the combination of *ola* 'LOW' and *o* 'ADDR' has given rise to an evidential-like function meaning 'patently, clearly'.

Chapter 9
Adnominal possession and related constructions

9.1 Introduction

Possession prototypically expresses an ownership relationship of a human possessor to an inanimate possessum. Yet, as in many languages, possessive constructions in Bunaq are not limited to such contexts. They have semantic extensions to refer to situations involving other relationships between entities, such as kinship, spatial, and part–whole relations, which do not involve one entity literally possessing another.

This chapter describes adnominal possession and related constructions in Bunaq. We will see that Bunaq has a contrast between indirect and direct possession encoded by free and bound possessive markers, respectively. Note that whilst each type of possession is associated with some prototypical semantics, there is not always a clear semantic motivation for the split. As such, the labels "alienable" and "inalienable" are used here primarily for lexically, rather than semantically, defined classes of nouns. At the same time, Bunaq allows for some different degrees of semantic closeness in possessive relationships to be indicated by changes in the possessive word order and by double possessive marking.

The morphosyntactic realisation of an adnominal possessive relationship in Bunaq depends on which possessive class (alienable or inalienable) the noun belongs to and, to a lesser extent, on the possessive relationship between possessor (PSR) and possessum (PSM). Table 9.1 overviews the patterns for the encoding of possessive relations. The labels and categories are explained below the table.

Table 9.1: Structural characteristics.

Class of noun	Locus of person inflection for possessor	Ordering of possessor and possessum
ALIENABLE	indirect: PSR$_x$ AGR$_x$-e PSM	PSR PSM, or PSM [PSR]$_{PRED}$
INALIENABLE	direct: PSR$_x$ AGR$_x$-PSM, or no prefix	PSR PSM

Nouns belonging to the alienably possessed class have their possessors marked "indirectly", that is, by means of a free form inflecting for the person of the possessor. The majority of nouns are indirectly possessed, and therefore belong to the alienably possessed class. The possessor of a noun belonging to the alienably possessed class normally precedes the possessum. However, the possessor can in certain circumstances be postposed to the possessum; in this case, the possessor in no longer strictly adnominal, but rather constitutes a predicate, either of a clause or of a relative clause. Even though postposed possessor constructions are predicative, they are discussed here because they make use of the same matter as adnominal possessor constructions, and their semantics are best understood when compared to the related preposed possessor constructions.

Nouns belonging to the inalienably possessed class are "directly" possessed, meaning that the possessed noun hosts a prefix inflected for the person of the possessor. On a small subset of nouns belonging to the inalienably possessed class, an INANIMATE 3rd person possessor receives no co-indexing prefixing; in these cases, the direct possessive construction is near indistinguishable from a right-headed compound.

In this chapter, possessive constructions for alienably possessed and inalienably possessed nouns are discussed in detail. Particular attention is paid to the description of variant constructions in which changes to the morphosyntactic coding of the possessor are used to denote differences in the semantics of the possessive relationship. I describe the expression of indirect possession in §9.2 and that of direct possession in §9.3. The relationship between direct possession and possessive compounding is considered in §9.4. The co-occurrence of free and bound possessive markers is treated in section §9.5. Section §9.6 summarises. For the use of existential verbs in the expression of predicative possession, see §10.6.2.

9.2 Indirect possession

Indirect possession typically expresses a variety of semantic relationships between a possessor and a possessum which are not of a permanent and inherent type, that is, in which no semantic dependency exists between the possessor and possessum (Chappell and McGregor 1989: 25). The majority of nominals in Bunaq belong to the inalienably possessed class.

Indirect possession is encoded with the free possessive classifier -*e* inflected for the person of the possessor. The inflections are given in Table 9.2. There is no specific INANIMATE inflection of the possessive classifier: there is only a single third person form, *gie* '3.POSS', which is used for both ANIMATE and INANIMATE possessors. Although the person inflections and the indirect possessive classifier are synchronically fused (see §2.6.1 on the irregularity of the prefixes in this paradigm), I avoid the use of the term "possessive pronoun" to describe the forms in Table 9.2. This is because the morphosyntactic behaviour of the inflected possessive forms parallels that of person inflections elsewhere in Bunaq, as seen in the ability of free nominal and pronominal elements to co-occur with the inflected possessive classifier to refer to a possessor of an alienably possessed noun (see §9.2.1 for illustration). The inflected forms of the indirect possessive classifier also lack the characteristics of pronouns described in §3.5.1.

Possessors of alienably possessed nouns either precede (§9.2.1) or follow the possessum (§9.2.2). The preceding possessor is non-predicative, i.e., part of the extended NP, while the possessor following the possessum is predicative. Not all types of possessors of alienably possessed nouns can appear in both positions, with the position

Table 9.2: Person inflections of the indirect possessive classifier.

nie	'1EXCL.POSS'
ie	'1INCL/2.POSS'
gie	'3.POSS'
die	'REFL.POSS'
tie	'RECP.POSS'

of the possessor depending to some extent on the possessor's properties: possessors that are animate and controlling typically precede and only rarely follow the possessum; possessors that lack prototypical possessor features only follow the possessum.

9.2.1 Preposed possessors

Possessors of alienably possessed nouns are usually expressed adnominally by an inflected form of the indirect possessive classifier which precedes the possessum (1). An NP explicitly expressing the possessor can precede the inflected classifier (2). See §6.2.1 on the obligatoriness of pronouns co-indexing agreement prefixes.

(1) a. *gie*   *zap*
         3.POSS   dog
         'his/her dog'
     b. *nie*   *turiq*
         1EXCL.POSS   knife
         'my knife'

(2) a. *Manek*   *gie*   *zap*
         Manek   3.POSS   dog
         'Manek's dog'
     b. *nei*   *nie*   *turiq*
         1PL.EXCL   1EXCL.POSS   knife
         'our knife'

Textual examples of this adnominal possessor construction are given below. In (3) we have a human possessor, in (4) an animal, *apa* 'cow', and in (5) an inanimate possessor, *desa* 'village group' (< Indonesian).

(3) *Bel*   *en*   *baqi*   *gu-huq,*   [*en*   *gie*   *tais*]   *h-apal*   *niq.*
     wind   person   NPRX.AN   3AN-blow   person   3.POSS   cloth   3INAN-open   NEG
     '(When) the wind blew that man, (it) didn't open the man's coat.'   [Bk-16.005]

(4) Hot   mil   sabtu   no   zal   [apa gie   luhan] mal.
    sun   DUR   Saturday   OBL   carry   cow   3.POSS   pen   go
    'On Saturday, we carried (it) to the cow's stable.'   [Bk-12.015]

(5) [Desa~desa   gie   hok   baqa]   mos=sa   tara
    REDUP~village.group   3.POSS   border   NPRX.INAN   also=EVEN   know
    haqal   niq.
    finish   NEG
    'The borders of the different village groups aren't even fully known.'   [Bk-67.088]

Examples (6) and (7) illustrate that a possessor of an alienably possessed noun can be expressed by a full NP marked by a determiner:

(6) Halaqi   gie   kaqa   [mete   [zon   bi   gie]_PSR   su   ba]_NP
    3PL   3.POSS   eB   NOW   pig   ART.AN   3.POSS   milk   ART.INAN
    gie   kauq   g-ege   hois.
    3.POSS   younger.sibling   3AN-give   suckle
    'Their older brother gave his younger sibling the milk of the pig to suckle.'
                                                                              [Bk-69.056]

(7) [[**Lusin**   **roi**   **gie**]_PSR   pagu-pilaq]_NP   hobel.
    Lusin   SPEC.AN   3.POSS   portion   not.exist
    'Lusin here did not get a portion.'   [Bk-67.225]

9.2.1.1 Associativity: Indirect possessor constructions without a possessum

A possessor encoded by an indirect possessive classifier can occur without a possessum expressed in the NP core (see §5.1 on the constituency of the NP core). In this construction, the possessum is not simply anaphorically elided. Rather the construction has a generic interpretation and conveys associative meaning, i.e., '(those things/people) associated with X'. The construction is represented schematically in (8).

(8) (PSR)   PSR-*e* [Ø]_NP.CORE   (DET)
    '(that) of (PSR)'

In (9) the 3rd person inflection of the indirect possessive classifier with the possessor expressed by the NP, *Timor Timur* 'East Timor', functions as the S argument of the verbal predicate *koleq* 'tired'. In (10) *rie* 'REFL.POSS' stands alone to act as the NP complement of the goal-encoding verbal postposition *a-ta* '3INAN-GL'.

(9) [*Timor Timur gie*] *koleq.*
    East Timor 3.POSS tired
    '(That) of East Timor is tired.', i.e., 'Everything about East Timor is worn.'
    [Bk-2.036]

(10) *Baqi* [*rie*] *a-ta tan~tan.*
     NPRX.AN REFL.POSS 3INAN-GL REDUP~more
     'He adds more and more to his own.', i.e., 'He just keeps on doing his own thing (and doesn't help anyone else).'
     [Bk-22.015]

In the above examples, the possessor is the only element of the NP that is expressed. In the majority of associative possession constructions, however, the possessor is itself possessed, as in (11) and (12), or the NP containing the possessor is determined, as in (13) and (14).

(11) *Ei Ø-ini* [**nie** *muk gie*] *r-ige.*
     2PL 1INCL/2-CAUS 1EXCL.POSS land 3.POSS REFL-learn
     '(I want) to make you learn all about my land.'
     [Bk-24.041]

(12) *Neto Ø-ege* [**rie** *tas gie*] *rale gie.*
     1SG 1INCL/2-BEN REFL.POSS village 3.POSS tell PROSP
     'I'm going to tell you all about my village.'
     [Bk-7.001]

(13) [*Tais gie* **baqa**] *en lele tara kuran.*
     cloth 3.POSS NPRX.INAN person nowadays know less
     'People don't know so much about those (things) of cloth nowadays.', i.e., 'People don't know so much about cloth and the things associated with it these days.'
     [OS-07.02]

(14) *Neto* [*a obon gie* **ba**] *sasi gie taq.*
     1SG food hang 3.POSS ART.INAN say PROSP CONT
     'Now I'm talking the (things) of the hanging food.', i.e., 'I am going to tell you about (the festival of) "the food hanging".'
     [Bk-18.043]

In these examples, both the possessor of the possessum and the determiner can be seen as acting as "reference-points" (cf. Langacker 1993) which aid in the interpretation and identification of the associative reference in the absence of an NP core.

9.2.2 Postposed possessors

An inflected indirect possessive classifier along with an NP expressing the possessor can follow the possessum to make a predicative possessor construction (see §4.3.3 on possessive clauses). In these constructions, the possessed noun is given, and is often marked by a determiner. Examples of the predicative use of the indirect possessive classifier are given in (15) and (16).

(15)   Atis=o   liqul   ba   [halaqi   gie]$_{PRED}$.
       loom.bar=AND   loom.backstrap   ART.INAN   3PL   3.POSS
       'The loom bar and backstrap are theirs.'   [LB-1.058]

(16)   Homo   [nei   gunung   nie]$_{PRED}$.
       CONTR.INAN   1PL.EXCL   mountain   1EXCL.POSS
       'That (type of cake) is ours, us mountain people's.'   [Bk-76.039]

The predicates in the above examples can also act as the predicate of a relative clause (RC) with the possessum as head of the NP, as in (17) and (18). In these examples, the possessor is encoded as an RC attribute of the N_{HEAD}. Note, however, that in (18) the head is elided. Pragmatically, the postposing of the possessor relative to the possessum functions to place weak stress on the identity of the possessor. Semantically, however, there is no difference in the nature of the possessive relation between the postposed possessors in these examples and those with the preposed possessor, described in §9.2.1.

(17)   [atis=o   liqul   [halaqi   gie]$_{RC}$ ba]$_{NP}$
       loom.bar=AND   loom.backstrap   3PL   3.POSS   ART.INAN
       'the loom bar and backstrap (that's) theirs'   [Not-07.01]

(18)   [[nei   gunung   nie]$_{RC}$ homo]$_{NP}$
       1PL.EXCL   mountain   1EXCL.POSS   CONTR.INAN
       'that (type of cake) is ours, us mountain people's'   [Not-07.01]

Whilst the above uses of a predicative possessor in the RC are possible, they are next to unknown in spontaneous discourse. The vast majority of instances of predicative possessors in the RC are not identificational in function, but rather are used to encode possessive relationships in which a 3rd person possessor lacks prototypical properties of "possessorship", like being the owner or controller of the possessum. Predicative possessors are further "removed" from their possessum than non-predicative, adnominal possessors in that they do not denote an actual, current possessive relationship, but potential or past ones.

Two types of predicative possessor are distinguished: (i) the possessor is construed as the intended *destination* of the possessum (§9.2.2.1); and (ii) the possessor is construed as the *origin* of the possessum (§9.2.2.2).[1] Both these types of predicative possession are only found with third person possessors.

9.2.2.1 Possessor as destination

Third person possessors of alienably possessed nouns are postposed where they express a "possessor" to which the possessum is intended to belong (19) or in connection with which it is intended to be used (20). In both cases, the postposed possessor does not own or have control over the possessum, rather it is the end-point or intended destination of the possessum. A postposed "destination" possessor also always has a non-specific, hypothetical reference (as in Radden and Dirven 2007: 94). A postposed possessor can be the predicate of a relative clause, as in (19), or the predicate of a main clause, as in (20).

(19) a. [*Tais* [*pana mil gie*]_RC *ba*]_NP *h-ini tais pana*.
cloth female COLL 3.POSS ART.INAN 3INAN-call cloth female
'A cloth for females is called a female cloth.' [Bk-24.026]

b. [*Tais* [*mone gie*]_RC *ba*]_NP *h-ini tais mone*.
cloth man 3.POSS ART.INAN 3INAN-call cloth male
'A cloth for men is called a male cloth.' [Bk-24.030]

(20) *Bai baqa* [*ru-bul gie*]_PRED, [*kalaq gie*]_PRED=*o*,
thing NPRX.INAN REFL-head 3.POSS neck 3.POSS=AND
[*r-on gie*]_PRED.
REFL-hand 3.POSS
'Those things are of the head, of the neck and of the hands.', i.e., 'Those (jewellery) items are intended for (being worn on) the head, the neck and the hands.' [Bk-24.024]

In the above examples, having the possessors preceding the possessum results in a change of meaning. The non-predicative possessors in (21) and (22) must denote a current possessive relationship in which the possessor is the owner/controller of the possessum and in which the possessor as owner has a specific referent.

(21) *kalaq bai gie baqa*
neck thing 3.POSS NPRX.INAN
'neck's things', i.e., the neck's features or characteristics.' [Not-07.02]

---

1 There are two further extensions of the postposed possessor construction, discussed elsewhere: extension to encoding NP with a reason role (§12.3), and extension to encoding prospective aspect (§14.3.3).

(22) mone   gie   tais   ba
      man   3.POSS   cloth   ART.INAN
      'man's cloth', i.e., 'the particular cloth possessed by a specific man'   [Not-07.02]

Some further textual examples of predicative "destination" possessors are given below. In (23) the possessor is the predicate of the RC modifying *mak-leqat* 'overseer', while in (24) there are two predicative possessor phrases acting as main clause predicates. In (23) the predicative possessor encodes the potential patch of the land to be managed by the to-be-elected overseers; a non-predicative possessor here would mean that the overseers own the land of the different *soron* 'land divisions', which is not the case. In (24) the predicative possessor encodes the potential sum of money which a bottle of each size could fetch; the possessor here cannot be non-predicative as a bottle is not the owner of the money it buys, i.e., does not have control over it.

(23) [Mak-leqat [soron   goniqil gie]_RC]_NP   go-poi   gie.
      overseer   land.division four   3.POSS   3AN-choose   PROSP
      '(We) will choose the overseers of the four land divisions.'   [Bk-19.026]

(24) Botil   uen   h-ini   nota   sogal   gonciet.   Homo   [botil
      bottle   one   3INAN-call   note   tens   five   CONTR.INAN   bottle
      legul   gie]_PRED.   Nota   sogo   homo   [botil   barak   gie]_PRED.
      tall   3.POSS   note   ten   CONTR.INAN   bottle   short   3.POSS
      'One bottle made 15 notes. That was for a big bottle. Ten notes, that was for a small bottle.'   [Bk-13.011]

9.2.2.2 Possessor as origin

Third person possessors of alienably possessed nouns are predicative where they express an entity in which the possessum originates. For instance, possessors referring to *bei mil* 'ancestors' are typically postposed in the corpus because they are construed as the origin of the many practices and stories. In (25) and (26) the predicative possessors refer to the ancestors in which the present *zapal* 'folktale' and *ton* 'marriage' originate. According to native speaker intuitions, the use of non-predicative possessors in examples like (25) and (26) would mean that the possessed items are alone the property of the Bunaq people of the past and not those of the present day, i.e., the ancestors are not the origin of an entity in the present day but the owners of an entity that no longer exists.

(25) [Zapal   [bei   mil   gie]_RC   uen]_NP,   roe   goet   on.
      folktale   ancestor   COLL   3.POSS   one   SPEC.INAN   LIKE   DO
      'One of the ancestors' folktales goes like this.', i.e., 'One of the folktales originating from our ancestors goes like this.'   [Bk-50.001]

(26) Tapi [ton   [en   bei   mil   gie]_RC]_NP
     but marriage person ancestor COLL 3.POSS
     h-alolo.
     3INAN-follow
     'But (we) follow the marriage of the ancestors.', i.e., 'We conform to the marriage traditions which come from our ancestors.' [Bk-62.021]

A predicative possessor may also encode an origin location. In (27) and (28) the NPs encoding the possessor are place names and refer to the origin location of the possessum. The use of a non-predicative possessor would mean that the location had ownership and control over the possessum. That is, that the church was owned and run by the people of Nualain in (27) and that the money was from the state of Indonesia in (28).

(27) [Reu   por   [Nualian gie]_RC]_NP a-ta   tama.
     house holy Nualain   3.POSS   3INAN-GL   enter
     '(I) entered into the church of Nualain.' [Bk-34.026]

(28) Neto [uang   [Indonesia gie]_RC]_NP g-osok.
     1SG   money   Indonesia   3.POSS   3AN-receive
     'I received money of Indonesia, i.e., Indonesian money.' [Bk-11.006]

Finally, the predicative possessor encoding origin is distinct from the non-predicative possessor construction in that it allows the possessum to be encoded with a pronoun, as in (29a) and (30a). In §3.5.1 we saw that a non-predicative possessor could not modify a pronoun, and we see that a non-predicative possessor in (29b) and (30b) results in outright ungrammaticality; speakers could not even assign semantically bizarre meanings to these clauses.

(29) a. Neto   Gewal   gie.
         1SG   Gewal   3.POSS
         'I am from Gewal.' [Bk-68.010]
     b. *Gewal gie   neto
         Gewal   3.POSS 1SG [Not-07.02]

(30) a. Halaqi Timor-Leste gie
         3PL   East Timor   3.POSS
         'They are from East Timor.' [Bk-11.013]
     b. *Timor-Leste gie   halaqi
         East Timor   3.POSS 3PL [Not-07.02]

9.3 Direct possession

Direct possession is used with inalienably possessed nouns and encodes possessive relations in which there is typically a more permanent and inherent semantic association between a possessor and possessum (Chappell and McGregor 1996). The inalienably possessed class of nouns includes prototypical inalienable referents such as human body parts and kin terms, as well as some animal and plant parts. In addition, nouns belonging to the inalienably possessed class include some "intimates" (Stolz 2008: 56), items aside from body parts and kin that a person cannot help having, e.g., a name, a language, and if one is a slave or an animal, a master and a price, and so forth.

The defining characteristic of nouns belonging to the inalienably possessed class is the ability to host a person prefix for the possessor. The prefixes are presented in Table 9.3. They are identical in form to the prefixes occurring on bivalent verbs co-indexing the P argument. See §2.5.1 for details on the prefixal allomorphy on such roots.[2]

Table 9.3: Person prefixes occurring on inalienably possessed nouns.

nV-	'1EXCL'
V-	'1INCL/2'
gV-	'3AN'
dV-	'REFL'
tV-	'RECP'

Inalienably possessed nouns form a closed class with only a small membership in comparison to the whole nominal lexicon. I divide inalienably possessed nouns into sub-classes based on other inflectional properties they exhibit. The properties I take into account are (i) the ability of the inalienably possessed noun to occur without a possessive prefix ("unmarked"); (ii) the hosting of an additional inflection (e.g., h- '3INAN' or n- 'LOC'); and (iii) the shape of the unprefixed root. Table 9.4 presents an overview of the five classes I distinguish and their inflectional characteristics. Each of the classes is treated in turn in the following sections.

---

[2] The majority of inalienably possessed nouns in Bunaq are vowel-initial. This has come about as a result of the vowels of the original prefixes becoming fused to the historical root. For example, the initial /e/ vowel in Bunaq -ewe 'tooth' (< PTAP *wasin 'tooth') is the historical vowel of a prefix that harmonised with the first vowel of the root.

Table 9.4: Possessive classes of inalienably possessed nouns.

	3ʳᵈ ANIMATE	Other inflectional properties	Kind of relation
CLASS I	g- '3AN'	–	body parts, kin terms, intimates
CLASS II	g- '3AN'	h- '3INAN'	body parts, intimates, plant parts
CLASS III	g- '3AN'	n- 'LOC'	intimates, plant parts, locational
CLASS IV	g- '3AN'	unmarked with initial t	intimates
CLASS V	gV- '3AN'	unmarked	body and plant parts, part–whole, locational

9.3.1 Class I

Class I contains obligatorily possessed nouns with only g- '3AN-' in the 3ʳᵈ person. This is the largest class of obligatorily possessed nouns in Bunaq. The person inflections of two members of this class are given in (31).

(31) a. *n-inup*   '1EXCL-nose'
       Ø-inup   '1INCL/2-nose'
       g-inup   '3AN-nose'
       d-inup   'REFL-nose'
       t-inup   'RECP-nose'
    b. *n-ol*   '1EXCL-child'
       Ø-ol   '1INCL/2-child'
       g-ol   '3AN-child'
       d-ol   'REFL-child'
       t-ol   'RECP-child'

Table 9.5 presents the known members of Class I; forms are cited with the 3ʳᵈ person inflection. The majority of this class designates parts of the body. Body part terms typically refer to either humans or animals, but sometimes differ in their translation between the different types of possessor, e.g., *g-ot* refers to 'body hair' for a human possessor, 'fur' for a mammal possessor, and 'feather' for a bird possessor.

Table 9.5: Class I inalienably possessed nouns.

gaban	'umbilical stump'	*giwitar*	'chest, breast bone'
gabaqul	'stomach'	*gizil*	'vagina'
gaqel	'shoulder'	*gobe*	'nickname, secret name'
gagar	'mouth'	*gobut*	'elbow'

Table 9.5 (continued)

gal	'rib, flank'	gol	'child'
galel	'great-great-grandchild'	goleq	'midriff'
gapuq	'lap, top of legs'	golep	'lower back, abdomen'
gaput	'spleen'	goli	'armpit'
gatal	'grandchild'	goloq	'spot, place'
gawal	'abdomen'	gomo	'master, owner'
gawas	'forehead'	gomoq	'udder'
gebol	'crotch'	gonos	'nail, claw'
gebu	'bottom'	gopil	'strength, ability'
gepal	'ear'	goral	'penis'
gesal	'cheek'	gorok	'coccyx, small of back'
gewe	'tooth'	gosil	'breath, spirit'
gewen	'face'	gosun	'wing'
gezel	'belly, womb (animal)'	got	'feather, fur, body hair'
gibis	'navel'	gotil	'cheek, spouse'
gibul	'ancestry, family'	gozul	'saliva, spittle'
giel	'nest'	gubel	'fat'
gigal	'gum'	gubu	'flesh (of humans, animals)'
gigo	'beak, snout'	gubulu	'fontanelle'
gilop	'underbelly'	gubuk	'great-grandchild'
gina	'inheritance'	gubut	'headless corpse'
gino	'tear'	guen	'heel'
gintili	'cousin'	guhin	'uterus, womb'
ginup	'nose'	guk	'joint'
gio	'shit, dropping'	guli	'scar'
gios	'vein, blood vessel'	gulik	'urine, semen'
gipe	'horn, tusk'	guloq	'tail; digit; youngest child'
giral	'eye'	guol	'back of knee'
giri	'leg'	gup	'tongue'
giwiq	'skin, body'	gupun	'breast (of bird)'
giwis	'male genitalia'	gut	'egg'

For those terms where the possessor is invariably an animal (e.g., *g-igo* '3AN-beak/snout', *g-ipe* '3AN-horn', etc.), the noun occurs most frequently with a 3rd person inflection; only when animals are anthropomorphised in folktales do we find other inflections of these items. For example, in (32), a bird menaces a child, threatening to peck it with its beak.

(32) *Eto   n-igo   bare   h-azal   milik=e   niq?*
     2SG   1EXCL-beak   PROX.INAN   3INAN-see   scared=AGREE   NEG
     'Are you scared of my beak or what?'   [Bk-49.020]

Several items in Class I refer to intimate possessions, such as *g-inil* '3AN-name' and *g-ina* '3AN-inheritance', *g-oloq* '3AN-spot, place', as well as *g-opil* '3AN-strength'. The class also includes items referring to bodily fluids and other bodily products: *g-ozul* '3AN-saliva', *g-io* '3AN-faeces', *g-osil* '3AN-breath,' and *g-ut* '3AN-egg'. The handful of kinship terms that are inalienably possessed are also members of this class; they refer exclusively to the child generation and below: *g-ol* '3AN-child', *g-atal* '3AN-grandchild', *g-ubuk* '3AN-great-grandchild', and *g-alel* '3AN-great-great-grandchild'.

9.3.2 Class II

In addition to ANIMATE 3rd person inflection with *g-* '3AN-', a small set of obligatory possessed nouns has a 3rd person INANIMATE form marked by *h-* '3INAN-' (paralleling the h-class of verbs described in §10.2.4.1). The complete set of these nouns in the corpus is presented in Table 9.6. Aside from ANIMACY, the agreement prefix taken by nouns in this class is affected by the alienation, or "closeness", of the relationship between possessor and possessum, by lexicalisation, and by loss of forms. Some further *h*-marked nouns that alternate with a prefix *n-* 'LOC-' are discussed in §9.3.3.

Table 9.6: Class II inalienably possessed nouns with *h-* '3INAN-'.

3rd INANIMATE		3rd ANIMATE	
hegil	'shade'	gegil	'shadow'
heruk	'thorn'	geruk	'thorn'
(hinil) †	'name, kind of'	ginil	'name, kind of'
hien	'louse'	gien	'louse'
ho	'source, centre'	go	'source, home'
hon	'hand'	gon	'hand'
(hotok) †	'liver'	gotok	'liver'
hua	'footprint, track'	gua	'footprint'
(hun) †	'back'	gun	'back'

† Dagger marks indicate a form which is rare and undergoing loss.

This class contains a mixed bag of items, ranging from canonical inalienables, such as body parts, to a range of items denoting intimates and plant parts. The person inflections of two members of this small class are given in (33).

(33) a. *n-egil* '1EXCL-shadow'
    Ø-egil '1INCL/2-shadow'
    g-egil '3AN-shadow'
    h-egil '3INAN-shadow'
 b. *n-ua* '1EXCL-footprint'
    Ø-ua '1INCL/2-footprint'
    g-ua '3AN-footprint'
    h-ua '3INAN-footprint'

The basic choice of form of a 3rd person possessor prefix depends on the ANIMACY and the perceived alienability of the possessor: a 3rd person ANIMATE possessor takes the *g-* '3AN-' marked form, while an 3rd person INANIMATE possessor takes *h-* '3INAN-'. This contrast is illustrated with the agreement on *h-un* '3INAN-back' in the temporal phrase *hun taru* 'appear once s.th./s.o. is over/gone' (34).

(34) a. Neto   inel   h-un   / *g-un   taru.
        1SG   rain   3INAN-back   3AN-back appear
    'I appear (at) the back of the rain', i.e., 'I appear after the rain is over.'
 b. Neto   eme   g-un   / *h-un   taru.
        1SG   mother   3AN-back   3INAN-back appear
    'I appear (at) the back of the mother', i.e., 'I appear after mother has left.'
                                                                    [Not-07.02]

In a few cases, the *h-* form is undergoing loss and is subject to replacement by the *g-* form, which is then used with both ANIMATE and INANIMATE agreement controllers. For instance, whilst *h-inil* '3INAN-name' is initially used with an INANIMATE possessor, *ipi* 'rice' in (35a), later in the same text the speaker uses *g-inil* '3AN-name' (35b). In fact, this is one of only two instances of *h-inil* '3INAN-name' in the corpus, with *g-inil* '3AN-name' appearing almost invariably regardless of the ANIMACY of its possessor.

(35) a. Ipi   h-inil   nego~nego?
        rice 3INAN-name   REDUP~what
    'What are the different sorts of rice?'   [Bk-90.01]
 b. Ipi   g-inil   baqa=na   neto   tara   ai.
        rice 3AN-name   NPRX.INAN=FOC   1SG   know   ONLY
    'Those are the only sorts of rice which I know.'   [Bk-90.10]

In other cases where a *h-* '3INAN-' is preserved, it is often only in specific constructions. For instance, the form *h-un* '3INAN-back' is limited to only a few temporal phrases, such as that in (34a); in locative contexts only *g-un* '3AN-back' is attested, as in (36):

(36) Neto   deu   g-un   / *h-un   gene.
    1SG   house   3AN-back   3INAN-back   LOC
    'I am at the back of the house.'   [Not-07.02]

The loss of the *h*-form in such cases appears to have to do partly with inalienability. That is, forms in *h-* '3INAN-' tend to have been lost more frequently in situations where there is a permanent, indissoluble relationship between the possessor and possessum. For instance, *h-un* '3INAN-back' is retained in temporal contexts, i.e., where there is no inherent relationship between possessor and possessum, but is lost in locative contexts, where the possessum is physically part of the possessor even if the referent is not ANIMATE.

Another example of this is provided in (37) with *h-egil* '3INAN-shade'. Whilst an ANIMATE possessor can only take the *g-* '3AN-' inflection of this noun (37a), an INANIMATE possessor can take either the *g-* '3AN-' inflection (37c) or the *h-* '3INAN-' inflection (37d). The different inflections correspond to a difference in degree of alienation between possessor and possessum. Example (37c) with *g-* '3AN-' inflection refers to the area of shade that is inherent to the rock itself: the rock creates the shade in that its overhanging form blocks out the sun. By contrast, (37d) with *h-* '3INAN-' indicates a greater alienation between possessor and possessum in that the shade is not an inherent feature of the rock, but rather an ephemeral characteristic caused by the sun striking the rock.

(37) a. en   g-egil
        person   3AN-shadow
        'person's shadow'
     b. *en   h-egil
        person   3INAN-shadow
     c. hol   g-egil
        stone   3AN-shadow
        'stone's shade (e.g., due to overhang, etc.)'
     d. hol   h-egil
        stone   3INAN-shadow
        'stone's shadow (cast by the sun)'

The difference between the use of *g-* and *h-* might also be explained by regarding the *h*-forms as uninflected. That is, whereas *g-egil* in (37a) and (37c) denotes a more inalienable relation with *hol* 'stone' encoded by means of a direct possessor prefix, *h-egil* in (40d) is the left-most noun in a possessive or right-headed compound (§3.2.1.2). As discussed for verbs in §10.2.4.1, the historical comparative evidence for viewing the initial /h/ as a 3rd person INANIMATE prefix is equivocal. The intersection of direct possession and possessive compounding is discussed further in §9.4.

9.3.3 Class III

A small subset of obligatorily possessed nouns are characterised by their taking the locative morpheme *n-* 'LOC-', a prefix homophonous with but distinct from the 1st person prefix, in that it is used with 3rd person possessors. While it is hard to characterise the meaning of *n-* 'LOC-' given its non-productivity, it appears to express that the referent of the noun it marks has an internal or central location. The location to which the referent of the noun is internal is encoded as a possessor and, as in other possessive constructions, precedes the possessum.³

The complete set of nouns marked with *n-* 'LOC-' that have been identified in the corpus is presented in Table 9.7. The morpheme has only been sporadically preserved. Notice that nouns with *n-* 'LOC-' vary in regard to what other inflections they are found with. Most frequently *n-* 'LOC-' alternates with *g-* '3AN-'; only a few *n-* 'LOC-' marked nouns have a *h-* '3INAN-' inflected form; one item, *il* 'water', can occur with *n-* 'LOC-', but also without any other prefix.

Table 9.7: Class III inalienably possessed nouns with *n-* 'LOC-' marked nouns.

LOCATIVE		3ʳᴰ PERSON ANIMATE		3ʳᴰ PERSON INANIMATE		UNMARKED	
nala	'remainder'	gala	'remainder'	hala	'rubbish'		
netel	'root'	getel	'root, sprout'	hetel	'medicine'	–	–
netiq	'bark'	getiq	'bark, scab'	–	–	–	–
nil	'inner juice'	gil	'sap, juices'	–	–	il	'water'
nilin	'centre point'	–	–	hilin	'halfway point'	–	–
niol	'sound'	giol	'voice, language'	–	–	–	–
noqet	'other side'	goqet	'other person'	–	–	–	–
noq	'flesh (of fruit)'	goq	'fruit'	–	–	–	–

Compare (38a) and (38b), illustrating the contrast between *n-* '1' and *n-* 'LOC-': the latter can be cross-referenced with a 3rd person, whereas the former cannot. In (38b) *n-* 'LOC-' indicates that the noise comes from a location internal to the motorbike, whereas in (38c), *g-* '3AN-' marks simply that the sound is that of a motorbike.

(38) a. *n-iol*
       1EXCL-voice
       'my voice'

---

3 Schapper (2020c: 427) relates this Bunaq locative prefix *n-* to a locative prefix occurring on vowel-initial verbs in the TAP languages of the Eastern Timor subgroup. Ultimately, both are likely to go back to a free form PTAP *na used in encoding locations.

b. *motor n-iol*
   motorbike LOC-voice
   'sound from (inside) the motorbike'
c. *motor g-iol*
   motorbike 3AN-voice
   'the motorbike's sound'

In (39a) we see *n-* 'LOC-' marking *il* 'water', referring to the water internal to the nut of the coconut palm (known as either 'coconut juice' or 'coconut water'). In (39b) *il* 'water' is marked with the prefix *g-* '3AN-' referring to an inherent part of the coconut plant, the vital fluid which circulates through it, i.e., its sap. In (39c) where there is no prefixation on *il* 'water', we have a possessive compound denoting a location at which the coconut is located.

(39) a. *hoza n-il*
        coconut LOC-water
        'coconut juice'
     b. *hoza g-il*
        coconut 3AN-water
        'sap of the coconut tree'
     c. *hoza il*
        coconut water
        lit., 'coconut water', i.e., 'water in a location with coconuts'

Lexicalisation and bleaching of the internal locative meaning of the morpheme *n-* 'LOC-' is apparent in the items *n-oqet* 'LOC-other side' and *n-ala* 'LOC-remainder'. On these items, the presence of *n-* 'LOC-' is only evident from the fact that it alternates with *g-* '3AN-', while *n-* 'LOC-' has the appearance of just another INANIMATE agreement form. Examples (40a) and (41a) show *n-* 'LOC-' marked forms co-indexing INANIMATE possessors, while in (40b) and (41b) *g-* '3AN-' respectively co-indexes a possessor with an ANIMATE referent, *en* 'person', and a possessor of ANIMATE noun class, *paqol* 'maize'.

(40) a. *deu n-oqet*
        house LOC-other.side
        'house's other side'
     b. *en g-oqet*
        person 3AN-other.side
        'other person', < *'person's other side'

(41) a. *ipi n-ala*
        rice LOC-remainder
        'leftover rice'

b. *paqol   g-ala*
   maize   3AN-remainder
   'small maize for giving away', *'leftover maize'

9.3.4 Class IV

Nouns belonging to Class IV can occur with a prefix for the possessor, but also without. Where they occur without, they have an initial /t/ which is not present on the prefixed root. The two nouns belonging to this class are presented in (42). We can see in the case of (42b) that some lexicalisation has occurred between the unprefixed and prefixed forms of the roots.

(42) a. *n-el*   '1EXCL-grave'
       Ø-el   '1INCL/2-grave'
       g-el   '3AN-grave'
       tel   'grave'
    b. *n-on*   '1EXCL-hand/arm'
       Ø-on   '1INCL/2-hand/arm'
       g-on   '3AN-hand/arm'
       ton   'branch'

Alienability plays a role in the choice between the unprefixed /t/-initial form and a specific person agreement form, such as *g-* '3AN-'. Consider the forms in (43). In (43a) where the possessor of *tel* 'grave' is encoded with *g-* '3AN-', the relationship between possessor and possessum is permanent: Mali is dead and occupying his grave. In (43b) we see that the unpossessed /t/-initial form refers to a grave without mention of a possessor, and in (43c) we see that it is unacceptable for this bare form to occur with a noun encoding possessor. It is, however, possible for *tel* 'grave' to have its possessor expressed with the indirect possessive classifier *-e* 'POSS', as in (43d). This can have a variety of readings, all of which involve a less permanent relationship between possessor and possessum than (43a), e.g., it is Mali's grave but he is not dead yet, or Mali owns the grave but it is not intended for him, etc.

(43) a. *Mali   g-el*
       Mali   3AN-grave
       'Mali's grave (he's dead)'
    b. *tel*
       grave
       '(a) grave'
    c. **Mali   tel*
       Mali   grave

d. *Mali   gie   tel*
   Mali   3.POSS   grave
   'Mali's grave'

Comparative evidence makes clear that the initial /t/ is original on both of the Class IV nouns: *tel* 'grave' goes back to PTAP *tar[i,u] 'bury, grave', while *ton* 'branch' goes back to PTAP *tana 'hand/arm, branch'. The loss of initial /t/ on prefixation is specific to these two nouns and not part of a generalised morphophonological pattern in the language, though the pattern is also evidenced on some verbs (see §10.2.4.3).

9.3.5 Class V

The final subset of nouns taking direct markers for the possessor have differential marking of 3rd person ANIMATE and INANIMATE possessors: ANIMATE possessors trigger *gV-* '3AN' on the possessum, while INANIMATE possessors trigger no agreement on the possessum; other persons are encoded with *nV-* '1EXCL' and *V-* '1INCL/2'. The person inflections of two members of this class are given in (44). This pattern of agreement class parallels that of bivalent verb Class II (§10.2.2).

(44) a. *na-wa*   '1EXCL-top'
        a-wa   '1INCL/2-top'
        ga-wa   '3AN-top'
        wa   'top'
     b. *ni-tin* '1EXCL-price'
        i-tin   '1INCL/2-price'
        gi-tin '3AN-price'
        tin   'price'

The full set of members of this class is given in Table 9.8. The class is composed of locational nouns, quantificational nouns indicating parts of wholes, and nouns denoting plant parts and some intimates. Notice that all but two members of the class are monosyllabic: *luel* 'peel' and *nuas* 'smell', however, do show the same agreement patterns as the other items and, like the other members of the class, they are disyllabic when prefixed due to the metathesis of the high front vowel (see §2.5.1.3).

Table 9.8: Class V nouns with differential possessor marking.

3RD INANIMATE		3RD ANIMATE	
bol	'cost'	gobol	'cost'
buk	'flower'	gubuk	'flower'
bul	'base, origin'	gubul	'head'

Table 9.8 (continued)

3ʳᵈ Inanimate		3ʳᵈ Animate	
lak	'place between'	galak	'place between'
luel	'peel, skin'	gulel	'peel, skin'
mil	'inside'	gimil	'feelings, thoughts'
nal	'stem'	ganal	'stem, earlobe'
nap	'side'	ganap	'side, flank (body)'
ne	'portion'	gene	'portion'
nes	'fleck, speck'	genes	'fleck, speck'
nor	'leaf'	(gonor)†	'leaf'
nuas	'smell'	gunas	'smell'
po	'foam, suds'	gopo	'lung, frog's spawn'
ter	'twig, stick'	geter	'upper arm'
tin	'price'	gitin	'price'
tul	'part'	gutul	'part'
wa	'top'	gawa	'top'
zup	'sliver, morsel'	guzup	'sliver, morsel'

† This form is only found in eastern dialects of Bunaq (§1.5).

As already seen for nouns in Classes II–IV, some lexicalisation of meaning can be observed between unprefixed and prefixed pairs in Class V. For instance, *bul* refers to 'origin, base', but with prefixes refers to the body part 'head'. Thus in (45a) we see that with the indirect possessor *nie* '1EXCL.POSS', *bul* denotes simply 'my origins'. By contrast, in (45b) with the direct 1ˢᵗ person possessor encoded with a prefix we get 'my head'.

(45) a. *nie   bul*
         1EXCL.POSS base
         'my origins, descent'
     b. *nu-bul*
         1EXCL-head
         'my head'

The differential marking of 3ʳᵈ persons with Class V nouns is illustrated in (46) on the basis of the plant part term *nal* 'stem'. In (46a) the possessor, *zo* 'mango', is INANIMATE and triggers no agreement on *nal* 'stem'. In (46b) where the possessor, *sabul* 'orange', is ANIMATE, agreement with *gV-* '3AN-' occurs on *nal* 'stem'. The absence/presence of the correct agreement for the particular controller results in ungrammaticality.

(46) a. zo   nal   / *ga-nal
       mango.INAN   stem   3AN-stem
       'stem of the mango'
    b. sabul   ga-nal / *nal
       orange.AN   3AN-stem   stem
       'stem of the orange'

Example (47) illustrates the use of a Class V noun with a non–3rd person, human possessor on *tin* 'price'. Examples (47a) and (47b) parallel the examples in (46a) and (46b), having INANIMATE/ANIMATE possessors and non-agreement/agreement on the possessum, respectively. In (47c) we have a 1st person possessor with the resulting meaning of 'bride price'.

(47) a. uer   tin
       pot.INAN   price
       'pot's price'
    b. apa   gi-tin
       cow.AN   3AN-price
       'cow's price'
    c. ni-tin
       1EXCL-price
       'my price', i.e., 'my bride price (said by a woman about the bride price attached to her for marriage)'

Examples such as (46a) and (47a) where the possessor is INANIMATE and therefore unmarked on the possessum are *prima facie* indistinguishable from possessive compounds, such as those in (48), where both nouns are grammatically INANIMATE. Discussed in §3.2.1.2 under the label "right-headed compounds", possessive compounds such as these express part–whole or spatial relationships. The only apparent difference with respect to the right-hand nouns of the compounds in the examples in (48), and with respect to Class V nouns is that the former never host a direct possessive prefix.

(48) a. reu   maten
       house   peak
       'house peak'
    b. mar   alan
       garden border
       'border/flank of the garden'
    c. zol   iti
       river   opposite
       'river's opposite (side/bank)'

d. *mok   pol*
   banana comb
   'comb of bananas'

The issue of distinguishing between possessive compounds and possessive phrases in relation to Class V nouns is taken up in the following section.

9.4 From possessive phrases to possessive compounds

In the previous section, we saw that Class V nouns with INANIMATE possessors seem to occur in possessive compounds, where the possessor noun precedes the noun denoting the possessum with no overt marking of the possessive relationship. In this section, I present evidence for viewing direct possessor constructions as representing a continuum of phrasal possessive constructions to possessive compound-like constructions. Table 9.9 (after Taylor 2000: 287–314, looking at possessives in English) presents syntactic and referential criteria which can be used to distinguish possessive phrases from possessive compounds in Bunaq.

Table 9.9: Characteristics distinguishing possessive phrases and compounds.

NP NP Possessive Phrases	NN Possessive Compounds
independent modification	no independent modification
possessor NP with determiner	possessor simple N
referential possessor (instance-specific)	non-/weakly referential possessor (type-specific)

The properties of possessive compounds in Bunaq are set out in (49). Both possessor and possessum are each expressed by a simple N (49a); the possessor N cannot be independently modified (49b) and any modifier following the possessum N has scope over the possessor and possessum as a whole (49c); the possessor N is only weakly referential and cannot be marked with a determiner (49d). Only with the inclusion of the indirect possessive classifier *gie* can the possessor and possessum be expanded to full referential NPs with the possibility of independent modification and determination (49e).

(49) a. *deu   puqup*
       house   roof
       'house roof'
    b. **deu   koen   puqup*
       house   nice   roof
       '[nice house]'s roof'

c. *deu   puqup   guzu*
   house   roof   black
   'black [house roof]'
d. **deu   ba   puqup*
   house   ART.INAN   roof
   '[the house]'s roof'
e. *deu   koen   ba   gie   puqup   guzu*
   house   nice   ART.INAN   3.POSS   roof   black
   '[the pretty house]'s [black roof]'   [Not-09.01]

By contrast, on an inalienably possessed noun, a possessor can always be encoded by a full NP where the possessum is marked with a 3rd person animate prefix, though this appears to be rare in actual discourse. Thus, the possessor nouns in *cie g-ut* 'chicken's egg' (50) and *en g-on* 'person's hand' (51) can be modified by a simple verbal attribute (50a, 51a), a determiner (50b, 51b), or both (50c, 51c).

(50) a. *cie   belis   g-ut*
        chicken   white   3AN-egg
        '[white chicken]'s egg'
     b. *cie   bari   g-ut*
        chicken   PROX.AN   3AN-egg
        '[this chicken]'s egg'
     c. *cie   belis   bari   g-ut*
        chicken   white   PROX.AN   3AN-egg
        '[this white chicken]'s egg'   [FB-250221]

(51) a. *en   heser   g-on*
        person   dead   3AN-hand
        '[dead person]'s hand'
     b. *en   bi   g-on*
        person   ART.AN   3AN-hand
        '[the person]'s hand'
     c. *en   heser   bi   g-on*
        person   dead   ART.AN   3AN-hand
        '[the dead person]'s hand'   [Not-09.01]

When Class V nouns are used without a possessive prefix, the possibility of independent modification of the possessor appears to be more restricted. In the corpus, we find that nouns of this class are used with a maximum of one nominal or verbal modifier, but no determiner. For example, we see in (52) the Class V noun *wa* 'top' has the possessor *tais* 'cloth' which is modified with the verb *lequ* 'wrap up'. Speakers that I consulted rejected inserting a determiner in between *wa* and *lequ* in example (52) and I also could not locate a determiner in such a position in the corpus with other Class V nouns.

(52) Homo=be,   kalo eto rasal=bu, sabul   bi
     CONTR.INAN=CONTEXP if 2SG stop=GIVEN orange ART.AN
     [**tais lequ** wa] no=na   ga-lai.
     cloth wrap   top OBL=FOC 3AN-place
     'But, if you stop, put the oranges on top of a wrapped-up cloth.' [Bk-4.043]

Class II inalienably possessed nouns occurring in their *h*-form with an INANIMATE possessor show the same restriction as unprefixed Class V inalienably possessed nouns. That is, a simple modifier, such as the N$_{MOD}$ *gol* 'small' can occur with the possessor noun before *hegil* 'shade' in (53), but speakers reject the possibility of including a determiner to mark *hotel* 'tree'. This could be taken to support the proposition raised in §9.3.2 that the *h-* prefix is not a referential prefix on a par with its ANIMATE counterpart *g-*.

(53) [**Hotel gol**   h-egil   uen], nor   baqa   no.
     tree   small 3INAN-shade one   without.purpose NPRX.INAN OBL
     '(They were) just (sitting) there, in the shade of a small tree.' [Bk-66.018]

All this leads us to the conclusion that possessive constructions of this kind with an INANIMATE possessor occupy a halfway position between true possessive compounds where no possessive prefixes are possible and directly possessed possessive phrases where the presence of a *gV-* prefix on the possessum licences the encoding of the possessor with a full NP. That is, they are semi-compounds which allow some independent modification of the possessor noun, but the apparently weak referentiality of these possessors means they cannot be determined.

9.5 Double possessor marking

Thus far in the discussion of Bunaq possession I have treated direct and indirect possessor marking as distinct phenomena. However, the corpus also includes multiple instances of double possessor marking where indirect *gie* '3.POSS' co-occurs with a direct prefix *gV-* '3AN' on a noun of the inalienably possessed class. Double marking is not obligatory in any context, but there are two related contexts where it tends to occur.

The first is where the referent of the inalienably possessed noun has been detached from its possessor. Double-marked detached possessors are attested in the corpus with reference to animal and plant possessors. In (54) the double possessive marking of *-oq* '-fruit' with direct and indirect markers is permitted because the fruits have been picked from their trees. In (55) the possessor of the skin and the ears is a cow which was slaughtered by a girl's parents. Double possessive marking can be used on the inalienably possessed body part nouns *-iwiq* 'skin' and *-epal* 'ear' in (55) because they have been cut from the cow's body.

(54) Hotel   gol   baqi   le hilereq   g-oq,   ei   ***gie***
     tree   small   NPRX.AN   future   3AN-fruit   2PL   3.POSS
     g-oq   bi   ge-neq=ka,   muk ukon   g-utu?
     3AN-fruit   ART.AN   3AN-divide=OR   ruler   3-COM
     'When the trees later fruit, will you share their fruits with the people in charge?'
     [Bk-65.061]

(55) Gie   eme   ama   mete   ***gie***   ***g-iwiq***=o   mete   ***gie***
     3.POSS   mother   father   NOW   3.POSS   3AN-skin=AND   NOW   3.POSS
     g-epal=o   bai   homo   hoto   a-ta   kama=na,
     3AN-ear=AND   thing   CONTR.INAN   fire   3INAN-GL   pile.up=FOC
     toqa   haqal.
     set.alight   finish
     'Her parents piled its skin and ears and other bits up on the fire and then set them all alight.'   [ApaGiriKereq-043]

Double marking of the possessor to signal its detachment is also attested in one case with an inalienably possessed noun which does not refer to a body or plant part. In (56) we see that the possessor, the ANIMATE noun *paqol* 'maize', is marked both by an indirect and direct prefix on the Class V inalienably possessed noun *nuas* 'smell'. According to my consultants, this is possible because the smell of the cooking maize has pervaded the whole house, i.e., it is not restricted to the immediate area where the cooking is taking place.

(56) Sekola   gene   tebe,   neto   ***paqol***   ***g-inik***   bi   ***gie***
     school   LOC   return   1SG   maize   3AN-cook   ART.AN   3.POSS
     g-unas   mobel.
     3AN-smell   like
     '(When I) return from school, I like the smell of the cooking maize.'
     [Bk-24.034]

The second context in which the indirect and direct possessive markers co-occur is on inalienably possessed nouns where, due to semantic extension, a semantically more alienable meaning exists alongside the original inalienable meaning. For example, in (57), *-ua* 'footprint' can be double marked by the direct and indirect possessive markers because it is not actual footprints being traced. Rather *-ua* is used here in the sense of journeys taken by Bunaq ancestors in settling Timor. The example of doubling marking on *-io* 'faeces' in (58) comes from a text in which the speaker describes the benefits of building terraces in the sloped gardens typical of the Bunaq area. Here -*io* obviously does not refer to actual faeces belonging to the soil, but instead denotes the manure or nutrients from the fertiliser that can be put into the soil without being washed away by rain once terraces are in place.

(57) *Makoqan tata g-atun ba,* **bei**
 poet ancestor 3AN-bring.down ART.INAN grandparent
 mil gie g-ua *rale.*
 COLL 3.POSS 3AN-footprint tell
 '(When) poets "bring down the ancestors", (they) recount the footsteps (i.e., journeys) of the ancestors.' [Bk-18.026]

(58) ... **muzuk gie g-io** *baqa hani il zal.*
 soil 3.POSS 3AN-faeces NPRX.INAN PROH water carry
 '... the nutrients in the soil cannot get carried away by the water.'
 [Bk-65.021]

In short, double possessor marking appears to be used by Bunaq speakers as a way to signal that the referent of an inalienably possessed noun shows a greater degree of semantic alienation from its possessor than its lexical class indicates. From this perspective, it is not so much the double marking which gives such inalienably possessed nouns a sense of alienation as the inclusion of the indirect possessive marker alongside the lexically required direct possessive prefix.

9.6 Summary

In this chapter, we have seen that Bunaq has a distinction between direct and indirect possession. The former is encoded by a free possessive classifier inflected for the person of the possessor. The latter is encoded by a prefix inflected for the person of the possessor that occurs on the possessum. Direct prefixation of the possessor on nouns of the inalienably possessed class in Bunaq accords with the iconicity principle (Haiman 1983). That is, it reflects the smaller conceptual distance between an inalienably possessed noun and its possessor, than between an alienably possessed noun and its possessor (cf. Croft 2003: 205–207 and Seiler 1983: 68 on this typologically widely attested phenomenon).

Also in accordance with iconicity is the word order variation observed in the encoding of possessors of alienably possessed nouns. A possessor which has prototypical possessor properties, such as being the owner or controller of the possessum, is almost always preposed to the possessum and thereby occurs within the extended NP. By contrast, possessors that lack these properties by virtue of being "removed" possessors (e.g., indicating an origin or an intended destination) are postposed to outside the NP where they head a possessive predicate.

Throughout this chapter I have emphasised that the Bunaq alienability contrast in possession is chiefly structural, rather than semantic. Inalienably possessed nouns form a closed lexical class defined by the ability of the nouns to host possessive prefixes. Still, the classes are not entirely discrete: an inalienably possessed noun can have its possessor encoded with an indirect possessive marker alongside the direct possessor prefix to signal a degree of alienation in the relationship with the possessor. What is more, a small number of inalienably possessed nouns can occur without a prefix where the possessor noun is grammatically INANIMATE, resulting in structures that are very similar to right-headed compounds, used for denoting partitive and spatial relations in Bunaq.

Chapter 10
Verbs

10.1 Introduction

The dominant morphosyntactic patterns in the encoding of arguments (S, A, P, T, R, and OBL) displayed by verbs in Bunaq were detailed in §4.2. This chapter is concerned with a closer categorisation of Bunaq verbs on the basis of a combination of morphosyntactic and semantic properties. The chapter details the major and minor verb classes, including groups of verbs whose distinct morphosyntactic behaviour sets them apart either within or from the major verb classes.

Bunaq verbs are classified primarily according to two properties:
(i) valency – the number of arguments (1, 2, 3 or a variable number) and the type of arguments (core or core and oblique) the verb takes; and,
(ii) prefixation – the set of prefixes the verb takes, in particular how 3rd person ANIMATE versus INANIMATE arguments are marked, and the argument (P, S, or R) the prefix agrees with.

For the most part, the classes defined by these properties result in semantically similar verbs being grouped together.

Table 10.1 provides an overview of the morphological behaviour of the different verb classes (see §2.5.1 on the morphophonemics of prefixation in Bunaq). A verb cannot host more than one prefix at a time. Verbs divide into four basic morphological types based on their prefixation patterns. This chapter concentrates on the person prefixes (1, 2, and 3); discussion of reflexive and reciprocal prefixes is reserved for Chapter 11.

Class I verbs take no prefixes regardless of the person or ANIMACY of the agreement controller. Class II verbs take no prefix when the agreement controller is 3rd person INANIMATE, but do take a prefix for 3rd person ANIMATE and other persons. Classes III and IV share the same inflectional pattern for 1st, 2nd, and 3rd person ANIMATE controllers, but differ in their treatment of 3rd person nouns of the INANIMATE class. Class III verbs do not, for the most part, take 3rd person INANIMATE arguments and therefore lack a 3rd person INANIMATE agreement form. Class IV verbs are characterised by having one of five initial consonants in their 3rd person INANIMATE P agreement form; the initial consonant is replaced with another prefix in other persons.[1]

---

[1] As noted for nouns in §9.3, the citation form of a prefix-taking verb is its 3rd person INANIMATE agreement form. Thus, a Class IV h-conjugation verb is cited as *h-ukat* '3INAN-lift'.

Table 10.1: Morphological summary of different verb classes.

	CLASS I	CLASS II	CLASS III†	CLASS IV†
1EXCL	unprefixed	nV-	n-	n-
1INCL/2	unprefixed	V-	Ø-	Ø-
3AN	unprefixed	gV-	g-	g-
3INAN	unprefixed	unprefixed	–	h-, s-, t-, d-, l-

† Note that Class III and Class IV verbs for the most part have vowel-initial roots and thus do not realise the unspecified vowel of the prefix as is found with Class II verbs.

The distribution of these four morphological patterns differs across verbs of different valencies. The vast majority of verbs taking prefixes are bivalent (§10.2). Most monovalent verbs (§10.3) are invariable in form (§10.3.1); only a few take prefixes agreeing with S (§10.3.2). Trivalent verbs take prefixes, but the class is small, having only two members (§10.4). Some labile verbs take prefixes in their bivalent frames (§10.5), while most verbs with unmarked obliques do not take prefixes (§10.6).

10.2 Bivalent verbs

The class of bivalent verbs is significant in size, with over 600 members listed in the corpus (containing 2000+ lexemes). Individual subclasses vary in size; some only have a handful of members and others over a hundred.

Bivalent verbs take an A and a P argument (distinct from verbs with an S and an OBL, discussed in §10.6). Prefixes on bivalent verbs index the P argument, and never the A. Bivalent verbs divide into the four classes seen above, with the division made chiefly according to the prototypical ANIMACY of the P argument and the manner in which it is co-indexed on the verb. In differentiating prefixing classes of bivalent verbs, the 3rd person inflectional pattern is diagnostic.

Class I bivalent verbs typically have INANIMATE Ps and do not take a prefix for any person of P (§10.2.1). Class II bivalent verbs take ANIMATE and INANIMATE 3rd person Ps; the former is prefixed with *gV-* '3AN' and the latter is unprefixed (§10.2.2). Class III bivalent verbs take ANIMATE Ps and have only an ANIMATE 3rd person prefix form (§10.2.3). Class IV bivalent verbs take ANIMATE and INANIMATE 3rd person Ps, the former again prefixed by *g-* '3AN', while the latter are realised with a range of different prefixes (§10.2.4). Finally, §10.2.5 looks at the handful of verbs showing distinct agreement patterns.

10.2.1 Class I bivalent verbs

Class I bivalent verbs do not take prefixes. In the corpus, there are just over 150 members of this class, examples of which are given in Table 10.2. The column on the left presents members of this class that are only attested with INANIMATE Ps, while in the column on the right are those verbs that are also attested with ANIMATE Ps.

Table 10.2: Examples of Class I bivalent verbs.

Only attested with INANIMATE P		Attested with ANIMATE P	
ari	'grind, sharpen (of knives, spears, etc.)'	balis	'break into segments (e.g., of a citrus fruit)'
cile	'pour (of liquids)'	ere	'plant a field with (e.g., maize, rice)'
es	'wear around shoulders (of clothes, blankets)'	eta	'wean, make accustomed to a new situation or place'
kali	'throw; strew (of seeds)'	hois	'draw milk from (of cows)'
koil	'whittle, scratch with a knife (of wood)'	kesi	'give birth to (of humans or animals)'
koin	'draw (of fire)'	koe	'stroke the belly of (a pig)'
kuku	'wear on head (of hats, cloths, etc.)'	koqus	'cradle, hold (of a child)'
murik	'sip, suck'	koto	'rouse from sleep (of a group of people)'
neti	'snatch, seize'	lohi	'cane'
pies	'clean, make clean'	seka	'castrate'
pulas	'make by twisting (of rope)'	seta	'spill, knock over'
sakat	'carry slung across chest (of bags, sacks, etc.)'	telen	'be bored of'
sekol	'lock (of a door)'	tenaq	'thieve'
zewen	'spread out (of mats)'	tuqal	'trade'

Example (1) illustrates that verbs of this class do not take prefixes with either INANIMATE or ANIMATE Ps.

(1) a. Neto   r-on   koqus.
      1SG   REFL-hand.INAN   cradle
      'I cradle my arm.'
    b. Neto   r-ol   koqus.
      1SG   REFL-child.AN   cradle
      'I cradle my child.'   [Not-07.01]

10.2.2 Class II bivalent verbs

Class II is the largest of the bivalent verb classes with over 200 members in the corpus. In this class, P arguments are differentially marked on the verb according to grammatical ANIMACY: INANIMATE Ps are uninflected, i.e., take no verbal agreement prefix, while P arguments of the ANIMATE noun class agree in person with a prefix on the verb. The full inflectional paradigms of 3 members of Class II are given in (2). Note that the prefix Ø- in (2c) represents *V-* '1INCL/2', which is deleted on prefixation to vowel initial roots, such as *iwal* 'pick' (§2.5.1.2).

(2) a. *ni-wit*   '1EXCL-fetch'
       i-wit   '1INCL/2-fetch'
       gi-wit   '3AN-fetch'
       wit   'fetch'
    b. *ne-tekeq*   '1EXCL-watch'
       e-tekeq   '1INCL/2-watch'
       ge-tekeq   '3AN-watch'
       tekeq   'watch'
    c. *n-iwal*   '1EXCL-pick'
       Ø-iwal   '1INCL/2-pick'
       g-iwal   '3AN-pick'
       iwal   'pick'

The differential P-marking pattern for Class II verbs is illustrated in (3) with the verb *wit* 'fetch'. In (3a) the ANIMATE P *zap* 'dog' triggers agreement on the verb, while in (3b) the INANIMATE P *il* 'water' does not trigger any agreement on the verb.

(3) a. *Neto   zap   gi-wit.*
       1SG   dog.AN   3AN-fetch
       'I fetched the dog.'
    b. *Neto   il   wit.*
       1SG   water.INAN fetch
       'I fetched the water.'   [Not-07.01]

10.2.3 Class III bivalent verbs

Class III is the smallest of the bivalent verb classes, with a total of 20 members in the corpus (Table 10.3). The P arguments taken by these verbs are of the ANIMATE noun class. In the 3ʳᵈ person, these verbs have only an ANIMATE agreement form with *g-* '3AN', and no distinct INANIMATE agreement form.

Class III bivalent verbs often denote events with a negative impact on an ANIMATE P, in particular humans and/or animals, such as striking or killing. The full paradigms for two verbs of this class are given in (4).

(4) a. *n-ue*   '1EXCL-hit'
       Ø-ue   '1INCL/2-hit'
       g-ue   '3AN-hit'
    b. *n-ume*   '1EXCL-kill'
       Ø-ume   '1INCL/2-kill'
       g-ume   '3AN-kill'

Also belonging to Class III are a number of verbs relating to practices with ANIMATE Ps referring to animals exclusively, such as *g-itil* 'remove (lice)', or *g-esi* 'shoo (animal)'. There are also a number of verbs in the class which occur exclusively with ANIMATE class nouns referring to certain plants (§5.2.3.2), such as *paqol* 'maize' and *hoqi* 'peanut'. As referents of this kind are not usually speech participants, i.e., 1st or 2nd persons, these verbs typically only occur in the 3rd person form marked by the ANIMATE prefix *g-* '3AN'; they can also, but do not typically, occur with *n-* '1EXCL' and *Ø-* '1INCL/2' inflections.

Table 10.3: Class III bivalent verbs.

g-agil	'eat (maize, hard foods)'	*g-ilan*	'bind (maize) into bundles'
g-ak	'hold (baby) away from oneself while it defecates'	*g-ine*	'call (dog)'
g-amaqil	'lead (animal)'	*g-iser*	'instruct, teach by demonstration (human)'
g-amaq	'murder (animate)'	*g-itil*	'remove (lice)'
g-asal	'search for, but not find (animate)'	*g-ohiq*	'rip off (maize husk)'
g-asu	'expel, exorcise (animate)'	*g-olo*	'bury (animate)'
g-atul	'carry (human) on upper back'	*g-omolale*	'persuade, coax (animate)'
g-elen	'make dizzy, nauseate (animate)'	*g-ulan*	'encourage (human)'
g-esi	'shoo (of animal)'	*g-ue*	'hit (animate)'
g-eweq	'deshell (peanuts)'	*g-ume*	'kill (human)'
g-iep	'hit (animate) with axe'	*g-uraq*	'beat (maize) to remove kernels from cob'
g-igin	'tell (person) off'	*g-ureq*	'pick (maize) by ripping from the stalk'

With one exception, 3rd person Ps of the INANIMATE noun class do not occur with class III bivalent verbs, i.e., the *g-* '3AN' inflection is not used in reference to 3rd person INANIMATE Ps. This is illustrated in (5) with the Class III verb *g-ue* '3AN-hit': with the ANIMATE P, *en* 'person', *g-ue* '3AN-hit' can be used as in (5a), but with the INANIMATE

P, *bai* 'thing', it is ungrammatical (5b).² By contrast, we see in (6) that the Class III verb *g-olo* '3-bury' can be used with both the ANIMATE P, *en* 'person' (6a), and the INANIMATE P, *bai* 'thing' (6b). Hence the gloss '3' is used rather than '3AN' for the *g-* inflection on this verb.³

(5) a. *Neto   en   g-ue.*
       1SG   person.AN   3AN-hit
       'I hit a person.'
    b. **Neto bai   g-ue.*
       1SG   thing.INAN   3AN-hit
       'I hit something.'

(6) a. *Neto   en   g-olo.*
       1SG   person.AN   3-bury
       'I bury a person.'
    b. *Neto   bai   g-olo.*
       1SG   thing.INAN   3-bury
       'I bury a thing.'

10.2.4 Class IV bivalent verbs

Like Class II bivalent verbs, Class IV bivalent verbs differentially mark 3rd person Ps. They differ in that, while Class III bivalent verbs do not prefix for 3rd person INANIMATE Ps, Class IV have distinct 3rd person INANIMATE P prefixes. Class IV bivalent verbs are divided into conjugation classes according to the consonant appearing on the root with a 3rd person INANIMATE P. Table 10.4 presents an overview of the five different conjugation classes and gives an example of each in their 3rd INANIMATE and 3rd ANIMATE P agreement contexts.

Class IV is a relatively small class of lexically specified verbs. Diachronically, the initial consonants of Class IV verbs represent, variously, historical prefixes in some cases, and initial consonants of the historical roots that were deleted on prefixation in others. Synchronically, neither the prefixes nor the replacing of initial consonants under prefixation are productive. As mentioned already in §2.6.2.3, irrespective of their historical sources, I segment initial consonants of the 3rd person INANIMATE P

---

2 *We* is the historically unprefixed form of *g-ue* '3AN-hit'. It has lexicalised and is now only used for 'beat a drum' and cannot be used for 'hit (an inanimate)'.
3 There are a few other instances in which the 3rd person ANIMATE prefix has come to be used with both 3rd person ANIMATE and INANIMATE agreement controllers. This is the case for the verbal postpositions, *g-utu* '3-COM' (§12.4.1) and *g-o* '3-SRC' (§12.4.4), as well as for the indirect possessive classifier (§9.2). See also the monovalent verb *gi-tip* '3AN-new' discussed in §10.3.2.

Table 10.4: Class IV bivalent verb conjugation classes.

Conjugation class	Example verb		Gloss	Section
	3rd INANIMATE	3rd ANIMATE		
h-class	h-azal	g-azal	'see'	§10.2.4.1
s-class	s-agal	g-agal	'seek'	§10.2.4.2
t-class	t-inik	g-inik	'cook'	§10.2.4.3
d-class	d-oenik	g-oenik	'forget'	§10.2.4.4
l-class	l-ual	g-ual	'bend'	§10.2.4.5

form of Class IV verbs as if they were prefixes in order to signal that the consonant is replaced when other person prefixes are used with the verb.

In the following subsections, I discuss the individual Class IV conjugations and the origins of their 3rd person INANIMATE forms in turn.

10.2.4.1 h-conjugation verbs

In the corpus, the h-conjugation of Class IV bivalent verbs has 95 members. In this class, 3rd person INANIMATE Ps have *h-* '3INAN' (7a), while 3rd person ANIMATE Ps are marked on the verb by the prefix *g-* '3AN' (7b).

(7) a. *Neto il   h-azal.*
        1SG water.INAN 3INAN-see
        'I see the water.'
    b. *Neto zap   g-azal.*
        1SG dog.AN 3AN-see
        'I see the dog.' [Not-07.01]

The paradigms in (8) illustrate the inflectional paradigm of verbs of the h-conjugation. We see that *h-* '3INAN' is found before vowels of all qualities.

(8) a. *n-ek*   '1EXCL-choose'
        Ø-ek   '1INCL/2-choose'
        g-ek   '3AN-choose'
        h-ek   '3INAN-choose'
    b. *n-iqil* '1EXCL-leave.behind'
        Ø-iqil '1INCL/2-leave.behind'
        g-iqil '3AN-leave.behind'
        h-iqil '3INAN-leave.behind'

c. *n-one* '1EXCL-hold'
   Ø-one '1INCL/2-hold'
   g-one '3AN-hold'
   h-one '3INAN-hold'
d. *n-uza* '1EXCL-chase'
   Ø-uza '1INCL/2-chase'
   g-uza '3AN-chase'
   h-uza '3INAN-chase'
e. *n-azal* '1EXCL-see'
   Ø-azal '1INCL/2-see'
   g-azal '3AN-see'
   h-azal '3INAN-see'

The historical status of the initial /h/ on verbs of this class as a 3rd person INANIMATE P agreement form is mixed. On some verbs, the initial /h/ appears to originate in a prefix *h(V)-* used for INANIMATE Ps. This analysis is supported by the existence of a number of roots which appear both with and without the putative *hV-* '3INAN' prefix. In (9) we see that unprefixed verbs are monovalent, while their equivalents with an *hV-* indexing 3rd person INANIMATE Ps are bivalent.[4]

	BIVALENT VERB, 3RD PERSON INANIMATE FORM		MONOVALENT VERB	
(9)	*he-beqen*	'3INAN-destroy'	*beqen*	'be squashed'
	h-erik	'3INAN-pin'	*erik*	'be pinned'
	hu-hukut	'3INAN-wrap up'	*hukut*	'be huddled up'
	ho-qon	'3INAN-make, do'	*on*	'DO'[5]

On other verbs, the initial /h/ does indeed appear to have been part of the root. The replacement of initial /h/ on prefixation appears to be part of an areal pattern in the languages of central Timor (e.g., Tetun Fehan, van Klinken 1999: 173–174). The presence of this in Tetun and the adoption of the replacive pattern for borrowed verbs with

---

4 Bunaq *h(V)-* '3INAN' may have its origins in a (pronominal) demonstrative **ha* that cliticised onto the verb, before becoming part of the inflection (as per the well-known grammaticalisation path described in Givón 1976). Reflexes of **ha* are found in all Bunaq dialects: for instance, in the Manufahi dialect, *habadi* is a distal demonstrative where initial /ha/ represents the demonstrative **ha* which has been "reinforced" with the newer demonstrative form *badi*, which is found on its own across the Bunaq area (cf. *bari* 'PROX.INAN' in Bunaq Lamaknen, §7.3); reflexes of **ha* are also found in two Bunaq Lamaknen sentence connectives, *habe* 'yet, however' and *hasi* 'so, therefore', which are composed of a reflex of **ha* plus *=be* 'CONTEXP' and *=si* 'REAS'. See Diessel (1999: 125–127) on the cross-linguistically common development of sentence connectives from a demonstrative plus some other element, such as an adverb or adposition.
5 This item is not strictly a monovalent verb. Synchronically, I analyse it as a 'performative' marker, but suggest that it has its origins in a lexical verb meaning 'do, make'. See the discussion in §14.3.2.

initial /h/ is likely to have reinforced the pattern in Bunaq. See the discussion of loan adjustment in what follows in section §10.2.4.1.1.

10.2.4.1.1 Note on /h/-initial items borrowed from Tetun

Verbs with initial /h/ borrowed from Tetun inflect either as Class II (9 verbs) or Class IV (25 verbs) bivalent verbs in Bunaq, or do not inflect at all (i.e., Class I: 2 verbs).[6] There do not appear to be hard and fast phonological conditions determining which inflectional class /h/-initial verbs from Tetun are assimilated into.

Borrowed items with initial-/h/ followed by a low non-front vowel, /a/ or /o/, always assimilate to the Class IV inflectional paradigm. Borrowed items with initial-/h/ followed by /e/ always inflect as Class II verbs. Finally, borrowed items with initial-/h/ followed by a high vowel, /i/ or /u/, may be assigned either to Class II or Class IV. Table 10.5 illustrates these patterns. The gaps observed in the distribution of /h/-initial borrowings may reflect insufficient sampling. However, given the size of the corpus, this seems unlikely.

Table 10.5: Assignment of /h/-initial Tetun borrowings to Class II versus Class IV.

		3rd INANIMATE	3rd ANIMATE		Tetun
Class II	/a/	–	–		
	/e/	heri	geheri	'spear'	hedi 'pierce'
	/i/	hiqit	gihiqit	'lift'	hiqit
	/o/	–	–		
	/u/	huq	guhuq	'blow'	huu 'puff'
Class IV	/a/	hakara	gakara	'love'	hakara
	/e/	–	–		
	/i/	hisik	gisik	'spray'	hisik
	/o/	hoban	goban	'soak'	hoban
	/u/	humul	gumul	'punch'	humul

Bunaq has also assimilated Tetun borrowings with the Austronesian causative prefix *ha-* 'CAUS' to the Class IV inflectional paradigm. However, it is not always clear what the underlying form and segmentation of such *ha*-marked borrowings are in Bunaq. For instance, Tetun *ha-tama* 'CAUS-enter' and *ha-tun* 'CAUS-fall' have been borrowed into Bunaq with regular penultimate stress (§2.4). The underlying representation in Bunaq could be taken to be *ha-tama* or *h-atama* in the one case, and *ha-tun* or *h-atun*

---

[6] At present I have only identified 36 /h/-initial verbs as borrowed from Tetun. It might be that more will be identified as Tetun borrowings in the future and that this could account for the surprisingly high number of verbs in the *h*-class.

in the other. As the Tetun verbs *tama* 'enter' and *tun* 'fall' have also been borrowed into Bunaq and they are regularly associated by Bunaq speakers with their Tetun causative-marked counterparts, *hatama* and *hatun*, I treat *ha-* as a '3INAN' prefix in Bunaq and *tama* 'enter' and *tun* 'fall' as the roots of these verbs.

10.2.4.2 s-conjugation verbs

The complete set of 16 Class IV bivalent verbs of the s-conjugation are given in Table 10.6.

Table 10.6: Class IV s-conjugation verbs.

3rd INANIMATE	3rd ANIMATE		3rd INANIMATE	3rd ANIMATE	
sagal	gagal	'search'	sili	gili	'prise off'
sapuq	gapuq	'nurse'	silik	gilik	'draw into'
salak	galak	'roast'	sorul	gorul	'drench'
sebuq	gebuq	'dig out'	suq	guq	'dig up'
selaq	gelaq	'arrange'	subeqen	gubeqen	'pinch'
seroq	geroq	'apportion'	sumak	gumak	'cover up'
sile	gile	'separate'	sumi	gumi	'hide'
sileqen	gileqen	'drop on'	susuk	gusuk	'agitate'

The inflectional paradigms of two of the members of the s-conjugation are given in (10).

(10) a. *n-agal*   '1EXCL-search'
       Ø-agal   '1INCL/2-search'
       g-agal   '3AN-search'
       s-agal   '3INAN-search'
     b. *n-umi*   '1EXCL-hide'
       Ø-umi   '1INCL/2-hide'
       g-umi   '3AN-hide'
       s-umi   '3INAN-hide'

In (11) we see that 3rd person INANIMATE Ps have *s-* '3INAN' (11a), and 3rd person ANIMATE Ps have *g-* '3AN' (11b).

(11) a. *Neto uor   s-agal.*
       1SG   vegetable.INAN   3INAN-search
       'I look for vegetables.'
     b. *Neto si   g-agal.*
       1SG   meat.AN   3AN-search
       'I look for meat.'   [Not-07.01]

Most of the /s/-initial verbs in this class do not have known etymologies. However, for the small number that do, the initial /s/ appears to have originally been the initial consonant of the root. For example, Bunaq s-*agal* 'search' is found both in nearby Austronesian and Papuan languages. In all languages with a related lexeme in the Timor area an initial /s/ occurs on the root (e.g., Makasae *saga*, Makalero *saka*, Termanu *saŋa*, Dadu'a *sana*, Leti *va-saka* 'search' – see Schapper, forthcoming, for more on this item).

10.2.4.3 t-conjugation verbs

The full set of 14 t-conjugation Class IV bivalent verbs is presented in Table 10.7.

Table 10.7: Class IV t-conjugation verbs.

3rd INANIMATE	3rd ANIMATE		3rd INANIMATE	3rd ANIMATE	
tabaq	gabaq	'hoe'	tirik	girik	'hold'
tao	gao	'pound'	tolo	golo	'put inside'
tereq	gereq	'beat (dust)'	toma	goma	'message'
tape	gape	'touch, feel'	tomon	gomon	'warm'
tapiq	gapiq	'sort, sift'	tubak	gubak	'gather'
ti	gin	'tie'	tuk	guk	'collect'
tinik	ginik	'cook'	turuk	guruk	'pierce'

The full inflectional paradigms of two members of the conjugation are given in (12).

(12) a. *n-ao* '1EXCL-pound'
   Ø-ao '1INCL/2-pound'
   g-ao '3AN-pound'
   t-ao '3INAN-pound'
  b. *n-ape* '1EXCL-touch'
   Ø-ape '1INCL/2-touch'
   g-ape '3AN-touch'
   t-ape '3INAN-touch'

In (13) we see a *t-* '3INAN' prefix in agreement with 3rd person INANIMATE P (13a), while *g-* '3AN' agrees with a 3rd person ANIMATE P on the same verb (13b).

(13) a. Neto   ipi   t-ao.
     1SG   rice.grain.INAN 3INAN-pound
     'I pound rice.'

b. *Neto paqol g-ao.*
   1SG maize.AN 3AN-pound
   'I pound maize.' [Not-07.01]

In several cases of verbs in this class, comparative data makes clear that the initial /t/ is part of the historical root. For example, Bunaq *t-inik* 'cook' has two cognates in its relatives on Timor and in both cases the roots have an initial /t/, i.e., Makasae *tina*, Makalero *tina* 'cook'.[7] In other cases, the initial /t/ appears to reflect a deponent use of the reciprocal prefix *tV-* 'RECP'. The presence of reciprocal prefixes on such verbs is part of a wider phenomenon of deponent uses of valency-reducing morphology. Verbs with deponent uses of the reciprocal prefix are discussed further in the subsections of §11.4.

10.2.4.4 d-conjugation verb
There is only one member of the d-conjugation of Class IV bivalent verb, given in (14).

(14) *n-oenik*   1EXCL-forget
      Ø-oenik   1INCL/2-forget
      g-oenik   3AN-forget
      d-oenik   3INAN-forget

Example (15) illustrates the appearance of *d-* on the verb to agree with 3rd person INANIMATE Ps (15a) and its replacement by other prefixes marking Ps of different types, in this case a 3rd person ANIMATE P (15b).

(15) a. *Neto ipi   d-oenik.*
        1SG rice.grain.INAN 3INAN-forget
        'I forgot the rice.'
     b. *Neto paqol   g-oenik.*
        1SG maize.AN   3AN-forget
        'I forgot the maize.' [Not-07.01]

Like some verbs of the t-conjugation, the d-conjugation verb goes back to a deponent use of the reflexive prefix, *dV-* 'REFL'. This is discussed further in §11.3.

10.2.4.5 l-conjugation verbs
The full set of nine l-conjugation Class IV bivalent verbs is presented in Table 10.8.

---

7 The forms and meanings of these items suggest that they may ultimately be borrowings of reflexes of PMP *tanek* 'cook by boiling'.

Table 10.8: Class IV l-conjugation verbs.

3ʳᵈ PERSON INANIMATE	3ʳᵈ PERSON ANIMATE	GLOSS	3ʳᵈ PERSON INANIMATE	3ʳᵈ PERSON ANIMATE	GLOSS
laba	gaba	'slice'	lobo	gobo	'pull out'
labak	gabak	'spread'	logo	gogo	'shake'
lebel	gebel	'chuck'	lorul	gorul	'aggravate'
lepek	gepek	'approve'	lual	gual	'bend'
lilik	gilik	'revolve'			

The full inflectional paradigms of two members of the conjugation are given in (16).

(16) a. n-aba   '1EXCL-slice'
       Ø-aba   '1INCL/2-slice'
       g-aba   '3AN-slice'
       l-aba   '3INAN-slice'
    b. n-epek   '1EXCL-approve'
       Ø-epek   '1INCL/2-approve'
       g-epek   '3AN-approve'
       l-epek   '3INAN-approve'

The use of the *l-* as the verbal agreement form with 3ʳᵈ person INANIMATE Ps and its alternation with other prefixes are illustrated in (17).

(17) a. Neto zo   l-aba.
        1SG   mango.INAN   3INAN-slice
        'I slice mango.'
     b. Neto si   g-aba.
        1SG   meat.AN   3AN-slice
        'I slice meat.'   [Not-07.01]

There are no established etymologies for the verbs in this class, so it is not known what the origin of the initial /l/ is.

10.2.5 Bivalent verb classes with distinct agreement patterns

The dominant pattern of prefixation of 3ʳᵈ person Ps seen in the above discussion on bivalent verbs involved ANIMATE Ps being prefixed by *gV-* '3AN' and INANIMATE Ps receiving either no prefixation or a different "prefix" (i.e., conjugation marker).

In this section, I look at a small number of bivalent verbs that do not display these canonical patterns of agreement between their P arguments and prefixes, allowing 3rd person ANIMATE Ps to be either prefixed or unprefixed. The presence/absence of the prefixal agreement corresponds to differences in the interpretation of the event denoted by the verb.

§10.2.5.1 looks at a set of two verbs denoting transport events, while §10.2.5.2 looks at a set of two verbs denoting keeping events.

10.2.5.1 Two transport verbs: *tula* 'move' and *penen* 'shift'

The verbs *tula* 'move' and *penen* 'shift' pattern morphologically with Class II bivalent verbs. The inflectional paradigms for these verbs are given in (18).

(18) a. *nu-tula*   '1EXCL-move'
       u-tula   '1INCL/2-move'
       gu-tula   '3AN-move'
       tula   'move'
    b. *ne-penen* '1EXCL-shift'
       e-penen   '1INCL/2-shift'
       ge-penen '3AN-shift'
       penen   'shift'

The conditions under which 3rd person ANIMATE Ps trigger agreement differ from those applying to other Class II bivalent verbs. Third person ANIMATE P arguments co-occur with both marked and unmarked forms of these verbs. Compare the following pairs of examples. The unprefixed verbal forms in (19a) and (20a) refer to an act of transporting a P from one location to another. By contrast, the prefixed verbal forms in (19b) and (20b) refer to non-translational motion events involving no significant displacement of the P argument, expressing instead their careful placement in a particular location.

(19) a. Nei   kura   g-erel   paqol   **tula**.
        1PL.EXCL   horse.AN   3AN-INS   maize   move
        'We transported the maize with the horse.'   [Not-07.04]
     b. Baqi   sabul   hiloqon   bi   tais   lequ
        NPRX.AN   orange.AN   two   ART.AN   cloth   wrap
        wa   no   **gu-tula**.
        top   OBL   3AN-move
        'He placed the two oranges on the wrapped-up cloth.'   [Bk-4.048]

(20) a. Halali   d-ege   cie   gol   uen   **penen**.
        3DU   REFL-BEN   chicken.AN   small   one   shift
        'They took a small chicken along for themselves.'   [LB-2.224]

b. *Biasanya   en   paqol   **ge-penen**.*
   usually   people maize.AN 3AN-shift
   'Usually people put some maize away (for safe-keeping).'   [OS-07.04]

A prefix cross-referencing a 3rd person ANIMATE P focuses on the A's particular choice of goal location for the P. The absence of a 3rd person ANIMATE P prefix indicates a transport event where the emphasis is on the movement from one location to another. This distinction is only found with 3rd person ANIMATE Ps; 1st and 2nd persons are always prefixed, 3rd person INANIMATE is always unprefixed.

In sum, prefixation with these verbs is not simply a matter of syntactic agreement, but rather also functions to change the interpretation of the action denoted by the verb.[8] In an alternative analysis, the different agreement patterns could be taken to mean that the forms *tula* 'move' and *penen* 'shift' each have two separate lexical entries: one with 3rd person ANIMATE agreement in the manner of a Class II bivalent verb, and one without, in the manner of a Class I bivalent verb.

10.2.5.2 Two keeping verbs: *lumaq* 'take care of' and *bilan* 'keep'

The verbs *lumaq* 'take care of' and *bilan* 'keep' display atypical agreement patterns in two ways: the form of agreement prefixes and the context triggering the agreement. The prefixal vowel with these verbs is the central back vowel /a/, thus *ga-* '3AN', etc. (see §2.6.1 on irregular prefixes). The inflectional paradigm of these verbs is given in (21). Note that 1st and 2nd person agreement forms are rare, as these verbs are used prototypically in reference to domestic animals.

(21) a. *na-lumaq*   '1EXCL-take care of'
        a-lumaq   '1INCL/2-take care of'
        ga-lumaq   '3AN-take care of'
        lumaq   'take care of'
     b. *na-bilan*   '1EXCL-keep'
        a-bilan   '1INCL/2-keep'
        ga-bilan   '3AN-keep'
        bilan   'keep'

As with the verbs of transport discussed in the previous section, 3rd person ANIMATE P arguments co-occur with both prefixed and unprefixed forms of these verbs; the differences in prefixation correlate with different verb meanings. Prefixation of a 3rd person ANIMATE P emphasises that the A actively engages in caring for and tending

---

8 This contrast is similar to that between directed motion verbs and manner of motion verbs, where directed motion verbs are morphologically more complex than manner of motion verbs. See Levin and Hovav (2001: 255 ff.).

to the referent of the P. In (22a) with unprefixed *lumaq*, the speaker states merely that animals are kept by his family. By contrast, in (22b) with the prefixed form of the verb, the inference is that the father personally and intimately nurtures his child.

(22) a. Reu   zigi   gene nei   sael=o   cie
        house underneath LOC   1PL.EXCL pig.AN=AND chicken.AN
        lumaq.
        take.care.of
        'Underneath the house we keep pigs and chicken.'   [Bk-24.019]
    b. Baqi   d-ege   ***ga-lumaq***,   baqi   g-ol.
        NPRX.AN REFL-BEN 3AN-take.care.of NPRX.AN 3AN-child.AN
        'He raised (the child) for himself, as his own child.'   [LB-5.025]

Similarly, in (23a) with unprefixed *bilan*, the suggestion is that the dog belongs to the household, but it is neither fed nor looked after in any way, instead being expected to fend for itself. In (23b) where the prefixed form of the verb is used, the named domestic animals are highly prized by their owners and are fed and generally cared for.

(23) a. Reu   gene   nei   zap   uen   ***bilan***.
        house   LOC   1PL.EXCL dog.AN   one   keep
        'At home we keep a dog.'   [OS-07.01]
    b. En   apa=o   pip   kura   bi   ***ga-bilan***
        person   cow.AN=AND   goat.AN horse.AN ART.AN 3AN-keep
        'People own and raise their cows and goats and horses.'   [Bk-19.001]

As with the verbs of transport, the different agreement patterns could be taken to mean that *lumaq* and *bilan* each have two separate lexical entries one with 3rd person ANIMATE agreement in the manner of a Class II bivalent verb and one without in the manner of a Class I bivalent verb. The differences observed with these verbs are also reminiscent of the transitivity alternations in agreement. The pattern is different, however, in that with these two verbs of keeping, Ps with semantically animate referents show agreement variation. This is not observed in the case of transitivity alternations on the agreement of other verbs, which are restricted to Ps with semantically inanimate referents. Variation in prefix agreement based on clausal transitivity is discussed in §4.7.3.

10.3 Monovalent verbs

The majority of monovalent verbs do not take agreement prefixes and are treated in §10.3.1. The handful of monovalent verbs taking agreement prefixes are discussed in §10.3.2.

10.3.1 Monovalent verbs without prefixes

There are over 500 monovalent verbs in the corpus. Each subcategorises for only an S argument (see §10.6 on verbs taking an S and an OBL) and takes no agreement prefix. The lack of agreement across persons by these monovalent verbs is illustrated with *wil* 'come down' in (24).

(24) a. *Neto   wil.*
        1SG   come.down
        'I came down.'
     b. *Eli   wil.*
        2DU   come.down
        'You two came down.'
     c. *Halaqi wil.*
        3PL   come.down
        'They came down.' [Not-07.04]

10.3.2 Monovalent verbs with prefixes

In the corpus, there are seven monovalent verbs which have agreement prefixes co-indexing their S argument. The S arguments of prefixing monovalent verbs are patientive, being low in properties such as control and volition.[9] Table 10.9 presents an overview of the distribution of prefixing monovalent verbs across inflectional classes.

Table 10.9: Classes of monovalent prefixing verbs.

CLASS	No.
II	4
III	1
IV h-conjugation	2
IV other conjugations	0

The full inflectional forms of three of the verbs following the Class II inflectional pattern are set out in (25). See §2.5.1.3 on the metathesis which takes place on the prefixation of these verbs.

---

[9] The presence of S prefixation on these verbs may be a remnant of an earlier system of split-S alignment. Semantic alignment is robustly attested in eastern Indonesia (Donohue 2004), including in many of the languages related to Bunaq (Klamer 2008).

(25) a. *n-uas*   '1EXCL-smell'
       Ø-unas '1INCL/2-smell'
       g-unas '3AN-smell'
       nuas   'smell'
    b. *n-unek* '1EXCL-stink'
       Ø-unek '1INCL/2-stink'
       g-unek '3AN-stink'
       nuek   'stink'
    c. *n-utek* '1EXCL-heavy'
       Ø-utek '1INCL/2-heavy'
       g-unek '3AN-heavy'
       tuek   'heavy'

The fourth prefixed Class II monovalent verb is *tip* 'new'. However, for this verb, prefixed and unprefixed forms of this verb differ in meaning. Unprefixed *tip* 'new' means 'recently made, acquired' of an item, and 'recently come into a particular state, position, or relationship' of a person; it can be used with an S of any person, as illustrated in (26a) and (26b). By contrast, prefixed *tip* means 'new' in the sense of an item or person which/who is of recent arrival or appearance and with which people are unfamiliar. The 3rd person prefixed form of *tip* 'new' can be used with both an INANIMATE P, e.g., *bai* 'thing' (26c), and an ANIMATE P, e.g., *en* 'person' (26d).

(26) a. *G-ol   tip.*
        3AN-child   new
        'Their child is new (i.e., newborn).'
     b. *Reu   por   tip.*
        house   holy   new
        'The church is new.'
     c. *Bai   bare   gi-tip.*
        thing   PROX.INAN   3-new
        'This thing is new (unfamiliar).'
     d. *En   bari   gi-tip.*
        person PROX.AN   3-new
        'This person is new (unfamiliar).'   [Not-07.04]

The one monovalent verb following the Class III inflectional pattern is *g-igaq* '3AN-content' (27). This verb is rare in Bunaq Lamaknen, but when used, is marked with *-wen* (see §11.5). In Bunaq Bobonaro, however, the verb is more common and need not be marked with *-wen*.

(27) n-igaq   '1EXCL-content'
    Ø-igaq   '1INCL/2-content'
    g-igaq   '3AN-content'

The two verbs with prefixation following the Class IV h-conjugation inflectional pattern are given in (28). The two verbs differ in that while *h-aziq* '3INAN-not visible' inflects for all persons (28a), *h-aqal* '3INAN-finished' is restricted to the 3rd person (28b). See §13.8.1 on the uses of *h-aqal* '3INAN-finished' and its agreement patterns.

(28) a. n-aziq   '1EXCL-not visible'
        Ø-aziq   '1INCL/2-not visible'
        g-aziq   '3AN-not visible'
        h-aziq   '3INAN-not visible'
    b. *n-aqal   '1EXCL-finished'
        *Ø-aqal   '1INCL/2-finished'
        g-aqal   '3AN-finished'
        h-aqal   '3INAN-finished'

10.4 Trivalent verbs

Trivalent verbs adhere to the prefixal pattern displayed by Class IV h-conjugation verbs. There are two members of the trivalent verb class in Bunaq: *h-ege* '3INAN-give' (29a) and *h-ini* '3INAN-call' (29b).

(29) a. n-ege   '1EXCL-give'
        Ø-ege   '1INCL/2-give'
        g-ege   '3AN-give'
        h-ege   '3INAN-give'
    b. n-ini   '1EXCL-call'
        Ø-ini   '1INCL/2-call'
        g-ini   '3AN-call'
        h-ini   '3INAN-call'

These two trivalent verbs are discussed in the following subsections.

10.4.1 *h-ege* '3INAN-give'

H-ege '3INAN-give' is the only true trivalent verb in Bunaq, with all three argument slots – A for the giver, R for the givee or recipient, and T for the gift or theme – realised as NPs, as in (30). The R argument is indexed by a prefix on the verb. A singular referent for R is often indicated simply with the verbal prefix and no free (pro)nominal elements, as in (31).

(30) Neto Manek g-ege   paqol.
      1SG   Manek 3AN-give maize
      'I gave Manek maize.'   [Not-07.04]

(31) Cio=na   Ø-ege   bai   n-iol   koen o   ba?
      who=FOC   1INCL/2-give   thing LOC-voice good ADDR ART.INAN
      'Who gave you that thing with the nice sound?'   [OrelZulo-13]

As the examples in (30) and (31) illustrate, the basic position for the NP encoding the T argument is after the verb.[10] However, it is also very common in Bunaq for an NP encoding T to occur in positions before *h-ege* '3INAN-give', as in (32) and (33).

(32) ..., eto   [kura   gu-bul   tobok roi   goet uen]_T n-ege.
            2SG   horse   3AN-head   twin   SPEC.AN LIKE one   1EXCL-give
      '..., you will give me a two-headed horse like this.'   [KuraTobok-49]

(33) [Bare]_T=bu   Ø-ege   niq.
      PROX.INAN=GIVEN   1INCL/2-give   NEG
      'As for this one, you cannot have it.'   [OrelBusaKawak-77]

See §4.2.3 for more on clauses with *h-ege* '3INAN-give'. See also §12.4.6 on its function as a beneficiary-adding verbal postposition and §13.4 on its function as a causative serial verb.

10.4.2 *h-ini* '3INAN-call'

H-ini '3INAN-call' is not a true trivalent verb in that its third, postverbal argument is itself an argument-taking predicate. That is, *h-ini* '3INAN-call' has the following argument structure: A for the caller, R for the callee, and T for the predicate denoting what is called. The S/A of a verbal embedded predicate or single argument of a non-verbal embedded predicate of *h-ini* '3INAN-call' is coreferent with the callee argument.

---

[10] Bunaq is the only language within the TAP family that has this word order (Klamer and Schapper 2012). Indeed, it appears to be extremely uncommon globally. In their typological survey of ditransitive constructions, Malchukov, Haspelmath, and Comrie (2010: 16) put it that the order ARVT does not occur in languages with SV/APV. Bunaq is an obvious counterexample to this claim. See Klamer and Schapper (2012: 202–204) for a scenario as to how this word order came about through analogical pressure from *h-ini* '3INAN-call'.

The callee argument is indexed by prefixes on the verb. In (34a) we have an equative clause where *Novi* is the predicate and *baqi* its subject (see §4.3.1 on clauses with nominal predicates). In (34b) *Novi* is the embedded predicate representing the third argument of *h-ini* '3INAN-call'; *baqi* 'NPRX.AN' is the argument of the embedded predicate and is identified as the person called. In its use of this verb to mean 'call', the A is frequently elided without any antecedent in the discourse to indicate who the caller is. Such clauses are commonly used to provide a person's name (34c)

(34) a. *Baqi*   [*Novi*]_PRED.
       NPRX.AN   Novi
       'She is Novi.'

   b. *En*   *baqi*   *g-ini*   [*Novi*]_PRED.
      people   NPRX.AN   3AN-call   Novi
      'People call her Novi.'

   c. *Baqi*   *g-ini*   [*Novi*]_PRED.
      NPRX.AN   3AN-call   Novi
      'She is called Novi.'   [Not-07.04]

H-ini '3INAN-call' also functions to introduce beliefs or suppositions on the part of the caller about the identity of the callee (i.e., 'say/think X to be Y') or about the conduct of the callee (i.e., 'say/think X to have Y'd'). This use is found particularly in contexts where the beliefs are erroneously held. For example, (35) was said to me by children in the house where I lived in Gewal village. Apparently, my lack of a skirt and long hair led some villagers to think I was male.

(35) *En*   *tas*   *gene*   *Ø-ini*   *mone.*
     person   village   LOC   1INCL/2-call   man
     'People in the village think you are a man.' (lit., people in the village call you a man').   [OS-07.09]

In (36) *n-ini* '1EXCL-call' is used to introduce two suppositions by the village head about the speaker having been responsible for the boy falling, suggesting that he committed the acts denoted by the embedded verb in (36c) and in (36d). Note that *g-ini* '3AN-CAUS' in (36d) is a causative use with the verb *topol* 'fall', and does not introduce a supposition. See below for more discussion and illustration of the causative use of this verb.

(36) a. *En*   *kepala*   *desa*   *nei*   *n-ege*   *seq.*
        person   head   village   1PL.EXCL   1EXCL-BEN   call
        'The village head called us.'   [Bk-1.033]

b. *Nei   n-o   sura,   nego   on=na   en   gol*
   1PL.EXCL   1EXCL-SRC   ask   what   DO=FOC   person   small
   roi   topol.
   SPEC.AN   fall
   '(He) asked us why that child fell.'   [Bk-1.034]

c. *Hele   nei   **n-ini**   gu-rumak.*
   perhaps   1PL.EXCL   1EXCL-call   3AN-push
   '(He) said that perhaps we pushed him.'   [Bk-1.035]

d. *Nei   **n-ini**   g-ini   topol   on.*
   1PL.EXCL   1EXCL-call   3AN-CAUS   fall   DO
   '(He) said that we made him fall.'   [Bk-1.036]

Similarly, in (37b) *n-ini* '1EXCL-call' is used to introduce a supposition about the speaker, which is then contradicted in (37c). In (37e) we see the inflections *n-ini* '1EXCL-call' and *h-ini* '3INAN-call' again used to introduce a range of suppositions about the health of the speaker.

(37) a. *Berita   huqe   mama   g-ege   sasi.*
        message   HERE   mother   3AN-BEN   say
        'A message told mother here (about the accident).'   [Bk-52.013]

  b. *Halaqi   zemal   gie,   **n-ini**   memel   baqis.*
     3PL   go.down   PROSP   1EXCL-call   sick   much
     'They were about to go down (to Atambua), thinking that I was really hurt.'
                                                                           [Bk-52.014]

  c. *Tapi   memel   baqis   niq.*
     but   sick   much   NEG
     'But I wasn't really sick.'   [Bk-52.015]

  d. *En   halaqi   ni-ta   holon.*
     person   3PL   1EXCL-GL   cry
     'The people were crying for me.'   [Bk-52.018]

  e. ***N-ini**   heser,   **n-ini**   memel   baqis,   nu-bul*
     1EXCL-call   dead   1EXCL-call   sick   much   1EXCL-head
     ***h-ini**   beqo,   n-on   **h-ini**   tol.*
     3INAN-call   crushed   1EXCL-hand   3INAN-call   broken
     '(They) thought I was dead, thought that I was really hurt, thought that my head had been crushed, thought that my hand was broken.'   [Bk-52.019]

In addition to being a lexical verb meaning 'call', *h-ini* '3INAN-call' is also used as a causative predicate and is the most highly productive and regular way in which causative meaning is expressed in Bunaq (see §13.4 on SVCs expressing causation). As a causative verb, it is glossed with 'CAUS' and has the same argument structure as *h-ini*

'3INAN-call'. That is, the S/A of the embedded predicate denoting the caused event is coreferent with the causee argument. Examples are given in (38)–(40).

(38) Nie   moen   roi   *g-ini*   matas mil   g-ege   *seq.*
     1EXCL.POSS friend SPEC.AN   3AN-CAUS   old   COLL   3AN-BEN   call
     '(We) made this friend of mine call to the parents.'   [Bk-1.045]

(39) *Sio=na*   en   bari   *g-ini*   tais   *h-apal...*
     who=FOC   person   PROX.AN   3AN-CAUS   cloth 3INAN-open
     'Whoever makes this person take off their cloth. . .'   [Bk-16.003]

(40) Eme   Yati   *g-ini*   *n-ege*   buku   bari.
     mother   Yati   3AN-CAUS   1EXCL-give   book   PROX.AN
     'Mother made Yati give me this book.'   [OS-06.07]

10.5 Labile verbs

Bunaq has a number of labile verbs (11 in my corpus) that can appear either with a single S argument or with an A and a P argument without any additional valency-changing morphemes.[11] Cross-linguistically, two types of labile verbs are widely attested (Kulikov 2003; McMillion 2006): A-preserving labile verbs, where the referent of the A in the bivalent frame is the S in the monovalent frame (e.g., English 'eat'); and P-preserving labile verbs, where the referent of the P in the bivalent frame is the S in the monovalent frame (e.g., English 'break').

Bunaq labile verbs largely conform to the P-preserving type. However, some labile verbs in Bunaq cannot be strictly classified as either A-preserving or P-preserving, since the S of the monovalent frame is simultaneously agentive and patientive, both initiating and undergoing the event denoted by the verb. There are no clear instances of A-preserving labile verbs in Bunaq.

That the verbs described in this section are labile is seen in the control properties of their different arguments in the monovalent versus bivalent frames. These properties have been discussed in §4.2, and are briefly reviewed here: the S of a labile verb in its monovalent frame controls agreement on the floating quantifier, binds the reflexive, and can be the P of the causative predicate; the A of a labile verb in its bivalent frame binds the reflexive and can be the P of the causative predicate, while the P controls agreement on the floating quantifier.

---

[11] Instead of "labile", some scholars use other terms such as "ambitransitive" (Dixon 1994) or "optionally transitive" (Miller 1993) to designate verbs of this type.

Labile verbs are discussed in classes according to their morphosyntax and semantics: verbs of setting (§10.5.1), verb of learning/teaching (§10.5.2), verbs of mixing (§10.5.3), and causative labile verbs (§10.5.4).

10.5.1 Verbs of setting

The two verbs of setting, *lai* 'set' and *lolit* 'set lengthways', are labile in Bunaq. In their bivalent frame, these verbs take person prefixes for P following the pattern of Class II verbs (§10.2.2): 3rd person ANIMATE P arguments trigger agreement with prefixes on the verb, but INANIMATE 3rd persons do not. In (41) the A is *neto* '1SG', while the P is the ANIMATE noun *buku* 'book' and shows verbal agreement with the prefix *gV-* '3AN'. In (42) the A is *neto* '1SG', while the P is the INANIMATE noun *botil* 'bottle' which does not trigger agreement on the verb.

(41) Neto   buku   ga-lai.
     1SG   book.AN   3AN-set
     'I set the book (down).'   [Not-07.01]

(42) Neto   botil   lolit.
     1SG   bottle.INAN   set.lengthways
     'I set the bottle (down).'   [Not-07.01]

Used monovalently, the S of *lai* 'set' and *lolit* 'lay' is never prefixed on the verb, as shown in (43) with an ANIMATE S and in (44) with an INANIMATE S. Both clauses denote a stative event and have a non-agentive S.

(43) Buku   lai.
     book.AN   set
     'The book is set (down).'   [Not-07.01]

(44) Botil   lolit.
     bottle.INAN   set.lengthways
     'The bottle is set (down).'   [Not-07.01]

Monovalent uses of *lai* 'set' and *lolit* 'lay' may also be active. Examples (45) and (46) have an S with an animate referent, and can have either an active – and thus necessarily agentive – reading, or a stative reading with ambiguity as to whether the S is controlling and volitional or not.

(45) Hos   meja   wa   no   lai.
     bird   table top   OBL   set
     'The bird sets itself (down) on the table.' or 'The bird is set (down) on the table.'
     [Not-07.01]

(46) Neto   muk   no   lolit.
     1SG   earth OBL   set.lengthways
     'I lay myself (down) on the ground.' or 'I lie on the ground.'   [Not-07.01]

10.5.2 Verb of learning/teaching

For many Bunaq speakers, the verb *hanorin* is a P-preserving labile verb.[12] In its monovalent frame, *hanorin* is a verb that is unchanging in form and means 'learn', i.e., the S argument encodes the person who is taught (47). It appears to be mostly speakers from the village of Dirun who use and accept *hanorin* in its monovalent frame. In its bivalent frame, Bunaq *hanorin* is a Class IV h-conjugation verb, meaning 'teach', i.e., the A argument encodes the teacher while the P argument encodes the person who is taught (48).

(47) *Meaq gol   iskola   gene   hanorin.*
     child   school   LOC   learn
     'The children learn at school.'   [Not07-02]

(48) *Guru   meaq gol   iskola   gene   g-anorin.*
     teacher   child   school   LOC   3AN-teach
     'The teacher teaches the children at school.'   [Not07-02]

Not all Bunaq speakers agree that (47) is acceptable. Several speakers I consulted said that the verb must have the form *g-anorin* to agree with *meaq gol* 'children', as in (49). For these speakers, this verb is not labile, but a bivalent verb meaning 'teach' that agrees with the P argument. The A argument may be elided where the referent is unimportant. These speakers use a reflexive-marked form of this verb for 'learn' (50), paralleling the pattern found with *g-ige* '3AN-teach' (discussed as "self-benefactive" marking in §11.3.2.2).

(49) *Meaq gol   iskola   gene   g-anorin.*
     child   school   LOC   3AN-teach
     'The children are taught (i.e., learn) at school.'   [Not07-02]

---

12 This verb is a borrowing of Tetun Belu *hanorin* 'teach'.

(50) Ei   t-erel   Gewal   no=na   d-anorin.
     2PL   RECP-INS   Gewal   OBL=FOC   REFL-teach
     'You are learning together in Gewal.'   [Bk-67.022]

10.5.3 Verbs of mixing

Verbs of mixing, *kahul* 'mix' and *soro* 'combine', have both a bivalent and a monovalent frame. In their bivalent frame, these verbs have an A and a P argument and denote an agentive event in which two or more substances are combined together. The verbs belong to inflectional Class I (§10.2.1), and do not change in form regardless of the ANIMACY of the P. Thus, in (51) the P is the ANIMATE noun *paqol* 'maize', but there is no agreement on the verb.

(51) Neto   paqol   kahul.
     1SG   maize   mix
     'I mix (different kinds of) maize (together).'   [Not-07.01]

In their monovalent frame, these verbs denote 'associate, keep company with'. The S argument has a plural human referent which is both agentive and patientive, that is, the referent both 'mixes' and 'is mixed with'. As seen in (52), there is no prefixation on the verb.

(52) Nei   iskola   gene   kahul.
     1PL.EXCL   school   LOC   mix
     'We mix (together) at school.'   [Not-07.01]

10.5.4 Causative labile verbs

There is a small group of six causative P-preserving labile verbs in Bunaq (Table 10.10). The monovalent frame of these verbs denotes 'be/come X', while the bivalent frame denotes 'cause X'. Morphologically, causative labile verbs belong to Class I, taking no prefixes in either of their frames.

Table 10.10: Causative labile verbs.

	BIVALENT	MONOVALENT
danu	'layer'	'be layered'
hokul	'puff up'	'be puffed up'
kapo	'stick to'	'be stuck to'

Table 10.10 (continued)

	BIVALENT	MONOVALENT
lequ	'wrap up'	'be wrapped up'
soran	'stir up'	'be stirred up'
uku	'tip'	'be tipped'

These verbs allow no agreement prefixes in any of their frames and their S is never agentive, as the S is with some of the labile verbs discussed in the previous sections. The two frames of the causative labile verbs are illustrated with *kapo* 'stick' in (53) for 'be X', and in (54) for 'cause X'.

(53) *Naka hotel gene kapo.*
    mud tree LOC stick
    'The mud stuck to the tree.' [Not-09.01]

(54) *Neto naka hotel gene kapo.*
    1SG mud tree LOC stick
    'I stuck the mud to the tree.' [Not-09.01]

The monovalent frame of a causative labile verb is distinguishable from situations where the A of a bivalent verb is simply elided for pragmatic reasons (§4.7.1.2) by the way in which it serialises with the causative verb *h-ini* '3INAN-CAUS'. If the S of a monovalent frame of a causative labile verb were in fact a P, it would not occur as the P of *h-ini* '3INAN-CAUS'. Yet we see that *naka* 'mud' of (53) unproblematically becomes the P of *h-ini* '3INAN-CAUS' in (55). Similarly, we see that the A, *neto* '1SG', of (54) becomes the P of *h-ini* '3INAN-CAUS' in (56).

(55) *Neto naka h-ini hotel gene kapo.*
    1SG mud 3INAN-CAUS tree LOC stick
    'I made the mud stick to the tree.' [Not-09.01]

(56) *Markus neto n-ini naka hotel gene kapo.*
    Markus 1SG 1EXCL-CAUS mud tree LOC stick
    'Markus made me stick mud to the tree.' [Not-09.01]

Contrast the pattern shown in the following examples. In (57) *naka* 'mud' is the P of the bivalent verb *siqil* 'deposit' whose A argument is unexpressed. *Naka* 'mud' as the P of *siqil* 'deposit' cannot be the P of *h-ini* '3INAN-CAUS' in serialisation (58), but must be an A (59).

(57) Naka hotel gene siqil.
     mud   tree   LOC   deposit
     'The mud was deposited on the tree.' [Not-09.01]

(58) *Neto naka h-ini   hotel gene siqil.
     1SG   mud   3INAN-CAUS   tree   LOC   deposit
     'I made mud be deposited on the tree.' [Not-09.01]

(59) Neto Markus g-ini   naka hotel gene siqil.
     1SG   Markus 3AN-CAUS   mud   tree   LOC   deposit
     'I made Markus deposit mud on the tree.' [Not09.01]

10.6 Verb classes with unmarked obliques

There are several sets of verbs in Bunaq that can occur with an unmarked oblique argument. The syntactic properties of unmarked obliques distinct from Ps are discussed in §4.2.4. Not all verbs which can take unmarked oblique arguments have an unmarked oblique in all their subcategorisation frames. Of the verb classes with unmarked obliques, only verbs of teaching have an A and P in addition to their OBL, and prefixation (for P); the remainder have S and OBL with no prefixes indexing any argument.

In this section, I look at the individual semantic sets of unmarked oblique–taking verbs. They are: saturation verbs (§10.6.1), existential verbs (§10.6.2), (some) motion verbs (§10.6.3), and a verb of teaching (§10.6.4).

10.6.1 Saturation verbs

The verbs *kaeq* 'filled', *liwe* 'brimming', *base* 'full', and *nur* 'empty' form a set in Bunaq. They are semantically unified by their expression of complete presence/absence of an entity (e.g., water) in respect to a location (e.g., a bucket). Syntactically the verbs share a distinct argument structure, subcategorising for two arguments: an S, expressing the entity which is present/absent, and an unmarked oblique, expressing the location of the entity, as illustrated in (60).

        S   OBL
(60) Ipi   hober kaeq.
     rice cave   fill
     'Rice filled the cave.' [Not-07.01]

Some speakers also allow the unmarked locative oblique to be encoded with a locative postposition, such as *no* 'OBL'. This PP can follow (61a) or precede (61b) the S.

(61) a.
```
     S     PP
     Ipi   hober  no    kaeq.
     rice  cave   OBL   fill
```
'Rice filled in the cave.'

     b.
```
     PP             S
     Hober  no      ipi   kaeq.
     cave   OBL     rice  fill
```
'In the cave, (it was) full (of) rice.'   [Not-07.01]

Textual examples show that the order of arguments with these verbs is quite free. That is, the oblique argument can regularly be observed to occur in positions in between the S and the verb (62) and preceding the S (63).

(62)
```
Pioq     [karon  hiloqon  homo]OBL    kaeq  haqal, ...
millet   sack    two      CONTR.INAN  fill  finished
```
'Millet filled the two sacks, ...'   [KuraGubulTobok.034]

(63)
```
[Bei          Luan  baqi     gie      leo     mil      bare]OBL
grandfather   Luan  NPRX.AN  3.POSS   yard    inside   PROX.INAN
molo          kaeq.
betel.vine    fill
```
'Bei Luan's garden was full of betel vine.'   [HosKakaqHitu.02]

10.6.2 Existential verbs

The existential verb *hati* 'exist' and the negative existential verb *hobel* 'not exist' have two subcategorisation frames: one with a simple S and one with an S and an oblique. Each of the frames is associated with a distinct function.

The first frame has a single S argument and expresses the (non-)existence of an entity encoded as S. A locative PP is often found in this frame (64), but it is not obligatory (65).

(64)
```
Gewal   gene   ewi       hati.
Gewal   LOC    soldier   exist
```
'There are soldiers in Gewal.'   [Bk-11.021]

(65) *Erenoq   masala   uen   hati.*
    yesterday problem   one   exist
    'Yesterday there was a problem.'   [Bk-21.001]

The existential verbs are also used in the expression of possession. In this function, the existential verbs have two sub-categorisation frames: a frame in which the possessed item is encoded as S and the possessor is a dependent constituent encoded with an inflection of the indirect possessive classifier -*e* 'POSS' (66a); and a frame in which the possessor is the S and the possessed item is an unmarked oblique (66b). These differ as to the type of possessor relationship they encode: (66a) expresses a straightforward ownership relationship, while in (66b) the S is the physical possessor or location of the money, but not necessarily its owner.

```
           S
(66) a.  [Nie          tumel]   hati.
         1EXCL.POSS    money    exist
         'I have money (and it is mine).'
           S            OBL
     b.  [Neto]       [tumel]   hati.
         1SG           money    exist
         'I am in possession of money (but it may not be mine).'   [Not-07.04]
```

Textual examples of the two different possessive frames of existential verbs are given in (67) and (68) for "ownership" possessive relations and in (69) and (70) for "locative" possessive relations.

```
         S
(67) [Gie      mar]    hati.
     3.POSS    garden  exist
     'S/he has a garden.'                                          [Bk-24.020]
```

```
         S
(68) [Nie         ama      gie      sore      legul   uen]   hati.
     1EXCL.POSS   father   3.POSS   machete   long    one    exist
     'My father owns a big machete.'                               [Bk-24.028]
```

```
         S                  OBL
(69) [En        waqen]    [mar]    hobel.
     person    PART.PL    garden   not.exist
     'Some people don't have gardens (i.e., to access to plant crops).'   [Bk-24.007]
```

	S	OBL	
(70)	[Nei]	[listrik]	hobel
	1PL.EXCL	electricity	not.exist

'We don't have electricity (i.e., available in the village).' [Bk-34.052]

10.6.3 Motion verbs

Four Bunaq motion verbs optionally subcategorise for an unmarked goal oblique: *mal* 'go', *saqe* 'ascend, rise', *pir* 'return home, reach', and *tama* 'enter'. These verbs may appear with an S argument (71a), or with an S argument and an unmarked goal oblique (71b).

(71) a. S
       Neto mal.
       1SG   go
       'I go.'
     b. S   OBL
        Neto   mar   mal.
        1SG   garden   go
        'I go to the garden.' [Not-06.01]

There are a range of alternative strategies for encoding the goal of a motion with these verbs with semantic differences (§13.9.1). For instance, either the goal-marking verbal postposition *a-ta* '3INAN-GL' (72a) or a postposition such as *no* 'OBL' (72b) can be used.

(72) a. S   PP
        Neto   [mar   a-ta]   mal.
        1SG   garden   3INAN-GL   go
        'I go towards the garden.'
     b. S   PP
        Neto   mal   [mar   no].
        1SG   go   garden   OBL
        'I go (and be) in the garden.' [Not-06.01]

Textual examples of *tama* and *pir* with unmarked goal obliques are given in (73) and (74), respectively. Examples of *saqe* with unmarked goal obliques are given in §4.2.4.

(73) ..., sael   zon=o   pip rusa   ai   g-uza,   g-erel
         pig   wild=AND   goat   only   3AN-chase   3AN-INS
     [mona   hatak]_OBL **tama**   liol.
      forest   dense   enter   continue
     '..., (the dog) chased the wild pig and the goat straight into the thick forest.'
                                                                              [BeiZap.055]

(74) Pana   gol   himo   [gie   reu]_OBL **pir**, ...
     female   small   CONTR.AN   3.POSS   house   reach
     'The girl reached her house, ...'   [BaloEnGakirik.021]

10.6.4 Verb of teaching

Morphologically the verb *g-ige* 'REFL-teach' belongs to Class III, i.e., it has no agreement form for INANIMATE Ps (for semantically obvious reasons), inflecting as *n-ige* '1EXCL-teach', *Ø-ige* '1INCL/2-teach', and *g-ige* '3AN-teach'. The A is 'teacher' and the prefix-marked P is 'recipient of the teaching'. The thing taught may be encoded either as an unmarked oblique (75a) or with an instrumental verbal postposition, *dele* 'INS' (75b). With *g-ige* '3AN-teach', the thing taught may also be left unspecified to denote the generic act of teaching without reference to the specific skill taught (75c).

(75) a. Nei   Bunaq   baqi   g-ige.
        1PL.EXCL   Bunaq   NPRX.AN   3AN-teach
        'We are teaching her Bunaq.'   [OS-06.02]
     b. Nei   baqi   Bunaq   dele   g-ige.
        1PL.EXCL   NPRX.AN   Bunaq   INS   3AN-teach
        'We are teaching her (with) Bunaq.'   [OS-06.02]
     c. Tues   ba   en   g-ige   niq.
        fine   ART.INAN   person   3AN-teach   NEG
        'The fines don't teach people.'   [Bk-53.103]

Chapter 11
Valency-reducing morphology and deponency

11.1 Introduction

Bunaq has two valency-reducing prefixes, *dV-* 'REFL' and *tV-* 'RECP'. These prefixes are in a paradigmatic relationship with the person-marking prefixes (discussed in §2.5.1), and do not themselves vary for number or person. The prefixes *dV-* 'REFL' and *tV-* 'RECP' are most frequently and productively used to express reflexive and reciprocal relations, respectively. Both *dV-* 'REFL' and *tV-* 'RECP' also have several other uses that are cross-linguistically well-known semantic extensions of reflexives and reciprocals. In addition to its reflexive functions, the Bunaq prefix *dV-* 'REFL' marks a wide range of "middle" situations, namely spontaneous natural events, self-benefactive events, cognitive events, and body action events, and is also used in impersonal contexts. The prefix *tV-* 'RECP' marks reciprocal relations, stative symmetrical relations, iterative motion, and a range of situations involving a plurality of participants. Extended uses of *dV-* 'REFL' and *tV-* 'RECP' often do not cause valency reduction and are treated as "deponent", that is, they show a mismatch between their morphological form and their actual function.

Bunaq also has a suffix *-wen* used in valency reduction. On bivalent verbs, *-wen* is an anticausative marker, functioning to delete the A argument and signal that the event happens spontaneously without a controlling participant. However, like *dV-* 'REFL' and *tV-* 'RECP', *-wen* is not always valency reducing. It can also appear as a moderative marker on non-agentive monovalent verbs and, more rarely, as a similative marker on verbs of any type.

In §11.2, the chapter begins with a discussion of deponency as it relates to *dV-* 'REFL' and *tV-* 'RECP'. Then, I discuss the functions of *dV-* 'REFL' in §11.3 and those of *tV-* 'RECP' in §11.4. Finally, in §11.5 the functions of *-wen* 'ANTIC' are discussed.

11.2 Prefixal deponency

Many of the items to be discussed in this chapter are "deponent", a term already mentioned in §10.2.4.3 and §10.2.4.4 for Class IV d- and t-conjugation verbs. Adopting Baerman's (2007) extended sense of the term, I take "deponency" to refer to a mismatch between the expected function of a morpheme and its actual function. Bunaq deponents are a subset of verbs marked with either *dV-* 'REFL' or *tV-* 'RECP'; these prefixes do not necessarily function to reduce the number of arguments in the clause, but rather have various non-referential, non-argument functions.[1] Deponent functions range from derivation-like alternations of the basic verb meaning to semantically empty conjugation markers.

Table 11.1 presents the different types of deponents. It represents them as intermediate stages on the continuum between fully productive valency-reducing occurrences of *dV-* 'REFL' or *tV-* 'RECP' and entirely unproductive uses whereby the prefix is fossilised onto the verb in all forms.[2] The "grey" area occupied by deponents represents different degrees of lexicalisation of the *dV-* 'REFL' or *tV-* 'RECP' prefixes. Thus, Type 1 represents the most productive and semantically transparent of deponent types, while Type 2 represents the less productive and more lexicalised deponent types, whereby the historical valency-reducing morpheme is synchronically little more than a conjugation marker.

Table 11.1: Continuum from productive to fossilised valency-reducing morphology.

Productive *dV-* / *tV-*		Deponent *dV-* / *tV-*		Unproductive *dV-* / *tV-*
	Type 1: Derivation-like alternations	←——————→	Type 2: Conjugation marker denoting semantics of *dV-* / *tV-*	
Always valency reducing	Sometimes valency reducing		Rarely valency reducing	Fossilised on verb

The two basic types of deponents that I differentiate are:

Type 1. Prefixes *dV-* 'REFL' and *tV-* 'RECP' appear on bivalent verbs to add some specification about the nature of the event denoted by the verb (e.g., 'for one's own benefit'); the valency-reducing prefixes alternate in a derivation-like way with ordinary P-marking forms of verbs that do not add any extra semantic specification;

Type 2. Prefixes *dV-* 'REFL' and *tV-* 'RECP' obligatorily mark the INANIMATE P agreement form of the verb alternating with person prefixes; the valency-reducing prefixes have apparent semantic motivation, but their presence/absence does not change the verb's meaning significantly.

---

[1] An additional minor deponent use of morphology in Bunaq is using the *gV-* '3AN' prefix for both ANIMATE and INANIMATE agreement controllers. See §10.2.3.

[2] Fossilised instances of *dV-* 'REFL' and *tV-* 'RECP' are apparent when comparing verb forms across dialects. For example, the monovalent verb *dipel* 'fast, not eat food' in Bunaq Lamaknen probably originates in a reflexive marked form, *d-ipel* 'REFL-fast'. This is suggested by the Bunaq Bobonaro form of the verb *nipel* 'fast, not eat food'. The initial /n/ appears to have been replaced by the reflexive prefix in Bunaq Lamaknen, as is common in Bunaq (see Class IV verbs as described in §10.2.4). Further support for this is seen in the fact that some speakers in Lamaknen have been heard to produce the form *g-ipel* '3AN-fast' with a third person S.

In §11.3 and §11.4, we will see that deponent verbs with *dV-* 'REFL' tend more towards Type 1 on the deponent scale, while those with *tV-* 'RECP' typically incline more towards Type 2 on the deponent scale.[3]

11.3 Reflexive *dV-*

The prefix *dV-* 'REFL'[4] canonically marks reflexive relations (§11.3.1). In addition, the prefix *dV-* has non-reflexive, or so-called "middle" functions (§11.3.2).

11.3.1 Reflexive situations

In this section, I illustrate the use of the reflexive on verbs and verbal postpositions (§11.3.1.1) and nouns (§11.3.1.2). In §11.3.1.3, I present some complexities of reflexive binding that are evident in clauses with serial verbs and complement clauses.

11.3.1.1 On verbs and verbal postpositions

On verbs and verbal postpositions, where there is coreference between an S/A and the P/R of a verb or the complement of a verbal postposition, the reflexive prefix must be used.

In (1) *hukut* 'wrap up' is marked with *dV-* 'REFL' and depicts a prototypical reflexive situation in which the referent is self-affecting. In (2) the A and P are also coreferential, but, following from the semantics and argument structure of the verb, self-affectedness is not a feature of the reflexive marking. That is, the reflexive of *tara* 'know' expresses the self-recognition and self-identification of the Bunaq people.

(1) En   uen   man   tais   rele **ru-hukut**.
    person one   come   cloth INS   REFL-wrap.up
    'A person came along wrapped up in a blanket (lit., wrapped himself with a blanket).'   [Bk-16.002]

(2) En   Bunaq mos=o   **da-tara**.
    person Bunaq also=AND   REFL-know
    'The Bunaq people also know themselves (i.e., have a sense of their own identity).'
                                                                        [Bk-15.012]

---

[3] Throughout this chapter I will gloss deponent instances of the valency-reducing morphemes *dV-* 'REFL' and *tV-* as 'REFL' and 'RECP', respectively. Elsewhere in this grammar, instances of these morphemes acting as a 3rd INANIMATE P agreement form are glossed as '3INAN' – see §10.2.4.4 and §10.2.4.5. For example, in this chapter *t-ubak* is glossed 'RECP-gather', but it is glossed as '3INAN-gather' elsewhere.
[4] Also *rV-*, cf. §2.2.3.2.2 on d~r allophony in Bunaq Lamaknen and its orthographic representation in this work.

On trivalent verbs the prefix *dV-* 'REFL' indicates coreferentiality between the A and R arguments. In (3) and (4) the trivalent verbs *h-ege* '3INAN-give' and *h-ini* '3INAN-CAUS' are marked with *dV-* 'REFL' and denote self-directed action.

(3) Neto ret **r-ege** die iskola gie urus.
 1SG alone REFL-give REFL.POSS school 3.POSS organise
 'I alone provided for my needs at school.' (lit., 'I alone organised my own school needs for myself.') [Bk-13.017]

(4) Berelikuq **d-ini** en.
 bird.sp. REFL-CAUS person
 'The bird made himself into (i.e., pretended to be) a person,' [LB-4.064]

The prefix *dV-* 'REFL' can also appear on some verbal postpositions (§12.4) to indicate coreference between the referent of the A/S and that of the complement of the verbal postposition. Examples (5) and (6) illustrate the use of *dV-* 'REFL' on verbal postpositions that are coreferent with an S and an A, respectively.

(5) Neto bai h-oqon loi niq, **ri-ta** paksa, r-on suel rele.
 1SG thing 3INAN-do good NEG REFL-GL force REFL-hand left INS
 'I couldn't do a thing, (but I) forced myself, (I did it) with my left hand.' [Bk-46.021]

(6) Baqi **r-otol** sabul hiloqon bi tais lequ wa
 NPRX.AN REFL-WITHOUT orange two ART.AN cloth wrapped top
 no gu-tula.
 OBL 3AN-transport
 'He without (concerning) himself transported the two oranges on top of a wrapped up cloth.' [Bk-4.048]

11.3.1.2 On nouns

The prefix *dV-* 'REFL is used with nominals to express coreference between an A/S and a possessor of an NP with a non-A/S role. Possessors that are coreferent with A/S are not obligatorily marked with *dV-* 'REFL'. Obligatoriness depends on whether the noun is inalienably (directly) possessed or alienably (indirectly) possessed.

Where an A/S argument is coreferent with a possessor of an inalienably possessed noun expressed by a prefix on a bound noun (§9.3), the possessive relation must be marked as reflexive. This is illustrated in the examples below with the inalienably possessed noun *g-on* '3AN-hand'. In (7a) the A must be the referent for the possessor of the P *r-on* 'REFL-hand'. In (7b), the use of the 1st person exclusive marking on 'hand' implies that the A is not coreferent with the possessor of P and that the A is unexpressed; the pronoun *neto* is in "strong" agreement (§6.2.1) with the possessor of the P.

(7) a. *Neto* **r-on** *doq.*
    1SG REFL-hand cut
    'I cut my hand.' [Bk-12.019]
  b. *Neto* **n-on** *doq.*
    1SG 1EXCL-hand cut
    '(Someone) cut *my* hand.' [Not-07.01]

In (8a) the possessor of the complement of *gene* 'LOC' is marked as reflexive and must be coreferent with the A. In (8b), the 3rd person possessor cannot be coreferent with the A.

(8) a. *Baqi* *mun* **r-on** *gene t-olo haqal.*
    NPRX.AN rope REFL-hand LOC 3INAN-put finished
    'He finished putting the rope in his hand.' [Not-07.01]
  b. *Baqi* *mun* **g-on** *gene t-olo haqal.*
    NPRX.AN rope 3AN-hand LOC 3INAN-put finished
    'He finished putting the rope in someone else's hand.' [Not-07.01]

Where a possessor is marked indirectly with an inflection of the free possessive classifier *-e* (§9.2) and is coreferent with the A/S, then the possessive relation is only optionally marked as reflexive. In (9a) the reflexive-marked possessor of the P, *pana* 'woman', can only be interpreted as coreferent with the A. In (9b) the possessor can be interpreted as coreferent either with A or with another 3rd person referent, if one is available in the discourse context.

(9) a. *Baqi* **rie** *pana g-ege sal.*
    NPRX.AN REFL.POSS woman 3AN-give wrong
    'He$_i$ does his$_i$ own wife wrong.' [Bk-21.017]
  b. *Baqi* **gie** *pana g-ege sal.*
    NPRX.AN 3.POSS woman 3AN-give wrong
    'He$_i$ does his$_{i/j}$ wife wrong.' [Bk-21.018]

In (10a), the addressee (S) of the imperative is coreferent with the reflexive-marked possessor of the NP complement of the comitative verbal postposition *g-utu* '3-COM'. In (10b) the S encoded by *neto* '1SG' is also coreferent with the possessor of the NP complement of the comitative, but the agreement for the possessor is marked *n-* '1EXCL'.

(10) a. Eto   rie   matas   mil   g-utu   man   naq!
       2SG   REFL.POSS   old   COLL   3-COM   come   PRIOR
       'You come with your parents!'   [Bk-38.005]
    b. Neto   nie   ama   g-utu   mar   mal.
       1SG   1EXCL.POSS father 3-COM   garden go
       'I go to the garden with my parents!'   [Bk-24.010]

The only circumstance in which coding of an indirect possessor with reflexive *die* 'REFL.POSS' appears to be obligatory is where there is the possibility of referential ambiguity. As expected, in (11a) the coreferent of the reflexive-marked possessor of *reu* 'house' is the A, *halaqi* '3PL', and not the P, *Suri Guloq*. However, if the possessor is encoded with a 3rd person inflection, the coreference is determined by linear ordering. That is, the antecedent is the nearest preceding NP with the appropriate person feature. In (11b) only the P, *Suri Guloq*, as the NP adjacent to the possessive inflection, can be coreferent with the possessor, not the A. In (11c), where *Suri Guloq* appears after the goal PP, the possessor of *reu* 'house' can only be interpreted as coreferent with the A, but not with the P.

(11) a. Halaqi   Suri Guloq   rie   reu   a-ta   gi-al.
       3PL$_i$ Suri Guloq$_j$ REFL$_{i/*j}$.POSS house 3INAN-GL 3AN$_j$-carry
       'They carried Suri Guloq to their house.'   [Bk-21.005]
    b. Halaqi   Suri Guloq   gie   reu   a-ta   gi-al.
       3PL$_i$ Suri Guloq$_j$ 3*$_{i/j}$.POSS house 3INAN-GL   3AN$_j$-carry
       'They carried Suri Guloq to his house.'   [Not-07.02]
    c. Halaqi   gie   reu   a-ta   Suri Guloq   gi-al.
       3PL$_i$ 3$_{i/*j}$.POSS house 3INAN-GL   Suri Guloq$_j$ 3AN$_j$-carry
       'They carried Suri Guloq to their house.'   [Not-07.02]

11.3.1.3 Reflexive binding with complement clauses and serial verbs

In §4.2, as well as in the immediately preceding sections of this chapter, we have seen that the antecedent of a reflexive must be either the S/A of a verbal clause or the "subject" of a non-verbal clause. In this section, I look at several situations in which the binding of the reflexive is to an antecedent that is not strictly one of these arguments. Although rare, deviations from the normal binding pattern for reflexives can be observed in the corpus in a small number of specific constructions.

Normally, an S argument cannot have a reflexive possessor, because there is no antecedent to bind the reflexive. However, this does happen if the reflexive can find its antecedent outside of the immediate clause containing it. This is permitted in Bunaq when a reflexive occurs in a complement clause and finds its antecedent in the S/A of the matrix clause. Such a case is seen, for example, in (12) where the reflexive form *die* 'REFL.POSS' encodes the possessor of the S of the complement clause and has as its antecedent the A of the verb *sasi* 'say' in the matrix clause. The complement clause occupies the P argument position within the matrix clause. See §15.2.1.1 for more discussion of this type of complementation, including the use of the reflexive in this example.

(12) Neto   ei   Ø-ege   [die   tais   loi   niq]_COMP   sasi   oa.
     1SG   2PL   1INCL/2-BEN   REFL.POSS cloth good   NEG   say   IAM
     'I told you my clothes were no good.'   [BaiANeq-43]

Reflexives are permitted in Bunaq in cases of overlapping referents. That is, a reflexive may also have an antecedent whose referent is not identical to the referent of the clausal S/A in which it occurs. Such non-identical antecedents are seen in benefactive serial verb constructions with reflexive-marked *d-ege* 'REFL-BEN' where the referent of S/A is a member of a set of referents which form the antecedent for the reflexive. In (13), for example, we see that the S/A for the clause is *neto* '1SG', but that the antecedent for the reflexive on the benefactive serial verb is *ili* '1DU.INCL' and includes the addressee. Similarly, in (14), the referent of the clausal S/A is an elided 2nd person, while the antecedent for the reflexive on the benefactive serial verb is encoded with *ili* '1DU.INCL' and includes the speaker. In these clauses, the fact that the clausal S/A is included within the referents of *ili* '1DU.INCL' allows the binding of the reflexive to this antecedent.

(13) Neto   mal   ili   d-ege   bai   a   s-agal   naq.
     1SG   go   1DU.INCL   REFL-BEN   thing   eat 3INAN-search   PRIOR
     'I will go and find food for us.'   [GepalMasaq-041]

(14) Lirun   goniqil   ni   uer   gol   buleqen   ba   ili   d-ege
     corner   four   OBL   pot   small   gold   ART.INAN   1DU.INCL   REFL-BEN
     zal   naq.
     carry   PRIOR
     Fetch the small pots of gold at the four corners (of the house) for us.'
                                                                      [EnBaruq-061]

Besides being permitted with inclusive pronouns, this construction with *d-ege* 'REFL-BEN' is also found with nouns. For example, in (15) we see that *d-ege* is right-clefted together with the nominal antecedent of the reflexive, *en* 'person'. As a part of the group of people who will receive the food, the speaker is included in the referent of *en* 'person', and thus the use of the reflexive on *d-ege* is permitted.

(15) Hei!   Baqa=be,   neto   inil,   nei   bere   inil
     INTERJ   NPRX.INAN=CONTEXP   1SG   try   1PL.EXCL   CONTEXP.INAN   try
     lau~lau,   en   d-ege.
     often   people   REFL-BEN
     'Hey! Despite that, I am prepared (to distribute the food), I have often been prepared (to do it) for (us) people.'   [BaiANeq-032]

11.3.2 Middle situations

The reflexive prefix is also found in situations commonly subsumed under the label "middle". Middle situations are similar to reflexive ones in that the participant performing the action and the participant affected by the action have one and the same referent. Whilst middle and reflexive situations are similar in that they both involve self-directed action, they differ in the distinguishability of participant roles. In a reflexive situation, a single participant performs an action filling two distinct roles in the action. By contrast, in a middle situation, a single participant performs an action for which there is a low elaboration of roles (Kemmer 1993: 238). That is, the roles of the participant as initiator of the action and as its end point are not fully distinguishable.

The specific semantic event types associated with middle uses of *dV-* 'REFL' in Bunaq are outlined in sections §11.3.2.1–§11.3.2.5. For the most part, discussion will be of verbs, but some cases of middle marking on nouns will also be dealt with. Deponent behaviour of middle-marked forms will be discussed on an item-by-item basis, as the fossilisation and lexicalisation of *dV-* 'REFL' in particular prefix-root combinations is advanced to differing degrees in individual forms and constructions.

11.3.2.1 Spontaneous events

In Bunaq *dV-* 'REFL' is found on a selection of bivalent verbs to express physical processes or actions occurring spontaneously without the direct initiation of a human agent. For instance, in (16a) the bivalent verb *olu* 'remove' is marked with *dV-* 'REFL' and has a single inanimate, non-controlling participant *sesal* 'bone'; the clause denotes a spontaneous event whereby the bones are stripped of flesh naturally of themselves, without the intervention of a human causer. By contrast, in (16b) where the single participant is animate and controlling, the clause denotes a reflexive action in which a volitional entity acts on itself. So, in a middle situation, *dV-* 'REFL' marks a single participant that undergoes the event, but does not cause it, while in the reflexive situation *dV-* marks a single entity that acts on itself, as it is both agent and patient.

(16) a. *Sesal d-olu   haqal.*
       bone   REFL-remove finished
       'The bones were completely bare.'   [Bk-4.092]
    b. *Neto d-olu   haqal.*
       1SG   REFL-remove finished
       'I finished undressing myself.'   [Not-07.04]

On some verbs, middle *dV-* 'REFL' is not necessarily valency reducing. For instance, the *dV-* marked form of the Class IV h-conjugation verb (§10.4.1) *h-en* '3INAN-dry' can for some speakers be used in active bivalent clauses. In (17a) *h-en* '3INAN-dry' occurs with distinct referents for its A and P arguments, and agreement on the verb is with the P *ipi* 'rice plant'. In (17b) and (17c) we see that *h-en* '3INAN-dry' is marked reflexive and occurs with a single participant occupying both the A and P syntactic roles. However, whilst (17b) denotes a reflexive situation with a self-affecting participant in the agent and patient roles, (17c) denotes a middle situation in which a single non-agentive participant spontaneously undergoes a change of state without clear articulation of the participant as both agentive and patientive. Finally, in (17d) we see *h-en* '3INAN-dry' marked with *dV-* 'REFL' but with two participants. Example (17d) denotes indirect causation: Manek puts the rice out to dry but is not directly responsible for the rice becoming dry. By contrast, (17a) suggests greater agentivity on the part of Manek in the actual process of drying the rice, e.g., he turns it regularly to aid the drying process. That is, *d-en* 'REFL-dry' used bivalently with middle semantics is in a derivational-like alternation with the non-middle bivalent form *h-en* '3INAN-dry', which is behaviour consistent with a Type 1 deponent verb.

(17) a. *Manek ipi   h-en.*
       Manek rice.plant   3INAN-dry
       'Manek dries the rice.'
   b. *Manek d-en.*
       Manek REFL-dry
       'Manek dries himself.'
   c. *Ipi   d-en.*
       rice.plant REFL-dry
       'The rice is drying.', lit., 'The rice dries itself.'
   d. *Manek ipi   d-en.*
       Manek rice.plant REFL-dry
       'Manek lets the rice dry itself.'   [Not-07.04]

Note that only younger Bunaq Lamaknen speakers and speakers of northeastern Bunaq have been heard to produce sentences like (17c) and (17d); older Bunaq Lamaknen speakers tend to reject these examples in elicitation.

Instances of *dV-* 'REFL' encoding spontaneous natural events convey passive-like meanings, in that the role of the initiator of the event is downplayed or virtually non-existent (cf. Steinbach 2002: 307). Consider the uses of the reflexive-marked verbs *belek* 'turn' in (18) and *h-ini* '3INAN-call' in (19). The examples in (18) come from a text which tells the story of a man who has the power to change items into anything he wishes. In the example, we see *belek* 'turn' is marked with *dV-* 'REFL' to denote the spontaneous transformation of the slaves and wealth. By marking the verb in this way, the role of the owner of the ring who was responsible for the transformation is downplayed.

(18) a. *Gie   mila=o   d-ebek   loi   niq oa.*
       3.POSS   slave=AND   REFL-turn   good   NEG IAM
       'His slave could also not be turned back any more.'   [LB-5.189]

b. *Gie   osan   gewen~gewen **d-ebek**   loi   niq   oa.*
   3.POSS   money   all.sorts   REFL-turn   good   NEG   IAM
   'All his different kinds of money could not be turned back any more.'
   [LB-5.190]

Example (19) could be interpreted as denoting a reflexive or middle situation. The monkeys could have spontaneously become girls without knowingly initiating the transformation (middle), or they could have intentionally changed form (reflexive).

(19) *Orel   hiloqon   bi   **r-ini**   pana   gol   hiloqon.*
     monkey   two   ART.AN   REFL-call   woman   small   two
     'The two monkeys turned into girls.'   [LB-2.211]

Inalienably possessed nouns are also found marked with *dV-* 'REFL' in clauses denoting spontaneous events. In (20) *dV-* 'REFL' marks the inalienably possessed noun *g-io* '3AN-faeces', which is the P of the clausal verb *a* 'eat'. This combination of the verb and *dV-* marked noun is the lexicalised expression for the spontaneous event of 'rusting' in Bunaq. In (21) the inalienably possessed noun *g-urul* '3AN-moulted snake skin' is marked with *dV-* and used predicatively to denote a spontaneous event in which people on death "shed their skin", i.e., take on a new form.

(20) *Turiq   gol   **r-io**   a.*
     machete   small   REFL-faeces   eat
     'The knife rusts / is rusty.' (lit., 'The knife eats its own faeces.')   [OS-06.02]

(21) *I   heser   niq,   i   **d-urul**   on.*
     1PL.INCL   dead   NEG   1PL.INCL REFL-moulted.skin   DO
     'We don't die, we take on another form.'   [LB-10.041]

11.3.2.2 Self-benefactive events

The prefix *dV-* 'REFL' is used to mark self-benefactive middle situations in which a participant does not act on itself, but allows itself to be acted upon (i.e., passive causation) for its own benefit.

Consider the use of the bivalent verb *h-ariqa* '3INAN-repair' marked as reflexive in (22) and (23). The clause in (22) has a single participant and denotes not that the people literally repaired themselves, but that the people had improved their standard of living by following the directives of the government. This context is clear in the example from the same text in (23) where we find *d-ariqa* 'REFL-repair' again used to refer to the same self-benefactive action on the part of the participant. Here we do not have a single participant, however, but find a P, *u* 'life' along with self-benefactive *dV-* 'REFL' on the verb. The contrast between bivalent *h-ariqa* '3INAN-repair' and bivalent

'REFL-repair' meaning 'repair X for one's self' is the kind of derivation-like prefixal alternation typical of Type 1 deponent verbs.

(22) En   denu   bari   **d-ariqa**   oa.
     person   commoner   PROX.AN   REFL-repair   IAM
     'These common people have improved their lot.'   [Bk-65.051]

(23) En   muk   ukon   nei   n-ege   baqa   g-ua
     person land   govern 1PL.EXCL   1EXCL-give   NPRX.INAN   3AN-footprint
     rale,   nei   u   bisa   **d-ariqa**   loi.
     speak   1PL.EXCL life can   REFL-repair   good
     '(When) the government showed us how to do it (lit., told us its footprints), we could repair (i.e., improve) our lives.'   [Bk-65.091]

Absence of valency reduction in self-benefactive middle situations marked by *dV-* 'REFL' is relatively frequent. In (24) the Class IV t-conjugation verb *t-inik* '3INAN-cook' is marked with the reflexive prefix, but does not have reduced valency; it still occurs with two arguments, *nei* '1PL.EXCL' and *buakae* 'provisions'. The *dV-* marking on the verb is clearly self-benefactive: the referents of A do not cook themselves, rather they cook *for* themselves.

(24) Nei   Atambua   mal   gie,   misti   ene   no   mel
     1PL.EXCL   Atambua   go   PROSP   must   night OBL   wake
     buakae   **d-inik**.
     provisions   REFL-cook
     'If we want to go to Atambua, (we) must get up in the night and cook ourselves provisions.'   [Bk-37.011]

The lexicalisation of meaning and fossilisation of *dV-* 'REFL' can be observed on several verbs denoting self-benefactive middle events. The verb *h-ota* '3INAN-stab' marked with *dV-* has the self-benefactive meaning 'get an injection': in (25a) there is a single participant who does not literally stab themselves, but rather allows themselves to be "stabbed" for their own benefit, i.e., injected with a needle. The verb *d-ota* 'REFL-stab' has further extended its use to be able to denote active 'injecting' events: in (25b) there are two participants, an A who does the injecting and a recipient of the injection, encoded with the benefactive verbal postposition *h-ege* '3INAN-BEN' (§12.4.6).

(25) a. Neto   haqe   gene   **r-ota**.
        1SG   THERE   LOC   REFL-stab
        'I got an injection there.'   [Bk-40.005]

b. *Neto   meaq gol   g-ege   r-ota.*
   1SG   child   3AN-BEN   REFL-stab
   'I gave the child an injection.'   [OS-07.01]

One of the most frequently occurring self-benefactive middle marked verbs is *d-ige* 'REFL-teach', literally 'teach oneself' (see §10.6.4 on this verb's argument structure). This form of this verb is used in contexts where the participant is clearly not self-instructing, but rather learning. The school context of (26) indicates that the children are not responsible for their own instruction. In (27), by contrast, the participant may be understood as self-instructing given the absence of study materials for the Bunaq language.

(26) *Iskola   gene   meaq gol   hasaq   r-ige.*
     school   LOC   child   count   REFL-teach
     'In school the children learn counting'   [OS-06.01]

(27) *Baqi   Bunaq   r-ige.*
     NPRX.AN   Bunaq   REFL-teach
     'S/he is learning Bunaq'   [OS-06.01]

Note that the regular and productive way of denoting self-benefaction is with a *dV-* 'REFL'-marked form of the benefactive verbal postposition (§12.4.6), *d-ege* 'REFL-BEN'.

11.3.2.3 Cognitive events

The prefix *dV-* 'REFL' is used to form predicates describing events involving cognition, belief, and feeling. In the examples below, *dV-*marked forms of the verbs *mak* 'hear' (28) and *ilek* 'listen' (29) denote the participant's mental state or process. In each case, there is no distinguishability of participants; the experiencer is both the initiator and endpoint of the mental event.

(28) *Eme   da-mak   koen   niq.*
     mother   REFL-hear   beautiful   NEG
     'Mother isn't feeling well.'   [OS.07-02]

(29) *Neto   r-ilek,   nie   muk   bare   muk   hotu~hotu*
     1SG   REFL-listen   1EXCL.POSS   land PROX.INAN   land   all
     g-o   lesin   liol.
     3-SRC more   continue
     'I think that my land is better than all other lands.'   [Bk-24.042]

When directly possessed, the topological noun *mil* 'inside' is metaphorically extended to denote the seat of emotion and thought, e.g., *gi-mil* 3AN-inside 'his/her feelings, emotions, inner thoughts' (see §9.3.5 on this pattern of nominal prefixation).

When marked with *dV-* 'REFL', the directly possessed form of this noun root acts as a predicate describing a cognitive event 'think', as in (30).

(30) *Halali* **ri-mil** *ate niq, baqa h-ua*
3DU REFL-inside far NEG NPRX.INAN 3INAN-footprint
gene=na h-oqon besik.
LOC=FOC 3INAN-do exact
'The two of them didn't think for long, (but) just did exactly as they were told.'
[Bk-4.091]

The cognitive process verb *d-oenik* 'REFL-forget' is a Type 2 bivalent deponent verb: 3rd person INANIMATE Ps and complement clauses always take a form of the verb marked by *dV-* 'REFL' (31a); Ps of other persons replace this prefix and are marked on the verb, e.g., *nV-* '1EXCL' (31b) and 3rd person ANIMATE *gV-* '3AN' (31c).

(31) a. *Novi taka masak baqa d-oenik.*
Novi basket big NPRX.INAN REFL-forget
'Novi forgot the big basket.' [OS-06.061]
b. *Nona hani nei n-oenik.*
miss PROH 1PL.EXCL 1EXCL-forget
'May you not forget us.' [Bk-14.003]
c. *Halaqi sabi g-oenik.*
3PL key.AN 3AN-forget
'They forgot the key.' [OS-06.01]

Dialectal evidence shows that *d-oenik* 'REFL-forget' is originally a Class IV h-conjugation bivalent verb with the INANIMATE agreement form *h-oenik* '3INAN-forget', still evidenced sporadically in the southwest dialect (§1.5).

11.3.2.4 Body action events

A range of body action events, including change of posture, non-translational motion, self-induced motion, and excretion events are denoted by *dV-* 'REFL'. Events of this kind are both reflexive-like in that they denote an action in which an entity acts volitionally on its own body, and middle-like in that the participant is both the beginning and endpoint of the action.

In (32) and (33) we see reflexive marking on the bivalent verbs *h-onen* '3INAN-lean' and *obon* 'hang', respectively, to denote change of posture events. Middle situations of this kind can have both active and stative readings.[5]

---

[5] The fossilisation and lexicalisation of middle marking on a posture verb has occurred in the case of *duqat* 'stand' in Bunaq Lamaknen. This is an innovative form based on a reduction of *du-huqat*

(32) Eme   meja   g-o   d-onen.
    mother table 3-SRC REFL-lean
    'Mother leans onto the table.' or 'Mother is leaning onto the table.' [Not-07.01]

(33) Neto hotel gene d-obon.
    1SG   tree   LOC   REFL-hang
    'I hang myself from the tree.' or 'I'm hanging from the tree.' [Not-07.01]

In (34) we see *dV-* 'REFL' marking the bivalent verb *h-oter* '3INAN-snatch' to denote a self-induced motion event 'getting away'. In (35) *d-ese* 'REFL-split' is used with a plural participant to denote their parting of ways in a motion event, not to indicate that they are themselves literally split.

(34) Halaqi hitu   bi   d-opil   no   d-oter   gie.
    3PL   seven ART.AN REFL-power OBL REFL-snatch   PROSP
    'They seven with all their might tried to snatch themselves, (i.e., get away).'
    [Bk-6.051]

(35) Neli   d-ese   oa.
    1DU.EXCL   REFL-split IAM
    'We go our separate paths now.' (lit., 'We split ourselves already') [OS-09.01]

Examples (36) and (37) illustrate *dV-* 'REFL' occurring on predicative inalienably possessed nouns to mark non-translational motion events. In (36) the noun *g-omoq* '3AN-resting place' is marked with *dV-* 'REFL' and functions predicatively (in an RC) to denote the event of 'settling one's self down'. In (37) the noun *luel* 'skin (of fruit), peel' is used predicatively and is marked by *dV-* 'REFL' to denote an event in which the participant figuratively creates a new skin for himself out of charcoal.

(36) Ola   hol   g-egil   no   d-omoq   bi
    LOW   stone 3AN-shade OBL REFL-resting.place ART.AN
    nei=bu   g-azal.
    1PL.EXCL=GIVEN   3AN-see
    'The (one) down there (who) has settled himself in the shade of a stone, we saw him.'
    [LB-4.109]

'REFL-erect' (§1.5). Today in Bunaq Lamaknen *du-huqat* 'REFL-erect' can still be used represent either a stative or active event, 'be standing' or 'stand up', but it is rare.

(37) Guzel   mil   no   d-ulel,   g-iwiq   tomak   guzu.
     charcoal inside OBL   REFL-peel 3AN-body whole   black
     'He covered himself (lit., peeled himself) in charcoal, (until) his whole body was black.' [Bk-6.021]

Finally, in (38) we observe the use *dV-* 'REFL' on the bivalent verb *h-isik* '3INAN-spray' to denote a body excretion event. *D-isik* 'REFL-spray' is a common, polite expression for 'urinate' in Bunaq Lamaknen.

(38) Neto   r-isik   gie   taq!
     1SG   REFL-sprinkle PROSP   CONT
     'I'm just going to the toilet!', lit., 'I'm just going to sprinkle myself.' [OS-07.03]

11.3.2.5 Impersonal middles

The *dV-* 'REFL' prefix is also found on inalienably possessed or "bound" nouns (§9.3) in contexts where there is no referent for a possessor, but where the grammar requires a possessor prefix to be present.

For instance, in (39) and (40) there is no semantically coherent antecedent for the reflexive prefixes on the inalienably possessed nouns *-bul* 'head' and *-on* 'hand'. Syntactically, the antecedent of the reflexive is *bai* 'thing' in (39) as "subject" of the possessive clause (§4.3.3), and *keke* 'bracelet' in (40) as S of the oblique-taking verb *kaeq* 'fill' (§10.6.1).[6] However, neither 'things' nor 'bracelets' have 'heads' or 'hands', such that they cannot be the semantic antecedent of *dV-* 'REFL' on the "bound" nouns in these examples. Rather, *dV-* 'REFL' here denotes an impersonal possessive relation, e.g., 'one's head', 'one's hand'. In the same contexts where impersonal reflexives are found on bound nouns, alienably possessed nouns occur without any expression of a possessor, as in *kalaq* 'neck' in (39).

(39) Bai   baqa   **ru-bul**   gie,   kalaq gie=o   **r-on**
     thing NPRX.INAN   REFL-head   3.POSS   neck   3.POSS=AND   REFL-hand
     gie.
     3.POSS
     'These things are for the head, for the neck and for the hands.' [Bk-24.024]

---

6 Note that the impersonal reflexive in these examples, although lacking a semantic antecedent, still requires a syntactic antecedent. That is, an impersonal reflexive – or any other kind reflexive, for that matter – cannot occur on a bound noun in the S function in the clause, as then there is no syntactically "higher" (verbal S/A or non-verbal "subject") antecedent to bind the reflexive.

(40) Keke   **r-on**   kaeq.
      bracelet REFL-hand   fill
      'Bracelets were bunched on one's (i.e., everyone's) arms.'   [Bk-68.044]

Impersonal *dV-* 'REFL' also appears to be present on the Type 1 deponent verb *sa* 'sweep'. This verb is unusual in that its 3ʳᵈ person INANIMATE agreement form can occur without any prefixation (41a) or with a *dV-* 'REFL' (41b). The contrast between these two forms appears to be related to genericity: whilst (41a) has a specific reading, e.g., sweep a specific location, (41b) has a general one, e.g., sweep a general area. No other verbs evidence a semantic alternation of this kind.

(41) a. *Yati hala   sa.*
         Yati rubbish sweep
         'Yati sweeps the rubbish (specific).'
     b. *Yati hala   da-sa.*
         Yati rubbish REFL-sweep
         'Yati sweeps up rubbish (general).'   [Not-06.01]

11.4 Reciprocal *tV-*

The morpheme *tV-* 'RECP' is used most productively to denote reciprocal situations (§11.4.1). In addition, Bunaq *tV-* 'RECP' is used to mark symmetrical states (§11.4.2), iterative motion (§11.4.3), and semantic plurality of relations (§11.4.4). Finally, *tV-* 'RECP' has non-predictable syntax and semantics in uses with some verbal postpositions, discussed in §11.4.5.

11.4.1 Reciprocal situations

A reciprocal situation is one with at least two participants, X and Y, where the semantic relation between X and Y is symmetrical, i.e., is the same as the semantic relation between Y and X (König and Kokutani 2006). As with the reflexive, the antecedent/binder of reciprocal *tV-* 'RECP' must be either the S/A of a verbal clause or the "subject" of a non-verbal clause.

11.4.1.1 On verbs

On bivalent verbs, *tV-* 'RECP' prototypically denotes a reciprocal event involving multiple participants, in which each participant is linked to two identical thematic roles. In this function, the antecedent of the reciprocal prefix is A/S, while the role filled by the prefix is a non-A/S role, either as a P (42) or as the complement of a verbal postposition such as *g-ege* '3AN-BEN' (43).

(42) *Pana   gol   mone gol   ta-tara.*
     female small   male small   RECP-know
     'The girl and the boy know each other.' [Bk-38.001]

(43) *Ola   gene nei   t-ege   bai   g-olo.*
     LOW   LOC   1PL.EXCL   RECP-BEN thing 3-bury
     'We bury stuff for each other.' [Bk-11.010]

11.4.1.2 On nouns

On nouns, *tV-* 'RECP' denotes that a reciprocal relation holds between a plural A/S and the possessor of an NP with a non-A/S role. In (44) an inalienably possessed noun (§9.3) and in (45) an alienably possessed noun (§9.2), both in P function, are marked with *tV-* 'RECP', where their possessors are coreferent with the A and in a symmetrical relationship.

(44) *Halali t-on   h-one.*
     3DU   RECP-hand   3INAN-hold
     'They held each other's hands.' (i.e., 'They shook hands.') [LB-8.187]

(45) *Halaqi tie   lisan   tara.*
     3PL   RECP.POSS   character   know
     'They knew each other's character.' [Bk-66.091]

In (46) *tV-* 'RECP' marks a Class V inalienably possessed noun, *nap* 'side' (§9.3.5), which is the complement of the postposition *ni* 'OBL' and denotes reciprocal relations between the plural participants. In (47) the alienably possessed noun *pana* 'woman' is marked as possessed with the reciprocal form of the indirect possessive classifier. The reciprocal has the A, Manek and Hiro, as its antecedent.

(46) *Halali ta-nap   ni   mit.*
     3DU   RECP-side   OBL   sit
     'The two of them sit at each other's side.' [OS-07.01]

(47) *Manek Hiro tazuq tie   pana   gi-ta   taqa.*
     Manek Hiro door   RECP.POSS   woman   3AN-GL   close
     'Manek and Hiro closed the door on each other's wives.' [Not-07.01]

11.4.2 Symmetrical states

Some bivalent verbs marked with *tV-* 'RECP' may be interpreted as denoting either a reciprocal event, or a non-agentive, stative event in which two participants are in a symmetrical relation to one another (48). This differs from non-reciprocal uses of the verbs with distinct referents for A and P, as these uses have active readings.

(48)

	Reciprocal			3rd person INANIMATE form	
tobok	'be doubled, twinned' 'bind each other'	<	bolok	'bind'
toli	'be complete, in full' 'pursue each other'	<	h-oli	'3INAN-pursue'
talik	'be tied together' 'tie each other up'	<	h-alik	'3INAN-wrap'
terik	'be squashed together' 'pin each other down'	<	h-erik	'3INAN-wedge'

Two examples of such uses of *tV-* 'RECP' are given below. In (49) the children are in a symmetrical relation to one another; as twins they are equally figuratively "bound" to one another. Similarly, in (50) the participants are both squashing and being squashed by the other, but they are not actively doing so.

(49) Meaq gol   halali   **t-obok**.
     child   3DU   RECP-bind
     'The two children are twins.' (lit., 'the two children are doubled together')
     [OS-07.01]

(50) Neli   kursi   no   mit   **t-erik**.
     1DU.EXCL   chair   OBL   sit   RECP-wedge
     'We two sit squashed up together on the chair.'   [OS-07.03]

11.4.3 Iterative events

In Bunaq, the prefix *tV-* 'RECP' is used on bivalent verbs to denote iterative motion (a common polysemy of reciprocals – see Nedjalkov 2007: 247–249). In this function, *tV-* 'RECP' marks a single participant event with no symmetrical sharing of roles. In (51), we see the Class IV l-conjugation bivalent verb *logo* 'move' marked with *tV-* 'RECP' to denote the shaking of the singular participant, *neto* '1SG'. In (52) the bivalent verb *h-iqit* '3INAN-lift' marked with *tV-* 'RECP' is used to denote iterative 'lifting' on the part of the participant. In (52) the participant can be interpreted as singular or plural;

where it denotes an iterative event, where the participant is plural, each individual participant acts discretely and distinct from other "jumpers".

(51) Neto **t-ogo,** mel loi niq.
1SG RECP-move rise good NEG
'I was shaking, (and) couldn't get up.' [Bk-40.007]

(52) Meaq gol **t-iqit** bukuq.
child RECP-lift play
'The child/children bounced around playfully.' (Also, reciprocal interpretation: 'The children lifted each other playfully.') [OS-07.01]

Iterative events marked by *tV-* 'RECP' can involve a controlling or non-controlling participant, with the interpretation depending on context. Compare the instances of *t-ipi* 'RECP-bend' (< *pili* 'bend') in (53) and (54). In (53), the participant *kebokoq* 'caterpillar' writhes uncontrollably as it burns in the fire, while in (54) the mouse Dia Laho is the instigator and controller of his shaking as he emerges from the ground.

(53) Kebokoq hoto no **t-ipi**.
caterpillar fire OBL RECP-bend
'The caterpillar writhed in the fire.' [OS-07.01]

(54) Dia Laho o gene **t-ipi**.
Dia Laho nowhere LOC RECP-bend
'Dia Laho (appeared) out of nowhere shaking (himself off).' [Bk-50.019]

The reciprocal and iterative meanings of *tV-* 'RECP' overlap in that both describe situations involving multiple discrete events.

11.4.4 Situations with plurality of participants

The prefix *tV-* 'RECP' is also found in a variety of situations where it implies a semantic plurality of participants in the event without necessarily assigning the participants to distinct syntactic roles.[7] Several distinct subtypes of verbs with *tV-* 'RECP' marking

---

[7] The term "plurality of participants" is adapted here from Lichtenberk (2000) and Creissels and Nouguier-Voisin (2008). Lichtenberk (2000) refers to Oceanic *paRi- as a marker of "plurality of relations", encoding not only reciprocal events but also chaining, collective, distributive, and repetitive events. Creissels and Nouguier-Voisin (2008) use the term "co-participation" to describe the meaning of a (set of) morpheme(s) which express a range of meanings, but have in common that they denote events which require multiple participants.

unspecified plural participation are recognised. These are deponents belonging to Type 1 and 2.

11.4.4.1 Fighting events

Bunaq uses *tV-* 'RECP' on a selection of bivalent verbs in semantic derivation-like alterations (i.e., Type 1 deponents) to denote physical fighting events. Examples are given in (55):

(55)

Reciprocal verb reading		"Fighting" reading		3rd person form reading	
t-ete	'chop each other'	'make war'	<	*h-ete*	'3INAN-chop'
t-iep	'spear each other'	'fight'	<	*g-iep*	'3AN-spear'
t-oqon	'do each other'	'battle'	<	*h-oqon*	'3INAN-do'
t-usuk	'prick each other'	'clash'	<	*s-usuk*	'3INAN-pierce'

Verbs of this kind may appear with a plural or singular participant. Where only one reciprocant in the fighting event is mentioned, the interpretation is generic. In (56a) we see that the plural participant can be interpreted as representing either both reciprocants in the fighting event, or just one of them with the second reciprocant left unspecified. In (56b) there is a singular participant, with the second reciprocant also left unspecified.

(56) a. *Nei   t-oqon.*
       1PL.EXCL RECP-do
       'We fight each other', or 'We fight (other people).'
    b. *Neto   t-oqon.*
       1SG   RECP-do
       'I fight (other people).'   [Not-07.01]

This use of *tV-* 'RECP' has a derivation-like function in that it creates predicates with different semantics and different syntax from those expected for the prefix. The use of *tV-* 'RECP' is semantically motivated by the fact that fighting is prototypically an event in which multiple participants occupy symmetrical roles in relation to one another.

11.4.4.2 Physical contact events

Events involving contact require two participants, the contacter and the contactee. Two Bunaq verbs referring to close physical contact events are *tV-* 'RECP'-marked deponents: *t-eqe* 'RECP-have sex' and *t-ape* 'RECP-touch'.

The verb, *t-eqe* 'RECP-have sex' is marked with *tV-* 'RECP' and can have a generic or a reciprocal meaning. For instance, (57a) where we have a plural participant with *t-eqe* 'RECP-have sex' can be interpreted as reciprocal with the *tV-* 'RECP' marking symmetrical coreference between the plural referents of A. Alternatively, it can be interpreted as referring to 'sex' generically, with the *tV-* 'RECP' marking not reciprocity, but that there is an inherent plurality of relations in the act of having sex. Similarly, in (57b) the interpretation must be generic as the participant is singular. The *tV-* 'RECP' on *t-eqe* 'RECP-have sex' thus marks semantic, but not necessarily syntactic, plurality of participation.

(57) a. *Nei* **t-eqe** *mobel.*
1PL.EXCL RECP-have.sex like
'We like having sex with each other.' or 'We like having sex.'
b. *Neto* **t-eqe** *mobel.*
1SG RECP-have.sex like
'I like having sex.' [Not-07.01]

Where there is asymmetrical involvement of participants in a sex event, the agentive participant is encoded as A and the patientive one as P. The P is then indexed on the verb by *gV-* '3AN' in place of *tV-* 'RECP'. Example (58) illustrates this pattern.

(58) *Baqi pana bi* **g-eqe**.
NPRX.AN female ART.AN 3AN-have.sex
'He had sex with the woman (she did not reciprocate).', i.e., 'He raped her.'
[Not-07.01]

Whilst the *tV-* 'RECP'-marked form of *t-eqe* 'RECP-have.sex' does not allow the inclusion of a syntactic P argument, *t-ape* 'RECP-touch' is always bivalent, as it has an A and a P. Where the A participant is plural, the *tV-* 'RECP'-marked form of the verb can be interpreted as reciprocal or as the agreement form for 3rd INANIMATE Ps with the P elided, as in (59a). Where the A participant is singular, *tV-* 'RECP' can only be interpreted as the agreement form for an 3rd INANIMATE P, as in (59b). Prefixes indexing Ps of other persons replace *tV-* 'RECP' on the verb (59c).

(59) a. *Nei* **t-ape**.
1PL.EXCL RECP-touch
'We touch each other.', or 'We touch (s.th.)'
b. *Neto zo* **t-ape**.
1SG mango RECP-touch
'I touch the mango.'
c. *Neto zap* **g-ape**.
1SG dog 3AN-touch
'I touch the dog.' [Not-07.01]

11.4.4.3 Gathering events

In Bunaq, verbs denoting gathering events are bivalent and semantically denote a plurality of P participants being gathered into one place or group. These verbs are similar to the verbs denoting symmetrical ("together") relations discussed in §11.4.2. However, they differ from them in that the verbs of gathering depict active and agentive events in which there is symmetricality between the P participants. Verbs of this kind are either Type 1 or Type 2 reciprocal deponents.

There are two Type 1 deponent gathering verbs: *duk* 'collect' and *ul* 'pull out'. On these verbs, *tV-* 'RECP' may function to reduce valency and denote reciprocal relations, as in (60a). 3rd person INANIMATE Ps may be un-indexed on the verb, following the expected agreement pattern of a Class II bivalent verb, as in (60b). Alternatively, *tV-* 'RECP' may index 3rd person INANIMATE Ps to denote that multiple P participants are gathered together into a single location, as in (60c). Ps of other persons must take the appropriate agreement form on the verb, as with the 3rd person ANIMATE P in (60d).

(60) a. *Neli* **tu-ruk**.
     1DU.EXCL RECP-collect
     'We two collect each other.'
   b. *Neto zo* **duk**.
     1SG mango collect
     'I collect the mangoes.'
   c. *Neto zo* **tu-ruk**.
     1SG mango RECP-collect
     'I collect the mangoes together.'
   d. *Neto zap* **gu-ruk** / **tu-ruk*.
     1SG dog 3AN-collect RECP-collect
     'I collect the dogs.' [Not-07.01]

There are also two Type 2 deponent gathering verbs: *t-ubak* 'RECP-gather' and *t-uk* 'RECP-pile'. On these verbs, *tV-* 'RECP' neither denotes reciprocity nor causes valency reduction; instead, it functions as the agreement form for 3rd person INANIMATE Ps (61a). Ps of other persons cause the replacement of *tV-* 'RECP' by the relevant person prefix, such as *gV-* '3AN' (61b).

(61) a. *Neto zo* **t-ubak**.
     1SG mango RECP-gather
     'I gathered the mangoes.'
   b. *Neto zap* **g-ubak**.
     1SG dog 3AN-gather
     'I gathered the dogs.' [Not-07.01]

11.4.4.4 Verbs of (un)joining

Events of (un)joining involve two or more participants with identical participation with respect to one another, i.e., that which is (un)joined and that with which it is (un)joined. There are three verbs denoting events of this kind that are reciprocal deponents in Bunaq.

The Class IV h-conjugation bivalent verb *h-ilin* '3INAN-undo' is a Type 1 deponent verb. On this verb, a 3rd person INANIMATE P can be encoded on the verb either by the expected, unmarked form *h-ilin* '3INAN-undo', or with *tV-* 'RECP'. In (62), we see that these different prefixes depict different types of 'undoing' in relation to the INANIMATE P, *mun* 'rope'. In (62a), *h-ilin* '3INAN-undo' denotes the unravelling of the individual strands of the rope from one another such that they no longer make up a rope. In (62b) *t-ilin* 'RECP-undo' denotes the untying of the two ends of a rope that are tied to one another to hold another object.

(62) a. *Neto   mun   h-ilin.*
        1SG   rope 3INAN-undo
        'I undid (the strands of) the rope.'
    b. *Neto   mun   t-ilin.*
        1SG   rope RECP-undo
        'I undid the rope (e.g., holding the mat coiled up).' [Not-07.01]

Note that the *tV-* 'RECP'-marked form of *h-ilin* '3INAN-undo' may also denote straightforward reciprocal relations, i.e., 'untie one another'.

The two Type 2 deponent verbs denoting (un)joining events are *t-irik* 'RECP-hold together' and *t-i* 'RECP-tie together'. On these verbs, *tV-* 'RECP' never denotes reciprocity and does not cause valency reduction. Instead, it functions as the agreement form for 3rd person INANIMATE Ps (63a). Ps of other persons cause the replacement of *tV-* 'RECP' by the relevant person prefix, such as *gV-* '3AN' (63b). That is, the *tV-* 'RECP' on these verbs marks semantic but not syntactic plurality of participation.

(63) a. *Neto   zo   t-irik.*
        1SG   mango   RECP-hold.together
        'I hold the mangoes together.'
    b. *Neto   zap   g-irik.*
        1SG   dog   3AN-hold.together
        'I hold the dogs together.' [Not-07.01]

11.4.5 Uses of *tV-* 'RECP' on verbal postpositions

In §11.4.1 we saw that the antecedent of *tV-* 'RECP' is always the S/A of a verbal clause or the "subject" of non-verbal clauses. This is not always the case with reciprocal *tV-* 'RECP' marking on verbal postpositions. In this section, I will examine special uses of *tV-* 'RECP' on the instrumental verbal postposition (§11.4.5.1), on the goal-marking verbal postposition (§11.4.5.2), and on the source-marking verbal postposition (§11.4.5.3).

11.4.5.1 Joint action *t-erel* 'RECP-INS'

Where two or more participants are joint agents, their co-agentivity is expressed by *t-erel* 'RECP-INS', the reciprocal inflection of the instrumental verbal postposition *dele* 'INS' (§12.4.2). Examples (64) and (65) show *t-erel* 'RECP-INS' being used to denote co-agency with bivalent verbs. In (64) *t-erel* 'RECP-INS' occurs after the NP encoding the A, and in (65) following the NP encoding the P argument. In both cases, *t-erel* 'RECP-INS' can only refer to the co-participation of the A participants. That is, *t-erel* 'RECP-INS' is always bound by A such that (65) cannot mean that the referents of P were eaten together.

(64) Nei   goniqil t-erel   u   h-ozep.
      1PL.EXCL   four   RECP-INS   herbaceous.plant   3INAN-cut
      'We four cut the grass together.'   [Bk-12.013]

(65) Halaqi dik=o   balo s-alak   baqa   t-erel
      3PL   cassava=AND   taro 3INAN-roast   NPRX.INAN   RECP-INS
      a.
      eat
      'They$_i$ ate [the roasted cassava and taro]$_j$ together$_i$.' *'They$_i$ ate [the roasted cassava and taro]$_j$ together$_j$'.   [Bk-6.057]

T-erel 'RECP-INS' also occurs with monovalent verbs with an agentive S, exemplified in (66). It cannot refer to co-participation in a non-agentive event (67).

(66) Akirnya nie   moen   mil   nei   t-erel   teqa
      finally 1EXCL.POSS   friend   COLL   1PL.EXCL   RECP-INS   pray
      on.
      DO
      'In the end, my friends and I prayed together.'   [Bk-40.011]

(67) *Halali baqi   t-erel   memel.
      3DU   NPRX.AN   RECP-INS   sick
      'They two were sick together.'   [Not-07.03]

T-erel 'RECP-INS' does not combine with the generic motion verb *mal* 'go'. In the description of generic motion events with *t-erel* 'RECP-INS' where *mal* 'go' would normally appear, the verb is omitted, as in (68) and (69); context serves to carry the predicative meaning. Omission of the predicate with *t-erel* 'RECP-INS' does not occur in other, non-motion contexts.

(68) Hei,   ibu   bari   ei   Ø-utu   t-erel   gie.
     hey   Mrs   PROX.AN   2PL   1INCL/2-COM   RECP-INS   PROSP
     'Hey, Mrs here wants to (go) together with you.'   [Bk-37.020]

(69) Sampai   ene   nie   moen   bun   nei   t-erel.
     until   night   1EXCL.POSS   friend   INDEF   1PL.EXCL   RECP-INS
     'Until night, a friend of mine (and me), we (went) together.'   [Bk-61.084]

11.4.5.2 Uniting of participants: *ti-ta* 'RECP-GL'

Whereas *t-erel* 'RECP-INS' denotes two or more agents performing an action together *in unison*, the process of two or more participants *uniting* to perform an action together is denoted by *ti-ta* 'RECP-GL', the reciprocal-marked form of the goal-encoding verbal postposition *a-ta* '3INAN-GL' (§12.4.3).

Ti-ta 'RECP-GL' can refer to the S of a monovalent verb, as illustrated in (70) and (71). *Ti-ta* 'RECP-GL' in these examples denotes that the participants were united together in a single location to perform the described action. The use of *t-erel* 'RECP-INS' in place of *ti-ta* 'RECP-GL' in these examples would indicate that the participants performed the action of crying/sitting simultaneously, and not that they came together in a single location to perform the action.

(70) Baqa   goet   ti-ta   holon.
     NPRX.INAN   LIKE   RECP-GL   cry
     'Like that, they cried to one another (i.e., together).'   [LB-2.151]

(71) Halali   baqa   ni   ti-ta   mit.
     3DU   NPRX.INAN   OBL   RECP-GL   sit
     'They two sat by one another (i.e., together).'   [LB-3.121]

Ti-ta 'RECP-GL' also differs from *t-erel* 'RECP-INS' in that it refers to the uniting of its nearest conjunct, whereas *t-erel* 'RECP-INS' can only refer to an agentive S/A. Binding of the reciprocal on *ti-ta* 'RECP-GL' is determined by linear order. That is, it refers to the P of a bivalent verb where it follows the P (72) and the A of a bivalent verb where it precedes the P (73).

(72) Neto   paqol   **ti-ta**   g-uk.
     1SG   maize   RECP-GL   3AN-collect
     'I collect the maize to one another (i.e., together).'   [OS-07.03]

(73) Halali   t-erel   kolun   t-ul   ba   ni,   **ti-ta**
     3DU   RECP-INS   fallow   RECP-pull ART.INAN   OBL   RECP-GL
     zipil   kama.
     garden.rubbish   pile
     'While they₁ two were working together clearing the fallow land, (they)₁ piled leaves₁ onto one another₁.', not *'While they₁ two were working clearing the fallow land, (they)₁ piled leaves₁ onto one another ⱼ.' [Bk-50.006]

It is common for comitative *g-utu* '3-COM' (§12.4.1) to be used together with *ti-ta* 'RECP-GL' to conjoin distinct sets of referents for a single argument. In (74) ANIMATE *paqol* 'maize' is the P and triggers agreement on the verb, while *uor* 'vegetable' is the complement of *g-utu* '3-COM'; *ti-ta* 'RECP-GL' follows both the P and the verbal postpositional phrase headed by *g-utu* '3-COM' and refers to the maize and the vegetables as being cooked together. Similarly, in (75) the S argument *neto* '1SG' is conjoined with *en* 'person' plus *g-utu* '3-COM'; *ti-ta* 'RECP-GL' follows both to denote that the participants were in a symmetrical relationship to one another, equally meeting and being met.

(74) Paqol   baqi   uor   g-utu   ti-ta   g-inik.
     maize   NPRX.AN   vegetable 3-COM   RECP-GL   3AN-cook
     '(They) cook the maize together with the vegetables.'   [Bk-24.032]

(75) Neto   en   g-utu   ti-ta   sai.
     1SG   person   3-COM   RECP-GL   exit
     'I met together with (some) people.'   [Bk-61.027]

Finally, *ti-ta* 'RECP-GL' can serve as a clausal predicate where it describes a stative situation of 'being in unity, being together'. Other inflections of the goal-marking verb do not have such a stative meaning and cannot be used as independent clausal predicates (§12.4.3). For instance:

(76) I   ti-ta   gie   oa!
     1PL.INCL   RECP-GL   PROSP   IAM
     'We will be together!'   [LB-5.051]

(77) Bare   no   ili   ti-ta   hori~hori   loi   niq.
     PROX.INAN   OBL   1DU.INCL   RECP-GL   eternally   good   NEG
     'Here we two cannot be together eternally.'   [LB-8.009]

11.4.5.3 Symmetrical participation: *t-o* 'RECP-SRC'

The reciprocal-marked form of the source-marking verbal postposition (§12.4.4), *t-o* 'RECP-SRC', is used to denote that two or more entities come or are brought together in the performance of an event.

T-o 'RECP-SRC' is used with a range of agentive monovalent verbs denoting "naturally reciprocal events" (defined by Kemmer 1993: 127), such as meeting and greeting. With these verbs, *t-o* 'RECP-SRC' denotes that the event has symmetrical involvement of participants. Consider the different encoding of the participants with the monovalent verb *botus* 'meet' in (78). In (78a), where the plural S of *botus* 'meet' is encoded with two zero-coordinated NPs, there is no special implication of (a)symmetricality in the meeting of participants. In (78b) *t-o* 'RECP-SRC' refers to the two zero-coordinated NPs and carries the implication that both participants equally met and were met with, either accidentally or deliberately. By contrast, in (78c), where Markus is S and Anto the complement of comitative *g-utu* '3-COM', there is an implication of asymmetrical involvement, with Markus being more the "meeter" than the "met".

(78) a. *Markus Anto botus.*
       Markus Anto meet
       'Markus and Anto met.'
    b. *Markus Anto t-o botus.*
       Markus Anto RECP-SRC meet
       'Markus and Anto met each other.'
    c. *Markus Anto g-utu botus.*
       Markus Anto 3-COM meet
       'Markus met Anto.' [Not-07.01]

T-o 'RECP-SRC' is only attested in the corpus bound by the P of a bivalent verb, as in (79a). That *t-o* 'RECP-SRC' is bound by the P here, *kacamata* 'glasses', and not the A, *halali* '3DU', is shown by two points. Firstly, it is grammatical to have a singular A, as in (79b); this would not be possible if *t-o* 'RECP-SRC' had the referent of A as its antecedent. Secondly, speakers judge it ungrammatical to have *t-o* 'RECP-SRC' preceding the P, as in (79c); this ungrammaticality results from a violation of the linear ordering constraint (Bresnan 1995), i.e., that *tV-* 'RECP' cannot precede the argument it refers to, indicating that P is its antecedent.

(79) a. *Halali kacamata t-o tuqal.*
       3DU glass RECP-SRC exchange
       'They two exchanged the glasses one in place of the other.'
    b. *Neto kacamata t-o tuqal.*
       1SG glass RECP-SRC exchange
       'I exchanged the glasses one in place of the other.'
    c. **Halali t-o kacamata tuqal.*
       3DU RECP-SRC glass exchange [Not-07.01]

It seems unlikely that the reciprocal on *t-o* 'RECP-SRC' cannot be bound by A at all; rather, it is probably the case that the semantically appropriate context is simply yet to be identified.

Finally, it is possible to use *t-o* 'RECP-SRC' and *ti-ta* 'RECP-GL' together with mixing verbs, as in (80). Here, *ti-ta* 'RECP-GL' refers to putting the coconut and turmeric together e.g., in a single container, while *t-o* 'RECP-SRC' refers to them being mixed into one another.

(80)   *Hoza=o*   *kirun*   **ti-ta**   **t-o**   *kahul.*
         coconut=AND   turmeric   RECP-GL   RECP-SRC   mix
         'Mix the coconut and the turmeric together.'   [Bk-83.004]

11.5 Anticausative *-wen*

In addition to the two prefixes discussed in this chapter, there is also a valency-reducing suffix, *-wen*. On agentive bivalent verbs, *-wen* is an anticausative marker, functioning to delete the A argument (§11.5.1). However, like *dV-* 'REFL' and *tV-* 'RECP', *-wen* is not always valency reducing. It can also appear on non-agentive monovalent verbs where it functions as a moderative marker (§11.5.2), and on verbs of any type as a similative marker (§11.5.3).[8]

11.5.1 Anticausative use

The most common use of Bunaq *-wen* is as an anticausative marker on bivalent verbs with an agentive A participant. That is, *-wen* 'ANTIC' signifies that the event denoted by the verb occurs by itself without the action of an agent. Compare the use of the bivalent verb *kakin* 'scatter, disperse, spread out' in the examples in (81). Without any marking, we see in (81a) that *kakin* is an event caused by an agent, *halali* '3DU' in the A argument role, and affecting a patient, *tuat* 'cake' in the P argument role. When marked with *-wen* in (81b), *kakin* lacks a causing argument and denotes a spontaneous event in which the flesh of the recently devoured girl scatters about the room when the engorged caterpillar explodes.

---

[8] The array of meanings associated with Bunaq *-wen* is not typologically usual for anticausative markers cross-linguistically (see, e.g., Haspelmath 1987). How the different functions of *-wen* relate to one another remains a question for future research.

(81) a. Causative: *kakin* 'scatter, disperse, spread out'
       Tuat homo   halali gol uen~gol uen hik   gene
       cake CONTR.INAN 3DU   REDUP~a.little path LOC
       kakin   liol,   liol,   liol,   liol,
       spread continue continue continue continue
       liol,   liol,   mete r-ua   ba   ni.
       continue continue NOW REFL-footstep ART.INAN OBL
       'The two of them scattered those cakes, piece by piece, all along the path in their tracks.'   [FetoUnuBauk-103]
   b. Anticausative: *kakin-wen* 'be scattered, dispersed, spread out'
       Toren wa   gene hilaq   balo   bi,
       attic   top LOC   surprisingly caterpillar ART.AN
       roi=na   paqa=na, gol   pana   g-ubu
       SPEC.AN=FOC burst=FOC 3AN-child female 3AN-flesh
       minak=na **kakin-wen**.
       entire=FOC spread-ANTIC
       'Up in the attic the caterpillar, he exploded and all the girl's flesh became scattered about.'   [BaloBiGakirik.065]

Syntactically, marking with *-wen* 'ANTIC' causes the A argument of the bivalent verb to be deleted. At the same time, the remaining argument retains agreement properties consistent with its original P status. Compare the clauses in (82). In (82a) we have a straightforward bivalent verbal clause with A and P expressed and the ANIMATE P, *buku* 'book', marked by agreement on the verb. In (82b), where *-wen* marks the verb, the action happens by itself; there is no A, but the original P argument of the bivalent verb is retained with agreement on the verb. In (82c) we see that it is ungrammatical to include the A when the verb is marked with *-wen*, while (82d) shows that the verb continues to agree with the original P in the presence of *-wen*.

(82) a. Neto buku g-apal.
       1SG   book 3AN-open
       'I open the book.'
   b. Buku g-apal-wen.
       book 3AN-open-ANTIC
       'The book opens.'
   c. *Neto buku g-apal-wen.
       1SG   book 3AN-open-ANTIC
   d. *Buku h-apal-wen.
       book   3INAN-open-ANTIC   [Not-09.01]

That valency reduction has taken place when *-wen* 'ANTIC' marks a bivalent verb is clear from the impermissibility of the reflexive marking of a possessor of the remaining argument. Consider the prefixal marking of *-ewe* 'tooth' when used with *leket* 'bare (of teeth)' in (83). Where the verb is used without any marking, it is bivalent and its P argument can be marked as reflexive, i.e., *d-ewe* 'REFL-tooth', as in (83a). However, when marked with anticausative *-wen*, the reflexive form is not permitted and the appropriate person inflection is used, that is, *g-ewe* '3AN-tooth' in the case of (83b).

(83) a. Causative: *leket* 'bare'
     Zap meaq gol g-ege   **d-ewe**   leket.
     dog child   3AN-BEN   REFL-tooth   bare
     'The dog bared its teeth at the children.' [Not-09.01]
  b. Anti-causative: *leket-wen* 'be bared'
     Dia Karawa=na   **g-ewe**   leket-wen,   lelek   heser.
     Dia Karawa=FOC 3AN-tooth   bare-ANTIC   ?   dead
     'Dia Karawa's teeth were bared, (he was) dead as a door nail.' [Bk-50.029]

Most commonly, *-wen* marks accidental events that occur involuntarily, that is, outside the control of the participant. Examples of *-wen* 'ANTIC' used for encoding accidental events with animate participants are given in (84) and (85), and with inanimate participants in (86) and (87). Note that in (87) *g-oq* '3AN-fruit' is a grammatical ANIMATE.

(84) Asa Paran tirin gene **koqe-wen** rebel,   Asa Paran heser.
     Asa Paran cliff LOC   roll-ANTIC   descend   Asa Paran dead
     'Asa Paran rolled down from the cliff to his death.' [Bk-4.079]

(85) Topol rebel   homo,   **ga-hake-wen**.
     fall   descend   CONTR.INAN   3AN-push.over-ANTIC
     'As he fell down, he flipped over.' [Bk-1.042]

(86) Oto   zol   lak   gene **h-abit-wen**   on
     car   river between   LOC   3INAN-wedge-ANTIC   DO
     bere,   zol   lak   gene.
     CONTEXP.INAN   river between   LOC
     'The car became wedged in between the river (banks).' [Bk-46.007]

(87) ..., g-iral   g-oq   **g-ebek-wen**,   mien   hati
          3AN-eye   3AN-fruit   3AN-turn-ANTIC   immediately exist
     g-osil   tun.
     3AN-breath   collapse
     '..., his eyes rolled back (in his head), and immediately his breathing became difficult.' [Puan-044]

Agentless events marked by -wen 'ANTIC' differ from spontaneous natural events with middle marking by dV- 'REFL' (§11.3.2.1) in that -wen is not used to refer to natural events, such as decaying or rusting, in the way the middle does. Rather, -wen is reserved for more "unnatural" events that would normally be expected to involve an agent, but that happen unexpectedly or without specific intent on the part of individuals. For example, in (88) the marking of -wen on dara 'erect' signals that the village of Lakus was not intentionally established but grew unexpectedly as refugees from East Timor accumulated in Lamaknen. In (89), the marking of -wen on l-ogo '3INAN-move' denotes the generalised tumult and agitation experienced by Lamaknen due to its position on the border with East Timor.

(88) Lakus   bare   bare   no   **dara-wen**.
     Lakus   PROX.INAN   PROX.INAN   OBL   erect-ANTIC
     'This (village) Lakus came about in this place on its own.'   [Bk-29.002]

(89) Meren   s-ileqen   niq   oa,   tan   muk   **l-ogo-wen**
     gun   3INAN-release   NEG   IAM   because   land   3INAN-move-ANTIC
     gie   ba=si.
     PROSP   ART.INAN=REAS
     'They don't fire guns anymore (during the *loro saen* ritual), because the country is in turmoil (lit., is being moved).'   [Bk-18.033]

In some situations, the surrounding discourse makes clear who or what caused the event denoted by a verb marked with -wen 'ANTIC'. In these cases, the event denoted by the verb marked with -wen occurs either non-volitionally, as in (90), or because there is no logical causative relationship and the event appears to occur spontaneously (91).

(90) Homo=na,   Bei   Usik   himo   s-obaq,
     CONTR.INAN=FOC   ancestor   crocodile   CONTR.AN   3INAN-grab
     mete   pip   g-iri   homo   **s-ileqen-wen**.
     NOW   goat   3AN-leg   CONTR.INAN   3INAN-release-ANTIC
     'Then, the crocodile grabbed hold of (the branch), (and) the goat's leg came free (lit., was released).'   [UsikPip-021]

(91) Hae,   o   roe,   ili   r-ebu   h-ini
     INTERJ   ADDR   SPEC.INAN   1DU.INCL   REFL-buttock   3INAN-CAUS
     sai   hik   goniqon=bu   ret   **ul-wen**   liol.
     exit   path   three=GIVEN   alone   pull.out-ANTIC   continue
     'Ha, this (door), if we make ourselves fart three times, it will just open on its own.'   [GolSogalHiloqon-045]

As also happens with the two valency-reducing prefixes, verbs marked with anticausative -*wen* often have lexicalised meanings. For example, when used with an animate participant and marked with -*wen*, the verb *h-opol* 'scoop up, take hold of' is used for 'startled' (92). *T-ilin-wen* '3INAN-undo-ANTIC' denotes the breaking of the day when used in respect to *pan le* 'light sky' (93), while *t-olo-wen* '3INAN-put-ANTIC' denotes ringing out when used with respect to sound (94).

(92) Keu   **g-opol-wen**=o   he   liol.
quail   3AN-take.hold.of-ANTIC=AND   run   continue
'The quail was startled and ran right away.'   [KeuOrel-011]

(93) Koak   doqon,   pan   le   **t-ilin-wen.**
helmeted.friarbird   make.sound   sky   light   3INAN-undo-ANTIC
'The helmeted friarbird squawked, as the day dawned.'   [LaqoKoak-022]

(94) Baqa   goet   ba   g-epal   gene
NPRX.INAN   LIKE   ART.INAN   3AN-ear   LOC
t-olo-wen   *t-olo-wen*.
3INAN-put-ANTIC   3INAN-put-ANTIC
'Like that it rang and rang in his ears.'   [FetoUnuBauk-089]

For at least two verbs in my corpus, *bore-wen* 'slide off, spill out' (95) and *halok-wen* 'be smelt' (96), there is no causative form of the verb. That is, -*wen* is fixed on these two verbs, though speakers still recognise *bore* and *halok* as the roots.

(95) Hoqi   nawa   no   **bore-wen**   gaqal
peanut   basket.type   OBL   slide.off-ANTIC   all.AN
'All the peanuts spilled out of the basket.'   [Not-07.02]

(96) Bai   nuas   o   ba   n-inup   gene   **halok-wen**   porsa.
thing   stink   ADDR   ART.INAN   1EXCL-nose   LOC   smelt-ANTIC   very
'The smell of it gets up my nose.' (lit., 'the smelly thing is smelt very greatly in my nose.')   [FB-220721]

11.5.2 Moderative use

On monovalent verbs with non-agentive meanings, -*wen* is moderative, that is, it expresses moderation of the basic meaning, i.e., 'be somewhat X' or 'be rather X', where X represents the state denoted by the verb. With this meaning, -*wen* is glossed 'MODER'; it does not cause valency reduction. Textual examples of this use of -*wen* are given in (97) to (100).

(97) a. Baqi **muda-wen** taq.
        NPRX.AN young-MODER CONT
        'She was somewhat young still.' [Bk-47.041]
    b. Tapi **matas-wen** gie oa.
        but old-MODER PROSP IAM
        'But (she) was getting a little old.' [Bk-47.042]

(98) Muk **res-wen** oa.
     land calm-MODER IAM
     'The country is somewhat calm now.' [Bk-66.041]

(99) Ai! Hina **boqal-wen**.
     INTERJ domestic.animal big-MODER
     'Wow! The animal is rather big.' [OrelBusaKawak-052]

(100) Tas Nualain **legul-wen**.
      village Nualain high-MODER
      'Nualain village is at rather high elevation.' [Bk-34.046]

In the above examples, the verb marked by moderative -wen is the sole predicate of the clause. However, such verbs marked with -wen can also appear as V₂ in event-oriented manner serial verbs (§13.6.2) encoding the manner in which the event denoted by V₁ occurs. Examples include (101) and (102).

(101) Orel himo g-ini mele **ate-wen**, ...
      monkey CONTR.AN 3AN-CAUS walk far-MODER
      'The monkey was made to walk rather far, ...' [OrelNisPipLoko-033]

(102) ..., hul tomol bi zol **g-iqal-wen**=o niq.
      month six ART.AN grow 3AN-be.advanced-MODER=AND NEG
      '..., the six-month-old didn't get even a bit bigger.' [Bk-46.044]

11.5.3 Similative use

A third, much less common function of -wen is as a similative marker, glossed here as 'SIM'. Textual examples of this use of -wen are given in (103) to (106). We see in these examples that -wen occurs on the verb, but introduces a whole clause. This clause itself forms a predication denoting a similarity or likeness to the subject.

(103) Ø-iwiq=o   [mun **lolan-wen**]_PRED doe,   n-ege   oa.
      1INCL/2-body=AND   rope slender-SIM   SPEC.INAN 1EXCL-give IAM
      'Your body is as slender as a rope, you will be mine.'   [HulTopol-040]

(104) Ei   bare   [keren   **doqon-wen**]_PRED.
      2PL   PROX.INAN bird.sp   make.sound-SIM
      'You are squawking like birds.'   [Not-12.01]

(105) Waqen   ola gene tei,   [pan **kumur-wen**]_PRED
      PART.PL LOW LOC dance sky   thundering-SIM
      'Some others were dancing down there, (making a sound) like the sky
      thundering.'   [RikHotel-037]

(106) ..., g-iral   suel heten no   pao   bon   lai,
           3AN-eye left right OBL bean.sp   box.bean   place
      hasi, [en   heser g-iral   **tekeq-wen**]_PRED, ...
      so   person   dead   3AN-eye look-SIM
      '..., (he) placed beans on both his eyes, so, they looked like the eyes of a dead
      person, ...'   [OrelMaMil-022]

The postposition *goet* 'LIKE' (§12.2.3) differs from similative *-wen* in that *goet* takes NPs as its complement and denotes that one entity has characteristics or qualities similar to those of some other entity.

Chapter 12
Expressing peripheral NPs

12.1 Introduction

This chapter is concerned with items used to express peripheral NPs, i.e., NPs that are not subcategorised for by the predicate (non-arguments). Core and unmarked oblique arguments of verbs have been discussed in Chapter 4. See §4.4 for an overview of the position of peripheral NPs in the clause.

Three kinds of items are used in expressing peripheral NPs in Bunaq: (i) postpositions (§12.2); (ii) possessive *gie* '3.POSS' (§12.3); and (iii) verbal postpositions (§12.4). This chapter focuses on the semantics of the different items used to express peripheral NPs. The difference between postpositions and verbal postpositions is discussed in §3.6.1.

12.2 Postpositions

Bunaq has three postpositions: *no* 'OBL', *gene* 'LOC', and *goet* 'LIKE'. Their properties as a class are the absence of inflection, the ability to act as a predicate head, and the inability to elide or front their NP complement (see §3.5.6 for illustration of the word class properties of postpositions). The individual functions of *no* 'OBL' and *gene* 'LOC' are discussed in §12.2.1 and §12.2.2, respectively, while *goet* 'LIKE' is discussed in §12.2.3.

12.2.1 *no* 'OBL'

The postposition *no* 'OBL' is used to encode NPs with locative and temporal roles. This postposition has the dialectal variant form *ni* 'OBL'.

As mentioned in §4.2.4, the gloss 'OBL' refers to the postposition *no/ni* which encodes NPs with locative and temporal roles, while the category label 'OBL' refers to a non-core argument.

12.2.1.1 Locative function
Marking locative NPs, *no* 'OBL' has a broad range of meanings, and is used to express many types of locations, 'in', 'on', 'at', 'into', etc. *No* 'OBL' may introduce a clause-initial locative-setting NP, i.e., an NP providing information about the location where the event denoted by the clause takes place, as in (1) and (2). Relevant PPs are bracketed.

(1) [*Il baqa no*], *pana gol hitu il ho.*
    water NPRX.INAN OBL female small seven water scoop
    'At the water(hole), the seven girls drew water.' [Bk-6.023]

(2) [Reu   mil   no],   keke=o   g-on   kaeq.
    house   inside   OBL   bracelet=AND   3AN-hand   fill
    'Inside the house, bracelets also filled her hands.'   [Bk-68.026]

Clause-medial locative NPs introduced by *no* 'OBL' have "inner" reference, giving locative information about a participant in the event rather than that of the event or state as a whole (Andrews 2007: 140). The locative PPs introduced by *no* 'OBL' in (3) and (4) refer to the location of the preceding participant, P and S, respectively.

(3) Nei   en   [kelompok   mil   no]   g-ubak.
    1PL.EXCL   person   group   inside   OBL   3AN-gather
    'We gather the people in a group.'   [Bk-65.002]

(4) En   [il   bul   uen   no]   rasal.
    person   water base   one   OBL   stop
    'The person stopped at a water spring.'   [Bk-69.110]

Unlike setting locatives which invariably refer to a static location, non-setting locatives often identify the direction of motion of a participant rather than a static location. In (5) and (6), *no* 'OBL' introduces an NP following the P referring to the goal location of a P as part of the act of setting. See §4.7.2 on pragmatically marked variations on this word order.

(5) Baqa   [hoto   wa   no]   lai.
    NPRX.INAN   fire   top   OBL   set
    '(You) set that on top of the fire.'   [Bk-76.069]

(6) Sabul   bi   [tais   lequ   wa   no]=na   ga-lai.
    orange ART.AN   cloth   wrapped   top   OBL=FOC   3AN-set
    'Set the oranges on top of a wrapped-up cloth.'   [Bk-4.043]

With motion verbs, an NP marked by *no* 'OBL' encodes a source location when it precedes the motion verb (7), and a goal location when following the motion verb (8). Schapper (2011c) describes this as a kind iconicity of sequence in source/goal encoding. See §13.9 for more on the encoding of complex motion events.

(7) [Zol   gol   no]   zemal.
    river   small   OBL   go.LOW
    'Go down from the small river.'   [Bk-67.042]

(8) Neto zemal   [mo alan   no].
    1SG   go.LOW   sea border OBL
    'I went down to the sea side (lit., (was) at the sea side).' [Not-06.02]

12.2.1.2 Temporal function

The postposition *no* 'OBL' also marks NPs providing information about time. Temporal setting NPs marked with *no* 'OBL' typically appear in clause-initial position (9), but they may also occur in a clause-medial position (10).

(9) [To   1987 mil no],   neto nie   moen   goniqon g-utu,
    year   1987 DUR OBL   1SG   1EXCL.POSS   friend three   3-COM
    nei   sirubisu   s-agal.
    1PL.EXCL   work   3INAN-search
    'During the year of 1987, I with my three friends, we were looking for work.'
    [Bk-12.001]

(10) N-ol   uen [hul   tomol no]=na   heser.
     1EXCL-child   one month   six   OBL=FOC dead
     'One of my children died in the sixth month (i.e., June),' [Bk-46.040]

The postposition *no* 'OBL' is occasionally dropped when marking a temporal setting, as in (11).

(11) Nei=na   n-on   rono   [hot   mil   uen] lesin gol
     1PL.EXCL=FOC 1EXCL-hand   tardy   sun   DUR   one   more   small
     uen   ai.
     one   ONLY
     'We who were slow-handed (in) one day would (do) only a little more.'
     [Bk-12.010]

A temporal setting introduced by *no* 'OBL' may also be a clause nominalised by a determiner. A nominalised setting clause marked by *no* 'OBL' always occurs clause-initially, as in (12). See §7.8.2 for more on the "domain-creating" function of the definite article.

(12) [Ipi   lete ba   no], en   denu,   pana
     rice.plant   step ART.INAN   OBL   person commoner   female
     mone hati.
     man   exist
     'During the threshing of the rice (lit., stepping of the rice), the whole population was there, men (and) women.' [Bk-70.049]

12.2.2 *gene* 'LOC'

Like *no* 'OBL', the postposition *gene* 'LOC' is also used to express a broad range of location types. The locatives *no* 'OBL' and *gene* 'LOC' can occur almost interchangeably. The difference between the two is that whilst *no* 'OBL' provides a specific location, *gene* 'LOC' introduces a more general one. In particular, *gene* 'LOC' can be used with a complement consisting of an elevational locational (13; see §8.3.1) or place locational (14; see §8.3.2), with both items having only vague locative reference, whilst *no* 'OBL' cannot: *ola no and *haqe no.

(13) [Ola gene] nei t-ege bai g-olo.
 LOW LOC 1PL.EXCL RECP-BEN thing 3-bury
 'We bury stuff for each other.' [Bk-11.010]

(14) En [haqe gene] gereja tekeq.
 person THERE LOC church look
 'People in that (place) were looking at the church.' [Bk-34.064]

Example (15) illustrates *gene* 'LOC' introducing a locative setting NP in clause-initial position. Example (16) shows *gene* 'LOC' introducing a stative locative NP in clause-medial position denoting the location in which the S lives. Example (17) shows *gene* 'LOC' introducing a non-stative locative NP with "inner" reference, denoting the location in which the P is planted.

(15) [Hik gene], baqi pit saq.
 path LOC NPRX.AN throat dry
 'On the way he got thirsty.' [Bk-4.046]

(16) Neto [Lamaknen gene] mit.
 1SG Lamaknen LOC sit
 'I live in Lamaknen.' [Bk-24.003]

(17) En bei mil biasa r-on g-onos
 person ancestor COLL usually REFL-hand 3AN-nail
 koil, tais tul roq, [muk gene] pelek.
 shave.off cloth piece cut.off earth LOC plant
 'The ancestors used to shave off (a bit of) fingernail, cut off a bit of material (and plant (them) in the ground.' [Bk-23.059]

In the same manner as *no* 'OBL', an NP introduced by *gene* 'LOC' encodes an origin location when it precedes a motion verb (18), and a goal location when following a motion verb (19). More detail on the expression of complex motion events is provided in §13.9.

(18) Nei   [kampung gene] sai.
    1PL.EXCL village   LOC   exit
    'We left the village.'   [Bk-1.013]

(19) Tebe   sai   [tas   Gewal gene].
    return exit village Gewal LOC
    '(He) came out back to the village Gewal.'   [Bk-1.051]

Unlike *no* 'OBL', the postposition *gene* 'LOC' is not typically used to introduce temporal NPs.

12.2.3 *goet* 'LIKE'

12.2.3.1 Similative function

Goet 'LIKE' is a postposition denoting that one entity has characteristics or qualities similar to some other entity. In (20) and (21), *goet* 'LIKE' heads a predicate phrase composed of it and its NP complement; the referent of the NP complement of *goet* 'LIKE' is equated with the referent of the first NP in the clause. In (20) a son, encoded by *baqi* 'NPRX.AN', is said to be similar to his father. In (21) and (22) the NP with which the complement of *goet* 'LIKE' is compared is elided, as it is retrievable from the previous clause.

(20) Baqi   **gie**   **ama**   **goet**.
    NPRX.AN 3.POSS   father   LIKE
    'He is like his father.'   [OS-07.01]

(21) Le   gol   uen halaqi gi-ta,   **senta** **goet**.
    light small one 3PL   3AN-GL   torch   LIKE
    'A little light struck them, (it was) like a torch.'   [Bk-47.112]

(22) G-epal   legul~legul,   **sael** **Makao** **goet**.
    3AN-ear   REDUP~long   pig   Macau   LIKE
    'His ears were really long, (they were) like a Macau pig('s).'   [Bk-47.100]

Goet 'LIKE' can also give information about a participant in an event. In this function *goet* 'LIKE' is the head of an RC predicate dependent on the N$_{HEAD}$ of a non-restrictive RC (§5.4.1). In (23) *goet* 'LIKE' is the predicate head of an RC modifying the head of the first NP in an equative clause; the complement of *goet* 'LIKE' is the demonstrative *bare* 'PROX.INAN' which refers to (the season) of the present time (§7.3.1.2). In (24) the RC predicate–headed *goet* 'LIKE' modifies *sore* 'machete', the P of *wit* 'fetch'; the complement of *goet* 'LIKE' is the demonstrative *baqa* 'NPRX.INAN', which refers back to the machete of the speaker's father mentioned in the previous clause. In (25), the N$_{HEAD}$ of the RC is elided, leaving just the RC predicate with *goet* 'LIKE' and its complement, *baqi* 'NPRX.AN'.

(23) [Pan   [bare   goet]_RC]_NP pan   porat.
     sky   PROX.INAN   LIKE   sky   dry.season
     'A season (which is) like this is a dry season.'   [Bk-7.014]

(24) Neto   ri-mil,   hot   mil   no   [sore   [baqa
     1SG   REFL-inside   sun   DUR   OBL   machete   NPRX.INAN
     goet]_RC]_NP   r-ege   wit   gie.
     LIKE   REFL-BEN   buy   PROSP
     'I think, one day I'm going to buy myself a machete like that.'   [Bk-24.040]

(25) [Ø   [baqi   goet]_RC]_NP   g-ek   haqal, ...
            NPRX.AN   LIKE   3AN-pick.up   finished
     '(When we have) finished picking up (stones) like those, ...'   [Bk-30.085]

Goet 'LIKE' can also take a stative predicate as its complement in place of an NP. This use of *goet* 'LIKE' functions to indicate that a participant experiences something similar to or resembling the state denoted by the complement of *goet* 'LIKE', as in:

(26) N-iwiq   ba   **mamut~mamut**   goet.
     1EXCL-body   ART.INAN   REDUP~soft   LIKE
     'My body was like (it was) really soft.', i.e., 'It was as if my body were really soft.'
                                                                        [Bk-40.003]

(27) N-osil   **hobel**   **gie**   goet   oa.
     1EXCL-breath   not.exist   PROSP   LIKE   IAM
     'My breath was already like (it was) about to not exist.', i.e., 'It was as if my breathing were about to stop.'   [Bk-40.009]

(28) Hoto   **naraka**   **mil**   **gene**   goet   on.
     fire   hell   inside   LOC   LIKE   DO
     '(I feel) like (I am) in the fires (of) hell.', i.e., 'It is as if (I were) in hell.'
                                                                        [Bk-46.053]

12.2.3.2 Demonstrative manner function

Goet 'LIKE' is frequently used with a demonstrative as its NP complement to denote the manner in which something is done, i.e., "like this", "like that", etc. The phrase introduced by *goet* 'LIKE' can precede the main verb of the clause (29), or follow it (30).

(29) Baqi   **baqa**   **goet**   liol   liol.
     NPRX.AN   NPRX.INAN   LIKE   continue   continue
     'He continued on and on like that.'   [Bk-70.015]

(30) Eto   g-ubeqen   **bare**   **goet**.
      2SG   3AN-pinch PROX.INAN   LIKE
      '(If) you pinch her like this.'   [Bk-38.025]

In (29) *baqa* 'NPRX.INAN' is an anaphoric discourse deictic demonstrative which refers back to the event described in the previous clause; in (30) *bare* 'PROX.INAN' is used because it is accompanied by a gestural demonstration of pinching by the speaker. The choice of the demonstrative to be the complement of *goet* 'LIKE' depends on the reference (see Chapter 7 on the functions of individual demonstratives).

Demonstrative complements of *goet* 'LIKE' may also be cataphoric. In (31) the proximal demonstrative *bare* 'PROX.INAN' refers forward to the description of the manner in which Bouq Memoq weaves in the following clause. Similarly, in (32) *doe* 'SPEC.INAN' refers forward to a description of how to spin cotton.

(31) Bouq Memoq   tais   selu   **bare**   **goet**   on.
      Bouq Memoq   cloth   weave   PROX.INAN   LIKE   DO
      'Bouq Memoq wove cloth like this.'   [LB-6.025]

(32) Gu-bul   hiliq   **roe**   **goet**.
      3-head   spin   SPEC.INAN   LIKE
      '(We) spin the ball (of cotton) like this.'   [Bk-64.001]

One of the most frequent uses of cataphoric demonstratives with *goet* 'LIKE' is in quotatives, described in the next section.

12.2.3.3 Introducing direct speech and thought

Goet 'LIKE' is frequently used with verbs of speaking to introduce direct speech and thought. In (33a) the verb of speech *sasi* 'say' occurs together with *goet* 'LIKE' whose complement is a cataphoric discourse deictic demonstrative, which refers forward to the quote in the following clause (33b). In (34) we find the same structure with the addition of an addressee encoded by *h-ege* '3INAN-BEN' (see §12.4.6.2) on the clause introducing the quote. The demonstrative and *goet* 'LIKE' may precede the verb of speaking (33a), but more frequently they follow it as in (34a).

(33) a. Naqi   **baqa**   **goet**   sasi:
         royal   NPRX.INAN   LIKE   say
         'The king said this: [Bk-72.033]
      b. Sio=na   hotel   gu-buk   bari   g-iwal
         who=FOC   tree   3AN-flower   PROX.AN   3AN-pick
         g-ere, ...
         3AN-reach
         "Whoever reaches (and) picks this flower, ..."'   [Bk-72.034]

(34) a. *Kepala desa g-ege   rale   baqa   goet:*
    head.village 3AN-BEN speak   NPRX.INAN LIKE
    '(We) spoke to the head of the village thusly: [Bk-1.039]
  b. *Nei   goniqo zo   baqa   saqe   gaqal.*
    1PL.EXCL three   mango NPRX.INAN ascend all.AN
    "All three of us climbed up the mango (trees)".' [Bk-1.040]

The verb of speaking in clauses such as in (33a) and (34a) is regularly omitted altogether; *goet* 'LIKE' with a cataphoric demonstrative as complement can function on its own to introduce the direct speech in the following clause, as in (35) without any encoding of the addressee, or (36) with an explicit addressee encoded by *h-ege* '3INAN-BEN'.

(35) a. *En   pana   gie   matas mil   baqa   goet:*
    person female 3.POSS old   COLL NPRX.INAN LIKE
    'The woman's parents (say) this: [Bk-38.005]
  b. *Kalo eto   n-ol   bari   g-akara   tepel, ...*
    if   2SG 1EXCL-child PROX.AN 3AN-love true
    "If you really love this child of mine, ..."' [Bk-38.006]

(36) a. *Neto mal Eta   g-ege   roe   goet:*
    1SG   go   Eta 3AN-BEN SPEC.INAN LIKE
    'I went (and said) this to Eta: [Bk-37.046]
  b. *Mama   Eta, en   gol   bari   bilat   o=nai.*
    mother Eta   person small PROX.AN hungry IAM=INFORM
    "Mother Eta, this person has got to be hungry already".' [Bk-37.047]

Goet 'LIKE' can function on its own to introduce direct speech, as in the following clause with an anaphoric discourse deictic demonstrative as a complement. In (37), *goet* 'LIKE' introduces *baqa* 'NPRX.INAN', a discourse deictic demonstrative referring back to the direct speech (an insult exchanged between school children) in the previous clause. Similarly, in (38) *doe* 'SPEC.INAN' refers back to the quotation of the previous clause, in which the speaker is asked to wait.

(37) *"Ei   ie   ama   g-oral   hai",   baqa   goet.*
    2PL 1INCL/2.POSS father 3AN-penis gape NPRX.INAN LIKE
    '"Your father's penis gapes", (they say) like that.' [Bk-30.016]

(38) *"Hainaq!",   roe   goet on.*
    INTERJ   SPEC.INAN LIKE DO
    '"Wait!", (he said) like this.' [Bk-19.002]

12.3 Reason *gie* 'BECAUSE'

The 3ʳᵈ person inflection of the indirect possessive classifier, *gie* '3.POSS' (§9.2), is used to introduce NPs denoting a reason with translation equivalents such as "due to" and "on account of".[1] In this function, *gie* '3.POSS' does not vary in form (i.e., no 1ˢᵗ or 2ⁿᵈ person inflections), and will be glossed as 'BECAUSE'.

Typically, the NP introduced by *gie* 'BECAUSE' is clause-initial (as in 39 and 40), but it may also be clause-medial (as in 41 and 42).

(39) **Adat   gie,**   *hiloqon   mit...*
      tradition   BECAUSE   two   sit
      'Because of tradition, two (people) sit...'   [Bk-38.070]

(40) **Teqa   gie=na,**   *nie   memel   bare   loi.*
      prayer   BECAUSE=FOC   1EXCL.POSS   sickness   PROX.INAN   good
      'It is on account of prayers that my sickness is better.'   [Bk-40.017]

(41) *Nei*   **milik   gie**   *he   tebe.*
      1PL.EXCL   fear   BECAUSE   run   return
      'We run back on account of fear.'   [Bk-47.013]

(42) *Nei*   *real   oto   terbalik   gie*   *ni-mil   susar.*
      1PL.EXCL   many   car   flip.over   BECAUSE   1EXCL-inside   be.afflicted
      'Us lot, we were worried (lit., insides were afflicted) on account of the car flipping over.'   [Bk-52.046]

Gie 'BECAUSE' also functions as a sentence connective in the construction given in (43). Following a final-intonation contour, *gie* 'BECAUSE' introduces a demonstrative which refers back to the preceding proposition, and indicates the relationship between the conjoined propositions: i.e., the event described in S_1 is the reason for S_2.

(43) S_1. DEM *gie*, S_2.
      'S_2 occurs on account of S_1'

The construction is illustrated in (44) and (45). We see in (44b) that the contrastive demonstrative, *homo* 'CONTR.INAN' (§7.6.2.2), is used to connect sentences,

---

[1] The use of possessive *gie* '3.POSS' to encode reasons seems to have developed out of the possessive's origin-encoding function (§9.2.2.2). If an event is precipitated by or occurs as a consequence of another event or entity, it can be seen to have its *origins* in that event. That is, the earlier event can be construed as the reason for the later one: i.e., 'from X' > 'because of X'. On the basis of this metaphor, *gie* '3.POSS' is seen to have come to encode reason NPs.

while in (45b) this function is performed by the non-proximal demonstrative, *baqa* 'NPRX.INAN' (§7.4.2.3).

(44) a. Gie   ama   g-awas=na   bagal, berelikuq g-iep
        3.POSS   father 3AN-forehead=FOC split   bird.sp   3AN-chop
        de   niq.
        true NEG
        '(He) split his father's forehead (open), not hitting the bird.'   [LB-4.055]
    b. **Homo**   **gie**, ama   himo   heser oa.
        CONTR.INAN BECAUSE father CONTR.AN dead   IAM
        'Because of that, the father was dead.'   [LB-4.056]

(45) a. Naran   nego=na   Suri Guloq h-oqon   ba,   gie
        every   what=FOC   Suri Guloq 3INAN-do   ART.INAN 3.POSS
        eme   h-ini   sal   minak.
        mother 3INAN-CAUS   wrong   complete
        'Everything that Suri Guloq did, his mother said was all wrong.'   [Bk-6.005]
    b. **Baqa**   **gie**=na,   Suri Guloq gi-mil   susar.
        NPRX.INAN BECAUSE=FOC   Suri Guloq 3AN-inside be.afflicted
        'It was because of that, Suri Guloq had a bad time of it.'   [Bk-6.006]

See also §12.4.3.3 on the encoding of reason-denoting NPs with *a-ta* '3INAN-GL'.

12.4 Verbal postpositions

Verbal postpositions form a restricted class of eight members in Bunaq (Table 12.1). Like postpositions, verbal postpositions function to introduce NPs with a range of different peripheral semantic roles into a clause.

Table 12.1: Verbal postpositions.

g-utu	'3-COM'
dele	'INS'
a-ta	'3INAN-GL'
g-o	'3-SRC'
h-otol	'3INAN-WITHOUT'
h-ege	'3INAN-BEN'
h-os	'3INAN-WAIT'
h-onogo	'3INAN-SEPARATE'

As we saw in §3.6.1, verbal postpositions differ morphosyntactically not only from verbs, but also from postpositions. They are distinct from postpositions in that they have inflection like verbs, allow the elision/fronting of their NP complement, and do not occur as an independent predicate head. They are distinct from verbs in that they lack the ability to occur clause-finally as an independent clausal verb, or at least differ significantly in meaning from their independent use. Some verbal postpositions also do not display the argument sharing restrictions which would be expected if they were serial verbs (see §13.2), while several verbal postpositions also show inflectional loss (extending their 3rd person ANIMATE agreement form to INANIMATES), or reduction in valency. If the hypothesis (floated in §3.6.1) that verbal postpositions originate in argument-adding serial verbs is correct, these are all signs of grammaticalisation away from a verbal status (Aikhenvald 2006: 45–47).

In §12.4.1–§12.4.8, I focus on the diverse semantic roles encoded by individual verbal postpositions. We will see that some verbal postpositions occur in combination with a few verbs with distinct lexical meanings. As mentioned in §4.4, this may be taken to indicate that the verbal postposition is subject to the lexical control of the verb, that is, it does not make a fully independent contribution to the meaning of the clause and that its NP is therefore a kind of oblique argument of the verb. However, the fact that there is no verb that absolutely requires a verbal postposition, and the broad semantic motivations that are evident in verbal postposition use, mean that overall, an adjunct analysis of verbal postpositions is favoured here, with only a very few constructional exceptions.

12.4.1 *g-utu* '3-COM'

The verbal postposition *g-utu* '3-COM' is synchronically the least verb-like of the verbal postpositions: it does not occur independently in final position as a main clausal verb, and is not bound by the A/S argument sharing restrictions of true serial verbs; it lacks reciprocal, reflexive, and a distinct 3rd person INANIMATE inflection (hence the gloss '3-' is used instead of '3AN-'). In the manner of a Class III verb (§10.2.3), *g-utu* '3-COM' inflects for 1st, 2nd, and 3rd person only.

The verbal postposition *g-utu* '3-COM' is used to express comitative relations. A comitative relation expresses that two separate entities participate in a single event jointly, in the same role. A comitative NP introduced by an inflection of *g-utu* '3-COM' follows the argument whose role it shares. In (46) and (47) *g-utu* '3-COM' introduces an NP which is the concomitant of the A argument in a bivalent verbal clause.

(46) *Baqi* **en** *g-utu si sael=na gi-a.*
 NPRX.AN person 3-COM meat pig=FOC 3AN-eat
 'He ate pig's meat with the people.' [Bk-70.171]

(47) **Nei** **n-utu** nei nie eme g-ua
     1PL.EXCL 1EXCL-COM 1PL.EXCL 1EXCL.POSS mother 3AN-footprint
     ba inil naq!
     ART.INAN examine PRIOR
     'Look for our mother's footprints with us!' [LB-3.025]

In (48) and (49), *g-utu* '3-COM' introduces an NP which denotes accompaniment to the S argument in a monovalent verbal clause. In these clauses the comitant participants could be realised together with a single noun or pronoun, but *g-utu* '3-COM' provides an alternative, allowing the participants to be construed as two separate sets of entities.

(48) Lakus **Duarato** **g-utu** hok.
     Lakus Duarato 3-COM border
     'Lakus borders with Duarato.' [Bk-29.058]

(49) **Gie** eme gie turunan baqi **g-utu** nor
     3.POSS mother 3.POSS descendant NPRX.AN 3-COM randomly
     ton niq.
     marry NEG
     '(They) don't just randomly marry one of their mother's family.' [Bk-18.013]

In the above examples, *g-utu* '3-COM' introduces an NP comitant with an A or S argument. *G-utu* '3-COM' can also be used to express an NP which accompanies a P. In (50) and (51), the NP complements of *g-utu* '3-COM' express a referent that goes together with the referent of the P in the event denoted by the verb. *G-utu* '3-COM' cannot be used to introduce an NP comitant with an R, T, OBL, or in a PP.

(50) Paqol baqi **uor** **g-utu** ti-ta g-inik.
     maize NPRX.AN vegetable 3-COM RECP-GL 3AN-cook
     '(They) cook that maize together with vegetables.' [Bk-24.032]

(51) Tun homo t-ubak haqal soq=bu, **mok**
     flour CONTR.INAN 3INAN-gather finished SEQ=GIVEN banana
     za **g-utu** kahul.
     ripe 3-COM mix
     'Once that flour has been gathered, then mix (it) with the ripe banana.'
     [Bk-76.011]

There is one instance in the corpus in which *g-utu* '3-COM' introduces an NP whose referent cannot be seen as a co-participant semantically equal to that with which it is conjoined. In (52) we see that *sendel* 'sandals' is conjoined with the S argument by means of *g-utu* '3-COM'. The semantically inanimate referent of *sendel* 'sandals' means that it cannot be an absolute equal of the animate S *nei* '1PL.EXCL'; instead, it must be regarded as an instrument, normally encoded by *dele* 'INS'. See §12.4.2.4 on the contrast between *dele* 'INS' and *g-utu* '3-COM'.

(52) **Sendel g-utu**, nei   roe   toman   oa,   mele.
     sandal 3-COM 1PL.EXCL SPEC.INAN used.to IAM walk
     'With sandals, we here were used to, (used to) walking (with).'   [Bk-37.033]

12.4.2 *dele* 'INS'

Dele 'INS' is used primarily to introduce NPs expressing instruments into a clause (§12.4.2.1). It can also introduce NPs denoting a cause (§12.4.2.2), manner (§12.4.2.3), or non-controlling comitant (§12.4.2.4).

The verbal postposition *dele* 'INS' inflects like a Class II verb (§10.2.2) and can have its complement elided/fronted. Both points are illustrated in (53) by the lack of inflection on *dele* 'INS' with an INANIMATE complement and by the fact that the postpositional phrase with *no* 'OBL' can intervene between *dele* 'INS' and its complement.

(53) Mais neto botil   baqa   r-opil   no   dele Weluli pir.
     but 1SG bottle NPRX.INAN   REFL-power OBL INS   Weluli reach
     'But I forced myself (to go) on to Weluli carrying those bottles.'   [Bk-13.009]

Dele 'INS' also cannot occur as an independent, clause-final verb. The exception to this is the reciprocal inflection, *t-erel* 'RECP-INS', which can occur as an independent verb denoting conjoint motion (§11.4.5.1), a function which is perhaps a remnant from an earlier verbal status.

12.4.2.1 Instrument

Dele 'INS' is used most frequently to introduce an NP encoding an instrument. The instrument introduced by *dele* 'INS' may be a tool (54) or, when combined with a verb of locomotion, a vehicle (55), or even an abstract force (56).

(54) **Rama rele** g-ao   gie.
     arrow INS   3AN-shoot PROSP
     '(They) intend to shoot him with arrows.'   [Bk-5.005]

(55) U=na   nei   h-ozep   baqa   hot   mil
    herbaceous.plant=FOC 1PL.EXCL 3INAN-cut NPRX.INAN sun DUR
    Sabtu   no=na   **oto rele** tula.
    Saturday   OBL=FOC car   INS   move.
    'On Saturday the grass which we had cut was transported with the car.'
    [Bk-12.015]

(56) Hot   g-iral   r-opil   ha-sai,   baqi
    sun   3AN-eye   REFL-power 3INAN-bring.out NPRX.AN
    rie   **cinoq** **rele** en   g-ini   sil.
    REFL.POSS   hot   INS   person 3AN-CAUS   sweat
    'The sun unleashed his power and with his heat made the person sweat.'
    [Bk-16.006]

The above examples represent prototypical situations involving instruments: there are three participants, an A working upon a P using an instrument (Stolz 2001: 591). However, *dele* 'INS' may also be used to express *the means by which* an event is achieved. For instance:

(57) En   **r-iol**   **rele** Makasai=o   Fataluku=na   rale.
    person REFL-voice   INS   Makasae=AND   Fataluku=FOC   talk
    'The people talk in their own languages, Makasai and Fataluku.'   [Bk-61.010]

(58) **Paqol   g-erel**=na   halaqi   u.
    maize   3AN-INS=FOC   3PL   live
    'It is maize which they live off.'   [Bk-7.025]

12.4.2.2 Cause

Dele 'INS' may also introduce an NP encoding a cause. An instrument can be interpreted as a cause in that the item with which an action is carried out can be seen to bring about the state resulting from that action (Durie 1988: 7). The cause NP encoded with *dele* 'INS' is always inanimate. In (59) *dele* introduces *milik* 'fear', the cause for the girl's crying. In (60) it is on account of the *soqat* 'poverty' marked by *dele* 'INS' that the children are forced to move about, while in (61) the hardship marked by *dele* 'INS' causes people to go to the speaker.

(59) En   pana   himo   milik,   die   tazuq   ube,   tebe
    person female CONTR.AN   fear   REFL.POSS door   close   return
    sai   heten niq,   loka   mil   gene   **milik** **rele** holon ai.
    exit   want   NEG   room   inside LOC   fear   INS   cry   ONLY
    'The girl got scared, she closed her door and wouldn't come out, but just cried in her room out of fear.'   [Bk-21.005]

(60) Gie   eme   ama   heser gaqal, tebe   susar,   **soqat** **dele**
     3.POSS   mother   father dead   all.AN return   be.afflicted poor   INS
     mele   liol   liol.
     walk   continue continue
     'Their parents were both dead and they fell on hard times and out of poverty
     were forced to keep moving about.'   [Bk-49.003]

(61) En=na   **susar**   **rele** i   i-ta   man.
     person=FOC   hardship   INS   1PL.INCL   1INCL/2-GL   come
     'People come to us out of hardship.'   [Bk-66.102]

12.4.2.3 Manner

Dele 'INS' is also found introducing NPs encoding the manner in which an action is performed. In this function, the complement of *dele* 'INS' is always inanimate and denotes an action or state (i.e., they are zero-conversion noun-verbs: §3.4), as in (62) to (64).

(62) **Cinoq** **dele**, neto   Ibu   Yip   g-o   mal.
     hot   INS   1SG   Mrs   Yip   3-SRC   go
     'Feverish (lit., with hotness) I went to Mrs Yip's.'   [Bk-40.005]

(63) Baqi   **sues**   **dele**=na   sasi.
     NPRX.AN   sit.with.legs.stretched.out   INS=FOC   say
     'She said (it) with her legs stretched out in front of her.'   [Bk-72.040]

(64) Gi-ta   tama,   **holon**   **dele**.
     3AN-GL   enter   cry   INS
     '(He) came inside to him, crying.'   [Bk-68.078]

12.4.2.4 Non-controlling comitants

Dele 'INS' is also used to encode NPs whose referents are concomitant in an action but whose role in that action is non-controlling and non-agentive. In (65) to (67), *dele* 'INS' introduces an additional NP denoting an entity that was taken along by the agentive S of the motion events denoted by the clause.

(65) Neto   **botil**   dele   Weluli   mal.
     1SG   bottle   INS   Weluli   go
     'I went to Weluli with the bottles (i.e., carrying bottles).'   [Bk-13.002]

(66) Hoza   bara,   nu   bara   **n-erel**   menal.
     coconut   short   coconut   short   1EXCL-INS   go.HIGH
     'Little coconut, little coconut, take me up.'   [Bk-6.011]

(67) Nie   kaqa   g-inat   nie   eme
    1EXCL.POSS older.brother   3AN-first   1EXCL.POSS   mother
    g-olep   no   **g-erel**   ciwal.
    3AN-belly   OBL   3AN-INS   flee
    'My mother fled with my oldest brother *in utero*.'   [Bk-29.067]

Dele 'INS' is also used with non-motion monovalent predicates to denote a participant to whom the predicate happened. In (68) *dele* 'INS' encodes the participant to whom the event denoted by the environmental condition predicate, *mon* 'evening', happened. Similarly, in (69), the participant encoded by *dele* 'INS' is the one to whom the shouting occurs.

(68) **Nei**   **n-erel**   mon.
    1PL.EXCL   1EXCL-INS   evening
    'We were overtaken by night.' (lit., '(it became) evening with us.')   [Bk-47.002]

(69) Eto   g-ubeqen   bare   goet,   en   **Ø-erel**   huk.
    2SG   3AN-pinch   PROX.INAN   LIKE   person   1INCL/2-INS   shout
    'If you were to squeeze her (hand) like this, people would make a fuss about you doing it (lit., shout with you).'   [Bk-38.025]

The contrast between comitative *g-utu* '3-COM' (§12.4.1) and comitative *dele* 'INS' is illustrated in (70). *G-utu* '3-COM' introduces Asa Paran, an agentive human accompanier of the A, Mau Paran. By contrast, *dele* 'INS' encodes *zap* 'dog', a non-human entity under the control of the A.

(70) Mau Paran   Asa Paran   g-utu   zap   g-erel   mele   zon=o
    Mau Paran   Asa Paran   3-COM   dog   3AN-INS   walk   game=AND
    zulo   g-agal   gie   mal.
    civet   3AN-seek   PROSP   go
    '(He) went walking with Asa Paran and the dogs to look for wild pigs and civets.'   [Bk-4.078]

12.4.3 *a-ta* '3INAN-GL'

The verbal postposition *a-ta* '3INAN-GL' has the verbal characteristics of inflecting (see §2.6.1 on its irregular inflection pattern) and allowing elision/fronting of its complement, as in (71); see also §5.4.3.2 on this.

(71) Hik=na   i   a-ta   mit   bare   h-azal   oa.
    path=FOC   1PL.INCL   3INAN-GL   sit   PROX.INAN   3INAN-see   IAM
    '(We) see that the path where we are sitting is this (one).'   [Bk-23.064]

The form *a-ta* '3INAN-GL' can appear as an independent predicate meaning 'shoot, aim'. As a verbal postposition, however, the meaning of *a-ta* '3INAN-GL' is semantically much more general: it is used primarily to introduce peripheral NPs expressing goals (§12.4.3.1), as well as ones denoting interest (§12.4.3.2) and motive (§12.4.3.3). An additional use of the reciprocal form of *a-ta* '3INAN-GL' is discussed in §11.4.5.2.

12.4.3.1 Goal

The verbal postposition *a-ta* '3INAN-GL' encodes an NP expressing the goal towards which a motion takes place. In (72) and (73), we see *a-ta* '3INAN-GL' used in conjunction with a verb of motion to denote movement towards an animate goal. Compare with other goal-encoding strategies discussed in §13.9.1.

(72) *Halaqi en* **Jepang gi-ta**=na *mal oa.*
3PL person Japan 3AN-GL=FOC go IAM
'They had gone to (i.e., sided with) the Japanese.' [Bk-29.010]

(73) *Baqa ni* **Berek**=*o* **Mauk gi-ta** *he.*
NPRX.INAN OBL Berek=AND Mauk 3AN-GL run
'At that, Berek and Mauk ran to her.' [LB-2.209]

Examples (74) and (75) illustrate the use of *a-ta* '3INAN-GL' to denote a movement towards an inanimate goal location.

(74) *Akirnya, halaqi rie* **muk a-ta** *tebe.*
finally 3PL REFL.POSS land 3INAN-GL return
'In the end they returned to their own land.' [Bk-29.014]

(75) *Nona* **Australia a-ta** *tebe=bu mele loi~loi.*
girl Australia 3INAN-GL return=GIVEN walk REDUP~good
'May you have a good trip back to Australia.' [Bk-14.009]

In the examples seen thus far *a-ta* '3INAN-GL' has denoted the goal of an S in a motion event. *A-ta* '3INAN-GL' is optionally used with bivalent predicates to denote a person or thing towards which the P is directed, as in (76) and (77).

(76) *Jepang gene Amerika* **Hiroshima**=*o* **Nagasaki**
Japan LOC America Hiroshima=AND Nagasaki
a-ta *bom g-ileqen.*
3INAN-GL bomb 3AN-drop
'In Japan, America dropped the bomb onto Hiroshima and Nagasaki.'
[Bk-29.011]

(77) Eli   hiloq   bare   zal,   **gi-ta**   **uku**.
    2DU   coconut.oil   PROX.INAN   carry   3INAN-GL   tip
    'You two take this coconut oil, (and) pour (it) on him.'   [Bk-4.071]

In the previous examples, the goal NP encoded by *a-ta* '3INAN-GL' is entirely optional: it is not required by any of the verbs at all. There is, however, a special collocation of the verbal postposition *a-ta* '3INAN-GL' and the verb *sai* 'exit' that has the lexicalised meaning 'find, come across'. This lexicalisation can be seen in that the collocation may be used in contexts where there is no "exiting" or even physical motion involved. In (78) two women search for their husband and "exit to him" already dead. In (79) a man lost in the forest suddenly "exits to the path", i.e., comes across the path he was looking for. In (80) the entity which is "exited to" is not a physical location but the abstract concept of "badness".

(78) Halali   **gi-ta**   **sai**   roe=bu,   heser   haqal   oa.
     3DU   3AN-GL   exit   SPEC.INAN=GIVEN   dead   finished   IAM
     'When they found him this time, he was already dead.'   [Bk-4.068]

(79) Tebe   hik   h-azal,   tebe   **hik**   **a-ta**   **sai**.
     return   path   3INAN-see   return   path   3INAN-GL   exit
     'He saw the path again, he found the path again.'   [Bk-23.58]

(80) I   en   g-ege   late   h-oqon=bu,   i=o
     1PL.INCL   person   3AN-BEN   bad   3INAN-do=GIVEN   1PL.INCL=AND
     late   **a-ta**   **sai**.
     bad   3INAN-GL   exit
     'If we do evil to others, we too come across (i.e., meet with) evil.'   [Bk-4.097]

12.4.3.2 Interest

A-ta '3INAN-GL' is used to encode NPs expressing a participant not directly involved in an action, but in whose interest or to whose advantage the action takes place.[2] This use of *a-ta* '3INAN-GL' is found with several different semantic class of verbs, including verbs of helping, managing, and praying, and is a metaphorical extension of the verbal postposition's goal-encoding use: the goal of a motion is the motion's endpoint and is the purpose for which the motion is undertaken, while a person in whose interest an action is performed can be construed as the purpose for which it is performed. See also §12.4.3.3 on the reason-encoding function of *a-ta* '3INAN-GL'.

---

[2] Kittilä (2005) calls this a "substitutive beneficiary". I reserve the term "beneficiary" for what Kittilä (2005) calls a "recipient-beneficiary". See §12.4.6.1.

In (81) *a-ta* '3INAN-GL' is combined with the monovalent verb *tulun* 'help' and expresses the party to whom assistance is given. In (82) *a-ta* '3INAN-GL' introduces *meaq gol* 'child', the person for whose sake the praying is undertaken. Similarly, in (83) *gi-ta* '3AN-GL' is used with verbs of speaking to denote the person on whose behalf the speaking was done, contrasting with *h-ege* '3INAN-BEN' which encodes the addressee of the speaking (see §12.4.6.2).

(81) Nie   eme=o   ama   gi-ta   tulun.
     1EXCL.POSS mother=AND father 3AN-GL help
     '(I) helped my parents.'   [Bk-13.012]

(82) Nei   meaq gol   gi-ta   timon.
     1PL.EXCL child   3AN-GL   pray.to.ancestors
     'We pray to the ancestors for the sake of the children.'   [Not-07.01]

(83) Hiro   halaqi g-ege   ni-ta   sasi.
     Hiro   3PL   3AN-BEN   1EXCL-GL speak
     'Hiro speaks to them on my behalf', i.e., 'Hiro defends me to them.'
                                                                                   [Not-06.01]

12.4.3.3 Motive

As the endpoint of a motion or action, a goal can also be interpreted as the grounds on which the action is undertaken, that is, the motive for the action. Accordingly, *a-ta* '3INAN-GL' can introduce an NP expressing a motive for the event expressed in the clause. Example (84) illustrates *a-ta* encoding an inanimate motive, and (85) illustrates the encoding of an animate motive.

(84) **Atis=o**   **liqul**   **ba**   **a-ta**=na   en
     loom.bar=AND backstrap ART.INAN 3INAN-GL=FOC person
     nei   n-ue.
     1PL.EXCL 1EXCL-hit
     'It is only because of the loom parts that the people hit us.'   [LB-1.056]

(85) Sael   senti atus uen   sok gonciet=na i   i-ta
     pig   cm   100   one   10s   five=FOC   1PL.INCL 1INCL/2-GL
     gi-a,   en   dato   mil.
     3AN-eat person noble COLL
     '(They) eat a pig (which is) 150cm (long) because of us, the nobles (do).'
                                                                                         [Bk-38.027]

Like *gie* 'BECAUSE' (§12.3), motive-marking *a-ta* can be used in sentence connective constructions with demonstratives (§15.4.2). Following a final-intonation contour, *a-ta* introduces an anaphoric demonstrative which refers back to the preceding proposition, and indicates that the event described in the first sentence is the reason for that in the second sentence, as in (86).

(86) a. *Halaqi   nie   atis=o   liqul   ba*
       3PL   1EXCL.POSS   loom.bar=AND   backstrap   ART.INAN
       h-ini   die=na   baqa   oa.
       3INAN-call   REFL.POSS=FOC   NPRX.INAN   IAM.
       'They say my loom parts are theirs, that's what.'   [LB-1.059]
   b. ***Baqa***   ***a-ta,***   *eli   Ø-oqon   loi.*
       NPRX.INAN   3INAN-GL   2DU   1INCL/2-do   good
       'Because of that, (they) can do (i.e., bash) you two.'   [LB-1.060]

12.4.4 *g-o* '3-SRC'

The verbal postposition *g-o* '3-SRC' cannot occur as an independent, clause-final verb, but it inflects like a Class III verb (§10.2.3), and, again like a verb, can have its complement omitted; see (87) and (88). The 3rd person ANIMATE inflection is used for 3rd person complements of both ANIMATE and INANIMATE class (hence the gloss '3').

G-o '3-SRC' functions to introduce NPs identified with the semantic role 'SOURCE', including: human sources (§12.4.4.1), points of relation/comparison (§12.4.4.2); maleficiaries (§12.4.4.3), and the addressees of verbs of questioning and answering (§12.4.4.4).

12.4.4.1 Human source

The verbal postposition *g-o* '3-SRC' most frequently introduces an NP denoting a human source. With bivalent verbs, *g-o* '3-SRC' marks a human referent from whom the P is taken, as in (87) and (88).

(87) *Baqi   il   ho,   gie   eme   h-ini   sikot,   **g-o***
     NPRX.AN   water   scoop   3.POSS   mother   3INAN-call   muddy   3-SRC
     uku   on.
     tip.out   DO
     '(When) he hauled water, his mother said (it) was muddy, took (it) from him, (and) tipped it out.'   [Bk-6.003]

(88) *Tais=na   en   aibaqa   olu   baqa   **g-o**   tebe*
     cloth=FOC   person   bride.giver   remove   NPRX.INAN   3-SRC   return
     wit   niq   oa.
     take   NEG   IAM
     'The weaving which the bride-giver removed can no longer be taken back from them.'   [Bk-18.041]

With verbs of motion, *g-o* '3-SRC' encodes the human referent away from whom the motion takes place, as in (89) and (90). Inanimate locations from which a motion takes place are encoded with preverbal postpositional phrases, see §13.9.1.

(89) Ari, **Loqu g-o** he on, Ø-ue=bu.
 Ari Loqu 3-SRC run DO 1INCL/2-hit=GIVEN
 'Ari, run away from Loqu, if (he) is hitting you.' [Bk-22.009]

(90) Nis ba dele he saqe loi niq, tebe **g-o** topol.
 mortar ART.INAN INS run ascend good NEG return 3-SRC fall
 '(She) couldn't run up with the mortar, (as it) fell back down from her.' [LB-3.005]

The normally bivalent motion verb *zal* 'carry' has a special lexicalised P-less use with *g-o* '3-SRC' to denote 'win over, defeat'. In (91), we see *g-o* '3-SRC' is used with the bivalent verb *zal* 'carry' to mark a human referent from whom the P, *hoto* 'fire', is taken. In (92), however, there is no P argument with *zal* 'carry'; the verb is used intransitively and *g-o* '3-SRC' denotes a defeated participant. The collocation of *g-o* and *zal* to mean 'win over, defeat' appears to have developed from bivalent *zal* 'carry' by means of a semantic extension whereby a person who is defeated is seen to suffer a loss in the same way as a person from whom an item is taken.

(91) Naqi **Lakabiruk g-o**=na hoto zal.
 royal Lakabiruk 3-SRC=FOC fire carry
 'The princess continued on up, carrying the fire away from Lakabiruk.' [LB-10.041]

(92) Hot **bel g-o** zal.
 sun wind 3-SRC carry
 'The sun defeated the wind.' [Bk-16.008]

12.4.4.2 Point of relation/comparison

The verbal postposition *g-o* '3-SRC' is also used to introduce a point in relation to which the A/S participant is located. This point may be physical or metaphorical: in (93) the rain is close in physical location to the speaker expressed by *n-o* '1EXCL-SRC'; in (94) the speaker's father is identified as being lower in social position in relation to the *dato* 'noble' marked by *g-o* '3-SRC'.

(93) Inel man oa, **n-o** reqin oa.
 rain come IAM 1EXCL-SRC close IAM
 'The rain was coming already, (it) was already close to me.' [Bk-13.021]

(94) Nie   bapaq gie   reu   roe   en   halaqi g-o
     1EXCL.POSS father 3.POSS   house   SPEC.INAN person   3PL   3-SRC
     zigi   no,   reu   dato.
     underneath OBL   house   noble
     'My father's house is beneath those people, (the people from) the noble houses.'
                                                                    [Bk-29.062]

A point of relation can also have a semantically inanimate referent. In (95), *g-o* '3-SRC' is marked as reciprocal and denotes that the gaming stones denoted by the ANIMATE class noun *bon* 'gaming stone' are located at a distance relative to one another. In (96) the town Maliana encoded by *g-o* '3-SRC' is the point relative to which the S, *tas* 'village', is located.

(95) **Bon**   *himo*   **t-o**   *ate*.
     box.bean   CONTR.AN   RECP-SRC   far
     'Those *bon* (gaming stones) are (spaced) far apart from one another.'
                                                                    [Bk-10.026]

(96) Kalo   i   Maliana   mal   gie   baqa,   nie
     if   1PL.INCL   Maliana   go   3.POSS   NPRX.INAN   1EXCL.POSS
     tas   **Maliana** **g-o**   reqin.
     village   Maliana   3-SRC   close
     'If you want to go to Maliana, my village is close to Maliana.'   [Bk-7.008]

In addition to marking points relative to one another, the verbal postposition *g-o* '3-SRC' is used in comparative constructions with the adverbs *lesin* 'more' and *kuran* 'less' (§14.3.1.3) to introduce a standard of comparison, as in (97) and (98).

(97) Hot   **bel**   **g-o**   solat   lesin.
     sun   wind   3-SRC   strong   more
     'The sun was stronger than the wind.'
                                                                    [Bk-16.008]

(98) Mila   bari   die   tais   h-ini   **n-o**   lesin
     slave   PROX.AN   REFL.POSS   cloth   3INAN-CAUS   1EXCL-SRC   more
     on   oa.
     DO   IAM
     'This slave has already produced more cloth than me.'
                                                                    [LB-6.042]

12.4.4.3 Maleficiary

The verbal postposition *g-o* '3-SRC' is also used to denote a variety of relations subsumed here under the label 'maleficiary'. In uses of this kind, *g-o* '3-SRC' denotes a referent against/counter to whom or to whose disadvantage an event takes place.

In (99) *g-o* '3-SRC' encodes that what is said is contrary to what is said by its referent. In (100) *n-o* '1EXCL-SRC' denotes that the death happens contrary to the efforts of the speaker, while in (101) *g-o* '3-SRC' encodes that the death deprived a family of their youngest sibling.

(99) Il   ho   man,   **g-o**   h-ini   sikot.
     water   scoop   come   3-SRC   3INAN-call   muddy
     '(He) came back from fetching water, (and his mother) called (it) muddy contrary to him (i.e., he said the water was not muddy).' [Bk-72.009]

(100) Baqi   **n-o**   heser.
      NPRX.AN   1EXCL-SRC   dead
      'He died on me.', i.e., 'He died and I was deprived of him.' [OS-09.01]

(101) Malaysia   gene,   **mete**   gie   kaqa   tuen~tuen   uen
      Malaysia   LOC   NOW   3.POSS   older.brother   several   one
      g-o   oto=na   g-eze   heser.
      3-SRC   car=FOC   3AN-crush   dead
      'In Malaysia, a car crushed him dead, depriving his several older brothers (of him).' [Bk-46.046]

Malefactive *g-o* '3-SRC' occurs in a lexicalised combination with the monovalent verb *de* 'right, accurate' to denote adverse bearing against a participant. In (102) and (103) the inanimate S argument of *de* 'right, accurate' has a negative impact on the referent of the NP complement of *g-o* '3-SRC'. Note that in (103) the NP complement of *g-o* '3-SRC' is fronted. See §4.7.2.3 on the effects of animacy on the word order of non-agentive clauses like these.

(102) Le   gol   uen   man,   **halaqi**   **g-o**   re.
      light   little   one   come   3PL   3-SRC   strike
      'A little light came, (and the light) struck them (i.e., some light fell on them).' [Bk-47.107-108]

(103) **Eme=o**   ama   bi   memel   **g-o**   re.
      mother=AND   father   ART.AN   sick   3-SRC   strike
      'Sickness struck the mother and father down.' [LB-7.004]

12.4.4.4 Addressee

The verbal postposition *g-o* '3-SRC' is used with verbs of asking and questioning to introduce an addressee, as in (104) and (105). Compare this encoding of addressee NPs with that of verbs of speaking in §12.4.6.2 with *h-ege* '3INAN-BEN'.

(104) **Hot esen g-o**=na   tulun   sura!
       God   3-SRC=FOC help   ask
       'Ask God for help!'   [Bk-61.022]

(105) Halali **g-o**   toquk.
       3DU   3-SRC   question
       'The two of them questioned him.'   [LB-3.042]

In addition, the normally Class IV bivalent verb *h-osok* '3INAN-receive' has a special P-less use with *g-o* '3-SRC' to denote the speech act 'respond'. In (106), we see *g-o* '3-SRC' is used with bivalent *h-osok* '3INAN-receive' to mark a human referent from whom the P, *bai a* 'food', is taken. In (107) *h-osok* '3INAN-receive' does not have a P and denotes 'respond', with *g-o* '3-SRC' encoding the party to whom the speaker responds. The collocation of *g-o* and *h-osok* to mean 'respond to' appears to have developed from bivalent *h-osok* 'receive' by means of a semantic extension whereby the person who is responded to is seen as the origin or source of the speech event. In its use to mean 'respond', the 3rd person inanimate prefix of *hosok* will not be segmented, but will be glossed 'respond' as a whole.

(106) Pengungsi **suster g-o**   bai   a   h-osok.
       refugee   nun   3-SRC thing eat   3INAN-recieve
       'The refugees received food from the sisters.'   [Not-07.02]

(107) I   en   g-ini   puan,   en   i
       1PL.INCL person 3AN-CAUS   cannibal person 1PL.INCL
       Ø-o   hosok   niq.
       1INCL/2-SRC   respond   NEG
       '(If) we call someone a cannibal, the person is not going to respond to us.'
                                                              [Bk-39.015]

12.4.5 *h-otol* '3INAN-WITHOUT'

The verbal postposition *h-otol* '3INAN-WITHOUT' does not occur as an independent, clause-final verb, but inflects like a Class IV h-conjugation verb (§10.2.4.1), and, like a verb, can have its complement omitted; see (108) and (109). *H-otol* functions to introduce NPs into the clause whose referents are excluded or removed from the event denoted in the clause.

Examples (108) and (109) come from procedural texts in which *h-otol* denotes an item that is left aside while another action is performed. In (110) the reflexive-marked *h-otol* denotes that the A "removes himself" from the P, *sabul* 'orange', by placing the oranges on the ground.

(108) *I* **g-otol** *il dara.*
1PL.INCL 3AN-WITHOUT water prepare
'We prepare the water without (adding the maize).' [Bk-44.021]

(109) *Tuban uen kaeq,* **h-otol** *hoto toqa.*
basket.type one full 3INAN-WITHOUT fire light
'(When) one basket is full (of flour), (we) leaving (the flour) aside light a fire.'
[Bk-76.027]

(110) *Baqi* **r-otol** *sabul hiloqon bi tais*
NPRX.AN REFL-WITHOUT orange two ART.AN cloth
lequ wa no gu-tula.
wrapped top OBL 3AN-put.on
'He, absenting himself, puts the two oranges on top of a wrapped cloth.'
[Bk-4.048]

H-otol can also introduce an NP whose referent was not aware of the occurrence of the event denoted in the clause. In (111) *h-otol* refers to the speaker being still asleep when her guest got up. Example (112) refers to the S returning to take over land belonging to Lusin, the person he has secretly left behind in the highlands.

(111) *Baqi* **n-otol** *mel.*
NPRX.AN 1EXCL-WITHOUT wake
'She got up without me (i.e., without my knowing/being aware).' [Bk-29.009]

(112) *Tebe* **Lusin g-otol** *rebel.*
return Lusin 3AN-WITHOUT descend
'(He) went back down without Lusin (knowing/being aware of her descent).'
[Bk-67.229]

H-otol is particularly common with monovalent verbs of anger where it denotes the individual with whom the S is angry, as in (113) and (114). The use of *h-otol* in these examples carries the implication that the anger is unexpressed and unknown to the referent, in contrast to examples such as (124), in §12.4.6.2 below, with *h-ege*

'3INAN-BEN', which introduces an entity which is the recipient of active verbal expressions of anger.

(113) Asa Paran **rie**   *kauq*   *g-otol*   hirus.
      Asa Paran REFL.POSS   younger.sibling   3AN-WITHOUT   furious
      'Asa Paran was furious with his younger sibling.' [Bk-4.094]

(114) En   mete   Belanda   g-ua   gene   g-ua   gene
      person   NOW   Dutch   3AN-footprint   LOC   3AN-footprint   LOC
      himo   **nei**   *nie*   matas mil   *g-otol*   na.
      CONTR.AN   1PL.EXCL   1EXCL.POSS   old   LOC   3AN-WITHOUT   angry
      'Those people who had been adherents of the Dutch were angry at our parents.' [Bk-29.009]

12.4.6 *h-ege* '3INAN-BEN'

The verbal postposition *h-ege* '3INAN-BEN(IFICIARY)' originates in the trivalent verb *h-ege* '3INAN-give' (§10.4.1) and maintains the Class IV h-conjugation inflectional pattern of the verb. The verbal postposition differs from the verb in that, whilst the verb always occurs with three participants, the verbal postposition can occur in a clause where there are fewer than three, i.e., with reduced valency; see below for illustration. The verbal postposition *h-ege* '3INAN-BEN' is also semantically bleached, showing conventionalisation of meaning in combination with verbs of particular semantic classes, and functions to encode: beneficiaries in bivalent and monovalent verbal clauses (§12.4.6.1); addressees with verbs of speaking (§12.4.6.2); and the themes of cognitive events (§12.4.6.3).

12.4.6.1 Beneficiary

H-ege is most frequently used to introduce an NP denoting a beneficiary, the person for whose benefit an action is carried out. In (115) and (116), the participants introduced by *h-ege* are not only the beneficiaries of the acts described, but also the intended recipients of the P of the bivalent verb.

(115) Nie   eme   **halaqi**   **g-ege**   sabi   g-iqil
      1EXCL.POSS   mother   3PL   3AN-BEN   key   3AN-leave.behind
      g-oenik.
      3AN-forget
      'My mother forgot to leave the key behind for them.' [OS-06.01]

(116) Sabul   bolu   hiloqon   bi   **g-ege**   g-iwal.
      orange   ball   two   ART.AN   3AN-BEN   3AN-pick
      '(He) picked the two round oranges for (them).'   [Bk-4.042]

Benefactive *h-ege* is also used in situations where no actual transfer of an item is implied. This is seen in (117) and (118) where no physical transfer of the P arguments of the clausal bivalent verbs can be seen to take place to the participant encoded by *h-ege*.

(117) Cio=na   **nei**   **n-ege**   tazuq   ul   gie   taq?
      who=FOC   1PL.EXCL   1EXCL-BEN   door   pull PROSP   CONT
      'Who is going to pull the door for us?'   [LB-1.088]

(118) Sejara   baqi   **n-ege**   g-apal   coba!
      history NPRX.AN   1EXCL-BEN   3AN-open   try
      'Try (and) open (i.e., reveal) that history for me!'   [Bk-67.146]

Similarly, in (119) and (120) *h-ege* cannot be regarded as encoding a recipient as the clausal verb in each is monovalent, with no possible P to transfer.

(119) Naqi   pana,   **n-ege**   debel   gie.
      royal   female   1EXCL-BEN   descend   PROSP
      'Princess, come down to me!'   [LB-10.013]

(120) Tapi   neto   ene   le   sirubisu,   **Timor Timur**   bare
      but   1SG   night day   work   East Timor   PROX.INAN
      h-ege.
      3INAN-BEN
      'But I worked night and day, for East Timor here.'   [Bk-2.003]

12.4.6.2 Addressee

H-ege is also used with verbs of speaking to encode an addressee, the person to whom speech is transferred. Examples (121) to (123) illustrate this usage with three different verbs of speaking.

(121) En   kepala desa   **nei**   **n-ege**   seq.
      person   head.village   1PL.EXCL   1EXCL-BEN   call
      'The village head called to us.'   [Bk-1.032]

(122) Mete   paq Donatus   bi=na   **ibu**   **g-ege**   rale.
      NOW   Mr.Donatus   ART.AN=FOC   lady   3AN-BEN   tell
      'It was Mr Donatus (mentioned just) now that told (it) to the lady.'   [Bk-70.101]

(123) Neli   **t-ege**   sasi, ...
      1DU.EXCL RECP-BEN say
      'We said to each other, ...'   [Bk-37.038]

We saw in §12.2.3.3 that, together with *goet* 'LIKE', *h-ege* can be used without a verb of speaking to denote the addressee of a speech event. Indeed, *h-ege* can be used to encode the addressee of verbal events of many different types which do not necessarily involve speaking. For instance, in (124) we see that the monovalent verb *na* 'angry' is used together with *h-ege* '3INAN-BEN' to denote a speaking event in which the participant introduced by *h-ege* '3INAN-BEN' received angry words (cf. §12.4.5, examples 113 and 114).

(124) Neneq   Eta roi   **Ela** **g-ege**   na.
      grandmother Eta SPEC.AN Ela   3AN-BEN   angry
      'Grandmother Eta was angry at Ela (i.e., spoke angrily to Ela).'   [Bk-30.051]

12.4.6.3 Theme of a cognitive event

The use of *h-ege* to encode the addressee of a verbal event is extended to include the theme of cognitive events: in the same way that an addressee is the entity to which words are directed, a cognitive theme is the entity to which thought is directed. In (125) and (126) the predicates are verbal, while in (127) the predicate is the reflexive-marked locational noun *mil* 'inside' which is frequently used predicatively to denote cognition (see §11.3.2.3 on this predicate).

(125) Nei   huqe gene **baqa**   **h-ege**   piar.
      1PL.EXCL HERE LOC   NPRX.INAN 3INAN-BEN   believe
      'We here believe in that.'   [Bk-8.038]

(126) Neto **keluarga** **g-ege**   hanoin.
      1SG   family   3AN-BEN   think
      'I was thinking of my family.'   [Bk-2.020]

(127) Nei   reu   Gewal gene **Nona** **g-ege**   ri-mil   los.
      1PL.EXCL house Gewal LOC   girl   3AN-BEN   REFL-inside   very
      'We (at) home in Gewal think a lot about Nona.'   [Bk-14.001]

A theme of the verb *piar* 'believe' can also be encoded with *g-o* '3-SRC' (128), in contrast to *h-ege* in (125). Used with *g-o* '3-SRC', *piar* 'believe' is seen to originate or stem from the referent of the NP introduced by *g-o* '3-SRC'. By contrast, with *h-ege*, *piar* 'believe' is construed as being given from the S to the referent of the NP introduced by *h-ege*.

(128) Berek=o   Mauk   **g-o**   piar   niq.
      Berek AND Mauk   3-SRC   believe   NEG
      'Berek and Mauk didn't believe him.'   [LB-2.054]

12.4.7 *h-os* '3INAN-WAIT'

The verbal postposition *h-os* '3INAN-WAIT' is related to the independent Class VI h-conjugation bivalent verb *h-os*, meaning 'wait for'. The waiter is coded as A, while the awaited is realised as P with verbal co-indexing, as in:

(129) Manek luron no   **n-os**   oa.
      Manek road   OBL   1EXCL-wait   IAM
      'Manek is already waiting for me in the road'   [OS-07.01]

The verbal postposition *h-os* has a semantically more general meaning than the verb of the same form. It functions to introduce an NP into the clause in whose absence the event denoted in the clause takes place, as illustrated in (130) and (131).

(130) Meaq gol bari   kesi,   mone mesaq=bu, **n-os**
      child   PROX.AN   give.birth   male if=GIVEN   1EXCL-WAIT
      g-ebeqen, ...
      3AN-kill
      'If this child (which you) give birth to is a boy, kill him before I get back, ...'
                                                                      [LB-8.005]

(131) Mon   pir=bu   gie   eme=o   ama   **g-os**
      afternoon   reach=GIVEN   3.POSS   mother=AND   father   3AN-WAIT
      hobel   oa.
      not.exist   IAM
      'When afternoon arrived, their mother and father had left in their absence.'
                                                                      [LB-2.036]

In (132) and (133), the events of "going" happen not so much in the absence of the participant denoted by *h-os*, but simply without them. The use of *h-os* '3INAN-WAIT' in these examples implies that the participant left behind is aware of being excluded. This differs from "excluded" participants encoded by *h-otol* '3INAN-WITHOUT', as seen in §12.4.5, in that they are not typically aware of their exclusion.

(132) **Ø-os**   mal!
      1INCL/2-WAIT   go
      'We're going without you!'   [OS-07.01]

(133) Neto   nona   **g-os**   mal   tut.
       1SG   miss   3AN-WAIT   go   first
       'I'll go on ahead without miss.'   [OS-07.01]

12.4.8 *h-onogo* '3INAN-SEPARATE'

The verbal postposition *h-onogo* '3INAN-SEPARATE' does not appear as an independent, clause-final verb in the corpus.[3] However, it inflects in the manner of a Class IV h-conjugation verb (§10.2.4.1) and, again like a verb, can have its complement omitted.

H-onogo '3INAN-SEPARATE' has a similar, but less extensive, range of functions to *g-o* '3-SRC' and its use is much less frequent. In (134) we see *h-onogo* '3INAN-SEPARATE' used to denote the source of the P in a bivalent verbal clause. In (135) it denotes the source of an S in a monovalent verbal clause. In (136) *h-onogo* '3INAN-SEPARATE' introduces the standard of comparison in a comparative construction with *lesin* 'more'.

(134) **G-onogo**   alan   a-ta   wa.
       3AN-SEPARATE   border   3INAN-GL   discard
       '(She) took it from (him and) threw (it) to the side.'   [Bk-72.012]

(135) Mit   haqal,   tebe   **g-onogo**   rebel   teni.
       sit   finished   return   3AN-SEPARATE   descend   again
       'After living (there), (he) went back down again from (him).' [Bk-67.245]

(136) Nei   nie   reu   maten   legul,   hotel   **g-onogo**
       1PL.EXCL   1EXCL.POSS   house   roof   tall   tree   3AN-SEPARATE
       legul   lesin.
       tall   more
       'The roof of our house is tall, taller than the trees.'   [Bk-24.013]

There appears to be little difference between *h-onogo* '3INAN-SEPARATE' and *g-o* '3-SRC' (§12.4.4) in the above contexts and speakers allow either verbal postposition to be used. However, unlike *g-o* '3-SRC', *h-onogo* '3INAN-SEPARATE' is not used as a locational noun, or to encode maleficiaries or addressees.

---

3 Note that in elicitation some informants allowed *h-onogo* '3INAN-SEPARATE' to be used as an independent verb, while other informants did not permit an independent use. In the absence of textual attestation of its independent use, I choose here to regard *h-onogo* '3INAN-SEPARATE' only as a verbal postposition.

Chapter 13
Serial verb constructions

13.1 Introduction

Serial verb constructions (SVCs) are a prominent feature of Bunaq as in many languages of eastern Indonesia and New Guinea (cf. Crowley 2002; Senft 2008). An SVC comprises a sequence of two or more verbs acting together as a single predicate in a monoclausal structure to describe what is conceptualised as a single complex event (Aikhenvald 2006; Bisang 2009; Durie 1997; Foley and Olson 1985).

Verbs are serialised together in diverse ways to express a wide variety of complex events. Following an overview of the properties of SVCs (§13.2) and the syntactic types of SVCs (§13.3), I discuss the individual semantic types of SVCs in Bunaq. The different types function to:
(i) express causation (§13.4) and resultative (cause-effect) relations (§13.5);
(ii) encode adverbial information including manner (§13.6), intensity (§13.7), and aspect (§13.8); and,
(iii) describe complex events involving motion and direction (§13.9).

13.2 Properties of Bunaq SVCs

SVCs involve verbs that are full lexical verbs which can head simple predicates in their own right.[1] Whilst SVCs encompass significant constructional diversity (see §13.3), there are a range of formal properties which warrant their treatment as a unified phenomenon. The properties that are shared by Bunaq SVCs and that separate them from other grammatical phenomena are:

(i) SVCs describe a single event with a close connection between subparts
Evidence supporting the view that SVCs comprise a single "verbal unit" is seen in the fact that SVCs contrast in meaning with multiclausal coordinated structures. Compare the meaning of the SVC and the multiclausal construction in (1). We see that the SVC in (1a) describes a single complex event with a close connection between subparts: the second verb, *rebel* 'descend', describes the direction in which the event denoted by the first verb, *wa* 'discard' occurs. By contrast, in the multiclausal construction in (1b), *rebel* does not further describe the act of throwing; rather, it is a separate motion event which occurs subsequent to it.

---

[1] This criterion synchronically excludes the verbal postpositions examined in §12.4, even though they otherwise share many properties with verbs; see §3.6.1.

SVC
(1) a. *Markus bola wa rebel.*
    Markus ball discard descend
    'Markus threw the ball away downwards.'
MULTICLAUSAL
b. *Markus bola wa, rebel.*
   Markus ball discard descend
   'Markus threw the ball away, (and he went) downwards.'

(ii) SVCs have the same intonational properties as monoverbal clauses

SVCs exhibit the same intonational properties as monoverbal clauses. A clausal boundary is marked by falling pitch and an intonation break. An SVC involves only a single falling intonation over the last elements of the construction with no dividing prosodic mark of a clause boundary, as with the SVC in (2a). By contrast, we see in the multiclausal construction in (2b) that there is a break in intonation between the first verb and the second verb. The first verb has a non-final "continuing" intonation characterised by a rise in pitch, while the second verb is accompanied by a final falling intonation contour. See §15.3.1 for details of clause conjoining by juxtaposition.

SVC
(2) a.
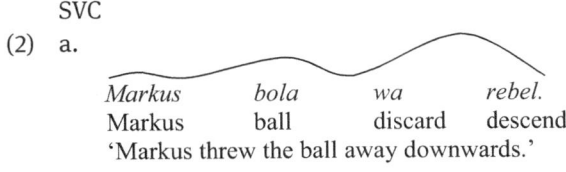
Markus bola wa rebel.
Markus ball discard descend
'Markus threw the ball away downwards.'

MULTICLAUSAL
b.

Markus bola wa, rebel.
Markus ball discard descend
'Markus threw the ball away, (and he went) downwards.'

(iii) SVCs have no intervening marker of subordination or coordination

SVCs have no intervening marker of subordination or coordination, and contrast in meaning with multiclausal structures which can include such markers. For instance, in (3) we see that the inclusion of the sequential clause conjoiner *soq* 'SEQ' changes the meaning of the SVC. Instead of the single purposive act of giving in the causative SVC (§13.4) in (3a), the multiclausal construction with *soq* 'SEQ' in (3b) denotes two separate acts: one of giving and one of drinking. What is more, whilst it is not possible to disrupt the iconic ordering of serialised elements in (3a), iconicity need not be observed in the multiclausal construction with *soq* 'SEQ', as in (3c). See §15.3.2 on Bunaq clause conjoiners.

SVC

(3) a. *Baqi   n-ege   il   a.*
       NPRX.AN   1EXCL-give   water   eat
       'He gave me water to drink.'

   MULTICLAUSAL

   b. *Baqi   n-ege   il   soq,   a.*
       NPRX.AN   1EXCL-give   water   SEQ   eat
       'He gave me water, then (I) drank (it).'

   MULTICLAUSAL

   c. *Neto   il   a,   n-ege   soq.*
       1SG   water   eat   1EXCL-give   SEQ
       'I drank the water, once (he) gave me (it).'

(iv) SVCs share scope for aspect and phasal polarity

Unlike multiclausal structures, the individual components of an SVC cannot independently select for aspect or phasal polarity. These markers must have scope over all verbs in an SVC. For example, we see that the prospective aspect marker, *gie* 'PROSP' (§14.3.3), can unproblematically follow the verbs in the causative SVC in (4a), but that it is ungrammatical for it to follow just the first verb in the SVC (4b). By contrast, in the complement clause constructions [bracketed] in (5), we see that independent aspect marking is permitted for both the matrix and complement clause. In (5a) the P-complement clause is independently marked with *gie* 'PROSP', while the main clause verb, *sura* 'ask', is followed by the continuative phasal polarity marker, *taq* 'CONT' (§14.3.5.1). Similarly, in (5b) we see that the complement-taking verb *heten* 'want' can have a complement independently marked with *gie* 'PROSP'.

(4) SVC

   a. *Baqi   n-ege   il   a   gie.*
       NPRX.AN   1EXCL-give   water   drink   PROSP
       'He is going to give me water to drink.'

   b. **Baqi   n-ege   gie   il   a.*
       NPRX.AN   1EXCL-give   PROSP   water   drink

   MULTICLAUSAL

(5) a. *Baqi   [teo   gene   neto   cier   gie   ba]   sura   taq.*
       NPRX.AN   where   LOC   1SG   sleep   PROSP   ART.INAN   ask   CONT
       'She is still asking [where am I going to sleep].'   [OS-06.01]

   b. *Baqi=o   [mal   gie]   heten.*
       NPRX.AN=AND   go   PROSP   want
       'She also wants [to walk].'   [Bk-37.023]

13.3 Syntactic types of SVCs in Bunaq

The different functional and semantic types of SVCs may be distinguished from one another according to the relationship that holds between the verbs in serialisation and between nominal arguments associated with each of the serialised verbs. There are three syntactic types of serialisation in Bunaq:

(i) **core serialisation**: core serialised verbs form independent phrasal units. This is seen in the fact that independent constituents, such as NPs, PP, or VpPs, can occur between the V_1 and V_2, thus: NP (NP) V_1 (NP. . .) V_2. Verbs in core serialisation share a single argument, either S/A (i.e., "subject"-sharing) or a non-S/A (i.e., non-"subject"-sharing), and occur within the scope of a single negator.

(ii) **nuclear serialisation**:[2] nuclear serialised verbs occur in a single phrase together. That is, the serialised verbs form a contiguous unit between which no constituents can intervene, thus: NP (NP. . .) V_1V_2. Verbs in nuclear serialisation share their S/A argument and occur in the scope of a negator.

(iii) **ambient serialisation**:[3] ambient serialised verbs do not share an argument; rather, V_2 describes a general predication, providing adverbial information about V_1 and the clause as a whole. A V_2 in ambient serialisation is distinguishable from a V_2 in nuclear and core serialisation in that it is possible for the negator, *niq* 'NEG',[4] either to intervene between V_1 and V_2 or to follow V_1 and V_2 with each order entailing differences within scope of the negation (discussed and illustrated in §4.5.1).

Table 13.1 presents an overview of the different properties dividing core, nuclear, and ambient serialisation from one another, and of how different semantic types of SVCs map onto them. We see that some semantic types of serialisation are split up across different syntactic types. For instance, SVCs expressing manner are core SVCs when they encode "participant-oriented" manner, and ambient SVCs when they encode "event-oriented" manner. These two different manner SVCs are discussed together in §13.6 so as to highlight their semantic differences. Similarly, complex motion events are encoded with different serialisation types depending on the component of the motion being expressed. The different types very frequently combine and are discussed together in §13.9.

---

[2] The "core" versus "nuclear" serialisation distinction originates in Foley and Van Valin (1984: chapters 4–5) and Foley and Olson (1985). It corresponds closely to the distinction between "non-contiguous" and "contiguous" serial verbs made by Durie (1997) and later by Aikhenvald (2006).

[3] The term "ambient serialisation" was developed by Crowley (2002: 41–42), after Chafe (1970: 101–102), in reference to serial verbs which do not refer to any participant in the clause, but rather function adverbially. The idea of argument sharing being a necessary criterion for verbs in serialisation has been the subject of some debate. See Baker (1989), and criticism by Durie (1997).

[4] Whilst all serialised verbs must share the scope of aspectual and phasal polarity markers, it is only verbs in nuclear and core serialisation that must share the scope of the negator. That ambient serial verbs do not have to share the scope of the negator is a typologically unusual property.

Table 13.1: Characteristics of different syntactic types of serialisation.

	Argument sharing		Intervening NP/PP/VpP	Negative sharing	See:
	S/A- sharing	Non-S/A- sharing			
Core					
Causative SVC	+	−	+	+	§13.4
Resultative SVC	−	+	+	+	§13.5
Participant-oriented manner SVC	+	−	+	+	§13.6.1
Origin-Motion-Goal SVC	+	−	+	+	§13.9.1
Reversive motion SVC	+	−	+	+	§13.9.2
Nuclear					
Directional SVC	+	−	−	+	§13.9.3
Ambient					
Event-oriented manner SVC	−	−	−	−	§13.6.2
Intensifying SVC	−	−	−	−	§13.7
Aspectual SVC	−	−	−	−	§13.8

13.4 Causative serialisation

Causative serialisation is a form of core serialisation expressing purposive causation in transfer events. The trivalent verb *h-ege* '3INAN-give' (§10.4) is the V_1 and combines with a bivalent V_2 which specifies the purpose of the transfer event. V_1 and V_2 share two arguments: the T of the V_1 is the P of the V_2, while the R of the V_1 is the A of the V_2. This construction is illustrated in the three examples below. In (6), the cakes are transferred for carrying, in (7) the water is transferred for drinking, while in (8) the land is transferred for use as gardens.

(6) G-otil   mone mal an   gene gie, **g-ege**   tubi
3AN-spouse male go   grass LOC   PROSP 3AN-give cake
baqa=na   zal.
NPRX.INAN=FOC carry
'When their husbands are to go hunting (lit., go into the grass), (wives) give them cakes to carry.' [Bk-76.042]

(7) Neto baqi **g-ege** il a.
    1SG NPRX.AN 3AN-give water eat
    'I gave him water to drink.' [OS-07.02]

(8) Muk bula, darau matas mil nie ama halaqi **g-ege**
    land pasture until old COLL 1EXCL.POSS father 3PL 3AN-give
    mar **h-one**.
    garden 3INAN-hold
    'The land was pasture, until the elders gave it to my father and his siblings to have as a garden.' [Bk-29.072]

In §13.2, we saw that the individual verbs in causative SVCs cannot independently select for aspect. This is also true for negation. We can negate a causative SVC, such as that in (7), with *niq* 'NEG' occurring clause-finally, as in (9a). It is not possible, however, for *niq* 'NEG' to occur between verbs of the causative SVC (9b), negating only one of the verbs of the SVC.

(9) a. Neto baqi g-ege il a **niq**.
       1SG NPRX.AN 3AN-give water eat NEG
       'I did not give him water to drink.'
    b. *Neto baqi g-ege **niq** il a.
       1SG NPRX.AN 3AN-give NEG water drink [Not-07.02]

Causative SVCs with *h-ege* '3INAN-give' are rare in the Bunaq corpus and are never found with monovalent verbs (see §10.4 on *h-ini* '3INAN-CAUS' for causatives with these verbs). Although mostly found in situations where a physical transfer takes place, causative serialisation with *h-ege* '3INAN-give' may, in fact, be a more general indirect causation construction in Bunaq. This is suggested by one example of causative serialisation with *h-ege* '3INAN-give' in my corpus where there is no actual transfer of the P of V₂. This example, presented in (10), has *h-ege* '3INAN-give' serialised with *h-azal* '3INAN-see'. If we were to substitute Ø-*ege* '1INCL/2-give' with the causative verb Ø-*ini* '1INCL/2-CAUS' in (10), this would denote that the causation is direct, that is, that the causee is made by the causer to look at the woman.

(10) Neto i bein Ø-ege d-ip g-azal oa.
     1SG 1PL.INCL lord 1INCL/2-give REFL-wife 3AN-see IAM
     'I now present a wife to your highness.' (lit., 'I give you your wife to see.')
     [KeleqMainuPintar-030]

That we are dealing in (10) with causative serialisation and not, for instance, benefactive serialisation (§12.4.6) is seen from the use of the reflexive possessive marking on the P of V₂, *d-ip* 'REFL-wife'. Normally, reflexive marking on a P or T argument is bound to an A argument (see §4.2.2 and §4.2.3). However, the context of the royal person seeking a wife makes it clear that in (10) the A, *neto* '1SG', is not the antecedent for the reflexive; that is, the speaker is not presenting his own wife to the royal for marriage. Rather, the referent of the R of *h-ege* '3INAN-give', the royal person, is the antecedent for the reflexive on the P of V₂. This binding of the reflexive can only be accounted for by seeing the construction as a case of causative serialisation, that is, a "switch subject" serialisation in which the R of the V₁ (*h-ege* '3INAN-give') is the A of the V₂ (*h-azal* '3INAN-see').

13.5 Resultative serialisation

Resultative serialisation is a form of core serialisation in which V₁ encodes a cause and V₂ the result of it. The V₁ is bivalent and agentive, while the V₂ is monovalent and stative. The P of the V₁ is the S of the V₂. In (11) *heser* 'dead' is an effect caused by the car on the child as the P. In (12) the *sore* 'machete' strikes the *gu-bul* '3AN-head' with the effect that it is *tol* 'broken'. See §13.8.1 on the third serial verb, *haqal*, in this example.

(11) *N-ol   uen   oto   **g-eze**   heser*.
    1EXCL-child one   car   3AN-crush   dead
    'One of my children was crushed dead by a car.'   [Bk-46.045]

(12) *Sore   rebel,   gu-bul   bere   **pak**   tol   haqal*.
    machete   descend   3AN-head   CONTEXP.INAN   strike   broken   finished
    'The machete descended (and) struck his head, splitting it completely.'
                                                                       [Bk-69.085]

That we are dealing with core serialisation here is seen in (13) where the series of V₁ *lai* 'set' and V₂ *ratu* 'stacked' is interrupted by the verbal postposition *t-o* 'RECP-SRC' (§12.4.4).

(13) *U   bilik   baqa   nei   **lai**   t-o*
    herbaceous.plant   bind   NPRX.INAN   1PL.EXCL   set   RECP-SRC
    ***ratu**   on*.
    stacked   DO
    'Those bales (of) undergrowth we set stacked against each other.'
                                                                       [Bk-12.006]

It is possible to negate a resultative SVC, such as that in (14), with final *niq* 'NEG' (14a), but the negator cannot occur between verbs of the SVC with only one of the verbs in its scope (14b).

(14) a. Nei   lai   t-o   ratu   **niq**.
        1PL.EXCL set RECP-SRC stacked NEG
        'We did not stack them against each other.'
    b. *Nei   lai   **niq**   t-o   ratu.
        1PL.EXCL set NEG   RECP-SRC stacked   [Not-07.02]

13.6 Manner serialisation

Manner serialisation involves a monovalent verb expressing the manner in which the event described by the main verb takes place. Two types of manner serialisation are distinguished:

(i) **participant-oriented manner serialisation** is a form of core serialisation in which the manner verb occurs as a monovalent V_1 between the S/A and the main verb/predication (V_2) and denotes a property of the S/A with respect to the performance of the event described by the main verb. Verbs in these SVCs share their S/A.

(ii) **event-oriented manner serialisation** is a form of ambient serialisation in which the manner verb is V_2 in the SVC and describes the manner of the performance of the event denoted by the V_1, rather than referring to any particular participant in the event.

The semantic contrast between participant- and event-oriented manner serialisation is illustrated in (15) using the monovalent verb *laun* 'quick'. In (15a) we have a participant-oriented manner SVC: *laun* 'quick' is V_1 and functions to denote quickness on the part of the agent in the act of eating, denoted by the V_2, *a* 'eat'. In (15b) we have an event-oriented manner SVC: *laun* 'quick' is V_2 and denotes that the act of eating happened quickly.

(15) a. Neto   **laun**   bai   *a*.
        1SG   quick   thing   eat
        'I am quick at eating.'
    b. Neto   bai   *a*   **laun**.
        1SG   thing   eat   quick
        'I eat quickly.'   [Not-07.01]

The participant-oriented and event-oriented manner SVCs are illustrated further in §13.6.1. and §13.6.2, respectively.

13.6.1 Participant-oriented manner serialisation

A participant-oriented manner serial verb refers to the S/A of the clause and the manner of its performance or experience of an action or state. The manner verb is monovalent and occurs between the S/A and the main verb, sharing its argument with the semantically main verb, which may be monovalent or bivalent.

In (16a) we see that the V₁ *omal* 'naked' refers to the condition in which the S undertook the V₂ *he* 'run'. By contrast, (16b) is semantically bizarre because nakedness cannot be understood as a property of running, but can be a property of a person who is in the act of running, as in (16a). Note that *omal* 'naked' is not a modifier within the NP denoting the S, since then it would have to appear to the left of the determiner, *baqi* 'NPRX.AN', which appears at the right periphery of the NP.

(16) a. *Baqi*   **omal**   *he.*
         NPRX.AN naked   run
         'She ran naked.'   [Bk-43.039]

     b. #*Baqi*   **he**   *omal.*
         NPRX.AN run   naked
         'She ran nakedly.'   [Not-07.01]

A verb that occurs frequently as a serial verb in participant-oriented manner serialisation is *det* 'alone'. In (17) we see that *det* 'alone' can appear as an independent clausal predicate. In serialisation *det* 'alone' occurs as V₁ and is used to indicate that the S/A participant is either unaccompanied (18) or unaided (19) in the context of the event denoted by the V₂.

(17) *Gie*   *ama*   **det**.
     3.POSS father   alone
     'His father was alone.'   [LB-5.166]

(18) *Neto* **ret**   *r-ege*   *die*   *iskola*   *gie*   **urus.**
     1SG   alone   REFL-BEN REFL.POSS school   3.POSS   arrange
     'I wanted to pay my own way through school by myself.' (lit., 'I alone was going to arrange my schooling for myself.')   [Bk-13.017]

(19) *Nego=na*   *sura,*   **det**   *hati.*
     what=FOC   ask   alone   exist
     'Whatever (they) asked for appeared by itself.'   [LB-5.041]

Another verb frequently occurring in participant-oriented manner SVCs is *han*, a verb denoting 'be no matter, of no import', illustrated in (20). In manner serialisation the meaning of *han* is paraphrasable as 'do nothing else but'. That is, it indicates that the participant does just that thing denoted by the semantically main predicate, as in (21) and (22). Notice in (21) that a PP intervenes between the manner V_1 *han* and the semantically main V_2 *lai*, as expected in core serialisation. See §13.8.2 on the third serial verb, *liol* 'continue', in (22).

(20) *Baqa*   ***han!***
    NPRX.AN   be.no.matter
    'It doesn't matter.'   [LB-4.035]

(21) *Oto   mil   no   **han**   kou   liol.*
    car   inside LOC   be.no.matter   faint   continue
    '(She) just kept fainting in the car.'   [Bk-43.010]

(22) *Hos   berelikuq   uen   **han**   nei   nie   ama*
    bird   bird.sp   one   be.no.matter   1PL.EXCL   1EXCL.POSS   father
    *g-awas   ni   **lai**.*
    3AN-forehead   OBL   set
    'The bird just goes landing on father's forehead.'   [LB-4.046]

As a form of non-contiguous serialisation, participant-oriented manner serial verbs must occur in the scope of a single final *niq* 'NEG', as in (23). It is ungrammatical for the negator to occur between verbs of the SVC.

(23) *Nei   det golaq   ta-tara   niq.*
    1PL.EXCL   all.alone   RECP-know   NEG
    'We didn't (get to) know each other all alone.'   [Bk-38.016]

13.6.2 Event-oriented manner serialisation

Event-oriented manner serialisation is a form of ambient serialisation used to describe the manner in which an action is performed. In event-oriented manner serialisation, there is no argument sharing between the semantically main V_1 and the manner adverbial V_2. The V_2 denotes the manner in which the event V_1 occurs. While V_2 is always monovalent, V_1 can be monovalent or bivalent.

Examples (24) and (25) illustrate event-oriented manner serialisation where the V_1 is monovalent. Examples (26) and (27) illustrate event-oriented manner serialisation where the V_1 is bivalent. There are no instances of event-oriented manner serialisation with trivalent verbs in the corpus. Recall from the discussion in §3.3.1 that there is no adjective class in Bunaq and that items such as *baqis* 'much' are monovalent verbs.

(24) *Meaq gol* **memel baqis**.
 child sick much
 'The child is really sick' [OS-07.01]

(25) **Leleq enoq~enoq**.
 flow REDUP~slow
 '(The water) runs really slowly.' [Bk-65.107]

(26) *Muk bare ei* **h-oqon koen**?
 land PROX.INAN 2PL 3INAN-do fine
 'Did you do (i.e., farm) this land well?' [Bk-29.070]

(27) *Sio* **g-azal milik**?
 who 3AN-see scared
 'Who (are you) afraid of?' (lit., 'Who (are you) seeing scaredly?') [OS-06.01]

In (28) and (29), we see the different placements of *niq* 'NEG' allowed in ambient serialisation. In (28) *niq* 'NEG' follows both V₁, here the nominal cognitive predicate *ri-mil* 'REFL-inside' (see §11.3.2.3), and V₂, *ate* 'far', and has scope over both. By contrast, in (29) *niq* 'NEG' intervenes between the V₁ *tara* 'know' and V₂ *masak* 'big'. The negator thus only has scope over the V₁, while the V₂ has both the negator and the V₁ in its scope.

(28) *Halali* **ri-mil ate** *niq*.
 3DU REFL-inside far NEG
 'They didn't think it through.' (lit., 'The two of them didn't think far.')
 [Bk-4.091]

(29) *Eto hilaq bai* **tara** *niq* **masak**=*o!*
 2SG surprisingly thing know NEG big=EXCLAM
 'Gosh, you know nothing!' (lit., 'Gosh, you don't know a thing greatly!')
 [OS-07.03]

13.7 Intensifying serialisation

Intensifying serialisation is ambient, with the intensifying V₂ providing general "adverbial" information about the preceding V₁. Several monovalent verbs can appear as a V₂ directly following a V₁ to express intensification. On non-verbal intensifiers in Bunaq, see §14.3.1.4.

The monovalent verb *tepel* 'true' is frequently used for the intensification of the meaning of V₁, which may be monovalent (30) or bivalent (31).

(30) Nie   koar   **tol**   **tepel**.⁵
     1EXCL.POSS neck   broken   true
     'My wrist was really broken.'   [Bk-67.216]

(31) Eto   n-ol   bari   **g-akara**   **tepel**, ...
     2SG   1EXCL-child   PROX.AN   3AN-love   true
     '(If) you really love this child of mine, ...'   [Bk-39.044]

The monovalent motion verb *liol* 'continue' also functions as an intensifier. In (32) and (33) it denotes that the state expressed by the preceding verb is "thoroughly" the case. Example (33) has double intensifiers, with *liol* 'continue' intensifying the preceding intensifying V, *tepel* 'true' (discussed above). See §13.8.2 on the use of *liol* 'continue' in aspectual serialisation. Context disambiguates whether the reading of *liol* 'continue' is intensifying or aspectual.

(32) Baqi   goet   bi=o   toek noq=bu   h-ini   **pisi**
     NPRX.AN   LIKE   ART.AN=AND   discussion=GIVEN   3INAN-CAUS   clean
     liol.
     continue
     '(Men) like that deal with everything in their discussions' (lit., 'The (men) like him also make the discussions completely clean').   [Bk-38.073]

(33) En   milik   **tepel**   **liol**.
     person   afraid   true   continue
     'The people were really, truly afraid.'   [Bk-66.012]

The monovalent verb *pisi* '(be) clean' is frequently used for intensification of the meaning of V₁ in the sense of 'thoroughly, completely', as in (34).

(34) Gie   g-ua~g-ua   ba   tara   **pisi**   oa.
     3.POSS   REDUP~3AN-footprint   ART.INAN   know   clean   IAM
     '(We) know the journeys of them thoroughly already.'   [Bk-65.076]

The monovalent verb *loi* 'good' is frequently used as a V₂ expressing intensification of the meaning of a non-agentive V₁, as in (35). Examples (36) and (37) illustrate the different placements of *niq* 'NEG' that are possible in intensifying serialisation. In (36), we see that *niq* 'NEG' follows both *loi* 'good' and the verb it intensifies, *buis*

---

5 For most Bunaq speakers I consulted, *koar* means 'neck'. As per the gloss here, 'forearm' was clearly the meaning of the speaker who showed me her visibly broken wrist/forearm as she recounted this story. For some speakers, *g-on koar* '3AN-hand/arm neck' or *g-on kalaq* 3AN-hand/arm', literally 'arm's neck', can be used for the forearm in place of *ge-ter* 3AN-hand 'forearm, branch'.

'vicious, brutal', while in (37) *niq* 'NEG' occurs between *loi* 'good' and the verb it intensifies, *iki* 'tiny'.

(35) *Nei   nie   sirubisu   koen   loi.*
     1PL.EXCL 1EXCL.POSS work   fine   good
     'Our work was very fine.'   [Bk-65.049]

(36) *Nei   nie   ama   bari   buis   loi   niq.*
     1PL.EXCL 1EXCL.POSS father   PROX.AN   vicious   good NEG
     'Our father is terribly vicious.' (lit., 'Our father here is not good vicious.')
                                                                           [LB-9.112]

(37) *Iki   niq   loi   oa.*
     tiny NEG good IAM
     'It was huge.' (lit., '(It) was already so not tiny.')   [Bk-71.048]

Intensifying *loi* 'good' differs from complement clause–taking *loi*, which expresses possibility and permission. See §15.2.1.2 for more on this other use of *loi*.

13.8 Aspectual serialisation

Serial verbs expressing aspect are ambient: they occur as V_2 after the semantically main verb of a clause, V_1, for which they express aspect; and they allow *niq* 'NEG' to intervene between V_1 and V_2. There are four serial verbs that are regularly used to denote aspect in Bunaq: *haqal* 'finished', denoting completive aspect (§13.8.1); *liol* 'continue' denoting continuous aspect (§13.8.2); *des* 'still', denoting frequentive aspect (§13.8.3); and *ciluq* 'stay', denoting persistent action (§13.8.4).

13.8.1 Serialisation with *haqal* 'finished'

The monovalent verb *h-aqal* '3INAN-finished' (§10.3.2) can be used as the sole verb in a clause. The agreement pattern of the verb is defective: 3rd person INANIMATE Ss are marked by *h-* '3INAN-' (38a), while ANIMATE Ss of all persons are marked by *g-* '3AN-' (38b) with an ANIMATE 3rd person (38c).

(38) a. *Pesta   h-aqal   oa.*
        festival   3INAN-finished   IAM
        'The festival was finished.'
     b. *Neto   g-aqal   oa.*
        1SG   3AN-finished   IAM
        'I was finished.', i.e., 'I was dead.'

c. *Zap g-aqal oa.*
   dog   3AN-finished   IAM
   'The dog was finished.', i.e., 'The dog was dead.' [Not-06.01]

In serialisation *haqal* 'finished' has three functions: (i) to indicate that the event specified by a non-stative verb is completed (§13.8.1.1); (ii) to indicate that the state is entered into completely (§13.8.1.2); or (iii) to act as a floating universal quantifier (§13.8.1.3). See Huber and Schapper (2014) for a discussion of the relationship between these uses. In its aspectual use, Bunaq *haqal* 'finished' will be glossed without segmentation.

13.8.1.1 Completed action

Haqal 'be finished' is used to indicate that an event denoted by a non-stative verb is finished. Completive *haqal* 'finished' can combine with monovalent verbs (39), bivalent verbs (40), and trivalent verbs (41). Notice in (41) that *oa* 'IAM' follows the SVC complex.

(39) *Pana mone ton haqal.*
     female   man   marry   finished
     'The woman (and) man have married.' [Bk-38.046]

(40) *En baqi g-olo haqal.*
     person   NPRX.AN   3AN-bury   finished
     'The person has been buried.' (lit., 'has finished being buried') [Bk-18.047]

(41) *Halaqi t-ege sal haqal oa.*
     3PL   RECP-give   bad   finished   IAM
     'They have stopped behaving badly to one another.' (lit., 'They have finished giving bad to each other.') [Bk-39.061]

In serialisation with motion verbs, *haqal* 'finished' indicates not that the motion event is finished but that it has begun. In (42) and (43), *haqal* 'finished' is serialised with the motion verbs *mal* 'go' and *liol* 'continue', respectively. In these examples, *haqal* 'finished' signals that the S participant has already departed; it says nothing about the completion of the event of going as a whole.

(42) *Gie moen himo ge-tekeq=bu, gie moen Atambua*
     3.POSS   friend   CONTR.AN   3AN-look.for=GIVEN   3.POSS   friend   Atambua
     roe mal haqal.
     SPEC.INAN   go   finished
     'When (we) went to look for that friend of his, his friend had gone (i.e., set off) to Atambua.' [Bk-37.108]

(43) Nona   Fulur a-ta   **liol**   **haqal.**
     miss   Fulur 3INAN-GL   continue   finished
     'Miss had continued on to Fulur.'   [Bk-63.007]

Haqal 'finished' is also used extensively to order events in clause conjoining. In (44) and (45), for example, *haqal* signals that the event in the following conjoined clause occurs after that in the initial clause with *haqal*. See §15.3.2.6 for more discussion and illustration of *haqal* in clause conjoining.

(44) Nei   iskola   **haqal,**   neto   botil   dele   Weluli   mal.
     1PL.EXCL   school   finished   1SG   bottle   INS   Weluli   go
     '(When) we finished school, I would go to Weluli with bottles.'   [Bk-63.007]

(45) H-ini   nigi   **haqal,**   tebe   pulas   rebel.
     3INAN-CAUS   fine   finished   return   twist   descend
     'After (the yarn) has been made fine, then twist it downwards.'   [Bk-64.017]

13.8.1.2 Complete state

In serialisation with verbs denoting a state, *haqal* 'finished' denotes not that the state is finished, but that it has been entered into completely (cf. Haspelmath 1995). In (46) the speaker questions the description of a person as having a bloody face, asking if it was completely bloody (*haqal* 'finished'). In (47), a bird shows some children its mouth, saying that it is completely (*haqal* 'finished') red (from the eating of flesh). In (48) the speaker's family say her hand is completely (*haqal* 'finished') broken, after she falls on her way home.

(46) G-ewen   **ho**   **haqal?**
     3AN-face   bloody   finished
     'Was her face completely bloody?'   [Bk-47.054]

(47) N-agar=sa   **buleqen**   **haqal.**
     1EXCL-mouth=EVEN   red   finished
     'My mouth is completely red.'   [Bk-49.028]

(48) N-on=o   bai   h-ini   **tol**   **haqal.**
     1EXCL-hand=AND   thing   3INAN-call   broken   finished
     '(They) said my hand or whatever was completely broken.'   [Bk-52.012]

In (49), the monovalent verb *boto* can be interpreted dynamically as 'disperse' or statively as 'dispersed'. Accordingly, in serialisation with *haqal* 'finished' it can have either the completed event or the complete state reading. A third reading is also possible: *haqal* 'finished' can be seen as a floated quantifier referring to 'all' the flames.

(49) Lili=sa   **boto**   **haqal**.
     flame=EVEN disperse   finished
     'The flames had finished dispersing'; or 'The flames had completely dispersed';
     or 'All the flames had dispersed.'   [Bk-43.006]

See §13.8.1.3 on the use of *haqal* 'finished' as a quantifier meaning 'all'.

13.8.1.3 "Complete" quantification

It was seen in §13.8.1.2 that in addition to indicating the temporal point at which an activity is completed, *haqal* 'finished' can also be used quantificationally to express that the event described by the verb is carried out completely. In this function, *haqal* does not specifically refer to any of the arguments of the predicate. However, *haqal* may also refer to an argument of the predicate, quantifying it universally. As a universal quantifier *haqal* is always floating; it never appears inside the NP that it quantifies, but rather remains in the post-V_1 position of the completive aspect verb.

The floating quantifier *haqal* can only refer to INANIMATE referents and is always ambiguous between its completive aspect, completive quantificational, and universal quantificational readings. For instance, in (50), *haqal* can be interpreted aspectually, or adverbially (i.e., meaning 'completely'), or as quantifying universally over the INANIMATE S, *zo* 'mango'. Note that in the first two readings the S may be interpreted as either singular or plural.

(50) Zo   baqa   za   **haqal**.
     mango   NPRX.INAN   ripe   finished
     'The mango(es) had finished ripening'; or 'The mango(es) were completely ripe';
     or 'All the mangoes were ripe.'   [Bk-1.016]

In contrast to its invariable form as an aspectual and adverbial modifier, as a floating universal quantifier, *haqal* inflects for the ANIMACY of the noun it refers to. The form *g-aqal* '3AN-finished' is used when the quantifier refers to non-singular NPs in the 1st (51a), 2nd (51b), or 3rd person ANIMATE (51c). In (51d), we see that *g-aqal* '3AN-finished' cannot be used with an NP headed by an INANIMATE noun. In serialisation, *g-aqal* '3AN-finished' can only be interpreted as a universal quantifier, and cannot denote completive aspect. For this, *haqal* 'finished' must be used, as in (51e).

(51) a. Nei   mal   *g-aqal*.
        1PL.EXCL   go   3AN-finished
        'We all went.'
     b. Ei   koleq   *g-aqal*.
        2PL   tired   3AN-finished
        'You are all tired.'

c. *Paqol   baqi   za   g-aqal.*
   maize   NPRX.AN   ripe   3AN-finished
   'All the maize was ripe.'

d. **Zo   baqa   za   g-aqal.*
   mango   NPRX.INAN ripe   3AN-finished
   'All the mangoes were ripe.'

e. *Paqol   baqi   za   haqal.*
   maize   NPRX.AN   ripe   finished
   'The maize has finished ripening.' [Not-06.01]

That we have agreement between a participant in the clause and the *haqal* as the V₂ suggests that we are no longer dealing with a case of ambient serialisation, but one of argument sharing where the S of *haqal* is held in common with the S/P/R of the V₁.[6] However, as with ambient serialisation, quantificational uses of *g-aqal* '3AN-finished' allow *niq* 'NEG' to either follow V₁ and V₂ (52) or intervene between V₁ and V₂ (53). As such, quantificational *g-aqal* '3AN-finished' is problematic to classify. Its mixed properties are perhaps a result of ongoing grammaticalisation from an SVC to a postverbal quantifier.

(52) *Sogo   baqi   **kou   g-aqal**   niq.*
     ten   NPRX.AN   slip   3AN-finished   NEG
     'Those ten didn't all slip.' [Bk-10.012]

(53) *Halaqi   sogo   baqi   **re**   niq   g-aqal.*
     3PL   ten   NPRX.AN   strike   NEG   3AN-finished
     'They didn't strike any of those ten.' [Bk-10.020]

13.8.2 Serialisation with *liol* 'continue'

Liol 'continue' is a motion verb meaning 'continue', as in (54). The verb is often repeated to denote iteration, as in (55).

(54) *Nei   liol   oa.*
     1PL.EXCL   continue   IAM
     'We continue (on moving) now.' [Bk-13.013]

---

[6] The floating quantifier is restricted to modifying the P of a bivalent clause, the R of a trivalent clause, the S of a monovalent verb, or the "subject" of a non-verbal clause. These restrictions are illustrated with *g-aqal* '3AN-finished' in §4.2, where, as elsewhere in this grammar, it is glossed as *gaqal* 'all.AN'.

(55) *Baqi   baqa   goet   liol   liol.*
     NPRX.AN NPRX.INAN LIKE   continue continue
     'He continued (moving) on and on like that.' [Bk-70.015]

In aspectual serialisation, *liol* 'continue' is used to denote continuous action (§13.8.2.1) and immediate action (§13.8.2.2). A third use in serialisation is as an intensifier; this was discussed in §13.7. See §4.5.1 for illustration of the different possibilities of combinations of the negator with *liol* 'continue', and thus demonstrating its status as an ambient serial verb.

13.8.2.1 Continuous action

Liol 'continue' can be used in serialisation to express a non-habitual event which is continued, prolonged, and maintained (Comrie 1985: 26). *Liol* 'continue' combines most commonly with verbs denoting motion events (56). However, it can be found in serialisation with verbs denoting all types of events with agents (57) and non-agents (58). See §13.6.1 on the meaning of *han* in this last example.

(56) *Meaq gol   hiloqon   **mele**   **liol**.*
     child   two   walk   continue
     'The two children continued to walk.' [LB1.020]

(57) *Neto   baqa=na   **h-oqon**   **liol**.*
     1SG   NPRX.INAN=FOC   3INAN-make   continue
     'It was these (terraces) that I continued to make.' [Bk-65.071]

(58) *Inel   debel,   han   muk   gene   **re**   **liol**.*
     rain   descend   be.no.matter   earth   LOC   strike   continue
     'The rain fell, just striking the earth continually.' [Bk-65.101]

Liol 'continue' can also serialise with verbs referring to states, in which case it denotes that the state is retained in place, condition, etc., as in (59) and (60).

(59) *Baqi   u   niq   oa,   baqi   **heser**   **liol**.*
     NPRX.AN   live   NEG   IAM   NPRX.AN   dead   continue
     'He didn't live anymore, he kept on being dead.' [Bk-4.093]

(60) *Muk   Timor-Leste   tekil   en   hobel,   muk   **nur**   **liol**.*
     land   East Timor   certainly   person   not.exist   land   empty   continue
     'The land (of) East Timor certainly had no people, the land continued to be empty.' [Bk-66.015]

As in its independent use, *liol* 'continue' can be repeated to indicate iteration when referring to an active event, as in (61) and (62).

(61) **Pese** *liol* *liol*, *baqa* *goet*.
squeeze continue continue NPRX.INAN LIKE
'Squeeze again and again, like that.' [Bk-64.014]

(62) *Nei* ***ge-lelu*** ***liol*** ***liol***.
1PL.EXCL 3AN-beat continue continue
'We keep beating and beating him.' [Bk-65.015]

13.8.2.2 Immediate action

Liol 'continue' can be used in serialisation to indicate that one event immediately follows another, denoted in a preceding conjoined clause. In (63) to (65), *liol* 'continue' signals that the event occurs immediately after the one denoted in the previous clause. Note in (65) that *liol* 'continue' is paired in the same clause with Indonesian *langsung* 'directly', emphasising the immediacy.

(63) *H-apal* *de,* *eli* ***tama*** ***liol***.
3INAN-open correct 2DU enter continue
'Open (the door) correctly, (and) you (will) enter immediately.' [LB2.143]

(64) *G-awas* *pak,* *baqi* ***rebel*** ***liol***.
3AN-forehead whack NPRX.AN descend continue
'(She) hit him on the head, (and) went on down immediately.' [Bk-43.75]

(65) *Ei* *g-azal,* *ei* *misti* *teqa,* ***langsung*** *teqa* ***liol***.
2PL 3AN-see 2PL must pray directly pray continue
'(When) you see them, you must pray, pray immediately.' [Bk-47.084]

13.8.3 Frequent action with *des* 'still'

The monovalent verb *des* [des ~ res] is an independent verb meaning '(be) still, unmoving, calm', as in (66).

(66) a. *Baqi* ***res***.
NPRX.AN still
'He was still.' [Bk-65.018]

b. *Baqi   lulai   niq   oa.*
   NPRX.AN move   NEG   IAM
   'He wasn't moving any longer.' [Bk-65.019]

As a V₂ in ambient serialisation, *des* 'still' is used to denote frequentive aspect. Depending on the context, the frequentive aspect denoted by *des* 'still' may be interpreted as either habitual or iterative in meaning.

The term "habitual" is taken here to refer to "a situation which is characteristic of an extended period of time" (Comrie 1985: 27). The use of *des* 'still' in habitual serialisation is illustrated below. In (67) *des* 'still' is used to denote an event that happens year in and year out. In (68) *des* 'still' denotes that the taking of bottles to Weluli on Sundays was habitual for the speaker. In (69) *des* 'still' is used to describe the ongoing paranoia of the A, following the death of her child.

(67) *To   ai   to   ai   baqa   goet   **h-oqon**   des.*
     year ONLY year ONLY NPRX.INAN LIKE   3INAN-do   still
     'Year after year, (we) do it like that all the time.' [Bk-8.048]

(68) *Neto hot mil   misa no   botil   Weluli   **mal**   des.*
     1SG   sun DUR   mass OBL   bottle Weluli   go   still
     'On Sundays (lit., on mass day) I would constantly be going to Weluli with bottles.' [Bk-13.013]

(69) *G-egil   **g-azal**   des.*
     3AN-shadow   3AN-see   still
     'She was constantly suspicious.' (lit., '(She) saw shadows constantly.')
     [Bk-39.042]

There is one example in the corpus where *des* 'still' is used to denote iterative rather than habitual aspect. Iterative refers to repeated occurrences of an event within a single situation (Declerck 1991: 277). In (70) we see that *des* 'still' occurs as V₂ with the monovalent verb *lulai* 'move' to denote the nervous shaking of the limbs of a just killed person.

(70) *G-on=o   g-iri   roe   **lulai**   res.*
     3AN-arm=AND   3AN-leg   SPEC.INAN   move   still
     'His arms and legs were constantly moving.' [Bk-52.028]

In some cases, the use of *des* 'still' as a V₂ in serialisation can be ambiguous. For instance, in (71) *des* 'still' can be interpreted either as referring to the manner in which the S is sitting (literally, 'sitting stilly') or as referring to frequentive (habitual) action ('sitting constantly'). Context serves to disambiguate the reading.

(71) Markus **mit** **des**.
 Markus sit still
 'Markus sits still.' or 'Markus is constantly sitting down.' [Not-07.03]

13.8.4 Persistent action with *ciluq* 'rest'

The monovalent verb *ciluq* denotes 'rest, relax' when used as a main verb in Bunaq.[7] This is illustrated in (72).

(72) Nei n-ol mil bari g-utu **ciluq**.
 1PL.EXCL 1EXCL-child COLL PROX.AN 3-COM rest
 '(He) hangs out with our children.' [Bk-22.010]

Ciluq 'rest' is occasionally used in serialisation, where it denotes persistent action. In both examples in the corpus, *ciluq* 'rest' is serialised with the motion verb *mal* 'go'. In (73) *ciluq* 'rest' denotes that the participant kept going to the cockfights. In (74) *ciluq* 'rest' is used to denote that the efforts of farmers to clear their gardens of undergrowth prior to planting are persistent.

(73) Baqi die zap g-ilan, mete baqa goet
 NPRX.AN REFL.POSS dog 3AN-tie NOW NPRX.INAN LIKE
 mal **ciluq**.
 go rest
 'He tied up his dog and like that kept going (to the cockfight).' [LB-8.178]

(74) U t-ul **mal** **siluq**.
 herbaceous.plant 3INAN-pull go rest
 '(They) keep going to clear undergrowth.' [Bk-3.008]

13.9 Motion serialisation

In Bunaq the serialisation of motion verbs to express complex motion events is highly productive. Motion SVCs follow a strictly ordered sequence such that a template with distinct slots can be used to describe the observed combinations and ordering of

---

7 *Ciluq* 'rest' appears to be a borrowing of Kemak *cilu* 'stay'. This verb is used in Kemak in serialisation to denote continuous aspect. The use of a verb meaning 'stay' as a marker of continuous aspect has been described for other Austronesian languages of Timor, such as Tetun Dili (Williams-van Klinken, Hajek and Nordlinger 2002: 79–80), and is a well-known grammaticalisation path cross-linguistically (Heine and Kuteva 2002: 277–278).

motion verbs in serialisation. This template is presented in Table 13.2. The elements in motion SVCs which appear leftmost following the S/A are shown in column 1, with items in other columns following in order until column 6, the items in which appear as the rightmost elements of the motion SVC. The ordering of the template is strongly iconic (Schapper 2011c): the origin of motion precedes verbs denoting the motion, with the goal of motion in turn following those verbs.

Lists in the columns of the template are complete, with the exception of column 4, which represents only a sample of the manner of motion verbs, albeit the most common ones, that can possibly occur in this slot. While there are some limited possibilities for using more than one item from the verbs in columns 4 and 5 in an SVC, only one item is included per clause from each of columns 1, 3, and 6. Specifically, if a goal is encoded in one way within the clause, it excludes the possibility of one of the other goal-encoding strategies being used in the same clause. This holds not only for goal-encoding strategies occupying the same slot in the template, but also across the two goal slots. For example, where a goal is expressed using a strategy from slot 3, it excludes the possibility of any additional goal being expressed by another form both in that slot and in slot 6.

In the following sections, I will illustrate and elaborate on aspects of this motion serialisation template. In §13.9.1, I look at the use of core serialisation to express origin and goal locations in motion SVCs, that is, the use of items in columns 1, 3, and 5 to add NPs (= 'X' in the template). In §13.9.2, I look at the encoding of reversive motion with the verb *tebe* 'return'. Finally, in §13.9.3 I look at nuclear serialisation with motion verbs from columns 4 and 5 in the template.

13.9.1 Origin-Motion-Goal SVCs

As mentioned above, the expression of goal and origin in a motion SVC is strictly iconic, with the origin (column 1) always preceding a verb denoting the motion or the goal of the motion, either one expressed in column 3 (75) or one expressed in column 6 (76).

Origin location + reversive + goal + deictic directional (1+2+3+5b)
(75) Nona **Australia gene** tebe   **Gewal a-ta**   man, ...
      girl   Australia LOC return   Gewal 3INAN-GL come
      '(When) Nona comes back from Australia to Gewal, ...'   [Bk-14.004]

Origin location + manner of motion + goal (1+4+6)
(76) **G-o**   he   reu   mal!
      3-SRC   run   house   go
      'Run away from (him) to home!'   [OS-07.01]

Table 13.2: Template of motion verb serialisation.

1. ORIGIN	2. REVERSIVE MOTION	3. GOAL	4. MANNER OF MOTION VERB	5. DIRECTIONAL VERB †		6. GOAL
				A. NON-DEICTIC	B. DEICTIC	
X *gene* 'LOC'	*tebe* 'return'	X *a-ta* '3INAN-GL'	*he* 'run'	*debel* 'descend'	*man* 'come'	X *gene* 'LOC'
X *no* 'OBL'			*mele* 'walk'	*sage* 'ascend'	*wil* 'come.LOW'	X *no* 'OBL'
X *g-o* '3-SRC'			*ciwal* 'flee'	*tama* 'enter'	*mina* 'come.HIGH'	X *pir* ‡ 'reach'
			topol 'fall'	*sai* ‡ 'exit'	*zemal* 'go.LOW'	X *mal* !! 'go'
			sikit 'leap'		*menal* 'go.HIGH'	X *a-ta mal* 'go towards'
			el 'crawl'		*honal* 'go.LEVEL'	X *a-ta sai* 'come upon'

† Column 5 gives a complete list of the directional verbs in Bunaq. Non-deictic motion verbs express motion inwards/outwards or upwards/downwards; the motion denoted by non-deictic motion verbs is not anchored to any deictic centre. Deictic motion verbs express motion events with reference to the speaker as the deictic centre: motion towards speaker ('come'), or motion away from speaker ('go'). Deictic motion verbs include an additional dimension of elevation: motion to lower elevation = 'down', or motion to higher elevation = 'up'. One verb, *man* 'come', is neutral as to changes of elevation in the motion, while another, *honal* 'go.LEVEL', denotes motion on a level plane ('across'); these two verbs lack deictic opposites in the paradigm, i.e., **'come across' and **'go'. The non-deictic directional verbs, *debel* 'descend' and *sage* 'ascend', are used instead of elevationally marked deictic motion verbs where vertical displacement is greater than horizontal displacement, e.g., when climbing a tree, getting out of a truck, or even ascending a very steep path. See §8.3.1.1 for more discussion of elevation-marked terms in Bunaq.

‡ The verbs *sai* 'exit' and *pir* 'reach' have additional motion meanings – 'go down to garden' and 'go up to home', respectively, when used independently without any specification for origin and/or goal location. Gardens are typically located on sloping ground in valleys below villages, while villages are located on ridges.

!! The verb *mal*, glossed as 'go' in column 6, has no deictic ground; it can be used in describing motions both to and from the deictic ground (cf. Wilkins and Hill (1995) on the cross-linguistic meaning of 'go' verbs relative to 'come').

The items used to express goal and origin NPs in motion SVCs constitute a mixed bag of postpositions, verbal postpositions, and verbs. The postpositions *no* 'OBL' (§12.2.1) and *gene* 'LOC' (§12.2.2) can head predicates (§3.5.6). Their role in motion SVCs (in columns 1–6) constitutes a clear form of serial predication in which there is S/A sharing between the motion verb and the PP, thus: $_{PRED1}[_{PP}origin]$ $_{PRED2}[_V motion]$ $_{PRED3}[_{PP}goal]$. Goal-encoding strategies using postpositions following a motion verb are resultative: the motion is completed and the result is that the participant is *at* the goal location, as in (77) and (78).

Origin+ deictic directional + goal (1+5b+6)
(77) Sun Gewen gene honal   [Ukaq Getel gene]$_{GOAL}$.
     Sun Gewen LOC   go.LEVEL   Ukaq Getel   LOC
     '(You) go across from Sun Gewen (and be) at Ukaq Getel.'   [Bk-34.001]

Deictic directional + goal (5b+6)
(78) Halaqi mina   [ola Lakus   mual   bare   no]$_{GOAL}$.
     3PL   come.HIGH   LOW   Lakus   low.land   PROX.INAN   OBL
     'They came up (and were) at this low land (of) Lakus.'   [Bk-29.019]

Alternatively, verbal postpositions can be used to express origin, in the case of *g-o* '3-SRC' expressing human origin locations (illustrated in 76), or to express a goal, in the case of *a-ta* '3INAN-GL', which introduces the location *towards* which a motion takes place, for both semantically animate (79) and inanimate (80) goals.

Goal + manner motion + non-deictic directional (3+4+5a)
(79) [Toren wa   a-ta]$_{GOAL}$ he   saqe.
     beam   top 3INAN-GL   run   ascend
     '(He) ran up to the top of the beam.'   [Bk-47.132]

Human goal + motion (3+5b)
(80) Baqi   [ei   i-ta]$_{GOAL}$ man   niq?
     NPRX.AN   2PL   1INCL/2-GL   come   NEG
     'He didn't come to you?'   [Bk-47.026]

Given their inability to head predicates (§3.6.1), the appearance of verbal postpositions in an SVC template could be considered syntactically problematic. However, because their appearance expressing origin and/or goal location blocks other true serial predications – which express those same roles – from appearing in a clause (as described in §13.9), they must be considered to be part of the motion template.

There are two verbs, *mal* 'go' and *pir* 'reach', which are used to express goal in column 6 of the template. i.e., following the verb of motion, in motion SVCs.⁸ *Mal* 'go' is neutral as to the "achievedness" of the motion to the goal location, i.e., the participant may or may not have arrived at the goal (81). *Pir* signifies an achieved goal, i.e., that the motion occurs *right up to* the goal location (82).

Deictic directional + goal (5b+6)
(81) Neto   rele   zemal   [Weluli   mal]_{GOAL}.
     1SG   INS   go.LOW   Weluli   go
     'I went down with (them) to Weluli.'   [Bk-13.005]

Reversive + deictic directional + goal (2+5b+6)
(82) Baqi   tebe   man   [deu   pir]_{GOAL}.
     NPRX.AN   return   come   house   reach
     'She came back (and) reached the house.'   [LB-5.180]

Finally, we see in column 6 that there are two complex goal-encoding strategies in which the verbal postposition *a-ta* '3INAN-GL' is nested as the complement of the verbs *mal* 'go' and *sai* 'exit'. That *mal* 'go' and *sai* 'exit' form a unit together with *a-ta* '3INAN-GL' is seen in the fact that, when co-occurring with *mal* 'go' and *sai* 'exit', *a-ta* '3INAN-GL' follows a manner and/or direction motion verb, as in (83) and (84). This contrasts with the expected order in which a goal encoded by *a-ta* '3INAN-GL' alone must precede a manner (column 4) and/or direction motion verb (column 5).

Manner motion + goal (4+6)
(83) En   baqis   loi   he   [haqe   a-ta   mal]_{GOAL}.
     person   much   good   run   THERE   3INAN-GL   go
     'A good many people run to there.'   [Bk-66.013]

Manner of motion (x2) + non-deictic directional + goal (2+5a+6)
(84) Baqi   he   sikit   rebel   [an   gol   uen   a-ta   sai]_{GOAL}.
     NPRX.AN   run   leap   descend   grass   small   one   3INAN-GL   exit
     'He ran down leaping (and) came onto a patch of grass.'   [Bk-6.019]

Like other verbs in column 6, the units *a-ta mal* 'go towards' and *a-ta sai* 'exit towards' not only appear in SVCs, but can also occur as independent clausal predicates. Seman-

---

8 Both these verbs can also occur as independent clausal predicates with the goal location NP encoded as an unmarked oblique (§10.6.3). That is, their ability to encode goals is not restricted to an SVC. As independent main verbs, *mal* 'go' and *pir* 'reach' can also appear without goal obliques. In the case of *mal* 'go', this means that the goal of the motion is simply left unspecified.

tically, *a-ta mal* 'go towards' denotes the direction towards which another motion is directed, with seemingly little difference between simple uses of *a-ta* '3INAN-GL' in column 3. The combination *a-ta sai* refers to a goal location which is simply 'come upon'.

13.9.2 Reversive motion SVCs

The verb *tebe* 'return' occurs before any verb denoting motion, with or without intrinsic direction. Examples of the different combinations of *tebe* 'return', with verbs from other slots in the template filled in various manners, are given in (85) to (87):

Reversive + goal (2+6)
(85) Nei   **tebe**   rie   iskola   mal.
     1PL.EXCL   return   REFL.POSS   school   go
     '(We) return to our school.'   [Bk-1.052]

Origin + reversive + non-deictic directional (1+2+5a)
(86) En   huqe   gene   **tebe**   saqe.
     person   HERE   LOC   return   ascend
     'The person ascended back from here.'   [Bk-10.019]

Reversive + deictic directional (2+5b)
(87) Belanda   **tebe**   man   teni   oa.
     Holland   return   come   again   IAM
     'The Dutch had already come back again.'   [Bk-29.015]

There is one notable deviation from the template presented in Table 13.2, involving *tebe* 'return'. As the template depicts, *tebe* 'return' occurs in serialisation before a goal location (in column 3 of the template) where a manner and/or directional motion verb follow, as illustrated in (88). However, when *tebe* 'return' is the only motion verb of a clause, it occurs after the goal encoded by *a-ta* '3INAN-GL', as in (89). This constraint is a reflection of the verbal postpositional status of *a-ta* '3INAN-GL' and of the fact that it cannot occur as an independent, clause-final predicate.

Origin location + reversive + goal + deictic directional (1+2+3+5b)
(88) Nona   Australia   gene   **tebe**   Gewal   **a-ta**   man, ...
     miss   Australia   LOC   return   Gewal   3INAN-GL   come
     '(When) you come back to Gewal from Australia, ...'   [Bk-14.004]

Goal + reversive motion (3+2)
(89) Akirnya,   halaqi   rie   muk   **a-ta**   **tebe.**
     finally   3PL   REFL.POSS   earth 3INAN-GL   return
     'In the end, they went back to their own land.'   [Bk-29.014]

Note also that *tebe* 'return' is not limited to denoting reversive motion. *Tebe* 'return' may also be used to denote any action that involves a restoration or return to a previous state, as in (90) and (91).

(90) Pana   gol   himo   **tebe**   g-ariqa.
     female small   CONTR.AN   return   3AN-repair
     '(He has to) repair back that girl.', i.e. '(He has to) restore that girl's reputation.'
                                                                        [Bk-21.029]

(91) Homo=na,   baqi   **tebe**   loi   soq, ...
     CONTR.INAN=FOC   NPRX.AN   return   good   SEQ
     'After that she returned (to being) good, ...'   [Bk-43.036]

Tebe 'return' may also introduce an event that happens "in turn", i.e., in sequence, to the event in the previous clause, as in (92). In this function, *tebe* 'return' occurs at the beginning of the clause in the manner of a sentence connective, and, unlike when *tebe* 'return' denotes a motion event, does not follow an origin of motion where one is expressed.

(92) **Tebe,**   Jepang   man.
     return   Japan   come
     'Then, the Japanese came.'   [Bk-29.007]

This function of *tebe* is discussed further in §15.4.3.

13.9.3 Directional SVCs

Directional serialisation is nuclear: the verbs share the S/A argument and form a tight unit together, with no other constituents – including the negator – able to occur between the serialised verbs. Manner of motion verbs lack directional orientation. As the template depicts, direction may be specified for these motion verbs by a following directional verb, either a non-deictic directional (93 and 94) or a deictic directional verb (95 and 96).

Manner of motion + non-deictic directional (4+5a)
(93) Mel   ba,   ciwal   sai.
     awake   ART.INAN   flee   exit
     '(When she) woke up, (she) fled outside.'   [Bk-43.056]

Origin + manner of motion + non-deictic directional (1+4+5a)
(94) Tirin   g-ewen   gene   topol   rebel.
    cliff   3AN-face   LOC   fall   descend
    '(She) fell down from the cliff face.'   [Bk-4.066]

Manner of motion + deictic directional (2+5b)
(95) He   mina.
    run   come.HIGH
    '(She) came running up here.'   [LB-3.127]

Manner of motion + deictic directional (2+5b)
(96) Mele   mele   zemal.
    walk   walk   go.LOW
    '(You) keep walking down.'   [Bk-34.037]

The direction of non-motion actions may also be specified by means of serialisation with directional verbs. The action verb is V_1 and may be monovalent (97) or bivalent (98). The second verb may be drawn either from the class of deictic directional verbs (97) or from that of non-deictic directional verbs (98).

(97) Gie   en   huqe   gene   g-ege   **hape**   **honal.**
    3.POSS   person   HERE   LOC   3AN-BEN   mobile.phone   go.LEVEL
    'Her people here mobile-phoned across to her.'   [Bk-43.004]

(98) Lolo   wa   gene=na   **g-ete**   rebel,   **g-iep**   rebel,
    mountain   top   LOC=FOC   3AN-hit   descend   3AN-axe   descend
    g-ota   rebel.
    3AN-stab   descend
    'From the mountain top (they) hit down, chop down, and stab down.'
                                                              [Bk-5.004]

There are only a few examples in the corpus of non-deictic directional verbs (column 5A) and deictic verbs being serialised together (column 5B). The attested combinations are given in (99) to (101). Notice that the non-deictic verb always precedes the deictic verb.

(99) Mali Gel Pur Masak   a-ta   **saqe**   **menal.**
    Mali Gel Pur Masak   3INAN-GL   ascend   go.HIGH
    '(You) ascend going up to Mali Gel Pur Masak.'   [Bk-34.007]

(100) *Homo   soq   naq=na,   tebe   **tama   man**.*
 CONTR.INAN SEQ PRIOR=FOC   return   enter   come
 'Once that was (done), (he) came back in.' [Bk-67.127]

(101) *Uen   o   gene   **debel   man**.*
 one   nowhere LOC   descend   come
 'One (bird) came down out of nowhere.' [LB3.082]

It is also possible for pairs of non-deictic directional verbs (column 5A) or pairs of deictic motion verbs to be serialised together (column 5B) in cases where the paired verbs denote the opposite motion, i.e., 'to and fro'. In (102) and (103), we see similar pairings of deictic motion verbs to denote 'go back and forth' and 'go up and down', respectively.

(102) *I   **honal   man**.*
 1PL.INCL   go.LEVEL   come
 'We go (and) come.' i.e., 'We go back and forth.' [Bk-39.020]

(103) *Baqi   **menal   wil**   gie.*
 NPRX.AN   go.HIGH   come.LOW   PROSP
 'He is going to go up (and) come down.' [OS-06.01]

The final form of nuclear serialisation observed is with two manner of motion verbs, though this is rare. In (104) the V₁ *he* 'run'[9] is serialised with the V₂ *sikit* 'leap' to denote that the running was done in a leaping manner, with *rebel* 'descend' following to describe the direction. Similarly, in (105), the V₁ *borus* 'move through' is serialised with the V₂ *ciwal* 'flee' to denote that the moving through was done in a fleeing manner.

(104) *Baqi   **he   sikit**   rebel   an   gol   uen   a-ta   sai.*
 NPRX.AN   run   leap   descend   grass   small   one   3INAN-GL   exit
 'He ran down leaping (and) came onto a patch of grass.' [Bk-6.019]

(105) *Tebe   tama   sai,   **borus**   ciwal   liol.*
 return   enter   exit   move.through   flee   continue
 'In turn (she) went in (then) out, continuing through in flight.'
  [Bk-43.077]

---

9 The meaning of *he* is better characterised as 'move at speed', as it can refer to 'fly' of a bird or 'swim' of a fish. It is the usual verb describing the motion of a motorbike, but it is only used with reference to the motion of buses or cars when they move at high speed.

Chapter 14
Verbal and clausal modifiers

14.1 Introduction

This chapter is concerned with items which function to modify elements other than nouns. Items with this function constitute a semantically and syntactically heterogenous group (§3.6.3), which can be variously characterised as "adverbs", "verbal modifiers", or "clausal modifiers". These items will be discussed together here as a matter of descriptive convenience. For the most part, I focus on individual items which occur with high frequency in Bunaq speech, but some discussion of phrases with adverbial functions is also included.

The main distinction to be made between the modifying items and phrases discussed in this chapter is between those that occur before the clausal predicate (here, "preverbal": §14.2) and those that occur following it ("postverbal": §14.3). There is often considerable freedom for an item to occur in different preverbal and postverbal positions with differences in scope and meaning between positions. Throughout this chapter, I concentrate on the semantics of the items with only brief reference to their possible positions.

14.2 Preverbal modification

Preverbal modifiers in Bunaq typically occur between any of the preverbal constituents, as in Figure 14.1. The different preverbal positions give rise to differences in scope and meaning. A preverbal modifier has scope over clausal constituents to its right. So, for example, a modifier preceding the S/A has scope over the whole clause, while a modifier occurring immediately before the predicate (V) has scope over the predicate alone.

(MOD_1)   S/A   (MOD_2)   P   (MOD_3)   V

Figure 14.1: Possible positions of preverbal modifiers.

Temporal modifiers are barred from the position between P and V (MOD_3), while other preverbal modifiers are barred from the pre-S/A position (MOD_1). There is no restriction on the number of preverbal modifiers that are permissible, though it is rare for more than one to occur in any of the positions in Figure 14.1.

Bunaq preverbal modifiers encode modality (§14.2.1), manner (§14.2.2), time (§14.2.3), and emphatic negation (§14.2.4).

14.2.1 Modal adverbs

Modality is the linguistic expression of a speaker's attitude towards a proposition, including its likelihood, necessity, and desirability. In Bunaq, modality is expressed by means of the set of adverbs given in Table 14.1.[1]

These adverbs appear in a position before the clausal predicate. They can also occur without a verb, if it can be understood from context, e.g., *misti!* '(you) must (do it)!'. The majority of modal adverbs can occur between any preverbal constituents from before an A/S to directly before the verb itself; only two are not found to occur prior to an A/S.

Table 14.1: Modal adverbs.

		Pre-A/S?
misti	'must'	N
sala	'should'	Y
asal	'necessarily'	Y
hilaq	'surprisingly'	Y
hele	'perhaps'	Y
kalaq	'maybe'	Y
hani	'PROH'	N

Bunaq speakers also regularly use modals from contact languages, Indonesian and Tetun, some of which are: Tetun *bele* 'can, may', Indonesian *bisa* 'can', and Indonesian *harus* 'must'. In §14.2.1.1–§14.2.1.7, only the modal adverbs which Bunaq speakers identify as belonging to Bunaq are discussed, although some of these are borrowings.

14.2.1.1 *misti* 'must'

The modal *misti*, also for a small number of speakers *musti*, is used to express a deontic modal meaning 'must, have to'. This item is probably a borrowing from Tetun *musti* 'must', but ultimately originates in Malay *mesti* 'must'. It is not considered a loan by most Bunaq speakers and it is found across all dialects of Bunaq.

Misti 'must' always follows the A/S of a clause, as in (1), and occasionally also follows the P (2).

---

[1] The term auxiliary is not used here, since the ability of modals to be placed in between a P and the verb suggests that the Bunaq modals are not located in a structural position above VP as is typically posited for an auxiliary, cf. Barbiers (2006).

(1) Ei   g-azal,   ei   **misti**   teqa.
    2PL   3AN-see   2PL   must   pray
    'If you see (them), you must pray.'   [Bk-47.084]

(2) Baqa   **misti**   h-one   tama.
    NPRX.INAN   must   3INAN-hold   enter
    'That must be held when entering.'   [Bk-70.082]

Where the A/S is elided, *misti* 'must' may come as the first element in a clause, as in (3) and (4). Alternatively, *misti* 'must' may follow the P, as in (5) and (6).

(3) **Misti**   ene   no   mel,   buakae   d-inik.
    must   night   OBL   wake   provisions   REFL-cook
    '(We) must wake in the night (and) cook provisions for ourselves.'   [Bk-37.011]

(4) **Misti**   baqa   h-oqon.
    must   NPRX.INAN   3INAN-do
    '(We) must do that.'   [Bk-23.007]

(5) Heruk   g-iri   gene   ba   **misti**   sukit.
    THORN   3-leg   LOC   ART.INAN   must   extract
    'The thorn in his leg must be pulled out.'   [Not-12.01]

(6) Kura   roi   **misti**   haqe   gene   g-ini   hati.
    horse   SPEC.AN   must   THERE   LOC   3AN-CAUS   exist
    'Those horses must be put there.'   [Bk-37.116]

There are a few instances in the corpus in which *misti* 'must' is used to express epistemic rather than deontic modality. For instance, in (7) *misti* 'must' is used in a hypothetical description of what to do when one encounters a *muk gomo* 'earth spirit'; *misti* 'must' expresses the speaker's factual certainty that the spirit would flee, if the addressee prayed when he saw the *muk gomo*.

(7) Baqa   goet   h-oqon,   baqi   **misti**   he   g-aziq.
    NPRX.INAN   LIKE   3INAN-do   NPRX.AN   must   run   3AN-disappear
    '(When) you do like that (pray), he must run (and) disappear.'   [Bk-47.086]

14.2.1.2 *sala* 'should'

Sala 'should' is a deontic modal that is used in strong statements of duty, obligation, or propriety. Typically, it follows the A/S of a clause, as in (8), but it may also appear initially where A/S is elided (9), or following P (10).

(8) Eto **sala** mal, ...
    2SG should go
    'You should go, ...' [LB5.145]

(9) Tapi **sala** hol rele ganjal.
    but should stone INS support
    'But (you) should have propped up (the car) with stones.' [Bk-52.038]

(10) D-agar **sala** tais.
     REFL-mouth should cloth
     '(I) should (tie shut with a) cloth my mouth.' [Bk-67.110]

Sala is used to denote a necessary condition, referring to what would occur or would have occurred under certain hypothetical conditions in the past or present. In (11) sala is used in the first clause to express an unreal condition, whose fulfilment would have meant the avoidance of humanity's mortality. In (12) sala stipulates that the speaker would marry the caterpillar were he to become human.

(11) **Sala** hoto wit ai, i heser niq.
     should fire fetch only 1PL.INCL die NEG
     'Should (she) have just fetched the fire, we would not die.' [LB10.041]

(12) **Sala** en on gie=bu, neto g-utu ton ai.
     should person DO PROSP=GIVEN 1SG 3-COM marry ONLY
     'Should (the caterpillar) become a human, I would just marry him.' [Bk-71.009]

14.2.1.3 *asal* 'necessarily'

Asal 'necessarily' is used to denote deontic modality in which the speaker expresses how the world ought to be, according to a certain norm or their own expectations. In (13) *asal* is used to indicate that *mal* 'going' is an action whose fulfilment is required. In (14) *asal* is used to refer to the changing standards in modern society whereby marriages cannot be arranged blind, but the couple must also like each other for the marriage to take place.

(13) Neto **asal** mal.
     1SG necessarily go
     'It is necessary that I go.' [OS.07-01]

(14) Ton, en **asal** to-mobel.
     marriage person necessarily RECP-like
     '(In) marriage (these days), it is necessary for the people to like each other.'
     [Bk-62.028]

Asal may occur either before or after the clausal A/S. The difference between these two positions is illustrated by the pair of minimally contrastive examples in (15). In (15a) *asal* follows the S and emphasises that it is the referent of S who needs to work. In (15b) *asal* is initial and has scope over the whole clause, with the pragmatic focus being on the necessity of working in general.

(15) a. *Baqi   asal   sirubisu.*
       NPRX.AN necessarily   work
       'For him/her to work is necessary.'
    b. *Asal   baqi   siribisu.*
       necessarily   NPRX.AN   work
       'It is necessary for him/her to work.' [Not.07-01]

14.2.1.4 *hilaq* 'surprisingly'

Hilaq 'surprisingly' is an evaluative modal adverb which denotes that the proposition expressed by a clause is against either the expectation of the speaker or some general expectation. *Hilaq* can occur clause-initially or following the S/A argument and is often accompanied by a rising intonation.

In (16) *hilaq* is used to highlight the circumstance that the surprising event of a person talking to a turtle really did happen. In (17) clause-initial *hilaq* highlights surprise at the fact that it was a monkey who had stolen the child.

(16) *Zol   gene   **hilaq**   lenuk   g-utu   rale.*
     river LOC   surprisingly   turtle   3-COM   speak
     'At the river (she) spoke with a turtle, it was a surprise.' [Bk-72.017]

(17) ***Hilaq***   *mete   orel   himo   g-ini   gie.*
     surprisingly   NOW   monkey   CONTR.AN 3AN-CAUS   3.POSS
     'What a surprise, the monkey (mentioned just) now had made her his.'
     [Bk-68.010]

Hilaq is frequently used in presentational clauses (§4.3.1) identifying an individual. In (18) and (19), *hilaq* is used to express surprise at the person's identity.

(18) *Berek=o   Mauk   **hilaq**   bari.*
     Berek=AND   Mauk   surprisingly   PROX.AN
     'What a surprise, these are Berek and Mauk.' [LB-3.158]

(19) ***Hilaq***   *gie   eme=na   baqi.*
     surprisingly   3.POSS   mother=FOC   NPRX.INAN
     'What a surprise, it's her mother.' [Bk-72.019]

14.2.1.5 *hele* 'perhaps'

Hele 'perhaps' is used in the expression of epistemic possibility, denoting the speaker's subjective belief in the possibility of the proposition in a clause. *Hele* occurs either preceding the A/S (20) or following the A/S (21). In elicitation, *hele* was also seen to be able to occur between P and V, but this is not attested in any natural language examples in the corpus.

(20) **Hele**   en   halaqi lekot   baqi   misa niq=be,
     perhaps person   3PL   busy   NPRX.INAN   mass NEG=CONTEXP
     ota   o   Nualain gie=bu   ate.
     LEVEL   ADDR   Nualain 3.POSS=GIVEN   far
     'Perhaps those busy people don't go to mass, but it is far to Nualain.'
     [Bk-34.094]

(21) En   **hele**   zonal   gene man, ...
     person   perhaps succession   LOC   come
     'People perhaps come in succession, ...'   [Bk-67.319]

Hele is also regularly used in questions, as in (22) and (23). The inclusion of *hele* functions to "soften" the speech act of questioning by framing the question as a possibility.

(22) **Hele**   hosu   hati?
     perhaps other exist
     'Perhaps there's something else?'   [Bk-44.014]

(23) Ei   **hele**   nei   nie   eme=o   nei
     2PL   perhaps 1PL.EXCL   1EXCL.POSS   mother=AND   1PL.EXCL
     nie   ama   g-azal?
     1EXCL.POSS   father 3AN-see
     'Have you perhaps seen our mother and father?'   [LB1.013]

Finally, *hele* is used in Bunaq to express the speaker's fear that an undesirable event might come to pass. Apprehensive uses of *hele* are illustrated in (24) and (25).

(24) Ili   bei   gie   mok   a,   bei   **hele**   i
     1DU.INCL   sir   3.POSS   banana   eat   sir   perhaps 1PL.INCL
     Ø-one.
     1INCL/2-hold
     '(If) we eat the human's bananas, he **might** catch us.'   [OrelLenuk.06]

(25) Nei=bu   neq=o   loi,   nei   n-omil
     1PL.EXCL=GIVEN divide=AND   good   1PL.EXCL 1EXCL-palm
     bekaq=si,   homo=be,   nei   n-uloq
     broad=REAS   CONTR.INAN=CONTEXP   1PL.EXCL 1EXCL-palm
     legul bere,   **hele**   ei   Ø-iral   kisu sal.
     long   CONTEXP.INAN   perhaps   2PL   1INCL/2-eye poke wrong
     'I could distribute (the food), because our palms are broad, but my long tail **might** poke you in the eyes.'   [BaiANeq.70]

Hele 'perhaps' and *hani* 'PROH' (§14.2.1.7) are often both translated by Bunaq speakers with Indonesian *jangan sampai* 'don't let it happen that, may it not happen that'. The difference between the two Bunaq items is that while *hele* expresses apprehension that an undesirable event might come to pass (26a), *hani* is precautionary, that is, aimed at preventing an undesirable event from happening (26b).

(26) a. I   **hele**   bilat.
         1PL.INCL   perhaps   hungry
         'We may hunger.'
     b. I   **hani**   bilat.
         1PL.INCL   PROH   hungry
         'May we not hunger.'   [FB-020821]

More examples of precautionary *hani* are given in §14.2.1.7 below.

14.2.1.6 *kalaq* 'maybe'

Kalaq, borrowed from Tetun *kala* 'maybe', expresses uncertainty or ambivalence on the part of the speaker. *Kalaq* 'maybe' is relatively infrequent in Bunaq, appearing in the speech of only a few older speakers in the corpus.

As an adverb, *kalaq* 'maybe' is attested in clause-medial position following an A/S (27), as well as clause-initially (28).

(27) Bari=na   **kalaq**   bare   h-oqon.
     PROX.AN=FOC   maybe   PROX.INAN   3INAN-do
     'It was maybe this (person) who did this.'   [Bk-72.046]

(28) **Kalaq**   en   n-azal   oa.
     maybe   person   1EXCL-see   IAM
     'Maybe people have seen me already.'   [Bk-72.021]

14.2.1.7 *hani* 'PROH'

Hani 'PROH' expresses prohibitive modality, i.e., that the proposition denoted by a clause is not permitted. *Hani* typically follows the A/S in declarative clauses, illustrated in (29) and (30).

(29)   *Baqa*   *h-oqon,*   *tan*   *homo=na,*   *baqi*   ***hani***
       NPRX.INAN   3INAN-do   because   CONTR.INAN=FOC   NPRX.AN   PROH
       bis=o   *bin*   *h-arat.*
       seed=AND   seed   3INAN-destroy
       '(We) do that, because then, they may not destroy the seeds.'   [Bk-8.006]

(30)   *Ini*   *mesaq=bu,*   *hoto*   ***hani***   *rene.*
       set.alight   GIVEN   fire   PROH   spread
       '(When they) burn (their garden), the fire is not permitted to spread.'   [Bk-3.023]

As mentioned already in §14.2.1.5, *hani* 'PROH' is often used precautionally, that is, with the aim of preventing an undesirable event from occurring. For example, in (31), *hani* 'PROH' is used in its precautionary function: by ensuring that the fertiliser enters into the soil (as opposed to sitting on the surface), the undesirable event whereby the rain washes the fertiliser away is avoided.

(31)   *Baqi*   *muk*   *mil*   *a-ta*   *tama*   *on,*   ***hani***   *leleq.*
       NPRX.AN   earth   inside   3INAN-GL   enter   DO   PROH   flow
       'That (fertiliser) enters into the earth, (it) may not run off.'   [Bk-65.108]

As mentioned in §4.6.1, *hani* is also used in negative imperatives. In imperatives, *hani* may follow a second person pronoun (32), or, where the pronoun is omitted, it occurs in clause-initial position (33). *Hani* may occur after a P (34) where the focus of the negation is on the predicate. In this example, the speaker is chastising the addressee for bringing hot water from the house, when in fact the addressee should have prepared the hot water in the place where it was needed.

(32)   *Ei*   ***hani***   *liol!*
       2PL   PROH   continue
       'Don't keep going.'   [Bk-29.041]

(33)   ***Hani***   *hik*   *gene*   *muk*   *ni*   *ga-lai.*
       PROH   path   LOC   earth   OBL   3AN-set
       'Don't on the way lay it down on the ground.'   [LB2.229]

(34) Il   cinoq   **hani**   reu   gene   zal.
     water   hot   PROH   house   LOC   carry
     'Don't carry the hot water from the house.'   [Bk-4.089]

14.2.2 Manner adverbs

There are two preverbal manner adverbs in the corpus: *nor* 'without reason/purpose, aimlessly' (§14.2.2.1) and *naqi* 'simply' (§14.2.2.2). Neither adverb can occur independently as a clausal predicate, nor can they occur without the predicate, even where it can be contextually understood. These manner adverbs can occur between any constituents following the A/S and following P prior to the verb.

14.2.2.1 *nor* 'aimlessly'
Actions which are performed without reason, purpose, or motivation are expressed by the preverbal adverb *nor* 'without reason/purpose, aimlessly', as in (35) and (36).

(35) Baqi   **nor**   kakolo   on.
     NPRX.AN   aimlessly   wander   DO
     'He wanders around aimlessly.'   [Bk-18.020]

(36) Ligi   ba,   **nor**   g-ue.
     be.sleepless   ART.INAN   aimlessly   3AN-hit
     '(During the time of) sleeplessness, (she) would hit people without reason.'
                                                              [Bk-43.022]

14.2.2.2 *naqi* 'simply'
An action performed "simply" for itself without any other thought or opinion is expressed with *naqi*, as in (37).

(37) Nona   **naqi**   Fulur   a-ta   liol   haqal.
     miss   simply   Fulur   3INAN-GL   continue   finished
     'Miss had simply continued on to Fulur.'   [Bk-63.007]

Naqi 'simply' patterns syntactically in the same way as *nor* 'aimlessly' and is close in meaning to it. *Naqi* is much less common than *nor*. *Nor* and *naqi* can on occasion be used together in the same clause, as in (38).

(38) Biasa   baqi   g-otok   sia=bu,   **nor**   **naqi**
     usually NPRX.INAN   3AN-liver burn=GIVEN   aimlessly   simply
     nei   n-ue   n-ue.
     1PL.EXCL   1EXCL-hit 1EXCL-hit
     'Whenever she gets angry, (she) just randomly hits and hits us without thinking.'
     [Bk-30.057]

14.2.3 Temporal adverbs

A non-exhaustive list of preverbal temporal adverbs is given in Table 14.2. Many of these are multi-word expressions.

Table 14.2: Bunaq preverbal temporal adverbs.

erenoq	'yesterday, day before'
hilerenoq	'day before yesterday, two days prior'
noqi	'currently, at the moment'
le gie	'tomorrow, next day'
hilere	'day after next'
inanoq	'last night, the previous night'
meten	'recently, just now'
metensi (~ metenti)	'very recently (past or present)'
nare-wen	'after a little while'
tekil-tekil	'suddenly, all of a sudden'
lalo-en	'in a while'
sal~sal-en	'in a little while, shortly'
hori~hori	'eternally'
hotin	'occasionally'
hocinoq	'in the daytime'

Temporal adverbs such as those given in Table 14.2 typically occur clause-initially (39) and can be separated from the clause by an intonation break (40). They may also follow an NP in S/A function (41). They do not occur between P and V.

(39) **Erenoq**   masala   uen   hati.
     yesterday   problem   one   exist
     'Yesterday there was a problem.'
     [Bk-21.001]

(40) **Tekil~tekil**, i   ie   moen   roi   topol rebel.
     suddenly   1PL.INCL 1INCL/2.POSS friend SPEC.AN fall   descend
     'All of a sudden this friend of ours falls down.'   [Bk-1.041]

(41) Neto   **hocinoq** he=o   los.
     1SG   day.time   run=AND   fly
     'In the daytime I run and fly.'   [Bk-49.018]

14.2.4 Negative reinforcers

As mentioned in §4.5.2, there are two negative reinforcers, *ozol* and *nen*, which are used with the standard clausal negator, *niq* 'NEG' (§4.5.1). While *niq* occurs postverbally, *ozol* and *nen* occur pre-verbally. The negative reinforcers serve to emphasise the negation with respect to the item that direct follows them. Neither *ozol* nor *nen* can be used without *niq* 'NEG'.

Examples of the use of *ozol* 'NEG' are given in (42) to (44). In (42) *ozol* 'NEG' emphasises the negation of the comitative phrase introduced by *g-utu* '3-COM' in order to assure the Muslim addressee that the food is safe to eat. In (43) *ozol* emphasises the negation of the A, *nei* '1PL.EXCL'. Finally, in (44) *ozol* precedes the clausal verb, *baqis* 'much', emphasising its negation.

(42) I   **ozol** minaq sael g-utu   **niq**.
     1PL.INCL   NEG   oil   pig   3AN-COM   NEG
     'We don't (cook) with pig's oil.'   [Bk-37.054]

(43) **Ozol** nei   tumel   bini   **niq**.
     NEG   1PL.EXCL   money   steal NEG
     'Not us, (we) didn't steal the money.'   [OS-07.01]

(44) Na   **ozol** baqis   **niq**.
     anger   NEG   much   NEG
     '(Her) anger was not much at all.'   [LB-4.036]

Nen 'NEG' (borrowed from Tetun *neen* 'not, neither…nor' < Portuguese *nem* 'nor') has the same syntax as *ozol*, but is far less frequent in my corpus. Examples are given in (45) and (46). In (45) *nen* reinforces the negation of the NP *nego uen* 'anything', the S of *dari* 'happen', emphasising that not a single thing transpired that related to the participant. In (46) *nen* occurs directly before the predication to emphasise that the event did not occur.

(45) G-ege **nen** nego uen=sa dari **niq** ai.
3AN-BEN NEG what one=EVEN happen NEG ONLY
'Not even a thing happened to them.' [LB2.010]

(46) Nie moen pip loko o bi, **nen** taru man
1EXCL.POSS friend goat male ADDR ART.AN NEG appear come
g-azal **niq** on oa.
3AN-see NEG DO IAM
'It seems that my friend Goat won't be turning up.' [OrelNisPipLoko.038]

While *ozol* always occurs to the left of the clausal predicate, *nen* can occur after the predicate directly preceding the standard negator *niq*, as seen in (47). Here the function of *nen* is simply to reinforce the negative meaning of *niq*, 'not at all'.

(47) A, eto, neto a-tara **nen niq**, ...
INTERJ 2SG 1SG 1INCL/2-know NEG NEG
'Ah! You, I don't know at all, ...' [BaloBiGakirik.014]

14.3 Postverbal modification

In many Papuan languages the verb is strictly clause-final, while in others the postverbal position is limited to a single locative/temporal nominal (Foley 1986: 168–169). Whilst being basically verb-final, Bunaq contrasts with both of these patterns, allowing a great many elements to follow the verb. These include items encoding aspect, phasal polarity, temporal duration, manner, addition, polarity, and information status. It is unusual for more than three or four elements to follow a verb, but there is no formal restriction on the number.

Figure 14.2 gives a template for the typical ordering of postverbal modifiers. The label 'ADVERBIAL' covers a broad range of elements encoding manner, time, aspect, and intensity, among others. These are discussed in §14.3.1. The other positions in the template refer to well-defined, closed positions filled by only one or two items: the performative *on* 'DO' (§14.3.2); the prospective *gie* 'PROSP' (§14.3.3); the restrictive marker *ai* 'ONLY' (§14.3.4); the phasal polarity markers ('PHASAL') *taq* 'CONT' and *oa* 'IAM' (§14.3.5); and the information markers ('INFO') *gin* 'REPORT' and *nai* 'INFORM' (§14.3.6). One final marker discussed here is the priorative *naq* 'PRIOR', a marker which does not co-occur with any other postverbal markers after the ADVERBIAL slot (§14.3.7).

V [ADVERBIAL DO PROSP NEG ONLY PHASAL] INFO

Figure 14.2: Template for postverbal modifiers.

Bunaq enclitic question tags (discussed in §4.6.2.2.2–§4.6.2.2.4) also occur in the 'INFO' position. The standard negator *niq* 'NEG' has already been discussed in §4.5.1. It is discussed in this chapter only insofar as it is used with other items such as those in the template in Figure 14.2. It should be noted that while the position of the negator given in the template is the most common, the negator very readily changes positions depending on the scope of negation. See §14.3.5 for discussion of the position of the negator, relative to the phasal polarity markers.

The "typical ordering" given in the template refers to the most commonly observed ordering of postverbal elements; it is not the only possible ordering. The bracketed elements in the template represent those elements whose ordering shows some degree of flexibility with respect to one another; elements outside the brackets must occur in those positions. Different orderings of these elements correspond to differences in scope, with a modifier on the right having scope over any modifier to its left. For instance, in (48a) *teni* 'again' occurs in the scope of *gie* 'PROSP' to mean that the speaker has the intention to again ascend, while in (48b) *gie* 'PROSP' occurs in the scope of *teni* 'again' to mean that the speaker again has the intention to ascend.

(48) a. *Neto* [[*saqe* ***teni***] ***gie***.]
       1SG   ascend   again   PROSP
       'I intend to again ascend.'
   b. *Neto* [[*saqe* ***gie***] ***teni***.]
       1SG   ascend   PROSP   again
       'I again intend to ascend.' [Not.07.01]

In the following sections, discussion will focus on the typical ordering of postverbal modifiers. The treatment of elements moves from left to right on the template, i.e., starting with those items appearing closest to the verb and ending with those farthest away.

14.3.1 Postverbal adverbials

14.3.1.1 Postverbal nominals

In addition to NPs encoding the T argument of a trivalent verb (§4.2.3), there are a small number of nominals that appear post-verbally with adverbial functions.

14.3.1.1.1 Duration/distance measure nominals

The distance or duration over which the event denoted by a predicate takes place is encoded post-verbally by a measure phrase, i.e., measure or temporal noun plus a numeral. This measure phrase plus numeral can be followed by a comparative adverb, a restrictive marker, and/or a phasal polarity marker.

Examples (49) and (50) illustrate a postverbal measure phrase denoting the distance over which the event denoted by the preceding verb takes place.

(49) Nie   tas   Atambua gene menal   **kilo**   sogo **goniqon**.
     1EXCL.POSS village   Atambua   LOC   go.LOW   kilometre   ten   three
     'My village is down from Atambua (by) 30 kilometres.'   [Bk-7.007]

(50) Gie   turiq   gol   homo   ret golaq topol, ret golaq
     3.POSS   machete   small   CONTR.INAN   all.alone fall   all.alone
     bitil-wen   **kira~kira**   **meter goniqo**.
     spin-ANTIC   approximately   metre   three
     'His small knife fell all by itself, (and) spun approximately three metres away.'
                                                                                     [Bk-1.043]

Examples (51) and (52) illustrate a postverbal measure phrase denoting the time over which the event denoted by the verb takes place.

(51) Hik   gene **tuku uen** ai,   mele   **tuku uen** lesin.
     path   LOC   hour   one   only   walk   hour   one   more
     '(We) are on the way for one hour only, (we) walk for more than one hour.'
                                                                                     [Bk-34.034]

(52) Mok   s-umak   **hot   mil   goniqil   gonciet**.
     banana   3INAN-ripen   sun   DUR   four   five
     'Ripen the bananas for four (or) five days.'   [Bk-20.009]

Frequency of occurrence is also encoded post-verbally, with the noun *hik* 'path' plus a numeral being used to denote the number of occurrences of the event of the verb, as in:

(53) Man   **hik**   **hiloqo**   oa,   hoqe   a-ta.
     come   path   two   IAM   SPCPLC   3INAN-GL
     '(He's) come here twice now.'   [Bk-63.020]

(54) Baqa   goet   **hik**   **goniqon**.
     NPRX.INAN   LIKE   path   three
     '(He did it) in that manner three times.'   [LB-5.163]

Measure phrases of this kind do not exclusively occur post-verbally, as seen in (55) and (56), but that is their most frequent and unmarked position. Measure phrases of duration and frequency that occur pre-verbally are weakly emphasised.

(55) Halaqi **to mil goniqon** Lebos bare gene.
    3PL   year inside three Lebos PROX.INAN LOC
    'They were three years in Lebos here.' [Bk-24.023]

(56) **Hik hitu** lai.
    path seven set
    '(He) sets (the goods) seven times.' [Bk-38.054]

14.3.1.2 Temporal/aspectual adverbs

A list of the temporal and aspectual postverbal adverbs in the corpus is given in Table 14.3. These adverbs appear directly following the verb/predicate they modify. They can also occur without a verb, if it can be understood from context, e.g., *teni!* '(do it) again!'.

Table 14.3: Postverbal temporal/aspectual adverbs.

teni	'again'
duquk	'always, constantly'
delele	'all night'
koto niq	'ceaselessly'
doli~doli	'at the same time, simultaneously'
gimen	'immediately'
dauq~dauq	'continually'
tut(u) ‡	'first, ahead'
niat ‡	'at first, earliest'

‡ These two items also appear as temporal nouns in PPs:
nominal *tut(u)* means 'past' and nominal *niat* means 'beginning'.

Examples of the postverbal temporal and aspectual adverbs are given in (57) and (58).

(57) Teras   koen=na   h-oqon   **gimen**?
    terrace good=FOC 3INAN-make immediately
    'Did you make good terraces immediately?' [Bk-65.066]

(58) Inel masak niq taq, **teni** gie   oa.
    rain big   NEG CONT again PROSP IAM
    'It wasn't raining much yet, (but) it was about to (rain a lot) again.' [Bk-13.020]

14.3.1.3 Adverbs of addition and comparison

Table 14.4 presents the greater or lesser degree to which the event denoted by the clause holds. With the exception of *kori* 'less', these adverbs are borrowings from Tetun.[2]

Table 14.4: Adverbs of addition/comparison.

lesin	'more'
kuran	'less'
kori	'less, not so much'
tuqan	'further, additionally'

These adverbs appear directly following the verb/predicate they modify. They can also occur without a verb, if it can be understood from context, e.g., *tuqan!* '(do it) further!'. Examples of the use of these items are:

(59) En   lele   gereja   gie   ukon   dele=na   mele   **lesin**.
     person   nowadays   church   3.POSS rules INS=FOC   walk   more
     'People nowadays walk more with the rules of the church.'   [Bk-62.030]

(60) Seq   **kori=e!**
     call   less=AGREE
     'Stop calling!'   [Bk-22.019]

(61) Lele   huqe   gene   tut   ba   h-oqon   **kuran~kuran**.
     nowadays   HERE   LOC   earlier   ART.INAN 3INAN-do   REDUP~less
     'Nowadays (they) do the (things of) earlier less (and) less.'   [Bk-38.019]

(62) En   tais   rele   ru-hukut   **tuqan**   on.
     person   cloth   INS   REFL-wrap.up   further   DO
     'The person wrapped himself up further with the cloth.'   [Bk-16.005]

In the above examples, the standard of comparison is not expressed. See §12.4.4.2 on the coding of these.

---

2 *Lesin* 'more' < Tetun *resin* 'more, extra'; *kuran* 'less' < Tetun *kuran* 'less', possibly < Indonesian *kurang* 'less'; *tuqan* 'less' < Tetun *tuʔan* 'grow'.

14.3.1.4 Intensifiers

In addition to the intensifying SVCs discussed in §13.7, Bunaq has a set of dedicated postverbal intensifiers (Table 14.5). With the exception of *dua* 'indeed', the Bunaq intensifiers have been borrowed from Tetun.[3]

Table 14.5: Postverbal intensifiers.

dua	'indeed'
porsa	'very'
los	'very, extremely, intensively'
tanan	'too, too much'
basuk	'too, very'

Intensifiers do not allow elision of the verb they refer to even where it can be contextually understood. Examples illustrating Bunaq intensifiers are given in (63) to (66).

(63) Tut   no   lilak   **rua**.
     past   OBL   crazy   indeed
     'In the past (she) was crazy indeed.'   [Bk-43.031]

(64) En   hiloqon=bu   g-on   laun   **porsa**.
     person   two=GIVEN   3AN-hand   fast   very
     'As for two of the people, their hands were really fast (i.e., they were fast workers).'   [Bk-12.011]

(65) Baqi   h-ota   **los**   oa.
     NPRX.AN   3INAN-plant   very   IAM
     'They really plant intensively.'   [Bk-3.021]

(66) En   bi   gie   lal   h-oqon   nare   **tanan**   niq.
     person   ART.AN   3.POSS   problem   3INAN-do   long.time   too   NEG
     '(They) dealt with the person's problem in not too long a time.'   [Bk-18.021]

---

3 *Porsa* < Tetun *forsa* 'force' < Portuguese *força* 'force'; *los* < Tetun *los* 'right, correct, well'; *tanan* < Tetun *tanan* 'bare, simple, plain'; *basuk* < Tetun *basuk* 'very, extremely'.

14.3.2 Performative *on* 'DO'

On 'DO' is a performative auxiliary which, broadly characterised, functions to give a clause an (additional) sense of active performance on the part of an S/A participant. Unlike "do" auxiliaries in many languages, Bunaq *on* is not obligatory in any context, e.g., in the presence of a negator, for instance, as in English *I **do** not know*. *On* 'DO' can mark clauses denoting both events with an agentive participant and events with a non-agentive participant. It can be used with predicates of all kinds: verbal, postpositional, nominal, etc. However, it cannot itself be a predicate or stand in for one, but always occurs with an overt predicate or with some other element which can stand in for a clause.

The diverse appearances of the performative auxiliary *on* 'DO' in Bunaq are treated here under three labels: emphasis (§14.3.2.1), durative/progressive events (§14.3.2.2), and causation (§14.3.2.3).

14.3.2.1 Emphasis

The performative *on* 'DO' is used very frequently to emphasise the way in which an event is done or happens, in contrast to some other possible way of doing it. The contrast may be contextually explicit or implied.

In (67) *on* emphasises what the fertiliser ought to do, while the paratactic clause without *on* tells us what it may not do. Similarly, in (68b) *on* is used to emphasise what the person did do, i.e., wrap themselves with a blanket as opposed to taking off the blanket (68a). In (69b) we see *on* used to emphasise how a non-agentive event did happen, as opposed to how it did not happen as in (69a).

(67) Baqi   muk   mil   a-ta   tama   **on,** hani   leleq.
     NPRX.AN   earth inside 3INAN-GL   enter DO   PROH   flow
     'That (fertiliser) **does** enter into the earth, (it) may not run off.'   [Bk-65.108]

(68) a. En   gie   tais   h-apal   niq.
        person 3.POSS   cloth 3INAN-open   NEG
        'The person didn't take off his blanket.'   [Bk-16.004]
     b. En   tais   rele ru-hukut   tuqan   on.
        person cloth INS   REFL-wrap.up   further DO
        'He **did** pull it tighter around him', i.e., 'Rather he pulled...'   [Bk-16.005]

(69) a. Nei   homo   ozol nego   uen=o   bai   niq.
        1PL.EXCL CONTR.INAN   NOT   what   one=AND   thing NEG
        'We didn't do a single thing.'   [Bk-1.046]
     b. Baqi   ret   topol   **on.**
        NPRX.AN   alone   fall   do
        'He **did** fall all by himself.' i.e., 'Rather he fell...'   [Bk-1.047]

In (70) and (71), *on* is used to emphasise the manner in which an event occurs without making any explicit contrast with another manner. In (70) *on* emphasises that when walking (to Atambua) one skirts the base of Mount Lakaqan. In (71) *on* functions to emphasise that the addressee simply receives their cows. In both cases, the use of *on* suggests that the manner in which the events occur contrasts with some other possible manner in which they could occur, e.g., keeping to the road when going by car, or buying cows.

(70) Mele,   nei   esen   Lakaqan bul   h-one   **on.**
walk   1PL.EXCL HIGH Lakaqan base   3INAN-hold DO
'Walking, we keep to the base of Lakaqan (as opposed to some other way of going).' [Bk-37.009]

(71) O   ie   kereq=o   hiloqon g-osok   **on.**
ADDR 1INCL/2.POSS single=AND two   3AN-recieve DO
'You receive your one or two (cows) (as opposed to some other way of acquiring them).' [Bk-19.012]

Emphatic *on* is also often used in questions and answers. In the questions in (72), *on* functions to contrast the two alternative propositions presented in the speaker's rhetorical questions. In (73) the speaker B uses *on* to emphasise that the entity in question was a ghost, objecting to the suggestion by speaker A that it was not a ghost.

(72) a. Indonesia a-ta   tama   **on** gie=ka?
Indonesia 3INAN-GL enter DO PROSP=OR
'Did (the East Timorese) want to enter Indonesia?' [Bk-66.003]
b. He   ret   ruqat **on** gie?
or   alone stand DO PROSP
'Or did (they) want to stand on their own?' [Bk-66.004]

(73) A. Hele   muk   g-omo   niq?
perhaps earth 3AN-master NEG
'Perhaps (she was) not an earth spirit?' [Bk-47.072]
B. Muk   g-omo   **on**=e!
earth 3AN-master DO=AGREE
'(She) *was* an earth spirit!' [Bk-47.073]

14.3.2.2 Durative/progressive events

On 'DO' is also used in a range of contexts to denote that an event happens over a period of time (durative) or is in progress at a specific time (progressive).

The use of *on* is common when describing a situation or event which holds of a period of time. In (74) *on* 'DO' emphasises that the participant wandered habitually. In (75) *on* 'DO' is used to indicate that the replacement is not a one-off event, but happens repeatedly over the course of a period of singing. In (76) the use of *on* denotes that the people spent a protracted period in the forest and were not simply there at a single point in time.

(74) *Baqi   nor   kakolo   **on**.*
     NPRX.AN randomly   wander   DO
     'She wandered on and on aimlessly.'   [Bk-18.020]

(75) *En   goniqon=o   goniqil   halaqi   biasanya   te-selu   **on**.*
     person   three=AND   four   3PL   usually   RECP-replace DO
     'Three or four people usually keep taking each others' (places).'   [Bk-18.027]

(76) *En   nor   mona   mil   gene   **on**.*
     person   aimlessly   forest   inside   LOC   DO
     'They were living in the forest.'   [Bk-66.017]

The performative auxiliary *on* is also used to denote actions which the A/S is in the process of carrying out. Compare the clauses with the motion verb *tebe* 'return' in (77). Example (77a) without *on* is the greeting given when one has returned home. By contrast, example (77b) with *on* can only be used when one is in the course of going home.

(77) a. *Tebe   oa.*
        return IAM
        'I'm back/home.' (lit., '(I am) returned.')
     b. *Tebe   on   oa.*
        return DO   IAM
        'I'm on my way back/home.'(lit., (I am doing) returning.')   [OS-07.01]

Further examples of the progressive use of *on* are given in (78) and (79).

(78) *Baqi   bupati   **on**   niq   taq.*
     NPRX.AN   governor   DO   NEG   CONT
     'He wasn't (doing the job of) governor yet.'   [Bk-29.035]

(79) *Baqi   heser   **on**, ...*
     NPRX.AN   dead   DO
     '(When) she was doing dying, ...' i.e., 'She was in the process of dying, ...'
                                                                  [Bk-46.037]

14.3.2.3 Causation

On 'DO' can be used to add a sense of causation to the clause and to focus on the achievement of the event or state denoted by the verb.

In agentive clauses, *on* 'DO' may serve to highlight the achievement of the event and underline the agentivity of the A participant. For instance, in (80) *on* 'DO' serves to heighten the sense of intentionality and volition on the part of the mother in tipping out the water and discarding the firewood fetched by her son.

(80) a. *Baqi   il   ho,   gie   eme   h-ini   sikot, g-o*
         NPRX.AN   water scoop 3.POSS mother 3INAN-call muddy   3-SRC
         uku   on.
         tip.out   DO
         '(When) he hauled water, his mother said (it) was muddy, (and taking it) from him, tipped (it) out.' [Bk-6.003]
    b. *Hotel=na   wit=o,   h-ini   ugar   minak,   g-o*
         wood=FOC   fetch=AND   3INAN-call green   complete   3-SRC
         wa   on.
         discard   DO
         '(When he) fetched wood, too, (his mother) said it was all green, took it from him and threw it out.' [Bk-6.004]

In clauses with stative verbs, *on* 'DO' indicates that the participant is actively experiencing the state denoted by the verb. Consider the examples in (81) with the stative verb *milik* 'afraid'. Example (81) without *on* 'DO' is neutral as to the nature of the *milik* 'afraid', denoting simply that the S participant experiences the state of being scared. In (81), however, *milik* 'afraid' is marked with *on* 'DO', indicating an experience in which the S participant is actively engaged and for which there is an unspecified stimulus/cause.

(81) a. *Neto   milik.*
         1SG   afraid
         'I am scared.'
    b. *Neto   milik   on.*
         1SG   afraid DO
         'I am made scared' (lit., 'I do being scared.') [OS-07.01]

The role of *on* in adding a sense of causation is also seen in its frequent use in clauses with the causative predicate *h-ini* '3INAN-CAUS' (cf. §10.4.2). In (82) and (83) *on* functions to emphasise the achieved causation of hungriness and laughing, respectively.

(82) In   ziek   baqa   n-ini   bilat   **on.**
     onion   fry   NPRX.INAN   1EXCL-CAUS   hungry   DO
     'Those frying onions make me feel hungry' (lit.,'Frying onions makes me do being hungry.')   [OS-06.01]

(83) Baqi   n-ini   higal   **on.**
     NPRX.INAN   1EXCL-CAUS   laugh   DO
     'She made me laugh' (lit., 'She makes me do laughing.')   [Bk-1.035]

14.3.3 Prospective *gie* '**PROSP**'

Gie 'PROSP' appears post-verbally denoting prospective aspect.[4] Prospective aspect is where a state is related to a subsequent future time (Comrie 1985: 64–65). *Gie* 'PROSP' cannot be used on its own without a predicate or some other element, such as a modal adverb, standing in for a predicate, even where the predicate can be anaphorically retrieved.

In Bunaq, prospective aspect with *gie* 'PROSP' includes the senses 'intend to', 'going to', and 'want to' and typically involves volitional and controlling human agents. Examples (84) to (86) illustrate these senses of *gie*. Note that while (84) and (85) denote prospective events in the near future, (86) refers to an event that is to take place at an undetermined future time.

(84) Teo   mal   **gie**?
     where   go   PROSP
     'Where (are you) going to?'   [LB-10.041]

(85) Neto   Ø-ege   rie   tas   gie   rale   **gie.**
     1SG   1INCL/2-BEN   REFL.POSS   village   3.POSS   say   PROSP
     'I'm going to tell you about my village.'   [Bk-7.001]

---

4 Schapper (2008) posits a diachronic relationship between a postposed possessive *gie* '3.POSS' and aspect-marking *gie* 'PROSP', and describes a grammaticalisation path from possession to prospective aspect. It is notable that several other nearby languages have identical forms for 3rd person possessive markers and similar aspect markers: in Wersing, a TAP language spoken on Alor, *ge* is both a possessive marker and a prospective aspect marker (Schapper 2020d). In Tetun, the imminent aspect suffix *-n* is homophonous with the 3rd person singular inalienable possessive suffix *-n*. However, van Klinken (1999: 239) points out that the imminent aspect suffix *-n* may simply be a reduction of the imminent aspectual marker *onan*.

(86) *Neto ri-mil,   hot mil no   sore   baqa   goet*
     1SG   REFL-inside sun DUR OBL machete NPRX.INAN   LIKE
     r-ege   wit   gie.
     REFL-BEN   fetch   PROSP
     'I feel, one day I would like to buy myself a machete like that.' [Bk-24.040]

In the above examples, the prospectivity marked by *gie* is relative to the time of speaking. However, *gie* may also mark an event as relative to time in the narrative. In (87b) the drinking of water is prospective to the time in the narrative when the participant got thirsty (87a). Similarly, in (88b) the eating of the mangoes is prospective to the going to the garden (88a).

(87) a. *Hik   gene, baqi   pit   saq.*
        road   LOC   NPRX.AN   throat dry
        'On the way he got thirsty.'   [Bk-04.046]
     b. *Baqi   il   a   gie.*
        NPRX.AN   water eat   PROSP
        'He wanted to drink water.'   [Bk-04.047]

(88) a. *Hot   mil   uen   no   nei   nie   moen   mil*
        sun   DUR   one   OBL   1PL.EXCL   1EXCL.POSS   friend   COLL
        g-utu   nei   goniqo   ola   mar.
        3-COM   1PL.EXCL   three   LOW   garden   go
        'One day we three, my friends and I, we went down to the garden.'
                                                                   [Bk-1.011]
     b. *Nei   mar   gene   zo   a   gie.*
        1PL.EXCL   farm   LOC   mango   eat   PROSP
        'We wanted to eat mangoes in the garden.'   [Bk-1.012]

Gie 'PROSP' can also be used in the context of past actions which were going to be carried out but which were not achieved due to intervening factors. In (89a) we see that *gie* marks a prospective event in which the participants attempt to escape their bonds. We learn in a later clause, (89b), that they were unsuccessful in their attempts to escape, being later released by Suri Guloq. Similarly, in (90a) *gie* marks a prospective event which does not take place, as the girl closes the door on the offending male (90b).

(89) a. *Halaqi   hitu   bi   d-opil   no   d-oter   gie.*
        3PL   seven   ART.AN REFL-power   OBL   REFL-snatch   PROSP
        'Those seven were wanting to getting themselves away.'   [Bk-6.051]
     b. *Suri Guloq   halaqi hitu   baqi   g-ilin.*
        Suri Guloq   3PL   seven   NPRX.AN   3AN-unleash
        'Suri Guloq unleashed those seven.'   [Bk-6.057]

(90) a. Baqi   en   pana   gol   bi   gu-sura, g-utu
       NPRX.AN   person female small ART.AN 3AN-ask   3-COM
       cier   **gie**.
       sleep PROSP
       'He propositioned the girl, wanting to sleep with her.' [Bk-21.004]

   b. Homo=na,   en   pana   himo   milik,   die
      CONTR.INAN=FOC person female CONTR.AN   scared   REFL.POSS
      tazuq ube.
      door   shut
      'With that, the girl got scared (and) shut her door.' [Bk-21.005]

Finally, where two clauses stand in parataxis, *gie* 'PROSP' marks a clause expressing the purpose for which the action depicted in the other clause is carried out. The marked clause expressing purpose typically follows the clause expressing the action that is done in order to achieve it, as in (91). However, this iconic ordering can also be perturbed when *gie* 'PROSP' is present, as in (92).

(91) Naqi   pana   gie   reu   mal, memel   ba   h-oqon
     royal   female 3.POSS house go   sickness ART.INAN 3INAN-do
     gie.
     PROSP
     '(He) went to the princess' home to cure her sickness.' [Bk-4.024]

(92) Reu   taqa   **gie**, hut   dele on.
     house cover   PROSP   kunai.grass INS   DO
     'To cover (i.e., roof) a house, (it is) done with thatch.' [Bk-24.012]

14.3.3.1 *gie oa* 'be about to'

Where *gie* 'PROSP' is followed by *oa* 'IAM' (see §14.3.5.2), the combination denotes imminence, i.e., indicates that an event or state is impending and will begin shortly. Examples (93) and (94) illustrate the use of *gie oa* with agentive bivalent and monovalent verbs, respectively, to signal that the action is about to take place.

(93) En   heser bi   g-olo   **gie** oa.
     person dead   ART.AN 3AN-bury PROSP   IAM
     '(They) were about to bury the dead person.' [Bk-18.010]

(94) Nei   nie   u   tula   **gie** oa.
     1PL.EXCL 1EXCL.POSS herbaceous.plant   transport PROSP   IAM
     'We were about to transport our undergrowth.' [Bk-12.017]

Examples (95) and (96) show the use of *gie oa* with two non-agentive verbs to denote imminent entry into a state.

(95) Eme   heser **gie**   **oa**.
     mother   dead   PROSP   IAM
     'Mother was about to die.'   [Bk-43.008]

(96) Inel   masak niq   taq,   teni   **gie**   **oa**.
     rain   big   NEG   CONT   again   PROSP   IAM
     'The rain was not yet much, (but it was) about to be (so) again.' [Bk-13.020]

14.3.3.2 *gie taq* 'just going to'

When *gie* 'PROSP' is followed by *taq* 'CONT' (see §14.3.5.1), it indicates that the event is just about to be in progress. This is typically used by a speaker to herald what they are about to do in continuation of an earlier event, as in (97) and (98). In (99) *gie taq* is used in a question to ask who is going to keep pulling on the door in the future.

(97) Bare   no,   neto   a   obon   gie   ba   sasi
     PROX.INAN   OBL   1SG   food   hang   PROSP   ART.INAN   say
     gie   **taq**.
     PROSP   CONT
     'Now, I'm just going to talk about the hanging of the food.'   [Bk-18.043]

(98) Neto   r-isik   **gie**   **taq**.
     person   REFL-sprinkle   PROSP   CONT
     'I'm just going to the toilet.'   [OS-07.01]

(99) Sio=na   nei   n-ege   tazuq   ul   **gie**   **taq**?
     who=FOC   1PL.EXCL   1EXCL-BEN   door   pull   PROSP   CONT
     'Who is going to keep pulling on the door for us?'   [LB1.088]

14.3.4 Restrictive *ai* 'ONLY'

The restrictive marker *ai* 'ONLY' serves to limit reference to the situation denoted by the clause. The restrictive marker cannot stand alone in a clause, even if the predicate is retrievable in the discourse; it always requires a predicate or some other item standing in for the predicate to be expressed in the clause preceding it.

In (100) and (101) we see *ai* being used to express that the event denoted by the predicate should happen 'precisely in that way, exactly in that manner'.

(100) Rie   loka mil   gene milik rele   holon **ai**.
      REFL.POSS   room inside LOC   scared INS   cry   ONLY
      '(She) just cried in her room out of fear.'   [Bk-21.006]

(101) I   r-ege   bai   wit=o   bai,   baqa=na
      1PL.INCL REFL-BEN thing buy=AND   thing NPRX.INAN=FOC
      a   **ai**.
      eat ONLY
      'We buy ourselves something to eat or whatever, (and it is) that alone (that) we eat.'   [Bk-30.089]

Examples (102) and (103) show *ai* 'ONLY' with stative predicates. Here, too, *ai* 'ONLY' functions to delimit reference to just that state denoted by the predicate.

(102) Nona bare   no   **ai**   oa.
      girl PROX.INAN   OBL   ONLY   IAM
      'Miss just be here now.', i.e. 'Don't move.'   [Bk-14.014]

(103) Meaq gol hiloqon   unu~unu   on   **ai**.
      child   two   REDUP~quiet   DO   ONLY
      'The children just kept really quiet.'   [LB-1.081]

Ai 'ONLY' occasionally appears with the negator *niq* 'NEG' in its scope, where it functions to reinforce the negation, as in (104) and (105).

(104) A. Ei   Ø-azal   nare   niq?
         2PL   1INCL/2-see   long.time NEG
         '(She) didn't see you for long?'   [Bk-47.030]
      B. Nare   niq   **ai**.
         long.time NEG   ONLY
         'For not a long time at all.'   [Bk-47.031]

(105) a. Gie   ama   heser o=si,   baqa   h-oqon
         3.POSS father dead   IAM=REAS   NPRX.INAN 3INAN-do
         liol   niq.
         continue NEG
         'Because her father had died, (they) didn't go on with that.'   [Bk-70.130]

b. *Baqa   ni,   malu-ai   h-oqon   liol*
   NPRX.INAN OBL   bride.exchange   3INAN-do   continue
   niq   ai.
   NEG   ONLY
   'At that (time), (they) didn't continue to do the uniting of houses at all.'
   [Bk-70.131]

Finally, the restrictive marker occurs in the construction *ai* V *ai* V to denote 'just keep doing V' where V represents the verb/predicate. In (106) we see this construction with an agentive verb and in (107) with a stative verb. See §5.7.4 on the same construction in the nominal domain.

(106) *Tuk   ai,   tuk   ai.*
       pile.up   ONLY pile.up   ONLY
       '(He) just kept piling up (the grass).'   [Bk-50.024]

(107) *Hoza   baqa   legul   ai,   legul   ai.*
       coconut   NPRX.INAN   tall   ONLY   tall   ONLY
       'The coconut tree just kept getting taller and taller.'   [Bk-6.018]

14.3.5 Phasal polarity markers

As is common across Indonesia, the basic aspectual distinction in Bunaq is one of phasal polarity. The Bunaq phasal polarity contrast is between the continuative marked by *taq* 'CONT' (§14.3.5.1) and the iamitive marked by *oa* 'IAM' (§14.3.5.2). These markers cannot stand on their own (108a) even where the predicate is retrievable in the discourse. They require a predicate or some other element, such as the negator in (108b), to precede them.

(108) a. **Oa!*
           IAM
           '(It's) already (done).'
       b. *Niq   oa.*
           NEG   IAM
           '(It's) not (the case) anymore.'   [Not-07.03]

Taq 'CONT' and *oa* 'IAM' typically occur to the right of the standard negator *niq* 'NEG', as in (108b) above. In elicitation, however, all informants accepted examples in which a phasal polarity marker preceded *niq* 'NEG' in the context of negating a question containing the phasal polarity marker, as in (109). In the absence of recorded spontaneous utterances with this ordering of a phasal polarity marker relative to the negator, it remains to be seen whether this is a truly natural construction in Bunaq.

(109) A. *Memel taq?*
    sick CONT
    '(Is she) still sick?'
  B. *Memel taq niq.*
    sick CONT NEG
    '(She's) not still sick.' [OS-07.01]

14.3.5.1 Continuative *taq* 'still'

Taq 'CONT' is a high frequency item in Bunaq, indicating the persistence of an already existing situation. Examples (110) and (111) illustrate the use of *taq* 'CONT' in agentive clauses in relation to an event that is persistent.

(110) *Le gie gol no, nei u h-ozep **taq**.*
    next.day small OBL 1PL.EXCL herbaceous.plant 3INAN-cut CONT
    'In the early hours of the next day, we were cutting undergrowth.' [Bk-12.018]

(111) *Le gol h-azal taq, g-ini kama ziqui **taq**.*
    light small 3INAN-see CONT 3AN-CAUS pile.up nevertheless CONT
    '(Whilst he) still saw a little light, (he) made him keep piling up (leaves).'
    [Bk-50.012]

Examples (112) and (113) illustrate the use of *taq* 'CONT' in non-agentive clauses to indicate that a state is still ongoing.

(112) *Lui Bert u **taq**.*
    Louis Berthe live CONT
    'Louis Berthe was still alive.' [Bk-70.116]

(113) *Ton baqa ton ho mil no **taq**.*
    marriage NPRX.INAN marriage blood inside OBL CONT
    'That marriage is still an incestuous marriage (lit., marriage within blood).'
    [Bk-62.006]

In procedural texts, *taq* 'CONT' emphasises that a marked event lasts for a period of time, illustrated in (114) and (115).

(114) a. *Homo   haqal,   mar   baqa   h-en   **taq**.*
       CONTR.INAN finished   garden   NPRX.INAN   3INAN-dry   CONT
       'After that, the gardens are drying.'   [Bk-3.013]
   b. *H-en   baqa,   kaleq   g-ini   saq   **taq**.*
       3INAN-dry   NPRX.INAN   plant.sp   3AN-CAUS   dried   CONT
       'That drying (means), the trees are being made to dry out.'   [Bk-3.014]

(115) a. *I   paqol   g-ao.*
       1PL.INCL   maize   3AN-pound
       'We pound the maize.'   [Bk-45.006]
   b. *Paqol   g-ao,   i   g-apiq   **taq**.*
       maize   3AN-pound   1PL.INCL   3AN-sift   CONT
       '(After) pounding maize, we are sifting it.'   [Bk-45.007]
   c. *G-apiq   haqal,   homo   soq,   i   a bokal*
       3AN-sift   finished   CONTR.INAN   SEQ   1PL.INCL   PORRIDGE
       *t-inik   **taq**.*
       3INAN-cook   CONT
       '(When) sifting is finished, then, we are cooking the coarse food (=maize porridge).'   [Bk-45.008]

14.3.5.1.1 *niq taq* 'not yet'

Taq frequently occurs following the negative *niq* to encode the continuing non-realisation of the event or state denoted in the clause, i.e., 'not yet, still not', as in:

(116) *Kalo   niq,   t-erel   mele   **niq**   **taq**.*
       if   NEG   RECP-INS   walk   NEG   CONT
       'If (it is) not (done), (they) cannot yet walk together.'   [Bk-38.010]

(117) *Bapaq   bari   mos   memel   nare   **niq**   **taq**.*
       father   PROX.AN   also   sick   long.time   NEG   CONT
       'Father here also was not yet long ago sick.'   [Bk-46.020]

14.3.5.2 Iamitive *oa* 'already'

The iamitive marker *oa* 'IAM' expresses that a situation has come to exist, that is, it indicates a change of polarity in that a non-existent situation comes into existence. Although often used in reference to past time events, *oa* is not limited to them and can be used in reference to present, future, and irrealis events (cf. its use with *gie* 'PROSP' in §14.3.3). Note that *oa* frequently reduces to [o=] when followed in the clause by another element (see, e.g., example 129 below).

Iamitive *oa* is used to encode that an event has 'already' begun by a reference time. A clause marked with *oa* may refer to an event that has begun by the time of speaking, as in (118) and (119). We see in these examples that *oa* indicates that the situation holds in the present.

(118) *Lele   moderen   tama **oa**.*
      nowadays   modernity enter IAM
      'Nowadays modernity has already entered.'   [Bk-29.030]

(119) *Reu   por   baru gene=na   misa h-oqon   **oa**.*
      house holy   new   LOC=FOC mass 3INAN-do   IAM
      '(They) already do the mass in the new church.'   [Bk-34.059]

A clause marked with *oa* 'IAM' may also refer to an event that has been brought into existence relative to some specified point in time in the narrative, as in (120) and (121).

(120) *Tan   n-on   hinal   **oa**, neto u   bilik*
      because   1EXCL-hand injured IAM   1SG   herbaceous.plant bind
      baqis-baqis,   baqa   h-iqil,   reu   mal.
      REDUP~much   NPRX.INAN 3INAN-leave.behind   house go
      'Because my hand had already been injured, I left behind the many bundles of undergrowth (and) went home.'   [Bk-12.020]

(121) *Jepang g-ini   i   ru-bul   ukon,   Jepang=na*
      Japan   3AN-CAUS   1PL.INCL   REFL-head   govern   Japan=FOC
      *nei   nu-bul   ukon   **oa**.*
      1PL.EXCL   REFL-head   govern   IAM
      '(We) made Japan our rulers, (and) the Japanese ruled over us.'   [Bk-29.008]

Used in stative clauses, *oa* 'IAM' indicates that the state has 'already' been entered into at the time of reference. The reference time may be the time of speaking (122) or some past time in a narrative (123).

(122) *Matas   **oa**=si,   basin   **oa**.*
      old   IAM=REAS   forgetful   IAM
      'Because (she) is old already, (she's) already forgetful.'   [Bk-30.061]

(123) *Baqa   no   neto   holon, tan   botil   tuek,*
      NPRX.INAN   OBL   1SG   cry   because   bottle   heavy
      *n-ezel=o   memel   **oa**.*
      1EXCL-belly=AND   sick   IAM
      'At that point, I cried, because the bottles were heavy and my stomach hurt already.'   [Bk-13.008]

Oa is also often used in reference to a present time event which is in the process of being brought into existence, with the sense 'now'. This use of *oa* is particularly common in exclamations and imperatives, as in (124) and (125).

(124) Mal **oa**.
 go IAM
 '(I'm) going now.' [OS-06.01]

(125) Ei sai **oa**.
 2PL exit IAM
 'Off you go.' (lit., You leave now.') [Bk-22.001]

Oa may be also used in irrealis contexts to denote that a hypothetical event/state has been brought into existence. Example (126) is an excerpt from a procedural text in which the speaker describes the way in which a kind of cake is made. *Oa* is used repeatedly to denote that some point in the preparation of the cakes is reached.

(126) a. Mete ubi mogor nor no homo hol beseq
 NOW tuber banana.leaf leaf OBL CONTR.INAN stone flat
 wa baqa no lai.
 top NPRX.INAN OBL set
 'Now the cassava on the banana leaf is set on that flat stone.' [Bk-76.030]
 b. Kalo mogor no homo lewen **oa**, ...
 if banana.leaf OBL CONTR.INAN wilt IAM
 'If those (things) on the banana leaves are already wilting, ...' [Bk-76.031]
 c. Lewen los **oa**, homo tekeq.
 wilt very IAM CONTR.INAN look.at
 '(If it's) already wilted a lot, have at look at it.' [Bk-76.032]
 d. Ten **oa**, h-atun **oa**.
 cooked IAM 3INAN-take.down IAM
 '(If it's) already ready, take it off already.' [Bk-76.033]

See also §14.3.3.1 on how *oa* can also be used in reference to events which are to be brought into existence in the future with *gie* 'PROSP'.

14.3.5.2.1 *niq oa* 'no more'
The negator *niq* 'NEG' frequently occurs to the left of *oa* 'IAM'. The resulting meaning of the combination is 'no longer, not any more'. For instance:

(127) Kalaq man=bu, g-azal **niq oa**.
 maybe come=GIVEN 3AN-see NEG IAM
 'If (he) has come, (I) didn't see him anymore.' [Bk-63.013]

(128) *Nei   matas   mil   gie   h-one   **niq**   **oa.***
      1PL.EXCL   old   COLL   3.POSS 3INAN-hold NEG   IAM
      'We don't hold to (the practices) of the elders anymore.'   [Bk-65.044]

14.3.6 Information markers

Bunaq has two markers that denote the nature of the information conveyed in the clause: *gin* 'REPORT' marking reported speech, and *nai* 'INFORM' marking that the speaker seeks to provide the hearer with information. The markers cannot be negated or followed by any postverbal adverbials and/or clause-modifying markers; only enclitic clause-final conjunctions follow an information marker, though their co-occurrence is rare. The markers do not co-occur and the clauses they mark cannot be elided under conditions of contextual anaphora.

14.3.6.1 Reportative *gin* 'REPORT'

The reportative marker *gin* 'REPORT' serves to denote that the information in the clause is reported by the speaker from a third party source beyond the speech situation. The third party source of the information is typically left unspecified, but is occasionally retrievable from the discourse context. In a semantic extension, *gin* can also be used for reported thoughts and for conjectured information.

In (129) and (130), *gin* 'REPORT' indicates that the information in the clause was obtained from a third party. The third party who was the source of the information is left unspecified; the identity of the informants is neither explicitly named nor contextually retrievable from the discourse.

(129) A. *Eto   roe?*
          2SG   SPEC.INAN
          'What's with you?' (lit., You here?')   [Bk-68.061]
      B. *Neto   nie   en   heser   o=**gin**.*
          1SG   1EXCL.POSS   person   dead   IAM=REPORT
          '(One of) my people has died {I'm told}.'   [Bk-68.062]

(130) *Lewat   loi   niq,   en   Dili   mil   kampanye,   kaco*
      go.via good   NEG   person   Dili   COLL   campaign   chaotic
      ***gin**=si.*
      REPORT=REAS
      '(We) couldn't go via (Dili), because the people (in) Dili were campaigning, (it was) chaotic {I was told}.'   [Bk-61.036]

In (131a), *gin* indicates that the speaker heard the information in the clause from a third party, but here the identity of the third party is known. In (131b) the speaker clarifies the source of the information as the woman under discussion by mentioning that the children had received the information from her.

(131) a. *Paq desa=i g-o gene=na ciluq **gin**.*
Mr village=HUM.PL 3-SRC LOC=FOC hang.out REPORT
'{It was said that} she was hanging out at the house of the village head's family.' [Bk-63.032]
b. *Baqi=na sasi, en meaq gol gol g-ege.*
NPRX.AN=FOC say person child small 3AN-BEN
'It was she who said that, (she said it) to the little children.' [Bk-63.033]

Gin is occasionally used to mark clauses whose information is supposed or conjectured. For example, in (132), *gin* marks the conjecture that the horse was still in the yard outside the house while the people slept. In (133), the conjecture marked by *gin* is that the addressee is most likely hunting, as that was his normal practice.

(132) *Homo ni, en real roi sier gaqal, kura*
CONTR.INAN OBL person many SPEC.AN sleep all.AN horse
*gu-bul tobok=bu leo homo ni **gin**.*
3.AN-head twin=GIVEN yard CONTR.INAN OBL REPORT
'Then, while all those many people were asleep, {it was thought that} the double-headed horse was in the yard.' [KuraTobok-055]

(133) *Mete hocinoq ba, ei ie kela*
NOW daytime ART.INAN 2PL 1INCL/2.POSS brother.in-law
Meta Puan gene Ø-agal, eli sala mete ene=bu
Meta Puan LOC 1INCL/2-search 2SG should NOW night=GIVEN
*zap g-utu mele gie taq **gin**, ...*
dog 3-COM walk PROSP CONT REPORT
'In the daytime, Brother Meta Puan was looking for you, {it was thought that} you would, now that it's night, be out hunting with the dogs, ...' [Puan-019]

There are a few instances in the corpus where a clause marked by *gin* 'REPORT' marks a clause preceded by a predicate of speaking or thinking, as in (134) and (135).

(134) *Kela Asa, eto **sasi=na**, Ø-ezel memel **gin**, ...*
brother.in-law Asa 2SG say=FOC 1INCL/2-belly sick REPORT
'Brother Asa, you say your stomach is sore.' [Puan-076]

(135) a. *Akir   Augustus   en   milisi=o   tentara   Indonesia*
        end   August   person   militia=AND   solider   Indonesia
        ri-mil:
        REFL-inside
        'At the end of August, the militia and Indonesian soliders thought:'
        [Bk-66.006]

   b. *En=na   Indonesia   tama   gie,   g-ini=na   baqis*
       person=FOC   Indonesia   enter   PROSP   3AN-CAUS=FOC   much
       *gie   **gin**.*
       PROSP   REPORT
       '(They) were going to make many people enter Indonesia.'
       [Bk-66.007]

Gin 'REPORT' originates in a verb of speech and is occasionally found as a verb, either independently (136) or together with *sasi* 'say' (137), in some older texts. When used as a verb, *gin* is glossed as 'say'.

(136) *Hot   mil   uen,   Orel   gie   moen   Pip   g-ege*
      sun   DUR   one   monkey   3.POSS   friend   goat   3AN-BEN
      *homo   **gin:**...*
      CONTR.INAN   say
      'One day, Monkey said this to his friend Goat: ...'   [OrelNisPipLoko-03]

(137) *Tazuq   ul-wen   oa,   g-utu   tama   hol   mil   homo   gene,*
      door   pull-ANTIC   IAM   3-COM   enter   stone   inside   CONTR.INAN   LOC
      *doe   **gin**   sasi:...*
      SPEC.INAN   say   say
      'The door opened and (he) went into the rock with her and said this: ...'
      [GepalMasak-036]

14.3.6.2 Informative *nai* 'INFORM'

The informative marker *nai* 'INFORM' serves to denote that the speaker intends to impart knowledge or communicate information to the addressee, often as part of a warning; possible translations of *nai* 'INFORM' include 'I'm telling you' and 'be warned'.

In (138) we see *nai* 'INFORM' used in a reply to a request for a person to go with speaker B. *Nai* 'INFORM' functions to impress on speaker A that the speaker B is walking and that if the lady also wishes to accompany them, she must also walk.

(138) A. *Hei   ibu,   ibu   bari   ei   Ø-utu   t-erel   gie.*
         hey   Mrs   Mrs   PROX.AN   2PL   1INCL/2-COM RECP-INS   PROSP
         'Hey Mrs, this lady wants (to go) together with you.'   [Bk-37.020]

B. *Nei   mele   on   **nai**.*
   1PL.EXCL walk   DO   INFORM
   'We're doing it on foot {be warned!}.' [Bk-37.021]

A. *Baqa   han=e!*
   NPRX.INAN   be.no.matter=AGREE
   'That's no problem.' [Bk-37.022]

In (139), *nai* is used to convey to the addressee that it is getting dark and it warns them not to be out at such a late hour. In (140) the speaker uses *nai* to warn the addressee that their companion is likely hungry, with the implication that the young person should be given some food.

(139) *Pan   mon   o=**nai**.*
       sky   evening   IAM=INFORM
       'It's getting dark! {be warned!}' (lit., 'the sky (is in its) evening (state) already') [OS-07.01]

(140) *Mama Eta,   en   gol   bari   bilat   o=**nai**.*
       mother Eta   person   small   PROX.AN   hungry   IAM=INFORM
       'Mother Eta, this young person is hungry already {I'm telling you}.' [Bk-37.047]

In the examples given thus far, *nai* marks situations that are occurring at the time of speech. But it is also possible for *nai* to be used in reference to events that are in the past or future. In (141) *nai* marks a clause referring to an event that occurred the previous night, informing the addressee that they failed to lock the door previously and warning that this should not be repeated. In (142) *nai* marks a clause referring to an event in the future: the crow warns the cockatoo that when he returns home after his seven days at the festival are over, his white features must be returned to him.

(141) *Inanoq   kunci   niq   **nai**.*
       last.night lock.up   NEG   INFORM
       'Last night (you) didn't lock up {I'm warning you not to do it again}.' [OS-07.02]

(142) *Baqa,   man=bu,   tebe   n-ege   **nai**!*
       NPRX.INAN   come=GIVEN   return   1EXCL-give   INFORM
       'But, when you come home, you will give (them) back to me {I'm warning you}.' [Bk-78.34]

Unlike *gin* 'REPORT', *nai* 'INFORM' does not have any known verbal uses.

14.3.7 Priorative *naq* 'PRIOR'

The priorative marker *naq* 'PRIOR' is used in exclamatory speech acts with a rising intonation to signal that the event denoted in the clause will be carried out as a matter of priority, before anything else is done. Examples of this with a 1st person singular S/A are given in (143) and (144).

(143) *We,   en   matas! Neto rebel   naq!*
      INTERJ person old   1SG   descend   PRIOR
      'Yes, sir! I'm coming down now!'   [UsikPip-019]

(144) *Neto mal   ili   d-ege   bai   a   s-agal   naq!*
      1SG   go   1DU.INCL   REFL-BEN thing eat 3INAN-search PRIOR
      'I will go and find food for us now.'   [GepalMasaq-041]

As already discussed in §4.6.1.1, *naq* 'PRIOR' is used with 2nd person and 1st person plural referents for S/A to denote imperative and hortative meanings, as in (145) and (146), respectively.

(145) *Eto   rie   matas mil   g-utu   man   naq!*
      2SG   REFL.POSS   old   COLL   3-COM   come PRIOR
      'You come with your parents!'   [Bk-38.005]

(146) *Nei   mal   naq!*
      1PL.EXCL   go   PRIOR
      'Let's go!'   [OS-07.02]

The priorative meaning of *naq* (i.e., that the event in the clause it marks occurs prior to another event) is most apparent when it is used to conjoin clauses. In clause-conjoining constructions, *naq* is always followed by =*na* 'FOC' (§4.7.3.2.3). For example, the clauses in (147) occur in a textual sequence: the proposition in (147a) is referred back to by *homo* 'CONTR.INAN' and marked as occurring prior to the event in (147b) by *naq* 'PRIOR'. See §15.3.2.1.4 for more illustration of this use.

(147) a. *Mone tumel   rele molo-pu   lai.*
         man   money   INS   betel-areca set
         'The man sets betel and areca down with money.' (figurative for 'The man pays a deposit of money for the bride-price.')   [Bk-38.008]
      b. *Homo   naq=na,   halali baqi   t-erel   mele.*
         CONTR.INAN PRIOR=FOC   3DU   NPRX.AN   RECP-INS walk
         'Once that (is done), then those two (can) walk together.'   [Bk-38.009]

Naq 'PRIOR' does not co-occur with postverbal modifiers like performative, aspectual, or phasal polarity markers. It can, albeit rarely, occur with postverbal adverbials like *teni* 'again' and the affirmative enclitic =*e*, as seen in (148).

(148) *Dia Laho, ni-ta   tuk   **teni**   **naq=e**!*
      Dia Laho, 1EXCL-GL pile.up again PRIOR=AGREE
      'Dia Laho, pile (it) up onto me again!'   [Bk-50.023]

Chapter 15
Multiclausal constructions

15.1 Introduction

This chapter deals with constructions that involve more than one clause. Based on differences in phonological and morphosyntactic characteristics, I distinguish three types of multiclausal construction in Bunaq.

The first type is clause complementation. This is where one clause acts as an argument of another clause. Unlike relative clauses (discussed in §5.4), complement clauses do not have heads. Additionally, clausal complements are only found with a restricted set of verbs in Bunaq. Clausal complementation is discussed in §15.2.

The second type is clause conjoining. This refers to the situation in which two or more clauses are linked to one another intonationally and/or by means of a marker of clause conjoining. Strategies for conjoining clauses are discussed in §15.3.

The third type of multicausal construction in Bunaq is sentence connecting. This refers to heterogenous devices used to create textual cohesion between phonologically and morphosyntactically independent utterances consisting of one or more clause. Bunaq sentence-connecting strategies are discussed in §15.4.

Throughout this chapter, as elsewhere in the grammar, the boundary between conjoined clauses is marked by a comma, while the boundary between sentences is marked with a full stop.

15.2 Clause complementation

Clause complementation is where one clause acts as an argument of another clause. Complementation is only found with a restricted set of verbs in Bunaq. There are two subtypes of complement clause in Bunaq: (i) clausal complements filling an argument slot of the verb in the matrix clause that can also be filled by an NP (§15.2.1), and (ii) clausal complements that can never be replaced by an NP (§15.2.2). A third type of complementation could be considered to occur with *h-ini* '3INAN-call/cause', but because of its structural similarities to *h-ege* '3INAN-give', I treat it separately as a trivalent verb in §10.4.1.

In order to be considered a complement clause, I require the clause to consist of more than a simple verb. It might, for instance, be a verb with one or more overtly expressed arguments, or a verb together with an aspect or phasal polarity marker. This requirement is a practical, rather than a theoretical one; it means that the ability of many lexemes to appear as verbs or nouns (e.g., *ton* 'marry, marriage', *mequ* 'give a kiss, kiss' – see §3.4 on noun-verb conversion) cannot confound the analysis of complement clauses.

15.2.1 NP-replacing complements

An NP-replacing clausal complement occupies an argument slot of the matrix clause which is normally filled by an NP. I discuss verbs taking clausal complements in place of an NP for P in §15.2.1.1 and in place of an NP for S in §15.2.1.2.

15.2.1.1 Complements as P

Complements acting as the P argument within a matrix clause occur with Bunaq verbs of speaking, perception, and liking, such as *sura* 'ask' (1), *mak* 'hear' (2), and *mobel* 'like' (3).

(1) Eme   [eto   teo   gene cier   gie]$_P$ sura.
    mother 2SG   where LOC   sleep PROSP   ask
    'Mother asks where are you going to sleep.'   [OS-07.01]

(2) Neto [topi bi   doqon]$_P$ ga-mak,   zap=bu   ga-mak   niq.
    1SG   owl ART.AN hoot   3AN-hear dog=GIVEN   3AN-hear NEG
    'I listen to the hooting of the owl, not the dog.'   [EnLoiEnPuanMoen-020]

(3) Neto [nie   ama   g-utu   mal gie]$_P$ mobel, ...
    1SG   1EXCL.POSS father 3-COM   go   PROSP   like
    'I like to go out with my father, ...'   [Bk-24.036]

In the above examples, the P complement clauses are structurally surrounded by the matrix clause, with the NP for A appearing before the P complement clause and the matrix verb after it. In natural speech, however, it is actually quite rare for a P complement clause to be preceded by an NP for A. Typically, the referent of A is already established in the discourse and is elided, such that the P complement clause is utterance-initial, as in (4) to (6). Alternatively, the NP for A can be right-clefted, as in (7).

(4) [En   ota   gene toek   roe]$_P$ mak   niq, ...
    person LEVEL   LOC   talk   SPEC.INAN   hear NEG
    '(I) couldn't hear the talking of the people over there, ...'
                                                                    [Zap-032]

(5) [En   g-ebeqen   gie   baqa]$_P$ h-azal   milik ...
    person 3AN-murder   PROSP   NPRX.INAN   3INAN-see   scared
    '(They) were scared of people being murdered ...'   [Bk-29.026]

(6) [Halaqi g-ini tebe honal gie]ₚ sasi.
    3PL   3AN-CAUS return go.LEVEL PROSP say
    '(We) said that they would be made to go back.' [Bk-66.042]

(7) [Ope   gi-al]ₚ sasi, nei   n-atal.
    pumpkin 3AN-carry say   1PL.EXCL 1EXCL-grandchild
    '(They) said that (you) should take a pumpkin, our grandkids did.' [Bk-22.022]

In a few cases, elements of the complement clause are clefted out to a topical position that is extra-clausal to the matrix clause. For example, in (8), the heavy NP encoding the P of the complement clause is topicalised, occurring in a left-cleft position.

(8) [Halaqi gie   il   kokoq no   ba]ᵢ,   Suri Guloq
    3PL   3.POSS water bucket OBL ART.INAN Suri Guloq
    [Øᵢ a   gie]ₚ sura.
         eat PROSP ask
    'Their water that was in the bucket, Suri Guloq asked to drink (it).' [Bk-6.024]

Complementation as P is not obligatory in Bunaq and such utterances can almost always be expressed through clauses conjoined by juxtaposition (§15.3.1). Thus, the P complement of *sasi* 'say' in (9a) can also be postposed into a juxtaposed clausal position, as in (9b). The choice of a complement clause versus a juxtaposed clause, however, is not without grammatical consequences. Notice the difference in the inflection on the indirect possessive classifer in the clauses in (9). In (9a) the reflexive form *die* indexes the possessor of the S of the complement clause. This is possible because in the complement position, the A of *sasi* 'say', the verb of the matrix clause, can act as the binding antecedent. By contrast, in (9b) where the clauses are conjoined by juxtaposition, the 1ˢᵗ person exclusive inflection of the indirect possessive classifier is needed. That is, the A of the preceding conjoined clause cannot bind the reflexive. Speakers I consulted judged such a use of the reflexive as bizarre. See §11.3.1.3 for more discussion of example (9a).

(9) a. Complement clause
       Neto ei   Ø-ege   [die   tais loi   niq]ₚ sasi oa.
       1SG 2PL 1INCL/2-BEN   REFL.POSS cloth good NEG   say   IAM
       'I told you my clothes were no good.' [BaiANeq-43]
    b. Juxtaposed conjoined clause
       Neto ei   Ø-ege   sasi oa,   nie   tais   loi   niq.
       1SG 2PL 1INCL/2-BEN   say   IAM   1EXCL.POSS   cloth good NEG
       'I told you my clothes were no good.' [Not-012]

The examples (4), (5), and (8) show that P complement clauses can be marked with an INANIMATE inflection of a determiner at their right edge in the same manner as a nominal argument (§5.1). This sets P complement clauses apart from S complement clauses, where determiners are not used in any examples in my corpus. This, and its analytical consequences, are discussed in the next section.

15.2.1.2 Complements as S

Complements occupying the S argument position within a matrix clause are known to occur with a small number of Bunaq monovalent verbs. In the present corpus, these are: *dari* 'happen' (10), *han* 'be no matter' (11), and *loi* 'good' (12). Of these, *dari* and *han* are relatively infrequent in their complement-taking use,[1] so the majority of examples in what follows will involve *loi*.

(10) [*Inel baqa man*]ₛ ***dari niq.***
 rain NPRX.INAN come happen NEG
 'The rain did not come.' (lit., 'It happened that the rain did not come.') [Bk-13.025]

(11) [*Hani, neli roe=bu mele=o*]ₛ ***han.***
 PROH 1DU.EXCL SPEC.INAN=GIVEN walk=AND be.no.matter
 'Don't, for us walking is not a problem!' [Bk-37.084]

(12) [*I bai a*]ₛ ***loi.***
 1PL.INCL thing eat good
 'We can eat the food.' (lit., 'It is good/possible that we eat food.') [Bk-15.002]

Complement clause–taking *loi* 'good' occurs with high frequency in Bunaq and is used in the expression of permission and permissibility. In (13), *loi* expresses that the burning of gardens is permitted only following a particular ceremony. In (14) *loi* is used with *niq* 'NEG' to denote the impermissibility of working during the pre-planting festival.

(13) *Homo haqal soq naq=na,* [*mar ini*]ₛ ***loi.***
 CONTR.INAN finished SEQ PRIOR=FOC garden set.alight good
 'Once that is finished, it is permitted to burn the gardens.' [Bk-8.003]

---

[1] The most common use of *han* 'be no matter' in the present Bunaq corpus is in participant-oriented manner serialisation constructions – see §13.6.1.

(14) Biasa   bon   g-ete,   karna   [sirubisu h-oqon]ₛ
     usually box.bean   3AN-whack   because   work   3INAN-do
     loi   niq.
     good   NEG
     'Usually (we) play the game *bon gete*, because it is not permitted to work.'
     [Bk-10.033]

Complement clause–taking *loi* is also used in the expression of judgements of potentiality and possibility. In (15), *loi* is used to denote the possibility of taking a road (15a) or a small path (15b) to church. In (16), *loi* together with *niq* 'NEG' expresses the impossibility of using traditional forms of payment, such as gold coins, for purchasing things from shops in the modern world.

(15) a. Kalo [Lolobul loron=na   h-alolo]ₛ   loi.
        if   Lolobul   road=FOC   3INAN-follow   good
        'As for Lolobul (people, they) can follow a road.'   [Bk-34.106]
     b. [Hik   gol=na   h-alolo]ₛ   loi.
        path   small=FOC   3INAN-follow   good
        '(Or they) can follow a small path.'   [Bk-34.107]

(16) Hatak,   tumel   buleqen, belak   baqa   en
     gold.coin   metal   red   silver.plate NPRX.INAN   person
     h-osok   niq,   tan   [baqa   rele bai   wit]ₛ loi   niq,
     3INAN-receive   NEG   because   NPRX.INAN   INS   thing fetch good NEG
     [baqa   rele toko mal]ₛ   loi   niq.
     NPRX.INAN   INS   shop go   good   NEG
     'Such coins, gold, and silver plates, people don't accept because with them (they) can't buy things, with them (they) can't go to the shop.'   [Bk-21.027]

The status of the bracketed portions of the preceding examples as clauses occupying the S argument slot needs analytical justification. As mentioned in §15.2.1.1, S complement clauses are not determined in natural speech as P complement clauses often are. Therefore, S complement clauses are not as "argumenty" as P complement clauses. In an alternative analysis, S complement clauses could be seen as a form of ambient serialisation (see §13.3 on the types of serialisation in Bunaq); that is, an SVC in which *loi* 'good' is serialised to the preceding verb, but is not associated with a specific referent, and describes a general predication. This analysis is not maintained here, however, because crucial restrictions applying to SVCs do not hold in relation to these constructions with *loi*. Most importantly, an S complement clause can be marked by a relator (17) or focus enclitic (18), both of which attach to the right edge of either an NP or a clause (see §4.7.4 on these enclitics as they appear marking NPs). Such a marker cannot occur between serialised verbs (see §13.2 on the characteristics of serial verbs).

(17) [Nei=o   neq]ₛ=**bu**   loi, ...
     1PL.EXCL=AND divide=GIVEN good
     'I can also do the dividing of food, ...' (lit., 'My dividing the food is possible')
     [BaiANeq-069]

(18) [Sogo lesin pir niq]ₛ=**o**   loi, ...
     ten more reach NEG=AND good
     'It is also ok to not reach 10 or more, ...'   [Bk-10.003]

Loi 'good' also appears in ambient serialisations, but there it has an intensifying function. See §13.7 on this kind of serialisation.

15.2.2 Non-NP replacing complements

Clausal complements that do not occur in place of an NP are found with two verbs: *heten* 'want' (19) and *ciaq* 'not want' (20).

(19) Moen, eto [zap g-erel   mele gie]_COMP heten=ka niq?
     friend 2SG dog 3AN-INS walk PROSP   want=OR NEG
     'Friend, do you want to go hunting (lit., walking with dogs)' [PuanHaeknau.04]

(20) [Tumel karon~karon g-ege   dusun]_COMP ciaq.
     metal REDUP~sack   3AN-BEN pile.up   not.want
     '(They) did not want to pile up sacks of metal for him.'   [EnBaruq-058]

Both verbs can only take a single argument NP. The impossibility of a second argument NP is seen in the impermissibility of the clauses in (21). Clauses including a second NP, such as these, were rejected by speakers in elicitation.

(21) a. *Baqi   buku heten.
        NPRX.AN book want
        Not good for: 'S/he wanted a book.'
     b. *Baqi   buku ciaq.
        NPRX.AN book want
        Not good for: 'S/he did not want a book.'   [Not-012]

To encode what is (not) wanted with these verbs, a complement clause is required, as in the above examples in (19) and (20). Alternatively, it can be inferred from the surrounding discourse. For example, the complement-less uses of *heten* 'want' in (22b) are possible because the preceding clause in (22a) makes clear that marriage is at issue in the discourse.

(22) a. Neto   i   bein   Ø-ege   d-ip   g-azal   oa.
       1SG   1PL.INCL   lord   1INCL/2-BEN   REFL-wife   3AN-see   IAM
       'I've already identified a wife for your highness.'   [KeleqMainuPintar-030]
    b. Guloq   bi=na   heten,   waqen   heten   niq   gaqal.
       last.child ART.AN=FOC   want   PART.PL   want   NEG   all.AN
       'The youngest child wants to (marry you), (but) all the others do not want to.'
                                                              [KeleqMainuPintar-031]

Similarly, in (23b) the complement of *ciaq* 'not want' is elided, as it is understood from the previous clause containing the offer of gold and silver in (23a). In (23c), we see that the noun *tumel* 'metal' is explicit, but occurs in an extra-clausal, left-cleft position. It would be ungrammatical for *tumel* to occur within the clause proper.

(23) a. "Buleqen   belis=na   Ø-ege   gie=o   loi".
       gold   silver=FOC   1INCL/2-give   PROSP=AND   good
       "We can even give you gold and silver."   [Bk-4.037]
    b. Mau Paran   siaq.
       Mau Paran   not.want
       'Mau Paran refused.'   [Bk-4.038]
    c. "Tumel=bu,   siaq".
       metal=GIVEN   want
       "(If it's) precious metal, (I) don't want to (have it)."   [Bk-4.041]

In examples (19) and (20) above, the complement clauses occur prior to the verb of the matrix clause. However, with *ciaq* 'not want', it is far more common for the complement clause to follow the matrix clause, as in (24). In the case of *heten* 'want', explicit complement clauses more frequently occur prior to the verb of the matrix clause, but can also follow the matrix clause, as in (25).

(24) Halaqi   g-ini   ciaq   [baqa   no=bu   mit]$_{COMP}$.
     3PL   3AN-call   not.want   NPRX.INAN   OBL=GIVEN   live
     'They said that (she) did not want to live in that place.'
                                                                            [Bk-39.050]

(25) Orel,   i-mil=sa   heten   [ret golaq=na   a]$_{COMP}$,
     monkey   1INCL/2-inside=EVEN   want   all.alone=FOC   eat
     n-ini   ri-mil   niq?
     1EXCL-CAUS   REFL-inside   NEG
     'Monkey, did you want to eat (them) all on your own without a thought for me?'
                                                                       [OrelPipMokBini.011]

Sometimes when the complement clause follows the matrix clause with these verbs, there is also an intonational break between matrix and complement clauses. In these situations, the original complement clause is treated as a right-clefted "clarifying" topic (§4.7.2.1.2). The reason for this analysis is explained further below.

In the examples examined thus far in this section, the S of the matrix clause and S/A of the complement clause have had the same referent. In situations where the S/A of the complement clause differs from the S of the verbs *heten* 'want' or *ciaq* 'not want' in the matrix clause, the verb *h-ini* '3INAN-call/cause' must be used to mark the switch of subject in the complement clause. *H-ini* '3INAN-call/cause' is inflected for the person of the underlying S/A of the complement, thereby converting that original S/A into a non-S/A argument role and maintaining the identity of the S/A across the matrix and complement clauses. For example, the underlying clause for the complement in (26) is *nei bai seqo* ('1PL.EXCL thing sell') 'we sell things', with *nei* '1PL.EXCL' as A. When this clause becomes the complement of the clause with *halaqi* '3PL' as the S of *ciaq*, *nei* '1PL.EXCL' is construed as a non-S/A argument by making it the second argument of *h-ini*, while the original predication becomes the third, postverbal argument of *h-ini*.

(26) Halaqi ciaq   [nei   **n-ini**   bai   seqo]_COMP.
     3PL   not.want   1PL.EXCL   1EXCL-CAUS   thing   sell
     'They don't want us to sell things.'   [Bk-11.008]

With *heten* 'want' in the matrix clause, the complement clause with an underlying non-identical S/A can occur before the verb of the matrix clause as in (27), but it is more common for it to occur following the matrix clause as in (28). Even where a postposed complement clause is separated from the matrix clause by an intonation break with a non-final (i.e., rising) contour, an underlying S/A in the complement clause that is not identical to the S of the matrix clause must be introduced by *h-ini* '3INAN-call/cause' (29). This suggests that the complement clause here is indeed still a complement clause. If it were simply a clause conjoined by juxtaposition, we would not expect to see the morphosyntactic requirement of subject identity across clauses. For this reason, as already stated above, complement clauses separated by an intonation break from matrix clauses with *heten* 'want' and *ciaq* 'not want' are still analysed as complement clauses, but ones which are right-clefted.

(27) Halaqi [n-ini   iskola]_COMP heten niq.
     3PL   1EXCL-CAUS   school   want   NEG
     'They didn't want me to go to school.'   [Bk-85.044]

(28) Nei   heten niq [baqi   **g-ini**   nei
    1PL.EXCL want   NEG NPRX.AN 3AN-CAUS 1PL.EXCL
    nie   naqi]COMP.
    1EXCL.POSS   royal
    'We don't want him to be our king.'   [BeiZap.014]

(29) Renu   heten niq teni, [kura g-ini   naqi   zal   gie]COMP, ...
    commoner want   NEG again horse 3AN-CAUS royal carry PROSP
    'The people also didn't want the horse to take on the position of king.'
                                                           [BeiZap.017]

Heten 'want' and *ciaq* 'not want' might reasonably be compared to *h-ini* '3INAN-call/cause', a trivalent verb whose third, postverbal argument is itself an argument-taking predicate. *H-ini* '3INAN-call/cause' differs from these two other complement-taking verbs in that its third argument can be a simple noun or NP, albeit analysed as a nominal predicate of an equative clause. See §10.4.2 for a full description of the argument structure and functions of *h-ini* '3INAN-call/cause'.

15.3 Clause conjoining

Clause conjoining is a situation in which two or more clauses are linked to one another intonationally and/or by means of a marker of clause conjoining. There are no particular grammatical correlates of subordination or coordination in Bunaq, and those terms are avoided here. Nevertheless, clauses conjoined with certain markers might be considered dependent in so far as they cannot occur independently of the conjoined clause. In §15.3.1, clauses conjoined by simple juxtaposition are discussed, and in §15.3.2, clause-conjoining constructions involving an overt marker of conjoining.

15.3.1 Clause conjoining by juxtaposition

In Bunaq, clauses are often conjoined by means of juxtaposition; that is, two clauses are placed side by side without an overt marker of conjoining. Intonation alone serves as the marker of their relationship: non-final "continuing" intonation signalled by a rising pitch contour accompanies the first clause in the pair, and there is a final intonation with a falling pitch contour at the end of the second (where this is itself not conjoined to another clause). For instance, in (30) and (31) the relation between the clauses is not overtly expressed in morphosyntax, but relies on iconic event ordering, together with the discourse context in which the utterance is placed, to clarify the relation between the clauses. The translations of 'if' and 'when' represent the least marked interpretations of the clauses.

(30) Nei   Timor-Leste gene, halaqi gie   polisi nei   n-one.
     1PL.EXCL   Timor-Leste LOC   3PL   3.POSS police 1PL.EXCL 1EXCL-hold
     '(If) we are in Timor Leste, their police will arrest us.'   [Bk-11.016]

(31) Pak desa   man, en   baqi   ge-sen.
     village.head come person NPRX.AN 3AN-show
     '(When) *Pak desa* comes, point (out who) these people (are).'   [Bk-19.028]

Juxtaposition of clauses is also widely found in situations of indirect thought and speech. Thus, in (32) and (33) the first of the juxtaposed conjoined clauses introduces the thought or speech event, while the second clause encodes what is thought or said.

(32) Zap baqi   ri-mil,   sael zon=o   pip rusa ai   g-uza, ...
     dog NPRX.AN REFL-inside   pig   wild=AND deer   only 3AN-chase
     'The dog thinks: (it would like to) chase the pig and deer, ...'   [BeiZap-055]

(33) Tabe   berita   huqe mama   g-ege   sasi, halaqi zemal   gie, ...
     greet message HERE mother 3AN-BEN say   3PL   go.LOW PROSP
     'The message given to my mother here said: they should go down, ...'
                                                                        [Bk-52.013]

As already discussed in §15.2.1.1, indirect thought and speech with these verbs can also be expressed as complement clauses in a P argument position.

In Bunaq, determiners are often found marking the first in a pair of clauses conjoined by juxtaposition. These determiner-marked thematic clauses (see §7.2 on this term) are "domain-creating constructions" (Reesink 1994); that is, they are nominalised clauses which are not arguments of a verb, but rather form the vantage point from which the following conjoined clause is to be viewed. As with other conjoined clauses, these nominalised clauses are linked to the following clause by a non-final intonation contour and can also be marked with overt markers of conjoining, such as those discussed in the previous sections. Determiners that mark clauses occur in their INANIMATE form. The following examples illustrate the "clausal frame" use of the different determiners: *baqa* 'NPRX.INAN' (34), *bare* 'PROX.INAN' (35), *doe* 'SPEC.INAN' (36), *homo* 'CONTR.INAN' (37), and *ba* 'ART.INAN' (38).

(34) En   halaqi hananu **baqa**,   baqi   g-ege   tais   zal.
     person 3PL   sing   NPRX.INAN   NPRX.AN 3AN-give cloth carry
     'While the people were singing, he was given a cloth to take.'   [Bk-34.067]

(35) Bai   toqan **bare,**   ene   goniqil ene   gonciet
    thing pray   PROX.INAN   night four   night five
    tergantung on.
    replace   DO
    'Doing this praying, (they do it for) four or five nights.'   [Bk-18.028]

(36) Ope   gi-al   gie   **roe**=bu,   mak   niq.
    pumpkin   3AN-carry   PROSP SPEC.INAN=GIVEN   hear NEG
    'When it came to carrying pumpkins just recently, he (pretended) not to hear.'
                                                                        [Bk-22.021]

(37) Nei   bai   pies   **homo,**   nei   n-erel   mon.
    1PL.EXCL   thing   clean   CONTR.INAN   1PL.EXCL   1EXCL-INS   twilight
    'While we were washing clothes, it got dark on us.'   [Bk-47.002]

(38) Sirubisu   sagal~sagal   **ba**   no,   nei   sirubisu
    work   REDUP~seek   ART.INAN   OBL   1PL.EXCL   work
    a-ta   sai.
    3INAN-GL   exit
    'We were looking and looking for work, then we came across work.'
                                                                        [Bk-12.002]

For information on the meanings associated with the different determiners marking thematic clauses, see the relevant sections on each determiner in Chapter 7.

15.3.2 Clause conjoining with overt markers

Bunaq has a large number of markers used in conjoining clauses. The different markers are not homogenous and display a range of morphosyntactic properties (see §3.6.4 for a concise statement of this). For descriptive convenience, I will use "conjunction" as a cover term for all types of markers used in clause conjoining. Most, but not all, native markers used in clause conjoining are enclitic to the clause. These and other clause-final conjunctions are discussed in §15.3.2.1. Markers of clause conjoining that are clause-initial are typically borrowed from Austronesian languages and are discussed in §15.3.2.2. On occasion, clause-final and clause-initial conjunctions mark one and the same clause, resulting in clausal "bracketing". This is discussed in §15.3.2.3. Adverbial clause conjoiners, (verbal) postpositions, and verbs used in clause conjoining are discussed in §15.3.2.4–§15.3.2.6.

15.3.2.1 Clause-final conjunctions

Table 15.1 presents an overview of the Bunaq markers used in clause conjoining that can be characterised as clause-final. With the exception of *soq* 'SEQ', clause-final conjunctions either are enclitic to the clause or are a combination of a free form and an enclitic. Of the simple conjunctions given in the table, only =*si* 'REAS' and *soq* 'SEQ' are dedicated to clause conjoining. *Soq* 'SEQ' is not strictly clause-final, as it can be followed by the iamitive marker *oa* 'IAM' and either a relator or focus enclitic. However, because it cannot co-occur with the other dedicated, native clausal conjunction =*si* 'REAS', *soq* is best treated here alongside =*si*. The other conjunctions are also found marking clausal constituents like NPs and PPs. These are the relator enclitics (=*bu* 'GIVEN' and =*be* 'CONTEXP'; see §4.7.4.1) and focus enclitics (=*o* 'AND', =*sa* 'EVEN', and =*na* 'FOC'; see §4.7.4.2).

As set out in Table 15.1, most clauses marked with a clause-final conjunction can either precede or follow the clause to which they are conjoined. Only where focus enclitics are used in the conjoining of clauses is it not possible for the clause marked by the conjunction to be postposed. The intonational contours that accompany conjoined clauses depend on the position of the clause marked with a conjunction. Where the clause marked by the conjunction is first in the pair, it is accompanied by a non-final intonation contour with a rising pitch at the end. Where second in the pair, the conjunction-marked clause is preceded by a short intonation break and characterised by clause-final intonation, that is, a sharply falling pitch contour.

Table 15.1: Clause-final conjunctions.

	Gloss	Position of marked clause
=si	'REAS'	[CLAUSE]=si, [CLAUSE] ~ [CLAUSE], [CLAUSE]=si
soq	'SEQ'	[CLAUSE] soq, [CLAUSE] ~ [CLAUSE], [CLAUSE] soq
soq oa	'SEQ IAM'	[CLAUSE] soq oa, [CLAUSE] ~ [CLAUSE], [CLAUSE] soq oa
=bu	'GIVEN'	[CLAUSE]=bu, [CLAUSE] ~ [CLAUSE], [CLAUSE]=bu
mesaq=bu	'GIVEN'	[CLAUSE] mesaq=bu, [CLAUSE] ~ [CLAUSE], [CLAUSE] mesaq=bu
=be	'CONTEXP'	[CLAUSE]=be, [CLAUSE] ~ [CLAUSE], [CLAUSE]=be
=o	'AND'	[CLAUSE]=o, [CLAUSE]
=sa	'EVEN'	[CLAUSE]=sa, [CLAUSE]
=na	'FOC'	[CLAUSE]=na, [CLAUSE]
naq=na	'PRIOR=FOC'	[CLAUSE] naq=na, [CLAUSE]

15.3.2.1.1 Reason conjunction: =si

The enclitic =si 'REAS' is used to express the rationale behind an event. That is, =si denotes that a causal relation exists between two events, such that one of the two represents the reason why the other event takes place. The enclitic =si attaches to the clause denoting the reason for the event/state expressed in the conjoined clause, as in (39) and (40).

(39) En   bei   mil=na   h-oqon=**si**,   nei=o
     person ancestor COLL=FOC   3INAN-do=REAS   1PL.EXCL=AND
     baqa=na   h-oqon.
     NPRX.INAN=FOC   3INAN-do
     'Because the ancestors did it, we also do it.'   [Bk-23.050]

(40) Matas oa=**si**,   basin   oa.
     old   IAM=REAS   forgetful IAM
     'Because (she's) old, (she's) forgetful.'   [Bk-30.061]

The above examples show the reason clause occurring as the first of the two clauses in the sequence. Whilst this is the most commonly occurring order, the clause marked by =si may also follow the clause with which it is paired, as in (41) and (42). Postposed reason clauses represent justificatory afterthoughts and occur where the speaker interrupts the sequence of events in the narration to insert the reason for the event in the prior clause. For instance, in (42), the speaker pauses in her narration of a story about walking to Atambua to explain why they had to dismount from their horses, before continuing with the account of events that followed their arrival in the city.

(41) Neli   mos=o   rebel   tebe   ge-tekeq,   baqi
     1DU.EXCL   also=AND   descend   return 3AN-look.at NPRX.AN
     zo   gene topol o=**si**.
     mango   LOC   fall   IAM=REAS
     'We also went down to look at him, because he had fallen from the mango tree.'
                                                                       [Bk-1.023]

(42) Ola   Atambua pir,   kura   kota mil   tama   loi   niq,
     LOW   Atambua reach   horse city inside enter good NEG
     kota mil   gene u   hobel=**si**.
     city inside LOC   herbaceous.plant   not.exist=REAS
     '(When we) reached Atambua, the horses couldn't enter the city, as there were no plants (for the horses to eat) in the city centre.'   [Bk-37.115]

The clauses conjoined by =si seen thus far represent factual, realis events between which there is a reason relation. In the preposed position, =si is also occasionally used to encode relations between irrealis events. In this case, =*si* marks a clause denoting an act performed where the *intended result* is the event expressed in the main clause. In the examples below, =*si* marks clauses denoting irrealis events that, if they do come to pass, give rise to the events described in the subsequent clauses. In (43) Suri Guloq's descent would give rise to his drinking of milk, while in (44) the constant observation of the mountain dwellers leads them to be in a position to strike down at potential attackers.

(43) Suri Guloq, rebel=**si**, rie su pata bare a
 Suri Guloq descend=REAS REFL.POSS breast worn.out PROX.INAN eat
 naq!
 PRIOR
 'Suri Guloq, descend in order to drink (from) this old breast.' [Bk-6.013]

(44) G-azal liol=**si**, lolo wa gene=na g-ete rebel.
 3AN-see continue=REAS mountain top LOC=FOC 3AN-strike descend
 '(They) would keep a look out for them in order to attack them from the mountain tops.' [Bk-5.004]

The enclitic =*si* does not co-occur with any other clause-final conjunction, enclitic or otherwise. This sets it apart from *soq* 'SEQ', discussed in the following section. *Hasi* 'so, therefore', a sentence connective related to =*si*, is discussed in §15.4.4.

15.3.2.1.2 Sequence conjunction: *soq* and *soq oa*

Soq 'SEQ' is used to conjoin events between which a temporally sequential relation exists. Occurring in a postverbal position, *soq* marks the clause denoting the first event in the sequence, and this typically occurs preceding the clause expressing the temporally later event, as in (45) and (46).

(45) A **soq**, il hobel
 eat SEQ water not.exist
 'Once (the child) drank (the water), then the water was gone.' [Bk-76.020]

(46) Baqi tebe loi **soq**, Malaysia mal.
 NPRX.AN return good SEQ Malaysia go
 'Once she was well again, then she went to Malaysia.' [Bk-43.036]

Although rare, it is also possible for a clause marked by *soq* to occur after the clause denoting the temporally prior event. The one clear example of this in my corpus is given in (47).

(47) ..., mete Bei Laho gi-ta   zipil   kama,   g-ini
         NOW Bei Laho 3AN-GL garden.cuttings pile.up 3AN-CAUS
    hoku   soq.
    curl.up SEQ
    '. . ., (he) piled up the garden cuttings onto Bei Laho, once he had got him to curl up.' [Bk-50.011]

The two dedicated clause conjunctions, =si 'REAS' and soq 'SEQ', cannot co-occur. This seems to be a matter of semantic incompatibility more than morphosyntax, since they have different distributional properties. Unlike =si, soq is not enclitic to the clause; it occurs in a clausal position following the prospective marker gie, but preceding the iamitive marker oa, as can be seen in (48). (For more on the template for the ordering of postverbal elements, see §14.3). A clause marked by soq can also be followed by enclitics other than =si. For example, soq occurs in a clause marked by the relator enclitic =bu 'GIVEN' in (49) (discussed further in §15.3.2.1.3) and by the focus enclitic =na 'FOC' in (50) (discussed further in §15.3.2.1.4).

(48) Gole   obon haqal,   tebe   sau   gie   soq oa.
    prohibition.marker hang finished return harvest PROSP SEQ IAM
    'Having hung the prohibition marker, (they) can straight away return to harvesting.' [Bk-76.020]

(49) Baqi   waktu nyonya Bert   gi-al   man   gie   soq=bu,
    NPRX.AN time girl   Berthe 3AN-carry come PROSP SEQ=GIVEN
    gi-al   man   niq ai, kaset.
    3AN-carry come NEG ONLY single
    'He was going to bring the Berthe girl, but then just didn't, he was alone.'
    [Bk-67.051]

(50) I   bai   a   soq=na,   mal.
    1PL.INCL thing eat SEQ=FOC   go
    'It is once we eat (that) we go.' [Bk-37.050]

The combination of soq 'SEQ' and oa 'IAM' is very common in the corpus. Where soq oa marks the second clause in a conjoined pair, it signals that the event in the marked clause happens immediately subsequent to the event in the preceding clause (51). Where it marks the first clause in a conjoined pair, it signals that as soon as the event in the marked clause occurs, it is followed by the event denoted in the following conjoined clause (52).

(51) Pan   h-iqit-wen,   legul   **soq**   **oa**.
     sky   3AN-raise-ANTIC   tall   SEQ   IAM
     'The sky lifted up on its own and immediately went high up'.   [LB10.003]

(52) Pan   mon   **soq**   **oa**,   lesiq.
     sky   afternoon   SEQ   IAM   argue
     'As soon as it's afternoon, (they) argue.'   [Bk-23.031]

15.3.2.1.3 Relator enclitics: =bu, mesaq=bu, and =be

The relator enclitics =*bu* 'GIVEN' and =*be* 'CONTEXP' have already been discussed in §4.7.4.1 in relation to their function marking NPs and PPs. This section discusses their functions in conjoining clauses, including the clause-conjoining collocation of =*bu* with *mesaq*.

A clause marked by =*bu* denotes an event that if/when realised, will be followed by the event in the conjoined clause. The most commonly suitable translations for =*bu* marking a clause are 'if' and 'when'. Clauses conjoined by =*bu* can express real or irreal events. Compare the following examples taken from a single text describing the same event from an irreal and real perspective, respectively:

(53) Ge-tekeq=**bu**,   eli   Ø-os   mit   oa.
     3AN-look.at=GIVEN   2DU   1INCL/2-wait   sit   IAM
     'When you (go) look at him, (he) will be sitting waiting for you.'   [Bk-4.074]

(54) Halali   mal   tebe   ge-tekeq=**bu**,   iu   gol=na   kaeq.
     3DU   go   return   3AN-look.at=GIVEN   maggot   small=FOC   full
     'When they went and looked at him again, (the body) was filled with maggots.'

In (53) the wives of a dead man are told that after a previously described treatment of the body, their husband will come back to life, as they will see when they go to look. Here, =*bu* conjoins clauses denoting irreal events (to take place in the future) and signals that the event in the second clause is the outcome of the fulfilment of the one in the first clause. By contrast, in (54) =*bu* conjoins clauses denoting past, realis events, namely what happened when the wives went out to look at their husband.

While it is most common for =*bu* to mark the first clause in a conjoined pair, it can also mark the second, as in (55).

(55) I   ho   goq,   hoqi,   pao   gol   soro,   hati=**bu**.
     1PL.INCL   bean   kernel   peanut   bean.type   small   mix.in   exist=GIVEN
     'We will mix in different types of beans and nuts, if they are available.'
                                                                                [BK-44.005]

When marking clauses, the enclitic =bu is often found attached to *mesaq*, a cranberry word only known in combination with =bu. *Mesaq=bu* has the same syntactic distribution as =bu, and can mark a clause that is either preceding (as in 56) or following (as in 57) the clause to which it is conjoined. Some speakers have remarked to me that there is a small semantic difference between using =bu and *mesaq=bu* to conjoin clauses. It appears that *mesaq=bu* tends to be used to mark a clause as expressing a more hypothetical proposition. It can typically be translated as 'in the event that' or 'should that'.

(56) *Lal   h-oqon   niq **mesaq=bu**, en   piar,   mete*
     matter 3INAN-do   NEG GIVEN   person believe NOW
     en   heser bi   bei   g-utu   ti-ta   bolu niq.
     person dead   ART.AN   ancestor 3-COM   RECP-GL unite NEG
     'Should (they) not perform the ritual, people believe that the dead person mentioned just now will not come together with their ancestors'.   [Bk-18.019]

(57) *Aibaq!   debel,   eto=na   baqa   **mesaq=bu**.*
     eldest.daughter   descend   2SG=FOC   NPRX.INAN   GIVEN
     'Daughter! Come down, should that be you.'   [LB-9.060]

The counter-expectational relator =be 'CONTEXP' is used to mark a concessive clause, that is, a clause which has unexpected, surprising, or contrastive content in relation to the event of the main clause. When the =be-marked clause precedes the clause to which it is conjoined, =be is typically translatable as 'although', as in (58) and (59).

(58) *Eli   tazuq nokar tama   gie=**be**,   eli   pioq   h-ek*
     2DU   door   gate   enter PROSP=CONTEXP   2DU   millet 3INAN-pick.up
     haqal   naq!
     finished PRIOR
     'Although you want to go in the door, first you must pick up all the grain.'
     [Bk-43.026]

(59) *Zulo=bu   muk   lete=**be**,   pan   ene   naq=na   sai, ...*
     civet=GIVEN   earth   step.on=CONTEXP   sky   night PRIOR=FOC   exit
     'Although the civet walks on the ground, it is night before it does so, ...'
     [HulTopol-085]

When the clause marked by =be follows the clause to which it is conjoined, it denotes an event which happened against expectation. For example, in (60) the postposed clause marked by =be denotes what unexpectedly happened when the event in the preceding clause was not realised.

(60) Uen   man   g-iwal   gie,   g-ere   niq,   tebe   rebel
     one   come   3AN-pick   PROSP   3AN-reach   NEG   return   descend
     muk   gene=**be**.
     earth LOC=CONTEXP
     'Someone came to pick (the flower), but didn't reach it, instead (he) returned
     to the ground.'   [Bk-72.036]

When the clause marked by =*be* has negative polarity, it denotes a clause whose non-occurrence goes counter to expectation. The clause to which it is conjoined denotes the event which actually took place, as in (61).

(61) Manek   Ela   g-ue   niq=**be**,   Eta   g-ue.
     Manek   Ela   3AN-hit   NEG=CONTEXP   Eta   3AN-hit
     'Manek didn't hit Ela, rather (he) hit Eta.'   [Not.01-07]

Habe 'rather, by contrast', a sentence connective related to =*be*, is discussed in §15.4.4.

15.3.2.1.4 Focus enclitics: =*o*, =*sa*, =*na*, and *naq=na*

The focus enclitics =*o* 'AND', =*sa* 'EVEN', and =*na* 'FOC' have already been discussed in §4.7.4.2 in relation to their function marking NPs and PPs. This section focuses particularly on their role in conjoining clauses. Focus enclitics differ from the clausal enclitics seen thus far in that a clause marked by a focus enclitic cannot be postposed to a position following the main clause. Prosodically, a clause marked by a focus enclitic is always accompanied by a continuing intonation contour.

The additive focus enclitic =*o* 'AND' conjoins clauses where the event expressed by the first clause is one of a set of alternatives which leads to or results in the event denoted in the next clause. Examples are given in (62) and (63).

(62) Hotel=na   wit=**o**,   h-ini   ugar   minak,   g-o   wa   on.
     tree=FOC   fetch=AND   3INAN-call   green   entire   3AN-SRC   discard   DO
     'Also when (he) fetched wood, (his mother) said that (the wood) was all green
     and threw it out.'   [Bk-6.004]

(63) Gie   eme   gie   ama   g-agal=**o**,   g-azal   niq.
     3.POSS   mother   3.POSS   father   3AN-seek=AND   3AN-see   NEG
     'Even (when they) looked for their mother and their father, they didn't see them.'
                                                                         [Bk-68.008]

A clause marked by the scalar additive focus enclitic =*sa* 'EVEN' expresses a proposition which is of low likelihood in relation to the proposition denoted by the conjoined clause. In (64) the use of =*sa* expresses the unexpected state of affairs that even after two car crashes, the speaker is still alive. In (65), =*sa* is employed to stress the fact that the stated boredom of the speaker is contrary to the presupposition that the eating of meat is a desirable activity.

(64) Hik   hiloqon oa=**sa**,   heser niq.
     path   two   IAM=EVEN dead   NEG
     'Even after (crashing) two times, (I'm) not dead.'   [Bk-61.070]

(65) Si   gi-a   gie=**sa**,   i   baruq oa.
     meat 3AN-eat PROSP=EVEN 1PL.INCL bored IAM
     'Even at the prospect of eating meat, we are bored.'   [LB8.153]

A clause marked by the restrictive focus enclitic =*na* 'FOC' denotes an event in particular relation to which the event in the following conjoined clause takes place. The following examples illustrate this use:

(66) Malaysia gene man=**na**, tebe   lilak   teni.
     Malaysia LOC   come=FOC return crazy   again
     'It was when she came back from Malaysia that she went back to being crazy.'
                                                                                                                               [Bk-43.037]

(67) Nei   g-os=**na**,   baqi   nei   n-ere.
     1PL.EXCL 3AN-wait=FOC NPRX.AN 1PL.EXCL 1EXCL-reach
     'It was while we waited for her that she reached us.'   [LB2.248]

A combination of the priorative marker *naq* 'PRIOR' (see also the functions of this in imperatives, discussed in §14.3.7) and =*na* is very common in Bunaq clause conjoining. *Naq*=*na* 'PRIOR=FOC' signals that the event described in the clause it marks occurs "first of all", that is, it happens prior to the event in the following conjoined clause. Examples (68) and (69) illustrate this.

(68) …, ie   kela   Asa Lesuq pir   **naq**=**na**, neto
          1INCL/2.POSS brother-in-law Asa Lesuq reach PRIOR=FOC 1SG
     g-ege   Ø-iol   bare   sasi oa.
     3AN-BEN 1INCL/2-voice PROX.INAN say   IAM
     'Once your brother-in-law Asa Lesuq returns from the garden, I will tell him what you said.'   [Puan.015]

(69) Orel   d-iwis   homo   tekeq   loi~loi   **naq=na**,
      monkey   REFL-genitals   CONTR.INAN   look.at REDUP~good   PRIOR=FOC
      homo   gin: ...
      CONTR.INAN   say
      'Once the monkey had a good look at his genitals, he said: ...'
      [OrelNisPipLoko-055]

15.3.2.2 Borrowed clause-initial conjunctions

Bunaq Lamaknen speakers use a wide range of clause conjunctions borrowed from the contact languages Malay/Indonesian and Tetun. In accordance with the word order typology of these contact languages, the conjunctions are clause-initial, a position which is in contrast to the clause-final position of Bunaq's native conjunctions. As a result, borrowed clause-initial conjunctions and native clause-final conjunctions are often found marking one and the same clause. See §15.3.2.3 for illustration of this.

In addition to =si 'REAS', reason clauses can be expressed in Bunaq using Tetun *tan* 'because' (70) or Malay/Indonesian *kar(e)na* 'because' (71). Whilst *kar(e)na* is still recognised as a borrowing, *tan* is not and is typically identified by Bunaq speakers as being native, even where those speakers are fluent in Tetun.

(70) **Tan**   n-on   hinal   oa,   neto   u   bilik
      because   1EXCL-hand   injured   IAM   1SG   herbaceous.plant   bind
      baqis~baqis   baqa   h-iqil,   tebe   reu   mal.
      REDUP~much   NPRX.INAN   3INAN-leave.behind   return   house   go
      'Because my hand was injured, I left my many bundles of grass behind and went.'
      [Bk-12.020]

(71) Biasa   bon   g-ete,   **karena**   sirubisu   h-oqon
      usually   box.bean   3AN-throw   because   work   3INAN-do
      loi   niq.
      good   NEG
      'Usually (people) play *bon gete*, because they are not allowed to work.'
      [Bk-15.006]

Conditionals may be expressed in Bunaq using the Malay conjunction *kalo* 'if, when, as regards' (cf. Indonesian *kalau*). For example:

(72) **Kalo**   botil   hobel,   neto   uor   dele   Weluli   mal.
      if   bottle   not.exist   1SG   vegetable   INS   Weluli   go
      'If there were no bottles, I took vegetables to Weluli.'
      [Bk-13.014]

Borrowed conjunctions expressing contrast are Portuguese/Tetun *mais* 'but' (73) and Malay/Indonesian *tapi* 'but' (74). Of these, only *mais* is not identified as a borrowing. Its use is largely limited to older Bunaq speakers in Lamaknen; in East Timor it is still widespread.

(73)   Halali   en   g-o   bai   a   sura   liol   liol,
         3DU   person 3AN-SRC thing eat ask   continue continue
         mais   en   halali   g-ege   niq.
         but   person 3DU   3AN-give NEG
         'The two of them kept asking them for food, but they didn't give them any.'
                                                                                                                   [LB7.061]

(74)   Gie   apa   sogo goniqil gonciet, **tapi** muzuk bare
         3.POSS   cow   ten   four   five   but   land   PROX.INAN
         h-arat   niq.
         3AN-destroy NEG
         'The number of his cows is in the forties or fifties, but they do not destroy this land.'   [Bk-19.015]

Less common conjunctions are Portuguese *depois* 'since', and Malay/Indonesian *supaya* 'so that' and *sampai* 'until'. While *depois* is widespread in all East Timorese dialects of Bunaq, the latter conjunctions are generally only integrated into the speech of the most Malay-influenced Bunaq speakers.

15.3.2.3 Clauses bracketed by multiple initial and final conjunctions

A conjoined clause can be marked simultaneously by clause-initial and clause-final conjunctions. These are cases of "doubling" (Muysken 2000: 104–105), where a borrowed, Austronesian clause-initial conjunction and a native Bunaq clause-final conjunction combine to create bracketing around a clause.

There are a number of common combinations of native Bunaq clause-final enclitic conjunctions and borrowed clause-initial conjunctions. Conditional clauses are frequently marked simultaneously by Malay *kalo* 'if' and clause-final *=bu* 'GIVEN', as in (75). Similarly, reason clauses may be marked simultaneously by Tetun *tan* 'because' or Malay *karna* 'because', and clause-final *=si* 'REAS', as in (76).

(75)   ..., memel   oa,   **kalo** sinoq lesin=**bu**.
              sick   IAM   if   hot   more=GIVEN
         '. . ., he would already be in pain, if (it were) hotter.'   [LuaWezun1-046]

(76) Gie   ba=na   h-alolo,   **tan**   reu   bare
     3.POSS ART.INAN=FOC 3INAN-follow because house PROX.INAN
     reu   suku=**si**.
     house   lineage.group=REAS
     'Accordingly (we) follow tradition, because this house is a lineage house.'
     [Bk-23.005]

15.3.2.4 Adverbial clause conjoiners

Bunaq has two adverbial clause conjoiners: temporal *helo* 'since' and temporal/locative *daurau* (or its variants, *darau* and *daro*) 'until'. The clauses introduced by these items provide "adverbial" information about the event described in the conjoined clause. They typically occur to the left of the clause with which they are conjoined, but can also occur to the right of it. The other functions of the adverbial clause conjoiners, as ways to introduce NPs and PPs, are illustrated in §3.6.4.

Helo 'since' introduces a clause denoting an event occurring in the past from which time on the event described in the following conjoined clause has occurred. This use is not frequent in the Bunaq corpus, but was produced without problem in elicitation by the speakers I worked with. Two such elicited examples of *helo* introducing a clause are given in (77) and (78).

(77) Eme   Eta   Atambua   gene tebe   **helo**, meaq gol skola   mal
     mother Eta   Atambua   LOC   return   since   child   school   go
     teni.
     Again
     'Since mother Eta came back from Atambua, the children are going to school again.'
     [Not.07-02]

(78) N-iri   tol   **helo**, neto mele   lomar   niq.
     1EXCL-leg   broken   since   1SG   walk   straight   NEG
     'Since I broke my leg, I don't walk right.'
     [Not.07-02]

Daurau 'until' (also realised as *darau ~ daro*) can be used to introduce a clause expressing an event that takes place up to the time of the event expressed by the conjoined clause. A clause introduced by *daurau* typically precedes the clause to which it is conjoined (79), but may also follow that clause, particularly where the clause marked by *daurau* introduces a motion towards a location which is the final destination (80).

(79) **Daro** hotel baqi   sia   mohu,   halaqi hoto koin.
     until   tree   NPRX.AN   burn   completely   3PL   fire draw
     'Until the trees are all burned, they spread the fire (throughout the garden).'
     [Bk-3.033]

(80) Loro   saen   reu   gene sai, **daurau** tel   pir.
    king send.off   house LOC exit   until   grave reach
    '(They do the) loro saen from (the time they) exit the house, until they reach the grave.' [Bk-18.031]

15.3.2.5 (Verbal) postpositions used in clause conjoining

Two postpositions in Bunaq have additional clause-conjoining functions. They are the oblique postposition *no* (or its dialect variant *ni*) 'OBL', and the goal-marking verbal postposition *a-ta* '3INAN-GL'. Clauses marked by one of these postpositions provide "adverbial" information about the event described in the conjoined clause. They typically occur to the left of the clause with which they are conjoined, but can also occur to the right of it.

The oblique postposition *no* 'OBL' (§12.2.1) is frequently used to introduce a clause denoting the setting in which the event in the following conjoined clause takes place. In (81) the setting expressed in the *no*-clause is temporal: it was *during* the speaker's childhood that he suffered from stomach aches. In (82), the setting expressed by the *no*-marked clause is circumstantial and refers to the people concerned being *in a state of fear* such that they fled.

(81) Neto   meaq gol taq   **no,** biasa   n-ezel   memel.
    1SG   child   IMP OBL   usually 1EXCL-stomach   sick
    'While I was still a child, I often used to get stomach aches.' [Bk-13.001]

(82) G-one   g-amaq   baqa   h-azal   milik   **no**=na,
    3AN-hold   3AN-murder   NPRX.INAN   3INAN-see   scared   OBL=FOC
    a-ta   ciwal   man.
    3INAN-GL   flee   come
    'It was when (they) were scared from having seen (people) being arrested and murdered, that (they) came fleeing towards (here).' [Bk-29.031]

Where *no* 'OBL' introduces a setting clause, the verb is often reduplicated. This emphasises that the event expressed in the clause marked by *no* was in progress when the event in the conjoined clause took place. For example:

(83) Sirubisu   sagal~sagal   ba   **no,** nei   sirubisu a-ta   sai.
    work   REDUP~seek   ART.INAN   OBL   1PL.EXCL   work   3AN-GL   exit
    'When we were looking and looking for work, we came across (some).'
    [Bk-12.002]

(84) Neto   mele~mele   **no,** kou   topol   duquk.
    1SG   REDUP~walk   OBL   slip   fall   always
    'When I'm walking, I always slip and fall.' [Not.01-06]

We see from (83) that a setting clause with *no* 'OBL' can also be nominalised with the article. See §7.8.2 for more examples of this.

In addition to introducing NPs (§12.4.3), the INANIMATE inflection of the goal-marking verbal postposition *a-ta* '3INAN-GL' can introduce clauses expressing the reason for the event denoted in the following clause. Examples of *a-ta* marking a reason clause are provided in (85) and (86).

(85) Halaqi   g-egil   g-azal   **a-ta**=na,   en   halaqi g-oqol.
     3PL   3AN-shadow   3AN-see   3INAN-GL=FOC   person   3PL   3AN-kill
     'On account of imagining things to themselves (lit., seeing shadows), those people killed him.'   [Bk-39.034]

(86) Gie   mone kalaq roq   gie   **a-ta**=na,   baqi   he   man.
     3.POSS   man   neck   cut   PROSP   3INAN-GL=FOC   NPRX.AN   run   come
     'On account of her husband wanting to slit her throat, she came running.'
                                                                                  [Bk-39.049]

15.3.2.6 Verbs used in clause conjoining

The verb *haqal* 'finished' (see §13.8.1 for a detailed description of this verb's monoclausal functions) is used extensively in clause conjoining where it indicates that the event described in the following conjoined clause occurs subsequent to that in the clause marked with *haqal*, as in (87) and (88).

(87) Nei   iskola   **haqal**,   neto   botil   dele   Weluli   mal.
     1PL.EXCL   school   finished   1SG   bottle   INS   Weluli   go
     '(When) we finished school, I would go to Weluli with bottles.'   [Bk-63.007]

(88) Molo   pu   lai   **haqal**,   tais   uen   mone   g-aqel   no.
     betel.vine   betel.nut   put.on   finished   cloth   one   man   3AN-shoulder OBL
     'After the bride price is negotiated (lit., the betel vine and betel nut is laid down), a cloth is (placed) on the man's shoulder.'   [Bk-38.008]

The related uses of *haqal* 'finished' in sentence connecting are discussed and illustrated in §15.4.1 and §15.4.2.

The second verb used in clause conjoining is *hali* 'go ahead'. This monovalent verb appears relatively infrequently as an independent predicate, but that this is possible can be seen in utterances such as *eto hali naq* 2SG go.ahead PRIOR 'you go ahead'. Most of the verb's appearances in my corpus are in clause-conjoining constructions where *hali* introduces a clause denoting an event that is chronologically prior to the event expressed in the conjoined clause. All examples of conjoined clauses marked with *hali* in the corpus also include the prospective aspect marker *gie* 'PROSP', as in (89) and (90).

(89) Nei   man   gie   **hali,**   il=o   hobel   oa,
     1PL.EXCL   come PROSP go.ahead   water=AND   not.exist IAM
     piral=o   hobel oa.
     rice.grain=AND   not.exist IAM
     'Before we arrived, both the water and the rice were already gone.'
     [LB5.186]

(90) Pan le   pisi   gie   **hali,**   mete balo   bi   el, ...
     sky light clean PROSP go.ahead NOW caterpillar ART.AN   crawl
     'Before the sky got properly light, the caterpillar (started to) crawl away, ...'
     [BaloBiEnGakirik.056]

15.4 Sentence connecting

A sentence is a unit of discourse consisting of one or more clauses that expresses illocutionary force. Sentences are phonologically and morphosyntactically independent utterances, but various devices pointing forward or back to another sentence exist in Bunaq to indicate a semantic or pragmatic relationship between two sentences.

Four types of sentence connecting are discussed in this section: tail-head linkage (§15.4.1), demonstratives used anaphorically in sentence connecting (§15.4.2), the verb *tebe* 'return' (§15.4.3), and a small class of dedicated sentence connectives (§15.4.4).

15.4.1 Tail-head linkage

Tail-head linkage is a common discourse strategy in the languages of the New Guinea area (de Vries 2005). Tail-head linkage involves the repetition of the "tail" or final part of one sentence at the "head" or beginning of the following sentence. The material repeated from the previous sentence is separated from the rest of the sentence by a distinct intonation contour, such as that which characterises clauses conjoined by juxtaposition (§15.3.1).

Procedural texts typically offer many good examples of tail-head linkage, such as that in the textual extract in (91). The tail and head are marked in bold. We see that the tail of the first sentence is repeated as the head of the next. In (91b) it is the verb and its P argument that are repeated in the "head", but once the referent of P is clearly established in the discourse, it is elided and the verb alone is used in the "tail" in (91b), the "head" and "tail" in (91c), and the "head" in (91d). Postverbal phasal polarity markers such as *taq* 'CONT' (§14.3.5.1) are not normally repeated from a "tail" into a "head", as can be seen in (91c) and (91d).

(91) a. *I   paqol   g-ao*.
         1PL.INCL   maize   3AN-pound
         'We pound the maize.'   [Bk-45.006]
     b. ***Paqol   g-ao***,   *i   g-apiq   taq*.
         maize   3AN-pound   1PL.INCL   3AN-winnow   CONT
         'Having pounded the maize, we winnow it.'   [Bk-45.007]
     c. ***G-apiq***   *haqal,   homo   soq,   i   a bokal*
         3AN-winnow   finished   CONTR.INAN   SEQ   1PL.INCL porridge
         t-inik   *taq*.
         3INAN-cook   CONT
         'Having finished winnowing, then we cook the porridge.'   [Bk-45.008]
     d. ***T-inik***,   *i   uer   dara*.
         3INAN-cook   1PL.INCL   pot   prepare
         'For the cooking, we get the pot ready.'   [Bk-45.009]

While it is most commonly verbs that are repeated from "tails" into "heads", this is not always the case. In repeating part of the "tail" in the "head", speakers can pick out what they see as the central information of the last part of the previous sentence. Consider the extract from a route description given in (92). Initially, the speaker repeats the whole clause in (92a) as the "head" in (92b), but for the subsequent "heads" in (92c) and (92d), the speaker only repeats the place names, as these represent the most important information for linking the stages in the journey.

(92) a. ***Pie Asa Toiq   a-ta   zemal***.
         Pie Asa Toiq   3INAN-GL   go.LOW
         'Go down towards Pie Asa Toiq.'   [Bk-34.016]
     b. ***Pie Asa Toiq   a-ta   zemal***   *haqal   soq,*
         Pie Asa Toiq   3INAN-GL   go.LOW   finished SEQ
         Pie Asa Toiq   homo   no   mele,   mele,   mele daro
         Pie Asa Toiq   CONTR.INAN   OBL   walk   walk   walk until
         *esen   o   **Duarato Pur Bul**   homo   pir*.
         HIGH   ADDR   Duarato Pur Bul   CONTR.INAN   reach
         'Having finished going down to Pie Asa Toiq, walk from Pie Asa Toiq until (you) reach Duarato Pur Bul.'   [Bk-34.017]
     c. ***Duarato Pur Bul***   *homo   no,   menal   **Leto Sun***
         Duarato Pur Bul   CONTR.INAN   OBL   go.HIGH   Leto Sun
         a-ta   sai.
         3INAN-GL   exit
         'From Duarato Pur Bul, go down until (you) come to Leto Sun.   [Bk-34.018-19]

d. **Leto Sun** homo no, menal teni.
   Leto Sun CONTR.INAN OBL go.HIGH again.
   'From Leto Sun, go up again.' [Bk-34.020]

There are two additional elements that are commonly used in the "heads" of tail-head linkage structures to order the sequence of linked events. The first is the conjunction *soq* 'SEQ' (§15.3.2.1.2). This is widely used in procedural texts where it functions to link the sequential steps of a process in tail-head linkage structures. The use of *soq* in the "heads" of sentences with tail-head linkage structures is illustrated in (93), an extract from a text describing the processing of cassava for storage.

(93) a. Dikotel saq himo, dikotel **gi-wil**.
   cassava dried CONTR.INAN cassava 3AN-dig.up
   'As for (making) dried cassava, dig up the cassava.' [Bk-76.054]
   b. **Gi-wil** soq, **g-aba**.
   3AN-dig.up SEQ 3AN-slice
   'Once dug up, slice (it).' [Bk-76.055]
   c. **G-aba** soq, **g-en**.
   3AN-slice SEQ 3AN-dry
   'Once sliced, lay (it) out to dry.' [Bk-76.056]
   d. **G-en haqal** soq, dikotel saq himo g-ipi,
   3AN-dry finished SEQ cassava dried CONTR.AN 3AN-break
   g-ini gol~gol.
   3AN-CAUS REDUP~small
   'Once finished drying, the dried cassava is broken up into small pieces.'
   [Bk-76.057]

Second, *haqal* 'finished' (discussed in §15.3.2.5) also frequently appears in the "heads" of texts where head-tail linkage is used. It signals that the event denoted in the following sentence follows on from the completion of the event denoted in the preceding one. We have already seen isolated examples of *haqal* in tail-head linkage in (91c) and (93d). The extract from a text describing gardening practices in (94) shows how *haqal* can be used in tail-head linkage structures over multiple clauses.

(94) a. Tapi nei tut no **mar se**.
   but 1PL.EXCL past.times OBL garden clear
   'But in the past, we would clear the gardens.' [Bk-65.034]
   b. **Mar se haqal**, ini.
   garden clear finished set.alight
   'Having finished clearing the gardens, (we) would burn (them).' [Bk-65.035]

c. ***Ini   haqal,***   inel   man.
   set.alight finished   rain   come
   'Having finished burning, the rain would come.'   [Bk-65.036]

15.4.2 Demonstratives in sentence connecting

15.4.2.1 Anaphoric demonstratives
We already saw in section §15.3.1 that determiners are used adclausally in Bunaq to create clausal "frames" for a following conjoined clause. In this section, we look at how the INANIMATE forms of some demonstratives are frequently used pronominally as sentence connectives to point back to the events in the preceding sentence. Demonstratives anaphorically connecting sentences appear at the beginning of a sentence, referring back to the immediately preceding sentence and linking it to the sentence in which it appears. The semantic or pragmatic relationship between the sentences linked by a connective demonstrative is typically made explicit by the inclusion of a marker of clause conjoining. Like the "head" in tail-head linkage structure, the demonstrative and the marker of conjoining, if any, are separated from the rest of the sentence in which they appear by a distinct comma intonation.

The unmarked choice of an anaphoric sentence-connecting demonstrative is the contrastive demonstrative *homo* 'CONTR.INAN' (see §7.6 for a full treatment of this demonstrative's functions). *Homo* occurs with extremely high frequency in this function in texts of all types. For example, in (95) we can see that with each new sentence from (95b) on, *homo* 'CONTR.INAN' is used to link together the sentences describing the sequence of events in the narrative.

(95) a. *Bel   en   baqi   gu-huq,   en   gie   tais   h-apal*
        wind   person   NPRX.AN   3AN-blow   person   3.POSS   cloth   3INAN-open
        niq,   en   tais   rele   ru-hukut   tuqan   on.
        NEG   person   cloth   INS   REFL-wrap.up   more   DO
        'The wind blew the person, (but) the person didn't take off the cloth, (rather) the person wrapped themselves up further with the cloth.'   [Bk-16.005]
    b. ***Homo   haqal,***   Hot   g-iral   r-opil   ha-sai,
        CONTR.INAN   finished   sun   3AN-eye   REFL-power   3INAN-exit
        baqi   rie   cinoq   rele   en   g-ini   sil.
        NPRX.AN   REFL.POSS   hot   INS   person   3AN-CAUS   sweat
        'Afterwards, the Sun unleashed his power, he made the person sweat with his heat.'   [Bk-16.006]

c. ***Homo=na,***   *en*   *gie*   *tais*   *olu.*
CONTR.INAN=FOC person 3.POSS cloth bare
'Then, the person removed the cloth.'   [Bk-16.007]

d. ***Homo***   ***no,***   *Hot*   *Bel*   *g-o*   *zal,*...
CONTR.INAN OBL sun wind 3-SRC carry
'With that, the Sun defeated the Wind, ...'   [Bk-16.008]

The non-proximal demonstrative *baqa* 'NPRX.INAN' is also occasionally used as a sentence connective (§7.4.2.3). In this context, *baqa*'s use is more marked than that of *homo* 'CONTR.INAN'; it is associated with greater topicality. Consider the extract in (96) from a text in which the speaker describes how to play the game *hol okoq*, known in Indonesian as *congk(l)ak*. The first sentences, given in (96a) to (96d), describe the sequence of actions involved in setting up and playing the game. These sentences are connected to the previous sentences by tail-head linkage in (96b) and then by connective structures with *homo* in (96c) and (96d). In (96e), the speaker brings the sequence of events to a close with a connective structure using *baqa*.

(96) a. *Hol*   *okoq*   *baqa,*   *i*   *okoq=na*   *wil*   *tut.*
stone dig NPRX.INAN 1PL.INCL hole=FOC dig first
'Concerning (playing the game) *hol okoq*, we first of all dig the holes.'
                                                                [Bk-9.001]

b. ***Okoq***   ***wil***   ***haqal***   ***soq=bu,***   *hol*   *g-oq*
hole dig finished SEQ=GIVEN stone 3AN-fruit
goniqil~goniqil   *g-olo,*   *okoq*   *baqa*   *no.*
REDUP~four 3AN-put.in hole NPRX.INAN OBL
'When finished digging the holes, (we) put the stones in fours, in the holes, that is.'   [Bk-9.002]

c. ***Homo***   ***haqal***   ***soq=bu,***   *i*   *bukuq*   *bare,*
CONTR.INAN finished SEQ=GIVEN 1PL.INCL play PROX.INAN
hol   *g-oq*   *baqi*   *g-olo,*   *g-olo,*   *g-olo,*
stone 3AN-fruit NPRX.AN 3AN-put.in 3AN-put.in 3AN-put.in
g-olo.
3AN-put.in
'When that's finished, we play by putting the stones (in the holes) over, over, over, and over.'   [Bk-9.003]

d. ***Homo***   *soq,*   *okoq*   *kosong*   *no*   *g-olo*   *ba=bu,*
CONTR.INAN SEQ hole empty OBL 3AN-put.in ART.INAN=GIVEN
heser   *oa.*
dead IAM
'Then, if (yours) goes in an empty hole, then (you're) out (of the game).'
                                                               [Bk-9.004]

e. **Baqa=bu,**   rasal,   main   niq   oa.
   NPRX.INAN=GIVEN stop   play   NEG   IAM
   'In *that* case, (we) stop, (we) don't play anymore.'   [Bk-9.005]

The proximal demonstrative may also occasionally be used pronominally in anaphoric sentence connecting, but this is even rarer than the use of the non-proximal demonstrative. See §7.3.2.3 for examples.

Interestingly, neither the non-proximal nor the proximal demonstrative are used pronominally in sentence connecting with the dedicated clause conjunctions =si 'REAS' (§15.3.2.1.1) and *soq* 'SEQ' (§15.3.2.1.2). By contrast, the contrastive demonstrative *homo* regularly occurs with these conjunctions in sentence connecting. Since all demonstratives otherwise have the same distributional properties (§3.5.4), this difference cannot easily be seen as a syntactic constraint, but seems rather to have to do with the semantics of *homo* as the unmarked sentence-connecting demonstrative.

15.4.2.2 Cataphoric demonstratives

The INANIMATE forms of some demonstratives can also be used pronominally as sentence connectives to refer forward to the events in the following sentence or, more broadly, to the following discourse as a whole. A proclausal demonstrative used cataphorically is always the complement of the postposition *goet* 'LIKE' (see §12.2.3 for more on this item).

There are two contexts in which cataphoric demonstratives with *goet* are found. The first is when they are used to introduce direct speech and thought, as illustrated in (97).

(97) a. Pir,   g-otil   pana   g-ege   **doe**   **goet** on.
       reach 3AN-spouse female 3AN-BEN SPEC.INAN LIKE   DO
       '(When he) got home, his wife (said) this:'   [EnBaruq-16]
    b. "Hae!   Baruq, eto   bai   a   masa gie=na   mal,
       INTERJ lazy   2SG   thing   eat   buy   PROSP=FOC go
       tebe   busa=na   gi-al."
       return cat=FOC   3AN-carry
       "'Huh! Lazy, when you were meant to go and buy food, (you've) returned with a cat.'"   [EnBaruq-17]

The second is at the beginning of an explanation of a procedure or manner in which something is done or has come about. In these contexts, the cataphoric demonstrative does not appear to be pointing simply to the following sentence or portion of text, but to the whole of the description. For example, the cataphoric specifier demonstrative in the first line of the text describing how to bake cakes in (98a) refers forward to the whole description, not just to the following sentence in (98b).

(98) a. *Tubi s-alak   **roe**   **goet** on.*
       cake 3INAN-roast SPEC.INAN LIKE DO
       'Roasting cakes is done like this:'   [Bk-76.001]
    b. *Niat   no   paqol=na   g-ao   tutu.*
       beginning OBL maize=FOC 3AN-pound first
       'In the beginning, first the maize is pounded.'   [Bk-76.002]

The specifier demonstrative, used in examples (97) and (98), is the most common demonstrative in cataphoric sentence connecting. However, the non-proximal, proximal, and contrastive demonstratives may also be used cataphorically with *goet*. See the relevant sections of Chapter 7 for examples of each of these demonstratives being used in cataphoric sentence connecting.

15.4.3 *Tebe* 'return' in sentence connecting

Tebe is a motion verb denoting 'return, go back' (see §13.9.2 on the use of this verb in serialisation). *Tebe* 'return' also has a sentence-connecting function where it means 'then, next'. Like other sentence-connecting devices, in this use *tebe* 'return' occurs sentence-initially, separated from the rest of the sentence by comma intonation. For example:

(99) a. *Homo   ni,   halali ata   lesiq.*
       CONTR.INAN OBL 3DU   further argue
       'At that, the two of them argued some more.'   [EnBaruq-021]
    b. ***Tebe**, minggu teni   gie,   pana   bi   die*
       return   week   again PROSP woman ART.AN REFL.POSS
       eme=o   die   ama   g-o   mal teni.
       mother=AND REFL.POSS father 3AN-SRC go   again
       'Then, for another week, the wife went to her parent's house again.'
                                                                [EnBaruq-022]

In some cases, connective *tebe* occurs between two conjoined clauses rather than sentences. For example, in (100) it occurs in between the two clauses it connects, but retains its distinct intonational properties.

(100) *Jadi paqol g-ota   haqal,   tebe,   paqol   sau.*
      so   maize 3AN-plant finished return maize harvest
      'So once the maize has been planted, then it is harvested.'   [Bk-8.041]

15.4.4 Sentence connectives

Bunaq has two dedicated sentence connectives: *hasi* [hasi ~ hisi][2] 'so, therefore' and *habe* 'rather, by contrast'.[3] Sentence connectives typically occur at the beginning of a prosodically and morphosyntactically independent sentence, connecting it with the previous sentence.

Hasi 'so, therefore' expresses that the event in the clause it marks is motivated by, or happens because of, the event denoted in the preceding clause. For instance:

(101) a. Neto   r-on   doq.
         1SG   REFL-hand   cut
         'I cut my hand.'
      b. **Hasi**, n-on   ho   pegar   los.
         SO   1EXCL-hand   blood bloodied very
         'Because of this my hand was covered in blood.' [Bk-12.019]

(102) a. Nei   reu   gene nona   g-ege   teqa.
         1PL.EXCL   house LOC   miss   3AN-BEN   pray
         'At home we have been praying for you.'
      b. **Hisi**, nona   hani   bai   memel.
         SO   miss   PROH   thing   sick
         'So, you won't get sick.' [Bk-30.104]

Of the two dedicated sentence connectives, *habe* 'rather, by contrast' is much less frequent than *hasi* 'so, therefore' in the Bunaq corpus. *Habe* signals that the sentence it introduces denotes an event or situation which is unexpected in relation to, or contrasts with, the one in the preceding sentence. For example:

(103) a. Neto   Yerusalem   a-ta=o   mal   niq.
         1SG   Jerusalem   3INAN-GL=AND   go   NEG
         'I didn't even go to Jerusalem.'
      b. **Habe**, neto muk   Arab   a-ta=na   mal   liol.
         rather 1SG   land Arab   3INAN-GL=FOC   go   continue
         'Rather, I went straight to Arabia.' [Bib-338]

---

2 There is a tendency, particularly among younger speakers, to harmonise the vowel of the initial syllable with the high vowel of the second syllable.
3 Schapper (2007) argues that *hasi* and *habe* have their origins in the fusion of a deictic *ha and the clause-conjoining enclitics =*si* 'REAS' (§15.3.2.1.1) and =*be* 'CONTEXP' (§15.3.2.1.3). Such diachronic sources for sentence connectives are very common cross-linguistically (Diessel 1999: 125–127). Today, *hasi* and *habe* still have very similar semantics to the combination of these enclitics with the sentence-connecting demonstrative *homo*, i.e., *homo=si* and *homo=be*.

(104) a. *Eto=bu   loi-wen,   laun~laun   hotel   saqe   loi=si.*
2SG=GIVEN good-MODER REDUP~quick tree ascend good=REAS
'You will be fine since you can quickly climb a tree.' [OrelNis PipLoko-09]

b. ***Habe**, neto=bu   heser,   u   d-iri   goniqil   bare*
rather 1SG=GIVEN dead life REFL-leg four PROX.INAN
g-o=na   sura   los.
3AN-SRC=FOC ask very
'By contrast, I am dead, (because) my life relies on these four legs.'
[OrelNis PipLoko-010]

As the preceding examples illustrate, *hasi* and *habe* are most commonly found in positions similar to those of other sentence-connecting devices, that is, in initial position and separated from the rest of the sentence by comma intonation. However, there are also examples in the Bunaq corpus of the sentence connectives occurring in non-initial positions. Examples are given in (105) and (106).

(105) *Baqi   **hasi**   g-ewen   ho~ho   on   bare.*
NPRX.AN so 3AN-face REDUP~blood DO PROX.INAN
'She thus had blood all over her face.' [Bk-47.074]

(106) *Eto   **habe**   cie   ti   gie?*
2SG rather chicken fight PROSP
'Are you going to fight chickens or what?' [LB-8.171]

Like connective *tebe* 'return' (§15.4.3), a sentence connective can sometimes also occur between two conjoined clauses rather than sentences. In (107), *hasi* occurs between the two clauses it connects, but it is noticeable that it is intonationally "comma-ed" off from them.

(107) *..., g-iral   suel   heten   no   pao   bon   lai,*
3AN-eye left right OBL bean.sp box.bean place
***hasi**, en   heser   g-iral   tekeq-wen, ...*
so person dead 3AN-eye look-SIM
'..., (he) placed beans on both his eyes, so, they look like the eyes of a dead person, ...' [OrelMaMil-022]

Text Appendix

Text 1: Planting vegetables

Told by Hendriana Bui from Gewal, aged 16 at the time, recorded in 2007. The text is procedural, describing the process of preparing plots and growing *uor* 'vegetable, leafy green'. It shows tail-head linkage structures, as well as sentence connecting using the contrastive demonstrative *homo*. Both are typical of Bunaq procedural descriptions and sequential narratives. As is common amongst the Bunaq, the speaker uses numerous Indonesian/Malay words and expressions (e.g., *tiap hari* 'every day', *pupuk* 'fertilizer', *siram* 'pour, water'), but also combines Indonesian/Malay words with their Bunaq equivalents (Malay *pertama* 'first' with Bunaq *tut* in line 2) or switches between equivalents in the text (Malay *bersikan* 'clean' in line 11 is substituted with Bunaq *h-anaul* 'weed, clean a garden' in line 12). The text illustrates the variable ANIMACY assignment that can be found with plants (see §5.2.3.2 on default assignment patterns on plant cultivars, and §5.2.4.3 on reassignment of normally INANIMATE nouns to ANIMATE): while *u* 'herbaceous plant, weed' is treated as INANIMATE in lines 2 and 3, *uor* is treated as ANIMATE in lines 8–15) because the emphasis is on the living plant that is being grown. Interestingly, the ANIMATE agreement of *uor* is continued in line 13, even when the vegetable has been picked and is to be eaten. Normally, Bunaq speakers treat *uor* as INANIMATE in this context.

(1) Neto hot mil uen no uor g-oloq h-oqon.
    1SG sun DUR one OBL vegetable 3AN-place 3INAN-make
    'I have at one time made vegetable plots (lit., make vegetable places).'

(2) Uor g-oloq h-oqon ba, pertama no
    vegetable 3AN-place 3INAN-make ART.INAN first OBL
    i u=na t-ul tut.
    1PL.INCL weed=FOC 3INAN-pull.out first
    'To make vegetable plots, first we remove the weeds.'

(3) U t-ul haqal soq=bu, muk belek, muk
    weed 3INAN-pull.out finished SEQ=GIVEN earth turn earth
    s-ebuq.
    3INAN-dig.up
    'When (we) have finished removing the weeds, (we) turn the soil, dig up the soil.'

(4) *Homo haqal soq=bu, i hala=o bai*
CONTR.INAN finished SEQ=GIVEN 1PL.INCL rubbish=AND thing
t-ubak.
3INAN-pile.up
'After that, we pile up the rubbish (i.e., the pulled-up weeds) and stuff.'

(5) *Homo soq, ti-ta toqa.*
CONTR.INAN SEQ RECP-GL set.alight
'Then, (we) burn (it) all together.'

(6) *Ti-ta toqa haqal, i siram ruquk,*
RECP-GL set.alight finished 1PL.INCL pour continuously
tiap hari.
every day
'Having burnt (it), we (have to) water (the plots), every day.'

(7) *I tiap hari siram haqal, pupuk lai.*
1PL.INCL every day pour finished fertilizer set.down
'Having watered every day, we put down fertilizer.'

(8) *Pupuk lai homo haqal soq=bu,*
fertilizer set.down CONTR.INAN finished SEQ=GIVEN
i uor himo g-olo.
1PL.INCL vegetables CONTR.AN 3AN-bury
'After having put down the fertilizer, we plant the vegetables.'

(9) *Uor himo g-olo haqal, i*
vegetables CONTR.AN 3AN-bury finished 1PL.INCL
le gie mel, mon gi-ta ruquk.
next.day morning afternoon 3AN-GL continuously
'Having planted the vegetables, we keep on (watering) them in the morning and evening.'

(10) *Homo soq, uor baqi boqal-wen=bu,*
CONTR.INAN SEQ vegetables NPRX.AN big-MODER=GIVEN
gi-ta pupuk teni.
3AN-GL fertilizer again
'Then, when the vegetables have grown somewhat, (we) again put fertilizer on them.'

(11) Gi-ta   pupuk   haqal   soq=bu,   bersikan   ruquk.
    3AN-GL   fertilizer   finished   SEQ=GIVEN   clean   continuously
    'After having put on fertilizer, (we) keep (the plots) clean (i.e., we weed the plots).'

(12) G-anaul   haqal   soq=bu,   masak   o=bu,   i
    3AN-weed   finished   SEQ=GIVEN   big   IAM=GIVEN   1PL.INCL
    r-ege   g-iwal   oa.
    REFL-BEN   3AN-pick   IAM
    'After having finished weeding, if (the vegetables) are already big, we pick them.'

(13) G-ul   haqal   soq,   i   gi-a.
    3AN-pull.out finished   SEQ   1PL.INCL   3AN-eat
    'Having finished pulling out (the vegetables), we eat (them).'

(14) Gi-a   haqal   soq=bu,   tebe   g-oloq   no
    3AN-eat   finished   SEQ=GIVEN   return   3AN-place   OBL
    g-olo   teni.
    3AN-bury   again
    'Having eaten them, (we can) again plant (vegetables) in the plots.'

(15) Baqa   goet   on=e,   i   uor   g-oloq
    NPRX.INAN   LIKE   DO=AGREE   1PL.INCL   vegetable   3AN-place
    h-oqon=bu.
    3INAN-make=GIVEN
    'That's how it's done, if we make vegetable plots.'

Text 2: Directions to Nualain

Told by Marieta Soi from Gewal, aged over 60 at the time, recorded in 2007. This text is a detailed route description of the path to be taken when walking from Gewal village to Nualain village. It shows the density of named places in the Bunaq landscape on the one hand, and the ubiquity of reference to elevation in Bunaq place- and path-descriptions on the other hand. The text also illustrates that for steeper gradients, *saqe* 'ascend' can be used in place of an elevation-marked verb like *menal* 'go.HIGH' – see lines 8, 23–24, and 40 for examples.

(1) Neto   Nualain   mal,   hik~hik   bare=na   h-alolo.
   1SG   Nualain   go   REDUP~path   PROX.INAN=FOC   3INAN-follow
   '(If) I were going to Nualain, (I would) follow this route.'

(2) *Reu   gene sai, Sun Gewen gene honal   Ukaq Getel gene.*
    house LOC   exist Sun Gewen LOC   go.LEVEL   Ukaq Getel LOC
    'Go out of the house, go across from Sun Gewen to Ukaq Getel.'

(3) *Ukaq Getel gene haqal   soq, Hur Gol Mil gene zemal,*
    Ukaq Getel LOC   finished   SEQ   Hur Gol Mil LOC   go.LOW
    Bei Gutek gene zemal.
    Bei Gutek LOC   go.LOW
    'After Ukaq Getel, go down from Hur Gol Mil and from Bui Gutek.'

(4) *Kariq Gobon gene honal.*
    Kariq Gobon LOC   go.LEVEL
    'Go on the level from Kariq Gobon.'

(5) *Bokoi gene honal.*
    Bokoi LOC   go.LEVEL
    'Go on the level from Bokoi.'

(6) *Bokoi gene haqal,   Sele Lolo a-ta   zemal.*
    Bokoi LOC   finished Sele Lolo 3INAN-GL   go.LOW
    'After Bokoi, go down to Sele Lolo.'

(7) *Sele Lolo   a-ta   zemal   haqal   soq,*
    Sele Lolo   3INAN-GL   go.LOW   finished SEQ
    mele mele, tebe,   Sele Lolo gene zemal,   honal
    walk walk   return Sele Lolo LOC   go.LOW   go.LEVEL
    ota   o   Bele Boso Nokar gene tama.
    LEVEL ADDR Bele Boso Nokar LOC   enter
    'After having gone down to Sele Lolo, walk on and on, then, go down from Sele Lolo, go on the level and enter into Bele Boso Nokar.'

(8) *Homo   haqal   soq, Il Mok a-ta   zemal,*
    CONTR.INAN   finished   SEQ   Il Mok 3INAN-GL   go.LOW
    Naka Nuaq a-ta   saqe,   Mali Gel Pur Masak a-ta
    Naka Nuaq 3INAN-GL   ascend Mali Gel Pur Masak 3INAN-GL
    menal,   tebe   zemal   hik   sorun Lakus a-ta   mal.
    go.HIGH   return go.LOW   path   fork   Lakus 3INAN-GL   go
    'After that, go down to Il Mok, ascend to Naka Nuaq, go up to Mali Gel Pur Masak, then go down towards the fork in the road to Lakus.'

(9) *Homo   h-alolo.*
    CONTR.INAN 3INAN-follow
    'Follow that (i.e., that fork in the road to Lakus).'

(10) *Homo   haqal   soq, hik   sorun.*
     CONTR.INAN finished SEQ   path fork
     'After that, (there's a) fork in the road.'

(11) *Homo   haqal   soq, Ma Sorun a-ta   zemal,*
     CONTR.INAN finished SEQ   Ma Sorun 3INAN-GL   go.LOW
     Ma   pir.
     Ma   reach
     'After that, go down to Ma Sorun (lit., the fork in the road at Ma) (until you) reach Ma.'

(12) *Ma ba   pir,   baqa   no   zemal   teni.*
     Ma ART.INAN reach NPRX.INAN OBL   go.LOW again
     'Having reached Ma, from there go down again.'

(13) *Hik   sorun a-ta   sai   teni.*
     path   fork   3INAN-GL exit   again
     '(You'll) again come across a fork in the road.'

(14) *Homo   Lakus   a-ta   tama   gie,   hik   sorun baqa.*
     CONTR.INAN Lakus   3INAN-GL   enter PROSP   path fork   NPRX.INAN
     'This is the fork in the road that goes to Lakus.'

(15) *Lakus   a-ta   tama   gie=na   baqa,   Pie Asa Toiq*
     Lakus   3INAN-GL   enter PROSP=FOC   NPRX.INAN   Pie Asa Toiq
     a-ta   zemal.
     3INAN-GL   go.LOW
     'That's the one to go Lakus, (but) go down to Pie Asa Toiq.'

(16) *Pie Asa Toiq a-ta   zemal.*
     Pie Asa Toiq 3INAN-GL   go.LOW
     'Go down to Pie Asa Toiq.'

(17) *Pie Asa Toiq a-ta   zemal   haqal   soq, Pie Asa Toiq*
     Pie Asa Toiq 3INAN-GL   go.LOW finished SEQ   Pie Asa Toiq
     Homo   no   mele   mele   mele,   daro   esen   o
     CONTR.INAN OBL   walk   walk   walk   until   HIGH   ADDR

Duarato Pur Bul homo pir.
Duarato Pur Bul CONTR.INAN reach
'After having gone down to Pie Asa Toiq, from Pie Asa Toiq walk on and on and on until reaching Duarato Pur Bul.'

(18) *Duarato Pur Bul homo no menal, Leto Sun*
Duarato Pur Bul CONTR.INAN OBL go.HIGH Leto Sun
a-ta sai.
3INAN-GL exit
'From Duarato Pur Bul go up (until you) come to Leto Sun.'

(19) *Leto Sun homo no menal teni.*
Leto Sun CONTR.INAN OBL go.HIGH again
'From Leto Sun go up again.'

(20) *Duarato tas mil gene honal soq, Il Tuen*
Duarato village inside LOC go.LEVEL SEQ Il Tuen
a-ta zemal.
3INAN-GL go.LOW
'From inside Duarato village go on the level, then go down towards Il Tuen.'

(21) *Il Tuen a-ta zemal haqal soq, tebe,*
Il Tuen 3INAN-GL go.LOW finished SEQ return
menal menal.
go.HIGH go.HIGH
'After having gone down towards Il Tuen, then, go up and up.'

(22) *Mele menal teni.*
walk go.HIGH again
'Walk up again.'

(23) *Baqa no, saqe=si Sie Giseq a-ta saqe.*
NPRX.INAN OBL ascend=REAS Sie Giseq 3INAN-GL ascend
'From there, ascend in order to get up to Sie Giseq.'

(24) *Sie Giseq a-ta saqe haqal soq, honal*
Sie Giseq 3INAN-GL ascend finished SEQ go.LEVEL
honal, daro Nualain Railubu pir.
go.LEVEL until Nualain Railubu reach
'Once you've ascended to Sie Giseq, go on and on on the level, until Nualain Railubu.'

(25) *Nualain Railubu pir,   reu   por   Nualain gie   a-ta*
     Nualain Railubu reach house holy Nualain 3.POSS 3INAN-GL
     tama atau reu   por   Nualain gie   a-ta   sai oa.
     enter or   house holy Nualain 3.POSS 3INAN-GL exit IAM
     'Having reached Nualain Railubu, (you can) go into the church of Nualain or (rather you) come upon the Nualain church.'

(26) *Tebe, Basal a-ta   zemal.*
     return Basal 3INAN-GL go.LOW
     'Then, go down to Basal.'

(27) *Homo   haqal   soq, liol   il   gene.*
     CONTR.INAN   finished SEQ   continue water LOC
     'After that, continue to the water.'

(28) *Il   baqa   h-ini   Boleton.*
     water NPRX.INAN   3INAN-call   Boleton
     'The water is called Boleton.'

(29) *Boleton Il gene liol.*
     Boleton Il LOC   continue
     'From Boleton Il continue on.'

(30) *Boleton Il gene liol,   Nualain=na   baqa.*
     Boleton Il LOC   continue Nualain=FOC   NPRX.INAN
     'Having continued on from Boleten Il, that's Nualain.'

(31) *Homo   soq, Nualain no   zemal.*
     CONTR.INAN   SEQ   Nualain OBL go.LOW
     'Then, go down from Nualain.'

(32) *Mele zemal   zemal   zemal, Zoil Toiq=o   bai*
     walk go.LOW   go.LOW   go.LOW Zoil Toiq=AND thing
     a-ta=na   sai   oa.
     3INAN-GL=FOC exit IAM
     'Walk down and down and down, (until you) come upon Zoil Toiq or whatever it's called.'

(33) *Hik   gene tuku uen ai.*
     path LOC   hour one ONLY
     '(It's) only an hour on the road.'

(34) *Mele tuku uen lesin.*
 walk hour one more
 'Walking, (it is) more than an hour.'

(35) *Kilo gonciet ai.*
 kilometre five ONLY
 '(It is) only 5 kilometres.'

(36) *Mele mele zemal.*
 walk walk go.LOW
 'Walk down.'

(37) *Mele mele menal.*
 walk walk go.HIGH
 'Walk up.'

(38) *Mele mele honal.*
 walk walk go.LEVEL
 'Walk across.'

(39) *Mele mele zemal.*
 walk walk go.LOW
 'Walk down.'

(40) *Mele mele saqe.*
 walk walk ascend
 'Climb up.'

(41) *Mele tuku mil uen lesin ai.*
 walk hour DUR one more ONLY
 'Walking, (it is) only (a little) more than an hour.'

(42) *Honal on, tuku mil uen lesin.*
 go.LEVEL DO hour DUR one more
 'Going there (it is) more than an hour.'

(43) *Man on, tuku mil uen lesin ai.*
 come DO hour DUR one more only
 'Coming back, (it is) only (a little) more than an hour.'

(44) Mete   nei   jam   sebelas no   man, jam   duabelas lesin
     NOW   1PL.EXCL   hour 11   OBL   come hour 12   more
     huqe   pir.
     HERE   reach
     'Now if we were to leave at 11 o'clock, we would get here after 12 o'clock.'

Text 3: The founding of Lakus village

Told by the Dato of Lakus village, aged approximately 60 at the time, recorded in 2007 in Lakus village. It tells the story of how his parents, along with other families from Lebos, came to Lamaknen at the end of World War II. Note the use of *i* '1PL.INCL' in lines 9 and 11 to politely include the addressee (myself, a non-Timorese) in the events, versus *nei* '1PL.EXCL' in lines 12–13, referring specifically to the speaker's parents' experiences; the speaker includes himself in the events even though he was not yet born at the time.

(1) Lakus bare   bare   no   dara-wen.
    Lakus PROX.INAN   PROX.INAN   OBL erect-ANTIC
    '(The village of) Lakus came about here all on its own.'

(2) Waktu man,   to   lihur   uen   atus   siwe   sogo goniqil
    time   come   year   thousand   one   hundred   nine   ten   four
    gal   gonciet no=na   man.
    plus   five   OBL=FOC   come
    'When (we) came, (it was) in the year 1945 that we came.'

(3) Bul~bul   haqe   gene man   baqa   ... tan   waktu en
    REDUP~origin   THERE   LOC   come NPRX.INAN   because   time   person
    g-iwiq   belis.
    3AN-skin   white
    'The reasons for (our) coming from there (was). . . because (it was the) time (of the) white people.'

(4) En   Belanda=o   Jepang.
    person   Holland=AND   Japan
    'The Dutch and Japanese people.'

(5) Waktu   Jepang Timor   mil   tama,   to   lihur   uen   atus
    time   Japan   Timor   inside   enter   year   thousand   one   hundred
    siwe   sogo   goniqil   gal   hiloqon   no.
    nine   ten   four   plus   two   OBL
    'When the Japanese entered Timor, it was in the year 1942.'

(6) Halaqi to mil goniqon Lebos bare gene.
3PL year DUR three Lebos PROX.INAN LOC
'They were three years in Lebos.'

(7) Homo=na, nei nie matas mil...
CONTR.INAN=FOC 1PL.EXCL 1EXCL.POSS old COLL
'Then, our parents...'

(8) En Belanda mit taq.
person Dutch sit CONT
'The Dutch people were still present.'

(9) Belanda=na i u-bul ukon.
Dutch=FOC 1PL.INCL 1INCL/2-head govern
'It was the Dutch who ruled us.'

(10) Tebe, Jepang man.
then Japan come
'Then, the Japanese came.'

(11) Tebe, Jepang g-ini i ru-bul ukon.
then Japan 3AN-CAUS 1PL.INCL REFL-head govern
'Then, the Japanese were made our rulers.'

(12) Jepang=na nei nu-bul ukon oa.
Japan=FOC 1PL.EXCL 1EXCL-head govern IAM
'It was now the Japanese that ruled us.'

(13) Homo ni, en mete Belanda g-ua gene
CONTR.INAN OBL person NOW Dutch 3AN-footprint LOC
g-ua gene himo, tebe, nei n-otol...
3AN-footstep LOC CONTR.AN then 1PL.EXCL 1EXCL-WITHOUT
'Then, those people who had been adherents of the Dutch, then (they) were (angry) with us...'

(14) Nei nie matas mil g-otol na, tan
1PL.EXCL 1EXCL.POSS old COLL 3AN-WITHOUT angry because
halaqi en Jepang gi-ta=na mal oa.
3PL person Japan 3AN-GL=FOC go IAM
'(They) were angry with our parents, because they had sided with the Japanese.'

(15) *Homo=na,   tebe   ota   gene.*
CONTR.INAN=FOC return LEVEL LOC
'Then, (they) went back over there (i.e., to East Timor).'

(16) *Waktu   to   lihur   uen   atus   siwe   sok   goniqil*
time   year   thousand one   hundred nine   tens four
gal   gonciet, hul   Augustus=ka, hul   baqa   goet,
plus   five   moon   August=OR   moon   NPRX.INAN LIKE
Jepang gene Amerika Hiroshima=o   Nagasaki a-ta
Japan LOC   America Hiroshima=AND Nagasaki 3INAN-GL
bom   g-ileqen.
bomb   3AN-drop
'(In the) year 1945 in August or thereabouts, America dropped a bomb onto Hiroshima and Nagasaki in Japan.'

(17) *Halaqi Jepang r-on   dara.*
3PL   Japan   REFL-hand   erect
'The Japanese surrendered (lit., put up their hands).'

(18) *R-on   dara.*
REFL-hand   erect
'(They) surrendered.'

(19) *Akirnya, halaqi rie   muk   a-ta   tebe.*
finally   3PL   REFL.POSS   land 3INAN-GL return
'Finally, they went back to their own country.'

(20) *Halaqi rie   muk   a-ta   tebe   haqal,   tebe,*
3PL   REFL.POSS   land 3INAN-GL return finished return
Belanda tebe   man   teni   oa.
Dutch   return come   again   IAM
'After they went back to their own country, then the Dutch came back again.'

(21) *Belanda tebe   man   teni,   homo   ni,   mete Belanda*
Dutch   return come   again   CONTR.INAN   OBL   NOW   Dutch
gi-ta   mal   himo,   en...
3AN-GL   go   CONTR.AN people
'(When) the Dutch came back again, at that point, those who had supported the Dutch, the people...'

(22) *Himo=na   tebe   nei   nie   matas   mil*
CONTR.AN=FOC return 1PL.EXCL 1EXCL.POSS old   COLL
g-ege   h-oqon   gie   oa.
3AN-BEN   3INAN-do   PROSP   IAM
'Those (people) now wanted to do (harm) to our elders.'

(23) *Homo   no=na,   halaqi ciwal   man.*
CONTR.INAN   OBL=FOC   3PL   flee   come
'It was at that point that they fled (and) came here.'

(24) *Halaqi ciwal   man,   meten   no   zol… ola   zol   alan   gene*
3PL   flee   come beginning OBL   river   LOW   river side   LOC
taq.
CONT
'(When) they had fled, in the beginning (they stayed) down there by the river.'

(25) *Tebe   hul   uen   hiloqon   goniqon,   halaqi mina   ola*
then   moon one   two   three   3PL   come.HIGH LOW
bare   no.
PROX.INAN   OBL
'Then, (after) one, two (or) three months, they moved up to a higher location (but still lower than the present village).'

(26) *Tebe,   hul   goniqil gonciet   tomol   baqa   goet   teni,*
return   moon   four   five   six   NPRX.INAN LIKE   again
halaqi   mina,   tas   bare   a-ta.
3PL   come.HIGH village   PROX.INAN 3INAN-GL
'Then (after) four, five (or) six months in the same manner again, they came up to where this village is now.'

(27) *Baqa=na   h-ini   Lakus.*
NPRX.INAN=FOC   3INAN-call   Lakus
'Lakus was (what they) called it.'

(28) *Lakus   bare,   tan   lolo   masak   bun   esen   gene*
Lakus   PROX.INAN because mountain big   INDEF   HIGH   LOC
h-ini   Lakus.
3INAN-call   Lakus
'This (name) "Lakus" (was chosen), because of a big mountain up there called Lakus.'

(29) *Esen baqa, wa gene, esen baqa.*
    HIGH NPRX.INAN top LOC HIGH NPRX.INAN
    '(It is) up there, on the top up there.'

(30) *Tan haqe gene=na man, baqa gie=na,*
    because THERE LOC=FOC come NPRX.INAN BECAUSE=FOC
    muk bare h-ini Lakus.
    land PROX.INAN 3INAN-call Lakus
    'Because it was there (that they) came from, on that account, this land is called Lakus.'

Text 4: A fall

Told by Manek Rofinus from Gewal, aged around 40 at the time, recorded in 2007. The text is a personal narrative of how one of his friends broke his leg falling from a mango tree. The village head accuses the speaker and his friend of pushing the other boy from the tree. In line 29, we see the speaker uses the verb *h-ini* '3INAN-call, cause' to signal the accusation of this action against them by the village head.

(1) *Tutu no, nei iskola taq, seminari gene, biasnya*
    past OBL 1PL.EXCL school CONT seminary LOC usually
    nei... hul sogal hiloqo, nei libur.
    1PL.EXCL moon ten.plus two 1PL.EXCL holiday
    'In the past, when we were still in school, at the seminary, usually in December, we would have holidays.'

(2) *Nei, waktu nei libur, nei biasnya*
    1PL.EXCL time 1PL.EXCL holiday 1PL.EXCL usually
    kampung a-ta mal, kampung Kewar baqa gene.
    village 3INAN-GL go village Gewal NPRX.INAN LOC
    'We, when we were on holidays, we would usually go to the village, to the village of Gewal.'

(3) *Nei nie matas mil baqa gene, nei*
    1PL.EXCL 1EXCL.POSS old COLL NPRX.INAN LOC 1PL.EXCL
    g-utu ti-ta bolu.
    3AN-COM RECP-GL united
    'We spent time together there with our parents.'

(4) *Hot mil uen no, nei nie moen mil g-utu*
sun DUR one OBL 1PL.EXCL 1EXCL.POSS friend COLL 3-COM
nei goniqo ola mar mal.
1PL.EXCL three LOW garden go
'One day, me and my friends, the three of us went to a garden down there.'

(5) *Nei mar gene zo a gie.*
1PL.EXCL garden LOC mango eat PROSP
'In the garden we wanted to eat mangoes.'

(6) *Le gie mel kira~kira tuku hitu nei*
next.day morning approximately hour seven 1PL.EXCL
kampung gene sai.
village LOC exit
'The next morning at approximately 7am we left the village.'

(7) *Mar baqa mar ate, h-ini Hol Taqol ola zol*
garden NPRX.INAN garden far 3INAN-call Hol Taqol LOW river
alan gene.
side LOC
'That garden is a distant garden, called Hol Taqol down by the river side.'

(8) *Hol Taqol baqa no nei nie zo masak*
Hol Taqol NPRX.INAN OBL 1PL.EXCL 1EXCL.POSS mango large
bul hiloqo.
base two
'At Hol Taqol we had two large mango trees.'

(9) *Zo baqa za haqal oa.*
mango NPRX.INAN ripe finished IAM
'Those mangoes were already completely ripe.'

(10) *Nei goniqo saqe.*
1PL.EXCL three ascend
'The three of us climbed up.'

(11) *En hiloqo zo bul uen no, en uen zo bul*
person two mango base one OBL person one mango base
uen no.
one OBL
'Two people climbed up one tree, and one person up (another) tree.'

(12) Nei   saqe,   h-atun.
    1PL.EXCL ascend   3INAN-take.down
    'When we climbed up, (we) lowered down (some mangoes).'

(13) Homo=na,   kira~kira   tuku sogal   hiloqo, nei   wa
    CONTR.INAN=FOC   approximately   hour 10.plus two   1PL.EXCL   top
    gene a.
    LOC   eat
    'Then, at about 12 noon, we were eating mangoes up top (i.e., in the tree).'

(14) Nei   wa   gene   a,   tekil~tekil homo   no,
    1PL.EXCL top   LOC   eat   suddenly   CONTR.INAN   OBL
    nie   moen   uen   baqi   zo   gene   topol.
    1EXCL.POSS   friend   one   NPRX.INAN   mango   LOC   fall
    'We were eating (them) up top, when suddenly, one of my friends fell from a tree.'

(15) Zo   gene   topol haqal,   neli   rebel.
    mango   LOC   fall   finished   1DU.EXCL   descend
    'After he had fallen from a mango (tree), the two of us climbed down.'

(16) Neli   mos=o   rebel,   tebe,   ge-tekeq,
    1DU.EXCL   also=AND   descend   return   3AN-look.at
    baqi   zo   gene   topol   o=si.
    NPRX.AN   mango   LOC   fall   IAM=REAS
    'We also climbed down, then, looked at him, because he had fallen from the tree.'

(17) Zo   gene   topol baqa,   g-iri   baqa   tugal,
    mango   LOC   fall   NPRX.INAN   3AN-leg   NPRX.INAN   broke
    g-iri   suel=na   tugal.
    3AN-leg   left=FOC   broke
    'When he had fallen from the mango tree, he had broken his leg, it was his left leg that was broken.'

(18) Homo=na   nei   t-ege   atur.
    CONTR.INAN=FOC   1PL.EXCL   RECP-BEN   arrange
    'Then, we organised ourselves.'

(19) Uen   g-ini   mal   matas   mil   gi-wit.
    one   3AN-CAUS   go   old   COLL   3AN-fetch
    'One (person) was sent to fetch the grown-ups.'

(20) Neto   roe   gi-ta   zaga,   baqa   no.
     1SG   SPEC.INAN   3AN-GL   watch.over NPRX.INAN   OBL
     'I watched over him, in that place.'

(21) Kira~kira   tuku   uen, matas mil   Gewal gene sai.
     approximately   hour   one   old   COLL Gewal LOC   exit
     'About an hour later, the grown-ups left Gewal.'

(22) Homo=na   en   topol himo   g-ukat.
     CONTR.INAN=FOC   person fall   CONTR.AN 3AN-lift.up
     'Then, (they) lifted up the person who had fallen.'

(23) G-ukat,   g-erel   Gewal gene.
     3AN-lift.up 3AN-INS   Gewal LOC
     'They lifted him up and took him to Gewal.'

(24) Gewal gene   haqal,   gi-al   reu   memel gene.
     Gewal LOC   finished 3AN-carry house sick LOC
     'Once in Gewal, they took him to the hospital.'

(25) Gi-al   reu   memel gene, haqe gene halaqi... perawat=na
     3AN-carry house sick LOC   THERE LOC   3PL   nurse=FOC
     g-ege   h-etel,   g-iri   homo   perban.
     3AN-BEN   3INAN-root 3AN-leg   CONTR.INAN bandage
     'Once he was taken to the hospital, there, they... the nurse gave him medicine, and bandaged his leg.'

(26) Homo   haqal   soq, en   kepala desa   nei
     CONTR.INAN   finished   SEQ   person village.head 1PL.EXCL
     n-ege   seq.
     1EXCL-BEN   call
     'After that, the village head called us.'

(27) Nei   no   sura, nego   on=na   en   gol   roi   topol?
     1PL.EXCL   OBL   ask   what   DO=FOC   person small   SPEC.AN   fall
     '(He) asked us why this child had fallen.'

(28) Hele   nei   n-ini   gu-rumak.
     maybe   1PL.EXCL   1EXCL-call 3AN-push
     '(He) said that maybe we pushed him.'

(29) Nei   n-ini   g-ini   topol   on.
     1PL.EXCL   1EXCL-call   3AN-CAUS   fall   DO
     '(He) said that we made him fall.'

(30) Baqa   gie=na,   en   kepala desa   nei   n-ege   seq.
     NPRX.INAN   BECAUSE=FOC   person   village.head   1PL.EXCL   1EXCL-BEN   call
     'Because of that (i.e., in order to ask us that), the village head had called us.'

(31) Nei   mos   kepala desa   g-ege   sasi,   g-ege   rale.
     1PL.EXCL   also   head village   3AN-BEN   say   3AN-BEN   talk
     'We replied to the village head, we told him.'

(32) "Tuen goet=na   baqi   ola   o   zo   gene   topol?"
     when LIKE=FOC   NPRX.AN   LOW   ADDR   mango   LOC   fall
     '(He had asked us) "How did he fall from the mango tree?"'

(33) Kepala desa   g-ege   rale   baqa   goet:
     head village   3AN-BEN   talk   NPRX.INAN   LIKE
     '(We) said this to the village head:'

(34) "Nei   goniqo zo   baqa   saqe   gaqal,   wa   gene   a.
     1PL.EXCL   three mango   NPRX.INAN   ascend   all.AN   top   LOC   eat
     '"The three of us all climbed up those mango trees, and were eating up top.'

(35) Waqen   h-atun,   tekil~tekil   i   ie
     PART.PL   3INAN-lower.down   suddenly   1PL.INCL   1INCL/2.POSS
     moen   roi   topol   rebel.
     friend   SPEC.AN   fall   descend
     '(We) were lowering some (mangoes) down, when suddenly our friend fell down.'

(36) Topol   rebel   homo,   ga-hake-wen.
     fall   descend   CONTR.INAN,   3AN-push.over-ANTIC
     'When he fell down, he just toppled over by himself (i.e., no one caused it).'

(37) Gie   turiq   gol   homo   ret golaq   topol,   ret golaq
     3.POSS   machete   small   CONTR.INAN   all.alone   fall   all.alone
     bitil-wen   kira~kira   meter   goniqo.
     spin-ANTIC   approximately   metre   three
     'His knife fell on its own, spinning about three metres away.'

(38) *Homo   haqal   naq=na,   baqi   topol o=si,*
CONTR.INAN finished   PRIOR=FOC NPRX.AN   fall   IAM=REAS
nei   zo   gene   rebel.
1PL.EXCL   mango   LOC   descend
'Only after that, because he had fallen, did we climb down from the mango trees.'

(39) *Homo=na,   nie   moen   roi   g-ini   matas*
CONTR.INAN=FOC 1EXCL.POSS   friend SPEC.AN 3AN-CAUS   elder
mil   g-ege   seq.
COLL   3AN-BEN   call
'Then, this friend was sent to call the grown-ups.'

(40) *Jadi, nei   homo   ozol nego   uen=o   bai   niq.*
so   1PL.EXCL   CONTR.INAN   NEG   what   one=AND   thing   NEG
'In the meanwhile, we had no idea what to do.'

(41) *Baqi   ret   topol   on."*
NPRX.INAN   alone   fall   DO
'He fell by himself (i.e., no one had done anything to cause it).'"

(42) *Homo   haqal,   gi-al   reu   memel   gene.*
CONTR.INAN   finished   3AN-carry   house   sick   LOC
'After that, he was taken to the hospital.'

(43) *Reu   memel   gene   ola   o   perawat   g-ege   h-etel,*
house   sick   LOC   LOW   ADDR   nurse   3AN-give   3INAN-root
g-iri   tugal   homo   perban.
3AN-leg   break   CONTR.INAN   bandage
'In the hospital, the nurse gave him medicine and bandaged his broken leg.'

(44) *Homo=na,   baqi   ota   reu   memel   gene,   kira~kira*
CONTR.INAN=FOC NPRX.INAN   LEVEL   house   sick   LOC   approximately
haqe   gene   hul   goniqo.
THERE   LOC   moon   three
'Then, he was in hospital for three months.'

(45) *Homo   haqal   soq,   tebe   sai.*
CONTR.INAN   finished   SEQ   return exit
'Afterwards, he came back out.'

(46) Tebe   sai, tas   Gewal gene.
     return exit village Gewal LOC
     'He came back out to the village.'

(47) Homo   haqal   soq, baqi... liburan haqal
     CONTR.INAN   finished SEQ   NPRX.AN holiday finished
     o=si,   nei   tebe   rie   iskola mal.
     IAM=REAS   1PL.EXCL   return REFL.POSS   school go
     'After that, because he... the holidays had finished, we had gone back to school.'

(48) Baqa   goet ai.
     NPRX.INAN   LIKE only
     'That's it.'

Text 5: Fire and Water

Told by Manuel Mela from Henes, aged 47 at the time, recorded in 2013. This text is a short exemplar of the Bunaq oral literature genre known as *zapal*. It tells the story of the emnity between Fire (*hoto*) and Water (*il*, also referred to in the story as *inel* 'rain' from line 5 on). This story is etiological, explaining why fire can be started by rubbing bamboo sticks together or striking stone on iron: because it was in bamboo, stone, and iron that Fire hid after its defeat by Water. In line 12 we see the formulaic phrase, literally, 'the pumpkin has fruited', used to end *zapal*.

(1) Nie   rale roe   goet on!
    1EXCL.POSS   talk SPEC.INAN   LIKE DO
    'This is my story!'

(2) Hoto=o   il,   tutu no,   hoto=o   il   bere   t-oqon.
    fire=AND   water   past OBL   fire=AND   water CONTEXP.INAN RECP-do
    'Fire and Water, once upon a time, Fire and Water were in conflict with one another.'

(3) Hoto=o   il   t-oqon,   hoto=be,   hoto=na   zal   gie,
    fire=AND   water   RECP-do   fire=CONTEXP   fire=FOC   carry PROSP
    il=be   il=na   zal   gie.
    water=CONTEXP   water=FOC   carry PROSP
    'When they fought, Fire maintained that he would win, while Water maintained that he would win.'

(4) *Halali t-oqon t-oqon t-oqon, terakir hoto kala, il=na menang.*
   3DU RECP-do RECP-do RECP-do finally fire lost water=FOC win
   'They fought and fought and fought, and, in the end, Fire was defeated, it was Water who won.'

(5) *E... inel... inel=na... inel=na menang, inel=na zal.*
   INTERJ rain rain=FOC rain=FOC won inel=FOC carry
   'Um... rain, it was rain, it was rain (i.e., water) who won the contest.'

(6) *Homo=na, hoto hotel tub... e... ma tubuk*
   CONTR.INAN=FOC fire tree hole INTERJ bamboo hole
   a-ta tama, besi tubuk a-ta tama, hol tubuk
   3INAN-GL enter iron hole 3INAN-GL enter stone hole
   a-ta tama.
   3INAN-GL enter
   'Then, Fire hid inside um... inside bamboo, inside iron, inside stones.'

(7) *Homo=na, hol uen besi uen pak, hoto sia.*
   CONTR.INAN=FOC stone one iron one strike fire burn
   'Then, (if you would) strike a stone and a piece of iron together, fire would come out.'

(8) *E... ma... ma minak h-ini to-ros, hoto sia.*
   INTERJ bamboo bamboo entire 3INAN-CAUS RECP-rub fire burn
   'Umm.... (if you) rub whole bamboo (pieces) together, fire comes out.'

(9) *Tan inel... inel=na zal, hoto... hoto kala, hoto...*
   because rain rain=FOC carry fire fire lost fire
   hoto zal niq o=si, hoto irak r-ege he,
   fire carry NEG IAM=REAS fire apart REFL-BEN run
   besi tubuk a-ta tama, hol tubuk a-ta tama.
   iron hole 3INAN-GL enter stone hole 3INAN-GL enter
   ma tubuk a-ta tama!
   bamboo hole 3INAN-GL enter
   'Because Rain won the contest and because Fire was defeated, Fire ran off in all directions to save itself, hiding inside iron, hiding inside stone, hiding inside bamboo!'

(10) *Baqa=na ma roq, hoto sia.*
   NPRX.INAN=FOC bamboo rub fire burn
   'That's why (if you) rub bamboo, fire comes out.'

(11) *Besi uen hol uen ta-taqek, hoto sia.*
 iron one stone one RECP-bash fire burn
 '(If you) strike a (piece of) iron and a stone together, fire comes out.'

(12) *Baqa no, ope g-oq – bouq g-oq.*
 NPRX.INAN OBL pumpkin 3AN-fruit gourd 3AN-fruit
 'That's the end.'

References

Abney, Steven. P. 1987. *The English noun phrase in its sentential aspect*. Cambridge, MA: Massachusetts Institute of Technology PhD thesis.
Aijmer, Karin. 2002. *English discourse particles: Evidence from a corpus*. Amsterdam/Philadelphia: John Benjamins.
Aikhenvald, Alexandra. 2006. Serial verbs in typological perspective. In Alexandra Aikhenvald & R. M. W. Dixon (eds.), *Serial verb constructions: A cross-linguistic typology*, 1–60. Oxford: Oxford University Press.
Alderete, John D. & Stefan A. Frisch. 2006. Dissimilation in grammar and the lexicon. In Paul de Lacy (ed.), *The Cambridge Handbook of Phonology*, 379–398. Cambridge: Cambridge University Press.
Ameka, Felix. 1992. Interjections: The universal yet neglected part of speech. *Journal of Pragmatics* 18. 101–118.
Andrews, Avery. 2007. The major functions of the noun phrase. In Timothy Shopen (ed.), *Language Typology and Syntactic Description. Vol. 1: Clause Structure*, 132–223. Cambridge: Cambridge University Press.
Badan Pusat Statistik Kabupaten Belu. 2019. *Belu dalam angka*. [Belu in figures]. Atambua: Badan Pusat Statistik Kabupaten Belu, Pemerintah Daerah Belu.
Badan Pusat Statistik Kabupaten Malaka. 2019. *Malaka dalam angka*. [Malaka in figures]. Atambua: Badan Pusat Statistik Kabupaten Belu, Pemerintah Daerah Malaka.
Baerman, Matthew. 2007. Morphological typology of deponency. *Proceedings of the British Academy* 145. 1–19.
Baker, Mark C. 1989. Object sharing and projection in serial verb constructions. *Linguistic Inquiry* 20(4). 513–553.
Barbiers, Sjef. 2006. The syntax of modal auxiliaries. In Martin Everaert & Henk van Riemsdijk (eds.), *The Blackwell Companion to Syntax Vol. 5*, 1–22. Oxford: Blackwell.
Bele, Anton. 2009. *Kamus bahasa Buna'–Indonesia* [Dictionary Bunaq–Indonesian]. Kupang: Gita Kasih.
Bellwood, Peter. 1998. The archaeology of Papuan and Austronesian prehistory in the Northern Moluccas, Indonesia. In Roger Blench & Matthew Spriggs (eds.), *Archaeology and Language, Volume 2: Correlating Archaeological and Linguistic Hypotheses*, 128–140. London: One World Archaeology Series, Routledge.
Bere Tallo, A. A. 1978. Adat istiadat dan kebiasaan suku bangsa Bunaq di Lamaknen (Timor tengah). Jilid III: "Sapal", Cerita dongeng rakyat [Traditions and customs of the Bunaq tribe in Lamaknen. Volume III: "Sapal", folk stories]. Unpublished manuscript, Kupang.
Berthe, Louis. 1959. Sur quelques distiques bunaq (Timor central). *Bijdragen tot de Taal, Land en Volkenkunde* 115. 336–371.
Berthe, Louis. 1961. Le mariage par achat et la captation des gendres dans une société semi-féodale: les Buna' de Timor central. *L'Homme* 1(3). 5–31.
Berthe, Louis. 1963. Morpho-syntaxe du Bunaq (Timor central). *L'Homme* 3(1). 106–116.
Berthe, Louis. 1972. *Bei Gua, itinéraire des ancêtres, mythes des Bunaq de Timor*. Paris: CNRS.
Berthe, Louis. 2020. Fonds Louis Berthe (1927–1968) (CNRSMH_Berthe). Centre de Recherche en Ethnomusicologie Sound Archive. http://archives.crem-cnrs.fr/fonds/38c
Bisang, Walter. 2009. Serial verb constructions. *Language and Linguistics Compass* 3(3). 792–814.
Blust, Robert. 2001. Thao triplication. *Oceanic Linguistics* 40(2). 324–335.
Bock, J. Kathryn & Richard K. Warren. 1985. Conceptual accessibility and syntactic structure in sentence formulation. *Cognition* 21(1). 47–67.

Bresnan, Joan. 1995. Linear order, syntactic rank and empty categories: On weak crossover. In Mary Dalrymple, Ronald M. Kaplan, John T. Maxwell & Annie Zaenen (eds.), *Formal Issues in Lexical-functional Grammar*, 241–274. Stanford: CSLI Publications.

Burenhult, Niclas. 2008. Spatial coordinate systems in demonstrative meaning. *Linguistic Typology* 12(1). 99–142.

Capell, Arthur. 1943a. Peoples and Languages of Timor. *Oceania* 14(3). 191–219.

Capell, Arthur. 1943b. Peoples and Languages of Timor. *Oceania* 14(4). 311–337.

Capell, Arthur. 1944. Peoples and Languages of Timor. *Oceania* 15(1). 19–48.

Capell, Arthur. 1972. Portuguese Timor: Two more non-Austronesian languages. *Oceania* 15. 95–104.

Capell, Arthur. 1975. The "West Papuan Phylum": General, and Timor and areas further west. In S. A. Wurm (ed.), *New Guinea Area Languages and Language Study*, 667–716. Canberra: Pacific Linguistics.

Capell, Arthur (collector) & Peter Newton (depositor). 1999. Arthur Capell's Pacific field notes. PARADISEC Archive. https://catalog.paradisec.org.au/collections/AC2

Chafe, Wallace L. 1970. *Meaning and the Structure of Language*. Chicago: University of Chicago Press.

Chafe, Wallace. L. 1976. Givenness, contrastiveness, definiteness, subjects, topics, and point of view. In Charles N. Li (ed.), *Subject and Topic*, 25–55. New York: Academic Press.

Chappell, Hillary & William McGregor. 1989. Alienability, inalienability and nominal classification. *Berkeley Linguistics Society* 15. 24–36.

Chappell, Hillary & William McGregor. 1996. Prolegomena to a theory of inalienability. In Hillary Chappell & William McGregor (eds.), *The Grammar of Inalienability*, 3–30. Berlin: Mouton de Gruyter.

Choi, Hye-Won. 1996. *Optimizing structure in context: Scrambling and information structure*. Stanford, CA: Stanford University PhD dissertation.

Clark, Herbert H., Robert Schreuder & Samuel Buttrick. 1983. Common ground and the understanding of demonstrative reference. *Journal of Verbal Learning and Verbal Behavior* 22. 245–258.

Comrie, Bernard. 1978. Ergativity. In W. P. Lehmann (ed.), *Syntactic Typology: Studies in the Phenomenology of Language*, 329–394. Austin: University of Texas Press.

Comrie, Bernard. 1985. *Aspect: An Introduction to Verbal Aspect and Related Problems*. Cambridge: Cambridge University Press.

Corbett, Greville. 2000. *Number*. Cambridge: Cambridge University Press.

Correia, Adérito J. G. 2011. *Describing Makasae: A Trans-New Guinea language of East Timor*. Sydney: University of Western Sydney PhD thesis.

Cottet, Fanny. 2015. *A phonology of Mbahám: Reduction and contrast*. Canberra: Australian National University PhD thesis.

Cowan, H. K. J. 1957/58. A large Papuan language phylum in West New Guinea. *Oceania* 28. 159–166.

Cowan, H. K. J. 1963. Le Buna' de Timor: une langue "ouest-papoue". *Bijdragen tot de Taal, Land en Volkenkunde* 119(4). 387–400.

Cowan, H. K. J. 1965. The Oirata Language. *Lingua* 14. 360–370.

Creissels, Denis & Sylvie Nouguier-Voisin. 2008. Valency-changing operations in Wolof and the notion of "co-participation". In Ekkehard König & Volker Gast. (eds.), *Reciprocals and Reflexives, Theoretical and Typological Explorations*, 289–306. Berlin/New York: Mouton de Gruyter.

Croft, William. 2003. *Typology and Universals*. Cambridge: Cambridge University Press.

Croft, William. 2005. Word classes, parts of speech, and syntactic argumentation. *Linguistic Typology* 9(3). 431–441.

Crowley, Terry. 2002. *Serial Verbs in Oceanic: A Descriptive Typology*. Oxford: Oxford University Press.

Cysouw, Michael. 2003. *The Paradigmatic Structure of Person Marking*. Oxford: Oxford University Press.
Cysouw, Michael. 2005. A typology of honorific uses of clusivity. In Elena Filimonova (ed.), *Clusivity: Typology and Case Studies of Inclusive-Exclusive Distinction*, 213–230. Amsterdam/Philadelphia: John Benjamins.
Declerck, Renaat. 1991. *Tense in English: Its Structure and Use in Discourse*. London: Routledge.
de Vries, Lourens. 2005. Towards a typology of tail–head linkage in Papuan languages. *Studies in Language* 29(2). 363–384.
de Vries, Lourens. 2006. Areal pragmatics of New Guinea: Thematization, distribution and recapitulative linkage in Papuan narratives. *Journal of Pragmatics* 38. 811–828.
Diessel, Holger. 1999. *Demonstratives: Form, Function, and Grammaticalization*. Amsterdam: John Benjamins.
Dik, Simon C. 1989. *The Theory of Functional Grammar. Part 1: The Structure of the Clause*. Dordrecht: Foris.
Dixon, R. M. W. 1982. *Where have All the Adjectives Gone?* Berlin: Mouton de Gruyter.
Dixon, R. M. W. 1994. *Ergativity*. Cambridge: Cambridge University Press.
Donohue, Mark. 2004. Typology and linguistic areas. *Oceanic Linguistics* 43(1). 221–239.
Donohue, Mark & John Charles Smith. 1998. What's happened to us? Developments in the Malay pronouns. *Oceanic Linguistics* 37(1). 65–84.
Dryer, Matthew S. 1986. Primary objects, secondary objects, and antidative. *Language* 62(4). 808–845.
Dryer, Matthew S. 2007. Clause types. In Timothy Shopen (ed.), *Language Typology and Syntactic Description. Vol. 1: Clause Structure*, 224–275. Cambridge: Cambridge University Press.
Durie, Mark. 1988. Verb serialization and "verbal prepositions". *Oceanic Linguistics* 27. 1–23.
Durie, Mark. 1997. Grammatical structures in verb serialization. In Alex Alsina, Joan Bresnan & Peter Sells (eds.), *Complex Predicates*, 289–354. Stanford: CSLI Publications.
Edwards, Owen. 2021. *Rote-Meto Comparative Dictionary*. Canberra: Asia-Pacific Linguistics.
Edwards, Owen. 2020. *Metathesis and Unmetathesis in Amarasi*. Berlin: Language Science Press.
Enfield, N. J. 2006. Heterosemy and the grammar-lexicon trade-off. In Felix Ameka, Alan Dench & Nicholas Evans (eds.), *Catching Language*, 297–320. Berlin: Mouton de Gruyter.
Ewing, Michael C. 2005. *Grammar and inference in conversation: Identifying clause structure in spoken Javanese*. Amsterdam/Philadelphia: John Benjamins.
Fillmore, Charles J. 1971. *Lectures on Deixis*. Stanford: CSLI Publications.
Foley, W. A. 1986. *The Papuan Languages of New Guinea*. Cambridge: Cambridge University Press.
Foley, W. A. 1998. Toward understanding Papuan languages. In Jelle Miedema, Cecilia Odé & R. A. C. Dam (eds.), *Perspectives on the Bird's Head of Irian Jaya, Indonesia*, 503–518. Amsterdam: Rodopi.
Foley, W. A. 2000. The languages of New Guinea. *Annual Review of Anthropology* 29. 357–404.
Foley, W. A. 2007. A typology of information packaging in the clause. In Timothy Shopen (ed.), *Language Typology and Syntactic Description: Clause Structure. Volume 1*, 362–446. Cambridge: Cambridge University Press.
Foley, W. A. & Mike Olson 1985. Clausehood and verb serialization. In Johanna Nichols & Anthony C. Woodbury (eds.), *Grammar Inside and Outside the Clause: Some Approaches to Theory from the Field*, 17–60. Cambridge: Cambridge University Press.
Foley, W. A. & Robert D. Van Valin 1984. *Functional Syntax and Universal Grammar*. Cambridge: Cambridge University Press.
Fox, James. J. 1988. *To Speak in Pairs: Essays on the Ritual Languages of Eastern Indonesia*. Cambridge: Cambridge University Press.
Fox, James J. 1989. To the aroma of the name: The celebration of a Rotinese ritual of rock and tree. *Bijdragen tot de Taal-, Land- en Volkenkunde* 145. 520–538.

Fox, James J. 1991. The heritage of traditional agriculture in eastern Indonesian: Lexical evidence and the indications of rituals from the outer arc of the Lesser Sundas. *Bulletin of the Indo-Pacific Prehistory Association* 10. 248–262.

Fox, James J. 2003. Tracing the path, recounting the past: Historical perspectives on Timor. In James J. Fox & Dionisio Babo Soares (eds.), *Out of the Ashes*, 1–27. Canberra: ANU E-Press.

Fox, James J. 2006. Genealogy and topogeny. In James J. Fox (ed.), *The Poetic Power of Place: Comparative Perspectives on Austronesian Ideas of Locality*, 91–102. Canberra: ANU-Press.

Francillon, Gerard. 1967. *Some matriarchic aspects of the social structure of the southern Tetun of middle Timor*. Canberra: Australian National University PhD thesis.

Fraurud, Kari. 1990. Definiteness and the processing of noun phrases in natural discourse. *Journal of Semantics* 7(4). 395–433.

Friedberg, Claudine. 1970. Analyse de quelques groupements de végétaux comme introduction à l'étude de la classification botanique bunaq. In Jean Pouillon & Pierre Maranda (eds.), *Échange et Communications, Mélanges offerts à Claude Lévi-Strauss*, 1092–1131. Paris: Mouton.

Friedberg, Claudine. 1971a. L'agriculture des Bunaq de Timor et les conditions d'un équilibre avec le milieu. *Journal d'agriculture tropicale et de botanique appliquée* 18(12). 481–532.

Friedberg, Claudine. 1971b. Aperçu sur la classification botanique bunaq (Timor central). *Bulletin de la Société botanique de France* 118(3–4). 255–262.

Friedberg, Claudine. 1972. Eléments de botanique bunaq. In J. M. C. Thomas & L. Bernot (eds.), *Langues et techniques, nature et société*, 375–393. Paris: Klincksieck.

Friedberg, Claudine. 1973a. Repérage et découpage du temps chez les Bunaq du centre de Timor. *Archipel* 6. 119–144.

Friedberg, Claudine. 1973b. Espace bunaq, pour une exploration naturaliste d'un paysage culturel. In Marc R Sauter (ed.), *L'Homme, hier et aujourd'hui, recueil d'études en hommage à A. Leroi-Gourhan*, 391–419. Paris: Cujas.

Friedberg, Claudine. 1978a. *Comment fut tranchée la liane céleste : et autres textes de littérature orale bunaq (Timor, Indonésie) recueillis et traduits par Louis Berthe*. Paris: Société d'Études Linguistiques et Anthropologiques de France.

Friedberg, Claudine. 1978b. The development of traditional agricultural practices in Western Timor. In J. Friedman & M. J. Rowlands (eds.), *The evolution of social systems*, 137–172. London: Duckworth and Co.

Friedberg, Claudine. 1978c. La cuisine bunaq. *Asie Sud – Est Monde insulind* 9(3–4). 215–227.

Friedberg Claudine. 1979. Socially significant plant species and their taxonomic position among the Bunaq of Central Timor. In R. F. Ellen & D. Reason (eds.), *Classifications in Their Social Context*, 81–101. London: Academic Press.

Friedberg, Claudine. 1980. Boiled woman and broiled man: Myths and agricultural rituals of the Bunaq of Central Timor. In James J. Fox (ed.), *The Flow of Life: Essays on Eastern Indonesia*, 266–289. Cambridge, MA/London: Harvard University Press.

Friedberg, Claudine. 1982. *Muk Gubul Nor: « la chevelure de la terre » : les Bunaq de Timor et les plantes*. 5 volumes. Paris: Université Paris V-René Descartes PhD thesis.

Friedberg, Claudine. 1986. Classifications populaires des plantes et modes de connaissance. In P. Tassy (ed.), *L'ordre et la diversité du vivant*, 22–49. Paris: Fayard.

Friedberg, Claudine. 1989. Social relations of territorial management in light of Bunaq farming rituals. *Bijdragen tot de Taal-, Land- en Volkenkunde* 145(4). 548–563.

Friedberg, Claudine. 1990. *Le savoir botanique des Bunaq, percevoir et classer dans le Haut Lamaknen (Timor, Indonésie)*. Paris: Muséum National d'Histoire Naturelle.

Friedberg, Claudine. 1991. Operative aspects of folk classification. In Andrew K. Pawley (ed.), *Man and a Half: Essays in Pacific Anthropology and Ethnobiology in Honour of Ralph Bulmer*, 102–109. Auckland: The Polynesian Society.

Friedberg, Claudine. 1999. Diversity, order, unity: Different levels in folk knowledge about the living. *Social Anthropology* 7(1). 1–16.
Friedberg, Claudine. 2014. Protéger les humains et les non-humains. L'exemple des Bunaq de Lamaknen. *Revue d'ethnoécologie* 6. 1–17.
Gawron, Jean Mark. 1986. Situations and prepositions. *Linguistics and Philosophy* 9. 327–382.
General Directorate of Statistics. 2020. *Timor-Leste Census 2020*. Dili: Statistics Timor-Leste.
Gil, David. 2001. Quantifiers. In Martin Haspelmath, Ekkehard König, Wulf Oesterreicher & Wolfgang Raible (eds.), *Language Typology and Language Universals I, II*, 1275–1294. Berlin: Mouton de Gruyter.
Gil, David. 2005. From repetition to reduplication in Riau Indonesian. In Bernhard. Hurch (ed.), *Studies on Reduplication*, 31–64. Berlin: Mouton de Gruyter.
Gil, David. 2008. Distributive numerals. In Martin Haspelmath, Matthew S. Dryer, David Gil & Bernard Comrie (eds.), *The World Atlas of Language Structures Online*. Munich: Max Planck Digital Library, chapter 54. URL: http://wals.info/feature/54
Givón, Talmy. 1976. Topic, pronoun and grammatical agreement. In Charles N. Li (ed.), *Subject and Topic*, 149–188. New York: Academic Press.
Givón, Talmy. 1983. *Topic Continuity in Discourse: A Quantitative Cross-language Study*. Amsterdam/ Philadelphia: John Benjamins.
Givón, Talmy. 1984. *Syntax: A Functional-typological Introduction*. Vol.1. Amsterdam/Philadelphia: John Benjamins.
Greenberg, Joseph H. 1971. The Indo-Pacific hypothesis. In Thomas A. Sebeok (ed.), *Current Trends in Linguistics, Vol. 8: Linguistics in Oceania*, 807–871. Berlin: Walter de Gruyter.
Greenberg, Joseph H. 1978. How does a language acquire gender markers? In Joseph Greenberg, Charles A. Ferguson & Edith A. Moravcik (eds.), *Universals of Human Languages, Vol. III*, 47–82. Stanford: Stanford University Press.
Haiman, John. 1978. Conditionals are topics. *Language* 54(3). 564–589.
Haiman, John. 1983. Iconic and economic motivation. *Language* 59(4). 781–819.
Haspelmath, Martin. 1987. *Transitivity alternations of the anticausative type*. (Arbeitspapiere, No. 5). Cologne: Institut für Sprachwissenschaft der Universität zu Köln.
Haspelmath, Martin. 1995. Diachronic sources of 'all' and 'every'. In Emmon Bach, Eloise Jelinek, Angelika Kratzer & Barbara H. Partee (eds.), *Quantification in Natural Languages*, 363–382. Dordrecht: Kluwer.
Haugen, Einar. 1957. The semantics of Icelandic orientation. *Word* 13. 447–460.
Hawkins, John A. 1978. *Definiteness and Indefiniteness*. London: Croom Helm.
Hawkins, Roger. 1981. Towards an account of the possessive constructions: NPs and the N of NP. *Journal of Linguistics* 17(2). 247–269.
Head, Brian F. 1978. Respect degrees in pronominal reference. In Joseph Greenberg (ed.), *Universals of Human Language. Vol. 3: Word Structure*, 151–211. Stanford: Stanford University Press.
Heine, Bernd & Tania Kuteva. 2002. *World Lexicon of Grammaticalization*. Cambridge: Cambridge University Press.
Hicks, David. 1983. A transitional relationship terminology of asymmetric prescriptive alliance among the Makassai of Eastern Indonesia. *Sociologus* 33(1). 73–85.
Himmelmann, Nikolaus P. 1996. Demonstratives in narrative discourse: A taxonomy of universal uses. In Barbara Fox (ed.), *Studies in Anaphora*, 203–252. Amsterdam: John Benjamins.
Himmelmann, Nikolaus P. 1997. *Deiktikon, Artikel, Nominalphrase: zur Emergenz syntaktischer Struktur*. Tübingen: Niemeyer.
Holton, Gary, Marian Klamer, František Kratochvíl, Laura Robinson & Antoinette Schapper. 2012. The historical relation of the Papuan languages of Alor and Pantar. *Oceanic Linguistics* 51(1). 86–122.

Holton, Gary & Laura C. Robinson. 2014. The linguistic position of the Timor-Alor-Pantar languages. In Marian Klamer (ed.), *The Alor-Pantar languages: History and Typology*, 155–198. Berlin: Language Sciences Press.

Hopper, Paul J., & Sandra A. Thompson. 1980. Transitivity in grammar and discourse. *Language* 56(2). 251–299.

Huber, Juliette & Antoinette Schapper. 2014. The relationship between aspect and universal quantification. Evidence from three Papuan languages from Timor and Alor. In Marian Klamer & František Kratochvíl (eds.), *Number and Quantity in East Nusantara*, 152–169. Canberra: Asia-Pacific Linguistics.

Hull, Geoffrey. 2004. The Papuan Languages of Timor. *Estudos de Línguas e Culturas de Timor Leste / Studies in Languages and Cultures of East Timor* 6. 23–99.

Jackendoff, Ray. 1990. *Semantic Structures*. Cambridge, MA: MIT Press.

Keenan, Edward L. & Bernard Comrie 1977. Noun phrase accessibility and universal grammar. *Linguistic Inquiry* 8. 63–99.

Kemmer, Suzanne. 1993. *The Middle Voice*. Amsterdam/Philadelphia: John Benjamins.

Kim, Alan Hyun-Oak. 1988. Preverbal focus position in type XIII languages. In Michael Hammond, Edith A. Moravcsik & Jessica Wirth (eds.), *Studies in Syntactic Typology*, 148–171. Amsterdam/Philadelphia: John Benjamins.

Kittilä, Seppo. 2005. Recipient-prominence vs. beneficiary-prominence. *Linguistic Typology* 9(2). 269–297.

Klamer, Marian. 2002. Typical features of Austronesian languages in Central/Eastern Indonesia. *Oceanic Linguistics* 41(2). 363–383.

Klamer, Marian. 2008. The semantics of semantic alignment in Eastern Indonesia. In Mark Donohue & Søren Wichmann (eds.), *The Typology of Semantic Alignment*, 221–251. Oxford: Oxford University Press.

Klamer, Marian & Antoinette Schapper. 2012. The history of 'give' constructions in the Papuan languages of Timor-Alor-Pantar. *Linguistic Discovery* 10(3). 174–207.

König, Ekkehard & Shigehiro Kokutani. 2006. Towards a typology of reciprocal constructions: Focus on German and Japanese. *Linguistics* 44(2). 271–302.

Koptjevskaja-Tamm, Maria. 2001. "A piece of the cake" and "a cup of tea": Partitive and pseudo-partitive nominal constructions in the Circum-Baltic Languages. In Östen Dahl & Maria Koptjevskaja-Tamm (eds.), *Circum-Baltic Languages: Their Typology and Contacts. Vol. 2.*, 523–568. Amsterdam/Philadelphia: John Benjamins.

Kulikov, Leonid. 2003. The labile syntactic type in a diachronic perspective: The case of Vedic. *SKY Journal of Linguistics* 16. 93–112.

Lakoff, George. 1987. *Women, Fire and Dangerous Things*. Chicago: Chicago University Press.

Lakoff, George & Mark Johnson. 1980. *Metaphors We Live by*. Chicago: Chicago University Press.

Lambrecht, Knud. 1994. *Information Structure and Sentence Form: Topic, Focus and the Mental Representations of Discourse Referents*. Cambridge: Cambridge University Press.

Langacker, Ronald W. 1993. Reference-point constructions. *Cognitive Linguistics* 4(1). 1–38.

Levin, Beth & Malka Rappaport Hovav. 2001. Morphology and lexical semantics. In Andrew Spencer & Arnold M. Zwicky (eds.), *The Handbook of Morphology*, 248–271. Oxford: Blackwell.

Levinson, Stephen C. 1983. *Pragmatics*. Cambridge: Cambridge University.

Levinson, Stephen C. 2003. *Space in Language and Cognition: Explorations in Cognitive Diversity*. Cambridge: Cambridge University Press.

Levinson, Stephen C. 2004. Deixis and pragmatics. In Laurence R. Horn & Gregory Ward (eds.), *The Handbook of Pragmatics*, 97–121. Oxford: Blackwell.

Levinson, Stephen C. & Niclas Burenhult. 2009. Semplates: A new concept in lexical semantics? *Language* 85(1). 153–174.

Libur por toma tip gie [New Testament of the Bible]. 1988. Atambua: Pusat Pastoral Keuskupan Atambua.
Lichtenberk, Frantisek. 1991. Semantic change and heterosemy in grammaticalisation. *Language* 67(3). 474–509.
Lichtenberk, Frantisek. 2000. Reciprocals without reflexives. In Zygmunt Frajzyngier & Traci Curl (eds.), *Reflexives: Forms and Functions*, 31–62. Amsterdam: John Benjamins.
Lyons, Joseph. 1977. *Semantics*. Cambridge: Cambridge University Press.
Lyons, Christopher. 1999. *Definiteness*. Cambridge: Cambridge University Press.
Malchukov, Andrej, Martin Haspelmath & Bernard Comrie. 2010. Ditransitive constructions: A typological overview. In Andrej Malchukov, Martin Haspelmath & Bernard Comrie (eds.), *Studies in Ditransitive Constructions: A Comparative Handbook*, 1–64. Berlin: Mouton De Gruyter.
Matthews, P. H. 2005. *Oxford Concise Dictionary of Linguistics*. Oxford: Oxford University Press.
Matthews, P. H. 2007. *Syntactic Relations: A Critical Survey*. Cambridge: Cambridge University Press.
McMillion, Alan. 2006. *Labile verbs in English: Their meaning, behavior and structure*. Stockholm: Stockholm University PhD thesis.
McWilliam, Andrew. 2006. Mapping with metaphor: Cultural topographies in West Timor. In James J. Fox (ed.), *The Poetic Power of Place: Comparative Perspectives on Austronesian Ideas of Locality*, 101–114. Canberra: ANU Press.
McWilliam, Andrew. 2007. Austronesians in linguistic disguise: Fataluku cultural fusion in East Timor. *Journal of Southeast Asian Studies* 38(2). 355–375.
Miller, D. Gary. 1993. *Complex Verb Formation*. Amsterdam: Benjamins.
Mushin, Ilana. 1995. Epistememes in Australian languages. *Australian Journal of Linguistics* 15(1). 1–32.
Muysken, Pieter. 2000. *Bilingual Speech: A Typology of Code-mixing*. Cambridge: Cambridge University Press.
Nedjalkov, Vladimir P. 2007. Polysemy of reciprocal markers. In Vladimir P. Nedjalkov (ed.), *Reciprocal Constructions*, 231–334. Amsterdam/Philadelphia: John Benjamins.
Oliveira, Nuno. V. 2008. *Subsistence archaeobotany: Food production and the agricultural transition in East Timor*. Canberra: Australian National University PhD thesis.
Pawley, Andrew K. 1973. Some problems in Proto-Oceanic grammar. *Oceanic Linguistics* 7. 103–188.
Pawley, Andrew K. 2000. Hunger acts of me: The grammar and semantics of bodily and mental process expressions in Kalam. In Videa P. De Guzman & Byron W. Bender (eds.), *Grammatical Analysis: Morphology, Syntax and Semantics. Studies in Honor of Stanley Starosta*, 153–185. Honolulu: University of Hawai'i Press.
Payne, Thomas. 1997. *Describing Morpho-syntax: A Guide for Field Linguists*. Cambridge: Cambridge University Press.
Quirk, Randolph, Sidney Greenbaum, Geoffrey Leech & Jan Svartvik. 1985. *A Comprehensive Grammar of the English Language*. London: Longman.
Radden, Günter & René Dirven. 2007. *Cognitive English Grammar*. Amsterdam/Philadelphia: John Benjamins.
Ramat, Paolo & Davide Ricca. 1994. Prototypical adverbs: On the scalarity/radiality of the notion of adverb. *Rivista di Linguistica* 6(2). 289–326.
Reesink, Ger P. 1994. Domain-creating constructions in Papuan languages. *Semaian* 10. 98–121.
Reesink, Ger P. 2002. The eastern Bird's Head languages compared. In Ger P. Reesink (ed.), *Languages of the Eastern Bird's Head*, 1–44. Canberra: Pacific Linguistics.
Renard-Clamagirand, Brigitte. 1982. *Marobo: une société ema de Timor*. Paris: SELAF.
Ross, Malcolm. 2005. Pronouns as a preliminary diagnostic for grouping Papuan languages. In Andrew Pawley, Robert Attenborough, Robin Hide & Jack Golson (eds.), *Papuan Pasts: Cultural, Linguistic and Biological Histories of Papuan-speaking Peoples*, 15–66. Canberra: Pacific Linguistics.

Ross, Malcolm. 2017. Languages of the New Guinea region. In Raymond Hickey (ed.), *The Cambridge Handbook of Areal Linguistics*, 758–820. Cambridge: Cambridge University Press.

Sacks, Harvey & Emanuel A. Schegloff. 1979. Two preferences in the organization of reference to persons in conversation and their interaction. In George Psathas (ed.), *Everyday Language: Studies in Ethnomethodology*, 15–21. New York: Irvington.

Sadock, Jerrold M. & Arnold M. Zwicky. 1985. Speech act distinctions in syntax. In Timothy Shopen (ed.), *Language Typology and Syntactic Description: Clause Structure, Volume 1*, 155–196. Cambridge: Cambridge University Press.

Sawardo, P., F. Sanda, H. Jehane, S. H. Nitbani & S. Kusharyanto 1996. *Fonologi, morfologi, dan sintaksis Bahasa Buna* [Phonology, morphology and syntax of the Buna language]. Jakarta: Departemen Pendidikan dan Kebudayaan.

Schachter, Paul. 1985. Parts-of-speech systems. In Timothy Shopen (ed.), *Language Typology and Syntactic Description: Clause Structure. Volume 1*, 3–61. Cambridge: Cambridge University Press.

Schachter, Paul & Timothy Shopen. 2007. Parts-of-speech systems. In Timothy Shopen (ed.), *Language Typology and Syntactic Description: Clause Structure. Volume 1*, 1–60. Cambridge: Cambridge University Press.

Schapper, Antoinette. 2007. Grammaticalization of demonstratives in the languages of Timor, Alor and Pantar. Handout from the fifth International East Nusa Tenggara Conference, Kupang, 1–3 August.

Schapper, Antoinette. 2008. From possessive to future. Conference talk given at the ANU Graduate Language and Linguistics conference, Canberra, 12 November.

Schapper, Antoinette. 2009. Possession in Kemak. Handout from the 9th International Conference of Austronesian Linguistics, Aussois, 22–26 June.

Schapper, Antoinette. 2010a. Neuter gender in eastern Indonesia. *Oceanic Linguistics* 49(2). 407–435.

Schapper, Antoinette. 2010b. *Bunaq, a Papuan language of central Timor*. Canberra: Australian National University PhD thesis.

Schapper, Antoinette. 2011a. Crossing the border. Historical and linguistic divides among the Bunaq in central Timor. *Wacana, Journal of the Humanities of Indonesia* 13. 29–49.

Schapper, Antoinette. 2011b. Finding Bunaq. The homeland and expansion of the Bunaq in central Timor. In Andrew McWilliam & Elizabeth G. Traube (eds), *Life and Land in Timor; Ethnographic Papers*, 163–186. Canberra: Australian National University Press.

Schapper, Antoinette. 2011c. Iconicity of sequence in the coding of source and goal in two Papuan languages. *Linguistics in the Netherlands* 2011. 101–113.

Schapper, Antoinette. 2014. Elevation in the spatial deictic systems of Alor-Pantar languages. In Marian Klamer (ed.), *The Alor-Pantar Languages: History and Typology*, 247–285. Berlin: Language Science Press.

Schapper, Antoinette. 2015a. Wallacea, a linguistic area. *Archipel* 90. 99–151.

Schapper, Antoinette. 2015b. *Cerita dongeng dari Bunaq Lamaknen* [Folktales from the Bunaq of Lamaknen]. Volume 1. Jakarta: Yayasan Pustaka Obor.

Schapper, Antoinette. 2016. *Cerita dongeng dari Bunaq Lamaknen* [Folktales from the Bunaq of Lamaknen]. Volume 2. Jakarta: Yayasan Pustaka Obor.

Schapper, Antoinette. 2017. Introduction to the Papuan languages of Timor, Alor and Pantar. Volume II. In Antoinette Schapper (ed.), *Papuan Languages of Timor, Alor and Pantar. Sketch Grammars: Volume 2*, 1–54. Berlin: de Gruyter Mouton.

Schapper, Antoinette. 2019. Zapal, an oral literature genre of the Bunaq Lamaknen. London: SOAS, Endangered Languages Archive. https://elar.soas.ac.uk/Collection/MPI1029743

Schapper, Antoinette. 2020a. Introduction to the Papuan languages of Timor, Alor and Pantar. Volume III. In Antoinette Schapper (ed.), *Papuan Languages of Timor, Alor and Pantar. Sketch Grammars: Volume 3*, 1–52. Berlin: de Gruyter Mouton.

Schapper, Antoinette. 2020b. Linguistic Melanesia. In Yaron Matras & Evangelia Adamou (eds.), *Routledge Handbook of Language Contact*, 480–502. London: Routledge.
Schapper, Antoinette. 2020c. The origins of isolating word structure in eastern Timor. In David Gil & Antoinette Schapper (eds.), *Austronesian Undressed: How and Why Languages Become Isolating*, 391–446. Amsterdam: John Benjamins.
Schapper, Antoinette. 2020d. Wersing dictionary. *Dictionaria* 11. 1–1430. https://dictionaria.clld.org/contributions/wersing
Schapper, Antoinette. forthcoming. Papuan influence on the Malayo-Polynesian languages of Southeast Asia. In Sander Adelaar & Antoinette Schapper (eds.), *Oxford Guide to the Malayo-Polynesian Languages of Southeast Asia*. Oxford: Oxford University Press.
Schapper, Antoinette, Juliette Huber & Aone van Engelenhoven. 2012. The historical relations of the Papuan languages of Timor and Kisar. *Language and Linguistics in Melanesia: Special Issue on the History, Contact & Classification of Papuan Languages*, 194–242. Port Moresby: Linguistic Society of Papua New Guinea.
Schapper, Antoinette, Juliette Huber & Aone van Engelenhoven. 2014. The relatedness of Timor-Kisar and Alor-Pantar languages: A preliminary demonstration. In Marian Klamer (ed.), *The Alor-Pantar Languages: History and Typology*, 99–154. Berlin: Language Science Press.
Schapper, Antoinette & Lila San Roque. 2011. Demonstratives and non-embedded nominalisations in three Papuan languages of the Timor-Alor-Pantar family. *Studies in Language* 35(2). 378–406.
Seiler, Hansjakob. 1983. *Possession as an Operational Dimension of Language*. Tübingen: Narr.
Senft, Gunter. 2008. *Serial Verb Constructions in Austronesian and Papuan Languages*. Canberra: Pacific Linguistics.
Silverstein, Michael. 1976. Hierarchy of features and ergativity. In R. M. W. Dixon (ed.), *Grammatical Categories in Australian Languages*, 112–171. New Jersey: Humanities Press.
Sneddon, James N. 1996. *Indonesian: A Comprehensive Grammar*. London: Routledge.
Sowash, W. B. 1948. Colonial rivalries in Timor. *Far Eastern Quarterly* 7(3). 227–235.
Steinbach, Markus. 2002. *Middle Voice: A Comparative Study in the Syntax-semantics Interface of German*. Amsterdam/Philadelphia: John Benjamins.
Stokhof, W. A. L. 1975. *Preliminary Notes on the Alor and Pantar Languages (East Indonesia)*. Canberra: Pacific Linguistics.
Stokhof, W. A. L. (ed.). 1983. Marae. In W. A. L. Stokhof (ed.), *Holle Lists: Vocabularies in Languages of Indonesia Volume 6: The Lesser Sunda Islands (Nusa Tenggara)*, 101–113. Canberra: Pacific Linguistics.
Stolz, Thomas. 2001. To be with X is to have X: Comitatives, instrumentals, locative, and predicative possession. *Linguistics* 39. 321–350.
Stolz, Thomas. 2008. *Split Possession: An Areal-linguistic Study of the Alienability Correlation and the Related Phenomena in the Languages of Europe*. Amsterdam/Philadelphia: John Benjamins.
Taylor, John R. 2000. *Possessives in English: An Exploration in Cognitive Grammar*. Oxford: Oxford University Press.
Tea Buna [Bunaq prayers]. 1961. Atambua: Heinr. Jassen Vicarius Delegatus Atambua.
Therik, Tom. 2004. *Wehali. The Female Land*. Canberra: Pandanus.
Tomlin, Russell S. 1986. *Basic Word Order: Functional Principles*. London: Croom Helm.
Trask, R. L. 1993. *A Dictionary of Grammatical Terms in Linguistics*. New York: Routledge.
Trubetzkoy, N. S. 1936. Die phonologischen Grenzsignale. In Daniel Jones & D. B. Fry (eds.), *Proceedings of the 2nd International Congress of the Phonetic Sciences*, 45–49. Cambridge: Cambridge University Press.
Unterladstetter, Volker. 2020. *Multi-verb Constructions in Eastern Indonesia*. Berlin: Language Science Press.

Usher, Timothy & Antoinette Schapper. 2018. The lexicons of the Papuan languages of Onin and their influences. *NUSA: Linguistic studies of languages in and around Indonesia* 64. 39–63.
Usher, Timothy & Antoinette Schapper. forthcoming. The Greater West Bomberai Family. *Oceanic Linguistics* 61(1).
van der Auwera, Johan, Nina Dobrushina & Valentin Goussev. 2013. Imperative-hortative systems. In Matthew S. Dryer & Martin Haspelmath (eds.), *The World Atlas of Language Structures Online*. Leipzig: Max Planck Institute for Evolutionary Anthropology.
van Klinken, Catharina. 1999. *A Grammar of the Fehan Dialect of Tetun*. Canberra: Pacific Linguistics.
van Nice, Kathy Y. & Rainer Dietrich 2003. Task sensitivity of animacy effects: Evidence from German picture descriptions. *Linguistics* 41(5). 825–849.
van Staden, Miriam & Ger P. Reesink 2008. Serial verb constructions in a linguistic area. In Gunter Senft (ed.), *Serial Verb Constructions in Austronesian and Papuan Languages*, 17–54. Canberra: Pacific Linguistics.
Vonen, Arnfinn Muruvik. 2001. Polynesian multifunctionality and the ambitions of linguistic description. In Petra M. Vogel & Bernard Comrie (eds.), *Approaches to the Typology of Word Classes*, 479–488. Berlin: Mouton de Gruyter.
Voorhoeve, C. L. 1975. West Papuan Phylum languages on the mainland of New Guinea: Bird's Head (Vogelkop) Peninsula. In S. A. Wurm (ed.), *New Guinea Area Languages and Language Study*, 717–728. Canberra: Pacific Linguistics.
Wälchli, Bernhard. 2005. *Co-compounds and Natural Coordination*. Oxford: Oxford University Press.
Wechsler, Stephen. 1995. *The Semantic Basis of Argument Structure*. Stanford: CSLI Publications.
Wilkins, David P. & Deborah Hill. 1995. When GO means COME: Questioning the basicness of basic motion verbs. *Cognitive Linguistics* 6(2/3). 209–259.
Williams-van Klinken, Catharina, John Hajek & Rachel Nordlinger. 2002. *Tetun Dili: A Grammar of an East Timorese Language*. Canberra: Pacific Linguistics.
Williams-van Klinken, Catharina & John Hajek. 2006. Patterns of address in Dili Tetum, East Timor. *Australian Review of Applied Linguistics* 29(2). 21.1–21.18.
Woertelboer, W. 1955. Zur Sprache und Kultur der Belu (Timor). *Anthropos* 50(1). 155–200.
Yeager, Ruth M. & Mark I. Jacobson 2002. *Textiles of Western Timor. Regional Variations in Historical Perspective*. Bangkok: White Lotus.

Index

Abbreviations and glosses XXI–XXIII
Accessibility Hierarchy (relativisation of NP roles) 206–208
Accidental events, marking of 417
Activation of referents 288, 308, 317, 319, 327
Adclausal determiners 256
Addition, adverbs of 496
Additive focus enclitic 180, 226
– scalar 181
Address
– honorific 241
– non-pronominal 245–250
– polite 243, 245, 559
– pronoun politeness hierarchy 244
– respectful 243, 249
Addressee locational 321–323
– combinations 325–327, 327
Addressee, verbs of questioning 445
Addressee, verbs of speaking 448
Adjectives, lack of an adjective class 91–94
Adverbial clause conjoiners 119, 539
Adverbial modifiers 493–497
Adverbs 117
– addition and comparison 496
– aspectual adverbs 495
– manner adverbs 489
– modal adverbs 482–489
– temporal adverbs 490, 495
Affrication 50
Agentivity
– agentive clauses 381, 414, 415, 501
– co-agentivity 411
– highlighting of 501
– non-agentive clauses 168, 419, 463
– non-agentive verbs 91, 94
– semantic transitivity 171
– spontaneous events 396
Agreement
– animacy (noun classes) 186–188, 188–195, 341–343, 347–350
– bivalent verb agreement 171–174
– N_{MOD} agreeing in animacy 202
Ainaro dialect of Bunaq 14
Alienably possessed nouns
– possessors of 331, 332, 335, 336, 354
– reciprocal marking 404

– use of "alienable" and "inalienable" labels 329
Alienation, degree of (possessor relationship) 341–343, 346, 354, 355
Alignment 131, 372
'All' (*hotu~hotu*) 221
Allomorphy 73
Allophony 46–51, 55, 82
Ambient serialisation 455, 461, 462–464, 464–472, 522
Ambitransitive verbs. *see* Labile verbs
Anaphora
– article (determiner) 297
– demonstratives 257, 259, 269, 277, 286, 545
– elision 154
Animacy 186
– agreement 186–188, 188–195
– animate group plural 218
– determiners 255
– effects on word order 168–170
– groups of animates 196
– inalienably possessed nouns 341–343, 347
– INANIMATE nouns reassigned to ANIMATE 195–199
– inanimates assigned to ANIMATE 189
– notation XXIII, 186
– noun class distinction 185, 188, 347–350
Animal and plant possessors 352
Animals
– group plural 219
– practices with ANIMATE Ps 360
– verbs of keeping domestic animals 370
Answers to polar questions 151
Anticausative *-wen* suffix 73, 388
– anticausative use 415–419
– moderative use 419
– similative use 420
Apprehensive modal adverb 486
Areal patterns 35, 363, 366, 507, 542
Argument sharing 115, 455, 468, 478, *see also* Serial verb constructions (SVCs)
Arguments
– alignment 131, 372
– argument types 122, 130–131
– differential P-marking 359, 361
– elision 154–157, 160, 437
– P complement clauses 519–521

- S complement clauses 521–523
- unmarked obliques (OBL) 122, 128–130, 383–387

Article (determiner) 104, 255, 297–301
- anaphoric use 298
- contrasted with non-proximal demonstrative 297, 298
- non-anaphoric use 299
- thematic use 300

"Ascriptive" clauses 131

Aspect
- aspect markers 94
- aspectual adverbs 495
- aspectual serialisation 464–472
- complete state 466
- completed action 465
- continuous action 469
- frequent action 470–472
- immediate action 470
- persistent action 472
- prospective 502–505
- serial verb constructions (SVCs) 454

Aspiration 45
Assertive discourse marker 326
Associative meaning, encoding of 332
Attributive verbs 203
Austronesian languages 2
- borrowing from 21–24, 29, 106, 364, 538
- compared to Papuan languages 33–35
- place names 6, 9, 12
- typology 32–36

Austronesian people 6, 10
Auxiliary, performative 363, 498–502

Backgrounded information 297
'BECAUSE' (*gie*) 430
Belu regency 5–8, 13, 312
Benefactive
- self-benefactive 380, 397–399
- serial verb constructions 394

Beneficiary 447
Bere Tallo, A. A. 37
Berthe, Louis 36, 38–39
Bible, Bunaq (*Libur por toma tip gie* 1988) 3, 39, 241
Bivalent verbal clauses 124–126
- pragmatic variation 171–174

Bivalent verbs 124, 357
- anticausative marked 415

- Class I: no prefixes 357
- Class II: differential P-marking 358
- Class III: ANIMATE P arguments 359–361
- Class IV: five conjugation classes 361–368
- prefixal deponency 389, 403, 405, 409
- serialisation 456, 458, 461
- spontaneous events 395
- with distinct agreement patterns 368–371

Bleaching, semantic 345, 447
Body action events 400
Body part terms, possession of 339

Borrowing
- Austronesian languages 21–24, 29, 106, 364, 537
- clause-initial conjunctions 537, 538
- consonant clusters 61
- Indonesian 54–56, 82, 193, 482, 537
- orthography 82
- phoneme adaptation 54–57
- Portuguese 3, 61, 538
- Tetun 24–28, 78, 82, 364, 496, 537

"Bridging" antecedent 299, 319
Bunak, spelling 3

Bunaq
- as a Papuan language 32–36, 77, 492
- dialects 14–17, 189, 363, 389
- language names 3
- language vitality 13
- proto-Bunaq 15, 23
- TAP language typology 310, 344, 375
- typology 31, 113, 378, 452, 455, 537

Bunaq Bible (*Libur por toma tip gie* 1988) 3, 39, 241
Bunaq culture 2, 30, 191, 193, 195, 251–253
Bunaq mythology 191, 195, 282
Bunaq personal names 251–253
Bunaq speakers 13
- dispersal of 4–12

Calling, verb of (*h-ini* '3INAN-call/cause') 126, 375–378, 525, 563
Cataphoric demonstratives 257, 263, 283, 428, 547

Causation
- causative labile verbs 381
- causative serialisation 456–458
- causative verb (*h-ini* '3INAN-call/cause') 377, 382, 391, 563
- NP encoding of cause 435

Index — 585

- performative auxiliary 501
Causative prefix, Austronesian 364
Causative serialisation 456–458
Causative verb (*h-ini* '3INAN-call/cause') 377, 382, 391, 563
Christian names 251
Classifier, free possessive 330, 334, 350, 392, see also Indirect possession
Classifiers, numeral 212
Clausal negation 139–141, 509, 511
Clause boundaries, notation of 518
Clause complementation 518–526
- Non-NP replacing complements 523–526
- NP-replacing complements 519–523
Clause conjoining 526, 528
- clause-final conjunctions 529
- "doubling" (clauses bracketed by initial and final conjunctions) 538
- juxtaposition 520, 526–528
- order of events 466, 516, 531, 536, 541
Clause conjunctions 118–120
- adverbial clause conjoiners 539
- borrowed clause-initial conjunctions 537, 538
- focus enclitics 535
- postpositions 540
- reason conjunction 530
- relator enclitics 533–535
- sequence conjunction 531, 544
- verbs 541
Clause structure 121
- argument realisation 154–160
- bivalent verb agreement 171–174
- reversibility 132
- word order 160–170, 492
Clauses
- complex character predicates 134–137
- exclamatives 152
- imperatives 142–145
- nominal clauses 131
- possessive clauses 133
- postpositional clauses 132
- thematic 257, 265, 276, 291, 527
- topicalised 163
- verbal clauses 121–131, 171–174
Clothing, noun classes (animacy) 193
Co-agentivity 411
Cognitive events 399, 527
- theme of 449

Collective, human, quantification 216
Comitants, non-controlling 436
Comitative relations 139, 432–344
Comparative constructions 93, 442, 451, 496
Comparative data 81, 347, 363, 367, see also Historical data
- areal patterns 35, 363, 366
Complement clauses
- reflexive binding with 393
- word order 524, 525
Complementation
- Non-NP replacing clausal complements 523–526
- NP-replacing clausal complements 519–523
Completive aspect 464–468
Complex character predicates 134–137
Compounds
- historical 62
- nominal 85–90
- possessive 86–88, 349, 350–352
- verbal 94
Conditional clauses 537, 538
Conjunction, nominal 225–228
Conjunctions
- borrowed clause-initial conjunctions 537, 538
- clause conjunctions 118–120, 529, 530, 531, 539, 540, 541
Consonant clusters
- loanwords 61
- native words 62
Consonant phonemes 43–54
Consonant replacement on prefixation 80
Constituents
- peripheral constituents 121, 137–139
Contact languages 21, 23, 29, 32, 482, 537
Content questions 146, 211
Continuative marker 507, 508
Continuous aspect 468–470, 472
Contrastive demonstrative
- contrastive use 285–287
- sentence connective use 292–294, 545, 547, 551
- thematic use 291
- topic shift use 287, 317
- used to mark sequentiality of multiple NPs 288–290
Contrastiveness
- borrowed conjunctions 538

- contrastive proximal deixis 279
- emphatic *on* 'DO' 499
- pronouns and person prefixes 232
- relator enclitics 179, 534
- restrictive focus enclitic 183
- sentence connecting 549
- specifier demonstrative 281

Conventions, glossing XXI–XXIV
Coordination. *see* Clause conjoining
Coordinative compounds
- nominal 88
- verbal 94

Co-participation. *see* Plurality of participants
Core serialisation 455, 456–458, 458, 460, 473–477, 477
Counter-expectation
- counter-expectational demonstrative 294–297
- counter-expectational sentence connective 549
- modal adverb (*hilaq* 'surprisingly') 485
- relation-marking enclitic 177, 294, 534

Currency, noun classes (animacy) 194

Data
- elicited 39
- Facebook group data 39
- fieldwork data 38
- overheard speech 39
- written texts 38

Deictic anchor (addressee locational) 321
Deictic verbs 474–480
Deictic projection 325
Deixis
- person 272–275
- spatial 258, 267, 278, 321
- symbolic spatial 325
- temporal 259

Demonstratives 104, 255
- contrastive 285–294
- counter-expectational 294–297
- manner function 427
- non-proximal 267–277
- proclausal 257
- proximal 258–266
- specifier 277–284

Deontic modal adverbs 482, 483, 484
Dependent, consideration of clauses as 526
Deponency, prefixal 367, 388

- reciprocal prefix 403
- reflexive prefix 390

Deponents, types of 389
Determiners 104, 255, *see also* Locationals
- adclausal 256
- article 297–301
- contrastive demonstrative 285–294
- counter-expectational demonstrative 294–297
- non-proximal demonstrative 267–277
- proclausal demonstratives 257
- pronoun combinations 234
- proximal demonstrative 258–266
- specifier demonstrative 277–284
- syntactic functions 256, 527

Diachronic change 113, 297, 361, 363, 502, 549
Dialects 14–17
- compared 15, 31, 107, 217, 279, 363

Dictionary project 39
Differential P-marking 359, 361
Diphthong phonemes 41–43
- orthography 81

Direct possession
- Class I: nouns with 3rd person *g-* '3AN-' 339–341
- Class II: nouns with 3rd person INANIMATE *h-* '3INAN-' 341–343, 352
- Class III: nouns with locative *n-* 'LOC-' 344
- Class IV: two nouns 346
- Class V: differential possessor marking for animacy 347–350, 351

Direct speech and thought, introducing of 428, 547
Directional serialisation 478–480
Discourse information structure
- backgrounded information 297
- first mention of referent 209, 300, 317
- new information 271, 272, 319

Discourse markers 174–183
- assertive 326

Discourse referent tracking 317–320
- anaphoric referents 259–261, 269–271, 298, 304
- different phases of a single referent 289
- first mention of referent 209, 263, 271, 300, 319
- locationals 304, 317–320, 322
- persisting referents 209, 272–275, 318–320
- specifier demonstrative 280

- topical referents 259–261, 269–271, 287
- zero anaphora 154

Disjunction with =ka 'OR', nominal 228
Dislocation 160
- left-dislocation 162
- right-dislocation 163–165, 525

Distal. see Non-proximal demonstrative
Distal place locational 314, 316, 323, 324
Distance/duration measure adverbial phrase 493
Distance-neutral place locational 314, 317
Ditransitive verbs. see Trivalent verbs
Documentation, previous work 36
Double possessor marking 352–354
"Doubling" (clauses bracketed by initial and final conjunctions) 538
Dual conjunction of NPs (reference to exactly two entities) 227
Dual pronouns 230
- versus plural 235

Duration/distance measure adverbial phrase 493
Durative/progressive events 499
Dutch colonisation 8
"Dvandva" compounds. see Coordinative compounds

East Timor 1, 14
- Bunaq speakers in 8–12, 13
- conflict in 7, 312, 418

Edible plant cultivars, noun classes (animacy) 190
Elevation distinction, three-way 310
Elevational locationals 308–314, 553
- combinations 324, 325–327

Elevationally marked motion verbs 310–314, 553
Elicitation 39
Elision of arguments 154–157, 160, 437
Emphasis (performative auxiliary) 498
Enclitics
- enclitic question tags 148, 150, 151, 493
- focus enclitics 179–183, 535
- reason clause conjunction 530
- relator enclitics 175–179, 533–535

Epenthesis 64, 65
Epistemic modality 483
Epistemic possibility 486
Equation, clauses of 131

Evaluative modal adverbs 485
Event chronology, clause conjoining 466, 516, 531, 536, 541
Event types
- durative/progressive events 499
- future events 502, 504
- negative impact 359, 444
- past events 268, 275, 283, 509
- persistent events 508
- present time events 511
- speech events 321, 325, 445, 527
- spontaneous events 395
- thought events 527
- transfer events 456
- transport events 369
- waiting events 450

Event-oriented manner serialisation 459, 461
Exclamatives 152
Exclamatory speech acts 516
Excluded referents from event, NP encoding of 446
Exclusive, distinction from inclusive 230
Existential verb
- negation 141
- unmarked obliques (OBL) 129, 384

Extension, semantic 353, 442, 512

Facebook group (community dictionary project) 39
Female speech 41
Fieldwork 37
- previous research 36
- recorded data 38
- written data 38

Fighting events 407
'Finished' (haqal) 464–468, 541, 544
Focus enclitics 179–183
- clause conjoining 535

Focus, unmarked (expressed in preverbal position) 167–168
Focused interrogatives 146–147
Folktales (Zapal) 37, 193
Fossilisation 389, 398, 400
Frequentive aspect 470–472
Fricatives 48
Friedberg, Claudine 36
Fronting (of clausal elements) 165, 233
Future events 502, 504

Gathering events, verbs of 409
Genealogical affiliations 17
Generalisations, expression of 236
Generic reference 236–239
Gewal (village in Lamaknen region of West Timor) 37, 242, 313, 325
Gie 'BECAUSE' 430
Glides 64
Global elevation, encoding of 309
Glossing conventions XXI–XXIV
Glottal stop 53
– as boundary marker 65
– phoneme 53, 60
– phonetic onset 58
Goal-encoding verbal postposition 412, 438, 475, 476
Grammaticalisation
– apparent 116, 432, 468
– paths 113, 363, 472, 502
Greater West Bomberai (GWB) family 17
– Proto-Greater West Bomberai (PGWB) 20

Habitual aspect 471, 500
h-ini '3INAN-call/cause' 126, 375–378, 382, 391, 525
Historical data
– compounds 62
– prefixes and roots 347, 361, 363, 366, 367, 389
Homeland of the Bunaq people 12
Honorific address 241
Hortatives (imperative clauses) 143
Human plurality 214–216
Human production, items of, noun classes (animacy) 192
Human source, NP encoding of 441

Iamitive marker 507, 509–512
Iconicity 354, 423, 453, 473, 504, 526
Immediate action, encoding of 470
Imperatives 142–145, 516
– responses to 145
Impersonal middles 402
Impersonal possessive relations 402
Inalienably possessed nouns
– as N_{MOD}s 200–202
– direct possession 338
– double possessor marking 352–354
– reciprocal marking 404
– reflexive marking 391, 397, 401, 402

– sub-classes 338, 339–341, 341–343, 344, 346, 347–350
– use of "inalienable" and "alienable" labels 329
Inanimate referents 188–195, see also Animacy
– assignment to ANIMATE 189
– INANIMATE nouns reassigned to ANIMATE 195–199
Inclusive–exclusive distinction 230
Indefiniteness, marking of 208–212
Indirect possession 330–337
Indirect thought and speech 527
Indonesian, borrowing from 54–56, 82, 193, 482, 537
Information (content) questions 146, 211
Information markers
– informative *nai* 'INFORM' 514
– reportative *gin* 'REPORT' 512–514
Information structure, discourse
– backgrounded information 297
– first mention of referent 209, 300, 317
– new information 271, 272, 319
Informative marker 514
Instrumental verbal postposition 411, 434
Intensifiers, postverbal 497
Intensifying serialisation 462–464
Intentionality, marking of 501
Interest or advantage of participant, NP encoding of 439
Interjections 111, 145
Interrogative clauses. *see* Questions (clause types)
Interrogatives 99–101
– as head of relative clause 205
Intonation contours
– clause conjoining 526, 529, 535
– complement clauses 525
– exclamatives 152, 516
– imperatives 142
– polar questions 148
– sentence connecting 548
– serial verb constructions (SVCs) 453
Intonation units
– glossing of XXIV
– locationals 102
– word-final voiceless stops 45
Intransitive verbs. *see* Monovalent verbs
Invitations (imperative clauses) 144
Irrealis events 511, 531, 533

Iterative meaning, encoding of 75, 405, 468, 470, 471

Japanese occupation 10
Jewellery, noun classes (animacy) 193
Joining and unjoining, verbs of 410
Juxtaposition (clause conjoining) 526–528

Kin terms 23, 246–250
- possession 341
- used with kin 247–248
- used with non-kin 249
Knowledge, shared (speaker–addressee) 322, 325, 327

Labile verbs 378–383
- causative labile verbs 381
Lamaknen (dialect of Bunaq) 14
- compared to other dialects 31, 107, 217, 279, 363, 396
- dictionary 37
Lamaknen (region of West Timor) 5, 7, 13, 37
- elevation in place- and path-finding 311–313
Language change
- bleaching 345, 447
- diachronic 113, 297, 361, 363, 502, 549
- fossilisation 389, 398, 400
- grammaticalisation 116, 363, 432, 468, 502
- lexicalisation 345, 348, 398, 400
- loss of forms 342, 432
- renewal 297
Language contact 21, 23, 29, 32, 482, 537
Language family 17
Learning/teaching, verbs of 129, 380, 387
Left-headed compounds 85, see also Compounds
Lexicalisation 345, 348, 398, 400, 419
Lineage groups, animacy 196
Literature, oral and written, noun classes (animacy) 193
Loanwords 24, see also Borrowing
- consonant clusters 61
- orthography 82
- phoneme adaptation 54–57
Location of origin, encoding of 134
Locationals 101–103, 302
- addressee locational 307, 321–323
- and possessors 303, 304
- combining locationals 323–328

- elevational locationals 308–314
- frequency of uses 307
- no N_{HEAD} use 306, 307
- place locationals 314–317, 323
- post-N_{HEAD} use 305, 307
- pre-N_{HEAD} use 303, 307
- temporal/discourse locational 306, 317–320
Locative morpheme n- 'LOC-' 344
Locative postpositional phrases 138, 425
- locative-setting NPs 422–424, 425
- NP complements as relative clause heads 207
- stative locative NPs 425

Male speech 46
Maleficiary 444
Manner
- demonstrative manner function 427
- manner adverbs 489
- manner of motion verbs 473, 478–480
- manner serialisation 459–462
- NP encoding of 436
Manner or procedure, explanation of 547
Manufahi dialect of Bunaq 14, 363
Marriage patterns 2
Maukatar enclave 8, 9
Measure adverbial phrases 493
Metaphorical extension 326, 399, 439
Metathesis 70–73
Mete 'NOW' (temporal/discourse locational) 305, 306, 308, 317–320, 327
Middle situations
- body action events 400
- cognitive events 399
- impersonal middles 402
- reflexive prefix 388
- self-benefactive events 397–399
- spontaneous events 395
Mixing, verbs of 381, 415
Modality (modal adverbs) 482–489
Moderative suffix 419
Modifiers. see also Preverbal modification, see also Postverbal modification
- adverbial 117, 481–492, 493–497
- nominal 116, 184, 199–203, 203
- verbal and clausal 481
Money, noun classes (animacy) 194
Monovalent predicates, non-motion 437
Monovalent verbal clauses 122
Monovalent verbs 122, 371–374

- anticausative marking 419
- reciprocal events 412, 414
- S complement clauses 521
- serialisation 458, 459, 460, 461, 462
- stative 91, 379, 458, 501, 510
- verbs of anger 446, 449

Morphology
- Papuan-Austronesian compared 34
- prefixation 69–73, 77–81
- reduplication 74–77
- root mutation 79
- root reduction 78
- suffixation 73

Motion events
- body action events 400
- continuous action 469
- goal-encoding 438
- human source 442
- iterative events 405
- non-translational 369, 401
- serialisation 465, 472–480

Motion verbs 129, 386
- elevationally marked 310–314
- sentence connecting 548
- serial verb constructions (SVCs) 465, 468, 472–480
- transport verbs 369

Motive, NP encoding of 440

Multiclausal constructions
- borrowed clause-initial conjunctions 537, 538
- clause conjoining 526–528, 539, 540, 541
- clause-final conjunctions 529, 530, 531, 533, 535
- complementation 518–526
- contrasted with SVCs 452, 453
- intonation contours 453, 525, 526, 529, 548
- sentence connecting 542–550
- types 518

Multiple participants. *see* Plurality of participants

'Must' (*misti*) modal adverb 482

Mythology 191, 195, 282

Names 251–253
- ancestral names 251
- Christian names 251
- name avoidance 253
- nicknames 253
- replacement names 252
- teknonyms 253

Negation 139–142
- *ciaq* 'not want' 523
- clausal 139–141, 509, 511
- in questions 148
- negative existential verb 141, 384
- negative reinforcers 142, 491
- prohibitive negator 141, 142
- serial verb constructions (SVCs) 455, 457, 458, 461

New discourse participant, reference to 209, 271

New information 271, 272, 317

N_{HEAD} (head noun) 184
- prosodic prominence 201

Nicknames 253

N_{MOD} (noun describing a property of an N_{HEAD}) 184, 199–203
- agreeing in animacy 202

Nominal clauses 131

Nominal compounds 85–90

Nominal conjunction 225–228

Nominal disjunction with =*ka* 'OR' 228

Nominalisations
- nominalised setting clause 424
- non-embedded 264, 275, 281–283, 296

Non-controlling comitants 436

Non-deictic verbs 311, 474–480

Non-pronominal person reference 245–253
- kin terms 246–250

Non-proximal demonstrative 267, 297, 298
- anaphoric use 269–271, 546
- non-embedded use 275
- referring to a new discourse participant 271
- sentence connective use 277, 546
- spatial use 267
- temporal use 268
- thematic use 276
- use in person deixis 272–275

Non-proximal place locational. *see* Distal place locational

Non-restrictive relative clauses 203

Northeast dialect of Bunaq 14, 48, 396

Noun class reassignment, animacy 195–199

Noun classes 185
- agreement targets 186
- animacy distinction 188, 202, 341–343, 347–350

- animate referents 186–188
- inanimate referents 188–195
- reassignment of INANIMATE nouns to ANIMATE 195–199

Noun phrases (NPs)
- dual conjunction 227
- template 184
- zero conjunction 225

Nouns
- nominal compounds 85, 88
- word class 83–90

Nouns, alienably possessed
- possessors of 331, 332, 335, 336, 354
- reciprocal marking 404
- use of "alienable" and "inalienable" labels 329

Nouns, inalienably possessed
- as N$_{MOD}$s 200–202
- direct possession 338
- double possessor marking 352–354
- reciprocal marking 404
- reflexive marking 391, 397, 401, 402
- sub-classes 338, 339–341, 341–343, 344, 346, 347–350
- use of "inalienable" and "alienable" labels 329

Noun-verb conversion 96, 436

'NOW' (mete), temporal/discourse locational 305, 306, 308, 317–320, 327

Nuclear serialisation 455, 478–480

Numeral classifier construction 212

Numerals 105–109
- the numeral uen 'one' 109, 209, 213, 217

"Object" grouping ("secundative" alignment) 131

Obliques, no 'OBL' postposition 422–424, 540

Obliques, unmarked oblique ('OBL') argument 122
- as relative clause heads 206
- contrasted with postposition gloss 'OBL' 128
- verb classes with 383–387

Older speakers 108, 487, 538

'ONLY' (ai) restrictive particle 505–507
- used to conjoin NPs 228

Oral literature 193, 569

Order of events, clause conjoining 466, 516, 531, 536, 541

Origin location, encoding of 134, 475

Origin-motion-goal SVCs 473, 475–477

Orthography 3, 81

Overheard speech as data 39

P complement clauses 519–521

Papuan languages 2, 19, 32
- alternative label ("non-Austronesian") 32
- and Austronesian languages 21, 23, 33–35, 33–35
- typology 32–36, 77, 492

Parallelism 30

Participant-oriented manner serialisation 459, 460

Partitive
- meaning 'one of a collective' 217
- plural 220

Part–whole relationships 86, 349

Past events 268, 275, 509
- recent past frame 283

Path-finding, real world locations 310–314, 553

Perception, verbs of 519

Performative auxiliary 363, 498–502

Peripheral constituents 121, 137–139

Permission
- expression of 521
- imperative clauses 144

Persistent action 472

Persistent events 508

Person
- dual versus plural number 235
- generic reference 236–239
- non-pronominal reference 245–253
- polite reference 239–245
- pronouns 230, 234

Person prefixes 231–233
- direct possession 338

Personal names 251–253
- ancestral names 251
- Christian names 251
- name avoidance 253
- nicknames 253
- replacement names 252
- teknonyms 253

Phasal polarity
- phasal polarity markers 118, 493, 507–511
- postverbal modification 492
- serial verb constructions (SVCs) 454

Phoneme inventory 31, 40

Phonemes 40
- adaptation in loanwords 54–57

- consonants 44–54
- diphthongs 41–43
- orthography 81
- phonotactic distribution 60
- vowel phonemes 40

Phonetic glide insertion 64
Phonological reduction 278, 509
Phonology, Papuan and Austronesian compared 33
Phonotactics
- glottal stop 65
- phoneme distribution 60
- syllable structure 57
- vowel sequences 63
- word templates 58

Physical contact events 407
Physical fighting events 407
Place- and path-finding, real world locations 310–314
Place locationals 314–317
- combinations 323, 324

Place names 8, 12, 314
- Austronesian 6, 9, 12

Plant possessors 352
Plants, noun classes of (animacy) 197–199
- edible cultivars 190
- nouns denoting plant parts 347, 348

Plural pronouns 230
- versus dual 235

Plurality
- animal group 219
- animate group 218
- human 214–216, 235

Plurality of participants
- fighting events 407
- gathering events 409
- physical contact events 407
- reciprocal marking 406–410
- verbs of (un)joining 410

Plurality, distributive, by reduplication 224
Point of relation/comparison 442
Polar questions 148–152
- alternative questions with =ka 'OR' 149
- answers to 151
- soliciting agreement 149
- unmarked 148

Polite reference 239–245
- honorific address 241
- polite address 243, 245, 559

- pronoun politeness hierarchy 244
- respectful address 243
- self-reference 239

Portuguese colonisation 8
Possession. *see also* Possessors
- alienably possessed nouns 329, 331, 332, 335, 336
- alienation, degree of 341–343, 346, 354, 355
- associative possession 332
- body part terms 339
- direct possession 338, 339–341, 341–343, 344, 346, 347–350, 352
- double possessor marking 352–354
- existential verbs 385
- impersonal possession 402
- inalienably possessed nouns 200–202, 329, 338, 352–354
- indirect possession 330–337, 352, 393
- predicative possessive 334–337
- types of constructions 329

Possessive classifier 330, 334, 350, 392
Possessive clauses 133, 330, 334–337
Possessive compounds 86–88, 349, 350–352
Possessive phrases 350–352
Possessors
- and locationals 303, 304
- animal and plant 352
- as destination 335
- as origin 336
- as relative clause heads 208
- reflexive 392, 393
- restriction on modifying a pronoun 98

Possibility
- epistemic 486
- expression of 522

Postpositional clauses 132
Postpositional phrases 137–139
Postpositions 110, 422, *see also* Verbal postpositions
- clause conjoining 540
- direct speech and thought 428
- *goet* 'LIKE' 132, 208, 426–429, 547
- locative 138, 207, 422–424, 425
- manner function 427
- oblique *no* 'OBL' 422–424, 540
- similative function 426
- temporal function 424, 540

Postverbal intensifiers 497
Postverbal modification 492

- adverbials 493–497
- information markers 512–515
- performative auxiliary 498–502
- phasal polarity markers 507–511
- prioritive marker 516
- prospective aspect 502–505
- template for typical ordering 492

Pragmatic variation in clause
- argument realisation 154–160
- bivalent verb agreement 171–174
- discourse markers 174–183
- word order 160–170

Precautionary modal adverb 488
Predicates 121
- complex character predicates 134–137

Prefixal deponency 388
- reciprocal prefix 367, 403
- reflexive prefix 390
- types of deponents 389

Prefixation 69–73
- affecting interpretation 369, 370, 373
- bivalent verbs 359, 361, 368
- initial consonant replacement 80
- irregularities 77–81
- metathesis 70–73
- monovalent verbs 372
- person prefixes 231–233, 338
- reciprocal prefix 367, 403
- reflexive prefix 135, 389, 390, 391, 395, 402
- valency-reducing prefixes 388
- verb classes 356
- vowel deletion 70
- vowel harmony 69

Present time events 511
Presentational clauses 132, 485
Preverbal modification 481–492
Primary stress. *see* Stress
Priorative marker 516, 536
Procedural text 551
Procedure or manner, explanation of 547
Proclausal demonstratives 257
Progressive/durative events 499
Prohibitive modal adverb 141, 142, 488
Pronouns 97, 230
- determiner combinations 234
- dual versus plural 235
- generic reference 236–239
- person prefixes 231–233
- polite reference 239–245

- politeness hierarchy 244

Prosody
- clause conjoining 526, 529, 535
- complement clauses 525
- dislocation 160
- locationals 102
- N_{HEAD} 201
- sentence connecting 548
- serial verb constructions 453

Prospective aspect 502–505
Proto-Bunaq 15, 23
Proto-Greater West Bomberai (PGWB) 20
Proto-Rote-Meto 29
Proto-Timor-Alor-Pantar (PTAP) 19, 23, 338, 347
Proximal demonstrative 258–266
- compared to proximal place locational 315

Proximal place locational 314, 323
PTAP (Proto-Timor-Alor-Pantar) 19, 23, 338, 347

Quantification 116, 212
- animal group plural 219
- animate group plural 218
- "complete" quantification 467
- distributive plurality by reduplication 224
- human collective 216
- human plurality 214–216
- numeral classifier construction 212
- numeral *uen* 'one' 213
- partitive plural 220
- plurality of 'kinds' 222–224
- temporal duration 217
- universal (*hotu~hotu* 'all') 221

Question tags 148, 150, 151, 493
Questioning
- "softening" the speech act 486
- verbs of, addressee 445

Questions (clause types) 146–152
- information questions 146
- polar questions 148–152

Raihat (district of Belu regency) 5, 7, 13
Reason clause conjunction 530, 538, 541
Reason, encoding of 430
Recent past 283
Recipient 447
Reciprocal prefix 367, 403
- on verbal postpositions 410–415

Reciprocal situations 388, 403
- iterative events 405

- marked on nouns 404
- marked on verbs 403
- plurality of participants 406–410
- symmetrical states 405

Reduplication 74–77, 109
- and repetition 74
- distributive plurality 224
- in-progress events 540

Reference, generic 236–239
Reference, non-pronominal person 245–253, 246–250
Reference, polite 239–245
- honorific address 241
- polite address 243, 245
- pronoun politeness hierarchy 244
- respectful address 243
- self-reference 239, 248

Referent (re)activation 288, 308, 317, 319, 327
Referent tracking 317–320
- anaphoric referents 259–261, 269–271, 298, 304
- different phases of a single referent 289
- first mention of referent 209, 263, 271, 300, 319
- locationals 304, 317–320, 322
- persisting referents 209, 272–275, 318–320
- specifier demonstrative 280
- topical referents 259–261, 269–271, 287
- zero anaphora 154

Reflexive prefix 135, 389, 390, 391
- middle situations 395–403, 402

Reflexive relations 388, 390
- impersonal reflexive 402
- marked on nouns 391–393, 457
- marked on verbs and verbal postpositions 390
- middle situations 395–403
- reflexive binding with complement clauses and serial verbs 393, 457

Reinforcers, negative 142, 491, 506
Relation/comparison, point of 442
Relative clauses (RCs)
- non-restrictive 203
- noun phrase Accessibility Hierarchy 206–208
- predicative possessive construction 334
- restrictive 205, 305

Relativisation 111

Relator enclitics 175–179
- clause conjoining 533–535

Removed referents from event, NP encoding of 446
Reportative marker 512–514
Respectful address 243, 249
Responses
- to imperatives 145
- to polar questions 151

Restrictive *ai* 'ONLY' 505–507
- used to conjoin NPs 228

Restrictive focus enclitic 146–147, 182, 536
Restrictive relative clauses 205
Resultative motion SVCs 475
Resultative serialisation 458
Reversive motion SVCs 477
Rhotic trill 46, 51
Right-headed compounds 86–88, *see also* Compounds
Ritual language 30
Rocks, noun classes (animacy) 195
Roots
- noun-verb roots 96
- root mutation 79
- root reduction 78

S complement clauses 521–523
Saturation verbs 129, 383
Scalar additive focus enclitic 181, 535
Secondary stress. *see* Stress
"Secundative" alignment ("object" grouping) 131
Self-benefactive 380, 397–399
Self-reference 239, 248
Semantic bleaching 345, 447
Semantic extension 353, 442, 512
Semantic–syntactic roles 122
Sentence connecting 542–550
- anaphoric demonstratives 545–547
- cataphoric demonstratives 547
- contrastive demonstrative 292–294, 545, 547, 551
- *gie* 'BECAUSE' 430
- non-proximal demonstrative 277, 546
- proximal demonstrative 265
- specifier demonstrative 283–284, 548
- tail-head linkage 542–545
- *tebe* 'return' 548

Sentence connectives 549

Sequence clause conjunction 531, 544
Sequence-marking (function of contrastive demonstrative) 288–290
Serial verb constructions (SVCs) 452–454, see also Serialisation
- ambient serialisation 455, 461, 462–464, 464–472, 522
- core serialisation 455, 456–458, 458, 460, 473–477, 477
- intonation contours 453
- motion SVC template 472–474
- nuclear serialisation 455, 478–480
- syntactic types 455
Serial verbs
- benefactive constructions 394
- reflexive binding with 393, 457
Serialisation
- aspectual serialisation 464–472
- causative serialisation 456–458
- directional serialisation 478–480
- intensifying serialisation 462–464
- manner serialisation 459–462
- motion serialisation 472–480
- resultative serialisation 458
Setting, verbs of 379
Shared knowledge (speaker–addressee) 322, 325, 327
'Should' (*sala*) modal adverb 483
Similative marker 420
Similative postpositional phrases 139, 426
Singular pronouns 230
Source verbal postposition 451
Source, human 441
Southwest dialect of Bunaq 14, 279, 400
Spatial deixis 258, 267, 278, 321
- symbolic 325
Speaker–addressee shared knowledge 322, 325, 327
Speaking, verbs of 428, 513
- addressee 445, 448
Specific place locational 314, 317, 324
Specifier demonstrative
- discourse use 280
- non-embedded use 281–283
- sentence connective use 283–284, 548
- spatial use 278
- thematic use 283
Speech events
- addressee 322, 325, 445

- exclamatory 516
- indirect 527
Speech, direct 428, 547
Spontaneous events, encoding of 395
Stative verbs 91, 379, 458, 501, 510
Stones, noun classes (animacy) 195
Stops (phonemes) 45–47
Storytelling, traditional forms 193
Stress 40, 63, 66–68
"Subject" grouping 131
Subordination. *see* Clause conjoining
Substitutive beneficiary 439
Suffixation
- anticausative -*wen* 73, 415–421
Syllables
- stress 40, 63, 66–68
- structure 57
Symbolic spatial deixis 325
Symmetrical participation, encoding of 413
Symmetrical states, encoding of 405
Synchronic processes
- metathesis 70
- prefixation 69, 81

Tail-head linkage 257, 291, 542–545, 546, 551
TAP (Timor-Alor-Pantar) language family 17–21, 310, 502
- Proto-Timor-Alor-Pantar (PTAP) 19, 23, 338, 347
Teaching/learning, verbs of 129, 380, 387
Teknonyms 253
Temporal adverbs 490, 495
Temporal deixis 259
Temporal duration 217
Temporal setting clauses 540
Temporal setting NPs 424
Temporal/discourse locational 306, 317–320
- combinations 327
Tetun (Austronesian language) 2, 9
- borrowing from 24–28, 78, 82, 364, 496, 537
Texts. *see* Data
Thematic clauses 257, 265, 276, 291, 527
Theme, cognitive event 449
Thinking, verbs of 513
Third party source, reporting of information from 512
Thought and direct speech, introducing of 428, 547

Thought events, theme of 449
Thoughts, reported 512, 513
Timor 1
- languages of 18
Timor-Alor-Pantar (TAP) language family 17–21
Timor-Leste. *see* East Timor
Topical elements 162–163, 260, 269, 276
Topic-comment structures 269
Topics
- clarifying 163–165, 525
- marked by contrastive demonstrative 287, 317
- marked by non-proximal demonstrative 269, 546
- marked by proximal demonstrative 260
Topography, conventionalised 314
Topological nouns 309
Topological relations, encoding of 309
Transfer events 456
Transitive verbs. *see* Bivalent verbs
Trans-New Guinea language family 19
Transport verbs 369
Trivalent verbal clauses 126–128
Trivalent verbs 126, 374–378
- reflexive marking 391
Typology 31
- Austronesian languages 113, 537
- labile verbs 378
- Papuan and Austronesian compared 33–35
- Papuan languages 492
- serial verb constructions (SVCs) 452, 455
- TAP languages 77, 310, 344, 375, 502

Uen 'one' (numeral) 109
- indefiniteness marking 209
- quantification 213
Uniting of participants, encoding of 412

Valency 90, 356, 375
- absence of valency reduction 158, 398, 419
- anticausative -*wen* suffix 388, 415–421
- labile verbs 378–383
- middle situations 395–403
- reciprocal situations 403–415
- reflexive relations 390–403
- types of deponents 389
- valency-reducing prefixes 388
Valency-reducing morphemes, glossing of 390
Verb classes

- bivalent verbs 357, 358, 359–361, 361–368, 368–371
- causative labile verbs 381
- classification of 356
- existential verbs 129, 384
- labile verbs 378–383
- monovalent verbs 371–374
- motion verbs 129, 386, 472–480, 548
- saturation verbs 129, 383
- trivalent verbs 374–378
- verbs of setting 379
- verbs of mixing 381, 415
- verbs of perception 519
- verbs of speaking 428, 445, 448, 513, 519
- verbs of teaching/learning 129, 380, 387
- verbs of wanting 523–526
- verbs with unmarked obliques 383–387
Verbal clauses 121–131
- bivalent 124–126, 171–174
- monovalent 122
- trivalent 126–128
- unmarked obliques 128–130
Verbal coordinative compounds 94
Verbal modifiers, postverbal 492–517
- template for typical ordering 492
Verbal modifiers, preverbal 481–492
Verbal postpositional phrases 137–139
Verbal postpositions 113–116, 431
- beneficiary, addressee, theme of cognitive event 447–450
- clause conjoining 540
- comitative 432
- goals, interest, motive 437–441, 540, 541
- instruments, cause, manner 434–437
- NP complements as RC heads 207
- reciprocal marking 410–415
- referents excluded or removed from event 445–447
- reflexive marking 391
- semantic role 'SOURCE' 441–445
Verbs
- attributive verbs 203
- used in clause conjoining 541
- verbal postpositions, compared to 113–116, 431, 441, 447
- word class 90–95
Voiced stops 46–47
Voiceless stops 45

Vowel deletion 70
Vowel harmony 69
Vowel phonemes 40
– orthography 81
Vowel sequences 63

Waiting events 450
Wanting, verbs of 523–526
Water, noun classes (animacy) 197
West Papuan language family 19
West Timor 4, 37, 312
– Bunaq speakers in 5–8, 13

Word order 31, 492
– animacy effects 168–170
– complement clauses 524, 525
– pragmatic variation 160–170
Word templates, phonotactic 58

Younger speakers 47, 396, 549

Zapal 'folktales' 37, 193, 569
Zero conjunction of NPs 225
"Zero pro" of A argument 157–160
Zero-conversion noun-verbs 96, 436

www.ingramcontent.com/pod-product-compliance
Lightning Source LLC
Chambersburg PA
CBHW081943230426
43669CB00019B/2903